DELAWARE

A Guide to the First State

DELAWARE

A GUIDE TO THE FIRST STATE

☆

Compiled and Written by the Federal Writers' Project
of the Works Progress Administration
for the State of Delaware

NEW AND REVISED EDITION
BY JEANNETTE ECKMAN
EDITED BY HENRY G. ALSBERG

AMERICAN GUIDE SERIES

ILLUSTRATED

HASTINGS HOUSE

Publishers   New York 22

FIRST PUBLISHED IN JUNE 1938
SECOND PRINTING IN DECEMBER 1948
SECOND EDITION EXTENSIVELY REVISED, MAY 1955

Printed in the United States of America

EDWARD W. COOCH
LIEUTENANT GOVERNOR

OFFICE OF LIEUTENANT GOVERNOR
DOVER, DELAWARE

The Delaware Guide is a welcome contribution to the understanding and appreciation
of this, the First State. It depicts present
conditions against a background of distinctive
history. The result is a revelation of the
State's individuality. Its publication at this
time is opportune in that it coincides with
Delaware's celebration of the three hundredth
anniversary of its first permanent settlement.

Edward W. Cooch

Lieutenant-Governor

State Motto

Liberty and Independence. Added to the Great Seal, 1847.

State Colors

Colonial Blue and Buff

State Flag

A background of colonial blue, surrounding a diamond of buff color containing the coat of arms of the State of Delaware in color. Below the diamond are the words, "December 7, 1787" indicating the day on which Delaware was the first State to ratify the Federal Constitution, thus becoming the first state in the Union.

Nicknames

"Blue Hen's Chickens"; "Diamond State."

State Song

"Our Delaware"—music by William M. S. Brown, and words by George B. Hynson. Adopted April 7, 1925.

State Flower—The Peach Blossom. Adopted May 9, 1895.

State Bird—Blue Hen Chicken. Adopted April 14, 1939.

State Tree—American Holly. Adopted May 1, 1939.

Foreword

THE "State Guide Books" published in the 1930's constitute a most valuable source of information for those people who would really know America. One of the best of these books is *Delaware, A Guide to the First State,* first issued in 1938 and now brought up-to-date and revised.

This revised edition should be eagerly read by the many new residents of the "First State" who seek knowledge of Delaware's history, development and current life along with a vivid and entertaining picture of its people, places and topography. This recommendation is founded upon personal experience. When I first came to the University of Delaware, I received a gift copy of the first edition from one of the editors, Mr. Anthony Higgins. He quite properly believed that I, as a newcomer, could best be oriented to my new environment with the help of this volume.

Now as one familiar with the State of Delaware, I can recommend it, also, to long-time residents who may be prone to overlook this systematic presentation of facts about their native state. We often rely upon half-forgotten tales told us in childhood by oldsters who themselves depended upon hearsay instead of such a reliable source of information. Young people raised in Delaware today, however, and especially those attending the University, do come to know their State through *Delaware, A Guide to the First State.* It is a basic text in the required course in Delaware History. This is tantamount to saying that our Department of History vouches for its authentic and stimulating approach.

Such knowledge of Delaware and its communities as this *Guide* offers is fundamental to intelligent citizenship. Such knowledge, too, will make more enjoyable the experience of those who are only visitors to Delaware.

JOHN A. PERKINS

Dr. Perkins came to the University of Delaware as President, November 1st, 1950.

Editors' Preface

(1938)

IN the preparation of the Delaware Guide the editors gratefully acknowledge the aid of Federal, State, and local governmental agencies, and of commercial and civic associations and appreciate the assistance of Arthur L. Bailey, librarian of the Wilmington Public Library, and his staff.

Among the many other individuals to whom the editors wish to express their gratitude for generous aid in special fields are: Julian Bacon, former U. S. Senator Thomas F. Bayard, the Rev. Robert Bell, Weston H. Blake, T. Leslie Carpenter, Lieutenant Governor Edward W. Cooch, Francis A. Cooch, W. S. Corkran, Charles M. Cullen, Judge Charles M. Curtis, Leon de Valinger Jr., Mrs. E. Paul du Pont, the Rev. Joseph H. Earp, Miss Mary Eastman, A. O. H. Grier, Mrs. Florence Hastings, Wilbert B. Hitchner, former Congressman Robert G. Houston, Dr. Frank Morton Jones, Miss Rosalie Martin, Mrs. Andrew Marvel, Miss Constance Moore, Judge John P. Nields, H. Geiger Omwake, Prof. Henry Clay Reed, Louis L. Redding, Mrs. Alden B. Richardson, Mrs. Henry Rockwell, Judge Richard S. Rodney, Laussat R. Rogers, James H. Semple, L. D. Shank, Mrs. Alice Steinlein, Secretary of State Charles L. Terry Jr., Francis Vincent, G. Morris Whiteside II, and Mayor J. Wallace Woodford.

> JEANNETTE ECKMAN,
> ANTHONY HIGGINS,
> WILLIAM H. CONNER,
> *Editors.*

THE author of this revision wishes to thank the many Delawareans who aided in bringing the State Guide up to date as far as technical limitations would permit. High cost of publication made it necessary to keep the paging of the original edition and avoid resetting as strictly as possible. A fuller index and some new illustrations are included.

Special recognition for invaluable help is due the original editors, Mr. Higgins and Mr. Conner; Mrs. J. Jesse Selinkoff, secretary of the former Federal Arts Projects, Charles Lee Reese, executive editor of the Wilmington daily newspapers, Professor H. Clay Reed of the University of Delaware, Hon. Leon de Valinger, Jr., State Archivist, Colonel and Mrs. Wilbur S. Corkran of Rehoboth, Mr. and Mrs. G. Marshall Townsend of Milford, Miss Catharine C. Maull of Lewes, Mrs. J. Thomas Robinson of Georgetown, Miss Ruthanna Hindes, librarian of the Historical Society of Delaware.

U. S. Census, 1950, has been used for population figures unless later were available.

> JEANNETTE ECKMAN, Wilmington, 1954

Miss Eckman was Director of the Delaware Federal Writers Project, 1935–1941.

Contents

I. Delaware: The General Background

II. Cities and Towns

III. Tours

IV. Appendices

Illustrations

All photographs not otherwise credited are by WILLARD S. STEWART, Wilmington. The drawings are the work of JOHN MOLL, Delaware artist.

Maps

NOTE: Current issues of State Highway Department official maps are a good supplement to State Guide information. They may be had by mail or personal inquiry at the Information Office of the Delaware Memorial Bridge, New Castle County, or the Traffic and Planning Division of the State Highway Department, 152 S. State Street, Dover.

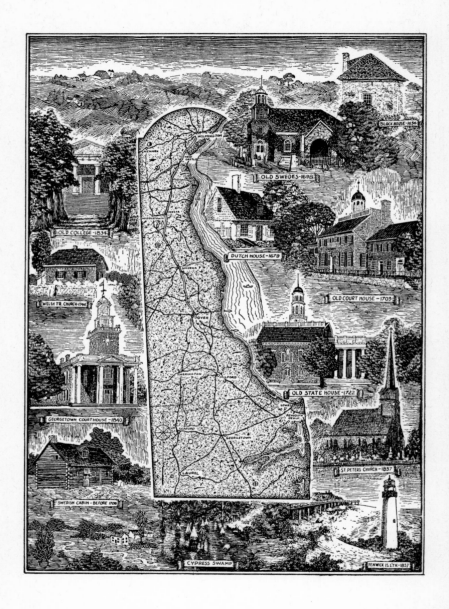

BLOCK HOUSE · 1654

OLD SWEDES · 1698

OLD COLLEGE · 1834

DUTCH HOUSE · 1679

WELSH TR. CHURCH · 1746

OLD COURT HOUSE · 1703

GEORGETOWN COURTHOUSE · 1840

OLD STATE HOUSE · 1722

SWEDISH CABIN · BEFORE 1700

ST. PETERS CHURCH · 1837

CYPRESS SWAMP

FENWICK IS. LT H · 1857

General Information

Railroads: Baltimore & Ohio, Pennsylvania, and Reading; latter does not carry passengers. Delaware Division of Pennsylvania system runs lengthwise through the State S. from Wilmington, affording connection through a second division to Cape Charles and Norfolk, Va.; branches serve southeastern Delaware and the Eastern Shore, with freight service only.

Highways: Four Federal highways: US 13, Trenton, N. J., to Cape Charles, Va., runs lengthwise through the State; US 113, Dover, the State capital, to Pocomoke City, Md., thus far an alternate route to US 13, runs nearer Delaware Bay and the Atlantic; US 40, Atlantic City to Baltimore and other points W., linked across Delaware River by Memorial Bridge, US 202, Wilmington to New England, runs due N. out of the State. Nearly all State highways are paved and rated excellent. State police patrol. State gasoline tax 5¢. Delaware River Bridge, all types of passenger cars, toll 75¢.

Bus Lines: Eight interstate: Greyhound, Red Star, Trailways, Short Line, Southern Pennsylvania Bus Co. (Between Wilmington and Philadelphia), South Jersey Coach Line, Public Service Line of New Jersey, Salem County Coach Line—all via Delaware Memorial Bridge. Intrastate are Delaware and Diamond State Bus Companies.

Air Lines: Scheduled aircraft service by 4 lines at New Castle County Airport near Hare's Corner. Charter service here and at Du Pont Airport, Wilmington. Scheduled service at Dover Army Air Base, at Rehoboth in summer; occasional at Georgetown and Seaford.

Waterways: Wilson Line steamboats ply regularly between Wilmington, Chester and Philadelphia.

Motor Vehicle Laws (digest): Minimum age for drivers, 16 years. Non-resident driver's license valid in this State while valid in his State (or country). Non-resident, whose State requires no licensing of drivers, may drive his car without a license in Delaware for 30 days of a calendar year, provided he displays tag or tags and carries registration card issued in his State. Non-resident may operate and permit operation of his non-commercial vehicle here provided it is registered in his State and displays tag or tags thereof.

Following are legal speed rates but only in safe driving conditions: 50 m. p. h. on two-lane, 55 on four- or more lane and divided roads; 25 in business or residence parts of cities and towns. Lights to be used, "from a half hour after sunset to a half hour before sunrise and at any other time when there is not sufficient light to render clearly discernible any person on the highway at a distance of two hundred feet ahead." Two auxiliary driving lamps and two spotlamps are permitted on motor-cars. Pass vehicles on left; in Wilmington pass trolley coaches on left. Stop at scene of accident, give proper identification and reasonable assistance to person or persons concerned, and within 24 hrs. report to nearest State police station, or in Wilmington to the department of public safety, accident resulting in personal injury (or death) or property damage apparently amounting to $50 or more.

Accommodations: Hotels and boarding houses, both white and Negro, in nearly all towns; city of Wilmington has also Y.M.C.A. and Y.W.C.A. Excellent motels and motor courts are near or within easy distance of all towns. Trailer parks and sites are convenient to towns and shopping centers. Camp sites are available near Delaware's 40 ponds and streams.

Climate and Equipment: Climate generally genial, though humid at times, especially in July and August. Seasonal clothing and equipment stores are plentiful. When drinking water from municipal systems is not readily available, pure water may be obtained at gasoline stations having the Blue Hen Seal of the State Board of Health.

Fishing: Chief bases for salt-water fishing are Bowers Beach, Lewes, Slaughter Beach, Little Creek, and Leipsic; power boats and necessary facilities may be secured at these towns. Salt-water fish more commonly caught are croakers or hardheads, trout or weakfish, channelbass or drum-fish, flounders, and kingfish. Large strips of State-owned land along the Atlantic, south from Cape Henlopen, are open to the public and offer opportunity for excellent surf fishing. Crabbing is excellent at Rehoboth Bay and Indian River Bay. Principal fresh-water fishing places, containing bass, pike or pickerel, yellow perch, carp, catfish, and crappies, are Nanticoke River, Broad Creek, Indian River, and many stocked mill ponds throughout the State. Boats are available for hire at most of these ponds, the better known of which are Noxontown Pond and Silver Lake near Middletown; Lake Como near Smyrna; Records Pond near Laurel; Milton

Pond at Milton, and the Red Mill Pond near Lewes. Licenses may be obtained from any justice of the peace. Non-resident, full term, $7.50; for residents the fishing license costs $1.25. No license is required to fish with hook and line in Delaware River, Delaware Bay, Atlantic Ocean, and Indian River Inlet. No license required of persons under age 16, or of women accompanied by persons who are legally fishing.

Bathing: Salt-water surf bathing at Rehoboth and Bethany Beach with life-guard protection. Lewes, Oak Orchard, and other beaches in lower Delaware offer excellent bathing facilities. In Wilmington are several large swimming pools in the public parks.

Boating: Canoeing on many tidal streams of the State, particularly Brandywine and Christina Creeks; motor-boating and sailing on the Delaware River and Bay, on Rehoboth Bay, and Indian River Bay.

Hunting and Trapping: Lower Delaware offers good gunning for rabbits, squirrels, bobwhite (quail), ducks, pheasants, and doves, which furnish the bulk of the bags, with a scattering of woodcock, snipe, rail, and geese. The last are obtained in diminishing numbers since 1935, when the Federal Law, prohibiting the use of live decoys, went into effect. Opossums and raccoons are trapped and also hunted at night with dogs. Scattered neighborhood clubs foster fox hunting. There is one officially recognized hunt, the Vicmead, near Wilmington. A number of small-game refuges have been set up throughout the State and an extensive restocking program is being carried on by the Board of Game and Fish Commissioners. Licenses for non-resident hunting-and-trapping, full term, $15.50; for resident hunting and trapping license, $2.25. Persons under age 15 may hunt without a license when accompanied by persons who are legally hunting. Persons over age 16 require a migratory bird hunting stamp when hunting ducks and geese. Stamps are issued at post offices and cost $1. *Note:* Conservation has required passage of elaborate game and fish laws and these are subject to change, so it is advisable to secure in advance detailed information (on open seasons, limits, and so on) issued without charge by the Board of Game and Fish Commissioners through the Chief Game and Fish Warden, Dover. This includes new deer hunting season. Wild turkeys and beavers cannot be killed at any time.

Trap Shooting: Several gun clubs, chiefly in New Castle County hold shoots each Saturday in the season. The Delaware Clay Target Events and the Delaware State Trapshooting Championship are important meetings that alternate between the State Clubs. Facilities for skeet shooting have been installed at many of the clubs.

Riding: Bridle paths, back roads, and open fields are used. Horses may be obtained at several riding academies, mostly near Wilmington.

Horse Races: Delaware Park, Stanton, conducts annual meets, totaling 32 days, under pari-mutuel betting system. Harness racing is a feature of the Kent and Sussex Fair at Harrington. 20-day pari-mutuel harness racing meets are held at Harrington (after the fair) and Brandywine Raceway.

Fairs: The only annual fair is the Kent and Sussex Fair, at Harrington, during a week in late July or early August.

Golf: Wilmington, Newark, Dover, and Rehoboth possess private country-club courses of 9 or 18 holes. Wilmington has a public course of 18 holes.

Tennis: While nearly all country clubs have courts, several public courts are maintained in the parks of Wilmington and permits are issued without charge. The Middle States Tennis Championship tournament is held annually at Wilmington.

Poisonous Plants, Reptiles, and Dangerous Insects: Poison-ivy common along fences and in clumps of brushwood. The copperhead is rarely seen, except in the upper part of New Castle County, where its numbers are so small as to cause little if any alarm. Potentially dangerous insects include malarial mosquito, dog tick (carrier of Rocky Mountain spotted fever), and black widow spider; this spider is very scarce, and the mosquito and tick are objects of systematic extermination. A tiny insect, known as chigger, jigger, or red bug, most often found on blackberries, is annoying but not directly dangerous.

Free Aid for Travelers: State police, both highway patrol and station personnel, are an excellent source of information for out-of-State visitors; stations are as follows: US 13 at Penny Hill (just N. of Wilmington), State Road, Dover and Bridgeville, and US 113 at Georgetown. All State policemen are trained by American Red Cross to render emergency first-aid and their stations are specially equipped for this purpose; over 30 fire houses along most traversed highways are also prepared to administer this type of public service. Information on roads, resorts, and accommodations may be secured at the office of Delaware Motor Club (AAA), 911 Tatnall Street, Wilmington; Delaware Automobile Association (AMA), 1310 Washington Street, Wilmington, and Delaware Memorial Bridge.

Calendar of Events

Note: "nfd" means *no fixed date*

Jan.	6	Sussex County	Old Christmas
	nfd	Wilmington	International Exhibition of Photography, sponsored by Delaware Camera Club
Feb.	nfd	Wilmington	Polish Day, in honor of Thaddeus Kosciusko
Mar.	24	Wilmington	Greek Independence Day
Mar.	29	State-wide	Delaware Swedish Colonial Day
Mar. or Apr.		Wilmington	Easter Sunrise Service in Rodney Square
		Cape Henlopen S. of Lewes	Easter Monday Pilgrimage to Cape Henlopen; egg rolling, games
Apr.	nfd	State-wide	Arbor and Bird Day
	nfd	New Castle	Antique Show
May	last or first Sat.	Hercules Farm Lancaster Pike	Dog Show of Wilmington Kennel Club
	whole month	State-wide	Delaware Festival of the Arts
	1st Sat.	Dover	Old Dover Day
	3rd Sat.	New Castle	A Day in Old New Castle
	nfd	Wilmington	Flower Market
	nfd	Wilmington	Garden Tour
	nfd	Wilmington	Women's Golf Tournament
	last Sat.	Stanton	Opening of Delaware Park Racing Season
	nfd	Indian River	St. George's Chapel Rogation Day

May or June	Trinity Sunday	Wilmington	Holy Trinity (Old Swedes) Church Anniversary
May or June	nfd	Longwood, Penna.	Savoy Opera Company
May	30 to Labor Day	Rehoboth	Fishing Tournaments
June	1st Sun.	Odessa	Old Drawyer's Church Anniversary
	3rd Sun.	Middletown	St. Anne's Church Anniversary
	nfd	Wilmington	St. Anthony of Padua Day, Italian Celebration
	nfd	Wilmington	State Lawn Tennis Invitation Tournament
	nfd	Milford Crossroads	Specialty Show of the Eastern Beagle Club
	nfd	Wilmington	Wilmington Country Club Invitation Golf Tournaments
	nfd	Town announced each year	Delmarva Chicken Festival
July	nfd	Rehoboth	Art Exhibition
	nfd	Rehoboth	Flower Show
	last wk.	Harrington	Kent and Sussex Fair
Aug.	last wk. 1st wk.	Longwood	Brandywiners' Opera
	nfd	Milford Crossroads	Pushmobile Derby, Sponsored by Delaware Association of Police
	nfd	Rehoboth	Cottage Tour of Art
	nfd	Georgetown	Sussex County Dairy Show
	last Sun.	Wilmington	Big Quarterly (Negro religious reunion)
	nfd	Naaman's Road	Harness Racing Meet

Sept.		Brandywine Raceway	
	Sat. before Labor Day	Arden	Arden Fair
	nfd	Harrington	Fall Harness Racing Meet
	nfd	Longwood	U. S. Marine Band Concert
	last Sun.	Frederica	Barratt's Chapel Anniversary
	nfd	Naaman's Road Brandywine Raceway	Fairfield Horse Show
Oct.	2nd Sun.	Odessa	Odessa Day
	11	Wilmington	Kazimerz Pulaski Day
	nfd	Wilmington	State Exhibition of Public and Private School Art
	nfd	Wilmington	Asbury Church Anniversary
Nov.	nfd	Wilmington	Trinity Christmas Shop
Dec.	7	State-wide	Delaware Day (anniversary of Delaware's signing of the U. S. Constitution)
	nfd	Wilmington	Civic Christmas Festivals
	nfd	Wilmington	Antique Show

Seasonal Events

Robinhood Theater—Arden. Summer stock, top Broadway hits. June-September.

New Castle Players—New Castle. June-August.

Fishing Tournaments—Rehoboth, May 30 to Labor Day.

Sailing Races—Dewey Beach, Rehoboth Bay. Weekly during summer months.

Museums

Old Town Hall. Wilmington. (Closed during August.) Silver, glass, ceramics, paintings, period furniture, maps and manuscripts.

Hagley. Early Du Pont Mills on the Brandywine. Restored as industrial museums.

Henry Francis du Pont Winterthur Museum. Arts of 18th Century America. Kennett Pike.

Delaware State Museum. Dover. Historical and contemporary.

Zwaanendael House. Lewes. Early settlement and Colonial exhibits.

Collections of Archaeological Society of Delaware are housed at the University of Delaware, Newark.

RECENT EVENTS OF INTEREST

The Sunday Star has ceased publication.

Mr. Pierre S. du Pont died, establishing by his will, foundations to carry on his Longwood Gardens and other projects in the interest of the public.

The Brick Hotel at Georgetown has been sold and is being razed for construction of an office building.

The Richardson Hotel at Dover has been torn down, not to be rebuilt.

Some Points of Interest on Tour 1, and other tours have been removed by improvements in highways, to make room for new industries.

The Tide Water Associated Oil Company has options on 4,500 acres of farm land and Delaware Rivershore just north of Delaware City for building a $100 million oil refinery.

New Castle County has extended its modern sewage disposal system to communities as distant from Wilmington as Newark.

The University of Delaware has received large gifts of money for new buildings.

Federalist Delaware, 1775–1815, by Dr. John A. Munroe, Chairman of the History Department of the University, was issued, 1954, by the Rutgers University Press—a major contribution to Delaware's history.

PART I
Delaware:
The General Background

John Moll

LITTLE DUTCH HOUSE, NEW CASTLE

Individual Aspects

DELAWARE is like a diamond, diminutive, but having within it inherent value," the Milford Bard, John Lofland, wrote in 1847. This was perhaps the origin of Delaware's popular name, the Diamond State. But it may have come from Thomas Jefferson's reference to Delaware as "a *jewel* among the States," probably because of its compact area and rich soil, certainly in tribute to the brilliance of its statesmen in his day.

One of the original thirteen Colonies and the first State—by adoption of the Constitution, December 7, 1787—Delaware is next to the smallest of the States in area. Its main landscape of farm, orchard, and tidal marsh stretches along the Delaware River and Bay, capped by hills in the north and bordered by ocean dunes in the south. For more than 300 years its inhabitants have played a significant part in the development of the nation. Swedes, Finns, Dutch, French, then English with an admixture of Scots and Irish, all, including the Negro, present from the early settlement days, and later the German, Italian, Polish, and other immigrants of the nineteenth century—all have contributed their share to the savor of local life.

Politically and in the life of the State as a whole the native Delawarean predominates. A tolerant friendly person in social relations, he may be liberal or extremely conservative in his active citizenship. The proportion of Delaware natives of native-born parentage has been decreasing as the population grows. In the rapid increase from 226,505 in 1940 to 318,015 in 1950 and a US Census Bureau estimate of 353,000 for 1953, a substantial part has been made up of newcomers from other states. These include office personnel of large corporations and employees of expanding industry. As many of the new residents join local and state-wide activities, they contribute to a cosmopolitan leaven that exists in a formerly intensely local-minded state community.

The one city in the State of more than 7,000 people, Wilmington, with 110,356 residents in 1950, is a prosperous manufacturing town, stimulated by the large home-office payrolls of big business. It stands near the head of the State, adjoined by suburban industrial and residence areas, which had, in 1950, a population of 77,000. Outside this urban area most Delaware towns are situated chiefly at the heads of navigation of tidal streams flowing east to the Delaware or west to the Chesapeake Bay.

After the Revolution, when the main routes of travel continued to turn away from the Delaware River at Wilmington or New Castle across the head of the Delaware and Chesapeake peninsula, much of the State south of the traffic routes was isolated. It remained an unspoiled rural paradise—called by some a backwash—of eighteenth century manners and customs. But the "backwash" belied its name by furnishing the greater number of statesmen, including governors.

The greatest recent contribution to transportation by the State was the opening of the $46 million Delaware Memorial Bridge in August 1951 connecting Delaware roads with those of New Jersey. This crossing of the Delaware River is linked by good Delaware and Maryland roads to the Chesapeake Bay Bridge from Maryland's Eastern Shore to Annapolis. Once more Delaware's northern county is a brief passageway in the main route of the north and south travel as it was in George Washington's time. Today, however, the State's 4,000 miles of excellent highways and improved rural roads keep every farm and hamlet connected with the main traffic ways of the Eastern States and invite the motorist to explore Delaware's three counties: New Castle, Kent and Sussex.

Each county has its individual personality in landscape, character of its towns and industries, buildings, parks and recreation areas; in crops, flora, and to some extent in climate. Fruit trees and shrubs blossom earliest in Sussex, the southern county, and in Kent two weeks earlier than in northern New Castle County. In all three counties there are notable areas of natural charm and beauty.

Since World War II, outdoor housekeeping in both urban and rural areas has greatly improved. Led by State and local departments, by public schools, garden clubs and the Delaware Roadside Council, outdoor seemliness is a goal for towns, villages and farms.

Each county has its individual problems. Recent large expansion of industry in New Castle County north of the Chesapeake and Delaware Canal has raised the question of how far desirable living conditions and human resources should be sacrificed to the drive for industrial development. The whole county has less than half the area of Sussex and outside Wilmington's town limits, has more than twice the number of people in the two counties. Including Wilmington, New Castle County has more than two-thirds of the population of the State. Controlling land use to preserve and protect residential, farm, and recreation areas in sufficient proportion to the industrialized districts is now a critical need in New Castle County.

The reactivation and huge expansion of a military air base in Kent

County near Dover, the Capital of the State, with thousands of military and civilian personnel, creates serious problems at the capital and in this small rural county. Among them is the danger that in the service of the base, unsuitable and misplaced housing, mercantile, and commercial-recreation projects may run ahead of an orderly development of these facilities. If the economic benefits from millions in military payrolls, local purchasing and rentals, can be enjoyed while maintaining the county's present attractive living advantages, Kent County will be of nation-wide importance.

Sussex County has a broad agricultural extent, its towns few and small, its leading industries on its borders east and west. The county needs and is acquiring small manufacturing plants to provide more employment for people of the towns. Its greatest need is zoning and a more vigorous conservation to keep unspoiled its streams, lakes, forests, road environment and its bay and ocean shore resorts.

As far back as today's oldest native can remember, an idea has been current that Delaware because of small size and natural and economic advantages could become the model state of the USA. The blueprints for its future, variously conceived, have always included corrections of governmental forms and operation and of land use; conserving natural resources, banishing menaces to health and morals, providing a decent home in wholesome environment for every family, constantly improving educational opportunities for children and adults, parks and open country of easy access to all the people; multiple well-maintained modes of transportation. And basic, of course, agricultural, business, and industrial soundness to insure well-paid jobs and adequate return on investment and operation. In short, the goal of humanitarians in every state.

Advocates of effective planning, immediate and long-range, and of co-ordinating constructive programs—as primary toward achieving a model state—have always been balked by inertia of many in favor as well as by strong opponents of any state-wide, state-financed planning. Meanwhile, notable among the achievements in separate programs is Delaware's rank near the top in public education, health, transportation advance, agricultural and industrial prosperity and employment opportunities. The State also authorizes cities and towns to zone, plan, and redevelop; combats soil erosion, water pollution; protects wild life; enables counties to adopt zoning codes and provide parks and recreation facilities with power of eminent domain.

With these and other advances, over-all planning and co-ordinating of programs remains essential to save unspoiled, and where necessary redevelop, Delaware's space for adequate living "from the hills of New Castle to the sands of Sussex."

Natural Setting

THERE existed as early as the year 1616 an illustrated essay upon Delaware geography, climate, and resources—the report of the Dutch navigator, Cornelis Hendricksen, to the High and Mighty Lords States General of the Free, United Netherlands Provinces. Captain Hendricksen had explored the Delaware in the first ship built by the Dutch in American waters, the *Restless,* had rescued from the Indians three Dutchmen, probably the first white men on Delaware soil, and had drawn a figurative map of the river with its tributaries. His report, illustrated by the map, is part of the pleasant source material of Delaware's earliest history. The "essay" is as follows:

"First, he hath discovered for his aforesaid Masters and Directors, certain lands, a bay and three rivers situate between 38 and 40 degrees.

"And did there trade with the Inhabitants; said trade consisting of Sables, Furs, Robes and other skins.

"He hath found the said Country full of trees, to wit: Oaks, hickory and pines; which trees were, in some places covered with vines.

"He hath seen, in the said country, Bucks and does, turkeys and partridges.

"He hath found the climate of the said Country very temperate, judging it to be as temperate as that of this country Holland.

"He also traded for, and bought from the inhabitants, the Minquas, three persons being people belonging to this Company; which three persons were employed in the service of the Mohawks and Mochicans; giving for them kettles, beads and merchandise."

Geography and Climate

The changing boundaries of the State of Delaware, now firmly drawn upon the map of the Chesapeake and Delaware Peninsula, could be represented by a series of tentative, more or less parallel lines, so drawn as to indicate a continuous shift between the opposing forces until the controversy subsided and left the lines in their present location. This uncer-

SUSSEX DUNE

tainty over boundaries goes back to the days of King James I of England, when the reports of English navigators and explorers were eloquent as to the noble beauty and economic prospects of the land and the watercourses of this region, but extremely vague as to geographic facts.

To the London Company for Virginia, to Lord Baltimore for Maryland, and to William Penn for Pennsylvania, King James and his successors gave overlapping grants of territory; and meanwhile the Delaware River region was claimed and settled by the Dutch and the Swedes as the "South River of New Netherland" and "New Sweden's River." The Dutch held the land against English claims until the dispute was well joined among the English claimants. This dispute with its intermittent sharp skirmishes affected the lives and fortunes of the settlers, leading to a separate colony, and then a separate State—one of the original thirteen. All these combats are significantly and inextricably a part of Delaware's whole history to the present day. As recently as February 4, 1934, as the outcome of a New Jersey-Delaware suit concerning fishing rights, the United States Supreme Court confirmed Delaware's control of the bed of the Delaware River to the mean low-water mark on the New Jersey side, within the "twelve-mile circle" about New Castle. The circle was originally surveyed in 1701 to define the extent of a grant to William Penn by the Duke of York, made in 1682.

Delaware is bounded on the north by Pennsylvania, on the east by the Delaware River and Bay to Cape Henlopen and from the cape south by the Atlantic to latitude 38 degrees and 27 minutes; and on the south and west by Maryland. The southern boundary was first surveyed by John Watson; the western boundary and one of the lines contributing to the northern boundary, by Mason and Dixon. The greatest length of Delaware is 110 miles, its greatest width is 35 miles, and its narrowest width is 9 to 10 miles. The land area is 1,965 square miles out of an approximate total area of 2,370.

The greater part of Delaware is almost level country, of sandy soil, in some places well forested. From the Christina Creek northward, it rises to the Piedmont Plateau and the foothills of southeastern Pennsylvania. The highest elevation in the State, 438 feet, occurs in this region at Centreville. Most of the land is under individual homestead cultivation or in estates with protected woodlands. South of the hilly section, the remainder of the State lies in the Atlantic Coastal Plain. Throughout this area, the elevation seldom rises to 60 feet above sea level; the soils are fertile and with cultivation yield an abundance of grain, vegetables, and fruits.

OLD FORD OF BRANDYWINE, WILMINGTON

The Delaware watershed, a slight ridge along the western boundary, turns in a southeasterly direction below the center of the State. The Appoquinimink, Smyrna (formerly Duck Creek), St. Jones, and Mispillion Rivers, each navigable for a considerable part of its course, empty into the Delaware River and Bay. On the west side of the watershed, the largest Chesapeake tributary is the Nanticoke River, fed by streams rising below the center of the State and flowing southwest across the Maryland boundary to the Chesapeake.

Rehoboth and Indian River Bays are shallow lagoons that lie behind the narrow and sandy coastal barrier along the sea, in the southeast corner of the State. A third lagoon, an arm of Assawoman Bay, extends west of Fenwick Island in the extreme south. This island, a strip of high dunes partly wooded, was called the "false cape" in the boundary disputes because from the sea it resembled a cape. Throughout the State are more than 50 fresh-water lakes and ponds and numerous abandoned mill sites where the restoration of dams would provide recreational facilities.

The waters of the Brandywine and Christina Rivers have been greatly diminished by the diversion of springs and the cutting of forests. With their tributaries these main streams converge from the arc of the boundary toward Wilmington, where their juncture provides a commodious harbor for that city. Other good harbors along the marshy coast are at New Castle and Lewes, the latter protected by the Delaware Breakwater.

The climate of the State represents an escape from the rigors of the north and the languor of the south, although it shares the excessive humidity of the Middle Atlantic Coast region in July and August. In northern Delaware the mean annual temperature is 52°F; the mean temperature in February is 31° and in July 73°. In southern Delaware the corresponding mean temperatures are from three to four degrees warmer. The extremes of cold and heat range from —5° to 102°. Spring frosts usually end April 1, but may run to the end of the month, while the first fall frost does not arrive until after October 10. The crop season, taken as the average period between killing frosts, ranges from the latter part of April to the middle of October, varying from 175 days in the north to 187 days in southeastern Sussex.

The rainfall is abundant and the average annual precipitation of 43 to 45 inches is uniform to a remarkable degree throughout the State, being least in late autumn and early winter. Occasionally, the average rainfall for a month arrives in one day.

The prevailing winds in winter come from the north and west, in summer from the south and southeast. Wind velocities seldom rise high enough to cause damage to crops and property; tornadoes and earthquakes are practically unknown.

The greater part of Delaware—the part lying within the Coastal Plain —is underlain by Cretaceous and Tertiary sediments that are covered to an average depth of 25 feet by unconsolidated Pleistocene sand and gravel. Exposures of these older sediments are rare. The northern part of the State—the Piedmont region—is composed of pre-Cambrian rocks on which are patches of coarse red sand and gravel of Pliocene age.

Kaolin, quartz, feldspar, mica, and the locally famous Brandywine blue granite are found in commercial quantites in the north. Iron has been mined at Chestnut and Iron Hills. Many choice specimens of garnet, tourmaline, and amethyst have attracted collectors to the region.

Cretaceous formations and clays important in terra cotta manufacture occur just to the south. The soil here is principally clay mixed with loam. Farther south are Tertiary white and blue clays underlying a sandy soil.

The outstanding reminder of past ages is the Great Pocomoke Swamp, an area of 30,000 acres that lies for the most part in Delaware and extends over Delaware's south boundary into Maryland *(see Tour 15)*.

FOREST NEAR TRAPPE POND

Flora

The location of Delaware on the Atlantic Coast midway between the zones of the north and the south, its position in a narrow peninsula between two great bays of the Atlantic Ocean, and the abundance of its watercourses, all account for the luxuriant vegetation described in the journals of early explorers and travelers. Trees of unusual height—pine, oak, walnut, hickory, and yellow poplar predominating—covered the whole mainland. A younger and richly varied growth bordered the shore marshes where Indians had burned off the woodland for hunting and planting. The hardwood forests, now mostly cleared of trees of ripe age, comprised much of the State's wealth before manufacturing developed. The virgin white oak, so esteemed for shipbuilding that lumbermen nearly exterminated it, now receives protection throughout the State, especially for the finest and oldest specimens, and is found frequently in present woodlands. Red, black, and pin oak, hickory, sycamore, walnut, tulip (yellow poplar), beech, sweet gum, maples, ash, and young chestnut are all common species.

The remains of the Brandywine Forest, chiefly bordering on the Brandywine Creek in the northern part of the State, contain hardwood growths that have been little cut during the past 50 years. Trees in the Ellendale Tract in the southern part of the State (not to be confused with the 40-acre State Forest of the same name), an area 16 miles square, vary from pine, or mixed pine and oak, to pure hardwood. A rectangle four miles square, south of Ellendale, shows less than 20 percent cleared. The Great Poco-moke Swamp section below Georgetown coincides with the northern limit of the bald cypress in the United States. All these areas, in the main, are covered with second-growth timber. Forest growth is rapid except in the extreme north, and trees reach merchantable size at an early period.

The presence of bald cypress *(Taxodium distichum)* and the occurrence of such plant forms as the muscadine grape *(Vitis rotundifolia)* and the sweet-leaf *(Symplococos tinctoria)* indicate the marked admixture of Southern (Lower Austral) forms in lower Delaware. Distinctly Northern species of plant life occur less frequently in the Piedmont Plateau area, which has flora essentially the same as that of southeastern Pennsylvania. The persimmon tree is common, along with wild cherry, beach plum, white dogwood, shadbush, sassafras, and laurel. The native walking fern and the blue-fringed gentian are now protected. The trailing arbutus, a native, has been almost extirpated.

Delaware has become a happy hunting ground for naturalists who seek rare plant forms and know how to protect their finds. The site of a single specimen of box huckleberry, for example, was known a dozen years ago to a number of naturalists and botanists, and a new station has been more recently discovered. Outside of this small group, probably few persons, eager to see what the box huckleberry looks like, have been able to find it. A favorite trek among local and visiting naturalists is made in May to the little known haunts of the "swamp-pink" (helonias), plentiful in isolated districts, chiefly in Sussex County. In fall and winter naturalists who know their location visit the few uncut holly trees, ancient in growth and of great size.

An account of unusual Delaware flora and conditions by Dr. John K. Small, Head Curator of the Museums for the New York Botanical Garden, is published in the *Journal of the New York Botanical Garden,* March 1929. The abundance of bloom in the summer months is especially noted by Dr. Small: open swamps that are showy flower gardens, high pinelands with several varieties of goldenrod coming into flower, ponds where water-lilies, spatterdocks, and floating-heart cover the surface—the edges surrounded with pickerel-weed and arrowhead. Other plants noted on this brief visit were three kinds of meadow-beauties, six of milkwort or candyroot, four kinds of orchids, the yellow foxglove, the turk's cap lily, and many asters; and of fruited plants, three kinds of blueberry and three of huckleberry—not including the box huckleberry. Among outstanding plants is the seaside-alder representing a vanishing type.

To the south, the tree range includes loblolly and spruce pines, oaks, maples, sweet and black gums, yellow poplar, and holly; the last named is commercially important. Magnolia, bristly sarsaparilla, spikenard (Aralia), sweet pepper bush (Clethra), high bush huckleberry, and cranberries (Vaccinium) are discovered in the undergrowth. In the sand bar land, the pitch and pond pine flourish, along with the willow and blackjack oak, the beach plum, red cedar, and wax myrtle. In swamp land, white cedar *(Chamaecyparis thoides)* predominates. Characteristic of the swamps are the sphagnum or peatmosses, the swamp magnolia, and the pink ladyslipper, or Noah's Ark. Somewhat rare orchids also exist in the swamp. Mistletoe is found throughout the State, but has been scarce in recent years.

One large bed of the American lotus *(Nelumbo lutea)* along the St. Jones River. near Dover, produces thousands of the huge blossoms each summer.

Fauna

The same favorable geographic conditions that gave the Delaware territory a varied and luxuriant flora also made the peninsula a special haven for wild life. The abundance of wild fowl and fish, with quantities of edible fruits growing near bodies of water, simplified the living problem of the first settlers. Wild life was ruthlessly slaughtered. The forests, cleared at first for planting, suffered from continuous cutting and the inroads of forest fires.

The beaver and larger mammals, like the black bear, the panther, the wildcat, and the wolf, have been extinct for a century or more. More persistent are the fox (red and gray), otter, mink, and muskrat, the last named being of commercial importance. The chipmunk and mole abound in northern districts. Deer, long missing from Delaware and surrounding territory, are now occasionally seen, and several families of beaver, recently imported, are increasing.

The State lies in the path of the annual migrations of wild birds and offers conditions favorable for residence. Such familiar birds as the robin, wood thrush, cardinal, catbird, wren, flicker, oriole (both orchard and Baltimore), purple grackle and redwing, brown thrush, meadow lark, and many others are abundant. An unusual feature is the habitual nesting in

Delaware, above their usual northern limit, of the prothonotary warbler, the yellow-throated warbler, and the summer tanager. Bald eagles, several colonies of the great blue heron, and large numbers of snowy egrets are found in Delaware. Black ducks, blue-wing teal, and wood ducks nest in the State. The turkey buzzard is seen the year around, and the black vulture of the South has been recorded more than once. Brown pelicans have been seen on Rehoboth Bay.

The ruby-throated humming-bird is to be found in all sections, coming even into the city gardens of Wilmington. The tufted titmouse, the Carolina wren, white-throated sparrow, nuthatch, downy and hairy woodpeckers, junco, winter wren, purple finch, chickadee, cardinal, and blue jay spend the winter and feed from window trays in suburban districts.

The reed and rail-birds, quail, woodcock, snipe, owls, hawks, and sandpipers abound in special localities. All the usual coastal plain and seashore species are present, in addition to the numerous migrants that follow the Delaware Valley and the Atlantic Coast on their lines of travel.

Among Delaware reptiles are the spreadhead (hog nose), a brown snake that puffs its head out when cornered, the pine snake, and the copperhead. The latter is classified as the only venomous snake, and is deservedly given a wide berth. There are no rattlers. The once abundant diamond-back terrapin is now rare. Snapping turtles inhabit every swamp.

Recent unofficial surveys of fish in Delaware waters indicate that as many species exist now as in former days. Among them are the shad, sturgeon, bass, pike, trout, catfish, eel, drumfish, and many others, in both the fresh-water and salt-water categories. Crabs (hard and soft shelled), oysters, and clams are of increasing importance commercially.

The Society of Natural History of Delaware has a large collection of specimens of Delaware wildlife including 30,000 of Delaware flora. The collection is in storage (1953) awaiting new permanent museum quarters. The Society meets once a month at Wilmington Public Library.

Conservation

After many years of waste and destruction of its natural resources, Delaware is belatedly protecting and conserving its wild life as well as the habitat of this life, the forests, lakes, marshes, and rivers of the State.

The State Forestry Department was created in 1927 upon the initiative of the late Coleman du Pont, who gave the first tract and for several years provided the services of a State forester. The department has jurisdiction of all matters pertaining to forestry and woodlands in Delaware. Its pro-

DAM AT TRAPPE POND
Credit: Waller Studio, Laurel

gram includes forestry education, roadside demonstration plots, distribution of forest—planting stock at nominal cost to landowners, and experiments in tree planting and growing. To encourage the planting and maintenance of trees to serve as windbreaks and shelterbelts in denuded areas, all reforested lands of five acres or more (maintained under the supervision of the State Forestry Department) are exempted from taxation for a period of thirty years.

In 1934, the Redden State Forest was secured by the department. This tract of 2,820 acres of forest land near Redden is Delaware's principal State forest. The State Forest Tree Nursery (four acres) near Milford was purchased in 1928 and is devoted to the production of forest planting stock. The Appenzeller Tract (45 acres), extending along both sides of the Du Pont Highway between the State Nursery and Ellendale Crossroads, has been utilized as an experimental and demonstration forest since its acquisition by Coleman du Pont's gift, 1928. In 1930 Mrs. Coleman du Pont gave a small tract in New Castle County. Since then Blackbird Forest in this County, 676 acres, has been created. In Sussex County are Owens Forest, 170 acres and Ellendale Forest, 993 acres, originally 40 acres turned over to the State Forestry Department by the State Highway Department for maintenance and operation. A public camp site and picnic area fronting on the Du Pont Highway is maintained here.

All State forest tracts are game sanctuaries. Improvements begun in the 1930's by the Civilian Conservation Corps under the direction of the State forester have been very greatly extended. Fire control is basic in the State Forestry Department's work. After a series of disastrous forest fires in the southern part of the State (38,000 acres burnt over in 1930), the General Assembly in 1931 passed forest protection laws, and established a modern organization and system of fire control. A corps of forest fire wardens is maintained, and five steel observation towers have been erected in Kent and Sussex Counties.

Wild life resources in the State are protected and augmented by the State Board of Game and Fish Commissioners, which was created in 1911. An act of the 1935 Assembly extended the powers of the commission and stipulated that 25 percent of its income be spent for game birds, animals, and fish for restocking purposes. Under this policy, pheasants, quail, partridges, and rabbits are released throughout the State; and the streams, lakes, and ponds are being stocked with game fish.

By a new game management plan (1936), absolute game refuges have been established by the commission on many farms scattered through the State. Land unsuitable for agricultural purposes is set aside and stocked with game. The owners are compensated for the use of the land, and are paid for planting feed patches and protecting wild life. Resident owners or tenants of these farm game preserves are commissioned deputy game wardens to protect the refuges.

During the Federal public works program, various conservation projects in the State had been inaugurated. Swamps in Sussex County have been drained to reclaim the flooded areas, preserve the standing timber, and lessen mosquito breeding. Under the supervision of the Delaware soil erosion commission and the mosquito control division of the State Highway Department effective work continues.

In 1936, the Land Utilization Division of the Resettlement Administration began the purchase of marginal and sub-marginal land in Kent and Sussex Counties, in order to release farmers stranded on the soil, and for purposes of reforestation, game and game food preservation, and recreation. The total acreage secured was 4,800 acres; the owners moved voluntarily. Three sites: Petersburg tract in Kent County, Trappe Pond and Assawoman sites in Sussex County have been leased to State agencies for maintenance and development as recreation areas (pp. 354, 512, 514).

The United States Biological Survey in 1937 purchased 14,000 acres of marsh and upland on the Delaware Bay east of Leipsic, and established the Bombay Hook Migratory Wild Fowl Preserve. The chief importance of this refuge, on the eastern "flyway" used by migratory wildfowl, is as a feeding ground and resting area for wild ducks and geese. The confirmation of Delaware's possession of the Delaware River bed within a twelve-mile radius from New Castle, brings within Delaware borders the large pool of the 1,400-acre United States Killcohook Migratory Bird Refuge, near the Fort Mott Military Reservation, Salem County, New Jersey.

By the terms of a general order against hunting, the State Rifle Range —300 acres of meadow and marshland along the Delaware River below New Castle—was made into a game refuge.

Ponds for fish hatcheries for the Delaware Fish and Game Commission have been constructed at Moore's Lake, two miles south of Dover, in the center of the Delaware fishing country. Game animals, English pheasants, black bass, and other birds and fish are distributed by the State Board of Fish and Game Commissioners.

Delaware is a member of the Interstate Commission on the Delaware Basin, formed in 1936 to abate and prevent the pollution of the Delaware River and to conserve and develop the natural resources of its watershed for the common advantage of the participating States—Delaware, Pennsylvania, New York, and New Jersey. Through this agency, known as INCODEL, reciprocal legislation has been secured in the several states providing treatment of wastes discharged into the Delaware. More far-reaching legislation is being sought and a comprehensive program of soil and forest conservation is making progress.

The Brandywine Valley Association, an organization of Delaware and Pennsylvania citizens working toward protection and improvement of natural resources in the watershed of the historic Brandywine River, has achieved remarkable success in freeing the stream from industrial waste, in soil conservation and restoring the recreational value of the Brandywine region.

The Red Clay Valley Association is undertaking a similar program for Red Clay Creek.

State agencies engaged (1953) in new or extended programs of conservation are the commissions on Soil Conservation, Water Pollution, Forestry, Game and Fish, Parks, Geological Survey, and the University of Delaware, whose programs include Agricultural Extension work in conservation, Conservation Workshops for teachers, and a Marine Laboratory at Lewes.

History

Backgrounds and Beginnings

RECORDED local history begins in 1609, on August 28, when Henry Hudson, an English navigator in the employ of the Dutch East India Company, discovered the present Delaware Bay and River. Sailing the *Half Moon* in search of a northwest passage to China and the Indies, he arrived off the coast of present Sussex County and "came to a point of land," now Cape Henlopen. Finding the bay shallow and having no small boat to take soundings ahead of him, Hudson departed and discovered farther north the river afterward named for him. This the Dutch called the North River, and the Delaware the South River. One year, lacking one day, after Hudson's visit, Captain Samuel Argall of the new English Colony of Virginia, sailing the pinnace *Discovery*, came to the entrance of the bay, and named the "point of land" Cape La Warre, for Lord de la Warre, Sir Thomas West, Governor of Virginia. Subsequently the English used this name for both bay and river, and finally for the land along their western shores.

Between 1614 and 1620 Dutch ships commanded by resourceful skippers explored the South River. Among these were Captain Cornelis Hendricksen in the *Onrust (Restless)*, built at Block Island in 1614, and Captain Cornelis Jacobsen May, of Hoorn, in the *Blyde Boodschap (Glad Tidings)*. In 1621, the Dutch West India Company was formed as the result of long effort on the part of William Usselinx, Dutch citizen, who advocated a program of permanent colonization. The company had plenary powers that practically made it an extension of the government itself, except the one of declaring war. Within three years the trading post at Fort Amsterdam (New York) on the North River had more than two hundred people, and a trading post, Fort Nassau, had been established on the South River near the site of Gloucester, New Jersey.

Urged by influential members, the West India Company in 1629 adopted a charter of freedoms and exemptions which gave the powers of feudal lords to patroons who would take up, settle, and cultivate tracts of land

John Moll

DAVID PIETERSEN DE VRIES OF HOORN

within New Netherland. In the interlocking directorates formed under it, each of the patroons became chief patroon in his own district, his associates having lesser shares of investment and correspondingly of profits. That year Samuel Godyn, president of the Amsterdam Chamber of the Company, sent Giles Hosset and Jacob Jansen as agents to buy land from the Indians. As chief of the South River patroons, Godyn chose land along the west shore from Cape Henlopen to Bombay Hook and formed a company that included Samuel Blommaert and Kiliaen Van Rensselaer. The purchase—the first within the limits of Delaware—was registered at Fort Amsterdam by Peter Minuit, July 15, 1630.

To secure the services of the experienced navigator, David Pietersen de Vries, of Hoorn, the patroons made terms of partnership with him and turned over to him the establishing of a whaling colony as their first bid to fortune on the South River. De Vries's ship, the *Walvis (Whale)* "of 150 lasts," sent out under command of Captain Peter Heyes, arrived near the site of Lewes on Lewes Creek in the spring of 1631, with twenty-eight men, whaling implements, cattle, and a large stock of supplies. The ship's ballast was building materials, "lime, brick, tiles, etc.," to be used in the construction of a large combination dwelling and storehouse within a stockade. The settlement was named Swanendael; the creek, Blommaert's Kill; and the bay, Godyn's Bay *(see LEWES)*. Giles Hosset and four others came from the North River to join the colonists. After the fields had been prepared and planted, Captain Heyes returned to Holland, leaving Hosset as commissary in charge of the settlement.

Early in 1632 Captain de Vries was ready to sail from Holland with a second expedition when Peter Minuit, returning to Holland, brought news to him that the colony on the South River had been massacred by Indians. De Vries sailed in the *Walvis* accompanied by a yacht, the *Squirrel,* and after spending some time in the West Indies reached the Delaware in December. There he found the settlers' house burnt and their bones, with those of their cattle, scattered over the fields. From the Indians he learned that one of their chiefs had taken from a post near the shore a tin coat-of-arms of Holland to make himself pipes; out of Giles Hosset's stupid handling of this incident, and possibly other misunderstandings, had come the savages' revenge. Competition between the traders of the Dutch West India Company and Hosset, as agent for the patroons, for the rich fur trade may well have been a cause of trouble with the Indians. Disagreement between the company and the patroons as to their respective rights at Swanendael continued until 1635, when the Dutch West India Company bought the land from the patroons for 16,500 guilders ($6,240).

Before de Vries left the river in 1633, he made friends with the Indians in the Delaware territory. These were of Algonkian stock, the Lenni-Lenape ("original people"). By other Indians they were called "Grand-fathers" out of respect for the tradition of their long descent from ances-tors who had emigrated from the far West. Of their several tribes the Unalachtigo, whose totem was the turkey, were found throughout Dela-ware territory, a few of the Unamis or Turtle tribe in the hilly region to the north. The Lenni-Lenapes were friendly and peaceful people, engaged in agriculture, hunting, and fishing. At the time of the first white settle-ments they were comparatively few in number, though the many village sites along most of the streams indicate previous and long-continued habitation by larger numbers. The Minquas Indians, from whom the Christina Creek took its original name, were of different stock, using the Iroquois language, a more warlike group living north of the Lehigh River in Pennsylvania and in the Susquehanna country. They came to the Delaware River to trade, and from them the white settlers obtained the largest and most valuable stocks of furs. The Nanticokes in the southwest part of the State were related to the Lenni-Lenape.

Subsequent to the Swanendael tragedy, there seems to have been another clash between traders and Indians, which gave rise to the name Murder-kill for a creek in middle Delaware. All other relations were friendly, and the Swedes, who arrived on the river five years after de Vries's first visit, became to the Indians a special people, beloved and befriended.

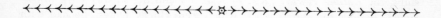

New Sweden

As the controlling directors of the Dutch West India Company showed a determination to play for immediate profits at the expense of permanent colonization in New Netherland, William Usselinx (who had first sug-gested founding the company) withdrew in 1624 and offered his services to Sweden. King Gustavus Adolphus, the outstanding ruler of his day, be-came deeply interested in promoting colonies for the advance of civiliza-tion in the New World as well as for profit. The Swedish South Company was formed in 1626–27, but, owing at first to the king's preoccupations with the Thirty Years' War in Europe and then to his death in 1632, no expedition was prepared.

By 1637 the work of Usselinx bore fruit in the New Sweden Company, supported by the Swedish Government through Chancellor Axel Oxenstierna (able regent during the young Queen Christina's minority) and Oxenstierna's assistant, Clas Fleming. Two Dutch citizens, Samuel Blommaert (formerly of the Swanendael company) and Peter Spiring (who had entered Swedish service), aided the plans for an expedition by raising half the money in Holland. Peter Minuit had offered his services to Blommaert in 1635, and from their common knowledge of the New World and common disgust with the controlling directors of the Dutch West India Company had come the proposal, ascribed to Minuit, of a Swedish-Dutch rival to that company. Minuit was engaged as Director of the first Swedish expedition, the preparations being kept secret in Holland until near the date of sailing.

The Minquas Kill (the Christina, flowing into the Delaware at Wilmington) was the intended site of the Colony, if conditions upon arrival permitted. The claim of Sweden to this territory was to be based upon valid purchase from the Indians as against the claim of Holland by right of Hudson's discovery. To avoid the Dutch West India Company's recently bought land extending from Cape Henlopen to Bombay Hook, Minuit was instructed to buy from the Minquas Kill to Sankikan (the Falls at Trenton). The purchase actually made by Minuit was from Bombay Hook to the Schuylkill.

In December 1637 Minuit set sail from Gothenburg with two Swedish ships, the *Kalmar Nyckel (Key of Kalmar)* and the smaller *Grip (Bird-Grip)*. Besides the ships' crews, which were chiefly Dutch, he had with him 22 Swedish and Dutch soldiers to man a fort and cultivate some land until a second expedition should arrive; he brought supplies for the Colony and for trade with the Indians and also a cargo of wines to be sold in the West Indies. Måns Nillson Kling was in charge of the soldiers, and Hendrick Huygen, a relative of Minuit, was commissary.

Early in March 1638 the ships arrived at Jamestown, Virginia, where Minuit made a ten-day stop "to refresh with wood and water." Jerome Hawley, Treasurer of the Virginia Colony, in writing to London, mentioned this visit. A second stop was made at "Paradise" in Delaware Bay, either at the site of Swanendael (Lewes) or further north. On the map (1654–55) of the Swedish engineer Peter Lindeström, the whole region in the neighborhood of Lewes is marked Paradijset (Paradise) and

G. Allen Pierce

KALMAR NYCKEL (KEY OF KALMAR)

a point south of the Murderkill, Paradijsudden (Paradise Point). Within a day or two of his arrival on the Minquas Kill late in March, Minuit secured a deed from the Indian chiefs, executed on board the *Kalmar Nyckel* and dated March 29 (probably Old Style, which would be April 8, New Style). It was signed by five chiefs, and by Minuit and his officers. A fort was built and named Christina for the young Queen of Sweden; and the *Grip* was dispatched to Virginia to trade. The Minquas Kill was first called the Elbe, but this name soon disappeared and Christina Kill took its place. Minuit sent the *Grip* upon a second trading expedition while he assembled a cargo of furs at the fort to take back to Sweden. He left the Colony in June, bound for the island of St. Christopher in the West Indies to trade his cargo of wine. There he visited a Dutch ship, which was blown out of the harbor in a storm during Minuit's visit and lost with all aboard. The *Kalmar Nyckel* returned to Sweden with Minuit's papers and reports (now lost).

Following a second expedition in 1640 in charge of Peter Hollander Ridder, the Swedish Government bought the shares of the Dutch investors in the New Sweden Company and satisfied all Dutch claims. But Dutch citizens in Swedish service, especially Samuel Blommaert, continued to assist in colonization. Governor Ridder (in Swedish service for some years) brought with him a few colonists, a new commissary, Joost van Langdonk, an assistant commissioner, Gregorius Van Dyck, and a Lutheran clergyman, Reorus Torkillus, the first of that faith to serve in America.

Fifty Dutch settlers from Utrecht arrived in the fall of 1640 in charge of Joost Van Bogaert under Swedish auspices; and in October 1641 the *Kalmar Nyckel* and the *Charitas* brought the first expedition of colonists qualified to create a self-reliant community. There were Swedish soldiers to serve as unskilled workers as well as guards; some Finns, who had deserted from the army or who had cut down trees against orders, but who came with wives and children and made good colonists; and there were farm laborers and skilled workmen—a bookkeeper, a tailor, a millwright, and a blacksmith (some of whom brought their families); and the preacher, H. Christoffer. Besides these, Gustaf Strahl, a young nobleman, was permitted by the Royal Admiral to sail for experience to the New World, and with him came the son of the mayor of a Swedish town, also bent upon adventure, and several youths of humbler family, one a baker's son. Måns Kling returned as lieutenant with wife, child, and maid.

Cattle, horses, sheep, and goats, and supplies of grain, implements, building materials, and small wares were unloaded from the two ships; new houses were put up and Ridder built a church at the fort during the year.

Reports of English encroachment—a settlement at Varkens Kill (Salem) across the river, and the attempted establishment of a trading-post on the Schuylkill—were sent to Sweden by Governor Ridder with the returning ships. The Swedish Council of State thereupon authorized a new expedition to reinforce the Colony. It was February 1643, however, before the sails of the *Swan* and the *Fama* were descried on the river. The ships brought a new governor in the commanding figure of Johan Printz, a former cavalry major of the Swedish Army, schooled in strategy on the battlefields of the Thirty Years' War. The Indians called him "the big tub" and he grew in size with the years, but the size of his person proved to be but a trifling symbol of the power and energy with which he defied and outwitted man and elements to bring the Colony through its testing period —years of neglect by the Government and friends at home. With him came his family, soldiers, servants, settlers, and the Reverend John Campanius.

The new Governor brought his own horses, doubtless "of brave size" like himself; brought, and added to by purchase from New Amsterdam, a larger supply of live stock than had yet come to the Colony, with feed to carry them through the winter; food for the settlers in substantial quantity; household equipment, clothing, and many packages of small articles needed by each settler. He had filled every crevice of the two ships with oranges and lemons during a stop at the West Indies.

Governor Ridder had bought from the Indians all the land on the western shore of the Delaware (including the Dutch West India Company's tract) from present Cape Henlopen to Trenton and on the east side from Raccoon Creek to Cape May. Adopting a suggestion of Ridder's, Printz built Fort Elfsborg on the New Jersey side below the mouth of the Varkens Kill, to control the trade and traffic of the Delaware.

Printz chose for his place of residence, where he built also a third fort, a location up the river at Tinicum Island (Essington), Pennsylvania, "about 3 Swedish miles from Fort Christina." At Upland (on Chester Creek, Pennsylvania), a blockhouse was built to protect the few settlers there and to make the site attractive to others.

Only two small expeditions, with few colonists and insufficient supplies, arrived during the time of Governor Printz. With no other help he so organized New Sweden as to maintain Sweden's control of the river territory for ten years against increasing intrusion of the English and the aggression of the Dutch. He built mills, houses, boats, wharfs, and trading-posts and encouraged all the industries of which the colonists were capable —cooperage, brewing, baking, weaving. But there were not enough colonists, cattle, or equipment, and especially not enough skilled workmen and artisans, to produce a comfortable surplus for the company's trade. Printz competed with English and Dutch in the Indian market and in lean years was forced to pay double to the English for essential supplies to sustain the Colony. Many of the colonists, feeling themselves cut off from Sweden and resenting the increasingly harsh regime into which the harassed Governor was forced, deserted the Colony to accept easier conditions under the Dutch or English.

Sweden's affairs at home demanded the close attention of her ablest ministers; the Queen was absorbed in the costly brilliance of her court, Blommaert had left Swedish service, Clas Fleming was dead. Although Printz's reports and appeals had led to the preparation in the early summer of 1649 of an additional expedition, the *Katt* on which it sailed was wrecked in the West Indies, and neither colonists nor supplies reached the Delaware.

Printz's weakness of defense was well known at Manhattan (New Amsterdam) to the able Peter Stuyvesant, Governor of New Netherland.

With men, money, and ships at his disposal and a larger and better fortified Colony behind him, Stuyvesant, in the summer of 1651, having secured from the Indians a deed for the land they had previously sold to Minuit and again to Ridder, sailed his fleet "drumming and cannonading" up and down the South River past the Swedish forts. Knowing that Printz had too little ammunition to provoke hostilities, he erected a fort at Sand Hook (New Castle), six miles down the river to control the traffic in the interest of the Dutch. He named it Fort Casimir in honor of Count Ernest Casimir of Nassau, for whom Fort Nassau had been named, moved to this new fort the Dutch soldiers and their families from Fort Nassau (site of Gloucester, N.J.) and abandoned that fort.

Printz made vigorous written protest to Stuyvesant and sent to Sweden urgent appeals to the Crown for the protection of the American Colony. Finally, early in 1653 he sent his son by an English ship to make a stronger plea, and hearing nothing, went himself at the end of the year, leaving the Colony in charge of his son-in-law, Johan Papegoja. By the time Printz arrived in Europe assistance for him had been arranged; a cargo, settlers, and an assistant governor, Johan Classon Rising, set sail in the ship *Orn (Eagle)* about February 10, 1654.

News of the arrival of Printz in Europe was not unexpected, and Rising had instructions, in case the Colony and lands had been taken by others, to get them back by peaceful means if possible, but if not to settle and fortify another place on the South River, or even to settle in Florida. Rising's ship was crowded with colonists and the *Gyllene Haj (Golden Shark)* was to follow with more; he had supplies and money and credit; so, although his instructions warned against hostilities, he came to anchor before Fort Casimir on Trinity Sunday, May 21, 1654, and demanded surrender under threat of his guns. As the little fort was entirely unprepared for defense, he won without bloodshed. Rising then manned the Fort, which he named Fort Trefaldighet (Fort Trinity), left Captain Sven Skute in charge, and sailed up the river to Christina.

Rising was well qualified by education and experience for his post as assistant governor. He was secretary of the Swedish Commercial College, had made commercial and economic studies at home and abroad, and had been knighted for his services. With him was an engineer of the caliber Governor Printz had long asked for, the "noble and well born Per Martensson Lindeström," whose *Geography of America,* translated by Dr. Amandus Johnson, is one of the most delightful sources of Delaware's early history.

By the following summer Rising had doubled the land under cultivation by organizing the loan of oxen and horses belonging to the freemen and to the company, and by planning a rotation of labor and volunteer help on the plantations of the freemen and on the company tracts. Roads between the settlements had been cleared and kept passable. Under Lindeström's supervision the village of Christina Harbor, behind Fort Christina, was expanded on a plan of rectangular blocks with streets crossing at right angles. Forts, blockhouses, and other buildings on the river were so well braced and strengthened that they withstood heavy floods and the ice of an unusually hard winter. In little over a year, the more than two hundred colonists brought by Rising and possibly a hundred he found under Papegoja had become a thriving community.

In the lives of the settlers throughout the Swedish period hard labor on their own account and in the interest of the New Sweden Company was the order of the day. But each of the governors, however vigorously he sought the financial success of the Colony, was primarily concerned with the welfare of the people.

The term of service for soldiers and servants, paid by the company, was usually for three years, after which they might receive land of their own and a start with its cultivation. Those coming as freemen, especially planters who took up land or farmed company land on shares, paid for their passage and land, and usually for cattle, on easy terms over a period of years.

After the first few years a majority of the freemen fared well and some became sufficiently prosperous to build larger houses and greatly extend their plantations. Trade with the Indians aided the individual settler as well as the company. To the latter the settler first offered his surplus of produce for sale and, if not taken by the company, sold it where the profit was greatest. Women, clever with the loom and the needle, made from cheap materials articles that sold well to the savages, especially caps with gay-colored tassels.

Suffering from lack of suitable food, clothing, and shelter, combined with overwork, took heavy toll of life in several years. Inexperience, failure of supplies from home, or misfortune in trade led to the discouragement of many. Yet the standard of living at which governors and colonists aimed was high. In good years, especially in the summer and early fall, there was an abundance and wholesome variety of foods that made festive their everyday living as well as the occasions of hospitality and sociability that the people enjoyed.

KEY OF KALMAR AT FORT CHRISTINA

John Møll

Dutch Rule

By seizing Fort Casimir Rising had made a false start, which Peter Stuyvesant was soon ready to make the Swedes pay for in drastic fashion. Conditions in Europe played into Stuyvesant's hands. Chancellor Oxenstierna, still the great statesman of Europe and in spite of his age a power in maintaining Sweden's prestige abroad, died the year Rising came to America, 1654; and in the same year Queen Christina gave up her throne. The Government of Holland, fearing the rise of Sweden's commercial power, made alliances against her.

A year and four months after Rising took Fort Casimir from the Dutch, Stuyvesant had it back, and the flag of Holland flew over Fort Christina as well. A month and a half later, the end of October 1655, Rising was on his way back to Sweden aboard a Dutch vessel. While the parley between Stuyvesant and Rising was still on, word had been brought to Stuyvesant by fast messenger that an Indian war was causing bloodshed and destruction at New Amsterdam. Had the messenger been swifter, Swedish colors might have continued to float at Fort Christina.

Stuyvesant left Dirck Smidt in command at Sand Hook, where Fort Trinity was given back the name Fort Casimir and became the Dutch capital on the river. The Swedes were permitted to keep their officers and their Lutheran clergyman, and were promised security in their lands and other possessions. Jean Paul Jacquet, a French Hugenot who had come to New Amsterdam from Holland well recommended by the Company's directors, arrived at Fort Casimir as vice-director on the South River under Peter Stuyvesant in December 1655. He governed with the aid of a council composed of the sheriff-and-secretary, Andries Hudde, former commissary for the Dutch at Fort Nassau, the commissary, Elmerhuysen Klein, and two sergeants. The chief Swedish officer up the river was Gregorius Van Dyck, sheriff, assisted by Sven Skute, Anders Dalbo, Jacob Swenson, Olaf Stille, Peter Rambo, Peter Cock, and others.

Vice-director Jacquet, following instructions from Stuyvesant, regulated trade with the Indians and the English, forbade sale of liquor and ammunition to the former, and sought to establish prevailing rates of exchange for skins and tobacco. The next year Swedes and Dutch were called

together at the fort to consider improvement of roads and bridges; ownership of land was confirmed and new grants made.

Important among the duties of the vice-director was the challenging of
all vessels on the river and collection of duty from those permitted to
trade. One of the first foreign ships to arrive, early in 1656, was the
Mercurius from Sweden with an expedition of colonists, mostly Finns.
The ship had sailed before news of the taking of New Sweden by the
Dutch had reached Stockholm. Hendrick Huygen, former commissary of
the Swedes, and Johan Papegoja, son-in-law of former Governor Printz,
were in charge. Permission to land settlers and cargo was refused by
Jacquet, and by Stuyvesant also when appeal was made to him. But the
Indians, offended at the Dutch for delaying the landing of the well-
provisioned expedition of their favorite people, went aboard the vessel
in numbers and piloted it past the guns of Fort Casimir, whose commander could not risk hostilities with the savages. The colonists landed
finally near Tinicum, and seem to have been taken care of by the local
Swedish officers, for there is no further record of trouble.

Because of the cost of Stuyvesant's conquest of the Delaware, added to
other losses and drains upon the resources of the Dutch West India Company,
the company in the summer of 1656 sold the settlement at Fort Casimir, together with the land between the Christina and Bombay Hook, to the rich
City of Amsterdam. Jacob Alrichs, the new director, who was responsible
to the burgomasters of that city, began development of the settlement at
the fort, called by them New Amstel, in the spring of 1657. In spite of
prevailing illness and a population of several hundred traders, clerks,
women, and children sent by the burgomasters instead of the needed artisans and farmers, Alrichs, with the help of Stuyvesant and the Swedes,
provided food and shelter for all of these people. At the beginning of the
next year New Amstel had nearly a hundred dwellings, a dozen or more
other buildings, and about 500 people.

After the surrender of Fort Christina in 1655, a few Dutch soldiers
were stationed there to keep an eye upon the Swedish planters and their
officers. But in this peaceful community the soldiers seem to have paid
more attention to their gardens and other interests than to the fort (called
Fort Altena by the Dutch), for the buildings became dilapidated and complaint was made of it as the haunt of smugglers of tobacco and other commodities. Upon the arrival of Governor Stuyvesant in the spring of 1658
to make a survey of conditions on the river, orders were given for the
repair of buildings and fortifications to serve as the West India Company's

seat of government. Later in the year William Beekman from New Amsterdam was put in command at Altena, as vice-director under Stuyvesant, and was made collector of customs for the whole river. The privileges accorded the Swedes, who now had plantations from the Appoquinimink to Tinicum and Wicaco (Philadelphia), were continued.

Meanwhile, at New Amstel, Director Alrichs, in good faith to the owners of the Colony, was enforcing many prohibitions against his settlers concerning trade, crops, and occupations. Though he seems to have labored early and late in the interest of the people as well as that of the burgomasters in Holland, the restrictions, together with enticements offered by the English of Maryland, caused many settlers to leave the Colony. Worn down by illness, overwork, and worry, Director Alrichs died in December 1659. At the time of his death Gerritt Van Sweringen was commissary, Cornelis Van Gezel, secretary. In command of the soldiers was Lieutenant Alexander D'Hinoyossa, an adventurer, who inherited Alrichs's office.

To protect the Swanendael region from trespass by English traders, Alrichs had stationed a guard at Blommaert's Kill—called by the Dutch the Hoerekill or Hoerenkill, within a few years after the destruction of the de Vries colony. Why the name was changed has not yet been discovered nor any certain origin of the Dutch form Horekill in its several spellings. As to whether it was a corruption of Hoorn, from which town some of the early explorers, and de Vries, and some of his colonists came, no evidence has been found in available records. The Dutch name continued in use until occupation by the English in 1664, when it became Whorekill.

Whatever the original name of Lewes Creek may have been, Delawareans now generally use the name Hoornkill in referring to the early stream and site, this form having been given official sanction by its use in the legislative and international ceremonies honoring the State's first white settlement.

D'Hinoyossa followed the practice of Stuyvesant, of the City of Amsterdam, and of Director Alrichs in giving privileges at the Hoerekill to settlers accepting Dutch sovereignty. But having established Peter Alrichs, nephew of the former director, in charge of trade there, and having given him sole right of trade on the bay, D'Hinoyossa devoted himself to plans for a trading-center and capital at Appoquinimy (near Odessa) for commerce with the English. He kept up a continuous quarrel with Beekman at Altena, who opposed his methods and complained bitterly to Stuyvesant.

In 1663 when the burgomasters of Amsterdam acquired the whole river from the Company, D'Hinoyossa persuaded them that only money and plenty of good Swedish farmers were needed to make the Colony a paying venture. He was made director of the whole river Colony and returned from a visit to Europe with a new appropriation of funds and as many Swedish settlers as could be persuaded to emigrate under the Dutch. To Beekman, D'Hinoyossa now offered a job as assistant in command, but Beekman refused to serve and left the river.

In spite of desertions to Maryland and the return of a number of settlers to Europe, the population along the river from the Schuylkill to the bay is believed to have been nearly a thousand at this time, the majority Swedes and Finns, the rest Dutch, with a few English and French. Besides Peter Alrichs, his associates and servants, a community of Dutch Mennonites, established in 1663 by Pieter Cornelis Plockhoy under Dutch protection, was settled at the Hoerekill along with other Dutch settlers, and perhaps a few Swedish, who had gone there after 1655.

Duke of York's Province

The land of present Delaware was not included in the grant made early in 1664, by which James, Duke of York, received from his brother, Charles II, territory in America extending from the St. Croix River to the east side of the Delaware. But because a powerful group in England, to which the Duke belonged, coveted the whole of the Dutch trade and colonies in America, it was decided to reduce to "submission and obedience" the Delaware Colony as well as New Amsterdam. This was easily accomplished when the impetuous Sir Robert Carr, representing the Duke's Deputy Governor, Colonel Richard Nicolls, appeared with two war vessels before the weak little fort at New Amstel (see NEW CASTLE). D'Hinoyossa, the officers Peter Alrichs and Gerritt Van Sweringen, and the soldiers were made prisoners. Their property was confiscated, and the soldiers and some of the Negroes belonging to the officers and other inhabitants were sold as slaves to the English in Virginia and Maryland. Other Negroes, together with the plantations of the Dutch officers and soldiers, were divided among Carr's men. D'Hinoyossa and the officers were later released, the former going to Maryland, where he unsuccessfully sought aid toward recovering his property. Alrichs signed the oath of allegiance and before long was appointed to public office and recovered most of his property. He was permitted to trade at the Whorekill and returned there in 1665 with six horses and a servant.

Other parts of the river were quickly made subject to the Duke's proprietorship. But Carr's harsh and autocratic control of this territory, without advice from New York, brought Deputy Governor Nicolls in person to enforce his authority and make peace with the colonists. He changed the name of New Amstel to New Castle, made Captain John Carr (son of Sir Robert) commander on the Delaware, and promised redress of grievances, tenure of lands, and new grants. By the Duke's orders the existing government was authorized to continue until further instructions were given.

English from Virginia, Maryland, and New Jersey, as well as from New York and Europe, came to settle among the Swedes and Dutch, and gradually made up in numbers for the loss of those who departed during D'Hinoyossa's rule and following the depredations under Sir Robert Carr. They settled also in the previously unoccupied territory from Bombay Hook south to Indian River. Trade developed again at the Whorekill, where Sir Robert had destroyed the houses of the Mennonites as part of his subjection of the whole settlement to the Duke's rule. Trade regulations under the Duke's government interfered at first with the opportunities of traders and farmers alike to barter in many articles. Governor Lovelace, who succeeded Nicolls in 1668, put a duty of 10 percent on exports and imports. The quit-rent in wheat charged for their lands was objected to by the Swedes, and many of them, because of the cost of survey, failed to have their titles to the land they cultivated confirmed. Owing to continuing dissatisfaction, aggravated by rumors that Sweden was sending ships to recapture the South River, many Swedes listened to a fomenter of rebellion who proposed an uprising against the English when the ships should appear. The arch-plotter, Marcus Jacobsen, who claimed to be a son of the Swedish General Konigsmarke and was known as "the Long Finn," was trapped by a Swedish officer and turned over to the Commandant. After the Long Finn's conviction in 1669 with a drastic sentence, and the fining of those who had given him aid and comfort, protests seem to have been limited to formal and informal complaint and petition. Smuggling increased, however, and the next year the tax on trade was removed.

Two years later, by order of the governor and council at New York, New Castle was incorporated a "bailiwick" and the government on the

Delaware was strengthened by a centralized authority there over the whole river. This was vested in a high sheriff, the English Edmund Cantwell, and a bailiff or chief magistrate, the Dutch Peter Alrichs, with six assistant magistrates. Both Governor Nicolls and Governor Lovelace had shown every disposition to carry out the Duke of York's injunction to treat the people "with all humanity and gentleness that can consist with the honor and safety" of the government.

While Lovelace was reorganizing the government on the Delaware in 1672, war was begun against Holland by France and England. In July of the next year, the Dutch Admiral Evertsen, successful on the seas, came to New York with a fleet and recovered the whole of the previous Dutch territory of New Netherland. Peter Alrichs was made commander on the Delaware. The government was otherwise undisturbed, the people being allowed to keep their property if they took the oath of allegiance—which they did. One major event during the interval of Dutch control, which lasted less than a year, was the establishment by Governor Colve of district courts at Upland (Chester), New Castle, and the Whorekill (Lewes). This laid the foundation for the counties of Delaware, and was a significant contribution toward the development of this small stretch of territory as a separate colony.

By the treaty of Westminster, which ended the Dutch and English war in 1674, each country gave back its conquests. In October of that year the Delaware Colony, used to sudden changes of sovereignty, swore allegiance to the English king. The local government was continued as it had existed before the interruption, except that the new English Governor of the Duke of York's province refused for a while to restore Peter Alrichs to office. No governor on the Delaware could long resist Peter's charm and ability, however, and by the next year he was back in favor and in office.

In 1676 Governor Edmund Andros re-established the courts set up by Colve, and affairs on the Delaware, better recorded from this time on, assumed the characteristics dominant throughout the Colonial and early State period. It was a sparsely settled community of individualists of differing ideas and temperaments. Everybody knew everybody else, each fellow spoke his mind, quarreled and protested when he believed his rights interfered with, accepted the established social order without being a truckler or much of a respecter of persons, and joined his dearest enemies in defense of the right of this small strip of territory to exist as an indivisible entity. The frequent changes of absentee ownership seemed only to cement this local conception of a special and peculiar privilege and destiny.

In 1680 the inhabitants of the upper part of the Whorekill court district or county petitioned Governor Andros for a separate court. This was granted, and the court and county of "St. Jones" was established with territory extending between Duck Creek and Cedar Creek in the center of the State. Among the first recorded motions of the magistrates of the new court was the disciplining of Thomas Williams, who had said he did not see why the Duke of York had been such a fool as to make them the judges. In this same year, the magistrates at the Whorekill petitioned for a change of name. Governor Andros complied by giving court and county the name Deal, after which both appear in records as "New Deal alias Whorekills" and "the Whorekill now New Deal." In this period a good many of the inhabitants who lived south and southwest of the Whorekill held their land (to the extent of 19,000 acres by 1682) under grants from Lord Baltimore, in territory claimed by Maryland (now lower Sussex, Delaware). The territory of New Deal alias Whorekill county was not at that time more definitely defined than "from Cedar Creek downwards."

Three Counties under Penn

The inhabitants of the Delaware Colony seem to have been fairly prosperous and contented when the English ship, the *Welcome,* appeared off New Castle on October 27, 1682. A messenger was sent ashore to announce the arrival from England of William Penn, newly made true and absolute proprietor of their land. Son of Admiral William Penn, whose service in the British Navy and in other public and personal offices had endeared him to Charles II and to his brother James, Duke of York, the younger Penn had not been saved thereby from prosecution and imprisonment for his active proselyting in the Quaker faith. Along with a considerable estate, Penn inherited a credit of £16,000 due the elder Penn from Charles II. The esteem in which his father was held and the royal indebtedness combined to produce a favorable answer to Penn's petition for a province in America. In this province Penn's "holy experiment" was to offer liberty of conscience and the peaceful pursuit of a livelihood in an ideal environment, under mild and just laws adopted with the consent of the freemen. That he came as lord of the soil, to receive quit-rents from the land and profit from commercial developments, was inherent in the proprietary system and consistent, in Penn's background, with his sincere and uncommon generosity toward all the inhabitants.

Penn had little doubt that his fair principles would meet with co-operation from the liberty-loving Swedes, the independent Dutch, and the courageous English, Scottish, and French Protestants who made up the population of the Duke's former Colony. But in these qualities and in the large degree of personal, political, and religious liberty that had long been enjoyed here (with and without legal or official sanction) lay the seeds of a new dissent.

Penn had in his possession two leases and two deeds of feoffment from the Duke of York, giving him all the territory within a twelve-mile circle about New Castle and from the circle south to Cape Henlopen—a stretch of territory "otherwise called Delaware." John Moll, the chief magistrate at New Castle, who with Ephraim Herman had been made the Duke's attorney conducted the ceremony of livery of seisin (see NEW CASTLE) at the fort on the Market Square. This was for the land within the twelve-mile circle only. To William Markham, Penn's cousin and his deputy-governor for Pennsylvania who had been on the Delaware since July of the previous year, Penn gave power of attorney to receive for him the lower counties as soon as the magistrates there could be visited. The delivery took place on November 7 at the home of Edmund Cantwell at Appoquinimy (Odessa). After receiving the allegiance of the people at New Castle, Penn reappointed the Duke of York's officers and authorized continuance of the Duke's laws for the time being.

William Penn had received his patent for Pennsylvania from Charles II on March 4, 1681, the leases and deeds for the Delaware counties on August 24, 1682, just before he set sail for America. The patent was a charter from the Crown, giving him wide powers of government as well as full proprietary rights of ownership in the soil. The leases and deeds made no mention of government, and the former proprietor, the Duke of York, had no paper or legal title to the land, but only as his secretary, Sir John Werden, frankly said, "a claim." Although the Duke of York, on March 22, 1683, received a grant for the Delaware territory from King Charles, this legalization of his claim was not retroactive and left Penn's title uncertain. In this defect of title the inhabitants of the lower counties, or "Territories" as Penn came to call the Delaware counties, found a convenient justification for the racial, religious, political, and temperamental incompatibility between them and Penn's upper counties in the years between 1682 and 1704.

At Penn's first assembly held at Upland (Chester) on December 6, 1682, the Delaware members in equal number with those of Pennsylvania accepted Penn's frame of government, and "petitioned" for union with the Province (which James Logan of Pennsylvania later said Penn "prevailed" upon them to accept). They were pleased to support Penn's naturalization of Swedes, Finns, and Dutch on the river and the confirmation of their land to all freeholders.

In 1683 the General Assembly of Penn's government was organized, consisting of nine members elected from each county, six to serve in the assembly and three in the council. The council acted with Penn or with his deputy-governors in the appointment of magistrates, judges, and other officials, and in proposing legislation. The assembly accepted or rejected the proposals but did not have the right of initiating legislation. From the first session, this restriction upon the assembly was resented by the representatives of all Penn's counties and the effort to nullify this obstacle to self-government was at the root of a growing contention against proprietary control. Penn strengthened the courts of the lower counties and provided a Provincial or Supreme Court. He changed the name of "Deal alias Whorekills" to Sussex for his own county in England, calling the county seat Lewes; and changed the name of St. Jones County to Kent.

One of the first open rifts between Penn's government and the lower counties was the refusal of a group of Kent County planters to pay quitrents. They claimed the rents belonged to the Duke of York, and that Penn had not kept his promise to treat the lower counties and the Province on equal terms. Another grievance was Penn's failure to protect the inhabitants along the southern and western parts of the lower counties from the depredations and attacks of Lord Baltimore's agents, who claimed the soil, collected tithes at the pistol point, started ejectment suits, and even seized property and imprisoned the owners. One other serious cause of resentment against the Quaker counties of the Province was the failure of the upper counties to provide a full share of means and men to protect the lower counties against the pirates who frequented the Delaware after 1685. Blackbeard (Teach), Avery, Canoot, Kidd, and many lesser characters brought terror to the inhabitants, as they rode at anchor off the capes or in the bay; and many unknown pirates and privateers plundered the inhabitants near the shores, and successfully preyed upon shipping in the bay and river. James II, the former Duke of York, sent ships to defend the coast and offered pardons to pirates who would give themselves up, pay a forfeit as security for their good behavior, and henceforth follow honest callings. Insufficient protection coupled with this policy created conditions easily imagined. Poor pirates who gave themselves up were jailed; those with stocks of treasure, especially gold, paid a large forfeit and went free, often to ply their trade again, or to settle in the respectable Quaker Colony as confederate informers to ships flying the black flag.

As the result of Penn's efforts upon his return to Philadelphia in 1699 after fourteen years in Europe, pirates were cleared from the river for the next eight years. But the bad reputation given his government by the pirate menace and the open breach between his upper and lower counties discouraged thousands of prospective immigrants. His right to govern the lower counties was called in question in England by the Board of Trade, and the Privy Council upheld a distinction between the Province and the lower counties, by which the lower counties saw themselves virtually a Royal Province. The governor of the Province and the governor of the counties might be the same person, but for the counties each governor had to be approved by the King.

The General Assembly for the Province and Territories had met at New Castle in 1684, in 1690, and again in 1700. In the latter year Penn reviewed the existing laws and put them in good form for printing so that the people might become familiar with them, and thus avoid the continual pleading of ignorance of the statutes. For weeks he labored, living in the little town, listening patiently to the long arguments of the Quakers from the upper counties and the conflicting ideas of the inhabitants of the lower ones. After this session, the Quaker Isaac Norris, member of Penn's Assembly from Pennsylvania, who lacked Penn's patience, expressed his relief at being home again from that "Frenchified, Scotchified, Dutchified place" (New Castle) where the delegates of the lower counties were "vociferous" and "teasing" in their demands.

The particular grievances and events which led to a separate assembly for the lower counties were interwoven with the long struggle between Penn's council and his assembly over their respective powers and rights, and between these two bodies and Penn himself. Appointment of officers for the lower counties without consulting the wishes of their representatives was the cause of several breaks. The Delawareans of that day left the General Assembly, and refused to return even when followed to New Castle with pleas and pledges; or they failed to elect members to the assembly under rules they objected to. In 1691 feeling ran so high over an arbitrary change in the method of making out commissions for the judges of the provincial court for the lower counties, that the minutes of both council and assembly for that year are believed to have been purposely destroyed.

The following year, to maintain his government in the lower counties, Penn was compelled to commission a separate governor for them—his cousin, William Markham. Among all Penn's officers up to this time "Cosin Markham" was the choice and favorite in the lower counties. He understood the people by long association and keen perception and was their "next friend" in the handling of many grievances.

In the 1701 charter, granted by Penn, the right to elect members of the council was taken from the freemen and power of appointment given to the Governor. This did not eliminate from the council members from the lower counties—New Castle, Kent, and Sussex—for both Penn and his deputy-governors sought through wise appointments to this office a closer tie with them.

For three years these counties cleverly refused to accept the charter of 1701 (to which Penn had reluctantly added a postscript giving the upper and lower counties the right to have separate assemblies if either desired), and thus put the government of the province into the position of demanding their retirement to form their own assembly. The lower counties and the Province then parted with mutual satisfaction and, so far as personalities were concerned, mutual good will. Arrogant and unreasonable as was much of the conduct of Delaware leaders, their actions were backed by the people and were grounded in the general trend of the times against proprietors and proprietary rights. They felt themselves entitled to self-government as subjects of the English Crown. Because the Duke of York had conducted all formal government in the King's name, they felt closer to the sovereignty they acknowledged under the Duke than under the personal proprietary control of Penn, however altruistic the latter's spirit. Practically, the inhabitants saw Penn's claim to revenue from soil and trade as a wedge introduced between them and the Crown, and Penn's development of richer and better populated counties to the north, with a fast-growing commercial center at Philadelphia, as a threat to their political and economic security.

The first separate assembly was held at New Castle in November 1704. No laws then or later were sent to England for confirmation. The counties accepted Penn's governors because these men were required to be approved by the Crown, and conducted their affairs as a Colony of the Crown until the Revolution. Though without an official name, the Colony was included after 1696, under the regulations of the Privy Council and Government of England, as subject to all sovereign powers and regulations including those of trade.

Boundaries

The disputes over boundaries as well as the claims to the soil itself, which made up the "dramatic relation" of the Delaware counties to the surrounding Colonies, began actively upon the landing of the Swedes at the Minquas Kill in 1638. Before that time Dutch traders and explorers had been charged by the English at Jamestown with usurping His Majesty's rights upon His Majesty's territory, and the *Grip*, sent to Virginia by Minuit to trade, was refused entry on that account. Governor Printz had been harassed by the efforts of English from New Haven to settle on the river at the same time that the Dutch Governor, Peter Stuyvesant, was threatening to wrest control of the whole river from the Swedes. Shortly after Stuyvesant made good his threat in 1655, the claims of Lord Baltimore of Maryland through Governor Fendall became aggressive. Colonel Charles Nathaniel Utie, representing Baltimore's claim, appeared at New Amstel in 1659 demanding the allegiance of the settlers and threatening destruction of the Colony.

The Director at New Amstel, Jacob Alrichs, who had offered no very spirited defense of the Dutch claim, was sharply rebuked by Stuyvesant; soldiers were sent immediately from New Amsterdam to New Amstel and to the Hoerekill. In the interest of the Dutch claim, Stuyvesant sent the astute emissaries and advocates Resolved Waldron and Augustine Herman, to confer with the officers of Lord Baltimore in Maryland. By an engaging reasonableness of manner they obtained for study a copy of the grant from King Charles I to Lord Baltimore's father, made in 1632, the year following the unhappy first settlement by the Dutch at Swanendael. In the preamble of the charter, Herman and Waldron found the portentous words, *hactenus inculta,* limiting the lands granted to Baltimore to those previously uncultivated (by white men). Upon this point, with the same reasonableness of manner plus tenacity of purpose, they made their stand—the west shore of the Delaware had been cultivated, even though the colony had been short lived, therefore this territory was excluded from the King's grant. Stuyvesant made good use of the discovery of the "flaw" in Lord Baltimore's grant. The conflict between Baltimore and the Dutch was well known in England and, if the issue had been fought out then, the lawyers for the Crown undoubtedly would have made short work of the *hactenus inculta* clause. But when James, Duke of York, wished to attach the Delaware Colony to his province of New York in 1664, the phrase became a horse of a different color. In his instructions to the commissioners sent over to take the territory, the Duke said, in effect, that if Lord Baltimore made objection, they were to say that it was only to assure possession by the English until the king's wishes could be known; but he added that Baltimore's title was very doubtful.

Since the Duke of York's control of the Delaware territory was by knowledge and consent of the king, the protests of Baltimore were not forcefully followed up, and they received slight attention at court. When part of William Penn's Province and all of "the territories" (Delaware) were carved out of Baltimore's express grant "unto that part of Delaware Bay on the north which lyeth under the fortieth Degree of Northerne Latitude," the gorge of Charles Calvert (third Lord Baltimore) rose. Unable to deal with Penn, he went to England in 1684 (followed as he had wished by Penn) to make a vigorous appeal for justice from Charles II. The king's death interrupted proceedings and put on the throne James II, who as Duke of York had been the original English invader of Baltimore's territory. Toward the end of 1685, the new king's commissioners ordered that the land between the Delaware and the Chesapeake be divided into equal parts by a line from the latitude of Cape Henlopen to the "fortieth Degree of Northerne Latitude," and that the eastern half "towards the Bay of Delaware be adjudged to belong to his Ma'ty." Upon this followed Penn's comment, "I endeavored to gett it, & have it, & will keep it if I can." The maps available at the time Penn's charter for Pennsylvania was being drawn had enabled the lawyers for the Crown to make no better guess at the "fortieth Degree," than twelve miles north of New Castle. This was more than eleven miles south of that latitude but it was at least an effort to avoid Baltimore's bounds. In the leases for the Delaware counties, bounds were based upon the possession of the soil by the Duke of York and upon the attitude of his secretary Sir John Werden that, since it was a matter of "claims," the Duke probably had the better one. Upon the death of William Penn in 1718 the boundary dispute was left to his heirs in conflict with the heirs of Charles Calvert, whose death had preceded Penn's. By 1732 the futile conflict had so far palled upon both sides that an agreement was reached with articles drawn and signed, stating that the parties were to abide by a line run west from Cape Henlopen to the exact middle of the Peninsula and from there northerly until it made a tangent point on the twelve-mile circle about New Castle, thence east by the arc of the circle. The reproduction of a map originally prepared by Maryland surveyors was attached, to which Calvert's representatives for Maryland paid little attention. On it Cape Henlopen was located at the old "false cape," now Fenwick Island where the present south boundary line of the State touches the ocean.

When Lord Baltimore's counsel charged the Penns with deceit in the effort to "hook in twenty miles more territory," the Penns pointed to the origin of the map. The mistake might have been expected, for the name (Hinlopen) was originally attached to just this point, and what was then Cape Henlopen, near Lewes, had been known by other names, Cape La Warre, Cape Cornelis, Cape James. Another difficulty was presented by the circle about New Castle, especially in adjusting its western end where the boundaries of Maryland, Pennsylvania, and Delaware meet. The fresh conflict resulting from these difficulties resolved itself into the case of Penn versus Lord Baltimore. A decree in favor of the Penns in 1750, assessing the costs against Lord Baltimore, did not settle the dispute, but established that the lines were to be drawn on the basis of the agreement of 1732. Later the bounds of Delaware were surveyed on the south line by John Watson (1750-51) and by Mason and Dixon (1763-67) on the south and west lines. The center of the circle ("ye end of ye Horse Dyke at New Castle," in the survey made for William Penn in 1701 by Taylor and Pierson) was changed to Court House spire. The difficult lines from the tangent point were temporarily adjusted, and the whole division of territory approved in 1769 by George III.

‹‹‹‹‹‹‹‹‹‹‹‹‹‹‹‹‹‹ ☼ ››››››››››››››››››››››

Colonial Development

From the year 1704, when the Three Lower Counties, choosing to be a colony of the Crown, set up their own assembly, to 1765, when these same counties defied King and Parliament by ignoring the Stamp Act, they enjoyed a high degree of freedom and self-government. They bore the brunt of the depredations of pirates and privateers on the Delaware, provided the major part of funds and manpower for defense of the shore, and gave more than their share of support to the King in the French and Indian wars. In this way they earned the favor of the governors, who were sometimes accused by the upper counties of too tender a feeling toward the lower. The lower counties had to maintain an orderly and self-supporting government or be swallowed up politically and economically by the adjoining provinces; this necessity bred the alertness and soundness of mind that produced the Rodneys, Dickinsons, Reads, McKeans, and many other distinguished men of the Revolutionary period.

In spite of the privateer menace from the river, especially during wars in Europe, and threats of sheriffs who claimed that taxes and allegiance were due Lord Baltimore, the inhabitants developed agriculture and fishing, built ships, and tanned leather. For export to Philadelphia and to the West Indies they prepared lumber, ship timber, beef, bread, butter, cheese, and grain. The assembly provided for internal improvements— clearing and maintaining roads, building bridges, protecting woodlands, "viewing" fences, and otherwise safeguarding life and property. Due attention was given to blue laws (those of 1719 were drastic), the encouragement of mills, destruction of wolves, and the administration of justice. Quakers were permitted to affirm instead of taking oath. Taxes were fairly heavy. The population in 1704 may have been 2,500; during the Revolution it was estimated at 37,000.

Development of the courts under able justices was one of the significant achievements of the Colonial period. Many of the early judges were laymen, men of integrity and good judgment, chosen for leadership and often for learning. Riding the circuit of the counties at least twice each year, as members of the Supreme Court for the Three Lower Counties after 1705, were such men as Henry Brooke of Lewes, whose ability and scholarship were regarded by James Logan, Secretary of Pennsylvania, as too great to be thrown away in an American colony; William Till of Sussex, who became Mayor of Philadelphia; Jehu Curtis of New Castle, whose epitaph, praising his uprightness, was written by Benjamin Franklin; and Col. John French of New Castle, whose influence with the Indians ranked with that of Penn. Colonel French was made Mayor of the "city of New Castle" in 1724, when Sir William Keith, the Governor of Penn's Province and of these counties, created a metropolitan area of forty square miles with New Castle as its center.

A special form of trial for Negroes was adopted as early as 1727. The first Negro in Delaware territory was Anthony, "an Angoler or Moor," captured by the skipper of the *Grip* in 1638, when Minuit sent him south to trade. Anthony was delivered at Fort Christina in 1639, and in 1648 was a special servant to Governor Printz. Some of the Dutch in Delaware territory owned slaves as servants and farm workers, and during the early English period English settlers in all three counties used slave labor to an increasing extent. But only on a few large estates in the two lower counties did any one person own a large number. The general feeling was against the increase of slavery and, before 1700, some slaves had been freed. Sentiment and the continued freeing of slaves did not prevent the sale of other Negroes to the inhabitants during most of the eighteenth century, but led to a declaration against slavery in the first constitution of the State in 1776. Finally by the law of 1787 any person bringing a slave into the State was subject to a fine of twenty pounds and the slave was declared free.

The separate Assembly enabled the lower counties to defend their population from importation of convicts from English jails and of mentally and physically defective paupers from English poorhouses. No restriction was put upon desirable individuals and families who offered themselves as servants for a term of years to pay their passage money, or who by misfortune after arrival were reduced to this expedient to get a start.

Beginning in 1723, the counties issued paper money secured chiefly by real estate. Because England accepted only coin and a limited number of staple products in exchange for the manufactured goods, hard money was drained from the counties which could export little of the chief staples—tobacco and furs. The paper currency, accepted by merchants in the adjoining Colonies, met the need for a medium of exchange. Efficiency in the handling of the issues of the bills of credit through county loan offices is one of the evidences of growing administrative ability in the government of the Three Lower Counties. Today specimens of the paper money are interesting for their charm of design and the signatures of citizens of the period.

Coincident with the development of finance and a growing economic independence among farmers was the spread of church and school. Every section had its subscription schools built and supported by farmers, and every hamlet where profit came from trade had one or more teachers or an academy. So eager were the people for their accustomed religious worship in the beginning of this period, that sometimes they had churches and assembled regularly with a lay reader several years before they secured a minister.

It is reported by a contemporary that in 1756 Dover, which was to become the capital of the State, had 100 houses, Lewes 100, New Castle 250, and Wilmington 260. Trade, including smuggling, was thriving in all the creeks and on the river. Wilmington had her own ships, built chiefly by Quakers, who had taken as their own the little village of Willingtown, laid out between 1730 and 1735 by the Swede, Andrew Justison, and his Quaker son-in-law, Thomas Willing.

In 1755 "the little government of New Castle, Kent and Sussex" had sent to General Braddock a herd of cattle and a consignment of provisions that indicated a high standard of living. The supplies included hams, cheeses, flasks of oil, raisins, spice and currants, pickles, vinegar, mustard; casks of biscuit, kegs of sturgeon and herring, chests of lemons, kegs of spirit, potatoes, and tubs of butter.

Assemblies sitting at New Castle continued to vote money and the people to raise companies of fighting men for the King throughout the French and Indian wars. Because of the hardships willingly endured for His Majesty's Service, the Stamp Act was the more resented. But there was no violence. The counties joined the non-importation agreement and waited for repeal. Jacob Kollock of Sussex, Caesar Rodney of Kent, and Thomas McKean of New Castle County were chosen by the assembly to represent the three counties in the Congress of 1765 at New York. Their instructions said: "If the Congress shall not . . . allow this Government an equal vote with any other Province or Government on this Continent, you are decently but firmly to urge the right of this Government to an equal vote in Congress with the other Colonies." When news of the repeal arrived, the Assembly appointed Rodney, McKean, and George Read to draw up an address of appreciation to the King. What they prepared was described in England as "wrote with the most natural, honest simplicity." The King read it twice.

Rodney, McKean, and Read were chosen the delegates to the Continental Congress of 1774. With John Dickinson and many other local leaders they reviewed for the people, in temperate, reasoned statements, the issues involved in the controversy with Great Britain. This spirit was embodied in the *Letters from a Farmer,* written by John Dickinson at his home near Dover *(see Tour 2B)* and published in the *Pennsylvania Chronicle.*

In 1774 money was raised to aid Boston when her port was closed, and by June 1775 the assembly had heard with approval the report of the representatives in Congress and resolved to bear whatever share for defense should be fixed by that body. In September the Council of Safety for the counties, of which John McKinly was President, reported "about 5,000 effective men in this government associated and determined to defend their just rights and liberties with their lives and fortunes." The following March a local fleet of row-galleys with guns in their bows succeeded in driving two British men-of-war out of the river, and this greatly reduced the fear of the war among the people and increased the confidence of the regiment under the command of Col. John Haslet.

Feeling and conviction against armed rebellion was apparently about to be organized on the side of the King, at the same time that Congress was moving toward the Declaration of Independence at Philadelphia. A thousand Tories were reported to be assembling in northeastern Sussex (above Lewes) on June 11. The militia of the counties was called to order for marching at short notice but, to prevent unnecessary civil conflict, members of the Council of Safety hastened to the Tory meeting place and talked with the leaders. These were all men who knew each other, and who could well share credit for Delaware's successful experiment in Colonial self-government. The talk resulted in the dispersion of the Tories. Individuals already had been arrested and their property confiscated. Many were released upon a declaration of regret and pledge of willingness to cooperate to the extent consistent with their conscience and religious principles. Though the patriots were dominant in the population, subdued but ardent Tories continued to argue that refusal to use tea would have been enough without making a great issue to disturb the peace and prosperity of these counties.

In Congress, Read believed too many of the people unready to support rebellion and that it was too early to vote for Independence; Rodney had returned to Dover to check the Tory activity and to stimulate recruiting. Since without him the vote of Delaware would be a tie between Read and McKean, the latter sent a messenger posthaste to Dover, and Rodney appeared on July 2, in time to give Delaware's vote for Independence *(see Tour 1, sec. c)*.

In September 1776 a convention of delegates from the three counties met at New Castle and framed a constitution for "the Delaware State." At last "the little government of New Castle, Kent and Sussex" had a name. No longer would the counties be mentioned in the royal records as "territories otherwise called Delaware." Loyalists, as Rodney had feared, were elected to the convention and to the first Legislature which met October 28, but the convention fully accepted the purport of the resolution that created it: that the members "immediately proceed to form a government on the Authority of the People of the State, in such Sort as may be best adapted to their Preservation and Happiness." From several drafts, one by Thomas McKean, the constitution was written. Both convention and Assembly made provision for vigorous promotion of the war.

Col. John Haslet's first Delaware regiment reported for duty in January 1776; in August 1781 the remnants of the third regiment were still fighting valiantly at Eutaw Springs, South Carolina. Although often referred to as "The Fighting Delawares," Haslet's regiment early won the sobriquet of "The Blue Hen's Chickens," which has come down as the proudly accepted nickname for all Delawareans. The name originated from the men of Capt. Jonathan Caldwell's company, who took with them game chickens celebrated for their fighting qualities, of the brood of a Kent County blue hen. The regiment fought at Long Island, White Plains, Trenton, and Princeton. In the latter battle, Colonel Haslet was killed while leading the advance.

The second regiment formed part of the Flying Camp; the third, organized in 1777 under Col. David Hall and known as the Delaware Line, won—with the Maryland Line—the reputation of being the crack regulars of the Continental Army. They fought at the Battle of Brandywine, and in the only engagement of the war on Delaware soil, a sharp skirmish at Cooch's Bridge on September 3, 1777. Here they were opposed by part of the forces of Gen. William Howe, who had landed at Head of Elk and was advancing toward Philadelphia. Gen. William Maxwell's light infantry, which included 100 men from each brigade, was forced to retreat after 40 were killed or wounded.

The day after Brandywine, General Howe sent troops to Wilmington, then a town of 1,250, and took possession. John McKinly, President of the Delaware State, was captured, and public and private records and money were confiscated.

In April 1780 the Delaware Line fought at Camden, where the regiment was almost annihilated—the 500 men being reduced to less than 175. The remnant became an independent company under Capt. Robert Kirkwood, and fought at Cowpens, Guilford Courthouse, Hobkirk's Hill, Ninety-Six, and Eutaw Springs. Kirkwood and his men were mentioned in almost every dispatch of General Greene, who said they would fight all day and dance all night. During the war enlistments totaled 3,763 out of a population of 37,000.

Delaware was one of the five States that sent delegates to the Annapolis Convention of September 1786 to consider general commercial regulations. John Dickinson, one of the Delaware delegates, was chosen President of the Convention. In February of the following year he presented in Congress the recommendation adopted at Annapolis for a new Convention in May to revise the Articles of Confederation. To the Constitutional Convention Delaware reappointed Dickinson and the other Annapolis delegates—George Read, Jacob Broom, Richard Bassett, and Gunning Bedford, Jr. Dickinson urged a new instrument rather than patching up the Articles of Confederation. Led by him, the Delaware delegates insisted that the States have equal representation in one house of Congress, and that the Representatives be elected by the people and the Senators by the State Legislatures. It was Dickinson also who effected the compromise in regard to slavery when the disagreement on that subject threatened to create a break. Being opposed to extension of slavery, he insisted that the power to prohibit importation of slaves must be left to the National Government.

Dissatisfaction with the Articles of Confederation had weakened allegiance in Delaware to the Union of States, and the Delaware leaders in favor of the Constitution feared this influence if delegates to the ratifying convention in their State were elected by the people. Upon the final motion, Delaware was the only State to vote against election of delegates by the people.

The leaders for the Constitution, including the delegates who had voted for it, then conducted a campaign for its support throughout the State, speaking and writing with eloquence and force. The convention elected by the people met at Dover, voted unanimously to ratify the Constitution, but left to a future Congress the adoption of a bill of rights which they believed the Constitution should include. By the ratification, which took place on December 7, 1787, Delaware led in the adoption of the Constitution and earned her proudest name: The First State.

Few loyalists left Delaware during the Revolution and those who remained became a strong and conservative element, controlling many elections. For a time their influence acted as a brake upon legislative response to the impetus toward internal improvements that followed the ratification of the Constitution. Conservatives as well as progressives favored a strong central government, however, and Delaware remained Federalist in politics longer than any other State. The party won its last victory in 1828 as the "Adams Party." Occasionally a Democrat had been elected to Congress, notably Caesar A. Rodney (nephew of the Revolutionary statesman) in 1802. He served as Attorney General of the United States in 1807. Twenty years later Louis McLane, the Bayards, Ridgelys, Coopers, Paynters, and some of the Rodneys became Jackson Democrats.

When President John McKinly was imprisoned by the British, Thomas

McKean and George Read succeeded him in office. Caesar Rodney, the fourth President, was followed by John Dickinson, who resigned as chief executive of Delaware in 1783, when he was elected President of the Supreme Executive Council of Pennsylvania. Both McKean and Dickinson held high office from Delaware and Pennsylvania throughout the Revolutionary and Constitution periods and had homes in both States. McKean, in fact, held several offices in both States at once. Joshua Clayton, the last President under the State constitution of 1776, became the first Governor under the new constitution of 1792. The constitutional convention in this year, which included among its members John Dickinson, Robert Coram, Richard Bassett, James Booth, Nicholas Ridgely, and Kensey Johns, called for the establishment of free public schools by legislative act. The State school fund was established in 1796, and after 1817 State aid was available for the education of "poor" children. In 1829 the first general free school act was passed.

From the early 1780's through the first decades of the nineteenth century, both the economic and cultural life in the State showed marked development. In and about Wilmington in 1791, manufacturing of flour, paper, carriages, furniture, iron, cotton and woolen cloth, and clothing employed 552 men and women. The previous year more than 300,000 bushels of grain were ground at the Brandywine mills. Total exports including lumber and agricultural products reached a value of $199,840. The first Federal census (1790) showed a population of 59,096 people, of whom 46,310 were white, 3,899 were free Negroes, and 8,887 were Negro slaves. The population was fairly evenly distributed, Sussex having 800 more inhabitants than New Castle County and 1,500 more than Kent.

Delaware, close to the center of Federal Government at Philadelphia and later at Washington, had outstanding citizens in the forefront of national life. Wilmington and Dover became forums for public discussion, attracting men of all shades of opinion. Distinguished European as well as native scholars and thinkers taught in their own schools or in the many excellent academies. In 1791 a noted Delaware teacher, Robert Coram, published the outstanding pamphlet of the period upon the issues of Democracy, with the proposal for a general system of free public schools for the Nation. His ideas, expressed with clarity and force, are pertinent today. A public library was established in the little village of Dagsborough in Sussex County, and Outerbridge Horsey, writing at Georgetown in 1799, mentions libraries planned for other Sussex towns, but urges that all efforts be united to provide one good library at the county seat, "where everyone comes at least once in two weeks."

Scientific groups, including James Madison, Benjamin Rush, Benjamin Franklin, and Benjamin Latrobe, met in Wilmington at various times to promote means of communication and progress in manufacture. A map that would show the best routes for canals between the Chesapeake and Delaware was advertised for and prepared in several editions between 1797 and 1801. In the latter year definite steps were taken toward the construction of the Delaware and Chesapeake Canal, which was completed in 1829. The New Castle and Frenchtown Railroad across the narrow neck of the peninsula was "open for transportation of persons and goods" in 1832.

The War of 1812 and the commercial embargo preceding it delayed both economic and educational progress and discouraged for a time the era of craftsmanship that had flowered in fine buildings, furniture, and silver during the 1790's and early 1800's. But along the creeks of upper New Castle County many small cotton and woolen mills were established.

Following the attack of the British warship *Leopard* upon the American frigate *Chesapeake* in 1807, protest meetings against "English aggression and outrage" were held in Delaware from Wilmington to Lewes. The Federalist leaders in the State restrained the war spirit in the interest of preparedness, and Senator James A. Bayard in Congress urged vigorous organization of Army and Navy before war should be declared.

After the engagement in October 1812 in which the sloop of war *Wasp*, commanded by Captain Jacob Jones of Delaware, captured the British *Frolic*, the Delaware River was blockaded by part of the British fleet under Commodore Sir John Beresford. At Lewes, Col. Samuel B. Davis refused the demands of the British for ship supplies, and withstood a bombardment with no loss of life and little property damage. With the victory at Lake Champlain in September 1814, won by Captain Thomas Macdonough of Delaware, State pride became overwhelming. General and vigorous efforts were made to revive the halted progress of manufacturing and commerce, and more scientific methods were introduced to promote agriculture. James A. Bayard of Delaware (1767–1815) was appointed a member of the Commission which negotiated the Treaty of Ghent, ending the war.

Lafayette on a visit to the State in 1824 wrote in a young girl's album: "After having seen nearly half a century ago, the banks of the Brandywine a scene of bloody fighting, I am happy now to find upon them the seat of industry, beauty and mutual friendship." During the years between Lafayette's visit and the middle of the century, a growing division of opinion and party allegiance in the State between the supporters of nationalist policies and the advocates of States' rights coincided with the division of interest between the agricultural area of most of the State and the small manufacturing area of New Castle County. Outside the latter area, except for tanneries, saw and bark mills, and the making of bar iron from bog ore, there was no manufacturing for more than immediate local consumption.

By 1850 the State had 91,532 inhabitants: 42,780 in New Castle County, 22,816 in Kent, and 25,093 in Sussex. Included in the total were 18,073 free Negroes and 2,290 slaves. For more than a century the freeing of slaves had been retarded by the legal requirement of an indemnity to be paid the county if the Negro should become a public charge. A succession of drastic laws to prevent the kidnaping of free Negroes did not stop the practice in Delaware *(see Tour 1A),* and in 1851 entrance of non-resident free Negroes into the State was prohibited.

Active Abolitionists in Delaware were comparatively few, but a group, chiefly Quakers, of whom Thomas Garrett was outstanding because of his impressive personality and moral conviction, conducted a link in the Underground Railroad by which thousands of fugitive slaves escaped to the North. The general antislavery sentiment existing from Colonial days contemplated the gradual freeing of the slaves by their owners or by State law and by the action of Congress to prevent further extension of slave territory. In the national election of 1860, the State vote for President, divided among four candidates, resulted in victory for the pro-slavery electors for Breckenridge, who polled 7,337. (The combined Lincoln-Douglas-Bell vote was 8,776.) But when a decision had to be made between Secession and the Union, the State supported the Union.

A serious disruption of life in this border State began when news of Fort Sumter was received. Families, life-long friends, associates in political and professional work, were separated in grief, bitterness, disappointment, and even hatred as the war progressed. Governor William Burton, a Democrat, conducted the government in the interest of the Union, as did his successor William Cannon, a former Democrat elected in 1862 on the Union ticket. Southern sentiment, which gained strength during the war, sent many sons of Delaware into the Confederate Army. The majority, following the State's tradition, contributed a large number of men in defense of the Union. Three-year service men totaled 10,303. More than 3,000 others served for part of the war. Delaware troops at Antietam, Fredericksburg, Chancellorsville, Gettysburg, and elsewhere upheld the reputation of the State for valor. General Thomas A. Smyth (last general officer killed in the war), Rear Admiral Samuel F. du Pont, General A. T. A. Torbert, and Colonel Henry A. du Pont were among the Delawareans who achieved renown.

Through Representative George P. Fisher, President Lincoln offered Delaware an emancipation proposal in 1861 by which the Federal Government would pay slave owners $500 for each emancipated slave. If Delaware accepted, other border States were expected to follow and thus lead to a peaceful settlement of the slavery issue. Delaware's refusal, together with the policing of polling places by Federal troops, became a weapon in the growing proslavery campaign in favor of the Confederacy.

Except for the election of a Republican congressman at the Special Election of 1863, the election of William Cannon as war Governor in 1862 was the last Republican success in the State until 1895. The local Democratic disapproval of Horace Greeley's attitude toward slavery caused many Democrats to cut the head of their ticket in 1872 and gave the Grant electors a substantial majority. After 1870 the Democrats campaigned as the White Man's Party. In 1878 and again in 1886 the Republicans failed to form a ticket. In the latter year the Temperance Reform Party, which polled a very small vote, offered the only opposition to the Democratic Party. A split in the Democratic Party in 1888, combined with new energy among Republicans, gave the latter a majority of one in the General Assembly.

At this strategic moment a new resident in the State, J. Edward Addicks, gas company promoter in several States, offered himself as candidate for the Senate. He met the consistent coldness of the Delaware electorate and politicians toward candidates not born in the State. Undaunted, he came back year after year, finally winning friends and splitting the Republican Party into the Union and Regular factions. In 1888 the Republican State Committee had a campaign fund of $5,000, and the total Republican vote was about 12,000. By 1903 the Republican vote had reached between 18,000 and 20,000, and the total funds expended were estimated in hundreds of thousands. Addicks was still a candidate for the Senate. Some of his Delaware-born friends won office, but Addicks finally lost after a twenty-year struggle (1905), during which his faction had caused a deadlock in the State Senate on several occasions, thus preventing the election of United States Senators.

The Republican ascendancy, gained during the Addicks period, continued, but with gradually smaller margins, to replace the long dominance of the Democratic Party, until the 1936 election.

In the era of general prosperity following the Civil War, industry developed rapidly and transportation expanded in the northern part of the State. The central and southern sections of Delaware for a time had both railroad and steamboat service in addition to the sailing sloops that continued to ply between town wharves and Philadelphia. By the 1880's, however, inadequate transportation facilities, high freight rates, and the competion of southern and western growers brought a decline in Delaware agriculture. Many of the large farms of the eighteenth and early nineteenth century had been divided among the inheriting generations, or broken up for sale in small holdings. Activities of agricultural societies and of several State agencies were beginning to spread improved methods among the more successful farmers, but the general low state of farm income made for backwardness in both economic and social welfare. Public education suffered as did public health, and the population declined in the more isolated districts. Comfortable circumstances in the northern part of the State led to a similar inaction and lack of social advance.

But throughout this period the State did not lack citizens of insight and civic spirit who continuously sought reforms and advantages for the people. Notable among these was Francis Vincent (1822–1884), who awakened and directed public sentiment, both as editor and publisher of *The Blue Hen's Chicken,* a weekly newspaper, and as historian of the State and leader of many progressive causes. One of his achievements (recorded by the *Breakwater Light,* published at Lewes) was the establishment of life-saving stations on the Delaware coast.

After the turn of the century, the Legislature finally ratified the thirteenth, fourteenth, and fifteenth amendments to the Constitution of the United States. With this milestone passed, measures for the public welfare and advancement in education were gradually adopted, and by the beginning of the First World War provision for modern roads and schools was well under way.

In that war, the Delaware soldiers were attached to many commands and their movements are difficult to trace. Of the 10,000 men mustered into service, the 59th Delaware Pioneer Infantry was the largest single group of Delaware men.

Highway development was inaugurated by the building of the first stretch of the Coleman du Pont Road, a State-long concrete highway, gift of the Delaware citizen for whom it is named *(see TRANSPORTATION).* The legislature of 1917 created a State highway commission, and provided for mothers' pensions, workmen's compensation, a State income tax, and a commission to study educational conditions and evolve an improved public school system. Many reforms followed, and new modern school buildings throughout the State were the gift of another Delawarean, Pierre S. du Pont.

An Americanization program, initiated by civic associations before the

First World War and later taken over by the State department of education, has brought to foreign-born residents unusual opportunities for becoming citizens and participating in community life. Among the State's foreign-born population, centered in Wilmington, few adults have failed to apply for citizenship papers. According to the United States census (1950), 4.4 percent of the total population, or 13,844 out of 318,058, were foreign-born whites. Italians, Poles, Irish and English predominate among the foreign born.

Of the 43,598 Negroes of Delaware more than 25,000 now live in urban areas. Leaders of the race have endeavored to obtain for them more cultural and economic opportunities, and Delaware Negroes have risen to distinction in public office, in the legal profession, in the church, and in the arts. Following a 1950 decision of the Vice-Chancellor that the State was not providing equal opportunities for university undergraduates, Negroes are admitted to the University of Delaware under the regular entrance requirements. The University had previously admitted Negroes to the engineering school and for graduate work.

The resilience of Delaware people when conditions began to improve after the hardships of the depression made notable this State's share in America's part in World War II. Industrial commodities from warships to wooden forks and spoons used by the armed forces were in high output. Freewill giving of money and services was on the same scale in civilian support.

Delaware had 33,000 men and women in the armed services, many injured and 798 dead. Since the war a $6,000,000 veterans hospital has been built at Elsmere, New Castle County and the Memorial Bridge across the Delaware River.

Postwar employment has been high, increasing from 92,026 registered in the state employment office in 1947 to 118,798 in 1953. Gross receipts of manufacturers for the same period averaged $377,000,000 and reached $805,000,000 in 1953.

In agricultural production, cash farm income from 1943 to 1951 averaged $92,604,000 annually and reached $112,958,000 in 1951.

Both rural and industrial Delaware have shown growing interest in cultural recreation—art, music, and the theater—and in the conservation and development of natural resources.

During the 1938-1953 period, interest of Delaware people in the State's past and present history has been marked by wide support of the agencies devoted to its study and publication.

Government

THE first colony in Delaware, at Swanendael (Lewes), was set up under a "Charter of Freedoms and Exemptions" issued to certain merchants of Amsterdam by the Dutch West India Company, and ratified by the States General of the Netherlands on June 7, 1629. This charter granted large tracts of land to any member of the company who, as a "patroon," should bring over to New Netherland within four years "fifty souls, upwards of fifteen years old," at his own cost and risk. The charter granted to the patroon the exclusive "fishing, fowling, and grinding" rights; civil and criminal jurisdiction; power to appoint all magistrates and other officials of his colony. The settlers sent out by a patroon were bound to him as subjects for a term of years. This modified form of feudalism existed for only a year on Delaware soil, ending when the colony, established in 1631 at the site of Lewes, was exterminated by the Indians.

In the Swedish settlements on the Delaware, founded under the charter and privileges granted in 1637 to the New Sweden Company by the Swedish Crown, a military form of government was established under instructions of a council of prominent shareholders in Sweden. The governor, appointed by the council, was given complete administrative and judicial powers, supported by his officers and soldiers. He was instructed to dispense justice according to Swedish law and to use his own discretion in all circumstances not covered by the council's rulings. In the rudimentary courts, the governor acted as judge (and sometimes also as plaintiff), assisted by a body of about twelve men chosen by him from the "principal and wisest" members of the colony, with whom he heard the evidence and decided the case, punishing by fine, imprisonment, or death. Until almost the end of Sweden's control of the Delaware, the people had no voice in the government. The last Swedish governor, Rising, called together the ablest men to draw up and adopt the ordinances his instructions authorized him to effect concerning trade, agriculture, hunting, preserving the forests, and other matters.

When the Dutch took possession of the settlements on the Delaware in 1655, they set up at Fort Casimir under a vice-director, Jean Paul Jacquet,

OLD COURTHOUSE (C. 1722), NEW CASTLE

an administration subject to the director-general, Peter Stuyvesant, and his council at New Amsterdam. Stuyvesant and his council had executive, legislative, and judicial authority over New Netherland, subject to the approval of the directors in Holland and as long as their acts did not violate the laws of that country. The instructions of the West India Company to Stuyvesant excluded any participation by the inhabitants in the selection of officers or in the determination of ordinances or taxes. Jacquet was given instructions by Stuyvesant accordingly. He was entrusted with "supreme command" over officers, soldiers, and freemen on the Delaware, but shared with a council of four—the secretary, military commander, and two sergeants, or two of the ablest freemen if the case was purely civil—the exercise of legislative and judicial power in petit affairs. All important cases and appeals were to be referred to Stuyvesant and his council at New Amsterdam.

After control of the settlement at Fort Casimir (over territory from the south side of the Christina to Bombay Hook) was transferred by the West India Company to the City of Amsterdam in the summer of 1656, Jacquet called the community together at the fort on several occasions, to nominate proper persons for tobacco inspectors and similar offices, and to consider ordinances. For inspectors, the people nominated four, from among whom the vice-director chose two, and in the adoption of ordinances the people seem to have had a determining voice.

When in April 1657, the City of Amsterdam's first expedition and new director arrived, the latter, Jacob Alrichs, put into effect the Amsterdam decree that the government and administration of justice in New Amstel should follow the Amsterdam model—the officers to be: a "schout" (who exercised the duties both of sheriff and of prosecuting attorney in the court), five or seven "schepens" (magistrates) appointed by the director from double the number nominated by the burghers, and three burgomasters selected by the burghers from the "honestest, fittest and richest" Dutch settlers in the community. These large concessions toward self-government represented a policy adopted to win and hold desirable settlers in sufficient numbers to make the colony pay. Alrichs died in 1659, and Alexander D'Hinoyossa succeeded him at New Amstel.

Meanwhile the government under Stuyvesant was maintained on the rest of the river, with its center under William Beeckman at Fort Altena. Beeckman, who in 1657 had succeeded Jacquet as vice-director, was customs collector for the West India Company and was required to go to New Amstel when ships arrived. Beeckman and D'Hinoyossa quarreled often over questions of conflicting jurisdiction, but after the formal transfer of the whole river to the City of Amsterdam, December 22, 1663, the West India Company's director withdrew and the New Amstel provisions were applied under D'Hinoyossa to the whole river. Though the colony suffered from the lack of judgment or neglect of duty of some of its officers, and from other causes, the form of government suited local conditions. Its representative character was emphasized at the close of Dutch control when the burgomasters signed, on behalf of all the inhabitants, the articles of capitulation to the English.

In 1664, after Sir Robert Carr had somewhat roughly ousted D'Hino-yossa from Fort Amstel and had established English authority on the river, Colonel Nicolls, Governor at New York, came down to the Delaware "to take special care for the good government of said place." By the Duke of York's instructions (1664) the Dutch officers—schout, burgomasters, and magistrates—were continued in power under a military commander, Captain John Carr, Sir Robert's son. The Dutch method of government with its magistrates' court was little changed during the first decade of the Duke's period. The first trial approximating English form was of the Long Finn in 1669. English customs and English laws, applied to some extent in 1672 under a high sheriff, a bailiff, and six magistrates at New Castle with authority over the whole river, were more fully introduced after 1673. In that year, during the brief return of Dutch control, three courts of justice were established: at New Amstel, Upland (Chester), and Whorekill (Lewes); the magistrates for each court were chosen by the governor at New York from double the number nominated by a "majority of votes" of the inhabitants. Upon resumption of control by the Duke of York the following year, these courts were continued. In 1676, an ordinance and proclamation on the establishment of the "Duke of York's Laws" were sent to the Delaware for enforcement; the same courts were again continued. At this period the courts had a broad jurisdiction; in addition to civil and criminal cases, they granted applications to take up land, received returns of surveys, had transfers of real estate acknowledged before them, regulated church affairs, directed construction and maintenance of highways and fences, made provision for the care of the poor, recorded sales of the time of servants, even recorded brand marks of cattle.

Popular government in Delaware received impetus from William Penn's "Frame of the Government of the Province of Pennsylvania," although at first—except in the council—the powers of the people's representatives did not include the initiation of legislation. Penn's first assembly, convened at Upland in 1682, passed the "Act of Union" joining the lower counties or territories (Delaware) with the Province; at Philadelphia in

1683, the "Act of Settlement" and the "Great Law" were adopted. These instruments provided for civil and religious liberty, for representative government through an elective council and assembly—the latter having the right to accept or reject but not to initiate legislation—and for a humane code for the administration of justice in the three counties of Delaware to be governed "in union" with the Province of Pennsylvania.

Penn's government included a deputy or lieutenant governor appointed by him, and a council of advisers to the governor called the Provincial Council; the members of the council and of the assembly were elected by counties by the freemen; the franchise was limited to land owners, "or any inhabitant" who paid "scot and lot to the governor." All elections were to be by ballot. How this last provision was carried out in Delaware is shown by a statement of Griffith Jones, a member of the council from Kent County. In a debate in council at Philadelphia in April 1689, Jones said: "Balloting . . . at upland & in all the Lower Countyes (is) by black & white beanes put into a hatt, wch is a balloting in his sense, & cannot be deneyed by the Charter, where it is demanded."

In 1701, Penn issued a more liberal charter, called "The Charter of Privileges," which confirmed the assembly's right to originate bills enjoyed under "Markham's Frame" since 1696, made the council appointive with executive power only, the Assembly to choose its own officers and the freemen of each county to elect sheriffs and coroners. This charter also permitted the "Territories" (Delaware) to hold a separate assembly from the "Province" (Pennsylvania) if either desired.

The Delaware counties did not at once accept the charter, but used it to bring to a head disagreements existing since Penn's arrival. The "three lower counties" separated from counties of the Province of Pennsylvania in 1704, and set up their own assembly at New Castle. They were still represented in the Council of the province and acknowledged the authority of the provincial governor of Pennsylvania, who after 1703 was to them a royal governor because his appointment had to be approved by the Crown. By their own assembly and the Governor and Council of Pennsylvania, the three Delaware counties were governed until a convention elected by the people adopted a separate constitution for the Delaware State in 1776.

Altogether Delaware has had four constitutions, adopted in the following years: 1776, 1792, 1831, and 1897. The constitution of 1776 provided that the general assembly should consist of two houses: an assembly of seven members from each county and a legislative council of three members from each county, to be elected by the freeholders. Only those freeholders were enfranchised "who owned 50 acres of land, with 12 acres of it cleared and improved, or were otherwise worth 40 pounds lawful money." The President of the State was chosen by joint vote of the two houses. To advise the general assembly there was provided a privy council, composed of four members, two elected by each house.

Penn had created a provincial court to sit in each of the counties during the year. By 1736 the local courts (developed by the separate assembly for the lower counties) were as follows: the county courts of general quarter sessions of the peace and jail delivery, the county courts of common pleas, and the supreme court of the counties of New Castle, Kent, and Sussex upon Delaware. The justices of the peace of each county formed the county courts; the supreme court consisted of three judges, who were empowered to try all appeals from the county courts and all civil and criminal matters not determinative by the county courts. The constitution of 1776 created a supreme court, consisting of three justices, one to be chief justice; and a court of common pleas for each county. There was also a court of appeals to "have all the authority and powers heretofore given by law in the last resort to the King in Council, under the old government."

Article 26 of this constitution is of unique historic interest. It provided that "no person hereafter imported into the State from Africa ought to be held in slavery under any pretense whatever, and no Negro, Indian, or Mulatto slave ought to be brought into this State, for sale, from any part of the world." Both this provision and the one relating to suffrage, mentioned above, were omitted from the constitution of 1792.

Under the 1792 constitution, the government was considerably less complicated. The executive power was no longer vested in a President but in a Governor to be chosen by popular vote; a voter must be free, white, and have paid a State or county tax. The Governor was given larger powers of appointment; the privy council was dropped; the Legislature became the senate and house of representatives. Radical changes were made in the courts. The court of common pleas, as well as the supreme court, was given State-wide jurisdiction. The justices of the supreme court, by virtue of their office, also constituted the court of oyer and terminer and general jail delivery. There was provided an orphans' court, a registers' court, and a court of quarter sessions of the peace for each county. The high court of errors and appeals, superseding the court of appeals, was set up as the court of last resort. A court of chancery was established, as a separate tribunal, presided over by a chancellor.

The third constitution, that of 1831, made the meetings of the Legislature biennial instead of annual; Presidential electors were to be elected by the people. The most important change in the judicial system was the abolishment of the supreme court and the court of common pleas; in their places the superior court was created, with the jurisdiction of the two former courts.

The present constitution was adopted in 1897, after many years of agitation for revision. Changing conditions—the abolition of slavery, the growing democratic spirit, the growth of population of the city of Wilmington—made numerous alterations desirable. The new constitution reapportioned representation according to election districts and thus partly in proportion to population. The judges were appointed by the Governor for twelve years instead of for life.

The constitution of 1897 has, in addition to the usual requirements as to age and residence, a provision that prospective voters, coming of age after 1900, must be able to read the Constitution of the United States in English. Those who have been prevented from receiving an education through a physical handicap are excused from meeting this test.

Delaware is the only State in the Union in which amendments to the constitution by legislative proposal or action of a constitutional convention do not have to be ratified by the voters before becoming effective. Amendments become part of the constitution by passing both houses of the Legislature by a two-thirds vote at two successive sessions.

The government of Delaware is divided into the traditional executive, legislative, and judicial branches. The Governor is elected for a term of four years and is ineligible for a third term. The Governor's appointments where emoluments exceed $500 must be confirmed by the senate, and his power to grant pardons is limited to those cases that have been recommended by the board of pardons. His veto power extends to separate items in appropriation bills, and a three-fifths vote of each house of the legislature is necessary to pass a bill over his veto. If he fails to sign or return a bill sent to him for his approval, such bill automatically becomes a law at the end of ten days, unless the general assembly shall, by adjournment, prevent its return, in which case it shall not become a law without the approval of the Governor.

Other executive officers include the Lieutenant Governor, State treasurer, attorney-general, insurance commissioner, and auditor of accounts, all of whom are elected at the general election. The terms of these officers are four years except those of the state treasurer and auditor of accounts, which are two years. The Governor appoints the Secretary of State.

Many of the administrative functions of the State government are vested in various boards and commissions set up by the General Assembly, whose members are appointed by the Governor. The members of these commissions, mostly unpaid, perform a great amount of work, solve administrative difficulties, and save the State money, while enabling it to assume necessary functions for the welfare of the people. The system has been carried somewhat to excess. A commission on reorganization of state government reporting in 1950, recommended consolidating 92 existing boards, commissions and agencies of the executive branch into 19 departments and agencies. The first step was taken 1951 by consolidating most of the state's welfare agencies into a state department of public welfare.

In the legislative branch of the government, the senate is composed of 17 members (the smallest State senate in the country), and the house of representatives, of 35 members. There are ten representative districts each in Sussex and Kent Counties and fifteen in New Castle County. The term of a representative is two years. The senatorial districts are allocated five each to Sussex and Kent Counties and seven to New Castle County. The city of Wilmington elects five representatives and two senators out of the numbers assigned to New Castle County. The senators serve for four years. This division of the State for election purposes is without regard to the proportion of population in Wilmington. With approximately one-half the inhabitants of the State, Wilmington is given only two of the 17 members of the senate, and five of the 35 representatives. So distinct is the city as a voting unit and in point of view, that it is customary to refer to the vote of Wilmington and rural New Castle County as being entirely separate.

The State retains the convention system of choosing candidates for State offices. The substitution of the direct primary has never been championed by either major party.

There is no requirement in Delaware for an individual to put himself on record as being a member of any particular party. Consequently, persons of all shades of political opinion may participate in the primaries of their adversaries.

The constitution provides that "the General Election shall be held biennially on the Tuesday next after the first Monday in the month of November, and shall be by ballot; but the General Assembly may by law prescribe the means, methods, and instruments of voting, so as best to secure secrecy and the independence of the voter, preserve the freedom and purity of elections, and prevent fraud, corruption, and intimidation thereat." The law making it possible for legal ballots to be distributed before election and previously marked ballots to be voted has been superseded (1953) by a law requiring use of voting machines. The permanent registration of voters was repealed and registration every four years required.

The judiciary procedure is still patterned largely after the ancient court system of England, and some forms of pleading long since discarded in England are retained in Delaware. Until 1951 the judicial functions of the State under the constitution of 1897, were exercised in seven major courts: Supreme Court, superior court, court of general sessions, court of oyer and terminer, court of chancery, orphans' court and register's court (probate). All except the register's court were held by seven judges, who were the chancellor and vice-chancellor (whose office was created in 1939), the chief justice and four associate judges.

The Supreme Court, the final court of appeal, consisted of the chancellor, chief justice and the four associate judges. In any appeal from a lower court only those members could sit who had not sat in the court below.

As the work of all the state courts increased during the half-century following adoption of the constitution of 1897, the burden of work upon the limited number of judges and the long delay in hearing appeals became a serious handicap in the administration of justice.

Agitation for an amendment to the constitution establishing a separate Supreme Court failed for many years to secure the necessary legislative support. Finally at two successive sessions of the General Assembly, 1949 and 1951, an amendment creating a separate Supreme Court became part of the constitution.

The Supreme Court consists of three justices one of whom is designated in his appointment as chief justice who when present presides at all sittings of the court which must always be of three judges. In case of vacancies, absences, or disqualification because of interest, the court is completed by designation of one or more judges from the other courts. The court determines questions of law certified to it by the other courts.

The amendment creating the Supreme Court eliminates two of the lower courts and otherwise simplifies the State judicial system. The major courts besides the Supreme Court are the superior court, court of chancery, orphans' court and register's court. The latter is held by the register, an elected county official. The others are held by seven State judges who are the chancellor, vice-chancellor, the president judge of the superior court and of the orphans' court and four associate judges of the superior and orphans' court, one of whom must be a resident in each county and the fourth appointed at large. All State judges are appointed by the governor with consent of the State Senate, for terms of twelve years. They are eligible for reappointment.

If for a case in any court there is no judge available to hold court, the Governor may appoint a judge "ad litem" for that one case.

STATE HOUSE, DOVER

The judges of the courts of common pleas of New Castle, Kent, and Sussex Counties, of the Wilmington municipal court, and the various magistrates constitute the minor judiciary, all appointed by the Governor.

The superior court, composed of the resident judge and four associate justices, may consist of one, two, or three of these five law judges. One constitutes a quorum, except in criminal cases, where three judges must sit. The superior court has jurisdiction over all causes of a civil nature, real, personal and mixed—at common law, and all major crimes. It has appellate jurisdiction from the minor courts.

The court of chancery, or equity, is entirely separate from the law courts. Presided over by the chancellor or vice-chancellor, it has "full power to hear and decree all matters and causes in equity."

The orphans' court in each county consists of the chancellor, vice-chancellor and the resident associate judge. One of them constitutes a quorum.

The court of common pleas is held at Wilmington for New Castle County, and at Dover for Kent County. This court has concurrent jurisdiction with the superior court in civil matters involving not more than $1,000, and with the magistrates' courts in criminal affairs. In 1953, the court of common pleas in Sussex County was created.

The register of wills court (probate court) is held in each county by the register of wills who is both judge and clerk of the court. All wills must be proved in this court. The register examines and approves the accounts of executors and administrators. Appeals from his decision are to the orphans court—with two judges sitting—whose decision is final.

There are two juvenile courts in the State; one at Wilmington, whose jurisdiction includes Wilmington and rural New Castle County, and the other sitting at specified times in and for Kent and Sussex Counties. In 1945 the family court for Wilmington and rural New Castle County was created to include the former juvenile court. It combines the powers and jurisdiction of a juvenile court concerning neglected, dependent, and delinquent children with jurisdiction within a family, civil and criminal, except felonies and wife-beating. No child under 18 years except for a capital crime may be taken to any other court. All hearings are required to be private. The staff includes trained investigators and probation officers.

The two judges of this court are appointed by the governor for twelve years. They must be attorneys having a knowledge of social problems and child psychology. The governor appoints one judge for Kent and Sussex Counties who must have the same knowledge but need not be an attorney.

The justices of the peace, or magistrates, are State officers appointed by the Governor. They have jurisdiction in minor criminal cases and in civil cases in which the amount does not exceed $500. By a law passed in 1935, the court of common pleas for New Castle County has the same jurisdiction and power in criminal matters as is now vested in justices of the peace for the county. The accused has the right to elect to have the case tried by the court of common pleas.

The municipal court of the city of Wilmington has jurisdiction over all cases involving violation of the city ordinances. The judge of this court has final jurisdiction as to some misdemeanors; and acts as committing magistrate as to others as well as to felonies committed in the city.

The elective governing bodies of the counties are the levy courts, the members of which, as provided for by the act of 1742, were first taken from three other county bodies: the justices of the peace, the grand jurymen, and the assessors. They met annually "for laying the levies," and to "settle and adjust the . . . money . . . to be raised yearly, to defray the charges of building and repairing courthouses, prisons, work-houses, or for destroying wolves, crows, and black-birds, with such other uses as may redound to the public service and benefit of the said counties. . . ." Their present duties are to administer the financial affairs of the counties, to supervise the assessing of property, fix the annual tax rate, levy the taxes, and appoint various county officials—the board of assessment, county engineer, constables, et al. County elective officials are sheriff, coroner, comptroller, receiver of taxes and county treasurer, register of wills, recorder of deeds, clerk of the peace, register in chancery and clerk of the orphans' court, and prothonotary.

The counties are subdivided into hundreds. This quaint political anachronism is still shown on all maps of Delaware, although for purposes of government the hundred is no longer of great importance. The constitution of 1897 divided the State into representative districts; five of these are in Wilmington; in rural New Castle County they are coextensive with the hundreds; and in Kent and Sussex with the hundreds or divisions and combinations of hundred areas. In New Castle County the jurisdiction of magistrates (in civil cases for debt) covers their own and adjacent hundreds; in Kent and Sussex it covers their respective counties. There is indication that the origin of the hundred system in Delaware dates from the Duke of York's period when the counties were divided into assessment districts; later this ancient political subdivision of the early Anglo-Saxons was confirmed by William Penn, whose charter from the British Crown authorized the dividing of his territory in America into hundreds.

Although the pillory was abolished in 1905, Delaware still maintains the whipping post in all three counties, its use legal for 5 to 60 lashes, "publicly by strokes on the bare back, well laid on," for robbery, assault, embezzlement, poisoning with intent to murder, arson, burglary, larceny, horse-stealing, wife-beating, and other offenses. Women and prisoners of "tender years" are exempt from the lash. In justifying retention of this form of punishment, its proponents, pointing to the State's freedom from serious crime waves, claim that fear of the lash keeps out-of-State criminals away, and that a very small percentage of offenders require a second whipping. Sentence of whipping is now at discretion of judges.

In Delaware, urban places are not classified and there are few general laws for municipalities. The legislature has granted an individual charter to each of the fifty-two incorporated cities and towns. In the larger towns, the mayor is chosen by the people. In the others, the town council or commissioners choose one of their number as presiding officer to act as executive head of the town government. Dover, the capital of the State, Milford, Harrington, Rehoboth and Seaford have the council-manager plan of government. Other town charters permit this form.

Wilmington received a borough charter from George II in 1739, granted in response to a petition of the inhabitants. It provided for the annual election of a chief burgess, second burgess, six assistant burgesses, high constable, and town clerk, and served until 1772, when the borough charter was amended by the general assembly to enlarge the town's boundaries and powers.

The present government of Wilmington is of the mayor-council type, operating under a charter from the State granted in 1832. In early days various committees of the council supervised the water supply, public safety, streets, and other facilities, but these functions were gradually turned over to the present boards, commissions, and departments. As is true of many of the towns of the State, a citizen must be a property owner in order to be eligible for the office of councilman. *(For Single-Tax Colonies, see Arden.)*

State and local revenues in Delaware come mostly from separate sources. The State obtains its revenues chiefly from business and corporation taxes, income, inheritance, and estate taxes, the gasoline tax, and various licenses and fees. The county and town revenues are principally derived from real estate taxes, supplemented by various license fees. There is no personal property tax in Delaware, no State real estate tax, no sales tax, no corporation income tax, and no tax upon intangible property.

The Delaware Corporation Law has a pertinent relation to State financing. Passed in 1899 (amended in 1903, and several times in later years) its liberal provisions have drawn many corporations here for chartering. The main attraction besides simplicity of the system and liberal provisions is that the law has been tested in the Delaware courts and its stability assured.

The constitution does not establish responsibility for a State fiscal system, but the present budget system created by legislative acts, provides a complete financial plan for the State, submitted biennially to the general assembly. Until 1941 State revenue was separated into special funds, according to source, earmarked as cumulative accounts for schools, highways, and other needs. State revenue is now paid into a general fund from which the general assembly makes annual appropriations. The State tax department headed by the State Tax Commissioner provides the governor, budget commission, and legislature with revenue estimates and detailed reports and records of moneys received and deposited.

Total receipts of the State at the close of the fiscal year, June 30, 1953 were $66,480,031. Cash balance at beginning of the year, $22,874,050. Expenditures were, $74,700,468. Gross debt (serial bonds for public improvements) $60,548,000; debt service (interest and redemptions) $3,148,107.

In recent years, Delaware has made rapid advance in the field of public education and in social legislation. The State school system especially has become modern in administration and facilities, and includes new, scientifically designed buildings.

The State Board of Charities began to function in 1919, to supervise the tax-supported charitable and corrective institutions and services. The Industrial Accident Board was set up in 1917 to administer the Workmen's Compensation Law; the Mothers' Pension Commission in 1917, to furnish pensions to widowed mothers for support of children under sixteen; the State Old Age Welfare Commission (1931), to grant and administer the old age pension, and to administer the State Welfare Home; the Labor Commission (1915), to enforce the provisions of the Child Labor Law, the Ten Hour Law for Female Employees, and the Sanitary Law for Female Employees; the Unemployment Compensation Commission (1937), to administer a system by which Delawareans will receive compensation during periods of unemployment.

State institutions include the Delaware State Hospital at Farnhurst; the State Training School for Feeble Minded, Stockley; the Blind Shop, Wilmington; the Governor Bacon Health Center, Delaware City; Emily P. Bissell Sanatorium (tuberculosis, general), Marshallton; Detention Home for Juveniles, Wilmington; Ferris School (industrial for boys), Marshallton; Woods Haven School (industrial for girls), Claymont; Kruse School (industrial for colored girls), near Marshallton; State Welfare Home, Smyrna.

From 1939 through 1953, most of the foregoing agencies and institutions have been developed and given improved facilities to meet the best modern standards and practices. Welfare agencies have been combined in a State department of public welfare. The tuberculosis sanatoria have been reorganized as one modern institution. A large State health center, on the site of the former Fort du Pont in New Castle County, cares for maladjusted children, chronically ill old persons, and other groups needing expert treatment and care.

Additional State agencies created in this period are the Commission on Children and Youth, State Development Department, Legislative Reference Bureau at Dover, State Archaeological Board, Geological Survey.

By amendment of the constitution a separate Supreme Court has been created and the State court system simplified. By constitutional amendment, also, zoning of counties may be authorized by act of legislature.

The State has provided surveys of the public school system by outstanding national authorities in this field and studies by similar authorities in the interest of reorganization of the State executive department.

Transportation

RIDGES of high land north of Wilmington in Brandywine Hundred, a mile or more away from the Delaware River, provide vantage ground from which to view most of the modern developments in transportation. Beyond the immediate slopes in the foreground and beyond the marginal lowlands lies an extensive sweep of the river with the shore and mainland of New Jersey visible in the distance. Through this area, between river and ridge, runs a series of high-speed transportation lines.

Close to the Delaware lie the multiple tracks of a main line railroad. Parallel with the railroad runs the new Governor Printz Boulevard for motortrucks, and parallel also, but further inland, runs US 13, with its heavy traffic of motor vehicles, including both local and trunk line buses. Electric coaches leave US 13 at Penny Hill and continue east of the highway, while, at the western edge of this belt of travel-ways and again parallel with the river, is another main-line railroad. Streamlined passenger trains and miles of freight cars pass continually along both railroads; also by the river, run electric and two-car Diesel trains for local traffic.

On the river, their speeds contrasted with one another's and with that of shore traffic, move liners, freighters, ocean-going yachts, and rivercraft: local steamboats and pilot boats, motorboats, ferries to and from New Jersey towns, and an occasional sailing vessel. Overhead the regular mail planes, seaplanes, and other aircraft follow the general direction of the land and water traffic.

At night this panorama of travel is displayed in the moving illumination of searchlights, beacons, and motor headlights, shining through spirals of smoke and steam; while the brilliant lamps along the New Jersey shore, and the patterned concentrations of innumerable facets of light from industrial plants on the Delaware side further illumine the landscape.

Still another railroad approaches Wilmington along the valley of Brandywine Creek, encircling the city west and south toward its river terminal at Pigeon Point, below the mouth of the Christina. Here a tugboat service of this road connects with the New Jersey shore.

The Wilmington Marine Terminal on the south bank of the Christina, close to the Delaware River, provides facilities for ships from all parts of the world. At the Terminal and at other points close to the industrial sections of the town, the Pennsylvania, the Baltimore and Ohio, and the Reading Railroads have adequate trackage for storing and for rapid classification and distribution of shipments, and operate many miles of freight siding service. The Reading is Wilmington's direct route to its anthracite supply in Pennsylvania. The line has no scheduled passenger service. The heavy passenger traffic of the Atlantic Coast route is carried by the Baltimore and Ohio and the Pennsylvania Railroads, and by the Delmarva division of the latter. On the Delmarva route, however, motor by far surpasses railroad travel. This division provides freight and refrigeration service for the perishable commodities and farm produce of the peninsula direct to Baltimore, Philadelphia, New York, and Boston markets.

South of Wilmington, the State-long Coleman du Pont Road (US 13 and US 113) is developing, as the founder intended, with two one-way lanes in each direction. Two double north and south roads, with a tree-planted parkway between, are now completed from State Road to Dover; and the Du Pont Road, with the diverging trunk line south of Dover, has become the backbone of an extensive system of paved highways connecting with the main Nation-wide systems and interconnecting all the towns and rural districts of the State.

Inland waterways, once all-important, are beginning to enjoy a return of former popularity. The Chesapeake and Delaware Canal, toll-free, owned by the Federal Government, crosses the State about 15 miles south of Wilmington, at sea-level, and unites the Delaware and Chesapeake Bays as part of the Intracoastal Waterway along the Atlantic and Gulf Coasts.

Creeks flowing into the Delaware south of the canal are navigable for fishing boats and a few small Diesel freighters; and on the west side of Sussex County, the Nanticoke River flowing into the Chesapeake carries small bay freighters to Seaford. The Lewes and Rehoboth Canal is an inland waterway for pleasure craft and commercial vessels of small draft from Delaware Bay south into Rehoboth and Indian River Bays. Another canal, now neglected except by the rowboats of naturalists, leads still further south to Chincoteague waters off Maryland and Virginia.

Airlines make scheduled flights, passenger, express and freight, from New Castle County Airport and Dover Air Base; at Rehoboth in summer. Private airports with commercial rating and a number of landing fields under private control offer accommodations to fliers. The Federal Government maintains large Army Air Defense bases, one at New Castle County Airport

Stanley M. Arthurs

MAIL STAGE PASSING CONESTOGA WAGON

and another at Dover Air Base. Seaford and other towns maintain airports or landing fields.

The Delaware River, a great natural highway, with numerous tributaries penetrating the forest-covered land, formed an ideal transportation system for the earliest colonists. Supplemented by a network of paths and roadways crudely leveled and ill-kept, this system served settlements, Colony, and State for nearly 200 years after the landing of the Swedes in 1638.

Meanwhile the inhabitants, as even the few surviving records show, established all the main travel routes followed by modern transportation lines. The Swedish, Dutch, and early English settlers went to market, to church, and to court by boat, or they used the Indian trails and the driftways for the cattle, until gradually the cartroads on the plantations of the Swedes and the cartroads and dykes of the Dutch, and later of the English, were joined with the driftways and paths between settlements to form a pattern of winding traffic lanes that became common rights-of-way, confirmed in land titles and road laws.

Beginning with an agreement in 1671 between "those of New Castle" and Augustine Herman of Bohemia Manor in Maryland, by which each was to clear half of a cartroad joining the two places, and the order of the Duke of York's court at New Castle in 1675 that "some convenient way bee made passable betweene Towne and Towne in this River," King's roads were gradually established, not of course "straight and commodious," as William Penn decreed in 1690, but along the established routes.

The first line of travel between north and south followed the river from Naaman's Creek to the ford or the ferry over the Brandywine, which is at present Wilmington, then south to New Castle, curving inland to Red Lion and "Appoquinimy" *(see ODESSA: Tour 1),* and south again, crossing all the streams near their headwaters, to Lewes and Cape Henlopen. From the ford over the Mispillion (now Milford) a branch ran to the ford of the Nanticoke (Seaford), and after 1791, when Georgetown became the county-seat of Sussex County, a road followed from Milford to Georgetown and south into Maryland. Today the Du Pont Boulevard runs through the State in the same general direction, but often cutting across the curves of the old road.

As early as 1684, there was an alternate route that curved west on high land to Newport, then south to the headwaters of the Christina Creek (later Christiana Bridge). From this point a road led west to Elk River in Maryland while the main route dropped south to meet the eastern route at Red Lion.

A colonial statute of 1752, and one of 1762—which declared that "straight roads are a credit and ornament to a country as well as an ease and advantage to travellers," and ordered a 60-foot right-of-way for main roads—had little immediate effect. It was 1796 before the King's roads, with some of their windings eliminated, became the continuous State Road from Wilmington into Maryland, with branches to Lewes and Seaford. In the settlers' day, the Minquas Indians, whose trade was most valuable, lived to the northwest. One of the chief Indian cross routes came by the Head of Elk along the Christina to the site of Wilmington with a branch route to New Castle; a second trail of importance led from Bohemia headwaters to "Appoquinimy" (Odessa); and others connected the Maryland waterways further down the Peninsula to points along the Delaware Bay.

Along these Indian trails the first cross roads were made and the Indian trading points were chosen for settlement. The trail between Bohemia headwaters and "Appoquinimy" was cleared of trees for a cartroad between 1666 and 1669 by Augustine Herman. The cartway between Bohemia Manor and New Castle was cleared at "noe great Labour or Charge" in 1671. Soon afterward a direct route from the Delaware, near the mouth of St. Augustine Creek, was cleared to Herman's plantation of St. Augustine adjoining Bohemia, and was described by travelers in 1679 as "a large broad wagon road."

Within a decade after the Revolution a new concentration of ships in

Delaware harbors and the expansion of water-borne commerce again absorbed interest and energy to the neglect of roads. Hundreds of sloops, schooners, brigs, and larger vessels plied the river, many of them built and owned by the merchants and transportation companies of Wilmington, New Castle, Smyrna, Dover, Milford, Lewes, and even the smaller villages. By the early 1800's an extensive trade with Atlantic States, Nova Scotia, and the West Indies was in full swing, and several Delaware-owned vessels were engaged in European trade. In addition to the local output, Pennsylvania counties made shipments of hundreds of thousands of bushels of grain annually from the wharves of Delaware creeks and rivers.

The hauling created a demand for better roads and gave prospect of making them pay. But even before the turnpike companies, chartered to build the New Castle-Frenchtown road, the Newport and Gap, and the Lancaster turnpikes, had their toll-roads completed, Delaware passengers and freight were being transported by steamboat. Perhaps because of faster and faster sailing vessels built at Delaware wharves, or because of the inventions of John Fitch and Oliver Evans *(see NEWPORT)*, Delawareans seem to have adopted steamboat transportation more readily than they did the railroads and later the modern highways. The first steamboat to ply regularly between Wilmington and Philadelphia was the *Vesta* (1812), which made the trip one way in 8 hours. In 1836 the *New Castle* was making the round trip in one day. Competition between steamboats on the river and the new railroad along the shore for the trip between Philadelphia and Wilmington became so keen that the boats reduced the fare, originally one dollar, to 25 cents. The railroad came down to 12½ cents, and for a while the boats countered with 10-cent fares.

Meanwhile the canal between the Delaware and the Chesapeake, originally proposed in 1654 by the Swedish Governor, Rising (the work started in 1804 was abandoned for lack of funds), was finally built through St. Georges Creek to Back Creek. It was opened for use in 1829, providing an all-water route from Philadelphia to Baltimore. From 1829 until the Federal Government bought it (1919) and made it a 12-foot tidal channel (1927), three locks maintained two water levels above tidewater. Between 1935 and 1938 Federal appropriations totaling $13,107,000 were used in enlarging the channel to the present 27-foot depth and 250-foot width. Thousands of pleasure craft passed through the canal, June, 1950 to June 1951; commercial vessels made 15,802 transits with 8,613,630 cargo tons. The lift bridge at St. Georges was replaced (1942) by a fixed span.

Steamboats on the Delaware River and Chesapeake Bay gave impetus to the finishing of turnpikes connecting with terminals on these two water-

DELAWARE MEMORIAL BRIDGE
Credit: Lubitsh & Bungarz

ways, and to the building of the State's first railroad, to form, like the canal and the New Castle Turnpike, a link in the cross-Peninsula trade and travel route.

Construction of the New Castle and Frenchtown Turnpike, chartered in 1809 and 1811, had proceeded very slowly until the commissioners put the steamboat *Chesapeake* of the Union Line into regular service in Chesapeake Bay to take the place of the sailing vessels that met the New Castle stages and packet wagons at Frenchtown. The new service was so successful that the promoters proposed a railroad to replace the stages. To permit its building, the charter rights of the turnpike company were increased in 1827 and 1829, and the New Castle and Frenchtown Railroad was finished in 1831 *(see NEW CASTLE)*. After a trial trip on July 4, passenger coaches drawn by horses made the 16½ miles between the Delaware River and the Elk River in 1 hour and 35 minutes.

The Baltimore and Ohio Railroad Company had run the first railway passenger cars in America, also horse-drawn, from Baltimore to Ellicott's mills some months earlier. On September 10, the following year, 1832, a steam locomotive made in England, with two passenger cars attached, opened the first regular steam railroad passenger service in this country, on the New Castle and Frenchtown Railroad. Most travelers between North and South, including the President of the United States and members of Congress, used this early railroad. What was to become an all-rail route to Baltimore and the South, composed of the Wilmington and Susquehanna (to the Maryland line), the Delaware and Maryland (the Delaware line to Elkton), and the Baltimore and Port Deposit, was opened in July 1837, and in 1838 was completed to Philadelphia by merger with the Philadelphia, Wilmington and Baltimore Company. As an independent company from 1838 to 1881, gradually acquiring by purchase or lease all the railroads on the Peninsula and in southern Pennsylvania, the P.W. & B. (in the latter year absorbed by the Pennsylvania System) played a major part in the transportation development of Delaware.

Before the opening of the Wilmington-to-Elkton Railroad, the New Castle and Frenchtown Company had met competition with the Delaware and Chesapeake Canal by purchase (1833) of the "Union" and "Peoples" lines of steamboats. The railroad continued to operate independently until 1840, when a controlling interest was sold to the P.W. & B. Upon completion of the Wilmington and New Castle railroad in 1852, the steamboat connection for the New Castle and Frenchtown Railroad was transferred from New Castle to Wilmington, and with it the commerce that had centered at New Castle; thus bringing to the site of Fort Christina— Wilmington—the convergence in traffic and trade Governor Rising had envisaged.

The new railroad fever which began about 1849 produced immediately the six-mile connection between Wilmington and New Castle. But shipping continued to flourish in the southern section, the chief agricultural area of the State. Rails were not to reach Lewes, over 85 miles of flat country, until the transcontinental railroad reached San Francisco.

As early as 1836, however, the founder of a railroad to serve the Peninsula from north to south, the Honorable John M. Clayton, then recently retired from the United States Senate in disapproval of the policies of President Jackson, had secured a charter from the Delaware Legislature to build the Delaware Railroad (see BUENA VISTA). Clayton saw in Maryland's recently proposed railroad down the west side of the Peninsula a possible diversion of trade, earnings, and investments from Delaware. Legislators responding to his eloquent campaigning granted practically without change the charter written by Clayton. Among the provisions were freedom from all manner of taxation for 50 years, ample and summary powers of condemnation, the power to exempt from taxation forever areas of private land belonging to free-will donors of rights-of-way, and payment by the State of the costs of survey and all expenses preparatory to actual organization of the company—in addition to a subscription of $25,-000. John M. Clayton, William D. Waples, and Richard Mansfield were appointed Commissioners.

The survey was made, but the skepticism of the farmers and the bank failures of the 1837-9 depression counteracted the eloquence of Clayton. Subscriptions could not be obtained and "the shortest and cheapest line between Norfolk and the northern cities" could not then be built. The charter was forfeited and the building of a north-and-south railway down the Peninsula delayed 17 years.

Chief Justice Samuel M. Harrington of Dover, in 1849, took up the railroad promotion (Clayton was serving as Secretary of State in the cabinet of President Taylor), and secured the renewal of the charter for the Delaware Railroad, with a modification permitting the building of a railroad from Dona Landing, 6 miles east of Dover, across the State to Seaford, as part of a transportation line from Philadelphia to Norfolk which was already successful by steamer and stage. Again subscriptions lagged until 1852, when the State subscribed half the money needed on condition that the commissioners raised the other half. The State's offer was met and the company organized at Dover, May 22, 1852. The Dona-to-Seaford route was abandoned, and, as soon as the Delaware Railroad was in operation, the company bought the steamboat *Zepher* of the Dona Line and sold her out of the river.

In 1853 Judge Harrington obtained from the Legislature authorization for the P.W. & B. Railroad to guarantee bonds of the Delaware Road, and by 1856 the Delaware Railroad was completed from a junction with the New Castle and Frenchtown Railroad at "Rodney Station" (now Porter), to Seaford. The road was immediately leased to the P.W. & B. The State had contributed many times the amount originally regarded by John M. Clayton as a wise limit, and the money had been wrung from a reluctant legislature.

The Delaware Railroad ran, for the most part, west of the center of the State and through long stretches of wooded country. Soon the carrying trade was withdrawn from the tidewater landings and new villages were created. The counties, because of agitation by railroad representatives and land-owners, made sufficient improvement in the roads to the railway stations to encourage sawmills, and new logging ventures arose among the few reserves of virgin hardwood along the western boundary. The quickness of delivery of perishable fruits to northern markets meant that Dela-

DU PONT PARKWAY
Credit: Brooks Studio

ware peaches could reach even Boston in prime condition. Fancy prices were offered by the buyers, the growers' profits went into increased acreage and better cultivation, and freight rates increased.

Then in 1863, the Delaware Railroad, unable to procure enough freight cars, failed to move a bumper crop. Many thousands of baskets of peaches spoiled and the growers sued the company. Local support for the growers was unexpectedly strong. There was some strongly-felt opinion that the State's money would have paid better if it had been spent on good roads to the wharves. A prominent director of the railroad resigned to aid the prosecution against the road. The growers won what railroad men considered an exorbitant award, and thereafter defense of the railroad's interests became an important factor in Delaware politics.

Even before the completion of the Delaware Railroad to the south boundary of the State, companies were being promoted to charter connecting lateral roads in Delaware and Maryland. The north-and-south railway for the Eastern Shore of Maryland had never been built, and, as John M.

Clayton had assured Maryland growers, the Delaware road served both borders of the Peninsula.

The Wilmington and Northern Railroad Company, absorbed by the Reading Company in 1900, was chartered in 1877, but the road had been in operation from Wilmington to Birdsboro, Pennsylvania, since 1870 and to Reading since 1874. Its development had come from the need of a direct route for carrying anthracite coal to manufactories at and near Wilmington. A passenger service was maintained until 1932 connecting at Chadds Ford with the Baltimore Central Railroad. The "Wilmington & Northern" is widely remembered because it carried thousands of Wilmington children annually to outings in Lenape Park.

Since the rapid development of the State's modern highways, many of the short branches of the three railroad systems, the Pennsylvania, the B. & O., and the Reading, have been closed, and the pattern of iron rails on the map of the State is gradually reverting to the simplicity of the 1850's.

The inauguration of the present superior highway system followed long lean years when wheels hardly turned on the rutted, bogged, or sand-drifted main and side roads of rural Delaware. Competition in the same markets with southern and western States—whose growers, because of competing transportation lines, could ship the longer distances more cheaply than could Delaware growers by the one railroad of the Delaware and Chesapeake Peninsula—played a major part in the decline of farm profit, as did the division of large farms into small. Neglect and the destruction of forests had permitted the silting up of tidewater creeks and the ruin of the never very good roads; farm equipment and draft animals had deteriorated, and the problem of hauling had so completely baffled many owners and tenants upon potentially productive soil, that they raised barely enough for their own frugal living. The "good roads" movement, spreading through the country in the early 1900's, so far affected Delaware as to bring State aid in 1903 (though only New Castle County responded at that time), and a legislative session in 1909 almost came to the point of voting to hard-surface the winding State road from Wilmington to Georgetown.

Then a Delaware citizen offered to build at his own expense a four-lane super-highway the entire length of the State. To the construction of this boulevard the foremost engineers and land-planners of Europe and the United States would contribute, and the road would be deeded to the State section by section as completed—the whole a free gift. The vision this offer gave of a prosperous and beautiful State was dramatically stimulating even to the "poor and contented" among the farmers. Among the politically minded there was some suspicion of so unheard-of a proposal. Also there was honest confusion, and honest attachment to a secluded life among other unresponsive citizens, but the majority were for the road.

Coleman du Pont (1863–1930), a great-grandson of the founder of the E. I. du Pont de Nemours Company and cousin of Pierre, Irénée, Lammot, and the late Alfred I. du Pont, had made the acquaintance of transportation problems at the age of five or six when he was first allowed to hold the reins on the horse-cars of his father's street railway lines in Louisville, Kentucky, and a few years later when he counted and wrapped nickels at the company office after school hours. The plan for the Delaware highway grew out of a survey made by Mr. du Pont in Europe and the United States to determine the ideal "road of the future" that would serve motor traffic, both passenger and freight, and conceal beneath bordering parkways, conduits for the electric and other services needed by farms and towns. He had a plan for maintenance based upon acquiring excess width of right-of-way, to be leased by the State under restrictions that would keep the character of the roadside under public control and at the same time pay an increasing revenue into the State treasury. He wanted to see his plans put into effect, but from experience in country-wide promotion of good roads, knew how slight the chances were at the time that a State Legislature would vote money for such a road. He also wanted to do something that would benefit all the people of Delaware, the native State of most of the du Pont family. As the two desires fitted together, Coleman du Pont asked Governor Pennewill to present his offer at the 1911 session of the Legislature.

Although the original plans had to be scaled down somewhat to secure legislative authorization to build the road even at private expense, the necessary law was passed, surveys were made, a road company was formed: The Coleman du Pont Road, Incorporated; and sufficient rights-of-way secured, 200 feet wide, to start the first lane of the road in Sussex County, in the fall of 1911. Much of the land for the road was given free, but where the owner was in need of money, Mr. du Pont paid 50 percent above the current selling price. Then some of the objectors to the route of the road and to the wide right-of-way were backed for a fight by political partisans. Condemnation proceedings and suits halted construction until well into the World War period, when costs of materials and labor were high. But in 1917 the first section of the road, from the Maryland line near Selbyville to the Appenzeller Farm within six miles of Milford, was completed and presented to the State.

The chief engineer of the Du Pont Road was Frank M. Williams of New York, who had been chief engineer of the New York Highway Department, and a builder of modern private roads. After the long interruption due to suits in court, Mr. Williams's associate, Dr. H. E. Breed, of New York, carried on the work. For consultation on construction Mr. du Pont brought to Delaware the Belgian engineer, Ernest Storms of Brussels, who had been chief engineer for King Leopold II, and Thomas Aitken of Cupper Fife, Scotland, the recognized expert of that country and England.

When Federal funds were made available to the States in 1916, the campaign for a modern State highway department (in which Mr. du Pont and the original few local leaders in the cause of good roads since 1900 had been joined by a great number of citizens) bore immediate fruit. The 1917 session of the Legislature established the State Highway Department, to which Mr. du Pont turned over the completion of his road with the agreement to pay up to $44,000 per mile for its construction. The State Highway Department abandoned the excess right-of-way policy but maintained the essential road-building principles of the founder of Delaware's good roads. The Du Pont Road was finished the length of the State in 1924, Mr. du Pont contributing a few thousands under four million dollars of the total cost. A State-wide celebration was held when the deed was turned over to the State (*see DOVER*), and a silver map, by Tiffany, with the Du Pont Road inlaid in gold was given to "the road-builder" by citizens of the State.

Today, the Du Pont Boulevard, US 13 and US 113, forms the backbone of an elaborate system of highways and secondary roads constructed of concrete and amiesite, with many additional miles of improved local roads. The State Highway Department has had control of all public roads since July 1, 1935. The Department maintains State highway police service day and night, which also renders ordinary police service to all parts of the State except Wilmington.

Bus lines were started before many of the hard-surfaced roads were built, chiefly for suburban service out of Wilmington. Opposition of steam and electric roads prevented the earliest company (1900) from securing a permit. The industrial expansion at Wilmington, New Castle, and other points during World War I brought into service a large "jitney bus" business. Opposition of the electric railway companies resulted in a franchise to the Delaware Power and Light Company to operate safe buses over regular routes.

Interstate bus service, beginning about 1924, now connects all parts of Delaware with the main bus routes of the country. The bus companies do no express business. The Peninsula Auto Express, a subsidiary of the Wilson Line, a pioneer in the motor-express industry, was organized with the purpose of furnishing shippers of Wilmington with "river-to-store" service, and later it was extended on down through Delaware and the Peninsula. The McCormick Transportation Company is a Delaware concern and operates a fleet of trucks between Wilmington and Philadelphia, New York, and Boston. Wooleyhan Transportation Company, Victor Lynn, Masten and other lines operate fleets of trucks in and through Delaware.

Numerous small express trucks, during the market seasons, gather the produce and fruits at the farms and transport them direct to the destination in Wilmington, and in cities outside the State.

Greatly increased traffic on Delaware roads since World War II has been met by an expanded program of road construction. New single, double, and divided highways have been built, many miles of traffic lanes widened or doubled, and several interchanges provided. The roads are excellent, well-policed, and safety measures enforced. But due to the great cost of the envisioned adequate program and the resistance of business and private property owners to proposed through-way routes, roadbuilding has not yet caught up with traffic needs in some sections of the State.

The greatest achievement of the State Highway Department has been the construction of the Delaware Memorial Bridge across the Delaware River between this State and New Jersey. The bridge is dedicated to the "men and women of the State of Delaware and the State of New Jersey who gave their lives in the armed forces of the United States of America during World War II." It was built by the State of Delaware at a cost of $46 million. Located between a point a short distance south of Wilmington and Deepwater Point, New Jersey, the bridge carries US Route 40. It joins Route 13 and Delaware 41 on the west with US 130 and New Jersey 44 on the east, connecting directly with the New Jersey Turnpike. When the Memorial Bridge was opened August 16, 1951, the ferry service at New Castle, which until then carried Route 40 traffic between that point and New Jersey, was discontinued.

The bridge is the sixth largest suspension bridge in the world, measuring more than two miles between abutments. Clearance under the center span is 190 feet above mean highwater, which permits the channel underneath to accommodate the largest naval and commercial ships.

The architect was A. Gordon Lorimer of Lorimer and Rose. The engineers were Howard, Needles, Tamen and Bergendoff. In the year ending May 31, 1953, 6,995,019 vehicles used the bridge. Tolls were $6,035,206.

Agriculture

FAVORED by climatic conditions and facing river, bay, and ocean as a part of the fertile Del-Mar-Va Peninsula, Delaware offers a rich field for diversified agriculture, a fact turned to good account by the State's progressive farmers. Under their scientific methods, aided by a fine system of roads, Delaware has become a veritable market garden, situated within 250 miles of approximately one-third of the population of the United States. Well-tilled farms, gardens, orchards, and diminishing woodlands cover the State. The towns, none of which, with the exception of Wilmington, exceeds 7,000 in population, serve as centers of rural trade.

Wheat, corn, hay, and other field crops are raised with ease, and the sandy coastal area grows practically all agricultural commodities known in the Temperate Zone. In the northern part of the State, the staple field crops predominate, but to the south, the farmers rely upon apples and peaches, upon truck-crops, small fruits, and poultry.

Most of the early settlers—Swedish, Finnish, Dutch, Scotch, Irish, and English—were accustomed to tilling the soil. Though many early English settlers, especially in the southern counties, had large estates or manors, these did not survive the first century after settlement, and small farm holdings predominated. The Swedes and Dutch established the cultivation of tobacco, a cash crop, on the partially cleared land, but concentrated on rye, barley, corn, and the native grasses, along with various fruits and vegetables, for home consumption. In time, wheat established supremacy over other grains, and clover and timothy supplanted the original grasses.

Sheep and cattle were raised extensively. An item of early importance was the importation by Eleuthère Irénée du Pont in 1801 of the famous Spanish Merino ram, Don Pedro, considered the father of all Merino sheep in America today (see p. 283). The slaughter of a 2,668 pound "Delaware ox" in Baltimore is mentioned in a news report of 1819.

An interesting experiment in early agriculture was the cultivation of white mulberry trees and silk worms to promote a native silk culture. Governor Johan Printz in 1642 was charged by the Swedish crown with investigation of the possibilties of silk production along the Delaware River.

He made no report, but from time to time thereafter the subject came up again. The minutes of the New Castle Agricultural Society of 1830 contain mention of a Silk Committee. Sometime earlier Thomas Garrett, Wilmington abolitionist, had planted mulberry trees on a tract south of the Christina River, and realized $7,500 from their sale. Passing from one purchaser to another, the trees finally sold for $18,000. The boom in mulberry trees brought visions of wealth to be gained in silk culture, and several acts were passed by the General Assembly to further the project, among them the incorporation of the New Castle County Silk Company in 1837, with a capital stock of $100,000. Silk farms were established, and in 1845 Delaware produced 5,500 pounds of cocoons. Unfortunately, the venture was on too small a scale for profitable returns. The Old World could manufacture and ship to America cheaper silks of much better quality than the local product. Soon the boom died, and farmers turned to less spectacular but more remunerative agriculture.

As in other pioneer colonies, bountiful crops were raised for a time, and nothing returned to the soil. By 1830, farming had fallen into decay. A writer in *The Plow,* farm magazine, states that on a visit to Delaware in the early 1830's he was shocked by the tottering farmhouses, starved cattle, worthless land, and dilapidated fences. On his return in 1852, he was amazed at the change for the better, attributed to "the liberal use of guano, lime, and plaster." Major Philip Reybold, Chauncey P. Holcomb, Anthony M. Higgins, and other progressive farmers organized agricultural societies, and through them spread the use of modern methods. The first New Castle County group was formed in 1804, and New Castle County continued to lead. John Lofland, an early Delaware writer, contrasted the bumper crops of New Castle in 1847 with the miserable yields of Kent.

The first State society was formed in 1849, with Peter F. Causey of Milford, later Governor of the State, its president. John M. Clayton, statesman and zealous worker for better farming throughout the State, demonstrated his theory that wornout farms could quickly be made profitable by rotation and variety of field and garden crops. Agricultural fairs, established under the auspices of the State and county societies, did much to advance Delaware farming. At one of these fairs held in Wilmington in 1843, 75 yokes of prize oxen were exhibited in line on French Street. The present Kent and Sussex Fair, held annually in Harrington, is the successor to a long line of such exhibitions.

The census of 1945 showed 9,296 farms in the State, comprising 923,-340 acres, or 72.9 percent of the total area, with cultivated land and all farm buildings valued at $72,693,794. Of these farms, 5,332 were be-

LAUREL LAKE
Credit: Waller Studio, Laurel

tween 20 and 300 acres in area; 691 of them owned or tenanted by Negroes. The number of agricultural workers in 1940 was 14,103. By 1950 the number had declined to 11,200; the number of farms to 7,448, but the average farm size had increased from 99.3 acres to 114.3 and the value of land and buildings to $93,613,812. Cash farm income increased from $95,029,000 in 1945 to $103,385,000 in 1952. In 1951, farm income reached an all-time high of $112,451,000, of which crops represented 20.7 percent, livestock and products, including broilers, 78.9 percent, and government payments 0.4 per cent.

Wheat ranked first among the field crops in financial return, with corn second. In 1937 the production of wheat was 1,376,000 bushels, valued at $1,050,000, and that of corn 4,147,000 bushels, valued at $950,000. The soybean crop was 352,000 bushels, valued at $225,000. In 1952 corn, 6,422,000 bushels, brought $5,810,000; wheat, 1,218,000, $2,953,000.

Delaware is one of the most extensive early-apple producing States in the Union, and is one of the few sections that can put this fruit on the market before the first of August. Kent and Sussex Counties lead in commercially important orchards of Yellow Transparent and Williams varieties. The State's late apples have a wide distribution through eastern United States, and during the season they are shipped in large quantities to Canada, South America, and Europe. The Delaware apple has an established rating for variety, flavor, and grade. Strict control is exercised over packing, branding, and marketing. Many orchards were over 500 acres in area, and the average annual commercial production of apples more than a million and a half bushels. In 1937, production reached the exceptional total, 2,750,000 bushels. Acreage, 1953, is much less but expanding again.

Peaches, once a bonanza crop when "the Delaware peach" ruled the eastern markets, are again grown with profit, and new orchards are being planted. From 1840 to the close of the century, the crop was harvested from millions of peach trees annually, and "peach-kings" and "peach-centers" sprang up. The once-dreaded "peach yellows" brought disaster to the State's orchards, and the growers turned to apples. Then, however, with the "yellows" under control, the acreage increased again. In 1937 398,000 bushels were produced but dropped again in 1953 to 141,000.

According to the estimates of the Bureau of Agricultural Economics, United States Department of Agriculture, 41,540 acres of truck-crops valued at $2,155,000 were grown in Delaware for commercial purposes in 1937. Strawberries and tomatoes headed the list in value, followed by cantaloupes, asparagus, cucumbers, green peas, and lima beans. Delaware ranked seventeenth among the States in the annual yield of strawberries. The largest producing areas lie across the southern section of the State.

The sweet potato is a profitable crop in Sussex County, and "sweet potato houses" dot lower Delaware. From them are shipped the much-favored "kiln-dried sweets." When the potatoes are placed in the houses they first go through a sweating process, after which the houses are heated and ventilated to maintain a given temperature. Although harvested in September and October, the sweet potatoes are sold chiefly through the period from December to April. But sweet potato production declined to 600 acres, $159,000 in 1952, vs. white potatoes, 6,600 acres, $2,115,000.

A growing source of farm income in recent years has been the poultry industry. In 1935 chickens and eggs alone netted $5,054,000, or 29 percent of the total farm income. The hatcheries of the State have a capacity of approximately three million eggs every three weeks during the hatching season, and baby chicks from certified, accredited, and blood-tested flocks are sold in large quantities. Broilers have recently gained special favor. These young chickens, weighing from two to four pounds, are placed on the market during every month of the year. While the poultry industry may be said to be state-wide in extent, the major output is from Sussex, which is ranked as first among the broiler-producing counties in the United States. The income from the broiler industry, 1952, was $56,990,000.

Dairying is a profitable and carefully conducted industry. All herds are tested for tuberculosis. The value of milk production alone was estimated at $3,048,000 in 1935. Seventy-five percent of the dairy products is exported, much milk being shipped to the Philadelphia section. The breeding of blooded cattle is a growing interest all over the State, especially among "luxury farmers." In 1952 farm income from milk was $10,194,000.

From the middle nineteenth century close co-operation has existed between the farm folk and agencies such as the Agricultural Experiment Station at the University of Delaware and the State Board of Agriculture. The Experiment Station was made possible through successive Federal acts receiving in 1928 the sum of $90,000 annually to carry on research work in the field of plant and animal production and the handling of products. The accomplishments of the Experiment Station have been significant, and through its work the farmers have been benefited greatly. The annual income, 1953, is $350,000. The Agricultural Experiment Station and its Extension Division share with the University School of Agriculture a modern building erected 1952, adjoining the experiment farm.

The Division of Agricultural Extension, connected with the University of Delaware, carries information on agriculture and home economics into the rural districts, and demonstrates its advantageous application. The aims are better farming, better farmhouses, more equitable distribution of farm products, and the inculcation in boys and girls of enthusiasm for country life. Ten thousand Delaware farmers take advantage of this extension service. A county agent is accorded each county to demonstrate the latest agricultural advances of special benefit to the Delaware farmer. The agents consult and advise on problems of farm management, drainage, construction of buildings, and crop rotation.

Home demonstration and 4-H Club programs are other phases of the extension service. In 1936 there were 51 organized home demonstration clubs in the State, with an enrollment of 1,373 women. Their projects included home management, food preservation, clothing, home furnishing, nutrition, beautification of home grounds, vegetable gardens, poultry, and co-operation. The total enrollment of the 4-H Clubs in 1936 was 1,977 boys and girls with 121 clubs in active operation. Club projects included crops, poultry and livestock, food and nutrition, farm management, food preservation, and clothing. In 1952, 2,000 boys and girls enrolled in 88 4-H Clubs engaged in a total of 1,642 projects. Sample results: 70,000 chicks raised, 1,249 acres of garden and field crops, 4,150 food packages frozen in quarts and pounds, 3,495 quarts canned. Special activities: the annual 4-H Club short course at the University; Kent-Sussex Fair; annual State 4-H Club camp, the national meeting to which 15 State 4-H Club members won trips in 1953 where they took national prizes and honors.

The work of the State Board of Agriculture has been especially valuable in eradicating tuberculosis among cattle, protecting hogs against cholera, and attacking plant diseases and insect pests through quarantine and other methods. The State Laboratory analyzes feeds, fertilizers, limes, and spray material free of charge. The Bureau of Markets offers market news, inspection service, and aid in transportation and co-operative marketing. The Poultry Department helps poultry raisers to fight disease, and supervises official certification of standards.

A four-year course in agriculture is offered at the University of Delaware and at Delaware State College (Negro). In the modern State high schools both white and Negro instruction is given in agriculture, and farm mechanics is taught in the agricultural shops connected with them. Credit is given to pupils for home projects. St. Joseph's Industrial School at Clayton offers instruction in agriculture to Negro boys *(see Tour 12)*.

Future Farmers of America are organized in twenty-one chapters at Delaware high schools, the group being confined to boys following vocational agriculture courses. The enrollment in 1953 was 800.

New Farmers of America (Negro) have three chapters, enrollment 147. Together, F.F.A. and N.F.A. raised 137,340 broilers, 422 swine and 391 cattle in one year. Members attend annual judging contests in livestock, crops, meat, tractor-driving. F.F.A. and N.F.A. are integral parts of the State Vocational Education system as are Future Homemakers of America (white) and New Homemakers of America (Negro), corresponding activities for girls.

The Grange has continued as a powerful influence since it was organized in 1874. Meetings are well attended and much has been accomplished in respect to better roads, schools, and progressive farming. There are 27 subordinate units, three Pomona Granges, and four juvenile units. The membership is approximately 2,300.

Farm co-operatives have not been especially successful in Delaware because of the close and ready market. Although favorable sentiment was aroused some years ago, finances were not sufficient to obtain expert managers. Nevertheless, several small co-operatives have operated profitably in Sussex County, including a cannery and a cantaloupe-marketing group. A farmers' exchange has been operating for years; the purchaser buys a share of stock and at the end of a year receives a share of the profits proportionate to the amount he has spent during that period. One large co-operative is an interstate milk producers' association.

Farm roadside stands along the main highways, usually family enter-prises, have been notably successful in Delaware. Some of these are per-manent stands conducted the year around, but the temporary type is more common—tables or racks placed under trees or at the sides of gasoline sta-tions or farm homes, with business confined often to week ends and holi-days.

The making and shipment of holly wreaths is a seasonal occupation among farmers in lower Delaware. From Thanksgiving until just before Christmas, the collecting of the twigs and berries and the preparation of wreaths occupies days and evenings. Extensive acreage is devoted to mod-ern nurseries by Delaware growers and in expansion by large growers in other states who are taking advantage of the favorable Delaware climate and economic conditions. Soil conservation methods are used.

Approximately two-thirds of Delaware farm property is operated by the owners, and the remainder by tenants, although the number of the latter has decreased in the last three decades. The usual type of rental is the share system whereby the landlord provides the farm and the tenant the operating equipment including livestock. The crop receipts are divided "share-and-share alike," with the tenant receiving returns in livestock and hay for use on the farm, unless the latter crop is sold, in which case the tenant receives one-half. The tenant pays costs of labor, machinery, thresh-ing, and similar expenses, repairs on his own equipment; the landlord is responsible for permanent improvements, taxes, and insurance. The cost of seeds and fertilizer is usually halved.

The trend is toward larger and fewer farms and increased use of ma-chinery which is cheaper than labor. The cost of the latter is high because of available jobs in the mounting number of new industries choosing rural and small-town sites.

In 1952 the gross farm income per farm family in Delaware was the second highest among the states east of the Mississippi. In less than a decade, 1943–51, the total cash income from agricultural production in-creased from $77,856,000 to $112,958,000. Delaware ranked third in the production of broilers—the Kent and Sussex County poultry industry that averages 60 percent of the total annual cash farm income.

Industry, Commerce, and Labor

THE present industrial and commercial life of Delaware grew naturally from the earliest adventures in trade and agriculture. The casual Dutch traders who first dealt with the Indians at the site of Wilmington established a market for pelts gathered by the tribes of Minquas over an extensive range of the Appalachian forests. The first permanent settlers profited from this market. The trifling money value of the kettles, rifles, match-cloth, and trinkets which the Swedish and Dutch settlers traded for valuable cargoes of beaver, otter, bear, mink, deer, and other pelts gave the European trading companies sufficient reason to finance the settler and give him his start. The monopoly of trade and commerce of the colonizing companies was, nevertheless, soon invaded by the individual settler.

Legally or illegally, the Swedish, Dutch, and later the English settler drove his own bargains with the Indians. Swedish freemen so thriftily cultivated the fertile soil that usually after the first harvest they could trade successfully beer, butter, cheese, and bread for pelts from the Indians or the tobacco raised by Maryland planters; and within a few years the women of Swedish households were producing woven cloth of wool and linen that served as the equivalent of money in reserve to see the families through seasons of bad harvest.

But more than the produce of the increasing agricultural acreage was needed for the success of the Colonies on the Delaware. Encouraged by the governors, companies of planters built grist and sawmills and in winter turned to the preparation of timber for the use of local coopers and for export. Until well into the English period, however, because of the shortage of labor, planks, clapboards, bricks, and other building materials had to be bought from the other Colonies to house the growing agricultural population.

Contrary to general opinion, Delaware in the early days did not produce tobacco in substantial commercial quantities. The absence of cheap labor restricted even the amount raised on company land under the Swedes

MARINE TERMINAL, WILMINGTON

and Dutch. Contemporary records show that in the seventeenth century the greater part of the tobacco exported from the Delaware was bought from Maryland and Virginia in exchange for food. It was probably this practical and convenient co-operation between the Delaware settlements and the Maryland planters that suggested to D'Hinoyossa, the last Governor of the Dutch, his proposed commercial center at "Appoqunime" (Odessa), where all the food supplies from the Delaware could be transported to Maryland by way of Bohemia Landing, and the tobacco received in exchange shipped to Europe, with a fat commission on both transactions to the ambitious Dutchman. Travelers in the early English period wrote that each settler along the river had his tobacco patch for private use. The Swedes were said to dry and twist the leaves and use them without further preparation.

Along with the building of canoes, shallops, sloops, yachts, and barges for local use, the first Dutch and Swedish colonists built vessels for coastwise trade; expert ship carpenters were never plentiful enough to meet the demand from planters and traders on the river for the swift seaworthy vessels they created. The great modern shipbuilding industry on the Delaware River had its beginning on Cooper's Island (later Vandever's Island) directly across the Brandywine from Fort Christina, where Lauris, the cooper, and Persson, the shipbuilder, were plying their crafts when Governor Printz arrived in 1643. Printz built at Christina the "beautiful large boat" of 90 or 100 tons burden that, for lack of the final fittings from Sweden, seems never to have been finished.

The abundance of navigable streams flowing into the Delaware and the Chesapeake, and the convenient wharves for loading under the very walls of the mills, led in short time to "the greatest concentration of mill industries in the Colonies." The final impetus to this development was given by the Quakers, who settled in Wilmington after 1735. Paper mills were established on the Brandywine and on the creeks flowing into the Christina. The number of flour mills increased with the successful cultivation of the important agricultural districts in the neighboring three Colonies—Delaware, Pennsylvania, and Maryland—and heavily laden wagon-trains began to converge upon the Christina and the Brandywine.

Christiana Bridge at the head of tidewater navigation on the Christina became the shipping point for the millers on the White Clay and Christina Creeks and on Elk River, Maryland. From Newport, on the same stream, several miles nearer the Delaware River, large quantites of grain, the product of Lancaster County farms, were shipped to Philadelphia.

After the development of water power on the north side of Brandywine Creek and the founding of the Brandywine Mills, the rapid growth of the milling industry followed. Wilmington soon became the flour center of the country and determined the price of wheat.

After the Revolution, Delaware liberalized its restrictions on commerce, so as to increase shipping to Wilmington. Trade with Cuba and the West Indies was greatly benefited by Delaware's invention of kiln-dried corn, by which method cargoes of meal were delivered in tropical ports free from mould or mustiness. The system of inspection in which the mills co-operated also assured excellent quality and correct weight. By general estimate at the period, the flour ground at the Brandywine Mills possessed an uncommon softness and whiteness. Fifty thousand barrels of this flour and 3,754 barrels of middlings and corn meal were made at the Brandywine Mills in the fall of 1789 and spring of 1790. About half of this total was exported. The importance of flour-milling in Delaware declined with the opening of the Erie Canal and of the railroads, which enabled western growers and millers to compete successfully with Delaware manufacturers.

By the middle of the eighteenth century commercial enterprises in Delaware had established a number of local trading companies with ships of their own. The voyages were chiefly to the West Indies, where foodstuffs and cooperage supplies were traded for rum, sugar, and molasses or, what was even more important in the economy of the community, for hard coin. An interesting reflection of the profit and conditions of this trade is contained in the journal of David Ferris, who was an original partner in the company, organized by William Shipley and others, which built the brig *Wilmington.* He claims that he was persuaded against his better judgment to join the company and that he withdrew because of his conscience. His description of his own merchandising establishment in Wilmington, with the statement that he charged less profit than others because he could not in conscience take the very high rates of profit enjoyed by his fellows, implies that the profits from the West Indies voyages were even higher. It may be that the general evasion of Great Britain's restriction upon American trade at that period was practiced by these local trading companies with unusual success. There are indications in surviving contemporary data that trade was heavy with the French islands, where the merchants not only avoided the duties and customs of Great Britain but bought at much lower prices. The impetus to local shipbuilding, gained during the flour period, carried the shipping industry over to the modern era.

For a hundred years, 1750 to 1850, many stout wooden vessels were built on the Christina, Brandywine, and other navigable streams throughout the State, for trade with the West Indies, Ireland, and Great Britain, in addition to the coasting trade. Nearly all of the leading citizens of Wilmington, from 1741 to 1775, owned or were interested in one or more sailing vessels, the majority of which were built locally. In the early 1840's, Samuel Harlan of the firm of Betts, Pusey, and Harlan, machinists, accepted a repair job on the steamer *Sun,* which led to the founding of the first iron shipbuilding yard in the United States. In May 1844, the firm (then Betts, Harlan, and Hollingsworth) launched the *Bangor,* the first iron sea-going propeller steamer constructed in this country.

The Pusey and Jones Corporation, founded as a machine shop in 1848, accepted its first ship contract in 1853. From its early days to the present time, this corporation has been one of the world's largest builders of papermaking machinery. Its foundries and machine shops have turned out a diversity of products from a "gold mill" weighing 14 tons for use in the California mines in 1850, to the anchors for the Brooklyn Bridge (1883), weighing 23 tons each.

Carbuilding and repairing, from its beginning in 1836, a few years after the opening of the first railroads, has been an important industry. Two of the firms which made history in the building of ships were also pioneers in carbuilding; cars constructed by the Jackson and Sharp Company and the Harlan and Hollingsworth Corporation have been shipped to many foreign countries. The plant of Bowers and Dure, afterwards purchased by the Pullman Company, was credited with building the first palace car east of the Ohio River. Chilled car wheels have been founded in Wilmington since 1836.

In early times great forests of white and black oak, yellow pine, cypress, tulip and gum trees provided the farmer with a cash crop, when his failure to fertilize his soil resulted in a poor yield. Later, masses of white oak were cut and used in local shipbuilding, and exported to Holland, Sweden, and England. The bark of the black oak, or quercitron, tree was in great demand for tanning and dyeing, and many tracts of forest were ruthlessly despoiled as the bark mills moved from place to place. The State's lumber production declined from 55 million board feet in 1909 to 5½ million in 1934. A State forestry department is now active in the conservation and replanting of timber.

Beginning before the Revolution in two small frame buildings on Market Street in Wilmington, the production of all types of horse-drawn vehicles increased until the town was celebrated throughout the country for the manufacture of carriages of superior quality and design. The industry was halted in the first year of the Civil War, but recovered quickly through Government orders for army wagons. Steam power for the preparation of wooden parts was used first in 1864, and the firm of McLear and Kendall was soon operating its large manufactory (1500 carriages annually) with steam-driven machines. Decline of the carriage industry began with the country's financial panic of 1873. About this time also, competition from the West was so keen that the Delaware product became a luxury.

Iron ore in Iron and Chestnut Hills in New Castle County, and bog ore at the heads of the streams in Sussex County, early brought furnaces and forges into the State. The Collins Forge, established in 1794, continued in operation by members of that family until 1850. Possibly the best known of the Sussex iron companies was the Millsboro furnace started in 1815, to which a foundry was added in 1822. Pipes for the Croton Water Works in New York and the railings formerly surrounding Independence Square in Philadelphia were furnished by this company. The furnace was abandoned in 1836, but the foundry was continued until 1879.

In New Castle County a forge was started by Samuel James at Iron Hill, which led to the founding there of the Abbington Iron Company in 1725. At the same period, a bloomery was operated by James M. Swank on the White Clay Creek, and Sir William Keith, Deputy-Governor of Penn's province, manufactured iron on the Christina before 1730. The smelting industry was not a financial success and, while the bog ore yielded 53 to 66 percent of iron, the process was found to be too expensive. By 1810, although five forges were operating in Sussex County, the blast furnaces had all disappeared. The owners of bog-ore producing tracts, however, continued their mining operations and shipped the material to New Jersey, where it was mixed with magnetic ore. The ore mined at Iron and Chestnut Hills, after the closing of the Abbington and other furnaces, was shipped to Maryland.

Slitting and rolling mills were operating near Wilmington as early as 1787 for the cutting and rolling of Swedish and Russian iron into strips for the manufacture of nails. After the close of the War of 1812, numerous forges, furnaces, and foundries were established in and near Wilmington, and after 1850 the founding of a number of large mills placed the State in the front rank for production in this industry. With the development of steel, and the subsequent formation of the large steel corporations through mergers, in the latter part of the nineteenth century, much of this industry was lost to Delaware. However, new heights in production were reached during the World War.

Machine shops have been an important branch of Delaware industry since the War of 1812, and today their products, together with those of the foundry, with which they are closely allied, head the list of the State's manufactured articles. Delaware machine shops now produce leather working machinery, tube expanders, hydraulic jacks (some of these were used in the construction of Boulder Dam), and many other specialties.

The leather industry assumed importance in Wilmington between 1825 and 1850. The manufacture of glazed kid is now the city's leading enterprise, although suffering a temporary eclipse, owing to the current popularity of suede.

Tanyards existed throughout the State before the eighteenth century, but the first record of leather manufacture in Wilmington is that of Francis Robinson, a Quaker, who commenced the preparation of buckskin and chamois leather in 1732. Moroccos were first manufactured in the State in 1823.

Because of the constantly changing hide market, fortunes were often quickly lost, and new firms, new partnerships, and amalgamations continued to appear up to 1890. At that time, the chrome process of tanning superseded the vegetable or sumach method. This process, the experiments of which were carried on in Wilmington factories, revolutionized the indus-

GLAZING KID

try, and the city became, with Philadelphia and Camden, one of the three glazed-kid centers of the United States. Mergers and consolidations have continued until today there are two great leather organizations in Wilmington and its environs, and less than a half-dozen smaller independent firms.

One leather firm in Wilmington was 74 years old when the Declaration of Independence was signed. J. E. Rhoads and Sons, belting manufacturers, began as a tanyard established in Delaware County, Pennsylvania, in 1702 by the ancestor of J. E. Rhoads. This Quaker firm makes no sales to manufacturers of munitions, or to distillers and brewers.

Pioneers in the local textile industry include Rowan, an Irish exile, who set up an establishment for printing and dyeing calico in Wilmington in 1790, and Jacob Broom, who built the first cotton mill on the Brandywine in 1795. In 1811 the du Pont-Bauduy woolen firm was founded in connection with the importation of Merino sheep. The Dean mills at Newark were the first in this section to manufacture clothing for the United States Army, and by 1860 were equipped for the large contracts they received. Bancroft, a Quaker from Lancashire, England, began the spinning and weaving of cotton in an old stone mill on the Brandywine. After 107 years of continuous operation and gradual expansion, the Joseph Bancroft and Sons Company is now actively engaged in the dyeing and finishing of cotton goods and the manufacture of book-cover cloths and window-shade material. It is the largest plant of its kind in the world. Other textile plants in Wilmington produce wool yarns, jute, and allied products. Near New Castle, there is a large plant for the production of imitation silk.

The manufacture of matches was once an important industry in Wilmington. In the employ of Edward Tatnall, who in 1853 had a small factory in which he made old-fashioned sulphur matches, was a young Englishman, Henry C. Courtney. In his small home near by, Courtney conducted a series of experiments, using kitchen utensils and a cooking-stove for apparatus, and evolved the parlor or cracking match. Keeping the secret to himself, he interested William H. Swift, Wilmington capitalist, and the firm of Swift and Courtney was formed. The firm later became Swift, Courtney, and Beecher, and in 1882, by merger with other companies, the Diamond Match Company. The plant in 1890 was moved to Oswego, New York. Meanwhile, Courtney's success incited other Wilmington mechanics to attempt match-perfecting methods and a sort of "match mania" ensued.

The three largest explosive manufacturers on the American continent—the Du Pont, Hercules, and Atlas Powder Companies—have their headquarters in Wilmington, although, contrary to general opinion, no explosives are manufactured in Delaware. One of the world's largest diversified chemical industries, the Du Pont Company, operates 81 plants in 27 States, three of them in Delaware. The other two companies have also entered the industrial chemical field, although first organized for the manufacture of explosives. The companies maintain extensive experiment stations.

The first paper makers in the State were Joshua and Thomas Gilpin, who had a mill on the Brandywine in 1787, where paper for books and banknotes was made. Thomas Gilpin in 1816 patented the first endless sheet paper machine in America, a great improvement on the old hand method. Modern paper-making in Delaware began in 1843. The Augustine mill, one of the largest and most complete at that time in the United States, made lithograph, map, and plate paper.

The fishing industry, including the dredging and packing of oysters, the catching of nonedible fish and crabs for fertilizer, as well as extensive food fisheries, is carried on in the lower part of the State. Lewes, at the entrance to the Delaware Bay, is an important commercial fishing center. Only one firm is engaged in the shucking and packing of oysters at Seaford. Ground oyster shells, once in great demand for road building in that locality, are now used by one firm in the manufacture of scratch feed for chickens. Bowers Beach and Little Creek, farther up the bay, lead in the business of providing for private fishing parties. Before World War II the hook-and-line salt-water fishing from licensed "party boats," rowboats, and shores in the Delaware Bay and on the Atlantic Ocean provided an annual income of between $400,000 and $500,000; the average annual catch of 5,000,000 fish has a food value of $250,000. Horseshoe crabs, collected at Bowers Beach, are dried, coarsely ground, and sold to fertilizer manufacturers. Commercial fishing as a food industry has suffered greatly in this century. The pollution of the Delaware River and Bay by sewage and chemicals practically annihilated the sturgeon and greatly reduced the number of the famous Delaware shad. Anti-pollution measures will aid their return.

In addition to these main industries, Delaware is noted for a number of specialties, some of them originally developed here. One of the latter is "vulcanized" hard fiber, developed in Delaware and employed in place of wood and metal. Northern New Castle County, and particularly Wilmington, has been the center of the vulcanized fiber industry. The first manufactory was the Vulcanized Fiber Company of Wilmington, established in 1873 by William Courtney and Caesar A. Rodney.

Braided rubber hose is also manufactured at Wilmington in one of the largest plants of its kind in the world and in the New Castle area, several

TEXTILE MILL, WILMINGTON

types of airplanes are manufactured. Snuff mills of the George W. Helme Company, founded in 1782, are located at Yorklyn. An industry of great importance in the lower part of the State is the manufacture of dental supplies and pharmaceutical preparations. To supply the demand for crates and baskets by the fruit industry in the lower counties, factories making these articles operate at Dover, Harrington, Laurel, and many other towns. Large quantities of gumwood, which is readily available in nearby forests, are used in the manufacture of small wooden spoons for mustard jars, picnic supplies, and ice cream service. More than thirty communities have one or more food canning and packing establishments. Among these are a nationally known chicken canning plant in Dover, and a cucumber-processing plant at Seaford. Small factories give permanent and seasonal employment to many workers, mostly women, in Middletown, Smyrna, Dover, Milton, Seaford, Dagsboro, Delmar, Milford and Georgetown.

In addition to these staple and special industries, manufacturing in the State produces such articles as automobile accessories, awnings, bakers' products, barrels, baskets, boxes, beds and bedding, beverages, bottle sealing devices, concrete products, felt base rugs, jute products, plumbers' supplies, refined oil, pyrites products, tanning extracts, and many others.

The State Tax Commissioner reports for the fiscal year ending June 30, 1953, 889 licensed manufacturers in the State with gross receipts of $805,-313,919. This shows recovery from the decline that followed the closing of war contracts in 1946–47. In the latter year, 807 manufacturers had gross receipts of $344,049,916.

The total number of employees under the unemployment compensation law, June 30, 1953, was 118,798. Total wages paid for the year were $440,-000,000. Unemployment compensation paid during this same fiscal year ending June 30, was $961,165.

Electric light and power, both for industry and domestic consumption, other than that furnished to a few sections by publicly owned plants, is distributed in the State by two major holding companies, one of which serves Wilmington and rural New Castle County, the other serving Kent and Sussex Counties. In some instances, towns purchase current from private corporations and distribute it to users. Gas is supplied to Wilmington and most of the towns of the State by private companies. In 1936, the Delaware Rural Electric Association was organized and petitioned the Rural Electrification Administration of the Federal Government for a loan to construct lines to supply electric power and light to outlying farms and communities. To lines built with the loan miles are added annually.

Free labor, slavery, and the system of indentured servants and redemptioners existed side by side in Delaware from the earliest days. The free labor was furnished chiefly by artisans, workingmen who owned their own tools and practiced their trades in small shops in the towns, or at the crossroads in rural sections. Negro slavery persisted in Delaware until the close of the Civil War, although the number of slaves had decreased from 8,887 in 1790 to 1,798 in 1860, at which time there were 19,829 free Negroes in the State.

At first, indentured servants and redemptioners were sold for passage money to the highest bidder immediately on arrival, but later they were permitted a month of grace in which to find a master willing to pay the passage costs. Many shiploads of immigrants were landed at New Castle, and as early as 1727 it was a common expression, when a ship arrived, to say: "Let us go & buy a School Master." A large number of Delaware's early schoolmasters were indentured servants. One notable example of an indentured servant's rise in life was Charles Thomson, Secretary to the Continental Congress, although Thomson ran away from his New Castle master soon after his arrival as a lad. The system was dying slowly at the time of the Revolution and had virtually disappeared by 1800.

The opportunities offered in a new country, especially the new and cheap land to the West when industrial employment failed at home, delayed the formation of labor organizations in Delaware. The first unions formed, early in the nineteenth century, were those of the cordwainers (boot and shoemakers) and the coopers employed in the Brandywine flour mills. They were interested at first in securing reforms and political rights. In its report of the memorial parade held July 28, 1834, at the death of Lafayette, the *Gazette and Watchman* (Wilmington), states:

"The Union Cordwainers Society came next in Citizen's dress, with the usual badges, and preceded their banner. They numbered about fifty.

"Then the Brandywine Coopers' Association, with black coats and white pantaloons, numbering about 45."

By August 1829, workingmen had organized the "Association of Working People of New Castle County" to agitate for the abolition of imprisonment for debt, a practice that had worked great hardship and misery on the wage earners. The *Delaware Free Press,* in part a free-thought paper and in part an organ for the workingmen's political movement, was established in Wilmington in 1830, the object stated being:

> To awaken the attention of the Working People to the importance of co-operating in order to attain that rank and station to which they are justly entitled by their virtue and industry.

The paper, continued for a couple of years, advocated abolition of imprisonment for debt and vigorously demanded free education.

The factory system was in full vigor in Wilmington by the middle of the nineteenth century. An item in the *Blue Hen's Chicken,* December 31, 1852, relates of the Franklin Factory, where muslins and ticking were made:

> *Struck.*—We are informed that the girls in the Franklin Factory are about striking on account of their being forced to work from 6 o'clock in the morning until 10 in the evening. This is too long for girls to work. The law especially should prevent minors from working that length of time. The law forbids it in England, and it should here.

Influx of skilled workers from other States and from Europe during the boom period of manufacturing (1840–1880) broke down many of the old ties between the employers and their employees, who formerly addressed each other by their Christian names and at times worked side by side in the mills. The employees were often content to work the long hours required, in the hope that the employer would come to their aid in case of need.

The Knights of Labor, a fraternal labor organization, was formed in Philadelphia in 1869. In its period of greatest influence during the 1880's, many converts were found in Wilmington, and the first recorded strike of organized labor unions in the State occurred during this time. On July 10, 1883, seventeen Negro workers for a Baltimore and Ohio Railroad contractor walked out at Wilmington, and were successful after one day in securing a small increase in wages. A little later in the same year, union telegraphers of the State joined the national strike of their craft to gain higher pay.

In March 1884, the 3,000 employees of ten Wilmington morocco plants struck for higher wages, and won their demands after being out six months. During that time subsistence money was paid by the union. In all, twenty strikes in various branches of industry were called in Wilmington between 1887 and 1893, most of them of short duration.

Labor stoppages grew more frequent in Delaware as the unions developed strength in the twentieth century. Between 1919 and 1934, a total of 71 strikes is recorded for the State, the high figure standing at 21 in 1934. Most of the strikes occurred in Wilmington, with an occasional stoppage of minor importance in the smaller towns.

The most bitterly contested labor conflict of recent years was the strike of Pennsylvania Railroad shopmen which began in Wilmington on July 1, 1922, as a part of the National Shopmen's strike. Within two weeks, 1,500 railroad men were out, chiefly at Todd's Cut, Wilmington, where the shops are located. The strike, not finally settled for a year, was turbulent, and tension ran high. At one time, strike breakers were compelled to remain in the shops for weeks before venturing to their homes. On September 13, four men were arrested in connection with an attempt to dynamite a railroad bridge at Fourteenth and Bowers Streets. Demand for higher pay and rectification of alleged inequities of employment were the causes for this strike, which eventually failed.

Among later strikes, that of truckdrivers and teamsters in Wilmington, was begun in March 1937 to enforce recognition of the union and uniform rates of pay. Six hundred drivers were idle for 23 days before a truce was agreed upon. On April 8, the union was recognized by 69 companies.

In recent years up to 1953, short strikes in the building trades have won increased wages. Other strikes have been minor. Union membership in the Wilmington area increased rapidly during World War II.

Most of the labor unions are affiliated with the American Federation of Labor and the Committee for Industrial Organization. The Delaware State Federation of Labor, Wilmington Central Labor Union, and Delaware State Industrial Union Council are leading central bodies.

Compulsory school attendance to the age of 16 years prevents employment of children under that age. The few who cannot benefit by being kept in school, may be given restricted permits if past their 14th year. Children are engaged for brief periods in berry-picking and other forms of industrialized agriculture when school is not in session.

The ten-hour day, or a maximum of fifty-five hours a week, for female employees is still legal in Delaware. Establishments canning and preserving perishable fruits and vegetables are exempted from the 55 hour limit. In practice, however, aside from seasonal employments only a minority of women work more than 40 to 48 hours per week. Women comprise about one-third of the total working force in the state: 36,223 out of 126,637 in 1950 (U.S. Census).

An Industrial Accident Board, established in 1917, awards compensation to workmen injured in industrial occupations.

Through the federal-state program of Vocational Rehabilitation and job-training, the State Board of Vocational Education is restoring more than 400 handicapped persons annually to paid employment.

Benefits paid by the State Unemployment Compensation Commission to persons who lose industrial jobs through no fault of their own, range from $7 to $25 per week for 11 to 26 weeks according to the job and wages. These benefits, raised by a tax on employers, and the services of the State Employment offices are without cost to the workers.

The trend toward establishing large industrial plants and large laboratories and office buildings on farm-sized suburban or rural sites has some notable examples in New Castle County, completed and under construction (1953). Recreation facilities, adequate parking areas, and landscaping are included. Outstanding are the $30 million Du Pont Experiment Station on the Brandywine, Hercules Experiment Station on the Lancaster Pike, General Motors Assembly Plant on Boxwood Road, Chrysler Motor Parts Depot and Tank Arsenal at Newark, a Du Pont administrative building north of that town, and a new Atlas administrative building on Concord Pike.

Folkways and Customs

FEW of Delaware's traditions and customs are reminiscent of the early Swedish or Dutch settlers, or of the aborigines they supplanted. Rather, they are overwhelmingly British whether English, Scotch-Irish, or Welsh, or else, particularly in Wilmington, the transplanted folklore of continental Europe and of comparatively recent arrival.

It is nearly two hundred years since the last of the Nanticoke tribesmen left Sussex County for the north, leaving none of pure stock, and at least as long since the last of the New Castle County tribes of the Lenni-Lenape trekked westward. Behind them were left a few Indian names, such as Appoquinimink, Naamans, Kiamensi, and Mispillion, but no legends or tales that may be classed as essentially Delaware Indian lore. While early writers recorded instances of naïveté, such as the Indians' belief that the **Reverend John** Campanius traveled overland to Sweden, his native country, **it seems** almost as if Indian folklore vanished with the Indians themselves.

John Lofland, the "Milford Bard," collected Indian legends of the Brandywine Creek at Wilmington and wove them into his romantic stories published in the early nineteenth century, but no one today can discover where the legends end and Lofland's vivid imagination begins. On the banks of the Brandywine one will look in vain for the names of Manitoo, the Indian beauty, and her white lover, Wild Harry of Wilmington, although Lofland says they are engraved in a secret pocket of the large flat rock "just opposite the upper dam," the rock from which the lovely Manitoo (as from how many rocks how many maidens!) leaped, protesting against Harry's perfidy. The rocks along the Brandywine might well be the scenes of romantic or tragic episodes, but if such occurred, no tale remains today.

Far down in Sussex County, at Riverdale on Indian River Bay, some of the descendants of the once powerful Nanticokes preserve a few of their native customs; and on Thanksgiving Day each year, through the interest of Dr. Frank G. Speck of the University of Pennsylvania, the dances, chants, folk arts, and customs of their ancestors are revived in tribal ceremonies.

The Swedes and the Dutch left a deep enough imprint upon the history and genealogy of Delaware, but of customs and traditions that were theirs, scarcely any may be found in their descendants.

Generations of insularity and self-sufficiency, especially in lower Delaware, permitted many English customs and habits to be strongly imbedded, although the radio, the motorcar, and modern education tend to destroy them. The customs, folklore, and speech forms that remain betray an Elizabethan origin, and the children's games are headed by such old English favorites as "Johnny's Not Home from the Fair" and "London Bridge Is Falling Down."

In Sussex County, where contact with other peoples has been slight, many local variants of English pronunciation may be heard, such as "carn" for corn, "caint" for can't, "aiout" for out, and "housen" for houses. Among friends and neighbors, "our folks" corresponds to the "you all" of the South. The question: "Our folks going somewhere today?" means "Going somewhere today, friends?" Addressed to one person, the question "You folks going to church?" means "Are you and your family going to church?"

Until recently, a mill in western Sussex was known as "Mung-em's Mill" because it was owned "among them" by a local group. A young male visitor in certain parts of the county may be flabbergasted to hear himself addressed by an older man as "Honey."

The native of Delaware uses flat "a's," and often fails to aspirate his "h's" in such words as "where" and "when" and "what." He usually refers to his homeland as "*Del*-a-wur," and winces when the outlander uses the harsh "Del-a-*ware*." His speech habits and mannerisms, handed down through generations, are sometimes so marked as to make him seem a character out of Shakespeare; he handles with fluency and appropriateness words and solecisms unfamiliar to modern ears. The late George Morgan, author and loyal son of Sussex County, caught a few phrases uttered by a trolley-car conductor in Philadelphia, and asked: "You're a Delawarean?" "Yes." "From Sussex County?" "Yes." "Northwest Fork Hundred?" "Yes."

Commonly accepted signs and portents, having their counterpart elsewhere, range from death warnings (upon which grim tales are hung) and the planting of crops according to phases of the moon, to the abundant household superstitions, such as that the dropping of a knife, fork, or spoon signifies respectively the coming of a man, a woman, or a child visitor. The vast and complex body of things that are lucky and unlucky at weddings would make a chapter in itself. In some parts of Delaware the family Bible and the salt-shaker are the first articles to be carried across the threshold of a new house. As in Indian days, the plaintive cry of the whippoorwill is believed to be the wailing of an uneasy spirit, mourning over things left undone in life, or over the failure of those living to carry out its wishes or render due respect to its memory. Some few even aver that whippoorwills are not birds at all, but disembodied spirits that can never be caught, the proof being that the sound retreats as a person approaches it.

Hunts for buried treasure are engaged in from time to time, usually at night and in secrecy. Pirates long plied their trade along river, bay, and ocean, and Captain Kidd, Blackbeard, and Blueskin are supposed to have buried some of their ill-gotten gains along the shores. The tales of shipwrecks, of which there have been many off Lewes, almost always report that fabulous sums were carried down to Davy Jones's locker. To aid in treasure hunts "gold-finders," which have arrows guaranteed to point to the spot where gold is hidden in the earth or under the sea, have been sold "on the quiet" about Delaware, the price reaching as high as $100. Zest is added to the hope of finding pirate or treasure hoards because coins (unfortunately usually of copper) are found frequently along the sands of the Sussex shoreline. The attempts to salvage the cargo of the British sloop-of-war *De Braak,* which went down off Lewes in 1798 with a store of gold, have attracted widespread attention, and it is at least indicative of the habits of mind of the treasure-seekers that when the *Liberty,* engaged in this work in 1935, was delayed for some time by unfavorable weather, a "bad weather witch" was burned, although burning weather witches is no part of the lore of the Delaware Bay or River.

Wells are often located by divining-rods, and in Delaware the peach twig is as powerful as the hazel twig elsewhere, and the results are in many cases as astonishing. Animals are believed to be able to see things invisible to human beings. The humble pig reputedly can see the wind; it is pointed out that he squeals before the blast strikes him. Purple martins build their apartment houses only where "good people" live, and quickly depart when "bad people" move in.

Herb cures also form a part of Sussex County folklore. The root of "Rassling Jack" is chewed to cure "risins and miseries" of the stomach; if the leaves are masticated, the chewer is given great strength for wrestling. "Conquerin' Tom" when rubbed on the body assures success in courting girls. "Old field balsam" and "horse mint" are fever cures. "Yaw weed" and "pipsiduary" (pipsissewa), thickened with resin, yield a popular salve for sore joints and often will quell the "risins." Burdock root is used in quinsy cases and the leaves of the burdock are a cure for boils.

Safety against spells and protection while traveling are obtained by wearing about the neck certain herbs tied in a heart-shaped bag made of red flannel. In Wilmington, Negroes are sold amulets to be worn about the neck or carried in the bosom, the object being to drive away bad luck. Sums of $5 to $25 are paid for the talismans, which, because of the voodooist's secret incantations, are depended upon to keep their owners out of police clutches, or, if by any chance the judge is faced, to insure that His Honor will dismiss the case. There are also those who believe a tarred rope bound about a patient's neck will stop nosebleed, and a bracelet of copper wire or of dried eelskin will cure rheumatism. Voodooism was long practiced at Belltown, an all-Negro settlement near Lewes. Devotees of the cult, no longer in existence, were known as "Devil Worshippers" and the casting of evil spells was one of their most feared claims (see Tour 14).

The tales of Fiddler's Bridge, of Patty Cannon, of the Moors, and of the haunted houses and ghosts in various parts of the State are told in other sections. Patty Cannon, Delaware's most notorious kidnaper of Negroes in ante-bellum days, "could stand in a half-bushel measure and lift five bushels of grain, weighing 300 pounds, to her shoulder." Her story, founded in gruesome fact but enlarged and expanded in its many tellings, has become a folk tale. There are as many versions of her demise as there are of the death of John Wilkes Booth.

The habit of "yarning" is a confirmed one in every rural and small-town section of the State, each community having its favorite yarn. A distinctive feature of Delaware yarn-telling is that the teller never steals another man's story and never tells a story as happening to himself if it happened to someone else. The story of how Fan Tingle stole a ham out of a smokehouse with the door locked is always told as Fan Tingle's story. The teller may spend five or ten minutes in the effort to recall the name of the hero, but only when the name is recalled does the narrator begin.

Most Delaware yarns are humorous or gruesome episodes dealing with the "smartness" of a victim or culprit in escaping blame or capture until someone still "smarter" outwits him. Even in the tall story, there must be a humorous slant or denouement to avoid "just plain lying."

Occasionally there is a sharp dig at the local storekeeper or miller. One oft-repeated tale relates how Old Daddy Joram, a poor man, took his bag of corn on mule-back to the local mill for grinding. As Daddy waited about for the grinding, the mill-owner happened to come along and asked the millhand: "Whose grist is that going through?" "Daddy Joram's," was the answer. "Did you toll it?" asked the miller. "Yessir!" said the millhand. "Joram's a poor man, isn't he?" "Poor as Job's turkey!" "Well, then, toll his grist again and keep him poor!" ordered the miller.

In no characteristic is the Delawarean so conspicuous as in his gregariousness. The centuries-old curbstone markets of Wilmington are thronged as much with gossipers as with bargain-seekers, and impromptu reunions are held in the midst of sidewalk traffic on busy Market Street. The reunion, in a thousand forms, is so nearly universal as to be practically a folkway. In summer, scores of large family gatherings are held in all parts of the State, sometimes attended by hundreds of descendants of a common prominent ancestor.

Church dinners and suppers have been popular and well attended for generations, and the dinner held annually at a rural church may have a history of a century or more. Harvest-homes, carnivals, fairs, turkey-shoots, and the fall hog-killings are other forms of reunion. A Sussex hog-killing is almost a social event. In some parts of the State, but more particularly in remote sections of Sussex County, the neighbors go "Sunday-visiting." The folks of the community, sometimes as many as fifty men, women, and children, gather at the home of one of the members on a Sunday to partake of a bountiful dinner and to inspect the crops and livestock. On the following Sunday, the visit is paid to another neighbor, and so on until the circuit is completed.

Camp meetings, almost the sole form of vacation in the earlier days of the nineteenth century, still hold much of the old favor, especially in the lower part of the State. Return Day, a custom now recently revived, was a monster reunion held in Georgetown, the county-seat of Sussex, two days after the biennial general election. The returns, district after district, were read to the crowd assembled in the Square.

The larger reunions of the present day are the time-honored celebrations at Bowers Beach and Oak Orchard, which are attended by thousands; and the Kent-Sussex Fair at Harrington, the successor to a long line of State fairs. In Wilmington, the Negroes have their picturesque reunion at the August Big Quarterly, an annual event since 1809, when a group led by Peter Spencer withdrew from Asbury Methodist Episcopal Church and established a church of their own.

A custom of early Delaware that survives, though feebly celebrated, is the Old Christmas of Sussex County. Observed on Twelfth Night, and formerly as the real Christmas, it represents the resistance of many families of old English descent to the change made in the calendar by Pope Gregory. It is still alleged by some that daffodils and elders shoot sprouts through the frozen ground, to remain visible until sunrise on Old Christmas.

Whether a Delawarean is such because of his habits of speech, his customs and traditions, or his ways, is open to question. There can be no doubt whatever that an intense State-consciousness exists in Delaware, the result of its small size and its compactness, its rather sparse population, and the unwillingness of the older native families to regard as of consequence those entering the State in recent times. An observant Episcopal Bishop once remarked sagely:

The ideal Delawarean is born in Sussex County, has Rodney and Burton grandmothers so that he is related to everybody, marries a Ridgely of Dover for his first wife and a Corbit of Odessa for his second, lives and practices law in Wilmington, eventually becoming Governor of Delaware or a Judge of the Supreme Court.

The Delaware Folklore Society, fostered by the Delaware Institute of History and Culture, was organized at Dover, June 5, 1950. The Society publishes at least one bulletin a year, which contains collections of Delaware sayings, of early customs and folk tales. The bulletin also contains scholarly and entertaining pieces of research in these fields.

Outdoor square-dancing on summer evenings in Wilmington's Rodney Square, initiated in 1953, met with such happy response that it is likely to become a custom. The onlooker could easily imagine in the absorbed dancers the recrudescence of a folkway of their ancestors.

The annual Wilmington Flower Market, in May, at Rockford Park, provides interest and accommodations for all ages from babies to grandparents; majors in flowers, plants, shrubs, and trees and equipment for gardeners and outdoor living, but sells also a wide range of appealing household items, from aprons to puppies. Profit goes to good causes, and the patronage of this market is such that it qualifies as a local custom.

Education

O NLY limitation of time under Dutch or Swedish control prevented Delaware from having an advanced educational system in the seventeenth century. Popular education had been planned for New Sweden long before the first expedition of colonists set sail from Gothenburg in November 1637. King Gustavus Adolphus proposed to support in his American colonies an adequate system of schools; education, from the King's viewpoint, would provide the test of fitness for economic and political advancement among the colonists.

Although the settlements came to be made on a much reduced scale after the King's death, education remained an essential part of administrative concern. Even the grant to the Dutch colonists from Utrecht, who arrived on the Delaware under Swedish auspices in 1640, contains the firm command in the name of the young Queen Christina, that "the patrons of this colony shall be obliged at all times to support as many ministers and schoolmasters as the number of inhabitants shall seem to require." In Sweden the importance of education was so generally accepted by this time that the country people, even if far from the parish school or church, felt disgraced if their children could not read. The children were taught in the home by their parents, or possibly by an older child or neighbor, between visits of the minister-teacher. Periodically the teacher gave them a thorough drilling and exhorted the parents to permit no relaxation in the practice of reading and speaking. Many Finns living in Swedish territory at the time understood Swedish and some could write and speak it.

During the seventeen years of Swedish sovereignty along the Delaware, seven clergymen, each for a part of the period, served the scattered settlements and plantations as both preachers and teachers. Reorus Torkillus from Mölndal, near Gothenburg, where he had taught in the High School, came to Fort Christina with Governor Ridder in 1640, the first Lutheran clergyman to have a charge in America. In a house at the fort and soon at a church built by Governor Ridder within the fort enclosure, Torkillus held services for the planters, workmen, soldiers, and their families. From November 1641 to April 1643 "Herr Christopher" shared the great amount of work expected of these clergymen, even in so small a settlement.

In September 1643, Torkillus died, leaving a wife and young child. He was buried at the fort by the Reverend Johan Campanius (Holm), who came with Governor Printz early in the year. Herr Christopher returned to Sweden on the ship that brought Printz and Campanius, but with this ship also had arrived a nephew of Governor Printz, the Reverend Israel Holg Fluviander. Campanius and Fluviander divided the shores of the Delaware between them until 1647, when Fluviander returned to Sweden. The next year, by his own request, Campanius also was permitted to go home and was replaced by Lars Karlsson Lock.

Lock was the only clergyman on the river from 1648 until 1654, when the Reverend Matthias Nertunius and the Reverend Peter Larsson Hjort arrived with Governor Rising. They returned to Sweden with Rising in 1655 after conquest of the Delaware territory by the Dutch, and Lock alone remained, a somewhat doubtful asset because of his troublemaking disposition. Years later, in the time of the Duke of York, he was involved in the rebellion led by the Long Finn. Governor Lovelace, writing from New York to Captain John Carr at New Castle, said: "I perceive the little domine hath played the trumpeter to this discord. I refer the quality of his punishment to your discretion."

Under the Dutch, after 1655, and under the English, after 1664, the Swedes were permitted to have their own clergymen and teachers. About 1663, New Amstel obtained the services of the Swedish clergyman, Abelius Zetskorn, as a teacher and reader in the church. Holland, long before the time of Dutch occupation of the Delaware, maintained at public expense schools that were open to all children. The patroons were required to furnish schoolmasters as one of the conditions for receiving grants in America. When the city of Amsterdam took over Fort Casimir and established New Amstel (New Castle) in 1656–57, the burgomasters of Amsterdam as a matter of course sent schoolmasters for whose salaries they assumed responsibility until such time as they expected the colonists to meet the cost by taxation. The burgomasters planned also for the immediate building of a church and a school, or a house that could be both school and residence for the teacher.

The first schoolmaster, Evert Pietersen, who arrived with Director Jacob Alrichs in the spring of 1657, had twenty-six pupils by summer. No school seems to have been built, but the small wooden church, erected on the Strand in that year, served the Dutch for religious worship, and the whole community for gatherings of a civic or social nature. Probably it also housed the school.

"EIGHT SQUARE" SCHOOL, COWGILL'S CORNER

The Dutch were less fortunate than the Swedes in securing clergymen. Domine Grassmeer of New Amsterdam conducted the first services in 1651. In 1657, Andries Hudde sold his house on the Strand to Director Alrichs for use as a church. Here Evert Peterson read sermons of the Reformed Dutch faith. The Reverend Everardus Welius who arrived with an expedition of colonists from Amsterdam in 1659, served only a year until his death. After conquest by the English, Domine Fabricius, a German Lutheran formerly in Dutch service at New Amsterdam, was pastor for a time at the Dutch church. He was in these years a frequent rebel against the authority of the magistrates and the laws of church and community. Later, Fabricius preached to both Swedes and Dutch at Crane Hook, near Christina, and in his old age acquired a reputation as a man of godly ways.

In 1678 the Reverend Peter Teschemaker was ordained minister of the Dutch Reformed church at New Castle. Early in the same year, before Peter Teschemaker came to New Castle, the Reverend John Yeo, the first Church of England clergyman on the Delaware, came to New Castle from Maryland, and was approved by the court and the Governor for the free will support of the inhabitants. There was some difficulty that resulted in the call to Teschemaker, and Yeo returned to Maryland.

From fifteen to twenty families of Welsh Baptists who had lived in Pennsylvania for two years came to Delaware in 1703, having secured from William Penn a tract of thirty thousand acres near Iron Hill *(see Tour 9)*, and there they established the Welsh Tract Meeting. Small wooden churches and meeting houses in many parts of the counties in the early 1700's represented the Church of England, the Society of Friends, and the Presbyterians, each of which became a center for the promotion of secular education.

As the English population increased, the well-to-do sent their sons to England or to New England, and their daughters to Philadelphia or elsewhere, to the best of the early schools and academies. Young children and sometimes the older ones were taught by tutors and governesses at home, or sent to a local private or subscription school in a teacher's house or in a small school house built by a group of subscribing parents. Slaves were often taught to read and write in the households of their owners, and the children of favored white servants and workmen were sometimes given free elementary education by employers. Until after 1800, there was no other free education, except by neighbors, friends, clergymen, or other professionals who sometimes gathered classes of "poor" children for instruction.

Beginning with the Duke of York's laws, the English authorities made statutory provision for some measure of education and for religious teaching in the Delaware territory. The Duke of York's laws specified that a church must be built in each parish, and that "although divers persons may bee of Different Judgments, Yett all shall contribute to the Minister Establisht and allowed of, which is in noe way judged to bee an Infringement of the Liberty of Conscience, to the which they may pretend."

The inhabitants were required to instruct their children and servants in matters of religion and in the laws of the country, and to bring them up in some lawful calling. If children and servants, sixteen years of age or over, should "refuse to hearken" and be unruly, the parents or masters might call upon the justice of the peace or the constable to administer corporal punishment to the extent of "ten stripes." The churches of the Dutch and Swedes were accepted as satisfactory to the law, and the court at New Castle readily passed the credentials of the ministers.

One of Penn's laws on education had more teeth than the Duke's, and was intended to bring about universal elementary education. This law required all parents and the guardians of those orphans who had "sufficient estates and ability so to do," to make certain that their children were able to read and write by the time they reached twelve years; and further required "that they be taught some useful trade and skill, that the poor may work to live and that the rich, if they become poor may not want, of which every County Court shall take care." There was fine or imprisonment for failure to comply.

Regarding religion, Penn's laws granted freedom of worship to all who lived peaceably, "who confess and acknowledge one Almighty and Eternal God. . . ." In contrast to the Duke's laws, Penn's law declared that the people would not be compelled to attend "or maintain any religious worship, place, or ministry." Persons of all faiths were included under the law requiring abstention "from their usual and common toil and labor on the first day of the week, called the Lord's day."

Beginning in the year 1696, the Swedish colonists enjoyed a revival of learning that crowned the long and painstaking efforts of the elder Swedes. In that year as an outgrowth of a visit (1690) to the Delaware by Andrew Printz, nephew of the former Governor, and through the interest of King Charles XI, Sweden reassumed responsibility for supplying well-educated Swedish clergymen to her former subjects. Cultured teachers also came to America at this period.

From 1749 to 1756, during the time of Israel Acrelius, Swedish clergyman, educator, student, and historian, and of the Swedish teacher, Nils Forsberg (1749–1758), educational influences in the village of Wilmington, developing in the midst of the plantations of prosperous Swedish farmers and of the glebe land of their church, made English education popular among the Swedes.

The Friends' meeting house, built in 1738, was given over wholly to use as a school in 1748, after the erection of a new meeting house. This marked the founding of the oldest continuously maintained school in the State. The Presbyterians had a brick church, built in 1740, that was long without a resident pastor; but it served as a center for educated Irish refugees, some of whom became teachers. The formation of a Library Company in 1754, and the arrival in 1761 of James Adams, first printer in Delaware, promoted English influences in education.

One of the first publications from the press of Adams was *The Child's New Spelling Book,* which sold for a shilling. The next year Adams issued a reprint of the popular English book entitled *A New Guide to the English Tongue,* by Thomas Dilworth. This work was illustrated and contained fables as well as word lists and "the rules of English grammar."

In 1767, two years after the building of a grammar school at Wilmington (later known as the Wilmington Academy), Newark Academy was established at the village of Newark, twelve miles away. Although Presbyterian in origin, it became, like the academy at Wilmington, a nondenominational secondary school and the forerunner of the University of Delaware. There had been a grammar school at Lewes before 1750, and a school was established in a new building in 1761.

Teaching went on with new vigor after the Revolution. Increasing travel through Wilmington, New Castle, and Newark across the northern part of the State resulted in the sojourn here of many educated persons attracted by the comfortable life of the towns ànd the stimulating interest in learning. At the end of the century, the Academy at New Castle, proposed in 1772, was finally built, and Brandywine Academy was opened at Wilmington, north of Brandywine Creek. Lewes had a new academy in 1795, and between 1801 and 1829 at least 31 educational institutions, chiefly academies and grammar and classical schools, were incorporated throughout the State. In 1810 was established the Dover Academy, where many of the State's ablest lawyers received their training.

Efforts to found a college in the State were advanced in 1818, when the Legislature authorized a lottery of $50,000 toward establishing a college at Newark. Three years later the fund was aided further by a tax upon the passengers of stage lines and steamboats. In 1833, "Newark College" was chartered for instruction in the languages, arts, and sciences, with power to give degrees; and college buildings were erected.

In 1796 the Legislature created a public school fund of all money from marriage and tavern licenses, and authorized the State Treasury to accept gifts, donations, and bequests from individuals. No use was made of the school fund until 1817 and 1818, when the Legislature appropriated $1,000 to each county to be used in the "hundreds" (corresponding to townships) for the education of poor children. Among institutions that could receive aid for teaching "poor children" to read and write were Sunday schools, at the rate of 20 cents per white scholar per year. The cost was to be met, not out of the school fund, but from taxes, which were not to exceed $200 per county per year and were to be raised by a county rate levied and collected with other county taxes—the first general taxation for school purposes in the State.

At this time Willard Hall, a lawyer, and later judge of the Federal District Court in Delaware, was devoting a great deal of time to the study and advocacy of public education. "An Act for the Establishing of Free Schools," drafted by him, was passed by the Legislature in 1829. This law, which brought its creator the title of father of public schools in Delaware, established a system under which the State matched, up to $300, the amount raised by local taxation, gift, or other method in any school district. If no money was raised, no school was opened. A district might have a poor school, a good school, or none.

In time the public school districts were permitted to raise substantial amounts in addition to the required sums, and to bond for permanent improvements. Incorporated town schools were freed from the financial restrictions of the law, and allowed to advance or decline according to the temper of the inhabitants. Wilmington schools, which were started in 1830 under the 1829 law, became independent of the State system immediately, and advanced more rapidly than those in other parts of the State.

In 1875, the school law was amended to provide for the appointment of a State superintendent, at a salary of $1800, and to prohibit the employment of any teacher in the districts who had not a certificate of fitness from the superintendent.

A series of experimental changes in the school law alternately promoted and retarded the opportunities of the pupil. But they failed to uproot the fundamental defect of assessing and collecting school taxes locally by 290 small independent districts. Responsible State control was advanced by the State constitution of 1897, which opened the way for uniform taxation for schools, and for compulsory attendance, first required by law in 1907. In 1911 a new State Board of Education was instructed to report on school conditions and suggest revision of laws.

To this board, and to the enlightened public support it received, is due the completely revised and modern system of education the State enjoys today. The members were Dr. George W. Twitmyer, then superintendent of schools in Wilmington; Henry Ridgely, attorney of Dover; George S. Messersmith of Lewes, Assistant Secretary of State of the United States; Professor Harry Hayward of the Delaware College Agricultural Department; John W. Hering of Milford; Henry Clay Davis of Laurel; and Frederick Brady of Middletown. Their report to the Legislature in 1913 was a candid factual survey of the educational conditions, good and bad, resulting from the Delaware system, together with recommendations for fundamental changes.

Special recommendations of the board achieved the result sought by earlier groups in regard to State responsibility for teacher-training. Delaware College was reorganized, and the Women's College established (1914) upon proposals of the State Federation of Women's Clubs. The trustees of these colleges were instructed to establish a Department of Education which should be a part of the State normal school system.

Although the chief school-system reforms failed in 1913, it was through the efforts of the board, of the State commissioner, Charles A. Wagner, and of numerous organized groups of citizens, that the system of local taxation in effect since 1829 was finally overturned.

Even the meager education available for white children during the earlier years of the State was denied to Negroes. Free Negroes sometimes bore the cost of their education and at other times accepted the patronage of philanthropic whites, while slaves were sometimes permitted to study with their masters' children. Instances were recorded where Negroes given such an opportunity used it to raise their own status and to improve the social and economic conditions of other Negroes. One such man was Adoniram Abrahams, born a slave in 1686 in Seaford Hundred, who secured an education through the aid of a Quaker in Philadelphia and became known in later years as one of the best educated men of his race. The society which he organized in Philadelphia to promote the welfare of Negroes developed into the first Negro Episcopal Church in America.

A school for Negro children with 34 pupils was in Wilmington as early as 1814, and in 1816 the African School Society bought a lot on Sixth Street between West and Tatnall Streets in Wilmington, where a good school building was erected at a cost of $800. But as late as 1867, there were only seven schools for Negroes in the State, three of them in Wilmington. Beginning that year, with the assistance of the Freedmen's Bureau and of Dr. James Carey Thomas of Baltimore, prominent white citizens of Wilmington established the Delaware Association for the Moral Improvement and Education of Colored People.

In 1875, the Legislature authorized the taxation of Negroes for the support of their schools, the funds to be turned over to the Association for equal division. In that year 67 Negro schools were reported in operation in the State, 28 of these outside of Wilmington. Supervision of the Wilmington schools was taken over by the local Board of Education. As the tax raised met about one-third of the cost, the remainder depended on subscriptions among Negro and white.

Beginning in 1881, the State made small appropriations. These were gradually increased, as was the extent of supervision over the schools until the duplicate system of Negro education was absorbed. By the school law of 1921, the State Board of Education was required to maintain separate schools for Negroes which should be uniform and equally as effective as those for white children. Pierre S. du Pont offered to build at his own expense schoolhouses for Negroes over the entire State. Under this program 87 schools were soon erected at a cost of $2,622,751.49, the greater part of which was contributed by Mr. Du Pont. Recent Negro elementary and high schools (1953) rank with the best in the country and are outstanding in architecture as well as in equipment and facilities.

The one institution of higher learning for Negroes is Delaware State College, near Dover, established in 1891 to take advantage of the Morrill Act for Agriculture Education. The college is directed by a nonpartisan board appointed by the Governor every two years. The faculty and administrative staff number 29 persons, and the student body approximately 153. Co-educational, "dedicated to cultural growth through curriculum and student activities," college offers besides liberal arts and science courses, premedical, teacher training, music, agriculture, home economics.

During thirty-five years since the appointment of a School Code Commission of 1917, most of the phases of public education in Delaware have been surveyed and studied with the aid of experts from educational foundations and from the United States Department of Education. The first code, adopted by the State in 1919–21 was later adjusted to local views and needs in the essential elements of a modern school system. Following its adoption a group of citizens (incorporated as the Delaware School Auxiliary to conduct studies for the improvement of the public schools) and a later body, the Delaware School Foundation, became the agencies through which Pierre S. du Pont spent approximately $10,000,000 toward modernizing and rebuilding the school plant. Mr. du Pont served as president of the State Board of Education for several years, and later as State Tax Commissioner.

At first under the code, income tax and other revenue was assigned to a special cumulative "School Fund," used only for the support of the school system. By act of 1949 this was replaced by annual appropriations from general revenue. Wilmington's schools are supported by local tax and State aid. Other districts may vote a tax for special needs.

The modern school code and system of financing provides for a comprehensive building program, the development of vocational training in rural as well as town schools, and the general inclusion of art, music, and crafts, even in one-room country schools. From a place somewhere between thirty-third and thirty-seventh in the general rating of the States in 1918, Delaware has achieved a place among the first ten. Invaluable contributions by a private citizen to public education were vocational schools at Wilmington, constructed and equipped to accommodate nearly a thousand students of industrial and commercial subjects (see page 294).

As a regular function of the public school system, a department of adult education conducts classes throughout the State in music, crafts, art, physical and vocational education, and in academic studies. Exhibits of work in the handcrafts, combined with musical and dramatic programs and forums on public affairs, are given in county assemblies at the end of each term. The cultural and economic gain by many individuals over a period of years has enriched community life throughout the State.

The school year is 180 days, attendance compulsory to the age of 16. In 1951–52 school year average attendance of all pupils was 172 days, enrollment 49,567; teaching, supervisory and administrative staff, 2,253. This staff and all employees receive starting salaries based upon qualifications and experience and advance by a schedule of increases in each category. Delaware salaries and expenditure per pupil rank high.

Wilmington schools have kindergartens and a school for crippled children. The State pays for education of a number of indigent deaf, dumb, blind and otherwise handicapped children through private schools and State commissions and institutions.

Two unusual characteristics mark the history of education in Delaware: the education of girls as well as boys from the earliest times (John Wilson, a learned Scotchman, teaching in Wilmington in the 1760's, seems to have raised a lone voice against taking the girls as far as the boys) ; and the inclusion of grammar and the classics and of French, painting, music, and dancing in many of the earliest schools.

Religion

MUCH of the early religious history of the State is an integral part of the history of the schools, because in each period the churches were the chief agencies of secular as well as religious education. The Swedish Lutheran and Dutch Reformed denominations founded both church and school on the Delaware, but no congregations in the State today are directly descended from these beginnings.

After 1696 Swedish clergymen were in demand among the early congregations of the Church of England, established by missionaries of the Society for the Propagation of the Gospel in Foreign Parts. Few of these congregations had settled clergymen. The Reverend Eric Bjorck, of Crane Hook and Christina, preached at most of the Society's churches in New Castle County. When Immanuel Church at New Castle was dedicated (1705), the Reverend Andrew Rudman from the Swedish church at Philadelphia preached the sermon at the invitation of the Reverend George Ross, the first settled minister. The continued sympathy and association between Swedish Lutherans and members of the Church of England brought about their union in Delaware in one denomination, the Protestant Episcopal Church. German Lutherans, settling in Wilmington about the middle of the eighteenth century, were not sufficiently numerous for nearly a hundred years to found a church, the Zion Lutheran, in 1848. Since that time English Lutheran congregations have been organized and the State now has three United Lutheran churches and three Evangelical Lutheran.

The Dutch Reformed, who must have held the first religious service on Delaware soil, in the short-lived colony at Swanendael in 1631, had only one church, at New Castle. It was built in 1657 and was absorbed about 1700 by the Presbyterians.

The Protestant English, Irish, and Welsh clergymen, with the Quakers, followed the Swedes and Dutch as the earliest preachers and teachers. During the late seventeenth and early eighteenth centuries they established the churches that have predominated since their day: Episcopal, Presbyterian, Baptist, and Society of Friends. Roman Catholic and Methodist congregations were organized before the Revolution, and Methodist churches

John Moll

OLD MEETING HOUSE, ODESSA

multiplied rapidly afterward. While by far the greater part of the church-goers belong to these six congregations, Delaware has 33 major denominations, and variations and separations within these bodies make 58 different forms of religious faith. The latest available census (1926) reports 110,142 church communicants out of a total population of 223,000.

An early religious group, the Mennonites, led by Peter Plockhoy, founded a colony in 1663 near the site of Lewes, under Dutch protection. They were uprooted the next year in the name of the Duke of York, by Sir Robert Carr, when he took the Delaware settlements from the Dutch. Carr boasted that he "destroyed the quaking colony of Plockhoy to a naile." The people were scattered, and later Plockhoy and his wife found friendly support among the Mennonites of Pennsylvania. One small Mennonite congregation, organized in 1930, now has a church at Richardson Park near Wilmington, and two groups of Pennsylvania Mennonites (Amish) are established in central Delaware, the Old Order near Dover, and the Conservatives near Greenwood.

Jews, except for special grants to a few individuals, were excluded from trade along the Delaware River during the Dutch period. Several individuals and later a few families settled at New Castle. Wilmington had several families at the end of the eighteenth century, but it was not until the late nineteenth that the first small synagogue was established. There are now five synagogues in Wilmington. In Kent County a congregation is centered at Dover, with a temple and full-time rabbi.

George Fox, the English Quaker, and some companions visited Delaware in 1672 and preached at New Castle. The first meeting houses, built soon after the arrival of William Penn in 1682, and others after the arrival of William Shipley and his group of followers at Wilmington in 1735, gave the Society of Friends a period of strong influence and growth. By the first quarter of the nineteenth century, however, the congregations outside Wilmington were few and widely dispersed. Efforts to maintain the meeting houses by combining services and other means failed, and all were finally closed except that at Camden in Kent County. In 1826, the controversy between the followers of Elias Hicks and those opposed divided the Delaware Quakers into Hicksite and Orthodox. The two branches of the Wilmington meeting, known as the Wilmington Monthly Meeting (Hicksite) and the Wilmington Meeting (Orthodox) still have separate meeting houses, but now frequently worship together.

The Church of England membership declined greatly during the Revolutionary period. Although several clergymen changed the service to leave out the prayers for the King, and thus kept their congregations together, most of the churches were closed until after the Revolution. After the Episcopal Church of the United Colonies was organized, Episcopal churches in Delaware increased in number, and the bitter feeling of the Revolutionary period subsided. In 1841, Delaware became a separate diocese by the election of Bishop Alfred Lee.

Following the organization of the first Presbyterian congregation at New Castle about 1698, new congregations were stimulated by the increased immigration of educated Irish, seeking freedom of worship because of persecution at home under Charles II. The tide of immigration flowed through New Castle and spread into the adjoining States of Maryland, New Jersey, and Pennsylvania. Presbyterian lay readers and clergy, who remained in Delaware, served jointly with those of the Church of England to bring about the "change in life and manners" that characterized many communities. The cultural heritage remains not only in the religious and educational life, but in the mellow architecture of the old churches at New Castle, Wilmington, Dover, and Old Drawyers (near Odessa). During the growth of the denomination, there was an early separation into "Old Side" and "New Side," and later separations and recombinations in matters of doctrine occurred, without greatly disturbing the development of individual churches. Most of the churches belong to the Baltimore Synod of the Presbyterian Church in the United States of America; two belong to the Philadelphia Presbytery of the United Presbyterian Church of North America; there are also Bible and Orthodox Presbyterian churches.

Beginning with the dramatic preaching of Captain Thomas Webb in 1766, Methodism, scorned at first, enlisted widespread support throughout the State and during the nineteenth century became the dominant church in the two southern counties. Captain Webb, a retired British naval officer who was converted in 1768 at the "Rigging Loft" church of Philip Embury in New York, wore his full uniform with scarlet cape when he preached along the Brandywine, at the old Academy grove in Wilmington, and later in improvised church quarters. With his sword resting beside a Bible on the table or pulpit, a black patch covering one blinded eye, Captain Webb inspired his hearers with pity and terror.

At Barratt's Chapel, a mile north of Frederica, known as the "Cradle of Methodism," Francis Asbury and Bishop Thomas Coke met and agreed to organize the Methodist Episcopal Church in America. This was accomplished a few weeks later at Baltimore. Members of the first Methodist Church in Wilmington, which was named Asbury, suffered more persecution than congregations elsewhere, but this appeared to strengthen belief among the faithful and to bring a great accession of members. The membership in the Methodist Church today almost equals the total of all other denominations in Del. It is now one church, M.E. and M.P. joined.

Most of the Negro congregations in the State, including the first one, Ezion, established in 1805 at Wilmington, were formed under Methodist auspices. The religious history of the Negro goes back to the early days of slavery, when certain pews in white churches were set apart for the slaves. Richard Allen, a slave owned by a planter near Dover, was the founder of the African Methodist Episcopal Church. He was converted in 1777 and began his career as a minister three years later. His master, who permitted him to conduct prayers and preach in his own house, was one of Allen's first converts; he made it possible for the young preacher and his brother to purchase their freedom for $2,000. Allen preached in Wilmington on September 13, 1783, the first sermon known to have been delivered by a Negro in that city. In 1786 he went to Philadelphia and began the work which resulted in the formation of Bethel, the first African Methodist Episcopal Church.

The majority of Delaware Negroes today are Methodists, in numerous small congregations. They are followed in numerical importance by the Baptists, whose largest church, Shiloh Baptist, was founded in Wilmington in 1875. St. Joseph's Catholic Church, parochial school, and orphanage and the Blessed Sacrament Church are in Wilmington. The St. Joseph's Industrial School is in Kent County. Other Negro sects in the State include Jehovah's Witnesses, the Church of the Nazarene, the Christian Spiritualist Churches, the Mormon Church, and the Disciples of Christ.

The first Roman Catholic services in Delaware are believed to have been held as early as the 1730's in the house of Cornelius Hallahan who owned the estate, "Cuba Rock," near the present hamlet of Mount Cuba in New Castle County. In the 1750's occasional services were conducted near Dover by a priest from Maryland, and an Appoquinimink mission is believed to have existed about this time near the road to Bohemia Manor. The first chapel was St. Mary's, built of logs in 1772 on the Lancaster Pike west of Wilmington. This chapel, near a stream called Coffee Run, was long known as Coffee Run Church. It was the forerunner of churches and schools in other parts of the State, notably St. Mary's College for boys at Wilmington founded by Father Patrick Reilly. Father Patrick Kenny, an early clergyman in this church, left records of interest to historians. A number of Roman Catholic priests and laymen came to Delaware in the 1790's as refugees from native uprisings in the French West Indies, and many records of Catholic Church history are written in French. The Wil-

FRIENDS' MEETING HOUSE, WILMINGTON

mington diocese was established in 1868 to include Delaware and the Eastern Shore counties of Maryland and Virginia.

From the Baptist congregation established at Welsh Tract near Newark in 1703 have developed all the early Baptist Churches of the State. These and most of the long established Baptist churches belonged originally to the "Primitive" or "Old School" faith, opposed to any formal administrative organization beyond the individual church with its pastor and deacons. Division and separation by groups desiring to take part in regional Baptist associations have diminished the number of "Old School Churches" until only six remain. The Northern Baptist Convention includes most of the thirty-two churches in the State.

Among the other denominations having one or more churches are: the Unitarian, Swedenborgian, The Church of Christ, Scientist, the Adventist, Spiritualist, Holiness, Mormon, Church of the Brethren (conservative Dunkards), and Undenominational.

Literature

TO IDENTIFY a certain body of American writing as Delaware literature is not entirely an arbitrary and illogical procedure. For it is true that the greater number of writers born or reared in this small State have influenced strongly its history or have recorded it; or else to Delaware, in poetry and prose, they have struck "the golden string of praise" (Milford Bard).

At the same time almost every field of literature has been entered by one or another of the more than three hundred writers of published volumes. To note two extremes in time and subject matter: Oliver Evans published in 1795 the *Young Millwright and Miller's Guide,* and in the 1920's Miss Annie Jump Cannon, distinguished astronomer at Harvard University, presented to science her great compendium of the stars, the *Henry Draper Catalog of Stellar Spectra* (1918–1924).

Possibly the Delaware writer with the strongest claim to literary genius is the first of a trio long dead who, as writers, are held almost without honor in their own State: John Dickinson, the "Penman of the Revolution," who though Maryland born was associated most closely with the States of Delaware and Pennsylvania; Robert Montgomery Bird, playwright and novelist; and John Lofland, the eccentric "Milford Bard." But recent and contemporary writers also have achieved national distinction: among them George Alfred Townsend (Gath), Howard Pyle, Henry Seidel Canby, Anne Parrish, and Christopher L. Ward.

John Dickinson (1732–1808) was born in Talbot County, Maryland, and in 1734 came with his family to Kent County in Delaware. Later he established himself as a lawyer in Philadelphia after several years of study in that city and in London. In his *Political Writings* (published by a Wilmington firm in 1801, as prepared by the author) may be found the documents that made Dickinson famous both as a brilliant statesman and as one of the most gifted writers of his day: the petitions to the King, presented at the First and Second Continental Congresses, the Declaration of Rights of the Stamp Act Congress, the celebrated *Letters from a Farmer in Pennsylvania to the Inhabitants of the British Colonies* (1767), and the series of letters signed "Fabius," written in support of the newly framed Constitution. In his *Letters from a Farmer in Pennsylvania,* directed against the Townshend Acts, Dickinson presented legal arguments, simply and lucidly developed, which were intended to bring about conciliatory action. Dickinson believed in constitutional procedure rather than revolution, and voted against the Declaration of Independence, even though he supported the military activities of the Colonies. In 1787–1788 the letters of "Fabius" appeared, and it is believed that the clear and forceful logic of this series did much to induce Delaware and Pennsylvania to ratify the Constitution.

After nearly a century of neglect Robert Montgomery Bird (1806–54), a native of New Castle, has been given decisive recognition in the authoritative *Dictionary of American Biography,* and this chiefly because a University of Pennsylvania student, Clement Edgar Foust, made Bird's life and works the subject of a doctor's thesis. "The fact that Bird's plays remained unpublished until 1917 prevented his sterling work from receiving its proper place in our literary history," declares the *Dictionary of American Biography.*

Bird was a physician who turned to literature because he disliked taking fees. He wrote four plays which were all accepted by Edwin Forrest, the reigning American actor. *The Gladiator* and *The Broker of Bogota* were immediate national successes, and the first-named became the subject of international discussion. Edwin Forrest's enthusiastic reception as Spartacus in *The Gladiator* inspired him to use the play as his opening vehicle on his first trip to London. By 1853 it had been played for the thousandth time, perhaps the first play written in English to be given so many times in the lifetime of the author. Forrest amassed a fortune from Bird's plays, but the author's pay for each was only $1,000. Actor and playwright broke in anger over the situation, Bird claiming he was promised additional sums if the plays proved successful. Unfortunately for Bird's later fame, Forrest blocked all endeavors of Bird and his heirs to publish them, asserting that he held copyrights. Not until 1916 was this statement found to be untrue, so that when the world got a chance to read the plays, included in Foust's life of Bird (1919), they were long outmoded.

Disgusted with the stage, Bird turned to novel writing and produced prolifically. *Nick of the Woods, a Tale of the Jibbenainosay* (1837), a story of the Kentucky backwoods, is notable for its genuine attempt to treat the American frontier realistically. In contrast to J. Fenimore Cooper's Indians, Bird's are primitives of flesh and blood. By 1900 this novel had been published ten times in London and four times in Germany. It was reprinted recently in this country. *Hawks of Hawk Hollow* (1835), which also was well received, is considered by some critics the best of Bird's novels.

Bird was editor-owner of the Philadelphia *North American* for a time, but the pressure of work brought a breakdown and he died of "suffusion of the brain" at the age of 48.

John Lofland (1798–1849), the "Milford Bard," was temperamentally akin to Poe and DeQuincey and, according to his own statement, a dipsomaniac and an opium eater. His body lies in a grave in the center of busy Wilmington traffic, unmarked until 1945.

Born in Milford, Lofland became a doctor, like his contemporary, Bird, and then, like him, relinquished practice for the precarious pathway writers trod in the America of those days. He wrote pleasing and facile poetry and prose, on themes drawn principally from his loved Delaware, and more specifically from the historic Brandywine at Wilmington, where the scene of many of his tales is laid. His chief claim to fame is as a poet of the lyrical Thomas Moore tradition. *Harp of Delaware,* a volume of poems, was published in 1828. His complete works were published in one volume in 1848, and a second edition in 1853. All are now collectors' items.

The financial straits of the writers of that day are illustrated by an advertisement published by Lofland: he would "write for any person in Wilmington or the United States on any subject connected with literature . . . confidential in all cases." His price list embraced lectures, orations, sentimental letters, inscriptions for tombs, medical theses, declamations, songs, and acrostics, ranging from $1 to $20. Poetry for albums was five cents a line. Many such commissions came his way, especially for sentimental letters at $3 each to be exchanged between lovers. All correspondents addressed him as "The Bard."

Aside from these three relatively prominent figures, early Delaware litterature was dominated by ministers, schoolmasters, and travelers, and much of their product was in the form of sermons and religious dissertations. The Reverend William Becket, missionary at Lewes from 1721 to 1743, may have been an exception as he is reputed to be Delaware's first poet. In addition to unpublished poems, Becket composed long epitaphs and obituaries in rhyme.

The diaries and correspondence of eminent Delawareans during the Revolutionary War period furnish a picture of the times that supplements the meager official records. In the main, each of the writers up to the middle of the nineteenth century wrote the one book that presumably everyone has it in him to produce, circumstances favoring, and many of the volumes have become items of Delawareana and prizes for collectors.

At least three Wilmington schoolmasters of this early period distinguished themselves as writers. The Pennsylvanian John Filson (1747–1788) taught school in Wilmington during Revolutionary days and then emigrated to Kentucky, where he wrote *The Discovery, Settlement, and Present State of Kentucke,* with the famous appendix purporting to be the autobiography of Daniel Boone. He rode back over the mountains to Wilmington where his now prized volume was published (1784) by James Adams, Delaware's first printer. In 1791, Robert Coram wrote and published a plan for the general establishment of schools throughout the United States. This was supported by a thesis on government, *Political Inquiries,* in which he demonstrated that only by general free education could a democracy survive. The pamphlet, a Delaware imprint, is now a rare historical document. Azariah Fobes, who taught in Wilmington early in the nineteenth century, published a collection of psalms and hymns, *The Delaware Harmony.*

Several historical writers of the middle and late nineteenth century are well remembered in the State. Elizabeth Montgomery's *Reminiscences of Wilmington* (1851; 2nd ed. 1872), is treasured in many Wilmington households. *A History of the Original Settlements on the Delaware* (1846), by Benjamin Ferris, is a valuable source of information. Emily Read, granddaughter of George Read the Signer, wrote *Two Hundred Years Ago, or Life in New Sweden* (1876), and Elizabeth Booth set down (1884) delightful *Reminiscences* (of New Castle).

Francis Vincent (1822–82), historian and editor, planned a State history which was to appear in several volumes. Only the first of these was published, *A History of the State of Delaware* (1870), which ended with the English occupation in 1664. Vincent, a man of ponderous girth, soft-spoken and courteous, was in his heyday a vigorous liberal. In his paper, *The Blue Hen's Chicken,* he favored courageously such reforms as abolition of slavery, a ten-hour workday, shorter hours for women workers, toll-free bridges, suffrage for Negroes, and establishment of life-saving service along the seacoast, all of which he saw come to pass in his lifetime. In 1868 he wrote an essay for the Cobden Club, London, advocating an Anglo-Saxon Confederation, and in 1870 presented a paper to the European Permanent League for Peace at Paris in which he proposed a league for peace in Europe that in some respects was similar to the League of Nations formed after World War I.

An amusing anecdote is told of Nathaniel Barratt Smithers, accomplished Dover scholar, who published *Translations of Latin Hymns of the Middle Ages* (1879). When Bret Harte's poem "The Heathen Chinee" first appeared, Mr. Smithers was delighted and translated it into Latin, afterwards sending it in a waggish mood to a Latin professor with the statement it had been found among some ancient ruins and that evidently Bret Harte was a plagiarist. It was not long before the news spread, and a prominent Kent County lawyer wrote to the New York *Herald* accusing Bret Harte of plagiarism and offering to furnish proof of the charge. The affair became sensational, the wise men insisting that the Latin translation by Smithers was the original poem. When Smithers had enjoyed the joke long enough, he acknowledged he was the guilty party, to the merriment of some and the chagrin of others.

Caleb Harlan, writer on varied subjects, is remembered chiefly for *Ida Randolph of Virginia* (1860), a poem in three cantos that went through a second edition. Three women writers popular in their day were Marian Calhoun Legare Reeves ("Fadette"), whose most popular novel was *Wearithorne, or, In the Light of Today* (1872); Harriet Pennawell Belt, who wrote *Marjorie Huntingdon* (1884); and Mary Jane Windle, author of *Truth and Fancy* (1850).

Toward the end of the nineteenth century and in the early years of the twentieth, Delaware's second group of more widely known writers began to be recognized. First among these was George Alfred Townsend (1841–1914), journalist and editor, who was born in Georgetown and early in life attained a Nation-wide reputation as a journalist, for his vivid reports of the Civil War. For forty years he wrote special articles to the journals of the country under the pseudonym of "Gath," derived from the initials of his name and the Biblical injunction: "Tell it not in Gath, publish it not in Askelon."

But Townsend's chief contributions to literature are his novels and short stories. *Tales of the Chesapeake* (1880), a collection of colorful folk stories of Delaware and the Eastern Shore of Maryland, was written in 1880. Then followed his best known novel, *The Entailed Hat* (1884), which deals with the notorious Patty Cannon of Sussex County, and the kidnaping of free Delaware Negroes into southern slavery. The fact that this novel has been reprinted recently testifies to its strong hold upon the reading public, in spite of its difficult and somewhat tedious style. No work depicts better the ante-bellum background of Delaware. Townsend's *Katy of Catoctin* (1887), a story of the conspiracy to assassinate Abraham Lincoln, gained moderate circulation.

Howard Pyle (1853–1911), nationally known as an illustrator, is rated by some critics to be as good a writer as an artist. Born in Wilmington, he made that city his home through the productive years of his life. When his first ventures in the field of the short story were unsuccessful, Pyle took up the work of illustration; as his reputation grew, he began publishing the books that have made him famous, illustrated by himself.

The Merry Adventures of Robin Hood appeared in 1883. It is safe to say that more American boys and girls have been introduced to Robin Hood through Howard Pyle's vigorous and imaginative re-creation of the outlaw than by any other means. *Pepper and Salt, The Wonder Clock, Otto of the Silver Hand,* and *Men of Iron* have all been popular with young people.

Howard Pyle had a warm spot in his heart for the freebooter, whether in the form of a pirate ravaging the seas or an outlaw robbing the rich to give to the poor. He is probably the foremost teller of pirate tales in America, and the assertion has been made that he created the buccaneer of modern fiction. Many of these tales are collected in *Howard Pyle's Book of Pirates* (1921); others are single volumes such as *Within the Capes, Rose of Paradise, The Price of Blood,* and *The Ghost of Captain Brand.* Unlike his other works, but not unexpected from the hand of an adventure seeker who leaned as heavily as most of his kind on pietistic teachings, is Pyle's *Rejected of Men* (1903). In this tale of Christ returned to men will be found the author's views on religion.

Christopher Ward (1868–1944), born in Wilmington, lived all his life in Delaware. He came to literature during a successful career at the law, publishing first a series of sparkling parodies, notably *The Triumph of the Nut.* In his first novel, *One Little Man* (1926), Ward used his native Wilmington for the setting. *Starling,* also a novel, was followed by a poetical mélange, *The Saga of Cap'n John Smith.* A series of period tales concerning the career of Jonathan Drew are collected in *Strange Adventures of Jonathan Drew* (1932) and *A Yankee Rover* (1932). Obedient to the urge toward local history that touches so many Delaware writers, Ward wrote in 1928 *The Dutch and Swedes on the Delaware.* This history of the early settlements is told with the wit and clarity of style that make his fiction notable. (For his later distinguished work see page 133.)

Henry Seidel Canby, born in Wilmington in 1878 and now living in New York City, is editor, essayist, and critic—more recently a historian of American culture. He founded the *Saturday Review of Literature* in 1924. As a very young man Canby went to Yale University as a lecturer in English, and his first published works were studies in the short story and in composition. *Our House,* a novel, was published in 1919. The two series of *Definitions* (1922 and 1924) were given national recognition. *Classic Americans* (1931) reviewed critically the work of important literary figures, and *Alma Mater, the Gothic Age of the American College* (1936), represents the point of view of an educator as well as a critic. *The Age of Confidence* (1934) portraying town life (Wilmington) in America of the 1890's received most favorable comment in both Europe and America. Before establishing the *Saturday Review,* Mr. Canby was assistant editor of the *Yale Review* and editor of the *Literary Review* for the New York *Evening Post.* Purity of style and sound scholarship characterize all his work.

Anne Parrish (widow of Charles A. Corliss), now living in New York City, was born of Delaware parentage in Colorado Springs, Colorado, in 1888, but came to Delaware early in life and attended school in Wilmington. The neighborhood of her home near Claymont is the scene of her most successful novel *The Perennial Bachelor,* which won the Harper's Prize in 1925 and became a national best-seller. Many other stories, some in collaboration with her brother Dillwyn Parrish, were written in Claymont. The craftsmanship of *All Kneeling* (1928) has been especially noted, but in all her work Miss Parrish shows great skill and humor in re-creating the little events and unique personalities of village life. This gift has been likened by some critics to that of E. M. Delafield in *The Diary of a Provincial Lady.*

Another recent novelist of importance is John P. Marquand, a native of Wilmington. In *The Late George Apley,* which received the Pulitzer Prize (1938), Mr. Marquand presents a study of a conservative New England gentleman, born before the Civil War period, whose life is linked with Revolutionary America through his family, and to the changing modern world through his descendants. Written largely in the form of diary notes and letters addressed to his son, the novel develops through the mind of a cultivated man as he attempts to comprehend his own period and to reorient himself toward the future.

George B. Rodney, author of the historical novel *In Buff and Blue* (1897), turned later to writing stories of western life. Judge John Biggs, like many a juristic native of Delaware, is also an author, with two novels favorably known—*Demigods* (1926) and *Seven Days' Whipping* (1928).

True to Delaware literary tradition, many contemporary writers have been attracted into the field of history. John Bassett Moore, distinguished jurist, is more than nationally esteemed for his six-volume *History and Digest of the International Arbitrations to which the United States Has Been a Party* (1898). Judge Henry C. Conrad is the author of a three-volume *History of the State of Delaware* (1908); and Judge Walter A.

Powell has contributed a compact but comprehensive one-volume *History of Delaware* (1928). *Colonial Finances in Delaware* and various other historical studies written by Judge Richard S. Rodney are both scholarly and entertaining. Anna T. Lincoln's *Wilmington, Delaware; Three Centuries under Four Flags 1609–1937* (1937) contributes materially to an understanding of the State's chief city.

In the related field of biography, George Morgan is remembered particularly for his *The True Patrick Henry* (1907) and *The True Lafayette* (1919). Edward Noble Vallandigham, a schoolmate of Morgan at Delaware College, was an educator and historian whose best-known book probably is *Delaware and the Eastern Shore*, subtitled *Some Aspects of a Peninsula Pleasant and Well-Beloved* (1922). Another biographer is Victor Thaddeus, of Arden, whose *Voltaire, Genius of Mockery,* was well received. Dr. John Janvier Black (1837–1909) surveyed the work of his own lifetime in *Forty Years in the Medical Profession* (1900). Lyman Pierson Powell (1866–1946), the author of a biography of Mary Baker Eddy (1930), is well known in the field of educational and religious writing. His *History of Education in Delaware* was published in 1893.

Among Delaware writers who have used their native State as the locale for their novels are Katharine Virden (Mrs. Clarence A. Southerland) in *The Crooked Eye,* and Gertrude Crownfield in *Where Glory Waits,* which deals with Mary Vining, Delaware Revolutionary belle, and General "Mad Anthony" Wayne; Ella Middleton Tybout in *Poketown People,* Anne Parrish in *The Perennial Bachelor* and other novels, Charles Wertenbaker in *To My Father.*

Christopher L. Ward's *The Delaware Continentals 1776–1783* (1941), an authentic history of the Delaware regiment in the American Revolution, presents much of the general history of the war, and is an outstanding work in this field in presentation and literary style. *Hey Day* (1953) by W. Mode Spackman, is mature and distinguished writing.

Delaware in each period of its history has had a few writers of good verse, usually poets aware of the quiet charm of their native State. Two recent poets of local reputation are Emily Bissell, author of *Happiness and Other Poems* (1907), written under the pen name of Priscilla Leonard; and George B. Hynson, who celebrated "Henlopen's jeweled finger" in the State song "Our Delaware." Present-day poetry is best known through the publications of the Wilmington Poetry Society. (See further mention of Delaware writers, page 538.)

The Press

EARLY Delawareans, residents of the Three Lower Counties of Penn's Province, usually arranged for their private and public printing to be done in Philadelphia. It was not until 1761 that a press was set up in Wilmington by James Adams (1725?–92), who was Londonderry born and trained, and had worked for seven years previously in the Quaker City printing house of Franklin and Hall. Many volumes published by Adams are extant.

During his career in Wilmington, Adams held almost a monopoly of the Delaware printing trade. His most notable publication (1784) was Filson's *The Discovery, Settlement and Present State of Kentucky* (mentioned above). His sons, James, John, and Samuel, carried on the business after his death in 1792.

Jacob A. Killen, James Wilson, Peter Brynberg, Samuel Andrews, and the firm of Bonsal and Niles were also early Delaware printers. Hezekiah Niles (1777–1839) removed to Baltimore where he established the much-quoted *Niles' Register,* a periodical of national importance.

The year of publication for Delaware's first newspaper is not definitely known. There is mention of the Wilmington *Chronicle,* supposedly published in 1760. Other commentators have asserted that James Adams established the Wilmington *Courant,* a weekly, in 1762, and that it was continued six months, but no copy of the paper has been discovered, and the commentators themselves qualify their statements. Adams may well have issued *Proposals* for an adventure that was not undertaken, or there may be confusion with the *Delaware Courant and Wilmington Advertiser,* issued in 1786–7 by Samuel and John Adams, sons of James. Jacob A. Killen published the *Delaware Gazette, or, the Faithful Centinel* in 1785, and the *Gazette* continued as a separate publication for 97 years, with Caleb P. Johnson as its last owner. Inasmuch as the plant, and probably the goodwill, was sold to *Every Evening,* now a part of the *Journal-Every Evening,* it may be possible to identify a newspaper of today with his 1785 publication.

Other newspapers, started before 1800, included *The Delaware and*

Eastern Shore Advertiser, the Wilmington *Mercury,* the *Mirror of the Times,* and the *Monitor, or, Wilmington Weekly Repository.*

The Progress of Delaware newspapers in the nineteenth century is marked by mergers, consolidations, changes of names every few years, and discontinuances. This is particularly true of Wilmington, where newspapers sometimes survived for years on the verge of bankruptcy, existing because of popular editorial columns rather than quality or scope of news. The list is too long to be given here, but mention must be made of the *Delaware State Journal* (1831), which in 1855 took over *The Statesman* (1854), the latter having previously taken over *The Blue Hen's Chicken,* a noteworthy publication of which Francis Vincent was long the able editor. The consolidated *Journal and Statesman* was sold to *Every Evening* (1871) in 1872; the *Delaware Republican* (1841), later the *Daily Republican,* was merged with the *Evening Journal,* first issued in 1886; the only afternoon journal in the State today is the Wilmington *Journal-Every Evening,* the result of a merger of these two papers in 1932. The frequent consolidation of failing or competitive rivals is shown in the case of *Every Evening,* which, having absorbed such notable papers as the *Journal and Statesman* and the *Daily Commercial* (1866), the first one-cent daily, itself succumbed to a merger with the *Evening Journal.*

The *Morning Herald,* Wilmington's first morning paper, was started in 1876. Its name was changed to Wilmington *Morning News* in 1880, and it is today Delaware's only morning daily. The *Sunday Despatch* (1878), first Sunday paper, failed, as did the *Sunday Mirror* (1880), but the *Sunday Star* (1881), with Jerome B. Bell as its energetic editor, endured. As the *Wilmington Sunday Star* it is Delaware's only Sunday paper.

Many journals were established at Dover, the State capital, which is also the county seat and the place of printing contracts for State and county work. The first newspaper was the *Federal Ark* (1802). Of the several that exist today, the *Delaware State News* (1901) has a wide circulation. In Milford, the Milford *Chronicle* (1878) is second in circulation only to Wilmington papers. All of the main towns of the State have weekly papers. In Dover, the *Delaware State News* has become a daily (1953).

Delaware journalism is extremely conservative, but the range and coverage in presenting news is broad and skilled. Controlling stock in the Wilmington dailies is owned by members of the Du Pont family through the Christiana Securities Company.

Art and Artists

TO DELAWARE came the earliest notable painter in America, Gustavus Hesselius of Sweden. His brother Andreas had been commissioned by King Charles XII to relieve Eric Bjorck, the rector of the Swedish congregation on the Delaware at the new church near the site of Fort Christina, now known as "Old Swedes," in Wilmington. The brothers Hesselius landed in the Carolinas in the spring of 1711 and came by way of Chesapeake Bay to Delaware. In the diary of Eric Bjorck we read: "Magister Hesselius' brother, Herr Gustaff Hesselius, a portrait painter, came up some days later with their belongings by boat from Appoquinimy [Odessa]." The brothers, who had a letter from William Penn written in London, paid a visit to Penn's deputy-governor, Charles Gookin, at Philadelphia, to present their credentials. Governor Gookin received them well, and it may be that through him the artist received his first American commissions. One of the early portraits by Hesselius is of George Ross, the Rector of Immanuel Church, of which the Governor was a patron. The year preceding the arrival of the painter, Governor Gookin had presented the church with a silver flagon made by Simeon Saumaine of New York.

Gustavus Hesselius came of a distinguished and scholarly family in Sweden and is believed to have studied in Italy before coming to America at the age of twenty-nine. He married within a few years after his arrival, and in 1716 "a son of Gustaf and Lydia Hesselius" was baptized at Old Swedes Church. Meanwhile, living in Philadelphia and traveling through Delaware, Maryland, and Virginia, Hesselius painted portraits full of character and individuality, and was given, on September 5, 1721, the first commission in America to do a painting for a public building. The record of the Church of St. Barnabas in Queen Anne Parish, Maryland, reads: "The Vestry agrees with Mr. Gustavus Hesselius to draw ye History of our Blessed Saviour and ye Twelve Apostles at ye last supper." The painting, which demonstrates the artist's considerable ability in its excellence of composition, skillful drawing, and characterization of the disciples, was lost for many years following the replacing of the old Maryland church building in 1773 by a new structure. Discovered by Charles Henry Hart in

Fredericksburg, Virginia, it came into the possession of Mrs. Rose Neel Warrington, of "Snowden," in Fredericksburg, and was exhibited in Delaware in 1931 by the Wilmington Society of the Fine Arts. (On loan at the Philadelphia Art Museum 1938.)

After twenty years of applying his brush to whatever work was offered, Hesselius bought a house in Philadelphia in 1735. Even then he did not devote himself entirely to portrait painting, for on December 11, 1740, the *Pennsylvania Packet* contained the following advertisement: "Painting done in the best manner by Gustavus Hesselius from Stockholm and John Winter from London, viz. Coat of Arms drawn on Coaches, Chaises, etc., or any kind of Ornaments, Land-skips, Signs, Shew-boards, Ship and House painting, Guilding of all sorts, Writing in Gold or Color, old Pictures cleaned and mended Ac." In addition, Hesselius was the first organbuilder in the Colonies. He speaks in his will of "my chamber organ"; and it is known that he had built a church organ for the Moravians at Bethlehem, Pennsylvania.

The connection of the Hesselius family with Delaware was continued by a second brother, Samuel, who relieved Andreas at Old Swedes in 1719; and through Gustav's own son John, who also painted portraits in Delaware and lived for a time at New Castle. John was the first teacher of Charles Willson Peale, whom John Dickinson of Delaware later aided and encouraged.

The research that revealed the record of the elder Hesselius was made possible through papers left by a later Swedish painter, Adolph Wertmuller, who spent his last years in Delaware. Wertmuller, born in Sweden in 1751, was taught in Paris, and became "First Painter to the King of Sweden." He came to Philadelphia some time before 1794, married Elizabeth Henderson, a granddaughter of Gustavus Hesselius, and in 1803 bought a farm on the Delaware River extending along Naaman's Creek opposite the Robinson property and the Swedish blockhouse. The deed is recorded in the name of "Adolph Ulrich Wertmuller, Gentleman, of Philadelphia." The price paid was $5,300 for 145½ acres. The artist seems not to have taken commissions for painting during the years on the Delaware farm, where he died in 1811. Through his wife the self-portrait of Gustavus Hesselius, her grandfather, and the portrait by him of her grandmother, Lydia Hesselius, were preserved along with Wertmuller's papers, which identified them. They are now in the possession of the Historical Society of Pennsylvania with other portraits by Hesselius. Wertmuller's portrait of George Washington, painted in 1794 and kept by himself, is owned by the Samuel Wagner estate in Philadelphia.

So far as is known, there were no painters in the settlements on the Delaware in the years before the arrival of Hesselius, 1638 to 1711. Appreciation of the natural beauty of the land was well expressed in contemporary writing, and a feeling for beauty and charm in the intimate accessories of daily life. Peter Lindeström, the Swedish engineer on the Delaware, 1654–1655, wrote of the calabashes or gourds used by the Indians for bowls, flasks, and cups: "They are worthy to be mounted with gold and silver on account of their excellence and beauty." From the days of Governor Printz to the present, the Swedes and their Scandinavian relatives have exhibited their long heritage in the art of shipbuilding. Early sailing vessels, constructed along the Delaware, were noted for their beauty of line and skillful craftsmanship.

The influence of the Dutch is recorded chiefly in architectural survivals, although the interest in painting in Holland during the years of colonization was in evidence on the Delaware in the possessions of the directors and well-to-do colonists. Even in a "little village full of trees with a few plank houses and a blockhouse" (New Amstel), there were paintings and at least one large mirror; and a Dutch director was concerned that the courtroom on the second floor of the blockhouse should have paintings, books, and furnishings as amenities that became the dignity of the court.

The elegance of some of the English deputy governors who represented the Penns—Governor Keith especially—had its influence upon New Castle, the court and assembly town, stimulating a taste for the beautiful interiors, with utensils and household equipment by the best craftsmen, which are still to be seen there. Dover, Lewes, and the tidewater hamlets showed similar taste; and a feeling for fine things in general came from the way of life of the successful planters, merchants, and professional men, whose sons frequently finished their education in Europe, and whose wives and daughters visited in Europe and in the fashionable centers in America.

During the whole of the eighteenth century there were local craftsmen, few at first but steadily increasing in number and in the perfection of their work, to meet the demands of persons of wealth, and—more important—to provide the plain people with pottery, silver, and other metalware, with furniture and fine cabinet work, in patterns and workmanship comparable to the best in the neighboring centers of Colonial culture. A recent writer on Colonial architecture in Delaware describes a local cabinetmaker, John Janvier, as "worthy to be remembered as an artist joiner whose touch was well-nigh magic upon the wonderful wood then known as 'walnut' and since as mahogany." Among the artist joiners of that century were George and Thomas Crow, clockmakers; Duncan Beard, clockmaker and silversmith; Jonas Alrichs, grandson of Peter Alrichs, who was commandant on the Delaware for the Dutch in 1673; George Whitelock, Samuel Young, David and William French; the Penny family, for whom Penny Hill near Wilmington is named; and Israel Stalcop, descendant of John Anderssen Stalcop, who in the seventeenth century owned half the site of present Wilmington. Another artist who worked in wood and metals was John Martin. In the last quarter of the century he made chariots, phaetons, coaches, chairs (horse-drawn), and sulkies. Notable silversmiths were Bancroft Woodcock, Joseph Warner, Thomas Byrnes, who made "Blue Hen's Chickens" spoons, and John Chandlee, who, in addition to silversmithing, painted miniature portraits for "twenty-four Dollars, one half to be paid at the first sitting,—the remainder on the delivery of the Picture."

The remoteness of the greater part of the State from the paths of travel favored the preservation to an unusual degree of family portraits and prints, silhouettes and samplers, the utensils of English and American silver and pewter, the needlework, woven fabrics, furniture, and metal work of periods preceding the decline of taste that came shortly before the Civil War. Even after the war, the average Delawarean who owned fine things from the earlier periods was slow to adopt the ornate Victorian or to have the family silver melted.

Only in the early 1900's did the collectors begin to carry off in quantity, along with valuable historic papers, records, and letters, the choice old silver and exquisite needlework, the handsome paneling, mantels, and stairways, and some of the portraits that had come down through many generations. Straitened circumstances, new tastes among the younger generations, and the automobile, which required increased spending money for the family and brought the commercial and private collectors to the door, all helped to deplete the unusual store of handicraft and art. But in the process came realization of the artistic and commercial values of these possessions, a realization that often led the owners to select among the new forms of household objects those that could dwell harmoniously with the old. So, though the collector lost his easy market, he stimulated respect for the taste and arts of forebears and an interest in the historic backgrounds that produced them.

Then followed the inauguration of the annual "Old New Castle Day," "Old Dover Day," and similar celebrations at Lewes and Rehoboth, where treasured examples of early art are exhibited in the owners' homes and in collections gathered from the surrounding countryside. The celebration of the three hundredth anniversary of the Dutch settlement at Lewes in

1931 included the creation of a museum, Swanendael House, where treasures that have come to it through bequest, as well as special exhibits, are shown to the public. The interest of local families and groups in Sussex County, many of whose members are descendants of the earliest settlers and owners of fine examples of early art, has increased the chances that examples of past and present arts will be preserved. The New Castle Historical Society has established Amstel House as a permanent museum, preserving, in addition to objects of art, the building itself, an interesting example of the work of the early builders.

In the village of Odessa, the Wilson House, an outstanding example of Delaware Georgian architecture, is a museum and library. Under the impetus of the revival of interest in the early arts and in papers, letters, and books of historic value, the Old Town Hall in Wilmington was restored as an important building in local history and as a library and museum for the State Historical Society. In this building is housed the largest single collection in the State of art and craftwork of the past. More recent are Historic New Castle, Inc., devoted to preserving New Castle's architectural heritage, and the State Museum at Dover which maintains exhibits of Delaware life, past and present. Winterthur Museum, with its 100 treasure-filled rooms covers the American domestic scene indoors and out, 1640–1840.

Through co-operation with Delaware owners, hundreds of examples of American handicraft, owned in Delaware households and not available for public inspection, have been photographed and reproduced in drawings and in full color by the Federal Art Project for the Index of American Design under the supervision of the Delaware artist, David Reyam. Delaware's contribution to this nation-wide permanent index, now published for the use of students, artists, and the public, includes local original designs of all periods, in objects ranging from quilts to iron gates, from silver christening bowls to ships' figureheads, from a doll's cradle to post chaises.

At the present time a few Delaware cabinetmakers maintain the ancient tradition of excellence and beauty of workmanship. Various handicrafts are still practiced by individuals and small companies throughout the State: ironwork, bookbinding, woodcarving, pottery, weaving, rug making, fish-net making, needlework, tapestries (at Frederica), and basketry. The better known artists are associated with the village of Arden.

Among notable art bequests within the State are four stained-glass windows designed by James H. Hogan of London, and executed by James Powell and Sons in their White Friars Glass Works, England. These windows, erected under the will of the late United States Senator Willard

Saulsbury in 1928, may be seen in Trinity Church, Wilmington, in Christ Church, Dover, and in St. John's Church, Milton, and St. Paul's, Georgetown, both in Sussex County.

During most of the eighteenth century and the early nineteenth, Delaware had no native painters of note. The portraits of statesmen and their families, and of other Delawareans, were either the work of itinerant artists—frequently unsigned—or were painted by the best painters of the day as guests in the sitter's household, or in sittings at Philadelphia and elsewhere. Paintings by Charles Willson Peale, Rembrandt Peale, Benjamin West, Gilbert Stuart, Thomas Sully, and other famous men have come down to present-day descendants of their subjects.

The first native-born painter of note was the Quaker, Henry Lea Tatnall (1829–1885), who was born in Brandywine Village in the house built by his grandfather, Joseph Tatnall. His landscapes celebrate the meadows, streams, and harbors of his native county. A contemporary of Tatnall and one of the notable American illustrators of the period, Felix O. C. Darley (1822–1888), lived at Claymont while he worked upon illustrations for special editions of James Fenimore Cooper, Charles Dickens, and many of Shakespeare's plays, and on his own *Sketches Abroad with Pen and Pencil.* Darley's vigorous characterization of American types and introduction of typical American humor mark all his work.

J. D. Chalfant (1856–1931), who studied widely abroad and lived at Ashley from 1880 until his death, displayed a gift for detail in his paintings of Delaware life. Robert Shaw (1859–1912), after studying in Europe the art of etching, went forth from his studio adjoining his home, the old Penny mansion on Penny Hill, to record the finest of early American and Colonial structures in Delaware: bridges, mills, churches, dwellings, and public buildings. He gave up etching after a temporary impairment of his sight, and painted in water colors. Claude Schuyler (1860–1920), of the old New York family (though he sometimes signed paintings "Schreyler"), who studied in Düsseldorf and Paris, lived in New Castle most of his life, and painted, among other Delaware subjects, the Old Tile House, a local architectural treasure *(see NEW CASTLE).* Clawson S. Hammitt (1857–1927), pupil of Eakins, of William Chase, and of Lefebvre in Paris, is known chiefly as a portrait painter—there are 25 portraits signed by him in the State House at Dover, uneven in quality but, at their best, forceful in treatment.

Since 1900, when a school was opened in Wilmington by the famous Delaware illustrator Howard Pyle (1853–1911), there has been a gradual widening and deepening of interest in art throughout the State. Pyle's teaching was free to talented students whom he selected from art schools in all parts of the country. His own work in the field of illustration is well known, particularly his successful interpretations of the children's classics —Robin Hood, the King Arthur cycle, and other favorites—and his portrayals of medieval figures and the pirates and buccaneers of early American history.

A memorial exhibit of Pyle's work led to the formation of the Wilmington Society of the Fine Arts in 1912. The Society owns, in addition to the Pyle collection, the Bancroft collection of Pre-Raphaelite paintings, manuscripts, and books *(see WILMINGTON)*, many valuable modern paintings and collections of prints. The Society's Art Center building on Bancroft Parkway, Wilmington, opened June 5, 1938. Each year the Center presents a notable and varied series of exhibits, sends out traveling exhibits, conducts a loan service, and gives at the Center, lectures, concerts and dramatics.

Appreciation of the fine arts and opportunity for creative work is being further developed in Delaware through the Art Center's co-operation with the adult education and art instruction of the public school system. Art Center classes for adults and children, including scholarship children of talent recommended by teachers in the public schools have increased greatly since 1943 when the teaching program began. In 1953 the enrollment of students was 763 of whom 339 enjoyed scholarships. Plans for an addition to the Center await funds.

The state-wide work of the Wilmington Society of the Fine Arts, the art colony centered about the Rehoboth Art League, and the annual Delaware Art Festival are logical expressions of the vitality of Delaware artists, demonstrated by a few painters in the late nineteenth century and since the 1920's by an increasing number who are represented in prominent exhibitions. The Federal Art Project did notable work in the 1930's.

The modern period may be said to have begun with Edward Willis Redfield, the great landscape painter, who, though most of his work has been done elsewhere, was born in Sussex County. Laussat R. Rogers, the architect and once conservative painter of Delaware buildings and landscapes, has exhibited a series of symbolic paintings rich in emotional qualities, and many canvases independent in spirit and individual in treatment.

More than a few of the pupils of Howard Pyle have become painters and illustrators of note. Among these is Newell Convers Wyeth, who died in 1945, has had a decided influence upon the work of younger artists. In the field of illustration he has taken the old fairy tales and stories of wonder and adventure out of their weak traditional rendering and given them a forceful interpretation. As a painter of murals he is represented by panels in the Missouri State Capitol, the Hubbard Memorial Building in Washington, D. C. (National Geographic Society), and in public buildings in New York City, Boston, and Philadelphia. In Delaware, his best known mural is in the Wilmington Savings Fund Bank. Three of Mr. Wyeth's children are painters of ability—his son Andrew of high merit.

Frank E. Schoonover shows the influence of the Pyle tradition in his competent portrayals of the Canadian woods and life among the Indians. The unerring draftsmanship of Gayle P. Hoskins gives spirit and authenticity to his illustrations, especially those of western life. Clifford Ashley makes interesting use of broken color in his marines, particularly in the painting of whaling ships and whalers. Another artist favorably known for his marine paintings and unusual treatment of atmospheric effects is Charles A. MacLellan, who is also an illustrator and portrait painter.

The work of the late Ellen B. Thompson Pyle (1874–1936), sister-in-law of Howard Pyle, is at its best in interpretations of children and young people. Her children, Walter Pyle, Jr., and Ellen Pyle Lawrence, display the family talent and individual merit in their paintings.

The paintings of Stanley Arthurs, which may be seen at the State House in Dover, at the University of Delaware, at St. Andrews School in Middletown, and in numerous private collections, show the Pyle tradition in their fidelity to historic detail. They reproduce painstakingly events of State and national importance. Andrew Doragh, one of the State's younger painters, is likewise known for his portrayal of historic subjects, although often in the form of panoramas recording the past and envisioning the future.

A modern painter whose work is having considerable influence upon the younger artists is Ethel Pennewill Brown Leach. She has been conspicuously successful in studies of small town life and, more recently, in flower paintings, which bear a kinship to modern French art.

Henryette Stadelman (Mrs. G. Morris Whiteside II) in 1928 founded the Wilmington Academy of Art, which enlisted the active support of many leading artists, some of whom joined the faculty, bringing their pupils with them. In 1943 the Academy dissolved and turned over its assets to the Society of Fine Arts. Mrs. Whiteside's painting, noted for the artist's sensitive use of color, has won a place in the Metropolitan galleries.

In addition the State Board of Education has provided public instruction in art for both town and country. Adult education, begun as part of an Americanization program during World War I, was soon expanded to meet the needs of native adults who, at all ages, were eager to enter courses in the arts and crafts. Marguerite H. Burnett, director of the program in Delaware, has given a sympathetic account of the work, which was published in part in *Enriched Community Living* (1936)—the title itself indicates the director's appreciation of the more intangible social benefits.

Not every school has a full-time art teacher, but with excellent state and local supervisory and consultant service, opportunities for creative work under wise encouragement are afforded to every child and the co-operation of parents is enlisted. Exhibits and community programs promote a healthy growth of interest among the latter.

The trend among serious artists is toward the fine arts—painting, drawing, sculpture. And the number of amateurs who spend leisure time in these occupations with and without help of accomplished artists, is a stimulating part of the Delaware art spirit.

The "Studio Group" of Delaware painters, organized 1935, sponsors the Clothes Line Fair on the steps of the Public Building, Wilmington, during the annual Delaware Festival of the Arts in May. Delaware artists sell to the public at this fair several thousand dollars' worth of paintings annually.

HENRY FRANCIS DU PONT WINTERTHUR MUSEUM (Entrance from the Kennett Pike, 5 *m*. N.W. of Wilmington. *See Tour 6*, pp. 423-27)

During many years of collecting and research, Mr. du Pont has brought together thousands of priceless objects of art and furnishings representing the American domestic scene from 1640 to 1840 in the Eastern colonies and states from New Hampshire to North Carolina. These he has arranged in 100 rooms that reproduce as nearly as it could be achieved the authentic lived-in setting of their day. Façades and other architectural elements have been transported and reset, including a lane of small shops and an inn courtyard.

Trained guides attend visitors through the museum. Admission is by reservation secured by writing well in advance. Only 20 per day can be accommodated. The museum is open daily except Sunday, Monday, and national holidays, from 10 to 4:30. The fee is $2.00.

The Theater

A PLEASURE house for the entertainment of the people" was built by Delaware's first Swedish Governor, Johan Printz, at Tinicum Island, at the present site of Essington, Pennsylvania. In the last days of the Swedish rule (1654–1655) Governor Rising transported it to Christina (Wilmington) as an alehouse and inn and here it undoubtedly became a center for singing and folk-dancing. Beyond this and the national fête day and religious festivals of the Swedes at Christina, no public dramatic or musical events are recorded until nearly a hundred years later.

In the 1740's fairs began to be held on market days in Wilmington, and developed into local counterparts of English fairs, with music, dancing, performances of tricksters and acrobats, and (seemingly) special educational features of a more dignified nature. Fairs were held also at New Castle, and were made legal by the Legislature of 1782. But upon complaint of the Quakers that the fairs had become a menace to peace and good conduct because of the many out-of-State fakers and vagrants, and that local merchants carried adequate supplies of things sold at fairs, the legislative blessing was withdrawn in 1785.

The earliest record of a professional theatrical troupe's appearance in Delaware is that of an operatic group in 1798 headed by John Bernard (1756–1828), English comedian and one of the earliest American managers. Bernard relates that the usual program of songs and recitations was given at "Dover, Lewiston and some other places, varying in size but agreeing so much in spirit that the pleasure of the trip soon began to overbalance its profit, and, like more eminent commanders, I was compelled, with chagrin, to give the signal for retreat."

Early in the nineteenth century, individuals, organizations, and especially literary and educational societies wrote and produced short dramatic episodes designed to point a moral. But the public in general enthusiastically patronized all the traveling troupes and individual entertainers until persons of tender conscience but strong political influence again besought the Legislature to preserve the respectability of the people. The result was the law of 1829, stating that "any circus rider . . . rope dancer, tumbler, mountebank or other persons" who gave exhibitions of "riding or managing a horse" or of "rope dancing, tumbling, tricks or puppet shows for the purpose of gain . . . shall forfeit and pay the sum of fifty dollars to any person who will sue for the same before any Justice of the Peace." Construction of tent, stage, or other place for such entertainment was also forbidden under penalty of from fifty to one hundred dollars' fine.

Despite ominous official frowns, "a full and efficient company" gave *The Merchant of Venice* in a building at Front and Orange Streets, Wilmington, in January 1834. The success of this company led to the organization of the Wilmington Theater Company, which erected the first theater building in the State in 1834 at the southwest corner of Sixth and Shipley Streets. It was 78 by 43 feet, had a gallery, and seated 600 persons. Boxes were 75 cents, the pit 37½ cents, the gallery 25 cents. The curtain rose at seven o'clock. *The Soldier's Daughter,* a comedy presented by Mr. and Mrs. Barns, made a successful opening on December 22. The managers of the company, taking advantage of the closing of the Philadelphia season for the summer, secured the best available players for a summer season.

Some of the leading actors of the day came to live in Wilmington during the prosperity of the Wilmington Theater. The mother of Joseph Jefferson was among these and during this time young Joseph went to a boy's school on Orange Street between Fifth and Sixth. In 1836 Mr. and Mrs. Ternan presented *The Bath Road,* followed by *Fazio or the Italian Wife,* and ending with a farce, *Personation or Fairly Taken In.* The opposition of religious zealots gave the theater much free advertising, which helped it for a time, but either the opposition gained strength, or the theater's failure to live up to its reputation for interesting wickedness discouraged the audience, for the State's first theater closed in 1839.

Meanwhile, Robert Montgomery Bird, the Delaware-born playwright (1806–54), was winning recognition. His play *The Gladiator,* starring Edwin Forrest, scored a success in New York in 1831. Spartacus, the leading character, exactly suited Forrest, and when *The Gladiator* was presented in Philadelphia, "the audience rose and cheered in their seats." Walt Whitman, then a drama critic in Brooklyn, also seemed favorably impressed. "This play," he commented, "is as full of 'Abolitionism' as an egg is of meat. It is founded on that passage of Roman history where the slaves— Gallic, Spanish, Thracian, and African—rose against their masters, and formed themselves into a military organization and for a time successfully resisted the forces sent to quell them." Though Robert Montgomery Bird's *The Gladiator* was performed 1,000 times during its run, it was never

played in Delaware. Bird's *The Broker of Bogota,* though not so popular
as *The Gladiator,* was Forrest's favorite.

Fraternal organizations in Wilmington did much to counteract official
and religious prejudices after the first quarter of the nineteenth century.
Temperance Hall on the south side of Fourth Street, built in 1842, was
the scene of many theatrical entertainments, its name no doubt allaying suspicion as to the respectability of the performances. Odd Fellows' Hall,
dedicated May 28, 1849, at that time the largest building in the State,
opened its auditorium to both amateur and professional players, and the
Wilmington Institute Hall, the old Public Library building, erected in 1860
on the site of the John Dickinson house at Eighth and Market Streets,
provided an auditorium for occasional plays and for many balls and entertainments.

When the Masons built the Masonic Temple on the east side of Market
Street south of Ninth in 1871, the major part of the large structure was
given over to the Grand Opera House. This theater, containing one of the
largest and best-equipped stages in the country, and with a seating capacity
of 1,400, secured the best theatrical and musical productions of the period.
It opened on Christmas Day, 1871, under the management of Proster &
Soulier of New York with the Caroline Richings Bernard Company in
Daisy Farm at the matinee and *Rob Roy* in the evening. Edwin Booth, the
Jeffersons, Helen Modjeska, Adelaide Neilson, Chauncey Olcott, De Wolfe
Hopper, Richard Mansfield, Maude Adams, James K. Hackett, Mrs. Fiske,
John Drew, William Faversham, George M. Cohan, Ethel Barrymore, Corse
Payton, and many other noted actors appeared here; also Patti, Homer,
Emma Eames, Tetrazzini, Schumann-Heink, and many operatic groups.

Interest in the theater was also developing in Newark, where a Shakespeare Club was organized before 1856. Following the first successful season of the Wilmington Opera House, students at Delaware College, Newark, presented Sheridan's *The Rivals* as a benefit for the college paper, and
followed this with other productions.

The Academy of Music opened in Wilmington at Delaware Avenue and
Orange Streets in January 1884. The builders were unable to finish the
interior for the opening night and there was no heat, but the opera scheduled was given for a whole week with performers, orchestra, and a near
capacity audience in overcoats. Between the scenes audience and performers
were thawed out with hot drinks, some on the spot, but most by quick
dashes to the nearest taverns. Upon this evidence of support the managers,
Lewis P. Buck and James H. Shoemaker, sought the best talent available.

For many years under various changes of name—Lyric, Bijou, and finally the Avenue Theater—this house continued as a rival of the Grand Opera House. Its last popular season was in 1909–10 when the Conness & Edwards Stock Company played for thirty weeks. The building was burned twice, and after the second fire in 1914 was not rebuilt. The Garrick Theater, devoted to vaudeville, built near the Grand Opera House by William L. Dockstader in 1903, was the only other Wilmington theater until the Playhouse, a part of the Du Pont Building in the block west of Rodney Square, was completed in 1913.

In Dover an Opera House, replacing an earlier meeting place, was built in 1902 as a community enterprise. Performances were given by local talent and there were occasional shows by traveling companies or minstrel troupes, but the enterprise was not a financial success. Opera houses were also built at New Castle, Newark, and Smyrna, and are now moving-picture houses.

In 1906, the Arden Players began the presentation of Shakespeare's plays in an outdoor theater, and between 1907 and 1919 the Green Room Club, of Wilmington, amateurs with professional quality, gave many plays at the New Century Club building and in the theaters. The Wilmington Drama League, in which membership is by invitation, is today the best known of the amateur dramatic organizations. Succeeding the earlier Aircastle Players, this community group presents an annual series of plays in its own theater at Market Street and Lea Boulevard.

The summer theater idea did not reach Delaware until 1931. In that year Edwin Ross, whose family was prominently associated with the original single-tax colony at Arden, founded the Robin Hood Theater with a resident professional cast in a converted barn at Ardentown. Ross, a young actor who both before and since the opening of the Robin Hood played in New York productions, presented a good cast each year in programs of well-known and popular plays. The popularity of the Robin Hood Theater has grown with each season. In 1937 Ross and his co-manager of several seasons, Robert C. Schnitzer, organized an apprenticeship group for advanced students under the direction of Esther Porter, former member of the Vassar College Experimental Theater staff, assisted by the resident theater summer company. Since World War II Robin Hood Theater, in charge of excellent stock-company producers, annually presents an outstanding summer program with well-known casts including New York stage favorites.

In 1936, a new and stimulating contribution to the drama was the opening in Delaware of the Federal Theater of the Works Progress Administration. Before its close in July 1937, it demonstrated the need for and the response to civic theater at popular prices. Many adults in the audiences, as well as young people and children, had never before seen performances on the legitimate stage. In Wilmington the project had its own Little Theater on the third floor of the Knights of Columbus Building.

The University of Delaware E52 Players, the campus honorary dramatic organization, offers ten or more theater programs during the school year. The excellence of performance by this group coincides with the high standards of the University Department of Dramatic Arts. In addition the University Dramatic Center at Mitchell Hall, Newark, conducts an extension service used by approximately 100 school and community theaters in Delaware and neighboring states.

The Wilmington Playhouse, under successful management offers a series of well-selected plays by New York companies each season.

The Strand Players, a new professional group in Wilmington, opened a summer season of well-produced plays in 1953 with such success that a year-round program is forecast.

The Arden Players have a year-round program of good plays at the Guild Hall, Arden (not connected with the Robin Hood Theater).

The "Brandywiners," a Wilmington group which started the study and production of Gilbert and Sullivan operas in 1932 just for the fun and interest of its members, has given annually since then at the Longwood open air theater of Mr. Pierre S. du Pont, performances of Gilbert and Sullivan or operettas of Victor Herbert and others to delighted capacity audiences. All profit goes to welfare organizations. Each performance runs for five days in late July and early August.

Dover and other towns have active dramatic groups. Kent County Theater Guild, organized early in 1953, gave its first production in September. All of the executive group had previous dramatic experience.

Music

THE "fiddle and dance," popular in rural gatherings and in Delaware taverns in the early eighteenth century, was a cause of concern later in the century to the Quaker town fathers of the Borough of Wilmington. The players, native and strolling, and the social gatherings that appreciated them survived the Quaker disapproval and suffered a decline only after the spread of Methodism in the next century. In many a village community before 1800 and in Wilmington, the Methodist "Singing Meeting," its hymns devoutly learned under the tuning-fork of the leader, and the secular singing school at the schoolhouse or the leader's home, were rivals of the lively tunes of the nearby taverns, while in the mansion-houses, young ladies—some of whom had been sent to Philadelphia for lessons—played gentle pieces for the entertainment of parents or beaux.

The singing teacher, Azariah Fobes, who styled himself "Teacher of Psalmody," published *The Delaware Harmony* in 1809, presenting methods and material that he had used for many years. Elkanah K. Dare invited "original and manuscript tunes" for his publication, *The Periodical Harmony* (1810), "a Collection of Celebrated and Original Pieces of Sacred Music and Church Tunes." Probably influenced by the work of Professor Dare and his contemporaries, the Harmonic Society was organized in 1814 in the old Academy on Market Street, Wilmington. The object of the Society was the study of sacred music, and its members, numbering 400 in 1816, helped to make concerts of instrumental music popular.

Musical instruments are mentioned in the seventeenth century wills; and throughout the eighteenth century, the fiddle, "my silver horn"—which was perhaps a hunting horn—the lute, harpsichord, spinet, and clarinet were bequeathed to descendants; toward the end of the century the clavichord, pianoforte, and parlor organ are mentioned. In 1805 a Wilmington music teacher advertised lessons "on the Pianofort, German Flute, Violin Guittar, &c."

In 1817, a concert arranged by Abel Sanders, singing teacher at the old Brandywine Academy, featured selections on the pianoforte, violin, "clarionette," flute, tambourine, triangle, basset horn, and "straw fiddle." The "straw fiddle" was described as a curious instrument of wood and straw that has a soft agreeable sound, "and is quite unknown in this country." A comparison of the Wilmington Directory of 1814 with the contemporary records of musical activities indicates that the craftsmen of the period were the active musicians. Abel Sanders is listed in the Directory as a carpenter and Elkanah K. Dare simply as a teacher.

Beginning at the time of the Revolution, band music was a leisure-time absorption for men in all groups and classes. Starting with only the fife and drum, these bands gradually developed to full instrumentation in every village community, as well as in Wilmington. In 1872 the City Cornet Band of Wilmington played at Richmond, Virginia, and was said to have been the first Northern organization of its kind to visit the South after the Civil War. In 1883, when the First Regiment Band was organized, nearly every Delaware town had a good band. Later, bands died out except in Wilmington. The prevalence of town bands throughout the State today has grown out of the instrumental instruction in the public schools, which began in 1928.

Music and choral societies kept pace with the bands in number and activity up to the end of the nineteenth century. In 1849 the Wilmington Sacred Music Society, composed of members of several church choirs, gave its first concert. The Delaware *Saengerbund* was organized in 1853 for the purpose of studying the musical productions of the best German composers. The Handel and Haydn Society of Wilmington gave concerts between 1863 and 1867.

An advance toward better music in Delaware was made by the organization of the Millard Club, a singing society which gave a concert on Delaware Day at the Centennial Exhibition, Philadelphia, in 1875. The club, a men's organization, presented several other concerts, among them one in 1872 to aid yellow fever sufferers of Louisiana. Later, women were admitted to membership, and the organization, under the name of the Philharmonic Society, presented Gilbert and Sullivan's *Trial by Jury* and *Pinafore* in 1879. A repeat performance of *Trial by Jury* was attended by an audience of 1,500, the largest crowd ever present at a musical performance in Delaware up to that time.

The Tuesday Club became a permanent organization in 1886 and a year later presented Haydn's *The Creation* in the Wilmington Opera House, the first complete rendition of an oratorio to be given in the State. Other outstanding musical events that year were the cantata, *Joseph's Bondage,* and the operetta, *Chimes of Normandy,* both presented by the Choral Club, another Wilmington amateur musical group.

Before 1900, a plan was tried out by which every teacher in the public school system of Wilmington taught music for a period of 15 minutes a day. However untrained the teacher was, each child had a chance to sing, an advance over the independent singing school of an earlier era. Today teacher training in Delaware includes instruction of every teacher in music. High school glee clubs are now developed to a high degree of excellence. The public school work in music and recently the adult education classes are giving form and direction to Negro singers and music groups. The Howard High School glee club in Wilmington has developed Christmas carol singing to so high a degree that this choral group plays a deservedly popular part in the civic functions during the holidays, and gives programs in costume at the Public Library, the Public Building, and the schools.

During the World War I period the Orpheus Club was organized in Wilmington (1917), and "community sings" were held. Later they were common throughout the State. Delaware's State song, "Our Delaware," was approved by the Legislature in 1925. The verses are by George B. Hynson, the music by Will M. S. Brown. There is also an official Wilmington song, "Hail Wilmington," with words by Mrs. Christine Haddock and music by T. Leslie Carpenter.

Kathryne A. Ross of Wilmington, the State's only opera singer, made her debut as Santuzza in *Cavalleria Rusticana* in Naples on October 3, 1926. Miss Ross, a dramatic soprano, made her first American appearance in 1927 as Aïda with the Philadelphia Opera Company. She sang later that year in Wilmington with the same company in *Cavalleria Rusticana*.

The establishment, beginning in 1926, of adult education centers in which emphasis is placed on choral music, has been a contribution to the development of better music in Delaware. A music division has been added to the State Department of Public Instruction, which directs music courses in the public schools and an annual County Music Festival. There are also music departments at the University of Delaware, Newark, and at Delaware State College (Negro), near Dover, where music teachers are trained.

In 1906, a serious effort was made to organize a symphony orchestra in Wilmington, and the first concert was given the following year. By 1909 there were 80 musicians in the orchestra but due to difficulty in arranging rehearsal periods, the organization disbanded that year. It reassembled once in 1910 for a benefit performance to raise funds for a silver service for the battleship *Delaware*. A symphony club, started in 1914, and two other groups, since merged, form the present Wilmington Symphony Orchestra, which is conducted by Harry E. Stausebach. The free concerts of this large local group, given at the Playhouse on several Sundays in the fall and winter, have devoted audiences among professionals as well as laymen.

Other organizations active in music are the Orpheus Club, the Capella Club, the Brandywiners, and three schools giving technical training to music students—all in Wilmington. The Wilmington Music Commission, organized in 1921 by the late Leroy Harvey, mayor of the city at the time, while not a governmental commission, comes nearest to being an official civic body devoted to the encouragement of music. The commission founded the Wilmington Music School, now operated independently as a non-profit school of music. Highly qualified instructors form the staff for instrumental music and voice. The scholarship fund of the school provides opportunity for many talented pupils. Regular student and faculty recitals are given. The school is backed by a large and active board of directors among citizens prominent for their cultural interests.

The Capella Club, founded by Frederick Wyatt in the 1920's "to study and sing good music" is the State's most distinguished choral organization. Two oratorios are given each year and a spring concert. These are free unless given to benefit a cause, when voluntary contributions are accepted.

Mr. Wyatt also founded the Wilmington Opera Singers, a more recent organization. Three full-scale operas were given in the 1940's after the war. Stars of New York and Philadelphia grand opera companies appeared with the local singers. The group has since been reorganized as the Wilmington Opera Society which is devoted to intimate opera. Opera scenes are given at Breck's Mill on the Brandywine.

The Wilmington Community Concert Association has a large subscription membership that enables it to provide a series of concerts each year by celebrated national and international artists.

An Artist Series of concerts is given annually at Mitchell Hall, University of Delaware in Newark. Talent for the series is obtained through the Metropolitan Opera Association and other leading musical organizations.

The Delaware Philharmonic Orchestra, a professional 24-piece group, gives a series of winter concerts at the Playhouse, in Wilmington.

Architecture

COMPARATIVELY few buildings remain in Delaware from the days of the Swedes, the Dutch, and the English settlers (a period extending from 1638 to 1682), but enough early architecture is standing to reveal the character of the life lived upon the soil as far back as the first permanent settlements. The first building erected within the State was the house at Lewes that sheltered the Dutchmen sent from Hoorn in Holland in 1631 to found a whaling colony. In very early records it is referred to as a brick house. Whether it was or not has been a subject of interesting historical controversy. Bricks similar to the "Friesian clinkers" imported from Holland by Governor Stuyvesant and other builders in Manhattan have been found, but they may have been taken there by later Dutch settlers; or the foresighted navigator, de Vries, may have sent in the *Walvis* (along with the settlers, the whaling implements, and the cattle) enough bricks for the chimney and ovens of a timber house which the settlers might well build in a "land full of trees." However, the Dutch were accustomed to use brick and tile at home rather than wood, a fact demonstrated in Lewes today by a recently erected reproduction of the medieval town hall of Hoorn. Enough bricks may have been imported to build a part brick and part timber house, or bricks may have been brought from Manhattan as they were to New Castle a score of years later.

The Swedes, who built their forts of logs, planks, and hewn timbers, also built in Delaware the first log houses on American soil, a type found so suitable for the pioneer in a forested country that it was adopted throughout the Colonies. It fitted harmoniously into the landscape, and as the settlers moved west the tradition spread that it was "a mode learned from the Indians." The logs were laid horizontally, notched and fitted at the corners of the house and the joints chinked with clay and straw, or plaster made from shell-heaps. Ovens and chimneys were built of stone or brick or, if these were lacking, of clay set very thick. The window openings had sliding wooden panels within and doubtless were covered with woven cloth both summer and winter until glass was available or could be afforded. The roofs were gambrel or pitched to permit a gallery or half story above the first floor.

Of the log houses described by contemporaries some remained intact well into the nineteenth century, and though no typical log house of the earliest period survives, it is believed that some, covered over with plaster or weather-boarding, have been incorporated in larger dwellings. Examples of these are the Judge Willey house near Dover, the Grubb store in Brandywine village, Wilmington, and two houses on the Irénée du Pont estate at Thompson's Bridge. Small log houses like the one at Price's Corner near Wilmington are probably representative of the earliest Dutch or English versions of the Swedish log dwelling, and many of the oldest houses in New Castle County and some in Kent have marked Swedish characteristics in the roofs and chimneys, and in general proportions and plan. For a good house, Swedes used planks, bricks, stone along with logs. In 1644 Governor Printz asked for 20,000 bricks from Sweden, presumably for chimneys and ovens, and bought of English merchants as much as 3,000 feet of oak plank and 2,300 clapboards at one time.

The blockhouse at Naamans must have been built much later than 1654, in Governor Rising's time, the date tradition gives it. It is of local stone, well preserved and has a well built corner chimney and brick oven. It has a narrow stairway leading from the first floor to a garrison room above. Old Swedes Church at Wilmington, also of rubble stone, was built at the end of the century by English workmen and has few Swedish characteristics. The Dutch, who began building houses on the present site of New Castle in 1651 and who had erected more than a hundred buildings there by 1658, used timber framing covered with planks or clapboards until bricks could be secured from Manhattan or manufactured locally in sufficient quantities. The oldest part of the Jacquet house on Long Hook farm, south of Wilmington, built about 1660, is of plank construction. The outside walls, now stuccoed, were covered with wide beaded boards set vertically. This part of the house has a ceiling height of only six feet five inches, wide floor boards, and a large brick fireplace and oven. Attached to the rear of several New Castle colonial dwellings are the original small houses on these sites, now kitchens. At least two of these are seventeenth century and one may be Dutch.

The early English dwellings, dating from 1664, were constructed of stone, brick, and often of frame covered with clapboards or shingles. They were rectangular in plan with a simple doorway in the middle of one long side, a story and a half or two stories in height, with pitched or gambrel

WOODWARD HOUSES, WILMINGTON

roof, dormer windows, and end chimneys. In the northern part of the State, especially, the house was often placed with a blank gable end to the north, though there might be a small window near the peak of the gable. South of Wilmington, summer kitchens are frequently separated from the house by a lattice-enclosed passageway or covered veranda. The superior craftsmanship of the early ship carpenters is evident in the detail of the earliest buildings of the coast regions from Wilmington to Lewes. The doorways, windows, stairways, fireplaces, and chair rails all exemplify their taste and skill.

In parts of Sussex County where the most frequent covering of outer walls has been the cypress shingle, the space between the studs was often filled with brick nogging, a protection against heat in summer and penetrating winds in winter. Exterior brickwork in Kent and New Castle Counties throughout the Colonial period was usually laid in Flemish bond, often with a strongly marked pattern of black glazed headers. Belt courses, watertables, cornices with moldings of vigorous design, decorative windowheads and door openings, all contributed to the harmonious design of the houses built in the first half of the eighteenth century. The fine color and texture of the stone houses in the northern part of the State are especially notable.

Many of the early small houses were converted into service wings of larger dwellings. In the northern half of the State, the new portion of the house, higher, broader, and of a more formal design than the older part, was usually so placed as to form an L- or T-shaped plan with the original dwelling. Examples are the Kensey Johns, Sr., house at New Castle, the Bringhurst house, Wilmington, and the Spruance house, Smyrna. There are numerous exceptions, however, in which successive additions have been made on the long axis of the original house, like the John England house near Ogletown and the Booth house, New Castle. In the southern half of the State this extension of the long axis is general, although the L- and T-shaped plans are frequent, as in the Collins house at Laurel, the Ingram house, Lewes, and the Lowber house at Magnolia. Houses of the late Colonial and the Classical Revival periods also followed the same general plan. Until the end of the eighteenth century there was little difference between urban and rural dwellings except in those town areas where building lots tended to become narrower as land costs increased. Toward the end of the eighteenth century, however, a final phase of the Georgian Colonial style was developed, chiefly in urban types. These later works represent the perfection of the builders' art in classical design and richness of detail.

From the Revolution until the 1830's all of the fine houses of the Fed-

John Moll

WOODLAWN, NEAR SMYRNA

eral period indicate familiarity with the academic orders in architecture, while exhibiting a wealth of individuality in the treatment of their exterior and interior details. The Corbit house at Odessa, "Woodburne" at Dover, and the Read house at New Castle are three masterly and varied examples.

The Revival period, which followed and lasted until the Civil War, is exemplified chiefly in the extensive use of Greek details: window frames with rosettes, temple porticoes, and classic cornices, moldings, and doorways. The rotunda type of dwelling, a fashion set by Thomas Jefferson, was popular for a time. Few of these houses remain, and almost the last of the monumental type of Greek Revival dwellings, the Draper house, was taken down a few years ago. Old College at Newark, and the Old Bank of Delaware—now the Delaware Academy of Medicine—are the only important buildings in this style.

In the last years of the eighteenth century and during the early part of the nineteenth, French influence affected the architecture of northern Delaware. This is evident in the details of the old Town Hall in Wilmington, for which Peter Bauduy was the architect, and in the admirable design of Regency house, known also as Swanwick Manor, on Stoeckles' Lane north of New Castle, built in 1820 for Jean P. Garesché.

The grand manner of building in Delaware as well as the simple and tasteful mode in small dwellings and other buildings gave way after 1850 to the confused and falsely prettified exteriors of which the Deemer house at New Castle is a most interesting example, and ended abruptly with the cessation of building during the Civil War. The grotesque Victorian type was developed chiefly in the towns. The era of the quick and the cheap, devoid of taste or any feeling for environment, marked the final deterioration of building that is everywhere apparent.

Almost without exception, the dwellings and other buildings of the eighteenth and a great deal of the nineteenth century represent the ideas of the owner or his friends and family in consultation with the master craftsmen. Both owner and craftsmen frequently used the books published in England as a guide in working out their problems. Long after the profession of architecture was well established, building in Delaware continued to be a partnership between the owner and the craftsmen and later between the owner and the master builder who employed "mechanics." The pride and skill of the latter in "workmanlike" performance was equal to that of the earlier craftsmen from whom they were directly descended, though the heritage of taste was gradually lost.

Nearness to Philadelphia meant dependence upon the architects of that city when a professional architect was to be employed. Not even Wilmington could support an architect before the middle of the nineteenth century, unless he had other means of income; and the employment of Philadelphia architects long worked to the disadvantage of developing local talent. Benjamin Latrobe seems to have been the first distinguished consultant for local public works. He lived in Wilmington for a time during the earliest surveys for the Delaware and Chesapeake Canal. Peter Bauduy, who built the Wilmington Town Hall, is not believed to have been an architect in the professional sense, but a gentleman of taste interested in the arts, like other good builders of the time.

Throughout the State, mills and wharves and old inns at country crossroads remain as part of the heritage from a time when men's handiwork reflected a feeling for design and beauty in everyday things. In town and country the simple and tasteful small house and substantial manorhouse still give pleasing evidence of the days when each beam and doorlatch was an object of the craftsman's devoted labor. Farmhouses and farm build-

John Moll

BARN AT BUTTONWOODS

ings, meeting houses and churches in all sections of the State—Old Swedes, Old Drawyers, Old St. Anne's near Middletown, Welsh Tract, Camden Meeting, Christ Church in Broad Creek Hundred, and many others—exert a subtle appeal in their dignity and charm.

The three early court towns—New Castle, Lewes, and Dover—one in each county, still show in varying pattern the relation to community life, of the green and the common, characteristic of the medieval village, where once the social and market center existed and where common land was assigned to the villagers for pasturage. In New Castle are to be seen the oldest and most interesting of these public buildings.

Several covered bridges are still in use in the State, and a few of the earliest academies and schoolhouses still serve their original purposes. The little octagonal or "eight square" schoolhouse, northeast of Dover, is especially interesting. Fort Delaware on Pea Patch Island in the river, built between 1850 and 1852 to replace the original fort built in 1814, has both a modern and an ancient aspect in its adaptation of form to function.

Outside of Wilmington, except for the suburban developments nearby, and the scattered small towns and villages accented by spires and occasional smokestacks, the Delaware landscape has little architectural interest. Well placed near the head of the State, the memorial carillon tower on the A. I. du Pont estate rises above hills and woodlands with its graceful belfry to a height of 210 feet; an occasional large dwelling or factory occupies a commanding position; a few tall lighthouses by the river, some airplane beacons, water towers, and the patterned steel lifts of the canal bridges pierce the sky line. Institutional groups are few, but the well-designed buildings of the State University at Newark are noteworthy.

The road system of the State forms the basis of a potential state-wide achievement in landscaping, for the State Highway Department is empowered to secure by purchase for the State five hundred feet of land on both sides of the roads, whenever it considers that roadside beautification or protection justifies it. New school buildings may be considered a state-wide architectural development, for as soon as sufficient roads were built, school buildings were set down everywhere—first the numerous small buildings for Negroes, and then the large consolidated schools and district high schools. The earlier buildings show a free adaptation of the Georgian Colonial style. A few create a factory-like impression of utility; and some buildings of the 1930's in the Georgian Colonial style with classic detail, ably planned from a technical and functional standpoint, are academic in design. Newer educational buildings throughout the State, indicate that the fresh and vigorous handling of school needs and architectural design demanded by Delaware's rapid advance in public school education have been admirably met by Delaware architects. This plane of excellence in elementary and high school structure and facilities spurs local pride.

Changing in character as the landscape changes from rocky hills in the north to flat sandy plains in the south, the architecture of the State, apart from the earliest log and frame construction, is expressed largely in stone in the north, in brick in the rolling country between Wilmington and Milford, and in wood in Sussex. The styles of building, affected by the use of native materials and climate, nearness to waterways, and by the traditions, tastes, and means of the builders, present a wide variation of individual treatment within a limited number of general types. This is true of seventeenth-, eighteenth-, and early nineteenth-century buildings; and all the surviving structures built before the middle of the nineteenth century, including even incidental buildings such as smokehouses and summer kitchens, demonstrate the amenities of the builders' art in ways that are good, pleasing, and often beautiful.

In Wilmington, the finest of the old structures as well as a few noteworthy late nineteenth-century buildings may be found along streets of business fronts and slum blocks. In semi-converted business areas, or in manufacturing districts, the surviving examples of early dwellings and those of the later Colonial period still reveal the dignity, beauty, and re-

IVY ROAD, WILMINGTON

finement created by the early master builders. Scattered through the city are some excellent modern public and business buildings: the Wilmington Public Library and the Nemours building, the uptown Farmers' Bank, First and Central Presbyterian Church, the Walnut Street "Y," and others.

Wilmington retains its traditional comeliness, in some of the older parts of town, in some tree-shaded streets lined with red-brick plain-but-comfortable residences. In a few outlying streets with more recent dwellings along parkways, in some restricted areas, and in industrial housing developments like Union Park Gardens, Woodlawn, and the early Bancroft village, both architecture and environment show the pleasing results of intelligent study and taste. But in the city as a whole, buildings of merit and distinction are the exceptions. A city without plan, with limited and elastic zoning regulations, with a minimum of open spaces and parked areas in its downtown and densely populated districts, Wilmington's economic expansion is marked chiefly by its blighted areas and by the spread of the small two-story brick house, in solid rows or in pairs with alleys or narrow yards between. In the older houses of this type the cornice hangs like a bang or stands up like a cowlick, and in later ones it was developed into a pompadour-like appendage that carries the front wall above the second story in a false half-story effect to permit a real or pretended air chamber above the second-story front bedroom. From the top of the façade the flat roof slopes to the rear over the diminishing height of the walls, much like a misshapen head behind a high forehead.

Approached from any of the converging highways or from the river, Wilmington looks like a garden city, its imagined long vistas closed at the center by a group of tall buildings forming a striking architectural composition. By day the play of light and shadow adds vivid interest to their forms and texture and at night the tall masses seem to stem from the lighted chalice of the city. Thus, from certain vantage points, Wilmington appears to be beautiful, spacious, and well-adapted to the work and leisure of its inhabitants—in a word, what its most hopeful citizens like to believe it will some day become.

Among Delaware architects and buildings singled out as of distinguished merit by leading American architectural and arts bodies and publications are: modern schools and business structures by Victorine and Samuel Homsey; modern schools and colonial restorations by Pope and Kruse; public housing communities, institutional and business structures by G. Morris Whiteside II; homes for modern living and functional, industrial, and institutional design by Massena & Du Pont; parks and community landscaping by Robert Wheelwright. Delaware fellows of the American Institute of Architects are: Walter Carlson, Samuel Homsey, Albert Kruse, W. William Martin and G. Morris Whiteside II. The State Chapter of the American Institute of Architects has stimulated a growing interest in the art of building, through exhibits and other activities, especially in relation to the environment and in the preservation and restoration of some of Delaware's superb examples of early architecture.

The Trustees of Historic New Castle, Inc. have had made an architectural and documentary study of the Old Court House at New Castle preparatory to a campaign for its restoration.

A log house near State Road, south of New Castle, mentioned in a will probated 1720 was still standing on its ancient site in 1952. The present owner of the land gave the house to the State Museum at Dover where it may be seen. Members of the Delaware Archaeological Society made a thorough study of the log structure on its site. Every part and piece was measured, cataloged, and specifications prepared for reassembling the whole in its original form.

For restoration of the John Dickinson House near Dover, see page 395.

A housing commission authorized by the 1931 Legislature to investigate housing conditions in Wilmington engaged the engineer Lawrence V. Smith as secretary and executive. His study, published December, 1932, portrayed in text, illustrations and statistics, the city's slum areas, resulting evils, and remedies needed.

In 1933 the commission secured the creation of the State Board of Housing. The Board, with the same engineer and a member of the previous commission, John K. Garrigues as chairman, continued the study of Wilmington—and completed similar surveys of Dover, Newark, Georgetown and Laurel, published in 1934. As a result of the board's work, housing authorities for counties, cities and towns were authorized and the Wilmington Housing Authority established 1938. Two attractively planned permanent low-rental housing communities were built in 1941–43, designed by G. Morris Whiteside II, architect, and Robert Wheelwright, landscape architect.

Eastlake, adjoining Price's Run Park in N.E. Wilmington, has 200 dwellings in 33 units. Southbridge, for Negroes, in south Wilmington west of New Castle Avenue has 180 dwellings in 32 buildings. Both are related to the surrounding areas on a community basis for convenience to schools, churches, and city parks. Having served the workers brought to Wilmington during the war effort, they have been returned to low-rental status.

Eastlake Extension, on the river side of the Governor Printz Boulevard, is a new low-rental public housing development of 200 dwelling units, not segregated. Southbridge Extension also doubles the original housing community by an additional 180 dwelling units.

In 1951 the jurisdiction of the Wilmington Housing Authority was extended to include the city metropolitan area. Wilmington and New Castle County planning and zoning, now under way (1953), a beginning of slum clearance in Wilmington and legislative authority granted the New Castle County Levy Court to condemn land for recreation areas afford city and county the opportunity for a thorough job of face-lifting, with high increase in living values.

<<<<<<<<<<<<<<<<<<<<<<<<✵>>>>>>>>>>>>>>>>>>>>>>>>

PART II

Cities and Towns

<<<<<<<<<<<<<<<<<<<<<<<<✵>>>>>>>>>>>>>>>>>>>>>>>>

Preface to Towns

Not all of the points of interest, the developing industries and civic affairs of the State's municipal communities could be included within the technical limitations of this revision.

Wilmington is increasingly a center whose residents can have a finger on the pulse of the whole State's business, social, cultural, and political life. Major state-wide organizations in these fields have their headquarters or principal meetings in this city. Their purposes and deliberations are well reported in the Wilmington daily newspapers and the facilities of the excellent Wilmington Public Library offer current state-wide information.

One of the newer state groups centered in Wilmington is the Delaware Academy of General Practice (in medicine), whose courses given by some of this country's outstanding specialists attract physicians from all parts of Delaware and from surrounding states.

Another new group is the Delaware Roadside Council whose state-wide membership and programs are winning acclaim outside the State as well as results within it.

Wilmington's first U. S. Post Office on the S.E. Corner of Sixth and King Streets, built 1855, may be of interest to architectural students for its style of the period and its unusually sturdy construction. It has housed the United States Custom Office since its erection.

At New Castle, recent research has established that a courthouse was erected on the site of the present building before 1689, that its first story, built of stone, was the jail with the courtrooms above and that a prisoner set fire to it and the whole was "burnt to the ground" in 1729–30. One wall of this early building remained and was incorporated in the present courthouse erected 1730–31, on the same site.

Landscaping has been completed on the beautiful site of the Nanticoke Memorial Hospital, east of Seaford on the Nanticoke River, built 1951.

A new town on State land, sold to individuals, has been incorporated by the legislature as Fenwick Island on part of the original stretch of the Atlantic shore near the Maryland boundary that has borne that name.

Arden

Buses: Regular service between Arden and Wilmington.

Accommodations: None.

Theaters: Gild Hall, Players' Gild; Robin Hood Theatre, summer stock productions.

Athletics: Semi-professional baseball and football teams; amateur basketball and tennis clubs.

Annual Events: Arden Day, May; Henry George Day, Sept.; Arden Fair, Sept.; Art Exhibition, June.

ARDEN (alt. 193; pop. three areas, 1500), on Grubb's Road, six miles north of Wilmington, a village lying between the Baltimore & Ohio Railroad and the West Branch of Naaman's Creek, has been given widespread national and international publicity as a Single Tax colony. Its homes, with those of adjoining Ardentown, founded upon the same principles, are scattered over a large acreage. Many are small cottages or cabins, some temporary in appearance. Of the larger homes a majority have grown from original smaller units.

Life in Arden centers about the Village Green, but its background is the woodland, uncut and undespoiled for a generation. Here are great numbers of the native dogwoods, wild azaleas, and other woods' growths. Winding paths and lanes with dwarf oak hedges add to the rural atmosphere.

Supporters of the Single Tax theory made a whirlwind third-party campaign in Delaware in the last years of the nineteenth century, attracted, no doubt, by the small size of the State and the close rivalry of the old political parties. In the campaign of 1896, Single Tax orators landed in Dover jail, which gave rise to a *cause célèbre* in the local annals of free speech. Among the campaigners, who gained not a single office, was (George) Frank Stephens, sculptor, pacifist, and idealist. On June 12, 1900, Stephens purchased from the Derrickson heirs three tracts of farmland comprising 163 acres on Grubb's Landing Road, a part of the original Grubb holding owned by that family for seven generations. The old Grubb mill is on the outskirts of Arden, and the Grubb burial ground is within Arden limits, on Grubb Road opposite The Sweep.

FRANK STEPHENS THEATER, ARDEN

Shortly after the purchase, a deed of trust was executed to Frank
Stephens and William L. Price, the latter an architect and the founder of
the village of Rose Valley, Pa. On the purchase price of $9,000 for the
land a cash payment of $2,500 was made, and a mortgage of $6,500,
applying only to the woodland, was taken by Joseph Fels, millionaire soap
manufacturer of Philadelphia.

The Arden land was laid out in lots of varying size, none less than one-
fourth of an acre, to be leased for 99 years at a rental based upon the
annual site value of the bare land without regard to improvements. Title
to the land was vested in the Arden trustees, three in number. The trustees
pay the State and local taxes and meet a few other expenses out of the
returns from the leaseholds. The balance is paid over to the community to
be used for such common purposes as a majority of the residents desire.
The community gathers in a monthly town meeting, where questions of
moment to the residents are discussed and decided. The "Ardenfolk," the
leaseholders and residents of the town, elect the trustees and elect also a
committee of five members as civic aids; the government operates with

the assistance of a town clerk, an accountant, and seven assessors. Only the town clerk is paid.

Growth was slight in the early years, but by 1909 every lot was taken and many additional applications were on file. The usual difficulties that beset such colonies arose. Ardenites living in cabins, tents, and cottages were regarded by the surrounding countryside as beings from another world. The press made the most of this circumstance, so that a village lad had only to build a small hideaway hut in a tree for the event to be heralded in metropolitan papers as "Arden Residents Roost in Tree-Tops."

One Arden episode involved Upton Sinclair, writer and publicist, when he "gamed on the Sabbath." In 1911, Sinclair, Scott Nearing, and other liberals, were residents of the village, along with fellow writers, artists, and professional men—some of them Single Taxers, some Socialists; and there was at least one Anarchist—a shoemaker. The latter was wont to explain his ideas of sex physiology at public meetings in the village. The Economic Club of Arden clamped down a censorship on the shoemaker, and when he persisted in his talk, had him arrested. That members of the Economic Club were also members of the baseball teams that played Sunday mornings on the Village Green gave the anarchist his chance for revenge. He went to Wilmington and swore out a warrant against the baseball players for violating a 1793 statute which forbade "gaming on the Sabbath." Sinclair was not a member of the club or a baseball player, but the warrant included him for good measure because he had played tennis that Sunday morning.

Eleven young men were arrested and haled before a Wilmington justice of the peace, in front of whose office the street was blocked by a curious crowd. The "Squire" refused to differentiate between gaming and gambling when Sinclair protested. Each offender was fined $4 and costs. All refused to pay and after serving an hour or two of their sentences partaking of ice cream in a nearby restaurant, the 11 were hustled off to the New Castle County Workhouse. They spent the night in cells and when released in the morning were greeted by 22 newspapermen and three camera men, and the story made the front page of every metropolitan daily in the country.

The group, led by Sinclair, was not hesitant in describing what they claimed were intolerable conditions at the Workhouse and the widespread publicity led to needed reforms. The Anarchist shoemaker still clamored to have the group jailed for a longer term, but the threat that detectives would be placed on watch at a popular Wilmington country club, where

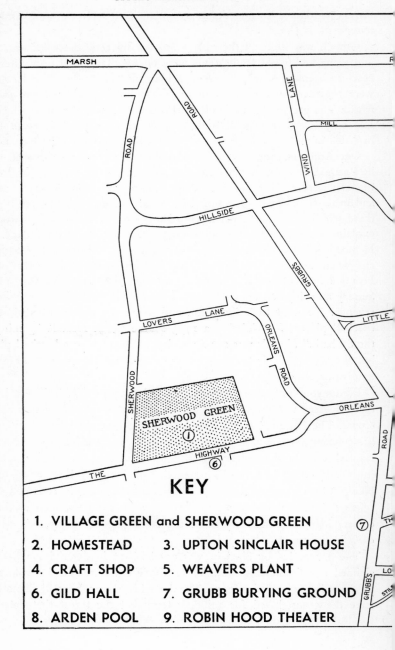

KEY

1. VILLAGE GREEN and SHERWOOD GREEN

2. HOMESTEAD   3. UPTON SINCLAIR HOUSE

4. CRAFT SHOP   5. WEAVERS PLANT

6. GILD HALL   7. GRUBB BURYING GROUND

8. ARDEN POOL   9. ROBIN HOOD THEATER

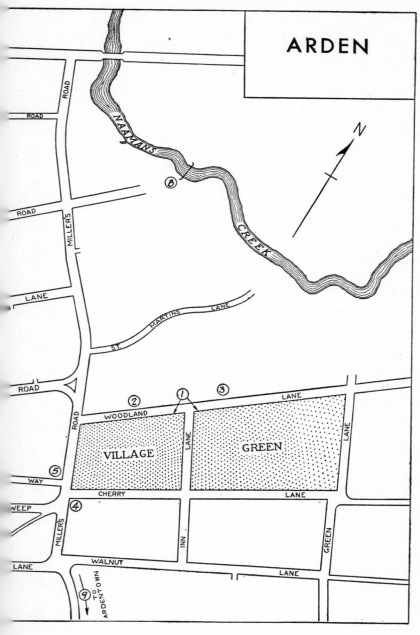

court officials and judges were accustomed to play golf on Sundays, brought a cessation of the contest.

The social and cultural life of the village is led by the Arden Club, its membership open to all residents. The club is divided into guilds among which are the Folk Guild Players, Gardeners, Housewives, Musicians, Athletic, and Craft "Gilds." The Crafts Gild, of which Frank Stephens was the leader, brought such substantial benefits to the village as the Arden Forge, the Weavers, and the handicrafts, such as woodcarving, designing and printing of greeting cards, and pottery making.

The village has had its ups and downs, its war days, its court days, and its local battles, yet living was comfortable enough until the depression. With only its handicraft industries, scarcely developed, to depend upon, when jobs ceased for its residents who had commuted to nearby cities, the depression was severely felt in the colony. The death of Frank Stephens, its founder, in 1935 was a severe blow, for Stephens kept both the handicrafts and the general economy at their best. Arden has returned slowly to normal conditions and to enthusiasm for the activities represented by its guilds.

The development of Arden led to a new movement to expand its area, and in 1922 a tract of 97 acres adjoining Arden was purchased with money advanced by Fiske Warren of Massachusetts. This new section was called Ardentown, and its leaseholds were soon taken up. Ardentown's system of land tenure and government is the same as that of Arden, but the two are not combined, although the Ardentown town meetings are held in the Gild Hall.

Arden, as well as Ardentown, has been in the Delaware Chancery Court for interpretations of the deed of trust. These cases have come from disagreements of the leaseholders with the trustees, and have resulted in clearer understandings as to the powers and duties of each. A third section called Ardencroft has developed since World War II.

The number of leaseholds in Arden totals 183; in Ardentown there are 149. Arden is one of five communities in the United States following, to the extent possible within the existing economic system, the Single Tax method proposed by Henry George. During its 53 years of existence, Arden has drawn within its boundaries persons of a wide range of political and economic opinion. For the most part, however, the Arden folk are believers in the Single Tax principle that all income from land value created by the community should be taken as a tax for community purposes and that no other tax should be levied.

Arden's campfires, its handicrafts, its Single Tax background, its woods' scenery, the Shakespearean plays, and the personality of Frank Stephens, who devoted his later life entirely to the colony he founded, as well as the unconventional simplicity of its life (in early years more a contrast to life outside its borders than now) have drawn thousands of visitors, some of whom have returned to become residents. Among members of the Arden art colony are Leander Leitner, landscape painter, and Marcus Aurelius Renzetti, sculptor, Ross Santee, artist-writer, and many other artists.

POINTS OF INTEREST

1. VILLAGE GREEN and SHERWOOD GREEN, large tracts of greensward, lie E. and W. respectively of Grubb's Road, and are dedicated to communal purposes. As the center of outdoor activities Village Green is the scene of athletic events and the annual Town Fair.

2. THE HOMESTEAD (*private*), Woodland Lane facing Village Green, a two-story, half-timbered and stuccoed dwelling with red slate roof, was built in 1909 by Frank Stephens (1859–1935), founder of Arden. Distinguishing features are the wood carving by Stephens, and the leaded glass of the casements. "Tomorrow Is Another Day" is the motto carved by Stephens on a crossbeam of the house. WOODLAND THEATER, adjoining the Homestead, was placed by Stephens in an outdoor setting; here for many years Shakespearean plays were produced by the Arden Players. Meetings were also held here, but of late years, all such plays and activities have been in Gild Hall. Beside a large rock on the natural stage, where Stephens often appeared in costume, his ashes are buried.

3. The UPTON SINCLAIR HOUSE, Woodland Lane and Theatre Path, was built in 1911 by Frank Stephens for Upton Sinclair and was occupied by Sinclair for several years. Then it was "painted brown on the outside, and stained on the inside." There was a living room in front with an open fireplace and a "chimney that smoked"; now, enlarged and remodeled, it is a prized home. Sinclair played a prominent role in early Arden, having moved there shortly after writing *The Jungle*. Not far from the Sinclair house is Scott Nearing's cabin, built about the same time and also used by Sinclair as a study. Its huge fireplace, built by Nearing, is still in use.

OPEN AIR STAGE, GILD HALL, ARDEN
Credit: Brooks Studio

4. The CRAFT SHOP, Cherry Lane and Miller's Rd., the seat of Arden crafts during the lifetime of Frank Stephens, was later used by an art class and sales department of the Arden Forge. It was in this shop that Stephens and his aides labored for years as craftsmen, turning out the art products for which the village was famous (see page 175).

5. The WEAVERS PLANT, Miller's Rd. and Milky Way, operated hand-looms in the manufacture of sport clothes, curtains, and draperies. The art of Colonial weaving and dyeing in Arden was originated by Miss Maude Rhodes in 1918 (see page 175).

6. GILD HALL *(open 9 a.m.-12 p.m. daily)*, Highway and Clubhouse Path, is headquarters for various Arden activities, notably the Arden and Ardentown Town meetings, vespers, and theatricals. It is a remodeled barn. Outside is the MOONLIGHT THEATER where plays are given by the Players Gild of Arden with natural background for scenery. Gild Hall is controlled by the Arden Club.

7. On Grubb's Rd., opposite The Sweep (a curved street), is the old GRUBB BURYING GROUND, containing graves of early Grubb and Talley pioneers, settlers of this section. Stones show burials as early as 1760.

When the Arden tract was purchased it was stipulated that the burial ground should not be disturbed. The Arden burial ground, called the Arden Memorial Garden, adjoins.

8. The ARDEN POOL *(use restricted to Arden residents),* where Hillside Rd. meets Naaman's Creek, is a large swimming pool formed by a concrete dam, braced by two large boulders in the bed of the stream. Successive enlargements have made the pool an adequate recreational spot for Arden residents and their friends, for whom the place is reserved. Night bathing became so popular that it was prohibited at the Arden Pool.

Along Naaman's Creek within Arden limits may be found impressive outcroppings of Delaware gabbro, an igneous stone used for building and road construction.

9. ROBIN HOOD THEATER, Miller's Rd. near the Mall in Ardentown is a barn transformed into a summer theater where professional dramatic productions are offered in the season. The theater, founded in 1931 by Edwin Ross of Arden, well-known actor in New York productions, attracts many visitors from Delaware and neighboring States.

Producer Windsor Lewis of New York made the 1953 season specially notable.

The Craft Shop and the Weavers Plant, points of interest 4 and 5 on the preceding page, are now apartment houses. During the early 1940's the craft workers went into war industries and did not re-establish their shops. But the Arts and Crafts Guild has an active year-round program of work and gives its annual Art Exhibition in June.

The Ardensingers give a Gilbert and Sullivan opera annually six nights in May.

The Folk Guild, proficient in programs of folkdances and costumes of many countries, is in demand for entertainments in Delaware and neighboring states. The Guild has made Arden the Delaware Valley capital of square dancing.

POINTS OF INTEREST IN ENVIRONS

Site of the Queen of France Tavern (Practical Farmer), *1.8 m.;* Grubb Homestead, *0.3 m. (see Tour 1).*

Dover

Railroad Station: Pennsylvania Station, W. end of Loockerman St., for Delmarva Division of Pennsylvania R.R.
Bus Station: 322 W. Loockerman St., for Greyhound, Trailways, Short Line, Red Star.
Airlines: Scheduled service at Dover Airforce Base, *3 m.* S. of U.S. 113.

Accommodations: Three Hotels (one for Negroes); tourist homes; no seasonal rates, good motels.

Information Service: State Development Department, Legislative Hall; Highway Building.

Motion Picture Houses: Two.
Hunting and Fishing: Areas and facilities within short driving radius.

Annual Event: "Old Dover Day," first Saturday in May, when many houses are opened to the public for an admission, proceeds used for further beautification of the city.

DOVER (20 alt., 6,500 pop.), capital of Delaware and county seat of Kent, borders St. Jones Creek and Silver Lake at the approximate center of the State. It is the market and shipping point for the fruit, vegetables, and other products grown in the low, fertile orchard and farm lands that surround it. Approached through this cultivated land, Dover has the aspect of a manorial park where houses and other buildings have been set down among oaks and elms and flowering trees. The town extends north and south between the creek on the east and the railroad on the west. State Street and Governor's Avenue, the main north and south arteries, and the streets parallel to them are bordered chiefly by residences. They are crossed at right angles by other residence streets and by the main exclusively business thoroughfare, Loockerman Street, near the center of the town. Two short blocks south of Loockerman Street, State Street runs into and through the Green, an open square, planted in grass under tall elms, and surrounded by old houses and public buildings.

Though US 13 follows Governor's Avenue and US 113 is a bypass east of town, State Street remains a popular route. One of the oldest streets, the section near the Green, originally part of the King's Highway, is broad, heavily shaded by tall elms and oaks. Here are many of the larger homes, outlined against shrubbery and trees affording glimpses into celebrated back gardens.

The older industries of Dover lie by the railroad tracks to the west,

COURTHOUSE, DOVER

with the exception of the nationally-known Richardson and Robbins Plant in the center of town. Several newer plants are in the east-central section. Dover industries include canning and the manufacture of silk hosiery, mattresses, baskets, auto bodies, cheese, plumbing supplies, and rubber products.

The biennial convening of the General Assembly, when its fifty-two members converge from all parts of the State, scarcely disturbs the flow of Dover life, except for the dignified bustle that pervades the streets and the mall adjoining the State buildings.

A lively scene is usually presented by Loockerman and other streets of the business district, lined with stores, banks, and markets. Here, Dover residents and crowds of people from the countryside throng the streets, especially on Friday nights. Occasionally one sees a Mennonite from the colony near Dover, in his severe black garb, his stiff-rimmed black hat, and his long beard; or a group of "yellow people," the so-called Moors of Cheswold who are related to the Moors of Indian River in Sussex County (see Tour 15). In the total of 6,322 inhabitants (1950 census), there were only 131 of foreign parentage.

The Negroes, numbering 1,643, or over 26 percent of the population, are with few exceptions natives of Delaware, mostly descendants of Delaware slaves. A few are in the professional class, but most are laborers, porters, and domestics. Those who can afford it reside on N. Queen Street; the remainder live in small frame houses of two and four rooms in the city's outskirts.

When the territory about Dover became a county separate from the Whorekill (Sussex) in 1680, with the name of St. Jones County (now Kent), the site of the town was a part of an estate of 800 acres, called "Brothers' Portion," belonging to John and Richard Walker. The Indian rights had cost the Walkers three match-coats, twelve bottles of drink, and four handfuls of powder. John Walker had been one of the petitioners for a separate court district or county, and was one of the first to receive a grant of land from the newly-appointed court at its session, November 17, 1680.

William Penn, in 1683, gave orders that a county seat, named Dover, be laid out along the King's Road with a broad cross street from the river, on which a courthouse and prison were to be erected, and in 1694 representatives of the county bought from William Southbee, who had bought the land from Walker, 200 acres for the town. Meanwhile, the court which had at first met at the home of one of the justices, Edward Pack, at Town Point near the mouth of St. Jones Creek east of the site of Dover *(see Tour 2A)*, was being held at James Maxwell's tavern on land adjoining the site for the county seat.

The courthouse and prison were built between 1694 and 1697 on the site of the present Kent County Courthouse. Nothing was done about laying out the town, however, until 1717, when the Delaware Assembly meeting at New Castle appointed three commissioners to lay out the town of Dover, the work to be finished on or before March 10, 1718. The commissioners so arranged the street from the creek running at right angles across the King's Highway that the courthouse stood in the spot appointed by Penn in the original plan, in the northwest corner of a courthouse square extending south and east.

For the town plot only about 125 of the 200 acres were used. Sixty-nine of the remaining 75 acres were bought by John Mifflin, who sold them to Nicholas Ridgely in 1748. This land is still owned by his descendants, and is known as "The Ridgely Farm."

The courthouse lot, including the courthouse and jail, was sold in 1722 to John Lindsay. A tavern, the King George, later occupied the site. A new courthouse was built on the site of the present State House probably about the time of the sale.

From its laying out in 1717 to the Revolution, Dover grew slowly. A schoolhouse known as the Academy was built on the present Governor's Avenue, south of Bank Alley, soon after the middle of the eighteenth century. As early as 1708, a wooden church existed near Dover in charge of a missionary of the English Society for the Propagation of the Gospel, and soon afterwards a Presbyterian clergyman was in residence. A Quaker meeting was organized later.

In 1738, Samuel Dickinson, father of John Dickinson, Signer of the Constitution and closely identified with the progress of Dover, became one of the magistrates of the Kent County court, later bought a town site, and lived but a few miles away *(see Tour 2A)*. On another large estate nearby, lived Caesar Rodney, who as a member from Delaware in the Continental Congress of 1776 was to save Delaware's vote for Independence. In June 1776, Rodney, who was Brigadier-General of Kent County militia as well as member of Congress, came home from the Congress at Philadelphia to help deal with a threatened Tory uprising. For the final vote on Independence, Rodney's vote was needed to break the tie between Thomas McKean "for" and George Read "opposed," so a messenger was dispatched to notify Rodney to return to Philadelphia. He was found at his farm, and rode the 86 miles back to Philadelphia without stop, except for change of horses. Upon news of the signing of the Declaration of Inde-

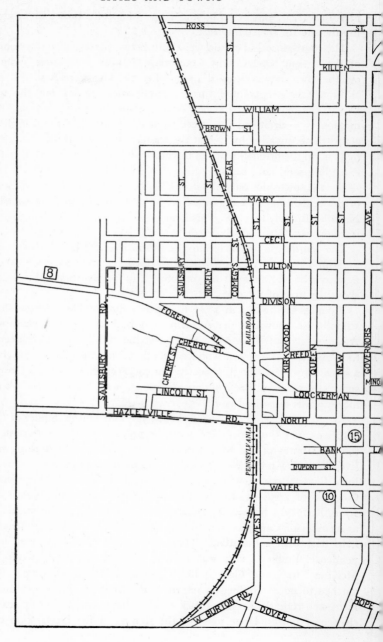

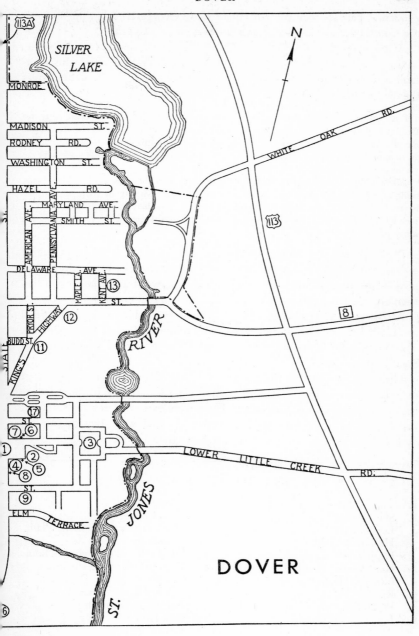

DOVER

pendence, patriots took the portrait of King George III from the walls of the Courthouse and burned it at a celebration on the Green.

At this period Louis Philippe, Comte de Ségur, kinsman of Lafayette, having come with the French squadron to Delaware Bay, made his overland way to the north. In his *Memoirs and Recollections,* he writes under the date of September 11–12, 1778:

> I set out early in the morning for Philadelphia, and I could therefore only see Dover in passing. It was the first American town to which fortune had conducted me. Its appearance struck me; it was surrounded with thick woods because there, as in other parts of the thirteen States, the population was still scattered over an immense territory, a small portion of which was cultivated.
>
> All the houses in Dover offered a simple but elegant appearance. They were built of wood and painted with different colors. This variety in their aspect, the neatness which distinguished them, the bright and polished knockers of the doors, seemed all to announce the order and activity, the intelligence and prosperity of the inhabitants.

Dover became the capital of the State on May 12, 1777, the seat of government being transferred from New Castle. Legislative sessions were held in the Kent County Courthouse, which between 1772 and 1776 had been enlarged and rebuilt at a cost of £800 or more.

At Dover on December 7, 1787, a convention of thirty delegates ratified the United States Constitution adopted in Philadelphia on September 17. This unanimous action brought Delaware the honor of being the first State in the Union.

Little change came in the picture of Dover during the first quarter of the nineteenth century, except that more houses, chiefly of brick, were built at a distance from the Green. Fears were expressed for the safety of the capital when the British fleet cruised in Delaware Bay during the War of 1812, but the conflict came no closer than Lewes.

KEY TO DOVER MAP

1. The Green
2. State House
3. Legislative Hall
3a. Hall of Records
3b. Highway Building
4. Kent County Courthouse
5. No. 49, The Green
6. Ridgely House
7. Parke Building
8. Loockerman House
9. Christ Church
10. Kent County Jail
11. Richardson and Robbins Plant
12. Woodburn
13. Elizabeth W. Murphey School
14. Wesley Collegiate Institute
15–16. Old Presbyterian Church now State museum
17. Post Office Building
18. City Hall

At the approach of the Civil War, Dover was the scene of active controversy between the majority for the Union and the minority whose sympathies were with the South. In 1862, Union troops disarmed some young Secessionists in the town and for a time kept the leaders under guard in the State House.

In 1873, the Courthouse containing the legislative hall and offices was sold to the State, and next year a new County Courthouse was erected on Penn's original site where the Courthouse of the 1690's and later King George Tavern stood.

Beginning in 1889, Dover was the scene of a hard-fought political battle over the attempt of the late John Edward Addicks of Boston and Philadelphia to win a seat in the United States Senate from Delaware. Until his final defeat in 1906, the biennial sessions of the General Assembly degenerated into sensational deadlocks, with vacancies in the Senate. The cry was "Addicks or Nobody" on one side; "Nobody," on the other.

In the twentieth century, the expansion of Dover has been notable. Population has doubled since 1920. Industry developed, and the business of government brought more and more residents to the town and also finer public buildings. One of the most important activities of the State government in Dover is the granting of corporation charters and the collection of fees and franchise taxes. About one-fifth of all the active United States corporations listed in Moody's *Manual* have been chartered in Dover *(see Government)*.

When the Du Pont Boulevard supplemented the Delaware Railroad, the capital came within an hour of Wilmington. To celebrate the completion of this modern highway, an important ceremony took place on the Green in 1924. Coleman du Pont presented the state-long road to the State, handing over the deed to the Governor. A map of Delaware in silver with the highway traced in gold was presented by citizens to Mr. du Pont.

In 1929, Dover adopted a modified form of city-manager government under a charter changing the corporate name from "The Town of Dover" to "The City of Dover." The mayor and council serve without salary. One mayor served fifteen successive terms and the town actually had only three mayors in 21 years. The city-owned electric generating plant is next to the largest on the Delmarva Peninsula, and, together with the efficient municipal government, has been a factor in the establishment of the present low city tax rate. The water supply and distribution system is also publicly owned, and in the summer of 1936, an incinerator and sewage disposal plant, sufficient to meet the needs of a population of 7,000, was completed.

Serving the needs of Dover and intended as an emergency hospital for middle Delaware, the Kent County General Hospital, west side of South State Street, near the city line, is thoroughly modern and well equipped and staffed. It was opened in October 1927, after a spirited campaign in which nearly everyone in Kent County participated, and represents an investment, including equipment, in 1953 of $771,700. Its medical staff includes all the physicians of the vicinity, and its capacity is about 96 beds. A property adjoining is used as a nurses' home. Support for this hospital comes in part from the General Assembly and the Kent County Levy Court, and in part from gifts and payment of fees by patients.

A 35-acre park on both sides of the St. Jones River from the mill dam to the wharf near the Legislative Hall was originally laid out and constructed by the Works Progress Administration. Adjacent is the new section laid out by the city for the new public buildings, of which the Post Office, Legislative Hall, Hall of Records, and Highway Building are a part. The St. Jones River has been widened to form a beautiful lake.

Among other parks in Dover at the present time is Richardson Park in the northwestern section of the city. This recreation ground, while privately maintained by the Richardson family, is open to the general public. Silver Lake at the north end of State Street is popular for fishing, boating, and outboard motor races held in the summer, and ice skating during the rare freezing weather.

POINTS OF INTEREST

1. THE GREEN, junction of State St. and Bank Lane, Dover's tree-shaded public square, is surrounded by office buildings, law and corporation offices, and private residences. Laid out in 1717 in accordance with William Penn's 1683 order, in the Green were held early fairs and markets including slave markets. Here during the Revolution, the First Delaware Regiment was mustered and marched to join Washington's army. Because much of the history of the State has centered about this quiet spot, fact and legend have peopled it with notables for 250 years.

Here took place, in 1745, the laying of the restless ghost of Chief Justice Samuel Chew by a public ceremony. Chew, born in 1693, was appointed Chief Justice of the Three Lower Counties in 1741, and retained that office until his death in 1744. Late one night a rustic on his way home over the Green was astonished to see a shadowy figure under a poplar tree. Upon drawing nearer, he recognized it as the late Chief Justice, standing in his favorite attitude, head bowed in deep meditation. By coincidence, the local miller crossed the Green at the same spot a few nights later, and there stood the dim figure of the Chief Justice under the same poplar tree. But this time the jurist beckoned to the miller.

So generally believed were these tales that Dover residents took to staying home of nights, to the dismay of the tavern-keepers and shopkeepers. Consultation resulted in a scheme to lay the ghost. A grave was dug under the old poplar tree, and on a sunny day a funeral procession of townspeople was formed, which moved across the Green to the grave. With bared heads they stood while a bell tolled solemnly and a clergyman intoned the burial service, consigning the spirit of Samuel Chew to everlasting peace and rest. The ghost of Samuel Chew never again disturbed late pedestrians.

The elms on the Green were planted in 1849 and the Green was stoutly fenced for more than ten years until the young trees were well established.

2. The STATE HOUSE *(open 8:30-4:30 Mon.-Fri.; 8:30-12 Sat.)*, E. side of the Green, is a two-and-one-half-story Late Georgian Colonial brick structure, with a classic doorway surmounted by a pediment and fanlight. At the second story, above the doorway, is a well proportioned Palladian window. An octagonal tower and cupola, with captain's walk, rises from the roof. This is claimed to be the second oldest State House in active use in America. In the 1870's, the building was enlarged and remodeled, and it was further restored and remodeled in 1910 with funds procured from the Federal Government as payment of interest on money given by Delaware toward financing the War of 1812. The east wing was added in 1921. Upon creation of a separate Supreme Court by constitutional amendment, 1951, second floor rooms at the building's south end, facing the Green, were appropriately remodeled for Supreme Court chambers. Architects' designs (Pope and Kruse, Wilmington) for the Georgian interior of the courtroom and its furnishings were skillfully worked out by able craftsmen. A distinguished period room resulted.

Bronze tablets on the rotunda walls of the first and second story honor distinguished Delawareans, including officers of the Revolution, framers of the American Constitution, signers of the Declaration of Independence, and James A. Bayard, signer of the Treaty of Ghent. Names of Delaware Governors are inscribed on tablets inside the main entrance. In the corridors are portraits of the Signers, of Delaware Governors, of Thomas West, Lord De La Warr, for whom the State, river, and bay are named, and of war heroes and statesmen from Colonial days to the present.

Paintings by the contemporary Delaware artist, Stanley M. Arthurs, are hung in the State law library on the first floor and in the rooms of the

State Budget Commission on the second floor: they are *The Troops Leaving Dover Green* (Revolutionary War), *The First Day of Peace* (Civil War), *The Crusaders* (World War I).

3. The LEGISLATIVE HALL *(open 8:30-4:30 Mon.-Fri.; 8:30-12 Sat.)*, E. of the Green, completed in 1933 as the newest state building, is designed in the Georgian Colonial style and constructed of handmade bricks in harmony with the State House. The architect was E. William Martin of Wilmington.

The House and Senate chambers, offices, and committee rooms occupy the first floor. The Governor's suite and offices of the Secretary of State are on the second floor. In the Governor's parlors hang two paintings by Thomas Sully: one of Commodore Thomas Macdonough, hero of the Battle of Lake Champlain (1814), and the other of Commodore Jacob Jones, distinguished in the War of 1812. Both were Delaware-born.

3a. HALL OF RECORDS *(open 8:30-4:30 Mon.-Fri.)*, N. of Legislative Hall, constructed and equipped to provide modern and effective means of preserving public records, is a storehouse of Delaware historical collections of wide range and content in charge of the State Archivist, with convenient provision for use by students and scholars.

3b. HIGHWAY BUILDING *(open 8:30-4:30 Mon.-Fri.; 8:30-12 Sat.)*, S. of Legislative Hall, administrative offices of the State Highway Department includes the engineering and map divisions and motor vehicle licensing.

4. KENT COUNTY COURTHOUSE *(8:30-4:30 Mon.-Fri.; 8:30-12 Sat.)*, SE. corner the Green and State St., a two-story brick structure with cupola, was built in 1874 and enlarged and remodeled in Georgian Colonial style in 1918. It occupies the site of the 1694 Courthouse and of the King George Tavern. This tavern originally displayed a likeness of George III, but the portrait of the King was painted over in 1776 and a portrait of George Washington was substituted. Time and weather faded out the colors so that both likenesses could be clearly seen.

5. NO. 49 THE GREEN *(private)*, a one-and-a-half-story frame office building covered with clapboards split by hand, is reckoned one of the city's earliest buildings, the precise date of erection unknown. It has served as Dover's first post office, as shop, and as law offices of Nathaniel B. Smithers and George V. Massey—leading attorneys of Dover.

6. RIDGELY HOUSE *(private)*, N. side of the Green, a two-and-a-half-story residence with thick walls of old-fashioned bricks, was the home of Thomas Parke, father of Col. John Parke (1754–89) of Revolutionary fame. The younger Parke, Oxford product, was author of a vol-

RIDGELY HOUSE: OLD DOVER DAY

ume of poems, *The Lyric Works of Horace translated into English to which are added a Number of Original Poems. By a Native of America.* Bibliophiles have called this one of the rarest and oddest of American books of poetry. Thomas Parke erected the oldest section of the house in 1728. The substantial old chimneys remain, but the original shingled roof is now covered with slate. Beneath the roof is a rafter bearing the date "1728." The back wing was added in 1764. Five of the rooms have original paneling, but bull's-eye doors and some interior paneling were obtained from other old houses.

The furnishings include a set of tables owned by Commodore Jacob Jones, and a Lowestoft china set given to Mary Vining, Revolutionary beauty, by Gen. Anthony Wayne, to whom she was betrothed. Much of the action of *Where Glory Waits,* Gertrude Crownfield's novel based on the Wayne-Vining episode, centers in and about the Ridgely house and garden. A copy of a miniature of Miss Vining, painted and presented to her by Major John André, is preserved here; the paintings include one of Mrs. Charles G. Ridgely by Charles Wilson Peale.

Charles Greenbury Ridgely, member of the Colonial and State legislative assemblies and a delegate to the first State constitutional convention of 1776, acquired the property in 1764, and it has since remained in the possession of the Ridgely family. A bronze tablet honoring the services of the Ridgely family is affixed to the front wall.

7. The PARKE BUILDING, NE. corner the Green and State St., a two-and-a-half-story brick office building, occupies the site of a tavern built by Thomas Parke. French Battell was the innkeeper here during the Revolution, and once gave a banquet in honor of the birth of the French Dauphin. Battell was a man of varied accomplishments, and became the official powderer to the General Assembly. The Battell family held possession of the property until 1820.

8. The LOOCKERMAN HOUSE (private), 419 S. State St., a large brick residence close to the sidewalk, was built in 1742 by Vincent Loockerman, descendant of Govert Loockerman, who came to this country from Holland. Vincent Loockerman was an active Whig during the Revolution, and other members of the family were prominent in Kent County affairs for over a century. The large square portion of the house is the oldest, the long wing being an addition. The interior contains elaborately hand-carved woodwork, and much of the furniture came from Holland and England. Prized among the china and glassware collection are two goblets, one inscribed, "A toast to the King of England"; the other, "Drink to His Majesty's Fleet." Loockerman Street is named for this family.

9. CHRIST CHURCH (Episcopal), SE. corner of S. State and Water Sts., had its beginnings about 1707, although the church structure was not built until 1734. The main entrance was originally at the center of the south wall; there was a slave gallery, and the floor was of brick laid in the ground. The church was unused during the Revolutionary period, but was restored for services about 1785. The principal entrance was then changed, the gallery removed, and the present flooring laid. The original high pews were removed in 1859–60; the tower added in 1876, and further changes made in 1913, so that much of the early character is lost. Treasured possessions of the church are a Bible presented in 1767 by Benjamin Wynkoop, and a silver chalice and paten by his daughter Esther, which bear the date of 1776.

In the front wall of the adjoining cemetery are two bronze tablets, honoring, respectively, Caesar Rodney and Nicholas Ridgely, Delaware patriots.

10. The KENT COUNTY JAIL (open on application), SW. corner Water and New Sts., a red brick structure built in 1932, is surrounded by

WOODBURN, DOVER

a jail yard in which stands one of Delaware's three whipping posts. Whippings take place at unannounced times, usually on Saturday mornings, and are public by law.

11. The RICHARDSON AND ROBBINS PLANT *(open on application)*, King's Highway near Budd St., a group of red brick factory buildings, produces nationally-known brands of boned chicken, chicken broth, and plum puddings. Founded in 1855 after Alden B. Richardson experimented for eight years with preserving fruits on a cook-stove, the first plant was a barn in the rear of what is now 29 South State Street. The business grew and a plant was erected on the site of the Hotel Richardson across the street. The 1856 pack was 600 cans of fruit. Now chicken is canned all through the year; puddings are produced in the spring and fall. Each can is packed, weighed, and labeled by hand.

The plant makes its own cans at sixty per minute, although some of the older employees still make cans by hand. One canmaker has been with the company for 51 years. White tile walls, painted cement floors, and men and women workers clad in spotless white characterize this large concern, whose storage plant has a capacity for $200,000 to $300,000 in finished food products at one time.

12. WOODBURN *(private)*, King's Highway and Pennsylvania Ave., a large brick mansion built about 1790 by Charles Hillyard, is a notable example of 18th-century Georgian architecture. The hall across the front of the house is 41 feet long and proportionately broad. Old Dutch doors open at either end onto the terraces added by a later owner. The interior contains hand-made paneling and in the drawing and dining rooms are paneled fireplaces with wall cupboards on either side. The present owner is restoring the few original details that had been modified. He bought the house after its fine Sheraton and Chippendale furnishings, chairs, desks, tables, highboys, chests, beds, clocks and other pieces had been sold recently at public sale. These pieces, originally owned by distinguished Delawareans and others brought record prices. Fortunately many of them were acquired by Delaware residents and can be seen on open-house days. Woodburn will be open on Old Dover Days.

This house is mentioned in George Alfred Townsend's novel, *The Entailed Hat, or Patty Cannon's Times*. Patty Cannon's raiders are said to have entered the house by a window on the stairway, interrupting a Negro dance for which the owners had given permission. The raiders were repulsed. The incident, however, is believed to have been invented by Townsend.

13. The ELIZABETH W. MURPHEY SCHOOL *(open on application)*, Division St. and Kent Ave., a group of Colonial type buildings on a 20 acre tract, is a home for dependent children, who attend Dover public schools. Sanford S. Murphey, son of a Dover minister, founded the school home in 1922 as a memorial to his mother, after he had made a fortune in a Western mining venture. His intention was to redress an abuse he had observed in youth respecting children bound out to farmers. While the Delaware law stipulated that such children should receive an elementary education, it was often violated.

Four cottages are used as living quarters, each building accommodating 16 children. Dependent children between the ages of two and ten years from the section of the State south of the Chesapeake and Delaware Canal are admitted.

14. The WESLEY COLLEGIATE INSTITUTE, State and Cecil Sts., a large red brick structure, was known formerly as the Wilmington Conference Academy, founded in 1874. A co-educational preparatory and commercial school, it was forced by economic reasons to close its doors in 1932; reopened 1942 as Wesley Junior College. Under Principal R. H.

Skinner, 1878 to 1884, it became an active missionary center for the cause of high school education. Professor Skinner spent his summers traveling from farm to farm and village to village over the peninsula, persuasively encouraging parents to make sacrifices, if necessary, for the better education of their children. Among the former pupils, distinguished today, is the former Curator of Astronomical Photographs at Harvard University, Miss Annie Jump Cannon. Miss Cannon, a native of Dover, had many degrees, including Doctor of Science from Oxford University, 1925. She had discovered more than 300 stars and many peculiar spectra.

15–16. OLD PRESBYTERIAN CHURCH, Governor's Avenue bet. North Street and Bank Lane with adjoining cemetery stands on "Meeting House Square," one of the two original plots marked out for churches in the town plot (1740–41). The first meeting house, built of logs, stood on the southwest corner of the Church Grounds at Governor's Avenue and Bank Lane. On Aug. 16, 1790, the "corner brick" was laid in the new building by the Reverend John Miller, pastor for 42 years. The old edifice was in constant use from the time of its erection in 1790 until Easter 1923. After standing unoccupied for a little over a quarter of a century the old church and adjacent Sunday School building had deteriorated so much that consideration was given to razing them. When the historic church, scene of ratification of Delaware's 1791 constitution under leadership of John Dickinson, was offered to the State, it was accepted and with funds raised by public subscriptions and by a supplemental appropriation from the Legislature, was restored by the Public Archives Commission and formally opened as the Delaware State Museum on December 15, 1950.

Notable interior features of the church are the circular stairway to the gallery and belfry, and the corner alcove furnished with old pews, a memorial tablet to the Reverend John Miller, communion silver and two of the five remaining original tin candle sconces. Early life in the State is shown through displays of period furniture, Delaware silver, costumes of an 18th century Dover belle, the Volunteer Firemen's exhibit and artifacts of Delaware Indians. In addition there are exhibits of Delaware's natural resources, industry, agriculture, commerce and transportation, old woodworking tools and spinning and weaving methods.

In the adjoining cemetery are the graves of Hon. John M. Clayton, U. S. Secretary of State under President Taylor; Governor Charles Polk and his wife; Colonel John Haslet, who was killed at the Battle of Princeton on January 3, 1777; and other noted Delawareans.

The Museum (on US Route 13 alternate) is *open daily, Tue.–Sat., 11:00-5:00; Sun., 2:00-5:00. Closed Mon.* Free parking at rear, by the New Street entrance. Admission free.

17. POST OFFICE BUILDING *(open 7:30-6 weekdays)*, Plaza E. of State St., a red brick structure with white trim, designed on modified Colonial lines, was completed in 1933. In 1938, five murals depicting Kent County life and industry were placed in the lobby. They are the work of William D. White, Wilmington artist, and were created under the direction of the U. S. Treasury Relief Art Projects.

18. The CITY HALL, N. side of Plaza E. of State St., a Victorian structure of red brick with stone trim, was formerly the Dover Post Office, erected in the 1870's. In exchange for the site of the new post office and

one dollar, the Federal Government deeded this building to the City of Dover in 1933. It formerly stood at the end of Loockerman Street, east of State, but was moved to its present site facing the new post office. City offices are on the first floor, and the Police Department has the basement. The second floor is occupied by the Public Library.

DOVER AIR FORCE BASE, three miles south of East Loockerman St. on US 113, was ready for its first military personnel February, 1952. Rapid development of the base in buildings and other accommodations has provided for eleven squadrons of Military Air Transport Planes among which are C-124's designed for troop or mechanized equipment transport. The C-124 can be converted into a 100-bed hospital. Though chiefly a key Military Air Transport service base, it maintains a fighter-interceptor wing, part of the East Coast Defense System.

Other Air Force units are expected to use parts of the 2,000-acre tract and the development of the base will have cost $42 million by the end of 1954.

As 30 percent of the enlisted men and 70 percent of the officers are married and live off the base, the housing demand of the 5,000 personnel has outrun facilities within convenient commuting distance of the base. Payrolls, expected to reach $2 million military and $185,000 civilian per month have had a stimulating but problem-raising economic impact upon Dover and neighboring small towns.

With the old Dover Airport closed, scheduled airline service, passenger, express, and freight is available at Air Force Base. Bus and taxi service connects with Dover. Private planes may land at field of U.S. Aeroplane Carriers, Inc., just north of Dover on US 13.

POINTS OF INTEREST IN ENVIRONS

Delaware State College (Negro), *2 m.;* Camden, *3.6 m.;* "Moor" colony, Cheswold, *6 m. (see Tour 1).* Barratt's Chapel, *11 m. (see Tour 2).* Kingston-upon-Hull, *5.6 m.;* Site of Byfield, Caesar Rodney's home, *7 m.;* Town Point, *8.7 m. (see Tour 2A).* Largest tree in Delaware (oak), *12 m.;* Bowers Beach, *13 m.;* King Crab plant, *13.4 m. (see Tour 2B).* Octagonal Schoolhouse, *4 m.;* Pleasanton Abbey, *4.6 m.;* Little Creek, *5.3 m.;* Wheel of Fortune, old house, *5.7 m.;* Cherbourg, *6 m.;* Port Mahon, oyster grounds, *7.8 m. (see Tour 10).* Ruins of Little Creek Meeting House, *4 m.;* Amish Mennonite colony, *4.9 m. (see Tour 13).* For description of Cherbourg, now destroyed, see p. 481. For description of John Dickinson House at Kingston-upon-Hull, see pp. 394-98.

Lewes

Railroad (no station): Pennsylvania R.R.; King's Highway; freight and express service; no passenger service.

Bus Station: Hotel Caesar Rodney, 2nd and Market, for the Short Line; Wyatt's Taxi Stand, 117 2nd St., for Trailways and Greyhound.

Wharves: Lewes Anglers Asso., NE. side of Canal Basin, wharves free to visiting yachts. Private docks furnish wharfage; 6 ft. depth at low water from Delaware Bay through the Inlet to the Basin, thence 5 ft. to Rehoboth Bay.

Airport: 4 m. S. for Rehoboth Airport on State 14. Scheduled service in Summer.

Traffic Regulations: All-night parking free; Sundays, all day; meters for business hours.

Accommodations: One hotel and tourist lodges in Lewes; hotel and lodges at Lewes Beach.

Information Service: Town Office, 120 2nd St.

Motion Picture House: One.

Bathing: In Delaware Bay at Lewes Beach.

Fishing: At wharf of Lewes Anglers Association, NE. side of Canal Basin, power cruisers furnished for deep-sea fishing parties, May 1st to Nov. 1st; rates, Mon.–Fri., $30, Sat.–Sun., $40 per day for party of 8 or less, $3 extra for each additional passenger. No license required for salt-water fishing. Fresh-water fishing in nearby millponds, license required.

Hunting: In season. Nearby uplands for quail and rabbits, nearby marshes for ducks. Hunting license required, also Federal Migratory Waterfowl stamp for duck-shooting.

Sailing: Lewes Yacht Club races on Delaware Bay, Sun. at 2, June to Labor Day.

Golf: 7 m. S. for Rehoboth Beach Country Club course, 9 holes, privileges extended visitors.

Annual Events: Egg-rolling at the Great Sand Hill, Easter Mon.; Labor Day swimming contest, amateur swimmers compete for prizes.

LEWES (15 alt., 3,000 pop.), pronounced *Lewis,* at the mouth of Delaware Bay, the saltiest town in Delaware, is known to every ship captain who has ever picked up a pilot for the river, or has ever rounded Cape Henlopen in a gale to find shelter behind Delaware Breakwater. As the home of Delaware pilots for at least 280 years, Lewes ("Lewestown" to older residents) has a tradition of the sea borne by every east wind that haunts its narrow streets and aged cypress-shingled houses. Its present is saturated with the drama of its past. There is a Fountain of Youth on Pilot Town Road, a Ship Carpenter St., a Mulberry St., and a Frog Alley. Lewes has been plundered by privateers and has bargained with Captain Kidd for his loot; it has been bombarded in war, and knows all about shipwreck and sunken treasure.

Because of the Dutch settlement here in 1631, Lewes is to Delaware what Plymouth is to Massachusetts and Jamestown is to Virginia. It has been a seat of Colonial and county government under four flags, and its residents have had much to do in the making of Delaware history.

From a vessel standing in from the Breakwater, Lewes is a low-lying scene of three diverse parts, all belonging inseparably to the whole. In the foreground, flanked on the east by the sand dunes of the Cape, are the gaunt structures of the fish-oil and fish-fertilizer plants, the bay piers, and the strung-out summer resort of Lewes Beach bordering the bay shore *(see Tours 14 and 14A)*. In the background, beyond a narrow strip of salt meadow, the spires and low-massed houses of Lewes proper are visible. Westward from Lewes there stretches the long curve of Pilot Town, a single row of houses facing the bay. From the west end of Lewes Beach the new Roosevelt Inlet cuts across the meadow to Lewes Creek, which, extending east past Pilot Town, becomes the Lewes and Rehoboth Canal.

The waterfront of Lewes itself is a row of old buildings and wharves dominated by the large brick bulk of the Postoffice and Customs House. Moving about the Canal Basin or made fast to the wharves are the dozens of craft that use this landlocked harbor as their base or as a port of call.

Most of the business houses of Lewes are contained within a single long block of 2d Street. Brick buildings of recent origin alternate with frame dwellings of unknown age whose ground floors are typical country stores with old-fashioned fixed awnings shading the sidewalk.

The ship pilots are still the central life and aristocracy of Lewes. Besides a few "mud pilots"—those who do not belong to the Pilots Association of the Bay and River Delaware—there are 63 Delaware River pilots of whom 33 live in Lewes, the rest in Cape May and Philadelphia. They look upon their calling as a gentlemen's profession and regard the dangers of bouncing skiffs and monkey-ladders as all in the day's work. A pilot sometimes fetches up in South America if high seas have prevented the pilot boat from making a pick-up at the Capes.

Formerly the pilots went off direct from Lewes on the pilot boat to board vessels near the Capes, or were taken off vessels by the pilot boats and brought back to Lewes to await their next turns. In 1935 the system was reversed. The pilot boats make a landing here only occasionally for supplies. A pilot now goes by road to Philadelphia or another river port where he boards an outbound ship, brings her down the river and bay, and is picked up by the pilot boat, which cruises about waiting for arriving vessels. The pilot boards one and takes her up; arriving at Philadelphia, he sets forth on the 120-mile trip down to Lewes again, by land.

So far, the love the pilots have for old Lewestown still holds them to the spot where generations of their ancestors are buried, but they sometimes mutter about moving to Philadelphia.

The pilots formerly worked in groups, each with its own fast sailing vessel, often racing 200 miles to sea to be first to hail an incoming ship. Since 1896, however, they have worked together on the pilot boats *Philadelphia* and *Delaware,* and pool all the fees received. To become a pilot, an apprenticeship of four years is required.

Lewes is situated on the oldest site of a white settlement within the Delaware river region, known to Dutch traders and adventurers since Henry Hudson's discovery of the bay in 1609. Capt. Samuel Argall of Virginia came close enough to shore inside the bay in 1610 to bargain for food with friendly Indians. Capt. Cornelis Hendricksen in the *Onrust* between 1614 and 1616 and Capt. Cornelis Jacobsen May in 1620 and in 1623 probably traded here. Giles Hosset and Jacob Jansen bought the land along this shore from the Indians in the spring of 1629 for the Dutch patroons, Samuel Godyn, Samuel Blommaert, Jan de Laet, Killaen Van Rensselaer, and Albert Conraets Burg, the first lords of the soil of Lewes. David Pietersen de Vries of Hoorn joined this group upon their willingness to grant him satisfactory terms of partnership, and prepared the *Walvis* expedition commanded by Peter Heyes, with 28 men and supplies to establish an agricultural colony and a whaling industry on the shore. Van Rensselaer later reports that in 1631 they "took possession of the bay of the South River (the Delaware) . . . engaged in whaling and farming and made suitable fortifications so that . . . their cows calved and their lands were seeded and covered with a fine crop."

The settlement, called Swanendael, was attacked by Indians, either in the fall of 1631 or early spring of 1632. Only one man escaped, Thunis Willemsen, whose affidavit that he was "left over" in Swanendael was later recorded at New Amsterdam. The place continued to be known by the name Swanendael, as well as the Indian name Sikonesse in a variation of spellings. The stream the Indians called Sikonessink, which appears in equally varied Anglicized spellings. The name's meaning remains uncertain in the opinion of place-name scholars. The Dutch traders, who continued to obtain large quantities of furs here after De Vries had restored friendship with the Indians, called the place the Hoerekill or Harlot's creek *(see HISTORY).*

In 1658 Governor Peter Stuyvesant ordered the site fortified to keep off English settlers. Vice-director William Beekman from Fort Altena (Wilmington) and Lieutenant d'Hinoyossa from New Amstel (New

Castle) came down and bought the land again from the Indians and a fort was built in 1659. In 1660 Peter Alrichs arrived from New Amstel, with sole trading rights south of Bombay Hook and free use of land. In 1663, the Dutch shipper, Peter Luckassen of the *St. Jacob,* landed "41 souls" here with their baggage and farm utensils. This was the Dutch Mennonite colony under the leadership of Peter Cornelis Plockhoy, one of the Quaker idealists of the age.

Like the first colony at the site of Lewes, the Mennonite settlement came to a sudden end, but this time without bloodshed. When Sir Robert Carr arrived in this part of the Dutch territory in 1664, to claim the land for the Duke of York, he destroyed or seized all the property of the Mennonites. Cornelis Plockhoy later swore allegiance to the English, and in 1680 a lot was granted him in this town where "he already has a house." Years later, Plockhoy and his wife found friends among the Mennonites of Germantown, Pennsylvania.

By 1673 the small community had developed into a port for ships and of trade in grains, meat, and timber for ships. In that year, magistrates of the first court endeavored to straighten out the land grants, and define the plot of the town. Edmund Cantwell, first High Sheriff under the English, seems to have planned the first streets. The first grant or confirmation under the English was to Hermanus Wiltbank, in 1672, who had long been settled here. Between 1671 and 1681, thousands of acres were surveyed and granted mostly to men with English names.

Called Deale in the early 1680's, the town became Lewes early in Penn's time—though it was more generally known as Lewestown.

William Penn ordered streets to be laid out 200 feet wide between the town plots, and inhabitants who encroached upon them were brought before the court and forced to remove obstructions. The common land— the marsh between the beach and the creek and the pine land toward the cape—was zealously and to large extent successfully guarded from private encroachment. Men from Lewes were selected for Penn's Council and for justices of the provincial court, among them being Henry Brooke, grandson of Sir Henry Brooke of Cheshire, William Till, and Ryves Holt.

During the years immediately preceding the Revolution, Lewes gave ardent support to the remonstrances against taxation without representation, and here on July 28, 1774 a large assemblage listened to Thomas McKean, Signer of the Declaration of Independence, present the case of the Colonies against England. Much sentiment was for settling the dispute by legal means. Both sides had leaders of high integrity and standing but the town finally aided the patriot cause and a company was formed under

Col. David Hall and did valiant service throughout the war. As usual Lewes bore the brunt of the menace to shore and shipping from the British war vessels and the privateers in the bay.

At the end of the century came a ship tragedy at the cape, the sinking of the British sloop-of-war, *De Braak,* capsized in a squall. Twenty-seven seamen, including Capt. James Drew, and a cargo of copper, gold and coin, the legendary worth of which ranges from $1,000,000 to $40,000,-000, were lost. The *De Braak* had taken two Spanish prizes and carried their wealth in her hold. That year and the next British frigates made vain efforts to raise the wreck. Eighty years later a group of Philadelphia and New York capitalists financed the unsuccessful Pancoast Expedition to salvage ship and treasure. Again in 1932, this time by improved modern methods, two companies vainly sought to establish the spot where the *De Braak* lay. To inhabitants of Lewes a jinx had been upon all efforts to find or raise this wreck, and the misfortunes of the salvaging companies confirmed their belief. This held for the recent (1935–36) efforts of the Colstad Expedition of Providence, R. I., though when a diver was hauled upon the deck of the *Liberty* with a piece of teak-wood in his hand and a silver Spanish coin fell from between the iron spikes of his diving shoes, the jinx seemed to have been lifted, but no further find was made.

In the War of 1812, Lewes refused the demands of British ships for provisions, and calmly defied threats of bombardment. Under command of Col. Samuel B. Davis, about 500 men, regulars and militia, were so drilled and marched in and out of the range of vision of the British fleet that they looked like thousands instead of a few. When the bombardment began, the men of the town crept through the marsh grass and over the sand to collect the cannon balls, which fitted the guns of their fort, and so returned the enemies' fire. The British gave up the attack, and though property was damaged, no inhabitant was hurt.

Construction of the Delaware Breakwater, begun in 1818, was the be-

---

KEY TO LEWES MAP

1. Zwaanendael House
2. David Hall House
3. Lewes Presbyterian Church
4. Bride-and-Groom Trees
5. Memorial Park
6. Ellis Building
7. David Rowland House
8. St. Peter's Episcopal Church
9. Holt House
10. Daniel Rodney House
11. Register House
12. Beebe Hospital
13. Collection of Firearms

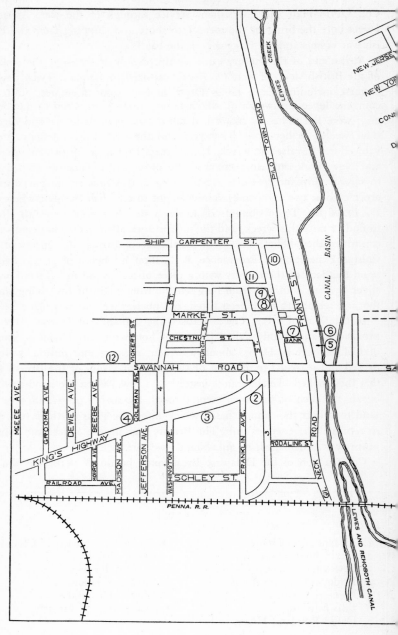

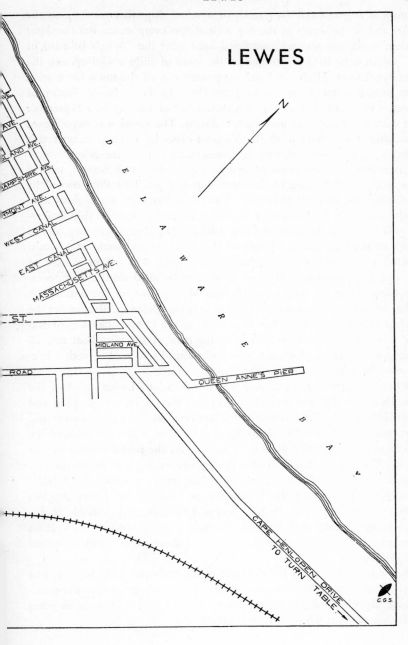

LEWES

N

D E L A W A R E

B A Y

AVE.

LAND AVE.

AMPSHIRE AVE.

RMONT AVE.

WEST CANAL

EAST CANAL

MASSACHUSETTS AVE.

ST.

MIDLAND AVE.

ROAD

QUEEN ANNE'S PIER

CAPE HENLOPEN DRIVE
TO TURN TABLE

C.G.S.

ginning of respite from the tragedy of wrecked ships that piled up on the shores and in the shoals of the bay with almost every storm. But the outer Harbor of Refuge was not completed until after the "March Blizzard of '88" claimed the lives of 70 men on the score of ships tossed up into the inner breakwater. High wind and deep snow cut off the town for a week from outside communication. In 1889 the pilot boat, *Enoch Turley* of Lewes, a two-masted schooner, was driven out of the bay in a September gale with five pilots and five seamen aboard. The vessel was never heard from after it was sighted off the Virginia capes by a tramp steamer that night; 43 vessels were piled up on Lewes beach in the same gale.

Lewes has been the scene of many exciting shipwreck rescues, one of these being the beaching of the steamship *Lenape.* This ship, owned by the Clyde Line, en route from New York to Jacksonville, was sighted afire off the Delaware on November 18, 1925 from the Burbage ship broker-age office. At the same time Capt. Charles H. Morris, cruising at the mouth of the bay, saw the plight of the ship. He and some of his men manned a boat and rowed to the *Lenape,* which had aboard a crew of 107 and 263 passengers. Most of these were huddled on the deck to es-cape flames from the hold when Captain Morris went on board and took charge of navigation. Heading the ship into the Delaware Breakwater, he beached her on a shoal as close as possible to the Lewes Coast Guard Sta-tion, where the guardsmen assisted by the crew of the pilot boat rescued passengers and crew. One man, who had jumped into the sea with a life-preserver, was lost.

When the branch railroad line was completed to Lewes in 1869, the main Delaware Railroad had already caused the decline of shipping and shipbuilding. The pilot business grew, however. So did a good tourist and sports trade and commercial fishing and processing. The 1953 catch of the famous menhaden fishing fleets from Lewes gave the port the major part of 360 million pounds, making Lewes the leading fishing port in the country.

Since 1930 Lewes has been one of the best known ports on the Atlantic Coast for salt-water fishing. Under the auspices of the Lewes Anglers Association, a co-operative body, a fleet of power boats is available at rea-sonable rates to take anglers out to the fishing grounds where there is an abundance of hardhead, trout, bluefish, and drum; also marlin, bluebass and porgies.

Industries of the town (1953) are: brush, tinware, nylon hosiery, and blouse factories; the latter make cotton, rayon, and nylon blouses; meat-packing, fish processing, sand shipping, clam cannery, electronics. A pure-bred cattle ranch is within the town limits.

ZWAANENDAEL MUSEUM, LEWES

POINTS OF INTEREST

1. ZWAANENDAEL HOUSE *(museum open Tues.-Sat., 10-5:30; Sun. 12:30-5:30; Mon. closed; public library 2d floor)*, S. corner Savannah Rd. and King's Highway, is a smaller-scale adaptation of part of the ancient Town Hall at Hoorn, Holland, ancestral home of Capt. David Pietersen de Vries, who sent here in 1631 the party of Dutchmen later massacred by the Indians. The original spelling was Swanendael, "Valley of Swans." On the site of the Lewes Academy, founded about 1795, this ornate brick building was erected in 1931 by the State as a tercentenary memorial. The richly-ornamented stepped-gable ends, the carved doorway, and the red-and-white shutters are designed in the traditional Dutch Renaissance style. A statue of De Vries tops the front gable. The architect was E. William Martin of Wilmington, who studied the building at Hoorn.

The museum contains permanent and loaned exhibits identified chiefly with the Colonial period of Lewes and lower Delaware. Over the vestibule door is a modeled coat of arms of the Town of Hoorn, and on an inside wall a portrait of the present Queen Wilhelmina at 18, both presented to Lewes by the Council of Hoorn in 1909 and brought back by the Rev. C. H. B. Turner, local Episcopal rector and historian.

Among the exhibits are an iron ladder from Henlopen Lighthouse, old Irish coins found on the ocean beach *(see Tour 2C)*, Indian relics, cannon balls of the bombardment in 1813, choice pieces of old chinaware and silverware, early documents including deeds and pilots' licenses; Captain Drew's sea chest from the *De Braak*.

2. The DAVID HALL HOUSE *(private)*, King's Highway opposite Zwaanendael House, shingled and painted gray, was the home of David Hall, Governor of Delaware 1802–5. Consisting of a tall main section and a lower wing, this house is one of the best preserved old homes of Lewes.

3. LEWES PRESBYTERIAN CHURCH, E. side of King's Highway between Franklin and Washington Sts., is a frame structure built in 1832, but later remodeled. The first Presbyterian Church was built on this site in 1707 and replaced by a second building in 1727. A silver communion service given the church by Col. Samuel B. Davis, leader of the troops here during the 1813 bombardment, is usually on display at Zwaanendael House. At this church in early days copper tokens were presented by communicants to indicate they were in good religious standing, and fit to receive the Sacrament.

4. The BRIDE-AND-GROOM TREES, W. side of King's Highway N. of Madison St., a pair of gigantic bald cypresses, once flanked the carriage entrance to the small cypress-shingled COLEMAN HOUSE on the next lot. Tradition says they were planted about 1812 by Miss Margaret Coleman in honor of her planned marriage to a young clergyman. She married another man, but the trees kept growing. There are several other pairs of bride-and-groom trees elsewhere in lower Delaware.

5. MEMORIAL PARK or the Battery, on the Canal Basin, is the site of one of the two defense batteries of Lewes during the War of 1812. (The other was at Pilot Town.) The two British-made naval guns at the water's edge, remounted here about 1915, were used in returning the fire from the British frigate *Belvidere,* April 6, 1813. Four large guns on the upper ramps were contributed by the Government. Between them is a small six-pounder believed taken from a pirate vessel abandoned in the creek; it was fired during the Civil War to celebrate Union victories, but when Lincoln was re-elected in 1864, Confederate sympathizers hid it on a farm where it lay for 50 years. A 3-in. naval gun on the lower terrace, used during the World War in the North Sea, was placed here by the American Legion in 1930. A granite monument set up by the U. S. Daughters of 1812 commemorates the bombardment.

6. The ELLIS BUILDING *(open by permission),* NE. side of Front St. next to the park, has a lookout turret on top, from which, before the days of radio, the arrival and departure of ships at the mouth of the bay were reported to Philadelphia by D. W. Burbage & Co., the ship-brokerage firm that operated here for 44 years until 1928. The large telescope is still mounted. An important part of the business was the relaying of sailing directions to ships that stopped at the Breakwater for instructions.

7. The DAVID ROWLAND HOUSE *(open by permission),* W. corner Front and Bank Sts., was erected prior to 1797 and is sheathed with cypress shingles. It has a sign indicating the patched place in the brick foundation where a shot struck during the Lewes bombardment. The house contains business offices.

8. ST. PETER'S EPISCOPAL CHURCH, W. corner 2d and Market Sts., is a brick structure of Gothic design, dedicated in 1858. A Church of England congregation, established here earlier, had William Black, a lay missionary, in 1706. In 1721, the Rev. William Beckett, a missionary of the Society for the Propagation of the Gospel, arrived and set about erecting a church building. A second frame building was erected in 1808 and used until 1853, when it was removed and turned into a barn *(see Tour 2C).*

The churchyard contains the graves of generations of Lewestowners; pilots, Governors, and others. The oldest stone is that of Margaret Huling, born in 1631. Elizabeth Cullen is recorded as having been born Feb. 30, 1760—several years after the adoption of the Gregorian calendar limiting the month to 28 days. At the foot of the grave of Capt. Henry F. Mc-Cracken, pilot, there is still visible the shank of the anchor of his last vessel. Here also is the grave of Capt. James Drew, of the treasure-ship *De Braak* that sank off Lewes in 1798. In a corner of the present church-yard stood the first Sussex County courthouses.

9. The HOLT HOUSE *(private)*, S. corner 2d and Mulberry (formerly Knitting) Sts., a plain, dignified shingled house painted yellow, the windows grouped unevenly, is said to have been built prior to 1685 and is one of the oldest buildings in Lewes. As one of the earliest inns of the region, it was operated for a time by Philip Russell, recorded as a "cup-bearer" to William Penn. The stairway and mantel are thought original.

This was the home of Ryves Holt (1696–1763), who settled at "Port Lewes," as he called it, in 1721 after quitting the West Indies and Portuguese trade out of Philadelphia. Here he became Naval Officer of the Port, many times Sheriff of Sussex County, and studied law. From 1745 until his death he was Chief Justice of Delaware. In Dec. 1750 he entertained John Watson, the Penns' surveyor and went with him to Fenwick's Island whence the Delaware-Maryland boundary was surveyed westward *(see HISTORY)*.

10. The DANIEL RODNEY HOUSE *(private)*, 231 2d St., a cypress-shingled house painted white with green trim, erected about 1800, was the home of Daniel Rodney, Judge 1793–1806, Governor of Delaware 1814–17. For many years a newspaper, the *Breakwater Light,* now defunct, was printed in the rear of the house. Daniel was a relative of Caesar Rodney, of Kent County, Revolutionary hero.

11. The REGISTER HOUSE *(private)*, N. corner 3rd and Knitting St., a long, low shingled dwelling, was used by the first Methodist congregation in Lewes. It was erected about 1790.

12. The BEEBE HOSPITAL, NW. side of Savannah Road bet. Mill St. and Beebe Ave., is an Emergency Relief Station of the United States Public Health Service. As such, its chief duty is to give emergency treatment to ill or injured persons that have to be sent ashore from ships entering or leaving the bay. When the Lewes Coast Guard station sights a ship that has raised a yellow flag, it notifies the hospital, and a doctor speeds out in a Coast Guard launch to treat the ill man aboard ship or rush him back to an ambulance waiting at the pier. If someone else wishes

to come ashore, the doctor makes a quarantine inspection of the entire ship's company.

Now a general hospital of the best modern facilities, with 104 beds and 16 bassinettes, the Beebe began with two rooms for patients and an operating room, comprised in an addition to their office building in 1916 by Drs. James and Richard C. Beebe. As soon as the young physicians, natives of Lewes, launched their small hospital, demand for its services required continued extension. After incorporation, 1921, by the two doctors and Benjamin F. Shaw, the modern hospital of 35-bed capacity was erected. Wings were added: one by Mr. and Mrs. Shaw in 1927; the Mary Thompson annex in 1939; and recently (1953) an extension to the laboratory.

TOUR OF PILOT TOWN—*1.2 m.*

(The entire settlement is on Pilot Town Road, an extension of Front St. from its intersection with Ship Carpenter St.)

For more than two centuries Pilot Town has been the name of a row of houses that border the southwest bank of Lewes Creek. In early times the creek entered the bay in this vicinity, and it was a business necessity for the pilots to have their headquarters where they could dash to their vessels, make sail, and be off without delay in a race to an incoming ship. Later the bay entrance filled up solidly and the creek made a new outlet into the Broadkill more than 3 miles northwest.

Though many of the old houses in Pilot Town have gone and new ones have been built by pilots and others, there are still a number of early dwellings facing across the meadow to Lewes Beach and the bay.

The ORTON HOUSE *(private)*, 0.1 *m.* (L) is said to have been erected about 1700.

At 0.2 *m.* (L) is the SITE OF THE LEWES STATION of the short-lived Queen Anne's R.R. *(see Tour 2)*, from Love Point, Md., built in 1895 in the hope of making Lewes a seaport for Baltimore and the central Eastern Shore of Maryland. The track crossed the creek here and extended to the Queen Anne's Pier at Lewes Beach, whence ferries plied for a while to Cape May, N. J. Station, track and piers have long been gone.

The WILLIAM RUSSELL HOUSE *(private)*, 0.5 *m.* (L), shingled and sedate, somewhat altered, was built about 1790 by William Russell, who hired William Virden to do the work at a salary of $100 a year. Virden finished the job within a year, and his fine workmanship appears in the walnut stairway and the rosewood door. The doorstep at the kitchen is a millstone from the bark mill of the tannery operated by one of the Russells long ago. Under the house are wine cellars where wine made by

MAULL HOUSE, LEWES

a shipwrecked Frenchman was stored. The Russells still own the house.

The FOUNTAIN OF YOUTH, 0.7 *m.* (R), is an ancient spring believed for more than 250 years to possess the virtue of restoring or preserving youth, especially if the water is drunk from that rarity, a right-handed conch shell. Most conches spiral so that they must be held in the left hand to drink from. After being neglected for 50 years, the spring was cleaned out in 1937 and a pavilion built over it. A proper conch shell hangs by a chain for use by youth-seekers.

Opposite the spring is the PETER MAULL HOUSE *(private)*, a little shingled house painted white, with a gambrel roof, built about 1750.

At the house occurred a brief but cherished episode in the famous romance of Jerome Bonaparte, brother of Napoleon, and the lovely Elizabeth (Betsy) Patterson of Baltimore. On their way back to France in 1803 their ship ran into a storm and was wrecked off Lewes. The bride and groom were taken in by the Maull family, and Mme. Bonaparte's soaked wardrobe was hung on the line to dry. A legend is that when they all sat down to a dinner of roast goose, Betsy's beauty was lighted by her own silver candlesticks—which she had sent a messenger to get from the stranded ship.

FISHER'S PARADISE *(private),* 1 *m.* (L) was the name of this large and delicately-styled house erected about 1725 by Dr. Henry Fisher, an Irishman of learning and influence. It is in a state of disrepair. Legend says that early in July 1776 his son Major Henry Fisher, a patriot, was host here to Caesar Rodney, and from here Rodney started his noted ride to Philadelphia to vote "aye" to the Declaration of Independence. Though most historians now agree that he started north from near Dover, the Lewes story is told and retold—how Rodney was infatuated with Sarah Rowland, the Tory daughter of the postmaster; how she seized letters from Thomas McKean frantically summoning Rodney to Philadelphia, and how finally a Negro maid in the Rowland house told him of the trick, giving him barely time enough to gallop the 120 miles to cast his vote in the Continental Congress.

The DE VRIES MONUMENT, 1.2 *m.* (R) is a granite block erected by the State in 1909 on what was believed to be the site of the fort built by the Dutch after landing at Swanendael in 1631. An inscription quotes the historian George Bancroft: "That Delaware exists as a separate Commonwealth is due to this colony."

ANCIENT BURYING GROUND, across the road from the monument, so called in a 1687 court record, believed by the Sussex Archaeological Assoc. to be approximate site of palisaded enclosure around first Dutch settlement on the Delaware, 1631. A competent research program is under way.

Beyond the monument is the temporary site of a MARINE LABORATORY opened 1951 by the University of Delaware Department of Biological Sciences. A permanent laboratory is being constructed at Roosevelt Inlet 3 miles up the beach.

At GREAT SAND HILL *(see page 497),* 3.2 *m.* is FORT MILES, a regular installation for coast defense during World War II; since the war an anti-aircraft training center for regular troops and reserve components.

POINTS OF INTEREST IN ENVIRONS

Red Mill Pond, fishing, *4.7 m.;* Mosquito Control Sod Monument, *13.4 m.;* Indian River Inlet, *14.2 m. (see Tour 2C).* Lewes Beach, *0.6 m.,* Belltown, all-Negro village, *3 m.;* Cool Spring Presbyterian Church, *6.8 m. (see Tour 14).* Lewes Coast Guard Station, *1.1 m.;* Consolidated Fisheries plant, *1.7 m.;* Fish Products Co. plant, *1.9 m.;* site of Cape Henlopen Light, Point o' Capes now within restricted area of Fort Miles *(see Tour 14A).* Burton's Pond, fishing, *8.8 m.;* St. George's Chapel *10.8 m.;* "Down Sockum," Moor or Indian community, *12-17 m.;* Millsboro pond, fishing, *18.2 m.;* Great Pocomoke Swamp, *30 m. (see Tour 15).*

Milford

Railroad Station: Lake Ave., for Pennsylvania R.R. No passenger service.
Bus Stations: S.W. Front St., for Eastern Shore Stages, Md.-Del. Stages, and The Short Line.
Wharves: Mispillion River below Walnut St.; 6 ft. depth at low water from bar at mouth of river at Delaware Bay. Mispillion Port, E. *6 m.,* wharfage and 35 party boats; meals, rooms available.
Traffic Regulations: All-night parking permitted.

Accommodations: Two hotels, tourist lodges.
Theater: Two motion-picture houses; one drive-in movie.
Bathing: Haven Lake, W. edge of Milford, no public facilities.
Fishing: Fresh-water angling at nearby millponds, license required; salt-water angling at nearby beaches, no license required.
Hunting: Fox-hunting in season, hounds followed by automobile and on foot, visitors welcome; nearby uplands for quail and rabbits, nearby marshes for ducks; hunting license required.

MILFORD (20 alt., 5,200 pop.), on both sides of the Mispillion River and 15 miles from Delaware Bay by water, is divided by the river into North and South Milford. The town, fourth largest in the State, is an industrial and trading center for lower Delaware.

As in other busy, prosperous towns of the Peninsula, the tradition of enterprise in Milford has resulted in the removal or alteration of nearly all of the oldest houses. The dwellings on the pleasant tree-lined streets are architecturally varied, comfortable and complacent, designed for large families.

A new trend for Lower Delaware is seen in the building of homes in the nearby open country that previously would have been built in Milford itself. Hitherto, despite the network of good roads and the spread of electricity, men who work in Milford have continued to build houses in town where they can talk across the fence to the neighbors, or their wives can run across the street to borrow a cup of sugar. As yet, however, only a few are making the departure. Most residents are still too close to the farm to forget mud, dust, frozen pumps, and hog-killing dinners. Meanwhile it is still the aim of most farm young people to get away. These families move into Milford as the smaller contingent moves out.

North Milford, the older part, stands on a tract formerly called Saw Mill Range, taken up by Henry Bowman in 1680. During the next cen-

GOVERNOR CAUSEY HOUSE, MILFORD

tury farms and plantations covered most of the countryside near the river, but no effort to establish a town was made until 1787, when Joseph Oliver, a landowner and merchant, laid out streets on his plantations at Oliver's landing. That year the Reverend Sydenham Thorne built a dam for a gristmill and sawmill at a ford on the stream—hence the name Milford. On the Sussex County side, South Milford was laid out in 1819 on the land of Henry Hudson.

Milford was early noted as a shipping and shipbuilding town. By the 1850's, before the railroad began to undermine water shipping, a dozen schooners and sloops of the port took away annually more than 300,000 bushels of grain in addition to tanbark, staves, lumber, cordwood, and other products. From Philadelphia and other ports they brought manufactured goods for a region extending well into Maryland on the west. In contrast to Frederica and other villages whose growth was also based largely on water transportation, Milford did not stagnate with the decline of shipping, but grew steadily larger and busier. Booming industries of the nineteenth century were the manufacture of fruit-drying machinery and an iron foundry, both established by an English ironmaster and inventor named George S. Grier. The last sailing vessel was launched here

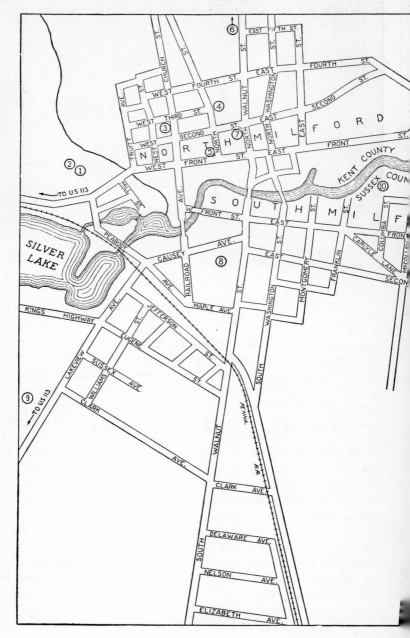

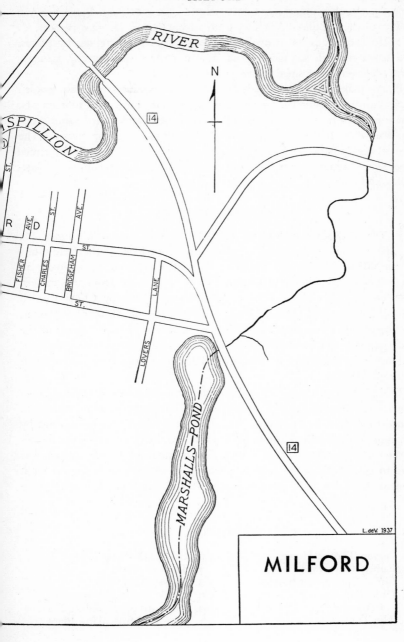

MILFORD

in 1917, the three-mast 195 foot schooner *Albert F. Paul.* Between 1920 and 1930 the population increased 38 percent, 1940–50, 22.9 percent.

Milford operates its own electric plant, also supplying nearby places, and has a modern sewage disposal system. It has had the city manager form of government since 1931.

Plants make dental materials, wood-veneer products, dresses, woolen yarn, building materials, bricks, fertilizer, flour, feed, and monuments. There are two boatyards, one building the expensive Vinyard cabin cruisers, the other building "party-boats" for saltwater fishing parties. The largest weekly paper in Lower Delaware, the *Milford Chronicle,* is printed here. Large canneries pack lima and string beans, peas, broccoli, other vegetables, and fruits.

POINTS OF INTEREST

1. The PARSON THORNE HOUSE *(private),* 501 W. Front St., N. Milford, was built about 1785 on a rise overlooking the headwaters of the Mispillion by the Reverend Sydenham Thorne (1747–93), an English-educated Church-of-England priest who came from the Eastern Shore of Virginia about 1773 to take charge of nearby Christ Church Mispillion Hundred. Besides being a co-founder of Milford, a planter, mill owner, and builder, Parson Thorne, as he was called, was one of the most popular and influential men in Kent County, despite his "political and religious principles of unconcealed loyalty to the King and Church of England."

Thorne built his house of brick in the style of Tidewater Virginia—a central part flanked by two smaller wings on the same axis, which are joined to it by walled passages. An arcade aspect is given each passage by a hanging triple-arch decoration of wood. As in other Delaware houses of the time, the window caps are wooden in imitation of stone, which was hard to get. Much of the interior paneling is original, with dog-ear trim. Sometime in the 19th century the walls and roofs of the wings were

---

KEY TO MILFORD MAP

1. Parson Thorne House
2. Family Graveyard
3. Christ Episcopal Church
4. Old Methodist Episcopal Cemetery
5. The Towers
6. Odd Fellows Cemetery
7. Torbert House
8. Causey Mansion
9. Caulk Dental Laboratories
10. Vineyard Shipbuilding Plant
11. John H. Mulholland Plant

raised and a sharp front gable put on each wing as well as on the main structure. Tenant farmers occupy the mansion.

2. The stone-walled FAMILY GRAVEYARD of the Thorne plantation, to the rear of the Thorne House, encloses a great white oak tree. A marble slab, askew on its crumbling foundation and overgrown with weeds and brambles, carries an inscription in memory of Parson Thorne.

Also in the graveyard is a monument erected by John M. Clayton, noted Delaware statesman, to his parents, James and Sarah Middleton Clayton, who are buried here. James Clayton, of Dagsborough, bought a 300-acre plantation from Peter Caverly, Thorne's nephew, and launched into such ambitious tanning, milling, farming, and other mercantile operations that he died a business failure in 1820.

3. CHRIST EPISCOPAL CHURCH *(open by permission)*, SW. corner 3d and Church Sts., much altered, retains part of the Flemish-bond walls erected in 1791 of brick paid for by the Rev. Sydenham Thorne, who also supplied the white-oak timbers from his woodland, having them sawed to shape in his own sawmill. The original groundsills are still in place. The plot was given by Joseph Oliver in laying out the town.

The congregation was so weakened by Thorne's death in 1793 that work on the church building was stopped, and it was not until 1835 that a simple two-story structure was completed, with box pews and Negro galleries. In 1866 this interior was torn out, the square tower added, and other alterations made that gave the present aspect to the church.

In the churchyard are the graves of William Burton, M. D. (1789–1866), Governor of Delaware 1859–63; William Tharp (1803–65), Governor 1847–51, and Joseph Oliver, the founder of Milford, who died in 1807 "aged about 80 years." The inscription on Oliver's tombstone, as if to offset the doubt as to the year of his birth, says that he died at "twenty minutes to seven in the morning."

4. OLD METHODIST EPISCOPAL CEMETERY, North and Third Sts., contains the graves of Peter F. Causey (1801–71), Governor of Delaware 1855–9, and of Maj. Gen. Alfred T. A. Torbert (1833–80). Oliver gave the site of this cemetery. A chapel, long since removed, was built here about 1788.

5. THE TOWERS *(private)*, NW. corner W. Front and North Sts., a red-and-green house of turrets and jigsaw trim, has stood since 1893 on the site of the birthplace of John Lofland, "The Milford Bard" (1798–1849), poet, essayist, and ghost-writer of speeches, love letters, and anything else that might be required by a large clientele. Though his verse generally followed the stilted and sentimental vogue of the day, his un-

happy romance with a Milford girl is reflected in some poems of merit. Lofland, famous in Delaware, led the life of the so-called Bohemian groups of Baltimore and Philadelphia. In a Baltimore saloon, the story goes, he once defeated his friend Edgar Allan Poe in a wager to see who could write the most verse in a given time. He is buried in the yard of St. Andrew's Church, Wilmington.

6. ODD FELLOWS CEMETERY, W. side of N. Walnut St. near the town limits, contains the graves of George Beswick Hynson and Col. Benjamin Potter. Hynson, lawyer, publisher, and poet, is best known for his homely, humorous verse about his own region entitled *Down Yan and Thereabout.* He also wrote the lyrics for *Our Delaware* (music by Will M. S. Brown), adopted as the official song of the State in 1925. Hynson's tombstone bears as an inscription, the closing words of one of his poems.

Colonel Potter, who bought the James Clayton plantation in 1820, bequeathed hundreds of acres and many town lots to be held in trust for the "poor white citizens of Kent County" and this bequest became known as the Potter Charity. In his will Potter stipulated:

I wish it to be clearly understood that no part of my bequest shall be applied to the use or benefit of any person or persons residing within the walls of the Poor House, but to be distributed amongst such only of the poor who, by timely assistance, may be kept from being carried to the Poor House and becoming subjects thereof.

The trustees named in the will were also the heirs-at-law of Colonel Potter. They refused the trusteeship and in 1847 unsuccessfully tried to have the trust declared invalid. Litigation went on for more than 50 years, impoverishing the estate until the total proceeds paid to the poor white citizens were only about $10 a year. Under Chancellor Charles M. Curtis the Potter Charity was put on its feet for the first time. In the fiscal year of 1937 the net income was about $1,200. The 12 farms of the estate include about 600 acres of tillable land.

Potter was buried just outside the wall of the Thorne family graveyard, but in 1926 the remains were re-interred in the Odd Fellows Cemetery.

7. The TORBERT HOUSE *(private),* SW. corner N. Walnut and Second Sts., a square brick house painted yellow, was built about 1825 by Benjamin B. Wadhams, of Connecticut, as a tavern. Originally a two-story house, a third floor was added by Daniel Currey from plans drawn by Alonzo Reynolds, of Port Deposit, Md. The house became the home of Maj. Gen. Alfred T. A. Torbert after his marriage to a daughter of Currey.

General Torbert was born in Georgetown, Del., and graduated from the U. S. Military Academy in 1855. Before the Civil War he served in various Indian campaigns in the West. His slave-holding, Southern-sympathizing relatives and friends pleaded with him not to fight for the Union, but he remained in the Army, and at the Battle of Fredericksburg, in 1862, demonstrated such ability that he was made a brigadier. At the time he was only 29. In recognition of his services during the Shenandoah campaign he was breveted Major General of Volunteers and in 1865 was made Brevet Major General of the Regulars. He resigned from the Army after the War, was appointed Minister to San Salvador, and later Consul-General in Havana and Paris. General Torbert was drowned in 1880 while attempting to assist rescuers when his steamer was wrecked off the Florida coast.

8. The CAUSEY MANSION *(private)*, facing the Plaza, S. Milford, a large and graceful yellow brick house set among trees on a pleasant lawn, was built in 1763 by an English architect named Mitchell, it is said, for Levin Crapper, a landowner and magistrate whose 1,500 acres included what is now South Milford. About 1855 the mansion was enlarged to its present form by Gov. Peter F. Causey. Following a current mode, the second architect gave the house a Greek Revival aspect modified by French simplicity and elegance, seen in the window caps and the intricate grillwork of the small third-story windows, and also in the general design of the house. The original pitched roof was replaced by a shallow third story and low-pitched roof, surmounted by a captain's walk. In front of the southwest wing are several tall square white pillars. The main wing has four large chimneys. The interior has been recently altered.

Preserved in good condition at one corner of the old-fashioned garden is one of the old brick SLAVE QUARTERS formerly used for house servants. The one lower room has a brick floor and a large fireplace. In the wall at the base of a ladder-like stairway is a large scooped-out dent—made there, it is related, to permit a stout Negro mammy to get up to her room. Other old brick quarters were removed by the present owner.

Governor Causey, like other successful down-State Delawareans, operated tanneries, mills, farms, and other enterprises. On his own Milford-built vessels he shipped to Philadelphia the grain and other products of the region. His schooners returned to Milford with pots, pans, drygoods, parlor organs, whiskey, and other articles for his general store. Until better ores were mined in Pennsylvania, Causey did a brisk business with bog iron ore from his land near Concord.

Before Causey bought the place it was the home of another Delaware governor, Daniel Rogers (1754–1806) of Accomac County, Va., who

SLAVE QUARTERS, CAUSEY HOUSE

served 1797–1799 to fill out the unexpired term of Gunning Bedford, who had died in office.

9. The CAULK DENTAL LABORATORIES *(open by permission)*, S. side of Lakeview Ave. near the town limits, one of the largest makers of dental filling materials in the world, was founded in 1877 by Dr. Levin D. Caulk who made his first products in his kitchen at Camden, Del. Products include synthetic porcelain, plastic materials for taking mouth impressions, and tooth cleansers. The research department is closed to the public.

10. The VINYARD SHIPBUILDING PLANT *(open by permission)*, foot of Columbia St., S. Milford, builds power yachts mostly 40-55 feet long, though up to 125 feet on order. Regular production models are standardized. Among the early employees were old-time ship carpenters who had worked on the last of the sailing ships.

11. The JOHN H. MULHOLLAND PLANT *(open by permission)*, foot of Marshall St., S. Milford, manufactures ice cream spoons, mustard paddles, lollypop sticks, and other wood veneer products. The gum-wood is brought by land and water from many parts of the Peninsula, and the visitor may see the processes from "cooking" the logs and shaving off the sheets of veneer to the finished article.

The MILFORD MEMORIAL HOSPITAL, on Clark Ave., opened in April, 1938. Enlarged since to 130-bed capacity, and having modern departments and facilities, it is an effective health center for a wide community.

This hospital is the direct descendant of the Milford Emergency Hospital whose starting fund was profits of a doll bazaar in 1907 conducted by Mrs. George Marshall and an interested group of citizens. Fêtes, balls, and parties continued to supplement a modest legislative appropriation. Successful from its start in two rooms of the Masonic Hall, in the top floor of the Windsor Hotel and in a building contributed by Dr. William Marshall, Jr., the war years changed the picture. Dr. William Marshall enlisted and by the end of 1918, Dr. Samuel Marshall who remained with the hospital was paying large deficits to keep the hospital open. The trustees closed it, raised funds, and reopened in a larger converted building, which served until the erection of the present building.

POINTS OF INTEREST IN ENVIRONS

Mordington, old house, *6 m.;* Ellendale Forest Camp Site, *8.8 m.;* Barratt's Chapel, *11.6 m.;* Redden Forest Picnic Shelter, *14.3 m. (see Tour 2).* Bowers Beach, *12.8 m. (see Tour 2B).* Diamond State Nursery, *1.7 m.;* Fort Saulsbury, *6 m.;* Cedar Beach, *6.4 m.;* Slaughter Beach, *9.1 m.*

Newark

Railroad Stations: Elkton Rd., near Main St., for B. & O. R.R.; ft. of St. College Ave. (Depot Rd.), for Pennsylvania R.R.
Bus Station: Boins Store, Elkton Rd., for Wilmington Coach Co., Wilmington-Newark, hourly schedule.
Daylight Saving Time: Generally observed, April–September.

Accommodations: Two hotels, tourist inns, boarding houses, motels.

Information: Clerk of Council office, 26 Academy St.
Motion Picture House: One.

Annual Events: Flower Show, Newark Garden Club, September; Memorial Day Vesper Service, American Legion, Sunday preceding Memorial Day; University of Delaware, scholastic and athletic events, dances, plays, etc.

NEWARK (135 alt., 6,731 pop.), pronounced New′-ark, is the second largest city in the State and seat of the University of Delaware. It is in the northwestern corner of the State, within three miles of the point where Maryland, Pennsylvania, and Delaware meet. White Clay Creek flows in a winding bed north of the town; Iron Hill, the other notable physical feature of the neighborhood, is directly south.

The town lies chiefly along State 2, known locally as the Capitol Trail. Main Street, coinciding with this highway as far west as the Baltimore & Ohio station, continues westward beyond that point as a tree-lined residential street. From the railroad-crossing at Main Street, New London Avenue, the center of the Negro population, strikes off at an angle.

The long narrow campus of the University of Delaware stretches at right angles across the Main Street axis of the town, and by day, during the college year, students dominate the town scene. Unpretentious shops, stores, and residences line the business part of Main Street, thronged on shopping days with people of the town and surrounding country. This trading area population is about 18,000. Town population doubled 1940–1950, and in 1951 the town site was enlarged from 1.54 to 5.46 sq. m.

Many of the inhabitants are descendants of the earliest English, Scotch, Irish, and Welsh settlers. The proportion of the foreign-born in 1950 was only 0.3 percent of the total white population. Negroes comprise 8.4 percent.

The site of Newark was one of the earliest crossroads meeting places for white travelers on the peninsula between the Chesapeake and the Delaware. An Indian trail from the Susquehanna country down the peninsula water shed, crossing a similar trail from the head of the Christina Creek to the Head of Elk, may have established its original importance. From a single house or tavern, where fresh horses could be secured, and messages and supplies exchanged, it grew into a village at the intersection of "two very Publick Roads." Mills, tanneries, and brickyards developed in the vicinity.

How "Newark," an English place-name of fairly common occurrence, came to be applied to this Delaware town is conjectural. A rather fanciful theory connects it with Valentine Hollingsworth, scion of an early Saxon family in old England. In 1683 he took out a patent for a tract of land north of Wilmington which he called New Wark, and later gave ground for a Quaker meeting house, also called New Wark, but later written Newark (see Newark Union Meeting, Tour 1, Sec. a). A Quaker meeting, aided by the New Wark group, was established near the present town. Valentine's son Henry inherited the New Wark homestead, and in 1712 acquired land in Maryland a few miles west of the present Newark. He and his sons traveled through this neighborhood on their trips to the headwaters of Christina, where their commercial and transportation enterprise centered, and may have suggested the name for the village.

Newark first received official recognition in 1758, when, at the request of residents, the village was empowered to conduct a semi-annual "fair" and a weekly market for the buying and selling of local produce. The old market house stood northeast of the present Academy lots, near where the Washington Hotel now stands.

Since the town had its origin at the junction of important highways, inns and taverns were early necessary. St. Patrick's Inn, a log structure which stood at what is now Daniel Thompson's residence, 34 West Main Street, dated back to 1747 and was the earliest of which there is record. Mason and Dixon are known to have had headquarters at St. Patrick's while making their surveys in the neighborhood. In 1760 a racecourse was built and horse-racing was a popular sport in Newark until after the Revolution. The army of the British General, Howe, passed through Newark in September 1777, just before the Battle of Brandywine, and General Washington's army also passed through the village in 1781, during his movement against Yorktown.

The first important industrial enterprise was the Meteer paper mill, established on the bank of White Clay Creek before 1798. In 1812 the Methodists built the first church in the village. In 1836 the Philadelphia, Wilmington & Susquehanna Railroad (now part of the Pennsylvania Sys-

OLD COLLEGE, UNIVERSITY OF DELAWARE

tem) extended its lines to Newark and in 1845 Joseph Dean, an Englishman, converted an old grist mill into a woolen manufactory.

In 1852 Newark received a town charter from the General Assembly and the Baltimore & Ohio Railroad entered the town in 1886. The town was reincorporated in 1887.

The first institution of learning in Newark was the Newark Academy. Established in New London, Pa., in 1743 by the Reverend Francis Alison, it was taken over by the Presbyterian Synod of Philadelphia in 1744, moved to Cecil County, Md., in 1752 and to Newark in 1765. In 1769 the school was granted a charter as the Academy of Newark by Lieut. Governor John Penn.

The academy functioned as the academic department of Delaware College from 1834 until 1859, but in the latter year when the college was temporarily closed by lack of funds, it again became a separate institution and operated as such until it closed its doors in 1898.

In 1818 the trustees of the academy were authorized by the Delaware legislature to raise $50,000 by means of a lottery for the establishment of a college at Newark, and the proceeds of certain taxes on steamboat and stagecoach lines were also turned over to them. In 1833 a new charter was granted and in May 1834, the college opened its doors. It was known as Newark College, however, until 1843, when it became Delaware College. Beset by financial difficulties from the start, the college struggled on until 1859, when it was forced to close, and eleven years elapsed before it was reopened.

When by the Morrill Act of 1862 the United States Government offered grants of Federal land to the States, the trustees of Delaware College persuaded the legislature to comply with the terms of the act, and deeded a half interest in the College to the State. The grant of 90,000 acres, which was sold for $83,000, enabled Delaware College to reorganize in 1869 and to reopen in 1870 as a "land grant college."

Under its new president, Col. William H. Purnell, a graduate of 1846, coeducation was introduced in 1872, but it was discontinued in 1885 and Dr. Purnell's resignation in that year resulted partly from his opposition to the change.

In 1913 the legislature appropriated money for the establishment of a women's college, under control of the Delaware College trustees, and the new school opened in the fall of 1914. In 1921 Delaware College and the Women's College were united to form the University of Delaware.

Negro education in Newark probably began with John Congo, who, about the time of the Civil War, taught such children as wished to learn in his house on the corner of Corbit Street and New London Avenue. The first school building for Negroes was erected on Corbit Street shortly after the Civil War of material from an army barracks shipped here by the government. A larger building on Cleveland Avenue was later used until the present structure of advanced design and equipment was erected on New London Road, the gift of Pierre S. du Pont.

The town was reincorporated, 1951, as the City of Newark, by a mayor and council charter with optional city manager operation. This accords with its responsibilities as a rapidly growing industrial, business, and cultural urban community.

Situated within the Greater Wilmington metropolitan area, Newark has a substantial economic and social relation to that city, where many of its residents work. An increasing number of Wilmington residents work and have business connections in Newark.

Industries include the large plants of the Continental-Diamond Fibre Company and National Vulcanized Fibre Company. Curtis Paper Company, a very old one, is noted for fine book paper. Among newer establishments are the Chrysler Corporation's motor parts plant and Tank Arsenal, the latter opened in 1951 with large government contracts; a large

Du Pont office building and research center and the Haskell and Stine laboratories give employment to several hundred persons. New construction under way includes shopping center, schools, dwellings and other buildings.

Townspeople provide community recreation and cultural programs and enjoy concerts, plays, athletic events and library of the university.

In addition to the *Newark Post,* a weekly, established 1910 by Everett C. Johnson, the town is served by Wilmington and other city dailies.

<<<<<<<<<<<<<<<<<<<<<<<< ☼ >>>>>>>>>>>>>>>>>>>>>>>>

University of Delaware

Situated on a 110-acre campus that bisects the town with a long ribbon of greensward and tree foliage, the University has 25 large buildings, mostly of red brick, of what may be called locally-inspired Colonial design, 20 smaller buildings, and several faculty residences. The two main divisions of the University—Delaware College, for men, and the Women's College—were merged September 1944 making the University coeducational in undergraduate and graduate studies.

Although the University of Delaware has only been in existence as such since 1921, it had its real beginning when Delaware College was reopened as a land grant college in 1870. The University receives an average annual appropriation of $2 million from the State in addition to funds for buildings and other permanent improvements. An endowment of $8 million is an added source of revenue and large gifts have come from the late Pierre S. du Pont and H. Fletcher Brown for buildings and facilities; also from H. Rodney Sharp, an alumnus, and other friends of the University. More buildings and facilities are still needed to serve the growing student body and deepening, broadening educational offerings of the University in the interest of enlightened citizenship.

The teaching staff of the University numbers more than 300 persons, including part-time instructors. There are about 75 others engaged exclusively in research or extension work of the Agricultural Experiment Station. Enrollment of full time students is over 1,800, about one-third girls. Summer sessions have been held regularly since 1913 and enroll from 700 to 900 students for the six-week terms. Summer sessions are paid for by

State appropriations, and are intended primarily for teachers, although many regular students and an average of 150 students from other colleges and universities also attend. A wide range of extension classes is conducted in towns throughout the State during the school year.

The University has five undergraduate schools: Arts and Sciences, Agriculture, Education, Engineering, Home Economics; and a Graduate School in which work leading to the master's degree is carried on in many fields. The degree of Doctor of Philosophy may be earned in chemistry and chemical engineering. Regular graduate courses are scheduled for evenings and Saturdays, available to men and women in educational, industrial and agricultural employment.

Among its goals and purposes the University stresses the importance of the Liberal Arts course as an invaluable background to profession or business, to graduate study or specialization, and to a rich personal life. The American Studies program brings together a number of courses in geographical, historical, economic, and cultural phases of American life, including collaboration with the Henry Francis du Pont Museum of American Decorative Arts and series of lectures by leading American scholars.

KEY TO NEWARK MAP
UNIVERSITY OF DELAWARE

1 Old College
2 Greenhouse
3 Military Laboratory
4 Military Shed
5 Taylor Gymnasium
6 Training House
7 Physical Education (Men)
8 Recitation Hall
9 Carpenter Gymnasium and Field House
10 Sigma Nu
11 Sigma Phi Epsilon
12 Elliott Hall
13 Purnell Hall
14 Alpha Tau Omega
15 Brown Hall
16 Harter Hall
17 Sharp Hall
18 Delta Tau Delta
19 The Knoll
20 Student Health Center

21 Economics and Business Administration
22 Wolf Hall
23 South Hall
24 Evans Hall Annex
25 Evans Hall
26 Mitchell Hall
27 Kappa Alpha
28 Hullihen Hall
29 Brown Laboratory
30 Memorial Library
31 Maintenance Center
32 Boiler Plant
33 Education and Home Economics
34 Academy Street Women's Dormitory
35 Cannon Hall
36 New Castle Hall
37 Kent Hall
38 Sussex Hall

39 Garages
40 Robinson Hall
41 Warner Hall
42 Boletus (Women's Dormitory)
43 Topsy (Women's Dormitory)
44 Turvy (Women's Dormitory)
45 Women's Gymnasium
46 Stenographic Services Center—Geography and Geology
47 Home Management House
48 Phi Kappa Tau
49 University Farm
50 Newton Poultry Building
51 Agricultural Hall
52 Delaware Stadium

OTHER POINTS OF INTEREST
(Not shown on map)

Newark Academy   Kells   Oaklands

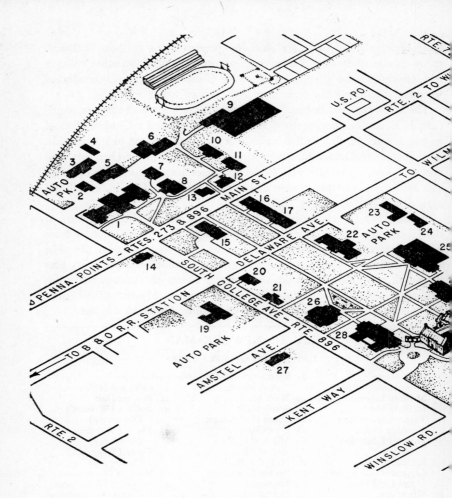

NEWARK

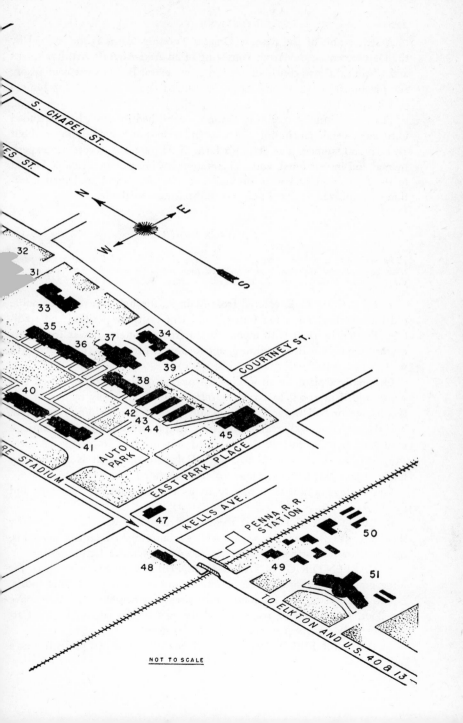

S. CHAPEL ST.

ES ST.

N

E

W

S

32

31

33

35

36

37

34

39

38

40

42

43

44

45

41

AUTO
PARK

RE STADIUM

EAST PARK PLACE

COURTNEY ST.

KELLS AVE.

47

PENNA. R. R.
STATION

50

48

49

51

TO ELKTON AND U.S. 40 & 13 —

NOT TO SCALE

A senior unit of the Reserve Officers Training Corps is maintained by the Department of the Army, consisting of an Anti-Aircraft Artillery Corps and Chemical Corps course divided into two parts: Basic course compulsory for Freshmen and Sophomores and advanced course optional for Juniors and Seniors.

The Agricultural Experiment Station, established in 1888, has expanded until its research (including teaching and extension) staffs number about 50 men and women. The Station's farm of 217 acres is devoted to experimental and instructional work. The Station has been of incalculable benefit to the farmers of Delaware through agricultural research and demonstration of improved farming practices and business methods.

CAMPUS TOUR

(The main entrance is at Main St. and College Ave. Points of Interest are listed in their geographical sequence and numbered to correspond with the numbers on the Campus map. Unless otherwise stated, all buildings are open during school hours.)

1. OLD COLLEGE, entered from Main St. through an avenue of noble old linden trees, dominates Campus and University by position and tradition. Erected in 1834 with money raised from a lottery, it was for a half century the only college building, and was used for a time for academic as well as collegiate instruction.

Originally a plain, cruciform brick structure of three stories, it had two wings added in 1902. In 1917 the interior was completely renovated and the steeple or bell tower (not originally part of the building) removed, but the exterior walls and portico were preserved, with just enough modification to accentuate the dignified simplicity of its design. A two-story granite stairway leads to the central portico, which is guarded by finely-proportioned, fluted Doric columns, painted white.

Old College is now used principally as a social center for students and faculty.

8. RECITATION HALL, a three-story red brick building, erected by the State of 1892 as the second college building, contains classrooms, offices of the Department of Physics, laboratories and a lecture hall.

9. CARPENTER GYMNASIUM and FIELD HOUSE, with space for large groups in physical education and indoor exercise and athletic sports, is 120 feet square, and its domed roof rises to a height of 40 feet above the floor. Completed in 1942, it was the gift of the late R. R. M. Carpenter, former member of the Board of Trustees.

9a. FRAZER FIELD, Delaware College Athletic field (presented as a

CAMPUS, UNIVERSITY OF DELAWARE

memorial to Joseph Heckart Frazer, '03), partly enclosed by a hollow-tile
stucco wall with a terrace at one side, this twelve-acre tract contains a
baseball diamond, football gridiron, and a cinder track.

12. ELLIOTT HALL, a two-and-a-half-story stone and brick structure,
long a private home, is used as residence apartments for members of the
teaching staff. It is one of the oldest buildings in Newark, erected probably at the outbreak of the American Revolution. It is a notable example
of late Georgian Colonial architecture with exterior walls of Flemish-bond
brick, well-proportioned dormer windows and fine interior woodwork.

13. PURNELL HALL, named for Dr. William H. Purnell (President
1870–85), is a two-and-a-half-story dwelling with ivy-covered exterior
walls of Flemish-bond brick. It was once known as the (John) Watson
Evans House, and in recent years has been used as a fraternity house, a
general library, and the eastern wing as a dentist's office. It now houses
Alumni Office and Placement Bureau. The architecture of the building is
distinguished by a dignified entrance doorway with arched and traceried
fanlight and by fine interior woodwork.

15. BROWN HALL, dormitory for men opposite Harter Hall, was built in 1941, the gift of H. Fletcher Brown. It accommodates undergraduate students and a number of bachelor members of the staff or graduate students.

16. HARTER HALL, a three-story brick dormitory for men, erected in 1917, accommodates 100 students. It is named for Dr. George A. Harter, President of Delaware College from 1896 to 1914, and Professor of Mathematics until his retirement in 1935.

17. SHARP HALL, built by the State and completed 1953, is continuous in structure and architecture and dormitory facilities with Harter Hall. It is named for H. Rodney Sharp, the alumnus who gave Mitchell Hall and many other fine gifts to the University.

22. WOLF HALL, which honors Dr. Theodore R. Wolf, Professor of Chemistry from 1871 to 1909, a spacious three-story brick building, was erected for the School of Agriculture in 1917. Several of the departments of Pure Science are in this building. The School of Agriculture moved in 1952 to the new Agricultural Building. Wolf Hall and Harter Hall were gifts of Pierre S. du Pont.

24-25. EVANS HALL, erected 1928–30, a large building of structural steel and brick, houses the divisions of Civil, Electrical, and Mechanical Engineering. It is named for George G. Evans and for his son, Charles B.

26. MITCHELL HALL, an auditorium with a seating capacity of almost 1,000, was erected and endowed by an alumnus, H. Rodney Sharp, class of 1900. Named for Samuel Chiles Mitchell (President 1914–20), the brick auditorium is an adaptation of the Georgian Colonial style of architecture. It is equipped with a stage for dramatic presentations and with a large pipe organ, the gift of Pierre S. du Pont.

28. HULLIHEN HALL, completed 1940, houses the Board Room of the Trustees which also serves as the President's office; the offices of the administrative staff, of Deans of several of the undergraduate Schools and the School of Graduate Study, besides other faculty offices and classrooms.

29. BROWN LABORATORY (formerly Chemistry Building), erected 1937, is a two-and-a-half-story brick structure with modern equipment and an auditorium with a capacity for 268 students. It has offices, classrooms, libraries, private laboratories in addition to the seven large ones, and many other rooms for special purposes. It is the gift of H. Fletcher Brown.

30. THE MEMORIAL LIBRARY *(open 8-5, 7-10 weekdays; 2-5, 7-10 Sundays, during the academic year; special hours during vacations and the summer sessions)*, erected in 1924 as a memorial to Delaware's dead in World War I, is the gift of the people of the State. A brick structure

of modified Georgian Colonial architecture with central dome and rotunda (Memorial Hall) and extensive east and west wings, it is the first unit of a larger structure to be completed when funds are available.

The main reading room seats 144, and the book collection totals 140,000 volumes. The building also houses the archives of the more-than-a-century old university as well as the libraries of the Athenaean and Delta Phi Literary Societies, which for decades supplied the deficiencies of the college library proper. On the top floor are university art exhibits.

In Memorial Hall, a Book of the Dead, 270 pages in all, one for each of the hero dead, rests upon an altar. A page is turned daily. On the walls are four bronze triptychs on which are inscribed the names of the men and women who died.

33. EDUCATION AND HOME ECONOMICS BUILDING, completed in 1953, harmonizing in architecture with the newer buildings on the campus, gives the Schools of Education and Home Economics modern, efficient quarters.

35. CANNON HALL, a new women's dormitory opened in 1952. It is named for Dr. Annie Jump Cannon, native of Delaware, who became a world famous astronomer. She died in 1941 at the age of 77.

36-38. SUSSEX HALL, a three-story fireproof brick dormitory, was erected in 1918, and NEW CASTLE HALL, corresponding in general plan, was erected in 1926. Each of these dormitories accommodates 62 persons. KENT HALL, a dining-hall, completed in 1926, contains three dining-rooms with capacity for 350 persons and kitchen.

40. ROBINSON HALL, erected in 1914 as one of the first two buildings constructed on a 19-acre plot purchased by the State of Delaware as the location for the Women's College, is a three-story brick structure, in which most of the recitation rooms, laboratories, and administrative offices of the College were located. Active and unremitting work by various women's organizations of the State was responsible for the building of the Women's College and the ending of inequity toward Delaware young women in pursuit of a college education. The building is named in honor of Winifred J. Robinson, Dean of the Women's College from 1914 to 1938, under whose leadership, Women's College had a remarkable development. It contains offices and classrooms.

41. WARNER HALL is a dormitory erected at the same time as Robinson Hall and corresponds with it in modern version of colonial architecture. Named in honor of Mrs. A. D. Warner (who died 1948), one of the Founders of the Women's College, the building accommodates sixty-five women and contains social rooms for students and faculty.

45. THE WOMEN'S GYMNASIUM, completed in 1931, contains exercise and locker rooms, showers, and a pool, as well as offices for the instructors. Fields for hockey, soccer, baseball, and track adjoin the gymnasium. Elsewhere on the campus is an archery range, and courts for tennis and croquet.

Not shown on the map is SMYTH HALL, a dormitory under construction, 1953–54, named in honor of Miss Alice P. Smyth, one of the founders of the Women's College, who established its library and has continued to support university development by an annual scholarship and other contributions.

49. UNIVERSITY FARM of 349 acres is a practical proving ground for solution of farm problems, where results of agricultural research and experiment may be seen and studied in crops, livestock, orchards, gardens, machinery and building upkeep.

51. AGRICULTURAL HALL, a large, well-designed brick building erected in 1952, adjacent to the Agricultural Experiment Farm and to the new Athletic Field, houses all departments of the School of Agriculture and also the offices and laboratories of the Agricultural Experiment Station and Agricultural Extension.

52. DELAWARE STADIUM, well-planned and equipped and set in large grounds, was completed 1952. This new facility has given a great lift to the Athletic Department's programs of collegiate and inter-collegiate games. It also provides a splendid field for many university events and celebrations.

(Further information concerning the buildings listed on the University map may be asked for at the Memorial Library.)

OTHER POINTS OF INTEREST

THE ACADEMY OF NEWARK buildings, plain, box-like brick structures, set well back on the Academy Lot, SE. corner of Main and Academy Sts., are now used as town offices and council rooms and as a home for the TOWN LIBRARY *(open 3-8 Mon., Wed., Fri.; 6:30-8:30 p.m. Sat.)*. Inscriptions on old books show that Newark had a library as early as 1763. The first Academy building, long since torn down, was of stone, erected in 1776 from funds raised in part in England. Of the present group, two date from the 1840's, while the third, built in 1872, completes a symmetrical ensemble.

When, in September 1777, it was apparent the British General Howe would march through Newark, the trustees sent the Academy funds to Wilmington for safekeeping. However, they fell into the hands of the British at that place, along with other valuables, including the New Castle County records and President John McKinly himself. After Howe's march, the Academy building was used as a shoe factory for the Delaware militia troops. Classes were resumed in 1780, and the Academy functioned, with some vicissitudes, for over a century, closing finally in 1898, although the trustees still meet.

Notable among visitors at Newark Academy was Edgar Allan Poe, who lectured here the evening of Dec. 23, 1843, holding the interest of the Academy and college faculty, students, and citizens for two hours. Said *Academicus* writing in the *Delaware State Journal,* January 2, 1844:

> The lecture was an eloquent production eloquently delivered by Edgar A. Poe, Esq.
> . . . His theme was the "Poetry of America"—a topic particularly appropriate to one who has himself acquired so honorable a place among the Poets of the land, and who has proven himself to possess in no small degree the high qualifications he demands of his brethren of the inspired pen.

KELLS *(open by permission),* 318 S. College Ave., a low rambling stone building with two large square towers, receives its name from the monastery of Kells, Ireland, where a copy of the Gospels, known as the *Book of Kells,* was produced in the eighth century. This volume, preserved in Trinity College, Dublin, was the inspiration for the name of the structure built in the decade 1910–20 by the late Everett C. Johnson, Secretary of State for Delaware (1916–20), as the home for his newspaper, the *Newark Post,* and as a place where distinctive printing could be produced. The building is now occupied by a fraternity house.

OAKLANDS *(private),* on Old Oak Rd., long the mansion house of Rathmell Wilson (1810–90), gentleman farmer and capitalist, was occupied until recently by members of the family. He had built Oaklands as a permanent home, but in late life removed to Philadelphia, and used the mansion as a summer residence. He was acting President of Delaware College during the suspension (1859–70), and one of its chief supporters during those critical days. The interior has fine walnut woodwork.

POINTS OF INTEREST IN ENVIRONS

Curtis Paper Plant, *1.1 m.;* White Clay Creek Presbyterian Church, *2.7 m.;* England House, *3.2 m.;* Delaware Park, racetrack, *5 m.;* St. James Episcopal Church, *5.9 m. (see Tour 8).* Welsh Tract Baptist Church, *2.5 m.;* The "Wedge," *2.9 m.;* Marker at E. end of Mason-Dixon Line, *3.5 m.;* Cooch's Bridge and old Cooch House, *3.6 m.;* Iron Hill, *5.4 m.;* Glasgow, *6.3 m.;* Summit Bridge at the Deep Cut of C. and D. Canal, *11.4 m. (see Tour 9).*

New Castle

Railroad Station: Eighth and South Sts., for Delmarva Division of Pennsylvania R.R.
Bus Station: Second and Delaware Sts., for Delaware Bus Co. (New Castle-Wilmington line).
River Crossing: Delaware Memorial Bridge, N. *2 m.* on Wilmington-New Castle road. Ferry service to New Jersey shore discontinued.
Airport: New Castle County Airport, W. *2 m.* to US 13; scheduled service by four lines.

Accommodations: One hotel, a few tourist homes, excellent motels on US 13.

Information: Amstel House, cor. 4th and Delaware Sts., Mayor's office, Old Courthouse.

Motion Picture House: One.

Annual Events: "A Day in Old New Castle," 3rd Saturday in May.

For further information regarding this city see *New Castle on the Delaware,* another of the American Guide Series, published (1937) by the New Castle Historical Society; revised edition (1950).

NEW CASTLE (20 alt., 5,400 pop.), on the Delaware, six miles south of Wilmington, the oldest town in the Delaware River Valley, lies in a curve of the shore, once a fine natural harbor for large vessels, with a commanding position and view. Along the first street, the Strand, parallel with the river, the houses face not the river, but each other. The streets and the broad Green preserve unspoiled the work of seventeenth-, eighteenth-, and early nineteenth-century builders. History, adventure, and romance are written in the doorways and roof lines, in the broad chimneys, and in glimpses of spacious rear gardens.

The inhabitants are predominantly American of long descent, many of families native for generations to the town or its environs. Irish as well as English, Dutch, and French extraction is represented in the oldest families. Negroes, present since the last period of the Dutch, are descended in part from slaves locally owned. They are employed not only as servants, but in the regular industrial occupations, skilled or unskilled. In an Italian group are highly skilled aircraft workers. A small Polish group includes industrial workers of varied skills.

The first settlement at New Castle's site was made by the Dutch in 1651, to regain the river trade usurped by the Swedes. Peter Stuyvesant—Governor for the Dutch West India Company—anchored two warships in the harbor and directed building of Fort Casimir on Sand Hook, a point of

NEW CASTLE'S BACK GATE

land now washed away that extended beyond the end of present Chestnut Street. Within the palisades of the fort, in a large blockhouse, lived Gerrit Bicker, the Commander, Andries Hudde, the Commissary, and some of the soldiers. Governor Stuyvesant left a large stock of supplies to lure the Indian trade, and when rain ruined the crops of the planters in 1652, the cream of this trade benefited the Company. With this exception, little is known of their activity between the fall of 1651 and May 21, 1654, when the new Swedish Governor on the Delaware, Captain Johan Classon Rising, in command of a large expedition, compelled the garrison to surrender.

Captain Rising found 22 houses by the Strand near the dilapidated fort. Hardly had he rebuilt the fortifications and repaired the houses under the direction of the Swedish engineer, Peter Lindeström, and the Swedish captain, Sven Skute, when the Swedish interlude was over. With Stuyvesant's permanent conquest of the Swedes in 1655, Fort Casimir became an established village, the Dutch capital on the South River of New Netherland. Rising had held a court early in that year and thereby initiated two and a quarter centuries of court history on the site. Jean Paul Jacquet, the first Vice-Director under Stuyvesant, extended the streets behind the fort, granting town lots 60 feet wide by 300 feet deep; each lot-holder was given as much land in the country roundabout as he would agree to cultivate—woods and marsh being held as a common. This system was continued under specific charter from the burgomasters of Amsterdam in Holland when that city took over the Colony from the Dutch West India Company in 1656. Fort Casimir then became New Amstel, named for a suburb of Amsterdam. The Vice-Director for the city, Jacob Alrichs, who arrived early in 1657 with about 200 colonists, built a town hall of logs, two stories in height, a wharf and store house, a bakehouse, guardhouse, a forge, and brick kilns, and so many dwellings that New Amstel was a town of 100 buildings at the end of the year.

Alrichs bought food from the Swedish farmers, received supplies from New Amsterdam, and made urgent appeals to Holland for the aid of the Colony, but exercised such a rigid oversight of the Indian trade to prevent loss to the owners of the Colony, that he antagonized many of the settlers. The unscrupulous D'Hinoyossa, Lieutenant at the fort, who inherited Alrichs' office at the latter's death toward the end of 1659, had broken all the Vice-Director's rulings, yet he made stricter rules when the power became his, and used the prohibitions against the trade of the colonists to protect his own buying and selling. Before his plans for a personal empire were well ripened, however, Sir Robert Carr arrived in the harbor with two frigates on September 30, 1664, demanding surrender of the town to the English. The fort was now in little better condition than when Rising captured it, but D'Hinoyossa, facing the end of his dreams, lost his head and prepared to use the guns. Then Carr, having fired into the little fort, wounding half of the twenty Dutch soldiers and killing three, took the town for the Duke of York.

Most of the old population, Swedes, Finns, and Dutch, remained, and English came from Virginia, Maryland, New Jersey, and New York, in addition to new colonists from England. Late in October 1664, Col. Richard Nicolls, the Duke of York's Deputy Governor for New York and the province on the Delaware, visited New Amstel and changed its name to New Castle, probably for William Cavendish, then Earl of New Castle, or for Newcastle-on-Tyne in England, which had a similar setting. Under the wise rule of the Deputy Governors, the community was permitted to keep its own officers for routine affairs, and English law, with necessary modifications, was slowly and imperfectly put in force. The Dutch recaptured New Castle in 1673, but it was restored to the English the following year, and the Duke of York's rule continued until the coming of William Penn. During the 31 years between the building of Fort Casimir and the establishment of Penn's province, New Castle had undergone five changes of sovereignty, and two additional changes of government—from the Dutch West India Company to the City of Amsterdam; from the Duke of York's province to that of William Penn.

When William Penn, with deeds from the Duke of York, arrived at New Castle, October 27, 1682, John Moll and Ephraim Herman, two magistrates of the court, accepted the Duke's power of attorney to transfer to Penn the land of the twelve-mile circle about New Castle. Through their influence, doubtless, the ceremony of taking possession, during which Penn on August 28, 1682, entered the fort alone, locked the door, and opened it again to receive a porringer of river water and soil with a twig upon it, was followed by a general swearing of allegiance on the part of the inhabitants and friendly pledges to Penn to cooperate in his new government. Grumbling and attack upon Penn's title began all too soon in New Castle as well as in the Delaware territory to the south, the Quaker spirit and ways being foreign to the much more liberal, urbane, and yet individualistic temperaments and tempers of the inhabitants. From 1704, when the counties of Delaware set up a separate Assembly from that of Penn's province of Pennsylvania, to 1776, New Castle was the seat of government of the "Lower Counties." Here were trained many of the patriot statesmen of the Revolutionary period. It was the self-government

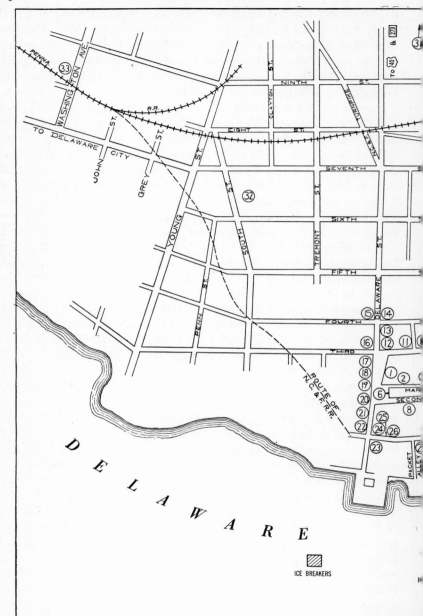

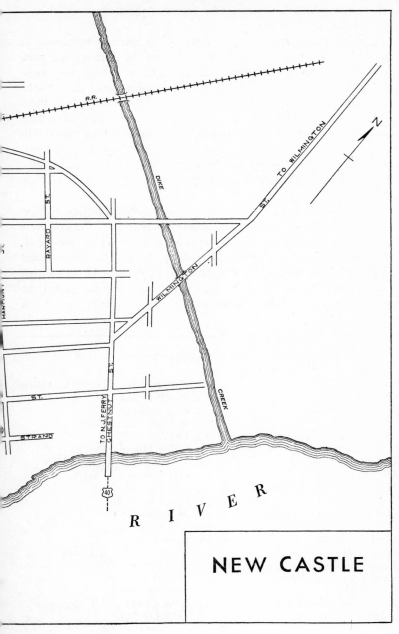

NEW CASTLE

of loyal British subjects, however, who regarded the three counties as a Crown Colony.

The acts of Parliament which later fostered the spirit of revolution in the colonies were also resented at New Castle; but the issue set up a conflict between the independent nature of the inhabitants and their long satisfaction in direct allegiance to the English sovereign rather than to the Provincial Governor. The conflict was resolved mainly on the side of independence, and pre-Revolutionary agitation in New Castle was at white heat when the port of Boston was closed by enforcement of the Port Bill. Under the leadership of Nicholas Van Dyke, the elder, and George Read, 200 pounds were raised locally for the aid of Boston's destitute citizens. (Boston returned the friendly service fifty years later at the time of New Castle's great fire, 1824.)

On September 21, 1776, a convention of the counties, meeting at New Castle, formed "The Delaware State." About a month later the first State legislature met here, but New Castle's period as State capital was brief. For although the town was never entered by the British, the constant threat of attack from the river and by land during General Howe's march across the peninsula and his later occupation of Wilmington, caused the officers of the State to meet elsewhere and, in 1777, the State capital was

---

KEY TO NEW CASTLE MAP

The Green
1. Old Courthouse
2. Old Sheriff's House
3. Old Arsenal
4. Immanuel Church and Immanuel Churchyard
5. Old Academy
6. Old Town Hall
7. New Castle and Frenchtown Monument
8. Old Presbyterian Church
9. Old Dutch House
10. Gemmill House
11. Rodney House
12. Kensey Johns House
13. Kensey Johns, Jr. House
14. Amstel House
15. Senator Nicholas Van Dyke House

16. Kensey Johns Van Dyke House
17. Booth House
18. Gilpin House
19. William Penn House
20. Delaware House
21. Colby House
22. Van Leuvenigh House
23. Old Jefferson Hotel
24. Old Farmers Bank
25. Gunning Bedford House
26. McIntire House
27. Old Stage Tavern
28. Read House
29. Immanuel Parish House
30. Aull Houses
31. The Hermitage
32. Deemer House
33. New Castle and Frenchtown Ticket Box

moved to Dover. But New Castle gained in travel through its port and by land what it lost in political assembly. Removal of the Federal Government to Washington in 1800 added to the already increased travel across the peninsula and up and down the river with New Castle as a transfer point. Inns and stage routes multiplied and the resulting prosperity led to the building of the New Castle & Frenchtown Railroad connecting the steamboat service of the Chesapeake Bay with the river travel and steam-packet service of the Delaware. The railroad, some distance south of the stage road and turnpike of the same name, began operations with horse-drawn cars on July 4, 1831. An English locomotive, on September 10, 1832, opened the first regular steam passenger line in the country. The old stone sleepers and wooden rails with iron strips nailed to their tops were replaced in 1833 by wooden ties and iron rails.

Incorporated in 1875 as a city with mayor and council, New Castle has had few changes in its governmental form. It retains its status as an endowed town with extra-municipal bodies serving as trustees for the Town Common, a tract of 1,068 acres, dating from the common land granted settlers in the earliest Dutch period, and confirmed by William Penn and his successors after a survey made between 1701 and 1704 at Penn's direction. The Trustees of the Common lease the land and spend the net profit for the benefit of the town. This income gave substantial support to early education, built the Town Hall, and continues to subsidize many a town improvement. A somewhat similar trust exercising control over the public buildings on the Green is chartered under the name of Trustees of the Market Square and Courthouse Square (The Green). The industries of New Castle include steel, rayon, fibre, and aircraft plants.

POINTS OF INTEREST

The GREEN, bounded by Delaware, Market, Harmony, and 3rd Sts., with its great elms and fine old public buildings and the adjoining Market Square between Market and 2nd Streets, where the Town Hall stands, was originally the Public Square, laid out under the direction of Peter Stuyvesant in the Dutch period. In the Duke of York's period, a log fort or blockhouse was built here "at the back of the town" and the square ordered to be stoutly enclosed as protection in case of Indian or other attack. After the courthouse was built and the town market later established on the river side of the plot, the whole was known as Courthouse Square. Not until the arsenal was built and leased to the Federal government in 1809 was the land considered as two plots and the Courthouse Square divided from the narrow Market Square by present Market Street. They are governed by the Trustees of Market Square and Courthouse Square, a body created by the legislature, independent of the city government, holding the property in trust for the citizens. This board, five members, elected one every ten years, replaces self-perpetuating trustees created 1772.

1. The OLD COURT HOUSE, N. side of Delaware St., on the Green, site of much of the activities of government of the Three Lower Counties from the early part of William Penn's period to the Revolution. The colonial State House-Court House still dominates both Green and old town. Of brick, built at various times during two centuries, it had removed in 1936 its nineteenth century stucco, a hopeful beginning of a final restoration then being planned. Signs of the decorative belt course of brick at the second floor level, that was "stepped" at the corner, are visible. A 20-foot square section of the east wing is the original east wing added to the central building in 1765 along with a similar wing on the west side. The tradition persists that here the ceremony of "closing upon himself the door" in token of proprietorship took place even though contemporary accounts use the word "fort," and the fort then stood upon the site of Immanuel Church.

The large Early Georgian Colonial central section of Flemish-bond brickwork with glazed headers was the original part of the building. Its large gambrel roof was replaced by the present one after a fire in 1771. Its arcaded octagonal cupola formed the center of "the 12-mile circle" that determined the location of the arc forming the north boundary of the Colony and State. Its original doorway, shown on an old drawing, in well-proportioned classical design with pediment and pilasters, was of fitting dignity. In 1845 the small west wing was removed and the present larger one of rough texture brick added. Its foundation stones are the granite sleepers of the old New Castle & Frenchtown Railroad.

2. The OLD SHERIFF'S HOUSE *(not open),* adjoining the Courthouse on Market St. on the site of an earlier jail and debtors' prison, was built in 1858 of red sandstone in the Victorian manner.

At the rear is the jail wing outside which stood the gallows and a whipping post, removed in 1901, as if to wipe from memory the gruesome scenes enacted there. The building, except that part of it within the north entrance, which is still the town lock-up, is rented by a private club.

3. The OLD ARSENAL *(open 9-5 Mon.-Fri., 9-12 Sat.)* on the Green, facing Market St. between Delaware and Harmony Sts., was erected in 1809 by the United States Government when the threat of war with England became serious. It was used in 1813 by Brig. Gen. John Stockton,

IMMANUEL CHURCH AND OLD ACADEMY, NEW CASTLE

and in 1831 lodged the garrison from Fort Delaware while the burned fort was being rebuilt. The fort was then in charge of Major Pierce, brother of Franklin Pierce who became President of the United States in 1853. The arsenal was used again in 1846 at the outbreak of the Mexican War.

Shortly thereafter it was discovered that the land, in common with the rest of the Green, could not legally be sold. A new deed was drawn, leasing the land but prohibiting, except with the town's consent, the storing of ammunition or the quartering of troops. Under these conditions the Government gave the building to the town. In 1852 the Trustees of the Common added a second floor and the cupola, closed the original wagon entrances at each end, and used the building for a schoolhouse until 1930.

It was repaired and remodeled in 1936, partly as a project of the Works Progress Administration. Used for offices, later again as a school, it is now temporarily the Church House of the Presbyterian Church.

4. IMMANUEL CHURCH (Episcopal; open 8-5 daily), on the Green at Market and Harmony Sts., originally designed in the manner of the traditional Anglican Church plan, with chancel at east end, is set without relation to street lines. The building, begun in 1703 and completed about 1710, is of brick, covered with buff stucco, and surrounded by a buff-stuccoed brick wall. The shingled tower and spire were added in 1820–22. At the same time the church was lengthened, the altar and chancel moved from the east to the west end, and a four-dialed clock placed in the tower. In 1848, the copper-covered wooden cross was added. Stones laid flat in the brick aisle mark four graves, the earliest inscription being dated February 12, 1717.

Immanuel Parish was organized in 1689, under the Society for the Propagation of the Gospel in America. Gifts of a "pulpit, altar cloaths, and a box of glass," now lost, were made by Queen Anne. Church silver, shown on Old New Castle Day, includes a flagon made in New York by Simeon Saumaine, and given to Immanuel by the Governor of Pennsylvania in 1710.

In the IMMANUEL CHURCHYARD, a few of the gravestones bear dates as early as 1707. The epitaph for Jehu Curtis, who died in 1755, is attributed to Benjamin Franklin. Among graves of noted Delawareans are those of Governor Gunning Bedford (1742–1797), Kensey Johns, Sr. (1759–1848), Chancellor of the State; Governor Thomas Stockton (1781–1846), Colonel John Stockton (1755–1822), James Booth, Sr. (1753–1828), James Booth, Jr. (1789–1855), Governor Nicholas Van Dyke, Sr. (1738–1789), Senator Nicholas Van Dyke, Jr. (1770–1826), and George

Read (1733–1798), Signer of the Declaration of Independence and of the Federal Constitution. Admitted to the bar at the age of nineteen years, Read became attorney-general of the "Three Lower Counties" in 1763. The same year he married the daughter of George Ross, rector of Immanuel Church. From this time he held successively all the highest offices within the elective or appointed power of Colony and early State, except Governor. He served in this office temporarily, however, during the time John McKinly, President of the State, was a prisoner of General Howe. Important not only to Delaware, Read was an outstanding personality and statesman throughout the formative period of the Nation.

5. The OLD ACADEMY *(open, apply the Rector of Immanuel Church)*, NW. corner of the Green, begun in 1798, completed 1811, is a long two-story brick building set off by a low garden wall. The broad entrance with its arch and fanlight is centered beneath a Palladian window and cupola. The building is being renovated and restored (1953) by a committee of Immanuel Church which holds a long term lease.

The Academy was planned in 1772 as "public seminary of learning" to replace the overcrowded old Quaker Meeting House, used as the first school, but the Revolution delayed construction until the end of the century. The Academy was the only school on a tuition basis until 1852, when New Castle Institute, a part tuition, part free school, a feature whereby the school could receive part of the State school funds, was opened.

6. The OLD TOWN HALL *(open 9-5 Mon.-Fri.; 9-12 Sat.)*, NW. corner Delaware and 2nd Sts., built 1823, of brick, three stories high, with square white tower and octagonal cupola, has an arcade through the center of its first story that originally led to the stalls of the town market at the rear. The market was held as early as 1682, and to make it successful the court restricted buying and selling elsewhere on market days.

7. The NEW CASTLE AND FRENCHTOWN MONUMENT, 2nd St., opposite the Green, is composed of the oblong stone "sleepers" first used to hold the track of the New Castle & Frenchtown R.R.

8. The OLD PRESBYTERIAN CHURCH *(open, apply pastor at Manse)*, E. side of 2nd St. between Delaware and Harmony Sts., replaced in 1707 the earliest church building in New Castle, the little old wooden church on the Strand dedicated by the Dutch in 1657, supporting the claim that this is one of the oldest Calvinistic congregations in the country.

Built of brick, the one-story church has a hipped roof above which a cupola tower was added after 1800, replacing a smaller one. Authentically restored, the church is a distinguished building. Its broad lawn stretching back toward the Strand includes part of the early Dutch burying ground of New Castle.

9. The OLD DUTCH HOUSE *(private)*, facing the Green on 3rd St. between Harmony and Delaware Sts., is thought by historians to have been built, probably 1698 to 1704. Of brick, with low pent eaves, an over-large central chimney, and two broad front windows, the house was bought in 1937 by the Delaware Society for the Preservation of Antiquities, for restoration. It is now a New Castle Historical Society museum.

10. The GEMMILL HOUSE *(private, open on Old New Castle Day)*, 18 3rd St., was built about 1801 for John Wiley by Peter Crowding. Constructed of brick, the house has marked simplicity and dignity. The well-designed fanlight above the entrance door, the broad windows of 24 panes, the single dormer repeating the motif of the eave pediment, are pleasing details. In the interior, the fine woodwork, now painted white, is of mahogany.

11. The RODNEY HOUSE *(private, open on Old New Castle Day)*, 16 3rd St., built 1831 by George B. Rodney, Member of Congress (1841–45) is of brick, with shuttered doorway and fanlight above. The proportions of the façade and interior are dignified. The house (still occupied by descendants of George Rodney) contains a very extensive collection of authentic Delawareana. Notable are portraits of George Read by Gilbert Stuart; George Ross, the elder, first Rector of Immanuel Church, by Hesselius; and Benjamin West's painting of George Ross, the younger.

12. The KENSEY JOHNS HOUSE *(private, open on Old New Castle Day)*, 2 3rd St. facing the Green, built 1789–90 by local craftsmen, is of brick on heavy stone foundation. The service wing, part of an earlier structure, is balanced by an office wing. The recessed and paneled doorway, without fanlight, is framed by gracefully tapering pilasters. The interior paneling is white pine; the mantels are of carved woodwork with marble facings; the stairway, with curved handrail and the repeated design in the wall molding, was designed by Lampson Sarrette. Two brass key plates and latches from this house were given to Mount Vernon for its restoration in 1910. With the exception of necessary replacements, the hardware and other details are all original.

Kensey Johns, Sr. (1759–1848) studied law under the elder George Read, and married a daughter of Governor Van Dyke in 1784. He served in many State offices, and became Chief Justice in 1798 and Chancellor in 1830.

13. The KENSEY JOHNS, JR. HOUSE *(private, open occasionally on Old New Castle Day)*, NE. corner Delaware and 4th Sts., was built in

FIREPLACE, AMSTEL HOUSE, NEW CASTLE

1823. Of brick with original treatment of cornice and roof, it has the characteristic restraint and elegance of its period.

Kensey Johns, Jr. (1791–1857) succeeded his father as Chancellor when the latter resigned in 1832.

14. The AMSTEL HOUSE *(open 10-5 weekdays, adm. 50¢)*, N. corner 4th and Delaware Sts., houses the museum of the New Castle Historical Society. Architects place the date of erection at 1730 or earlier, and it is believed that the present kitchen wing was the residence in 1706, date of the first recorded transfer.

The locally-made brick are laid in Flemish bond, with a belt course and water table. The house is broad, and heavy in design. No two windows are exactly alike, although two are symmetrically disposed on either side of the narrow fanlight doorway, five above and three in the broad gable. A wide cove cornice spanning the gable repeats the design of the main cornice. The rooms on either side of a central hallway are paneled in wood and furnished with museum pieces. The original Van Dyke furniture is scattered among descendants, but Mrs. Coleman du Pont, a great-great-granddaughter of Governor Van Dyke, had the music room furniture reproduced, and the walls of the room restored to their original soft green found under many layers of later paperings. In this room, standing upon the hearthstone, George Washington kissed the young bride of Kensey Johns, Ann Van Dyke, daughter of Governor Van Dyke, on the afternoon of the wedding, April 30, 1784; and, as Chief Justice James Booth wrote at the time, he kissed all the pretty girls—"as was his wont."

Cut with a diamond on the pane of a second-story window are the lines:

> Around her head ye angels constant vigil keep,
> And guard fair innocence her balmy sleep.

The author and date are unknown.

Exhibits at Amstel House include complete kitchen furnishings of Colonial times, and many examples of the arts and handicraft of early periods, including costumes, metal work, and paintings. Among the latter are portraits of Ann Van Dyke and Kensey Johns, Sr., and a large portrait of Mrs. Jehu Curtis, ascribed to John Hesselius.

15. SENATOR NICHOLAS VAN DYKE HOUSE *(private, open on Old New Castle Day)*, 400 Delaware St., built 1799, was the first of three residences built by Senator Van Dyke, son of the Governor, and resembles the Amstel House across the street. Instead of the broad gable, it has a pediment breaking the long line of the eaves, centered above the doorway and its graceful fanlight, in a symmetrical façade. The shutters of the doorway swing back into the curves of iron guard rails at the top of the stone stoop.

16. The KENSEY JOHNS VAN DYKE HOUSE *(private, open on Old New Castle Day)*, 300 Delaware St., built 1820, of brick, two-and-a-half stories high, like the older Van Dyke House, is in much more formal and severe taste than the earlier-built dwelling. Brick eaves relieve the plainness of the entrance façade. The broad door and the shutters of the first floor are in unusual geometric design. The interior is notable for its fine woodwork.

17. The BOOTH HOUSE *(private, open on Old New Castle Day)*, 216 Delaware St., built in part about 1730 and added to later, is of original brick, with a clapboard wing to the west. The classic main doorway with bull's eyes in the top panel is notable. Judge James Booth, Jr. who was born in the house in 1789, again lived there when he was Chief Justice. When the jury in the Courthouse across the street failed to agree,

ON THE STRAND

Judge Booth rested in his home and when called to hear the verdict, he would arrive in dressing gown and slippers, mount the bench and, if necessary, sentence the defendant.

In this house also was born Robert Montgomery Bird (1806–54), versatile author of romances and dramas, successful in their time, and recently acquiring a belated fame from the criticism of modern students of literature. Bird's best known tale is *Nick of the Woods (see Literature)*.

18. The GILPIN HOUSE *(private)*, 210 Delaware St., now a store and apartments, is one of the town's oldest buildings. A broad arched driveway through it to the garden and stables in the rear and other rare architectural details have been destroyed by remodeling. In 1797, it was the "McCullough Tavern"; in 1802, the "Arms of the United States"; in 1804, "Darragh Tavern." It continued as a hotel frequented by court attendants until recent years. The name is from Edward W. Gilpin, Chief Justice from 1857 to 1876, who lived here during that time.

19. The WILLIAM PENN HOUSE *(private)*, 206 Delaware St., with the original front brickwork replaced, but that on the sides and back remaining was built and sold by the Dutch Rynier Vanderculen in the early 1680's after William Penn had formally taken possession of New Castle in 1682. Tradition has it that Penn stayed here over night, and

"Penn's room," with its corner fireplace and original woodwork, is preserved.

20. The DELAWARE HOUSE *(private)*, 202 Delaware St., was the residence and hotel of John Crow, Revolutionary figure. It was chiefly through Crow's efforts that the dilapidated wooden market house and stalls were replaced in 1823 by the present Town Hall. The alley between this building and the William Penn House, originally the driveway to the stables of both, gives a view of the original brickwork and structure of both houses.

21. The ROSEMONT HOUSE *(private, open on Old New Castle Day)*, 110 Delaware St., restored by Miss Ruth Colby in 1936, is one of the typical New Castle houses incorporating in the structure Martin Rosemont's 1675 dwelling. In the back wing the ceiling rafters are heavy beams of oak covered with boards. Whitewash of so many layers that it resembled plaster was found on the boards when the ceiling was cut through in remodeling. The front section of the house was built in the early 1700's. Its unspoiled main features, the belt course three bricks deep, the denticulated band adorning the cornice, and its excellent proportions make this one of the most charming small houses in New Castle.

22. The VAN LEUVENIGH HOUSE *(private, open on Old New Castle Day)*, end of the Strand, was built (1732), of brick, now covered with stucco. French influence appears in the proportions of the house, its unusual gambrel roof, and the simple cornice with the rectangular modillions; it is traceable also in the fine woodwork and decoration of the fireplaces. Zachariah Van Leuvenigh, chief magistrate of New Castle during the Revolution, received here the post riders bearing news of the battles of Lexington and Bunker Hill, signed the messages, and bade the riders Godspeed to Baltimore.

23. The OLD JEFFERSON HOTEL *(private)*, NE. corner Strand and Delaware St., of brick, three and one half stories in height, with broad gable, is now converted into apartments. It was originally the office, hotel, dwelling, and supply center for the heads of one of New Castle's largest enterprises of the eighteenth and early nineteenth century—the general shipping and naval supply business of Riddle and Bird. The wharf on this property is public and affords an excellent view of the Delaware. The great fire of 1824 started in the rear of the building, but was swept up the Strand by the wind, leaving the main part toward Delaware Street unharmed. The name Jefferson, for an owner of the hotel in later years, is discernible beneath the iron initials of James Riddle.

24. The OLD FARMERS BANK *(private, open on Old New Castle Day)*, 4 Strand, is a square, flat-roofed brick building with brownstone

trim and quoins, built (1845) by the Farmers Bank, which opened that year with Kensey Johns, Jr., as president. The garden in the rear of the house is the site of stables for the horses that first drew the cars of the New Castle & Frenchtown Railroad.

25. The GUNNING BEDFORD HOUSE *(private, open on Old New Castle Day)*, 6 Strand, built about 1730 of brick, by John Van Gezel, was left high above the pavement when the Strand was leveled in 1804. A few years before his death in 1797, Gunning Bedford, Revolutionary patriot and soldier, and Governor of the State (1796–97) lived here. Caleb P. Bennett, Revolutionary officer and Governor (1833–36), opened an inn here, 1803. John Van Gezel, descendant of a Dutch founder, died here 1783.

26. The McINTIRE HOUSE *(private, open on Old New Castle Day)*, 8 Strand, one of the very old smaller houses, is notable for the harmony of design and beauty of execution in the paneling and fireplaces of the interior. Architects regard the date of the building as about 1690. The builder is unknown, but the house long bore the name of one of its occupants in pre-Revolutionary days, Richard McWilliam, Jr., who married Zachariah Van Leuvenigh's daughter, Rebecca.

27. The OLD STAGE TAVERN *(private)*, N. side of Packet Alley, on Strand between Delaware and Harmony Sts., is a brick structure now converted into a dwelling. It was erected as a store immediately following a fire in 1824 that destroyed a popular stage tavern, and the old name remains. PACKET ALLEY was once a crowded street down which notable visitors, ships' crews and immigrants, hastened to the packet boats docked below. It was also a thoroughfare for great Conestoga wagons hauling grain, and packet stages loaded with goods for western pioneers.

28. The READ HOUSE *(private, open on Old New Castle Day)*, NW. side of Strand, between Harmony and Delaware Sts., in the late Georgian Colonial mode, was built by George Read, son of the Signer of the Declaration of Independence.

Built of brick, two and a half stories, the house is broader than its height, its four basement windows with marble lintels and vertical iron bars flanking the flight of nine marble entrance steps. All of the elements of the exterior are symmetrical: two high broad windows on each side of the monumental entrance doorway with its great fanlight above and glazed panels at the sides; two similar broad windows on each side of the Palladian window on the second story, the latter window designed in proportion to the entrance doorway and immediately above it; two dormers in the roof set above the tier of windows on each side of the central

HALLWAY, READ HOUSE, NEW CASTLE

THE DEEMER HOUSE, NEW CASTLE

apertures; a balustraded platform extending along the ridge of the roof, stopped by chimneys in pairs at each end. Outside the Palladian window above the entrance doorway, a curved balcony of delicate ironwork forms an exquisite detail of the façade and harmonizes with the delicate tracery of ornament on much of the exterior woodwork.

A great Palladian window on the north side of the house is a striking feature of the interior, lighting the stairway. The interior is designed with vigor and restraint without over-emphasis of decoration. The long hall from entrance to garden door at the rear is broken by two archways. The fireplaces in the three great rooms on the first floor rival in striking effect the Palladian window of the stairs. A double doorway between the reception room and the living room, reaching the cornice of the 13-foot ceiling, is crowned by an arch in which the fanlight is composed of six concentric arcs, each glazed in panes of different shape, the whole a delicate traceried design. The swinging mahogany doors of comparatively simple paneling are nearly as wide as their height.

Peter Crowding, Philadelphia contractor, constantly supervised the construction and detail of the mansion during the several years of its building (1797–1801), and much of the material was brought from Philadelphia. The mason, James Traquair, was also from the Quaker city.

George Read, the younger, native of New Castle, was a jurist who served for 30 years as U. S. District Attorney. John M. Clayton, Secretary of State, under President Taylor, lived here for a short time while building Buena Vista, several miles south of New Castle.

29. The IMMANUEL PARISH HOUSE *(open by permission; open on Old New Castle Day)*, corner Strand and Harmony St., was built about 1801 by the contractor, Peter Crowding, for the Charles Thomas-Mc-Calmont family. This double entrance house, designed in the late Georgian Colonial style as a hotel and dwelling, was used mostly as a private residence before Immanuel Church received it as the gift of a descendant of the first owner. Its three and a half stories with a deck above on the peak of the roof made the house a landmark from the river and surrounding country.

30. The AULL HOUSES, E. side of the Strand, of considerable interest architecturally, are survivors of the fire of 1824. Of these, Nos. 49-51, built about 1797, are frame with flush clapboards; Nos. 53-55, built 25 years later, are of brick with stone belt course.

31. The HERMITAGE, W. edge of New Castle near the William Penn School, was named by Senator Van Dyke, who bought here "141 acres with brick messuage" of seventeenth century construction from David and Mary Finney April 1, 1801, and added the larger wing to make a summer home.

32. The DEEMER HOUSE, NW. corner 6th and South Sts., is a typical example of the Victorian period fine house.

33. The NEW CASTLE AND FRENCHTOWN TICKET BOX, on the south side of Delaware St. near wharf, is a small building in continuous use since 1832, when tickets were handed out through its window to passengers of the N. C. & F. R. R., one of the earliest in the country, later as a crossing watchbox. It is now restored, on its original site.

POINTS OF INTEREST IN ENVIRONS

Swanwick or Regency House, *2.6 m.;* Buena Vista, *5.2 m. (see Tour 1).* Bellanca Airplane Plant and flying field, *1.1 m.;* New Castle Common, *1.2 m.;* Boothhurst, *1.5 m.;* Glasgow, *11.4 m. (see Tour 4).* Newport, *4.3 m. (see Tour 7).* Delaware Park, racetrack, *9 m. (see Tour 8).* Deemer's Beach, *2.5 m.;* Lexington, *7 m.;* Delaware City, *9.7 m.;* Fort Du Pont, *10.1 m.;* Fort Delaware, *12 m.* via Fort Du Pont; Port Penn, *14 m.;* Augustine Beach, *14.6 m. (see Tour 10).*

Rehoboth

Railroad Office: Rehoboth Ave. for Pennsylvania R.R. (no passenger service).

Bus Station: Rehoboth Ave. for The Short Line, Greyhound, Trailways.

Airport: 2 *m.* W. on State 14; scheduled service in summer, large field for private planes.

Wharves: Public Wharf on Lewes-Rehoboth Canal, ft. Rehoboth Ave.; private yacht basin, Henlopen Acres, available to visiting craft on request; 6 ft. depth at low water from Delaware Bay.

Accommodations: Five hotels (one for Negroes), boarding houses, tourist lodges. Public trailer camp in Shaw Park, Rehoboth Ave., approved motels. Private trailer camp, Henlopen Acres.

Information: Office of Town Manager, Town Hall, Rehoboth Ave.

Motion Picture Houses: Three.

Bathing: Public bath house, Boardwalk at Rehoboth Ave.; undressing in automobiles forbidden; section of beach reserved for Negroes.

Camping: Permitted in sand dunes on State lands, N. and S. of Rehoboth.

Fishing: Surf fishing on beach; deep-sea fishing; power boats for hire at Dewey Beach, at Lewes and Indian River Inlet; fresh-water fishing, license required.

Hunting: In season; nearby uplands for quail and rabbits, marshes for ducks and geese; license required.

Riding: No riding on beach within town limits.

Sailing: Sailboats and motorboats for hire, sailing parties taken out, Rehoboth Bay, 1 *m.* S. on State 14.

Annual Events: Art Exhibit, Boardwalk; Art League Studio, July-Aug.; Invitation Golf Tournament, Aug.; Artists Costume Ball in July.

REHOBOTH (10 alt., 2,500 pop. in winter), on the Atlantic Ocean five miles south of Cape Henlopen, and the largest summer resort in Delaware, occupies one of the few spots along the South Atlantic coast where the mainland extends to the surf itself. Large stands of tall loblolly pine and holly, in the Pines section of town, approach within a city block of the sea, making an effective background to a widespread town of many pleasant cottages of all sizes, and typical resort hotels and boarding houses.

In summer, during the early part of the week, Rehoboth has the appearance of a quiet residential community. Then at the week-end, visitors arriving by automobile, bus, and airplanes tax the accommodations in the town, and holiday crowds sometimes cause an overflow into environs within a 10-mile radius. Though Rehoboth is often called "Delaware's Summer Capital," Delawareans are in the minority during the season. The largest single group comes by the Chesapeake Bridge from Washington, D.C. (to which this is the nearest ocean resort directly east) and includes

THE BEACH AT REHOBOTH

members of Congress, Government officials, members of foreign legations and their families.

Some vacationists spend their days on the broad white sandy beach, bathing in the surf or sun-bathing among the hundreds of brightly-colored beach umbrellas. Some are off fishing, sketching, sailing, playing golf, or playing bridge on front porches. As the evening progresses there is dancing in several public places, and the beach until long after midnight is dotted with driftwood fires.

Church denominations include Methodist, Presbyterian, Episcopal, and Roman Catholic. The annual Rehoboth Art Exhibits, showing the work of Delaware and other artists, are largely attended. The Rehoboth Art League has its studios at Henlopen Acres, a suburb; also a Colonial cypress-shingled farmhouse where classes are taught and exhibits are held from time to time. Flower shows and courses are held during the summer.

Mosquitoes are almost eliminated by an efficient State control of the nearby marshes. Fresh meats, poultry, pasteurized milk, fruit, vegetables, and seafood come into town daily from the surrounding region. The local supply of servants is not enough for the summer demand, and many families bring theirs along.

Rehoboth out of season is a pleasant place of green aromatic pines, holly trees bright with berries, and mild climate. Snow seldom lies more than a few hours, and there is no mud. Besides the native residents there is a small winter colony of persons who live here because of the woods, the sea air, the golf, fishing, and hunting, and the comfortable charm of Sussex County.

The Biblical name of the resort comes from nearby Rehoboth Bay, named by English settlers before 1675; it is said to mean "room enough" (Gen. 26; 22). The forest land of Rehoboth Neck, where the town stands, was taken up in great tracts about that time. During the next century larger and larger fields of corn, tobacco, flax, wheat, and other crops surrounded the cypress-sheathed plantation houses and the smaller slave quarters. Little account, however, was paid to the beach here as a summer-ing place until 1855, when the State granted five acres of beachland to the Rehoboth Hotel Company if they would build a hotel. The hotel was not built, and it was not until 1870 that Louis Tredenick opened a combination summer hotel and fall gunning-camp at Dewey Beach (see Tour 2C).

In 1872 a group, first calling themselves the Rehoboth Association and later the Rehoboth Beach Camp-Meeting Association of the Methodist Episcopal Church, bought a tract on the beach front and laid out streets. The next year two hotels were built and some cottages erected. (Houses dating from this period are recognizable by their sharp peaks and ginger-bread trim.) The camp-meeting grounds were a fine grove near the present canal bridge, to which in 1878 the railroad was extended from Lewes. The campers came in wagons, mostly, bringing everything needed for a two-weeks' stay and lived in small frame "tents" arranged in the usual circle. In 1881 the camp-meetings were discontinued, but despite the mosquito plague, more and more cottages were built and the summer population grew. Excursion trains brought Saturday and Sunday crowds, and regular trains were met by a half-dozen hotel hacks whose drivers were paid to corral as many customers as possible. Horn's Pier was a noted and garish emporium until the great storm of 1914 destroyed it and washed away the boardwalk, Surf Avenue, and many of the beach-front cottages as well. Horn's moved back half a block but Surf Avenue has not been given up by the sea.

In the early 1920's the railroad began to feel the competition of the new Coleman du Pont Boulevard down the State, and rail passenger traffic dwindled to nothing after the paved highway reached here from George-town in 1925. Between 1925 and 1929 a real estate and building boom skyrocketed the value of lots, and scores of cottages arose on fields, sand

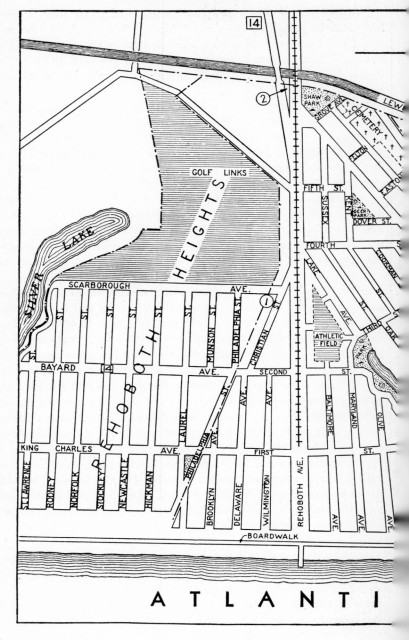

14

2

SHAW PARK

GROVE AV.

CEMETERY

LEW

FELTON

EASTON

FIFTH ST.

SUSSEX

KENT

DEER PARK

DOVER ST.

FOURTH

LOOKMAN

GOLF LINKS

HEIGHTS

SILVER LAKE

1

SCARBOROUGH AVE.

REHOBOTH ST.

ATHLETIC FIELD

PARK

ART

THIRD

OAK

SCARBOROUGH ST.

MUNSON ST.

PHILADELPHIA ST.

CHRISTIAN ST.

BAYARD AVE.

14

SECOND ST.

BALTIMORE ST.

MARYLAND ST.

OLIVE

LAUREL

PHILADELPHIA

AVE.

AVE.

KING

CHARLES AVE.

FIRST ST.

ST. LAWRENCE

RODNEY

NORFOLK

STOCKLEY

NEWCASTLE

HICKMAN

BROOKLYN

DELAWARE

WILMINGTON

REHOBOTH AVE.

AVE.

AVE.

AVE.

BOARDWALK

ATLANTI

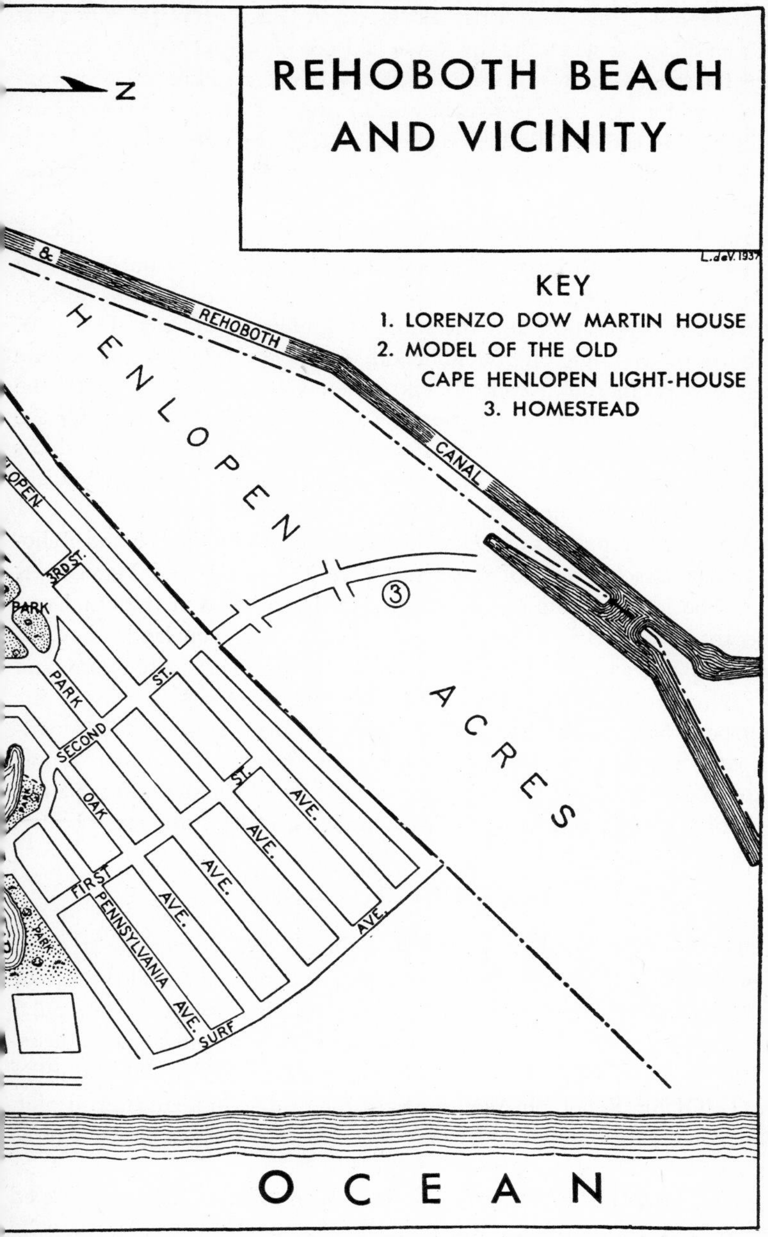

REHOBOTH BEACH
AND VICINITY
N
L. deV. 1937
KEY
1. LORENZO DOW MARTIN HOUSE
2. MODEL OF THE OLD
CAPE HENLOPEN LIGHT-HOUSE
3. HOMESTEAD
&
REHOBOTH
CANAL
HENLOPEN
ACRES
3
3RD ST.
PARK
PARK
ST.
SECOND
ST.
OAK
FIRST
PENNSYLVANIA
AVE.
AVE.
AVE.
AVE.
AVE.
AVE.
SURF
OCEAN

dunes, and in the Pines near little Lake Gerar. A large area of the Pines was made a public park when the town was laid out. Adjacent woods, recently offered for sale by the town, were bought by Irénée du Pont, of Wilmington, who sold a part to persons who would preserve as many trees as possible in placing cottages. Besides large holly trees, the Pines contains much dogwood flowering in May; one naturalist has reported seeing 275 species of birds in the area.

The first mosquito-control work here was undertaken half-heartedly in 1909 by the Rehoboth Board of Health, but lapsed, and not until the late 1920's did the town make another serious effort backed by the Village Improvement Association and the militant leadership of Mrs. Henry B. Thompson of Wilmington and Rehoboth *(see Tour 2C)*, through whose efforts, largely, mosquito control was undertaken in Delaware with the aid of the Civilian Conservation Corps, 1933. In the past 15 years, for the first time in Rehoboth's history, persons have been able to be out of doors at night in comfort. Since the abatement of the plague the resort has undergone vigorous development, especially since World War II.

Suburban developments of Rehoboth are Rehoboth-by-the-Sea and Rehoboth Indian Beach, south of the resort *(see Tour 2C)*, and HENLOPEN ACRES. The latter, adjoining the north side, lying between the canal and the ocean, contains 175 acres of woods, glades, and open land on which building is restricted to high suburban standards. The yacht basin and trailer camp are available to the public at reasonable fees.

Rehoboth has an adequate sewage system, also an efficient fire department, and has the city-manager form of government. The water supply is pure. Year-round activities include a laundry, clothes-cleaning plants, two dairies, a bank, and a large cannery, movies, roller rink, youth center.

POINTS OF INTEREST

1. The LORENZO DOW MARTIN HOUSE, SW. corner Christian St. and Scarborough Ave., was the farmhouse of the man who sold the site of Rehoboth to the Rehoboth Association in 1872. It is a small rectangular frame building, painted yellow, in the familiar style of old Sussex houses.

2. A ¼ scale wood MODEL OF THE OLD CAPE HENLOPEN LIGHTHOUSE, Rehoboth Ave. just E. of the bridge, in a landscaped plot, commemorates the famous old tower that fell into the sea in 1926 *(see Tour 14A)*.

3. THE HOMESTEAD *(private)*, Henlopen Acres, a cypress-shingled house with recent additions, was built about 1742 by Peter Marsh, who

THE HOMESTEAD, REHOBOTH

bought a tract called Young's Hope from "Richard Hinman, Gent." Marsh, it is said, settled here to be near the pirate gold he thought was buried in the dunes nearby. The walls of the main part and interior partitions are filled with brick in the manner of the day, and the framing is of hand-hewn walnut instead of the usual oak. Hand-made doors, the primitive paneling on the chimney breasts, the wide floor boards, and the other original details have been carefully preserved in the restoration by the architect-owner, Col. W. S. Corkran, who used the original style in the additions. The formal garden is a show-place of the county, with a salty flavor lent by salvaged anchors, capstans, and other old marine gear. By tradition the well on the front slope is a "wishing-well," sought in past times by young couples to make their vows to each other.

POINTS OF INTEREST IN ENVIRONS

Marsh Family Cemetery, *2.7 m.;* Indian River Inlet, *7.7 m.;* Red Mill Pond, fishing, *8.1 m.;* Fort Miles, U.S. Army, Anti-Aircraft, *9 m.* distant; Belltown, all-Negro village, *6.4 m. (see Tour 14).* Site of Cape Henlopen Light, Point o' Capes, *10 m.* by road, *5 m.* on foot by beach *(see Tour 14A).* Burton's Pond, fishing, *8.8 m;* St. George's Chapel, *10.8 m.;* "Down Sockum," Moor or Indian community, *12-17 m.;* Site of Nanticoke Indian Pow-wow, Riverdale Park, *15.4 m.;* Millsboro Pond, fishing, *18.2 m.;* Great Pocomoke Swamp, *30 m. (see Tour 15).*

Wilmington

Railroad Stations: B. & O. Station, Delaware Ave. and Dupont St., for Baltimore & Ohio R.R., Pennsylvania Station, Front and French Sts., for Pennsylvania R.R.

Bus Stations: Bus Center, Second and French Sts., for Greyhound, Short Line, Diamond State Lines, Trailways, South Jersey Coach Line, Public Service Line of New Jersey, Salem County Coach Line; Pennsylvania Station for Red Star Lines. Buses for Chester and Philadelphia stop at S.W. Cor. of 9th and Shipley Sts. New Castle buses (no station) stop on Fifth St. S. between Market and Shipley Sts.

Piers: Wilson Line, E. end of Fourth St., for steamboats to Chester and Philadelphia.

Taxis: Fare within first zone, approximately the city limits, for first passenger, 45¢, 25¢ for each additional passenger.

Streetcars: Trackless trolley coaches. Extensive service; 15¢ fare or 5 tokens for 70¢; free transfers when requested; no fare for children under age of 5.

Traffic Regulations: Speed limit, 25 m.p.h. Downtown parking is permitted for limited periods. Parking meters used in central business section. All-night parking is forbidden. Watch for numerous traffic signs and signals.

Accommodations: Eleven hotels; wide range of boarding houses and rooming houses. Good motels on US 13, S. of city.

Information Service: Travelers' Aid Society, Pennsylvania Station, Front and French Sts.; Delaware Motor Club (AAA), 911 Tatnall St.; Delaware Automobile Association (AMA), 1310 Washington St.; Delaware State Chamber of Commerce, 1114 King St.

Radio Stations: WDEL-AM-FM; WDEL-TV; WTUX; WAMS.

Theaters and Motion Picture Houses: The Playhouse, Du Pont Building, Broadway plays shows and concerts; Strand Theater, 2412 Market St., different play each week, professional. Four first-run motion picture houses; numerous neighborhood houses.

Golf: Rock Manor Course; 18 holes, greens fee $1.50; weekends during season $2.25.

Picnic Grounds: Special picnic grounds are set aside in Alapocas, Brandywine, Bringhurst, Canby, Eden, Rockford, and Sellers Parks, all of which are included in public park system. Permit required to build a fire. Park Commission, Public Bldg.

Races: See State GENERAL INFORMATION.

Swimming: Five swimming pools maintained by Park Commission and open to public either free of charge or for fees not greater than 25¢ (depending on day, time of day, and pool) are as follows: Price Run Pool, 23d and Church Sts., Canby Pool, S. Clayton and Oak Sts.; Brandywine Pool, Park Drive and Adams Sts.; Kirkwood Pool, 13th and Pine Sts.; Kruse Pool (for Negroes), 14th and Poplar Sts.

Tennis: Several courts are maintained in public parks and permits for their use are issued without charge by Board of Park Commissioners, City Hall, Tenth and King Sts.

Horseback Riding: Bridle paths are located in Brandywine Park, Alapocas Woods, Rockford Park, and Canby Park.

Walks: Public parks along Brandywine River afford opportunity for walks through picturesque scenery; Canby, Bringhurst, and Sellers Parks, also included in public system, are especially suitable for solitary rambles.

WILMINGTON LOOKING WEST ACROSS TOWN CENTER
Credit: Lubitsh & Bungarz

Annual Events: Sunnyfield Horse Show, 1 day in October, Brandywine Raceway, Concord Pike and Naaman's Rd.; Wilmington Flower Market, day in May, Rockford Park; Old Swedes Anniversary, Trinity Sunday, at the Church; Wilmington Country Club Invitation Golf Tournament, one day in June; Big Quarterly, Negro religious festival, last Sunday in August; Wilmington Kennel Club Show, one day in October, Hercules Farms, Lancaster Pike; Wilmington Symphony Orchestra Public Concerts, variable dates winter and spring.

WILMINGTON (alt. 225; pop. 110,356), only town of more than 7,000 population in Delaware, contains with the immediate suburban area more than half the State's 318,085 inhabitants. It is situated on the west bank of the Delaware River, and occupies a series of low, rolling hills overlooking the river at its broadest point, and a strip of low land, much of it formerly marshes, a mile to two miles in width between the river and the hills. From "The Rocks," landing place of the Swedes, first permanent settlers, the city extends fanlike between two streams—the Christina River and Brandywine Creek—and beyond these streams north into wooded highlands and south into undulating lowlands. From the lowlands, the slopes of the main central area of the city rise terrace-like to a crest crowned by several high office buildings observable for miles in all directions.

The banks of the Christina River, navigable to the heart of the city for vessels of 20-foot draft, are lined with ship and carbuilding plants, machine shops, warehouses, storage yards, and other industries for approximately three miles of the river's winding course through the southern parts of the city. On the south bank near its mouth, a modern marine terminal, constructed in 1923, makes Wilmington a seaport, as it was formerly, when a deeper and broader Christina accommodated sailing ships from all parts of the world.

The main city crowds densely about tiny, open Rodney Square near the tall buildings that mark its business center. A few blocks away at Brandywine Creek Bridge is the entrance to the one parkway that penetrates the solidly built-up central city. Other parked open spaces are at long distances from the center and the large area of parks lies chiefly on or beyond the city boundaries.

Wilmington's main streets run at right angles, those from north to south bearing the names of trees, personages, and presidents, and those running east and west bearing numbers. Market Street, the chief business thoroughfare, is also the dividing line of the east and west numbering of the lateral streets. Parallel with this street run the other main north and south business streets, King to the east and Shipley, Orange, and Tatnall to the west. From Market Street business has spread along many of the cross streets, notably West Ninth and West Tenth Streets. A number of avenues, generally wider than the streets, crisscross various sections of the city. Of these, Delaware Avenue comes nearest to the town center, joining West Tenth Street at Tatnall. Baynard Boulevard is a wide tree-lined avenue extending from the north end of Washington Street Bridge to the city line. From north to south near the western end of the town, the Bancroft Parkway, a double street with parked area in the center, extends from Union Park Gardens and the close-built, low-rental Woodlawn "flats" at one end to $50,000 houses on large plots at the other.

Motor traffic converging through all sections of the city into the narrow streets of the business section intensifies the effect of congestion created by the solidly built-up blocks, though vistas through the straight streets to the river, the creeks, and the hills, serve somewhat as relief to pedestrian and driver as they await their turns at the crossings.

Along King Street on Wednesdays and Saturdays is the street market that has continued without break from early days. Moved from Market to King Street when the first horse car line was established on the former street, it now occupies nearly nine blocks between Front and Tenth Streets and changes from east side in summer to west side in winter. Farmers back their cars of produce against the curb and sell directly to the consumer. The market is thronged on the appointed days; there is no room nor mercy for the mere loiterer. He is shoved in the back by huge market baskets or assailed from the front by housewives who move forward with eyes fixed upon the produce-covered stands. The displays are tempting, the farmers are jocular with their customers, there is constant making of change from shot-bags, and rosy-cheeked farm damsels bend over apple baskets and measure out produce. Market-day is not likely to lose its savor for the dyed-in-the-wool Wilmingtonian. Other street markets are on Madison Street, six blocks west of Market, and on Lincoln Street, 19 blocks west. Flower markets fill some of the down-town cross streets on the same days.

The people of Wilmington are still chiefly native Delawareans of an admixture of the early Swedish, Finnish, and Dutch strains and of the earliest Quaker and non-Quaker English, with a goodly infusion of French, Irish, and Scotch, especially since the middle of the eighteenth century. But native Americans from other States form a large and rapidly increasing part of the population. Italians and Poles are substantial groups having their own communities since the days of industrial growth following the Civil War. Ukrainians, also, though a much smaller group, have kept together in a neighborhood where they maintain their Old World culture. Germans, Russian and German Jews, Scandinavians, Greeks, and a few Asiatics form minority groups.

The Negroes, present from the earliest settlement, form slightly more than 15 percent of the population and are employed in industry and in service occupations and to a limited extent have entered the professions. They live in communities of generally bad housing at high rents, with a few better sections, and suffer from the lack of parks, playgrounds, and other recreation facilities. Despite disadvantages the Negroes in Wilmington play their part in the local life with interest and good humor.

A Negro custom prevailing since slave days, of holding the August quarterly religious meeting for the whole Middle Atlantic States in Wilmington on the last Sunday of the month, has given the city annually one of the most colorful religious festivals in the region—"Big Quarterly."

On that day, every available space within the building lines of French and Walnut Streets from Eighth to Ninth Streets is phalanxed with tables and concessions of varied types. Almost every house is an eating place for the day. The feasting starts upon arrival, early in the morning, and the menu consists in part of fried chicken, chicken potpie, ham and cabbage, hot corn pone, greens and side meat, frankfurters, watermelons, soft drinks, vari-colored "ades," pig's feet, and dishes of unknown origin. Barkers shout loudly the virtues of their wares. Every effort is made to inveigle the passers-by to partake.

To the casual observer "Big Quarterly" presents a kaleidoscopic mass of humanity, vari-colored in dress and hue of skin—sleek, slender, buxom and fat. Milling throngs of primitive folk are gathered to worship their God, shouting, singing, praying and giving vent to unbounded enthusiasms. To those taking part, this is a day of joy, gladness, and freedom. Those of more serious mien attend services in churches and outdoor meetings which run continuously from early morning till late at night.

The first Swedish expedition to the Delaware landed at The Rocks in 1638. Peter Minuit, the commander, conducted his parleys with the Indians, built Fort Christina and departed in the *Kalmar Nyckel*. During the building of the fort with its dwelling and storehouse inside the ramparts, the Indians came filing down the trails or gliding along the Christina in strings of canoes laden with pelts, and Minuit sailed with a rich cargo. As the successive Swedish expeditions arrived under the commanders, Peter Hollander Ridder, Johan Printz, and Johan Classon Rising, sections of the site of Wilmington along the creeks and up over the hills were cultivated. Near the fort the little hamlet of Christina Harbor showed new houses from year to year and in 1654–55 had a building boom, spurred by a town plan made by the Swedish engineer, Peter Lindeström, and by the many new settlers and supplies arriving with Governor Rising.

In 1655 Governor Stuyvesant brought his ships and soldiers into the Christina, surrounded the fort and hamlet by water and land, and after a series of conferences, took them over without bloodshed. The Dutch ships and soldiers were withdrawn, and Governor Rising and some other Swedes soon returned to Sweden. The name of the fort became Fort Altena, but otherwise life there was little changed. A few Dutchmen acquired land on both sides of the Christina near the fort, but the Swedes kept their officers, their land, and their clergymen.

Within ten years, Sir Robert Carr had stationed English soldiers at the

STREET MARKET, WILMINGTON

Fort, and the people swore allegiance to the English James, Duke of York. Some Englishmen acquired the land the Dutch officers had taken from Governor Rising on both sides of the Christina, but the Swedish, Dutch, and Finnish planters were undisturbed. The Duke confirmed their land titles if they paid a fee, and if not they often kept the land anyway. Trade restrictions were modified and quit-rents fairly well evaded during the nearly two decades under the Duke, so the wharves along the Christina were the scene of a thriving trade when William Penn, the new English proprietor, sailed by on his way up the river in October, 1682.

About 1690, a young visitor from Sweden, Andrew Printz, nephew of the former Governor, was so impressed by these Swedes who were prosperous under English rule, but in need of books and clergymen, that he told the story at home where it finally reached King Charles XI. As a result, three ministers arrived in 1697. One of them, Eric Bjorck (1668–1740), remained at Christina. On May 28, 1698, shortly after Bjorck's arrival, a new stone church, "Old Swedes," was begun at the graveyard near the old fort by English workmen, with most of the people helping, hauling stone, sand, and lumber.

At the time of its dedication, Old Swedes was one of a cluster of buildings near the old fort. In 1671, two Swedes, Johan Andersson Stalcop and Dr. Tymen Stidham, had owned between them all the land from the Christina River to the Brandywine, and from the neighborhood of The Rocks to Rattlesnake Run. Stalcop's land extended north from the Christina; Stidham's, south from the Brandywine. Across the Brandywine was the land of Jacob Vandever, a Dutch settler; across the Christina was a farm, owned by Jean Paul Jacquet, who had been first Dutch Director at Fort Casimir. North of the river was land, once Peter Alrichs's, nephew of Jacob Alrichs, the second Governor at New Amstel. Stalcop, who died before 1685, had granted half his land to Samuel Peterson and Lars Cornelison. He willed the remainder in two plots, one each to his wife and his son Andrew. Peterson kept his land; Cornelison sold his to Matthias de Foss, who sold it to Charles Pickering. The Pickering tract became the glebe of Old Swedes Church by purchase from John Stalcop, Jr. Peterson's son sold the Peterson land to Andrew Justison. These two tracts, the glebe and Justison's, adjoined, starting along the Christina and running diagonally in a broad band of cultivated fields, groves of hardwood trees and heavy forest, northwestward to Rattlesnake Run, a mile and a half distant, across the site of the main built-up section of present Wilmington.

About 1730 Andrew Justison had the eastern portion of his land surveyed for the purpose of laying out a town. The town plot began at French Street, extended along the Christina to West Street and north to Third Street. Some lots were sold in 1732, and in 1734, Thomas Willing, who had married Justison's daughter, Catherine, became associated with his father-in-law in the development of the town, that was then called Willingtown. In 1736 Justison deeded to Willing in two plots all the land along the Christina to Willing's original land. The latter was a ten-acre tract extending from present Monroe to Harrison Street between Fifth and Seventh.

Willingtown was meant for a farmer's town, a place of trade, and for the service of ships and mills. A ropewalk and a sail loft were among the immediate enterprises. Free ground for a markethouse which the townsmen might erect was offered the first group of lot-owners. The Swedes, much interested in the sale of lots, because their glebe land would be in demand as the town grew, made Charles Christopher Springer their attorney and trustee to act with the churchwardens in promoting their interests.

In the spring of 1735, William Shipley visited Willingtown, then a village of 15 to 20 houses. He bought a lot "in Second Street," came again in August and bought all of the town west of Market Street (bounded by Market and West, Christina Creek and Fifth Street). In the fall he moved with his family from Ridley Township in Pennsylvania to a small brick dwelling, set back from the south side of Fourth Street between Shipley and Orange, and lived there until his mansion house at the southwest corner of Fourth and Shipley was completed in the following year. An influential Quaker, a man of means and enterprise recently come from England (1725) with many families like his own, married to Elizabeth Levis after the death of his first wife, Mary Ann Tatnall, Shipley produced such a boom for the new town that the number of houses doubled within a year. Soon his building lots, market house, brewery, shipping wharf, all were in demand by Quaker families—the majority of whom came because of Shipley to live in the town or its environs and to contribute to its growth. Thus Wilmington became "a Quaker Town." Some Quakers and numerous other English, whose families had lived in the surrounding country from much earlier days, also bought lots as investments. Swedish and Dutch farmers were among the lot buyers who built town houses. Some of their sons married Quakers, and Quaker sons married the daughters of landowning Swedes, Dutch, and Finns.

Until 1739, there was no formal government. Consent of all the townspeople was sought to correct abuses and to make improvements. This did not prevent an open breach over the location of the first market.

Soon after his arrival, Shipley put up a large market house on his own land "in High Street" (Fourth) between Shipley and Market. Only two blocks away "in Second Street," running east from Market, was the site given by Willing for the town market. This had not been built because those interested did not provide the money until Shipley's market was up. Then a number of these "first families" protested the building of a privately-owned market. The disagreement hastened the incorporating of the town, already asked for, each side in the market quarrel appealing for support of its market site to Thomas Penn, proprietor of the Three-Counties-on-Delaware.

Meanwhile, the first of all first families, the Swedes and Dutch, came in strongly for letting Shipley's market be the town market and for letting a second market house wait upon need. In the end, Shipley's market was bought by 82 subscribers and made public. The die-hards for the other site built a handsomer market than Shipley's in Second Street, and when Thomas Penn sent a charter for the Borough in November, it provided that sites and market days in the future were to be decided by vote among the burgesses, freeholders, and such inhabitants as paid an annual rent of five pounds, or over. As the result of the first popular vote, the Saturday Market and Spring Fair were held at the market place in High Street; the Wednesday Market and Fall Fair at the market place in Second Street.

It was very likely the markethouse disagreement, with Thomas Willing on one side and William Shipley on the other, that caused the proprietor to change the name of the town from Willingtown to Wilmington. The name, Wilmington, enough like the original in the old script to look almost like an error, was given in tribute to Penn's friend, Spencer Compton, Earl of Wilmington (1673–1743), who had no local association until the writing of this charter. At the first election under the new charter, William Shipley became chief burgess. That same year, with David Ferris, Joshua Way, and others, he built a brig, the *Wilmington,* for trade with the West Indies. She was loaded chiefly with oak-staves, flour, beef, and butter, and with her sailing, rivalry with New Castle—shipping port and port of call six miles down the river—was established. Wilmington was already benefiting from its nearness to that long-established port. Travelers and immigrants who landed there en route to Philadelphia, usually stopped at Wilmington, and sometimes stayed, as did many Irish Protestant refugees at this time.

Ten years later, George Ross, minister at Immanuel Church at New Castle, writes to London of "the wretched Fate of the poor town" (New Castle), and adds: "This dying condition is partly owing to an upstart

THE PUBLIC BUILDING, WILMINGTON

village lying on a neighboring creek, which yields a convenient port to the adjacent Country."

Wilmington both profited and suffered from the attractiveness of its site to smugglers and the ease with which cargoes of rum, tobacco, and dress-goods could be loaded and unloaded along the navigable creeks. When illicit cargoes of incoming vessels had been disposed of, the crews sought the town to celebrate, and peace in the idyllic hamlet was shattered. The burgesses in feasance of their office built a "cage" or jail in this same eventful year, 1740, and put up stocks and a whipping-post in front of it. The newly-arrived Irish built the First Presbyterian Church (near present Tenth and Market) on the road from the Brandywine Ford to The Rocks; the Quakers had built a meeting house on West Street near Fourth in 1738, which probably, even that early, was used also as a school.

By 1754 there was a subscription library, and in 1761, James Adams established the first printing press. Within a few years an institution of higher education, the Wilmington Academy, had been built below Ninth

Street on Market, at the edge of a grove of ancient oaks beneath which pupils and instructors walked, and where meetings were held as in an amphitheater. Lawrence Girelius, the last Swedish-speaking minister at Old Swedes, was the first president of the board. In 1774 the town burgesses, among whom was John McKinly, Irish Presbyterian and future President of the Delaware State, met in a newly-built town hall—a second-story addition to the Second Street Market House. Shipley and Willing were dead; the town had so developed as to include both their market-houses in a well built-up and popular business and residence community.

Another profitable market, at the wharves of the Christina, that disturbed the conscience of many citizens, dealt in slaves, imported chiefly by Willing and Morris of Philadelphia. The sales were announced in Pennsylvania newspapers and most of the slaves were bought by large planters south of Wilmington. The few bought locally were usually given their freedom when they had worked out their cost at the prevailing rate for labor.

As the controversy with England sharpened during the few years before the Revolution, the peace-loving town became a center of the patriot cause. News of the Boston Port Bill stirred deeply the local merchants and shippers who could picture Wilmington in a similar plight. Protection of its mills, vital to the American cause, was a concern of the Congress, and for the raising of money and men the town's resources were soon called upon. This may have had something to do with the selection (February 12, 1777) of Dr. John McKinly of Wilmington, physician, four times chief burgess and four times second burgess, as the first President of the Delaware State under the first constitution, adopted by convention at New Castle, September, 1776. He was familiar with the finances of the State, having been a signer of the 30,000 pounds in paper money voted by the Assembly in 1775. (The bills, printed by James Adams, bore on their reverse side the legend: "To counterfeit is death.")

One of the first naval battles of the war was fought against the English frigates, the *Roebuck* and the *Liverpool,* by the schooner *Wasp* and several row-galleys off the mouth of Christina Creek, in May 1776. Fort Christina was again made a place of defense; the town and its environment were charted and mapped. The day of General Howe's landing at Elk River on the opposite side of the Peninsula, August 25, 1777, General Washington with his main army came to Wilmington. Most of his troops encamped beyond the town on the road through Newport, while Washington used as headquarters the house of Captain Joseph Bennett, a seaman, at 303 West Street. Here he received messages from scouting parties and set out upon his personal reconnoitering with Greene and Lafayette.

The major event of the war at Wilmington occurred on September 13, 1777, when the British in a surprise raid captured the President of the State, John McKinly, and also a sloop in the river containing county and State papers and public money. President McKinly was kept a prisoner until September, 1778, when Congress arranged for his exchange.

When the British took Wilmington following the Battle of Brandywine, they brought their wounded with them. The inhabitants, now calm in the certainty that they would not be bombarded from the river, gave competent attention to hospital facilities and care of the invalided until the English left at the end of October.

During the economic slump that followed the war, when even Delaware's unusually sound bills of credit failed as legal tender, the patriot business men who had exchanged their gold for Continental money had to borrow to start afresh. By 1800 the town owned many sloops, brigs, and schooners engaged in coastwide and European trade. A new Irish immigration through this port was in progress; the ship that brought passengers brought also glassware and Irish linens.

Closely following Irish refugees came French from Santo Domingo, driven out by the insurrection of the blacks. Several hundred of these new citizens had hardly settled and planned for houses of their own, when the refugees from yellow fever (1793) came in hundreds from Philadelphia. Strangely, no case of the disease appeared in Wilmington that year, though every house was crowded beyond comfort, and the masts of ships formed a veritable thicket along the Christina. The population was increased from 1,200 at the outbreak of the Revolution to 2,500.

House-room and all supplies, especially food, sky-rocketed in price. The Bank of Delaware opened its doors at the northeast corner of Fourth and Market Streets in 1795; a new Town Hall designed by one of the French refugees from Santo Domingo, Peter Bauduy, was built below Sixth on the east side of Market. In that year, the yellow fever was again rampant in Philadelphia. There was now an alert quarantine against vessels and persons coming to the town from the infected area, but the disease appeared in Wilmington and without respect of persons or neighborhoods, took off young and old.

Between the close of the Revolution and the War of 1812, while Wilmington was becoming a town of 5,000, it seems to have had its most cosmopolitan society, an intellectual and civic-minded era along with growing scientific interests and a new impetus both to manufacturing and to shipping. Robert Coram, teacher and librarian, published his plan for a general system of public education in the United States. The "Old Academy" building was the center of learning, of meetings attended by Benjamin Franklin, James Madison, and other persons from outside the State who were interested in science. With the Academy were associated also the Revolutionary leaders, Thomas McKean, Signer of the Declaration of Independence, Gunning Bedford, Jr., John Dickinson, and Jacob Broom, Signers from Delaware of the Federal Constitution, James A. Bayard, Louis McLane, and many additional distinguished citizens of the State. Educated political refugees taught school in Wilmington, especially the French who fled thither from the uprisings at Santo Domingo, 1791. Lewis Cass and William Cobbett also taught here. Robert Morris of Philadelphia spent summers at Eden Park. Archibald Hamilton Rowan, the Irish patriot, with a price of ten thousand pounds on his head, lived on the banks of the Brandywine with his dogs "Sallie" and "Charles." In a little stone house on East Sixth Street the son of the Marquise de Sourci made beautiful boxes out of gourds and perfected with whalebone and wood an automatic grasshopper, to earn means toward recovering position and fortune. John Dickinson, when his term as Governor of Pennsylvania expired in 1785, came home and built the largest private house in Wilmington at the northwest corner of Eighth and Market Streets, and there entertained the notable persons of the day. Hezekiah Niles, who later published *Niles' Register* at Baltimore, had a printing shop on Market Street, a center for the news and wit of the world. Benjamin H. Latrobe, the architect of part of the Capitol at Washington, lived here for a while on the same street. He was engineer for the first company organized to build a Chesapeake and Delaware Canal. About 1803 Willard Hall, graduate of Harvard, lawyer and teacher, arrived in Wilmington, to become the "father of public education" in the State.

Meanwhile Jacob Broom became the town's first postmaster and started the first cotton factory in this part of the country, in the Old Academy. The experiment proving satisfactory, he bought a mill-seat, two miles up the Brandywine, and erected the first cotton mill. Near the mill he built a mansion house, and in 1802 sold the shell of the mill, which had burned, with the mill-seat to the first E. I. du Pont, who started his powder making on this spot. In this period, also, Joshua and Thomas Gilpin established their paper-mill on the Brandywine at "Kentmere," part of the present Bancroft plant, and began their experiments toward perfecting the first continuous-roll paper-making machinery.

In the War of 1812, concern was paramount for the mill industries

WASHINGTON MEMORIAL BRIDGE, BRANDYWINE CREEK

and the safety of Wilmington. James A. Bayard, first of five Bayards to represent Delaware in the United States Senate, joined citizens in building Fort Union on the site of Fort Christina—the fourth time the old fortress had been used, always without bloodshed.

Local shipping suffered from the embargo declared by President Jefferson in 1808; after the war the cotton and woolen mills fared ill, and the whole range of mill-buildings on the creeks about Wilmington seemed to change hands and products continuously. Prosperity returned with the developing means of transportation. Wilmington had steamboat service of a sort before 1800, and from 1812 at least one packet and passenger steamer ran regularly between the town and Philadelphia. Within a few years every main road out of Wilmington, except the "down-state" road, had been improved as a toll-road. At this period, the so-called Wilmington conspiracy, opposition to the lowering of the tariff barriers said to have been secretly plotted with Washington officials, was charged against the mill-owners in a heated political campaign.

Until 1832, Wilmington lived under the Borough Charter, granted by the Proprietary Governor of the Three Lower Counties. In this year it was chartered as a city with mayor and council form of government. The mayor could hold court and perform marriages. Richard H. Bayard was elected first Mayor and the new lists of officers of the city looked like family names chosen at random from those that appeared on the earliest borough lists.

In 1835, a Wilmington company bought the *Ceres,* the initial vessel of a fleet to engage in whaling. The adventure lasted until 1845 and gave the city one of its most picturesque aspects in the departure and return of the vessels, each away to the Pacific around Cape Horn on voyages of two or three years. A shot was fired from Whalers' Wharf when a returning vessel was sighted. With the sound, most of the town stopped work and went to greet the fishermen and sailors. If the voyage had been successful the captain was "chaired." Husky sailors secured a chair at the tavern, seated the captain, and raised the chair on poles across their shoulders. Thus they bore him up one street, down another, and back to the inn, while he received congratulations of the inhabitants who lined the streets or joined the procession.

From 1832 to the Civil War the manufacturing and shipping that had created Wilmington's economic importance and furnished the money for its well-built brick houses continued to flourish, and were supplemented by a steadily increasing number of commercial and manufacturing undertakings that now followed the shores of the Christina rather than the Brandywine.

During this development, local statesmanship concerned itself with slavery and other public questions that stirred the Nation. Wilmington was chiefly anti-slaveholding, and the slaves, fleeing from sale and barter in the South, found developed here one of the most important links in the Underground Railroad. The fearless Quaker, Thomas Garrett, known from end to end of the Atlantic Coast States for his quiet but firm defiance of sheriffs, overseers, and posses, with the tacit consent of the local population, gave temporary shelter to the Negroes.

Following the financial panic in the decade after the Civil War, money was subscribed for a succession of railroads and transportation companies, new industries developed, and such long-established small manufactures as fibre and leather gave distinctive character to the local output.

Through the foresight of a group of citizens led by William P. Bancroft, a Wilmington Park Commission was created by legislative act in 1883 to preserve from industrial spoliation the banks of the Brandywine throughout the city limits, and to acquire additional tracts for park land.

During his lifetime, Mr. Bancroft made a series of gifts—Rockford Park, and numerous other tracts—and by active participation in its affairs, started the Commission upon a career of achievement in the life of the city.

Although Wilmington was an important shipping center for generations, its maritime base was confined to the winding shores of the Christina at a distance of several miles from the Delaware River. The Marine Terminal is the culmination of many years of effort on the part of progressive citizens and the municipality to turn to advantage the unused river-front. The Wilmington Board of Harbor Commissioners was created by the General Assembly in 1917 to operate the Terminal but construction was delayed until after the World War.

In 1917 the people began to respond to a program of social advancement promoted through the active unofficial statesmanship of some of the more thoughtful citizens. With official cooperation, the city joined the State in the reduction of infant mortality, the protection and promotion of public health, and the revamping of the school system.

The World War stimulated all the available industrial plants in the city; the blast furnaces and shipyards operated 24 hours a day. When the close of the war brought about the immediate cancellation of the industrial contracts, the city lapsed into a semi-industrial character. It became the wholesale buying center for the State and commercially the clearing house for the Delmarva Peninsula. It has become also a center for big business because of the number of large corporations maintaining offices in the city.

The transfer to Wilmington of the executive and clerical personnel of several of these industries, such as the Krebs and Grasselli Chemical Companies, which are part of the E. I. du Pont de Nemours chemical organization, and some smaller groups seeking the advantages of Delaware's tax system, brought appreciable gain to the office population in 1936-7. Before the war the majority of the gainfully employed were skilled workers and artisans, or semi-skilled labor employed in the many manufacturing plants, and although manufactures have recently increased in number and output, the proportion of less than one-fourth in the total working population engaged in industry in 1930 is probably even lower now. The site of the greatest concentration of mill industries in the early colonies has become in the twentieth century the locale of a similar concentration of great wealth in corporations.

Most of the younger workers, from choice and in response to the trend, have turned to preparation for white-collar jobs. The Wilmington

Board of Education, with the aid of local industrialists, has planned for increased trade-school facilities to meet the need for skilled workers by the manufacturing plants. More than a fourth of those gainfully employed are women, and the last census listed a few more females than males in the population.

For many years the celebrated case of the Springer Heirs has provided the city with thousands of lines of publicity in newspapers throughout the Nation. In relation to Wilmington property Charles Christopher Springer is known to his local descendants and to students of early Wilmington history as the legally constituted agent of the congregation of Old Swedes Church, charged with leasing and selling the glebe land, about the time Willingtown was laid out in 1731. He gave deeds in fee simple and also on lease at a low annual rental. During the eighteenth and nineteenth centuries, all of the glebe, the old Pickering tract, from the Christina to Rattlesnake Run in a broad diagonal strip, became incorporated in the city, remaining claims of the church being satisfied and clear title obtained by individual owners. Publicity in connection with a title-deed, soon after the Civil War, may have misled some of the many descendants of this original Charles Springer living at a distance from Wilmington. As a result of their efforts to establish a claim they honestly believed to be just, the claimants were eventually brought together by a group of shrewd promoters who saw in these unsuspecting persons an opportunity for a huge and widespread confidence game. The background of the scheme was well prepared. It was discovered that Charles Christopher Springer had been kidnapped in youth while attending an English school, brought to this country and during many years lost touch with his family in Stockholm, Sweden. To this was added a story that he bought from the Indians, at the site of Wilmington, land that was confirmed to him under a grant from William Penn. The supposed grant occupied a tract of some 1,900 acres of land, 228 of which ran through the center of Wilmington. The promoters elaborated on the scheme, held meetings, and talked of an estate which ran from $80,000,000 to as high as $150,000,000. The interest of the victims was kept alive by constant increases in the estimated value of the estate and the adding of fictitious tales, such as one relating that Charles Christopher Springer had been a Swedish Baron to whose credit $100,000,000 in treasure remained deposited in a Stockholm bank.

The scheme flourished in spite of many setbacks on the part of the "heirs," who were of great number and had been recruited from all sections of the country. Meetings were held and large sums of money ex-

OLD SWEDES CHURCH, WILMINGTON

tracted from the prospective millionaires to prosecute the claim, but to no avail. Court records proved conclusively that Charles Christopher Springer had not been a landed member of the original settlement and that the land reputed to have been his was actually the property of Old Swedes Church bought from heirs of John Andersson Stalcop, original Swedish owner. In Swedish Charles Springer's name was "Karrell Christofferson Springer."

The "heirs" continued their efforts for many years and it was not until a Chicago judge had refused to allow a meeting of the clan and one of the promoters had confessed his part in the scheme that the activity of the incorporated group was discontinued.

Letters are still received from individual Springer descendants all over the world, asking when the claims of the "Springer Heirs" will be settled.

POINTS OF INTEREST

1. OLD SWEDES (HOLY TRINITY CHURCH), *(open, apply to the sexton)* SE. corner 7th and Church Sts., formerly Swedish Lutheran, now Protestant Episcopal, is a gray stone structure of modest height and

proportions, with massive gabled side porch, hooded gable and delicate arcaded belfry topped with a low onion-shaped dome. Constructed in 1698, it is characterized by simplicity of lines and rugged strength. Approached from Church Street through an arched and ivy-clad gateway, Old Swedes stands in the midst of the dead of centuries, linking the present with the pioneers who landed at The Rocks nearby in 1638.

When the Reverend Eric Bjorck (1668–1740) arrived from Sweden in 1697 and took charge at Crane Hook, he bent his efforts toward the erection of this church. On May 28, 1698, the first stones of the foundation were "laid all around about one foot deep except a piece on the south wall and for here and there a grave—and some stumps." Joseph Richardson, mason, engaged on October 6, 1697 by Pastor Bjorck and the wardens to build the church, having broken his contract, Joseph Yard, of Philadelphia, assisted by his sons Joseph, William, and John, agreed to do the masonry for the sum of 86 pounds in silver money, in addition to "sufficient Meat, Drink, Washing and Lodging." The contract for the carpenter work was made with John Smart and John Britt of Philadelphia. Britt "failed" his partner, and Smart worked alone until John Harrison, also of Philadelphia, was engaged to do all the inside carpentry.

The following April, the "glazier from Holland" arrived and by the 28th of that month, the gable ends were up with "all the laths nailed to the arch of the roof." Matthias de Foss, "a smith of our own folk," prepared letters of wrought iron to be used in inscriptions on the west, east, south, and north walls, the letters being colored red.

The church was a plain, rectangular building with brick floor, shingled roof, hooded gable ends, but without tower or belfry, gallery or porches. Consecration was on Trinity Sunday, June 4, 1699.

Nine Swedish ministers followed Bjorck, who returned to Sweden in 1714, among them Israel Acrelius, who wrote a history of New Sweden, and Lawrence Girelius, the last to serve. During Girelius' pastorate, ending in 1791, the sermon was preached on alternate Sundays in Swedish and English, and the Holy Communion was celebrated in English. Since many of the congregation no longer understood the Swedish language, English-speaking pastors were engaged from this time, and by common consent the service became Episcopal.

About 1750, the arched south porch was erected. The gallery with outside chairs at the south porch was built in 1774. In 1802, the tower and belfry were built of brick, 12 by 14 feet and 34 feet high, in accordance with a drawing exhibited by Joseph Stidham.

After long failure to repair Old Swedes, a new building at Fifth and King Streets was first occupied on Christmas Day 1830. Twelve years later Old Swedes was re-opened for services, the pews were removed except in the gallery, wooden benches substituted, a wooden floor laid over the bricks, and the gallery stairway placed inside. In 1899, Old Swedes was restored, and the bicentennial celebration was held. The belfry was rebuilt, a new roof laid, the quaint stairs again placed on the outside, and the wooden floor removed from the original bricks.

The vicarage, the sexton's lodge, and the gateway were built in 1855;

the parish house in 1893. The first bell hung in a walnut tree near the church. The present bell has been in use since 1772, being recast in 1853.

Thousands of visitors from all parts of the world come to Old Swedes. Among those of the last half century have been Theodore Roosevelt, Grover Cleveland, and Crown Prince Gustavus Adolphus and Princess Louise, of Sweden.

The nave is entered through the tower at the west end of the church. The chancel occupies the hooded gable at the east, where the marble altar incloses the original altar of Old Swedes. On the north side is the aged pulpit; at the south, the baptistry. The gallery at the west is entered by outside stairs; at its rear is the pipe organ.

Box pews, the pulpit with octagonal sounding board, the square block of bricks in the floor of the main aisle, lifted out to receive the Christmas tree, and the original Church Chest are characteristic details. It is affirmed of the pulpit, built of black walnut in 1698, that "this is no doubt the oldest church pulpit in the United States." The chest, of walnut, was formerly the depository of church funds. On June 7, the record says: "Talked of a church chest in which the income of the church should be put." On June 4, 1713: "Resolved, that the church money shall be deposited in the chest given by Christian Joransson for that purpose which should always stand in the church."

On the north wall is a memorial to Captain Richard Brindley, killed at Gaines' Mill, Va. On the south wall is a tablet to the memory of Phoebe George Bradford and her son, Judge Edward Green Bradford. To the north of the chancel is a tablet to the memory of Thomas Francis Bayard.

Oil portraits of Pastor Israel Acrelius, Pastor Eric Bjorck, and Pastor Peter Tranberg are in the vestry. The Bjorck painting was sent by the Great Copperberg Mining District Joint Stock Co., Fahlun, Sweden, in 1899. In 1718, the Fahlun Company sent in tribute to Bjorck a silver chalice and paten still used annually on Trinity Sunday. Here also is a likeness of Gustavus Adolphus, as well as photographs of Bishops of the Diocese of Delaware and those of Vicars of Old Swedes.

Beneath the brick pavement and under the walls are interred the remains of early settlers. Directly in front of the chancel rail is the flat tomb of the Reverend Peter Tranberg. Here also his son Peter Tranberg, aged nine years, six months, two weeks, was buried July 29, 1750.

To the south of the altar are buried Petter Bjorck, died September 20, 1710, son of Eric Bjorck; Emmanuel Hesselius, died October 6, 1719, son of Pastor A. Hesselius; Petrus Hesselius, died November 25, 1716, son of Pastor Andrew Hesselius; and Brewer Seneke, died December 2, 1709, churchwarden. In the aisle leading to the choir room is a flat stone in memory of Peter Abraham Girelius, son of Pastor Girelius, buried September 18, 1786, aged 19 days. Peter was "born with the whooping cough," the church record recites.

It is recorded also that Aaron Johnson, who died July 13, 1708, is buried in the main aisle near the door. Johnson was the first to be buried in the church, and the first person to will property to it. At the funeral, in

INTERIOR, OLD SWEDES CHURCH

the presence of a large congregation, the old ceremony of standing on the bier during the sermon was followed.

Pastor Andrew Borell, who served from 1760 to 1767, was buried within the walls April 5, 1768, but the location of his grave is not recorded. Finck, in *Lutheran Landmarks and Pioneers in America*, says that the Reverend Reorus Torkillus, first Lutheran pastor in the United States, who died at Fort Christina in 1643, was buried at what later became the south wall. Benjamin Ferris, historian, says that Carl Christopher Springer (1658–1738), churchwarden and keeper of the records, was buried near the south wall, and, in 1762, the wall was extended over his remains.

Elizabeth Montgomery, author of *Reminiscences of Wilmington (1851)*, grew eloquent in describing OLD SWEDES CEMETERY. Here she is buried beside her father, Captain Hugh Montgomery, of Revolutionary War fame. The beautiful and accomplished Mary Vining, affianced to General "Mad Anthony" Wayne, lies in an unmarked grave, the fate of thousands buried here. Old marble tombstones have disintegrated, while rough field stones have become indistinguishable from ordinary ones as the rudely carved letters have weathered away. It is tradition that the nearby railroad trains thunder over the obliterated graves of many Swedish pioneers.

The earliest burial on the site dates from a short time after the building

CHALICE AND PATEN, OLD SWEDES CHURCH

of Fort Christina (1638), and the estimated number of burials is 15,000. The oldest decipherable stone is the tomb of William Vandevere (1656–1719), kinsman of Jacob Vandevere, sergeant at Fort Altena in 1660. The grave, under a buttonwood tree, is about 20 paces from the south porch. The next oldest are those of Brita and Katharina Cock; their markers are rough stones by the walk of the southwest corner of the church, that of Brita, marked "1726.B.C.," and that of her sister, who died two days later, marked simply "K.C."

Most of the early Wilmington families irrespective of race or religion have members buried in Old Swedes. To the southeast of the church is the French section where many of the refugees from Santo Domingo are buried. Here may be found the Bauduys, the Hamons, the Gareschés, the Verriers, the Ullmans, and others. The tomb of Ferdinand Bauduy, erected 39 years after his death, bears the inscription "Restituit Uxor A.D. 1853." Ferdinand, who married Victorine du Pont, November 9, 1813, after some opposition of her father, E. I. du Pont, founder of the powder mills, died on January 14, 1814, "of a fever." Peter Bauduy, father of Ferdinand, was a partner of du Pont at the time of the marriage; dissolution of the partnership came in 1815.

Revolutionary War heroes are likewise interred here, including the well-known Major Peter Jacquet, Major Daniel J. Adams, and Captain Joseph Stidham; statesmen, including James A. Bayard (the younger), Thomas F. Bayard, and Senator Samuel White (1770–1809); and the Right Reverend Alfred Lee, first Episcopal bishop of Delaware.

2. SITE OF FORT CHRISTINA, at THE ROCKS, foot of E. 7th St.,

is now a State park. Here, upon a ledge of rocks that formed a natural wharf along the Christina between Fourth and Seventh Streets, the first Swedish expedition, commanded by Peter Minuit, landed in late March 1638, built Fort Christina, named for the young Queen of Sweden, and established the first permanent settlement of Europeans in Delaware. A small stone monument, with informative inscription, erected by the Delaware Society of Colonial Dames March 29, 1903, marks the site.

Fort Christina was constructed of palisades and earth in the form of a square, at the four corners of which acute-angled bastions projected diagonally. Cannon were placed in three of these corners and within the enclosure two log houses were erected for the garrison and its supplies. The fort extended nearly to the Christina River. An incident in its late Swedish occupancy is described by the engineer, Peter Lindeström, in his *Geographia Americae,* translated by Amandus Johnson. Lindeström wrote:

Now, I will not withhold a ludicrous occurrence which happened one night on our first arrival at Fort Christina, namely, that one of our soldiers who had lately arrived at Fort Christina, gave an alarm in the fort, while he was on guard, because he saw Spanish flies (fireflies) shine bright, and close which he had not seen before, crying out with a loud voice, "Alarm, Alarm, the enemy is about." Thereupon the drummer beat the alarm. He was asked what he had seen. He replied: "The enemy is here close to the fort, see how many burning tapers there are." And when it was looked into, it was (found to be) nothing but Spanish flies, for which all the people in the fort had run to arms.

A two-acre tract surrounding The Rocks was purchased in 1937 by the State of Delaware as part of the preparations for the Swedish Tercentenary (1938). The Crown Prince and Crown Princess of Sweden with Prince Bertil attended the Tercentenary. Thirty thousand commemorative half-dollars were struck by the U. S. Mint as mementoes, and the Swedish people raised $50,000 for a monument of black Swedish granite to be erected here. The monument, a shaft designed by Carl Milles, Swedish sculptor, is surmounted by a stylized wave bearing a representation of the *Kalmar Nyckel (Key of Kalmar),* one of the Swedish vessels that landed the first expedition at The Rocks.

3. The ALRICHS HOUSE *(private),* standing on an embankment on the S. side of the Christina River near the Delaware, and facing the Marine Terminal, is a two-and-a-half-story brick-and-frame structure with dormers, and recalls the days of Dutch occupation when the Alrichs family, especially its many prominent members, played a large part in the government of the young Colony. High on the north wall of the brick section appears the S-face of an iron tie-rod through the chimney, and below it is the inscription in wrought-iron letters "L A" and the date "1785." While the significance of the initials cannot be traced with certainty, the property at the time was owned jointly by Sigfredus and Lucas Alrichs, sons of Peter Sigfredus Alrichs. For this reason, the S of the tie-bolt has often been read with the L and A for the initials of the two men. The frame portion of the building is believed to be 17th century.

The land, owned by the Poulson family, was bought by Peter Sigfredus Alrichs in 1751. Legend confuses him with the first Peter, whose land, north of the Christina, was one of the Dutch properties seized by the English in 1664 and granted to Ensign Stock. By 1667, Alrichs had prospered sufficiently to reclaim it from Stock, who in addition to selling him his own property, "did freely restore and bestow to the number of eleven negroes upon said Peter Alrichs as a guift."

4. MARINE TERMINAL *(open on application at office)*, S. bank of the Christina River near its junction with the Delaware, has been Wilmington's port since 1923, when the first unit was completed at a cost of $2,250,000. Expansion, especially of storage capacity invites heavy annual increase of tonnage handled at the port. Charges are favorable to shippers because of economical methods of operation.

Facilities at the Terminal include a quay, transit and cargo sheds, a twenty-five-acre open storage area, and seven miles of railroad track. Seven cranes move the cargoes shipped to the port from all parts of the world.

5. EDEN PARK, New Castle Ave. and F St., public recreation center of South Wilmington, is marked by the long stone wall fronting New Castle Ave. and by the pair of rams that surmount the entrance gate-pillars. The area of the park is 13.43 acres, although it was once an estate of 333 acres.

Known as Monckton Park before 1783, an early owner was George Haynes, merchant, who purchased it from John Malcolm, Gentleman, in 1780. Haynes was so neat in dress that every night he covered the fashionable silver buttons on his coat with tissue paper. He succeeded in having the first milestones placed on New Castle County roads, and one of them is imbedded in the pillar to the left of the entrance gate.

The next owner, Robert Morris, used it as a summer estate. Morris sold it in 1791 to Comte de Ségur, uncle by marriage of Lafayette, and like Lafayette, a supporter of the cause of the patriots. Peter Bauduy, associate of E. I. du Pont de Nemours in establishing the powder yards on the Brandywine, purchased it next, with General Alexandre Bauduy, aide to Napoleon, as guarantor.

Bauduy first turned Eden Park to account commercially in 1816 when he established powder yards here, after his break with du Pont. The mills were driven by horse power. Bauduy was not successful, but his sons-in-law, Jean Pierre and Vital Marie Garesché, continued the plant as partners. Jean Garesché afterward operated it alone. Serious explosions at Eden Park menaced Wilmington at intervals, until one in 1861 finally wiped out the plant.

Eventually the tract came into possession of the Lobdell Car Wheel Company, who sold 7.35 acres to the City of Wilmington in 1890, and an additional lot of 6.08 acres in 1909. The mansion house was demolished between 1892 and 1895, and other buildings later.

The rams on the gateposts represent the once well-known ram, "Don Pedro." Bauduy and du Pont were interested in the raising of merino sheep, and du Pont imported Don Pedro from Spain. The ram was well-known to sheep-raisers of this country, including Thomas Jefferson who wrote his regrets to du Pont on hearing of Don Pedro's death in 1811. Du Pont had a wooden image made of the ram, and Bauduy, raising sheep on a large scale at Eden Park, had two images made at the same time. These, of wood and partly hollow so that oil might be poured into the interior to preserve them, were set up at the entrance gates. They stayed there until a few years ago, when, quite dilapidated, they were taken down for preservation by Francis V. du Pont, descendant of E. I. du Pont, and concrete ones substituted.

Bauduy also imported a Spanish shepherd from the Pyrenees with his dogs to guard the Eden Park flocks, and the tale has come down that the shepherd used stilts to get about the marshy ground. The marsh may have been the cause of Bauduy's failure with sheep, for they were stricken with hoof-rot. Bauduy, financially embarrassed, left Wilmington for Cuba in 1819 to invest in coffee and sugar plantations, and died there.

6. The approximate SITE OF CRANE HOOK CHURCH, E. of New Castle Ave., approached through property of the Schock Independent Oil Co., *(open on application at office of the company)*, is marked by a stone of native granite, erected by the Historical Society of Delaware in 1896. The church was a little log building at the edge of a forest, built in 1667 and attended by Swedish and other Lutherans until 1699, when Holy Trinity (Old Swedes) was opened. The last service held at Crane Hook was on the fourth Sunday after Easter in 1699, with the new minister from Sweden, Eric Bjorck, officiating.

7. RODNEY SQUARE, covering the block bounded by Market, King, 10th, and 11th Sts., and surrounded by buildings housing the city's administrative, cultural, and business activities, is Wilmington's unusual civic center. Containing little more than 1½ acres, the plot, landscaped by Zantzinger, Borie and Medary, of Philadelphia, is in the form of a sunken garden. It was completed in 1917.

Two memorials stand at the Market Street side. The CAESAR RODNEY EQUESTRIAN STATUE, designed by James Kelly of New York, honors the Signer of the Declaration of Independence for whom the Square is named; a DRINKING FOUNTAIN is a memorial to William Poole (1853–1918), descendant of one of the early Quaker families who settled in Wilmington, and former head of the Wilmington Fountain Society.

8. The PUBLIC BUILDING of the City of Wilmington and County of New Castle, *(open 9-5 Mon.-Fri.; 9-12 Sat.)*, E. side of Rodney Square, King St., between 10th and 11th Sts., built of granite on classic lines, was completed in 1916. Designed by Palmer and Hornbostel of New York, with John D. Thompson as local associate, the exterior, of modified Graeco-Roman design, is dignified and austere. Between the entrance wings at each end of the main façade, massive fluted columns extend to the cornice of the three-story building. The interior is finished in pink marble and Indiana limestone. A wide arcade on the ground floor connects the offices of the City Hall, occupying the southern half of the building, with those of the county government in the northern half. Nearly all branches of both governments are represented. A basement and sub-basement house valuable records of city and county.

The Public Building takes the place of the County Courthouse, formerly occupying the site of Rodney Square, and serves the City government for offices moved from the old Town Hall between Fifth and Sixth Streets on Market, and other buildings. The cornerstone of the present structure was laid February 12, 1915, and the formal dedication took place May 27, 1916.

9. WILMINGTON PUBLIC LIBRARY *(open 9 a.m.-9:30 p.m. week-days)*, 10th St. facing Rodney Square, a gray-white structure of neoclassic design, is the work of Alfred Morton Githens and Edward L. Tilton, architects of New York. Of simple plan and mass, and commanding a broad frontage on the city square, the design of the building is ably adapted to the specific requirements of function and building site. The architects received the gold medal of the American Institute of Architecture for excellence of design of monumental public edifices. The exterior is a logical expression of the building plan. The symmetrical façade is designed with an imposing entrance motif—a solid wall surface, embellished with slightly-projecting Ionic pilasters, festoons and narrow grilled openings. In the center is a well-proportioned doorway enframed with architrave and cornice heading in the manner of the north portal of the Erectheon in Athens. Fenestration is concentrated at the ends of the façade where lofty fluted columns, separating the windows, rise in support of the elaborate main cornice. Beneath the classic cresting of the cornice is a colorful terra-cotta frieze, adorned with griffins and acanthus scrolls in shades of gray-brown and blue on a clear yellow background.

The interior color scheme is in harmony with the architectural traditions embodied in the structure, the decorations following the classic mode; black Doric columns and a bas-relief reproduction of the Parthenon's frieze around the gallery at the floor level are striking features. The first story is without corridors, its center opens to a glass skylight in the manner of a Roman atrium. A children's department is entered from the lower level of King Street.

The library has 212,000 volumes, and 95,000 pictures also are available for circulation. A continuous series of exhibits of cultural, educational, and historical material, chiefly of local production or ownership, is maintained on the main floor. The music department circulates 2,500 records.

The collection of Delawareana has been enriched by the purchase and gift of many items pertaining to the earliest settlements in Delaware. Among these is a contract, published in 1626 at Stockholm, between the Swedish South Seas Company and William Usselinx concerning the colonization that was finally achieved 12 years later on the site of Wilmington.

The Public Library is the outgrowth of a subscription library, "The Library Company of Wilmington," organized in 1788, which may have been the revival after the interruption of the Revolutionary War of an earlier "Wilmington Library." The date on the seal of the earlier library is 1754. It was still active in 1763. The library was conducted for some years at the homes of the librarians, among whom was Robert Coram, schoolmaster and writer; then in the Town Hall and in the quarters of literary organizations with which the library was merged. After a change of name to the "Wilmington Institute" and a new charter, the John Dick-

PUBLIC LIBRARY, WILMINGTON

inson property, northwest corner of Eighth and Market Streets, was bought and a library building erected (dedicated July 24, 1860), which included stores for rental and provided a large auditorium for public meetings. The library quarters were on the ground floor, entered from Eighth Street.

In 1893, William P. Bancroft offered to pay the debts of the library and provide an endowment if its facilities were made free to the public and the means of the Institute supplemented by annual contribution from the City. His offer was accepted, the Wilmington Institute Free Library was chartered by the Legislature, and the library opened to the public February 12, 1894, in the auditorium of the building at Eighth and Market Streets. By 1921 the space and facilities of this building were outgrown. Pierre S. du Pont contributed the site for the present building which was part of the graveyard of Old First Presbyterian Church acquired at a cost of $266,000; the public subscribed $325,000, and City Council issued bonds for $200,000. The building was completed in April and dedicated May 5, 1923. Mr. Bancroft continued his support of the Library for twenty years after it became free. The Public Library is still supported in part by the proceeds of his endowment and other gifts.

In the S. gallery is the headquarters of the New Castle COUNTY FREE LIBRARY *(open 9-5:30 weekdays)* founded 1927 by Miss Alice Smythe in memory of Mary H. Askew Mather. At first a privately financed experiment in rural library service, the library's "bookmobile" and "stations" were immediately in popular demand with the result that the county government supplemented the founder's fund. The county now provides the bulk of the steadily increasing budget, to which the founder also contributes. In addition to supplying frequently changed collections of books to 66 community stations, schools, and welfare organizations, the County Library cooperates with the rural organizations, granges, churches, women's clubs, by providing reference material for special activities and interests. It circulates 48,500 volumes of its own collection.

The Wilmington and the County Libraries are under the same Board of Managers with administration by a Director and Assistant Director of Libraries. The Wilmington Library has branches in three sections of the city. The County Library has its Mobile Branch.

A recently established separate division of the main library is the Business and Technical Department, primarily engaged in furnishing information and business services to people in business and industry and to students and home owners.

In the N.E. gallery, till 1938 devoted to the Wilmington Society of the Fine Arts collections, is the LINCOLN ROOM, opened 1941, to house a special collection of Lincoln material bequeathed to the Library 1938 by Frank Gifford Tallman. The collection now contains more than 2,000 books, many photographs, prints, medals, and miscellaneous materials.

The room has been furnished, through the efforts of the Delaware Lincoln Club, as a typical American living room of Lincoln's time. Since the opening of the Lincoln Room persons interested in the collection have presented books and manuscripts, also contributions to the furnishings. The collection contains an engrossed copy of the Thirteenth Amendment to the U. S. Constitution signed by Abraham Lincoln; Hannibal Hamlin, Vice President; Schuyler Colfax, Speaker of the House of Representatives; John W. Forney, Clerk of the House; a copy of the Emancipation Proclamation signed by Abraham Lincoln and William Henry Seward.

The Wilmington Library's Lecture Hall, second floor, is meeting place of the Delaware Society of Natural History, whose extensive collections are now stored (1953) awaiting permanent museum quarters; of the Archaeological Society of Delaware, whose museum collections are at the University of Delaware; and of many regular and special groups for discussion of public affairs and topics of general literary and cultural interest. Architectural, photographic, book and other exhibits are held here.

10. The DU PONT BUILDING, W. side of Rodney Square, and its companion structure, the NEMOURS BUILDING, Orange St. between 10th and 11th Sts., house the administration offices of the E. I. du Pont de Nemours & Co., Inc.

The Du Pont Building, 13 stories in height and covering an entire block, is designed in a modified Italian Renaissance style. The yellow-brick section at Tenth and Market Streets was completed in 1907. (In 1902 the Company had moved its offices from the banks of the Brandywine to the Equitable Building, Ninth and Market Streets.) Made up of a number of units, the building contains 1,500 offices (most of them occupied by the company), the HOTEL DU PONT, and the PLAYHOUSE, Wilmington's only legitimate theater, both opened 1913. The hotel exterior is of brick and stone; decorative window balconies at intervals relieve its vertical lines. The lobby is of travertine stone with a 14-carat gold leaf ceiling. The theater seats 1,200 comfortably and is equipped to present almost any type of performance.

The Nemours Building, 15 stories, modern in its vertical lines and setbacks, connected with the Du Pont Building by a tunnel under the street and by a lofty aluminum enclosed bridge, was completed in 1937. Built of steel and concrete faced with brick, except for the first two stories of limestone, the building is air-conditioned throughout. Photo-electric cells control all elevator doors as well as the doors at either end of the eighth floor bridge. Frederick A. Godley of New York City was the architect.

The story of the Company as a modern corporation dates from 1902, following the death of Eugene du Pont, then president. In that year Coleman du Pont (1864–1930), grandson of Alfred Victor du Pont, second company president, and great grandson of Eleuthére Irénée du Pont, founder of the organization, bought the company from its owners at their price, $12,000,000. His offer of a 24 percent bonus in common stock in the new company and payments in four percent notes had been accepted. Coleman was associated with his cousins, Pierre S. du Pont and Alfred I. du Pont, in the operation of the company. The reorganization, however, was his work.

The new president's first step was to arrange for the purchase of the Laflin and Rand Powder Company, which, with the du Pont Company, was joint owner of stock in about 100 other companies. The new organization also bought the International Smokeless Powder and Chemical Company of Canada. These were consolidated with the du Pont Company and scores of smaller companies were gradually absorbed, the greater part of their shares being exchanged for shares in the new du Pont Company.

In 1907 the Federal Government filed suit against the E. I. du Pont de Nemours Powder Company, charging that it was a combination in restraint of trade, in violation of the Sherman Anti-Trust Act. The final decree in this case, June 1912, ordered dissolution, but permitted the du Pont Company to retain its one monopoly, the manufacture of smokeless powder for the Government. Two new companies, Atlas and Hercules, were formed by agreement between the Court and the du Pont Company, these titles being used to preserve the names of two brands of explosives.

By 1915 the company's assets amounted to more than $200,000,000. In this year, Coleman decided to resign from the company and offered his stock for sale to younger executives who were to carry the company through the World War. Philip du Pont, Alfred I. du Pont, and others brought suit in Federal Court against Pierre S. du Pont, Lammot du Pont, Irénée du Pont, and others, in an attempt to prove sale of the stock should have been to the company, rather than to individuals. Stockholders approved the sale in a referendum ordered by the court, and on June 2, 1919, the U.S. Supreme Court refused to review a decision in favor of the purchasers made by the U.S. Circuit Court of Appeals.

At the entrance of America into World War I, the company offered its experience and facilities to produce the Government's estimated requirement of 115,000,000 pounds of powder for the army and navy. Construction of the world's largest smokeless powder plant was begun under Federal contract in March 1918 at Old Hickory, near Nashville, Tenn., and five units were in operation by the time the armistice was signed.

Dye works were built by the company at Deepwater Point, N. J., toward the close of the war. Later, a construction program was launched that included a huge Cadillac plant at Detroit for General Motors, in which company du Pont had become a large stockholder, and 1,500 homes at Flint and Pontiac, Mich. New rayon and cellophane plants were constructed in Buffalo, N. Y., and Old Hickory, Tenn. More plants followed including the first nylon manufactory at Seaford, Delaware, in 1939.

The company contributed a commensurately larger service to U.S. military effort in World War II. Since then it has developed immensely greater research and experimental facilities into broader fields, and has opened new manufacturing plants in a number of communities.

Through its own activities and the purchase of the Grasselli Chemical Company in 1928, and Roessler and Hasslacher in 1930, du Pont dominates the American chemical field. Wilmington, headquarters of many du Pont chemical units and important laboratories, is rated among the leading chemical centers of the world. In 1933, the company bought a controlling interest in the Remington Arms Company.

Du Pont has a pension system and maintains health services and recreation programs and buildings for employees.

11. The UNITED STATES POST OFFICE AND COURTHOUSE which is at N. side of Rodney Square, formally dedicated on March 27, 1937, completed the Wilmington Town Center. The architecture of the building harmonizes with that of the Public Library on the opposite side of the square. The massive limestone structure, symmetrical in plan, rises two full stories above a raised basement story of rusticated granite. Set behind the main cornice is a third or attic story. The façade is adorned with engaged Ionic columns. The designers of the building, especially incorporated for the purpose, were the "Associated Federal Architects," comprising E. William Martin, G. Morris Whiteside II, Robinson, Stanhope and Manning, and Walker and Gillette, consultants.

The post office occupies the first floor and much of the basement. Finished with terrazzo floors and marble wainscoting, two of its wall panels have been decorated by murals dealing with the manufacture and use of chemicals in agriculture. A competitive submission of design resulted in the selection of H. Zimmerman, of Cincinnati, to paint the murals.

Wilmington was one of the 75 post offices designated by the act of 1790. Receipts in 1791 were $204 as compared with $1,183,933.32 in 1937. There was no free delivery in Wilmington until 1863. During part of the preceding period, an agent named Roche delivered letters for one cent. As receipt, he pasted green glazed stamps on letters, stamps now valued at $200 each.

On the second floor is the Federal Court, often in the news because of

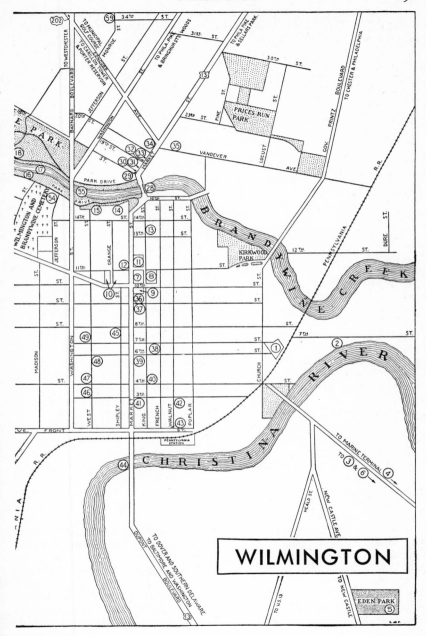

important cases arising from the great number of corporations chartered in the State. On the walls of the Court Room hang portraits of earlier District Judges. Above the judge's seat is a large mural, *Landing of the Swedes on the Rocks in 1638,* painted by Albert Pels of New York. On the third floor are offices of the Bureau of Internal Revenue, Bureau of Foreign and Domestic Commerce.

12. FIRST AND CENTRAL PRESBYTERIAN CHURCH *(open 9-4:30 Mon.-Fri.)* NW. corner 11th and Market Sts., is of modified Georgian-Colonial architecture. The design of the red brick building embodies many of the traditional forms found in the early architecture of the State. Designed by Brown and Whiteside, it was completed in 1930.

KEY TO WILMINGTON MAP

1. Old Swedes (Holy Trinity Church)
2. Site of Fort Christina
3. The Alrichs House
4. Marine Terminal
5. Eden Park
6. Site of Crane Hook Church
7. Rodney Square
8. The Public Building
9. Public Library
10. The Du Pont Building
11. The Post Office
12. First and Central Presbyterian Church
13. Jacob Starr House
14. Bishopstead
15. Colonial Dames House
16. Site of the Old Barley Mill
17. Old Brandywine Ford
18. Josephine Garden
19. Site of Encampment of Colonial Troops
20. Augustine Bridge
21. Delaware Academy of Medicine
22. Delaware Art Center
23. Thomas F. Bayard Statue
24. Canby Memorial Seat
25. Rockford Tower
26. Admiral Samuel F. du Pont Statue
27. William P. Bancroft Memorial
28. Brandywine Bridge
29. Derickson House
30. Joseph Tatnall House
31. Edward Tatnall House
32. William Lea House
33. William Smith House
34. The Cathedral Church of St. John
35. Old Brandywine Academy
36. The Delaware Trust Building
37. Wilmington Savings Fund Building
38. Dr. Didier House
39. Old Town Hall
40. Dr. Simms House
41. Sign of the Ship Tavern
42. Asbury M. E. Church
43. Capt. Thos. Mendenhall House
44. South Market St. Bridge
45. St. Andrew's P. E. Church
46. Washington's Headquarters
47. Friends Meeting House
48. St. Peter's R.C. Pro-Cathedral
49. The Woodward Houses
50. Cool Spring Park
51. Tilton House
52. Rodney Reservoir
53. Soldiers and Sailors Monument
54. Wilmington and Brandywine Cemetery
55. Washington Memorial Bridge
56. Canby Park
57. Banning House
58. Latimeria
59. Pierre S. du Pont High School

Four tall Doric columns support the roof of the portico, which, with the cupola tower and steeple, dominates the main façade on Market Street. Surmounting the steeple is a weather vane in the form of a large copper fish. A parish house, three stories in height, directly attached to the main church, extends westward on Eleventh Street; its smaller cupola is like the large one. Also on the Eleventh Street side stands the small but complete chapel, almost a duplicate of the larger church.

OLD BRANDYWINE WALK, Market St., between 10th and 16th Sts., part of a fashionable residence neighborhood in the early life of Wilmington, still retains on the west side a few of its stately mansions hemmed in by encroaching commercial development. In the block beyond Twelfth Street, the JOHN MAROT TWIN HOUSES *(private)*, Nos. 1203-1205 Market Street, are notable examples of early nineteenth-century domestic architecture. Reminiscent of early Quaker prosperity and refinement of taste are the four PRICE HOUSES *(private)* occupying the block from Thirteenth to Fourteenth Streets. Built in the decade, 1825–35, by James Price (1777–1840), for his three sons and a daughter, they have similarity of design, and in spite of modifications retain in various degrees the application of Greek motifs to Colonial design. The thick walls are of brick; broad chimneys with connecting wall mask the gable ends, and long service ells extend to the rear of each house. An iron hitching-post, surmounted by the model of a horse's head, and a large stone landing block stood before each house. In the park-like gardens at the rear, each dwelling had a stable and carriage-house. All of these homes were damaged in 1854 when some du Pont powder wagons exploded near Fourteenth and Market Sts. Since this was written No. 1301 has been torn down.

The maple trees along Market and Fourteenth Streets were planted by the late Judge George Gray (1840–1925), whose residence for many years was at 1317 Market Street, where his family still lives. Born in New Castle, member of an old Delaware family, Judge Gray, during a long life of many honors, served both State and Nation. He was for three terms United States Senator from Delaware, and was appointed Chief Justice of the United States Supreme Court by President Cleveland, an appointment that never reached the Senate because the group there in charge of the Administration's program insisted that his absence would jeopardize the passage of bills. Senator Gray later served for many years as Judge of the U.S. Circuit Court of Appeals in Philadelphia.

13. The JACOB STARR HOUSE *(private)*, 1310 King St., its marble front door sill worn almost to a razor's thinness by generations of footsteps, while occupied by members of the Starr family. Jacob Starr purchased the sturdy two-and-a-half-story brick house in 1806 from the builder, Thomas Van Kirk, and lived there until his death in 1845. Here also, for 40 years, lived his son, Captain Thomas Starr, owner of vessels plying between Wilmington, Philadelphia, and Virginia. Captain Starr's cargoes were chiefly flour from the Lea and Price mills on the Brandywine. At this home, he built a smokehouse and Dutch oven, still standing, where supplies for his crews were prepared.

Refinement is shown in the marble belt course on the street front, in the marble steps, and in the flat brick arches with marble key and end blocks. The marble mantelpieces within are light blue and white, carefully preserved, as are the glazed bare walls, broad Colonial stairway, and brass doorknobs. Broad cracks in the yellow pine doors on the first floor, the marks of the powder explosion at 14th and Orange Streets in 1854, have been filled up. Sold in 1946, the house has been carefully restored.

14. BISHOPSTEAD (*private*) 101 W. 14th St., a large gabled house with grounds sloping down to the Brandywine race, rises high among its trees on the south bank. Built in 1742 by Oliver Canby who bought the ancient gristmill site of Timothy Stidham, son of the original Swedish owner, Dr. Tymen Stidham, the house was acquired in 1841 as a residence by Bishop Alfred Lee, and was afterward bought by the Diocese of Delaware as a residence for its bishops. In poor condition. soon to be razed.

The YMCA building at N.W. cor. Eleventh and Washington Sts., was built in 1929 of Indiana limestone and tapestry brick in a modified north Italian architectural style, the architects Brown and Whiteside of Wilmington. Cafeteria, auditorium, gymnasium, reading, recreation and meeting rooms, are only part of the facilities devoted to a wide civic program.

The YWCA building at 908 King St. was erected 1923–24 at a cost of nearly half a million dollars. Five stories and basement in simplified Georgian design, house dormitories, auditorium, cafeteria, gymnasium, swimming pool and many meeting and class rooms. The YWCA provides educational courses and activities, also recreation and health programs.

The WALNUT STREET BRANCH, YMCA and YWCA (Negro) is at N.E. cor. Tenth and Walnut Sts., built 1939–40. The distinguished three-story structure was the gift of the late H. Fletcher Brown and Mrs. Brown of Wilmington. Its modern Swedish architectural style is eminently fitting as this site overlooks that of the first Swedish settlement, 1638. Thither, that year came the first Negro known to have lived in Delaware. Anthony, an "Angoler or Moor," worked as did many early Swedes for the Swedish Company. Of concrete and steel faced with brick and stone, the Walnut Street "Y" has two low-relief friezes of three panels each, depicting activities and contributions of famous Negroes. The architect was G. Morris Whiteside, 2nd. Like the main YMCA and YWCA branches, this is a civic and cultural center.

15. COLONIAL DAMES HOUSE (*private*), Park Drive at West St., a small Dutch Colonial red brick building with gambrel roof, was built in 1740 as the First Presbyterian Church on the east side of Market Street below 10th. Removed in 1919 from the original site, which had been bought for the Public Library, it serves as a meeting place for the Colonial Dames.

16. The approximate SITE OF THE OLD BARLEY MILL, Park Drive at Adams St., is designated by the large flat millstone near the little iron and cement bridge crossing the raceway. Near here Dr. Tymen Stidham, who came with the Swedish Governor Rising in 1654, is believed to have built the first Brandywine mill for cleaning barley. A mill on the site was later converted into a calico printing and dyeing establishment, which, in 1790, was operated by Archibald Hamilton Rowan, wealthy Irish exile, and William Alfred Rowan, who at first ran the mill alone, soon required

FIRST PRESBYTERIAN CHURCH (COLONIAL DAMES HOUSE), WILMINGTON

the services of two "experienced artists." A piece of calico printed at Rowan's mill is displayed in the Old Town Hall Museum.

Rowan, fleeing to America after a sensational escape from a Dublin prison where he was held on a charge of plotting against the English government, came to Wilmington in 1797 and occupied a cottage near this spot. Handbills headed "Rowan in the Smoke" offered ten thousand pounds for his recapture. During his sojourn in Wilmington he lived simply and made a pretense at working for a living by doing odd jobs and selling spruce beer in the street, although he evidently was well supplied with money from home. A jovial and friendly person, he won all hearts by his hospitality and the lending of books from his excellent library. Two gadgets, unusual for the time, he delighted in showing to his guests; a pedometer, made at his wife's direction, to check his mileage while exercising in prison, and a sword cane with a compass at the knob-end. When the Brandywine was ice-covered Rowan found amusement in the sport of curling, which Elizabeth Montgomery, in her *Reminiscences of Wilmington,* naïvely describes: "a Scotch game called golfing."

17. OLD BRANDYWINE FORD, near the foot of Adams St., identified by water-soaked planks in the Brandywine, was a crossing used by travelers prior to 1764 when the first bridge was built at Market St.

Across this ford on her tall horse in the early 1730's rode Elizabeth

Shipley, of Ridley Township, Pennsylvania, minister of the Society of Friends, on a religious tour of meetings on the Peninsula. She ascended the hill to the clearing of a Swedish settler, and stopped there in amazement as a glorious and strangely familiar view spread before her. In a moment she recognized the scene of a dream during which she had been accompanied by a guide who led her to this spot and said: "It is the design of Providence that the family of William Shipley settle here where the blessing of Heaven shall descend upon you and your labors." Her husband had not been impressed with the idea of moving a business and household because of a dream, but when his wife returned with a wide-awake description of the site upon which Willingtown was being laid out, William came, bought land on his first visit, moved his family and worldly effects, and thereafter prospered greatly.

18. JOSEPHINE GARDEN, NE. end of Van Buren Street Bridge, contains the Josephine Memorial Fountain, erected in 1932 by Gen. J. Ernest Smith in memory of his wife. The memorial is a reproduction of the Tribola Fountain, Florence, Italy. About the fountain is a lawn, each side of which is lined with Japanese cherry trees. The trees, while blooming in April, are floodlighted at night.

Across the road is the Brandywine Rose Garden, a gift of Jasper E. Crane.

To the left, on the little rise at the foot of Monkey Hill, is the red-brick Monkey House, part of the ZOO, at one time much larger but now limited to monkeys, guinea pigs, and parrots in the Monkey House; and bears, porcupines, prairie dogs, alligators, and ducks in nearby cages. Over the hill behind the Monkey House lies a flat stretch of land on which are football fields, baseball diamonds, hockey field, and three soft-ball diamonds. Baynard Field with a single cement bleacher and cinder track, lies one-quarter mile beyond. It was named for Samuel H. Baynard (1851–1925), Park Commissioner who devoted his declining years to the development of this playground area.

19. The approximate SITE OF ENCAMPMENT OF CONTINENTAL TROOPS (1777), Lovering Ave. near Broom St., is indicated by Historic Marker N.C. 7. Troops under General William Smallwood, ordered to Wilmington to prevent occupation by the British and protect four mills on the Brandywine, encamped here. The General aroused the ire of an elderly Quaker woman whose pasture he had used for army horses. Confronting him, she asked "Is thy name Billy Smallwood?" The General, surprised, said that was correct. "Well," the indignant Friend told him, "thee deserves small wood laid across thy broad shoulders, thee naughty man, for destroying my fine pasture!" The commander promised to make good the damage.

20. AUGUSTINE BRIDGE, crossing the Brandywine near Lovering Ave. and Dupont St., was built by the Baltimore & Ohio Railroad Co., in 1883, when it was ranked as one of the finest railroad spans in America. Abandoned as a railroad bridge in 1920, when a new one was built one hundred feet further downstream, the Levy Court of New Castle County converted it into a public bridge, after some remodeling, and gave

it its present name. North of the bridge can be seen what was formerly the DELAWARE PAPER MILL, familiarly known as the AUGUSTINE MILLS. The original mill dates back to 1843 when Bloomfield H. Moore entered into a partnership with his father-in-law, Augustus E. Jessup, under the firm name of Jessup and Moore, for the manufacture of paper on the Brandywine. They converted an old snuff-and-flour mill to their purpose. It is now a plant of the American Container Corporation.

21. DELAWARE ACADEMY OF MEDICINE *(open 10-5 weekdays; 10-12 Sat.)*, Lovering Ave. and Union St., was erected in 1816 at Sixth and Market Sts. It served 115 years as the Bank of Delaware, then was moved here in 1931, after $40,000 had been raised to prevent its demolition.

The square two-story building is of Federal style with mellow brick walls, set in Flemish bond with white stone trim. The architecture of the structure is typical of the early days of the Republic. The building is raised on a terraced lawn, protected on the front by a low brick retaining wall and iron picket fence. The exterior is designed with dignity and restraint. The slender proportions and simplicity of the architectural details—the narrow windows, the continuous line of the belt-course between the first and second stories, and the sharp lines of the stone lintels with their corner rosettes, are characteristic of the period. Especially notable is the well proportioned entrance loggia, arched and adorned with slender Ionic columns *in antis.*

The interior, slightly altered, provides a lecture room, library, and study. The hand-hewn rafters, wooden-pegged, the flooring, wood-framed fireplace, and trim are well preserved. On the second floor, which was equipped for study and research, is a display of early dental instruments. A library, covering all fields of medicine, contains more than 2,000 volumes, and 115 American and foreign periodicals are subscribed for. The building is used by the Medical Society of Delaware, founded 1789, third oldest medical society in the United States, and by the New Castle County Medical Society, and the Delaware State Dental Society.

22. DELAWARE ART CENTER of the Wilmington Society of the Fine Arts, Park Drive near Woodlawn Ave., a large brick structure with Vermont marble trim, conforms to the Georgian Colonial tradition of architecture in Delaware. It was designed by Victorine and Samuel Homsey and G. Morris Whiteside, II, of Wilmington. The exhibition rooms now house the Pre-Raphaelite group collected by Samuel Bancroft, Jr., and the Howard Pyle collections. There is a children's gallery and art academy.

Heirs of Samuel Bancroft, Jr., (1840–1915), gave to the Society of Fine Arts his Pre-Raphaelite collection of 46 paintings and 75 additional pictures, appraised at more than $300,000. A large library devoted chiefly to the Pre-Raphaelites, and also photographs, bronzes, and miniatures, are included in the gift in addition to a large tract of ground at this site.

At a formal dinner in London in the early '80's, the Delawarean, Samuel Bancroft, Jr., tried to make conversation, but could not take his eyes off a painting on the wall opposite—the *Fiametta* of Dante Gabriel Rossetti. Enchanted, he did not even eat, but rising abruptly, excused himself and ran to his hotel, where he told his wife she must see the painting as

FISHING SCHOOL, BRANDYWINE PARK

soon as possible. Upon viewing the *Fiametta*, she, too, was caught by its spell, and both agreed they would not be satisfied until they owned one of the master's paintings.

Unable to obtain the *Fiametta* at any price, they did acquire *Water Willow*, Rossetti's portrait of Mrs. William Morris. Then, for thirty years, the search and interest continued unabated until the Bancroft collection became world-famous.

Among the better known paintings of the collection are: *Romeo and Juliet*, by Ford Madox Brown (1821–93) ; *The Council Chamber*, and the water color *The Prioress' Tale* (first seen by Mrs. Samuel Bancroft on the easel and then contracted for), by Sir Edward Burne-Jones (1833–98) ; *A Highland Lassie* (portrait of Mrs. John Ruskin, later Lady Millais), *Master Mayor* and *The White Cockade* by Sir John E. Millais (1829–96) ; *Found*, *Hesterna Rosa* (water color), *La Bella Mano*, *The Lady Lilith*, *Mary Magdalene*, *Mnemosyne*, or *The Lamp of Memory*, *Veronica Veronese*, and *Water Willow*, by Dante Gabriel Rossetti (1828–82) ; *The Dead Rossetti* (pencil), and *William Blake's Workroom* (water color), by Frederick Shield ; *Mary Magdalene*, by Frederick Sandys (1833–1904) ; and *Jessamine*, by George Frederick Watts (1817–1904).

Constable's *Flatford Suffolk*, and Greuze's *Marquis de Mirabeau* are in the collection, and there are two paintings by Marie Stillman—*Love Son-*

nets and *The Messenger of Love* (water color). Mrs. Stillman was the model for the *Fiametta*. Her daughter, Effie Stillman, a young sculptress, executed the Thomas F. Bayard Statue in Wilmington *(see below)*, and her son Michael, the platform, base, and seat for the statue.

While the Pre-Raphaelite Collection is a memorial to Mr. Bancroft, it is also a memorial to his widow, born Mary Askew Richardson, who died in 1933.

23. The bronze THOMAS FRANCIS BAYARD STATUE, Woodlawn Ave. between Shallcross and Lovering Aves., was unveiled and dedicated June 22, 1907. The statue, sculptured by Effie Stillman, presents Bayard in the conventional dress of his day, cape on arm, scroll in hand. Bayard (1828–98), U. S. Senator, U. S. Secretary of State, and Ambassador to Great Britain, began the study of law in Wilmington at twenty. Son of James Asheton Bayard, the younger, and a strong Democrat like his father, he was elected to the U. S. Senate in 1869 and took the oath on the same day that his father left his seat in that house. He served three successive terms, and was last elected in 1881. In 1885, he was named Secretary of State by Cleveland, which office he relinquished in 1889 and retired to private life. In 1893, Cleveland appointed Bayard the first Ambassador of the United States to Great Britain.

Returning to America in 1897, Bayard lived in retirement until his death on September 28, 1898. He was buried in the family vault in Old Swedes Cemetery. In an era of political corruption, Bayard earned respect for his high ideals and unblemished character.

Three times Bayard was a candidate for the Democratic nomination for the Presidency, in 1876, 1880, and 1884, but the few electoral votes commanded by Delaware made it politically inexpedient to name him. In 1880, Bayard had 153½ votes to Hancock's 174, and in 1884, he gained 170 votes to Cleveland's 392.

ROCKFORD VILLAGE, a section of small brick houses on narrow streets, carries a slight flavor of Old England. It was built a century ago as a mill workers' community, and continues as such today. The JOSEPH BANCROFT & SONS CO. PLANT, *(open on application at office)*, foot of Rockford Road, was founded by Joseph Bancroft in 1831 as the Rockford Bleaching and Dye Works and Cotton Factory. The mills comprise the largest and oldest textile plant in the region. Joseph Bancroft, trained by his uncle, Jacob Bright, in Lancashire cotton-weaving mills, was the son of John and Elizabeth Wood Bancroft, of English Quaker families, who came to Wilmington in 1822, and bought a small flannel mill, on the Brandywine below Joseph Tatnall's house. Bancroft worked first at the Young paper mill at Rockland two miles further up the Brandywine. He was the father of Samuel Bancroft, Jr., and of William P. Bancroft. On the lands now held by the Bancrofts were located the mills of Thomas and Joshua Gilpin, once reckoned the country's most important producers of paper. The Gilpins, first in America to perfect the process of making paper in a continuous roll, commercialized the discovery in 1817, finding ready customers in publishers of books and newspapers. Thomas Gilpin patented the invention in 1816, but the importance of the discovery brought wholesale infringement. Added to this trouble was the work of floods and fires, and by 1825 the Gilpin Mills lay in ruins, abandoned.

The eastern part of this section, with its ivy-covered cottages, once known as Riddle's Banks, is now called KENTMERE. Here James Riddle started a cotton dress goods manufacturing plant. Its site is occupied by one of the Bancroft mills.

24. From the Barré granite CANBY MEMORIAL SEAT, N. of Rockford Tower, a clear view is had of the valley below. The seat was placed here in 1905 by the Board of Park Commissioners in memory of William Marriott Canby (1831–1904), first president of the board.

25. ROCKFORD TOWER (under repair), Tower Rd. N. of 19th St., 115 feet high, provides a panoramic view for many miles. Built of native stone and surmounted by a tile roof, the tower conceals a 500,000-gallon tank forming part of the city's water supply system. Far up the south side of the tower is a large sun dial. The observation platform, reached by a spiral stairway around the tank in the stone shell, is 75 feet above the ground. The interior walls are glazed white, and reflect the light let in by narrow slit windows.

The 15 stone archways about the platform mark off surrounding views. Directly through the third archway L. of the stairs is Tower Hill School, noted private secondary school. Views of Wilmington are secured through archways 4, 5, and 6; the Delaware River, and New Jersey, are seen through archways 7 and 8. The wooded regions of Brandywine Hills and the Alfred I. du Pont Memorial Carillon Tower at Nemours show through archway 9. Through archways 11 and 13 can be seen the Du Pont Experimental Laboratories, and behind it the Du Pont Country Club. Through archway 14, Henry Clay village and large estates are visible.

26. The bronze ADMIRAL SAMUEL F. DU PONT STATUE, S. of the Tower at the junction of Tower Rd. and W. 19th St., was first erected in Dupont Circle, Washington, D.C., in 1884. It was removed to this spot in 1920, when members of the du Pont family gave to the city of Washington a fountain by Daniel Chester French in its stead. Du Pont, (1803–65) was commodore of a squadron of 75 vessels at the capture of Port Royal, S. C., when the naval power of the Confederacy was partly broken. Promoted, du Pont was relieved at his own request when he failed to force a passage into the harbor of Charleston, S. C.

27. WILLIAM P. BANCROFT MEMORIAL, E. of Rockford Tower, which consists of a stone platform equipped with benches and a drinking fountain, with long stone flagged approach from the east, is a vantage point from which to survey the northern and western sections of Wilmington. A bronze tablet mounted on a huge boulder cites William P. Bancroft's services as president of the Park Commissioners (1904–23), and the fact that his gift of tracts of adjacent land inspired the purchase of much of the Brandywine valley and other areas as park land.

28. BRANDYWINE BRIDGE, N. Market St. at 16th, a steel-concrete structure completed in 1928, is the sixth bridge to span the historic stream at Market Street. The former bridges, of which the first was built in 1764, included the Old Covered Bridge made famous by the Delaware etcher,

ALONG BRANDYWINE PARK DRIVE, WILMINGTON

Robert Shaw. Two bridges were carried away by the "turbulent wild river."

Not far from this bridge, before the year 1670, a man named Andrew Brandwin, spelled also Brandwine, and Brainwinde in the old records, had a parcel of land adjoining the land of Jacob Van de Vere, and the stream is referred to in the indentures as Brandwyn's Kill, and Brandwine's Kill. In June 1670, Governor Francis Lovelace confirmed a patent to Robert Jones for a tract of land in Delaware "lyeing and being to ye South of Brainwend Kill or Creeke haveing a small run or ryvalett neare thereunto and lyeing adjacent to Jacob Vannivers island conteyning by estimation two hundred acres or thereabouts bee ye same more or lesse, which sd piece or parcell of land was bought and purchased by Robert Jones (in whoe tenure and occupation it now is), of Andren Brainwinde."

In succeeding deeds for land along the Creek the spelling gradually changes until "Brandywine" is established and appears on charts and maps. By this time the Finn had been forgotten, and the rotting hulk of an old vessel near the mouth of the stream gave color to a legend that grew, doubtless to explain the name Brandywine on the deeds and maps, of a cargo of brandy and wine lost by a Dutch master when his ship overturned in a storm. The Brandywine was called Wauwaset by the Indians, and Fiskiekylen (Fish Creek) by the earliest Swedes.

At the southeast end of the bridge the group of low brick buildings, facing East Sixteenth Street, comprise the BRANDYWINE PUMPING

STATION, the WILMINGTON WATER DEPÁRTMENT OFFICE BUILDING, and the city water filtration and purification plants. Since 1827, Wilmington has obtained its water supply from the Brandywine.

BRANDYWINE VILLAGE is the oldest and quaintest of Wilmington neighborhoods. It comprises the section north of the Brandywine from Sixteenth Street to Vandever Avenue, on either side of Market. Part of it near the Creek to the east was the Swedish neighborhood of "Bokton." A canoe to be used "for ferrying the church folk" of Old Swedes "was bought entirely new of Hendrik Tossa (Tussey) in Bokton on the other side of Brantwein's creek for 20 shillings country money," soon after the church was built. The village is built on the original grant to Jacob Vandever, early Dutch settler, part of it on land once owned by John Dickinson.

Since World War II, a few of the oldest small dwellings have been torn down or so remodeled as to lose their original character; but in several of the latter, parts of the early log or stone structure are visible.

Near the bridge was the mill colony of the Tatnalls and the Leas, facing that of the Canbys and the Prices opposite. These mills, which furnished flour and meal for the American troops during the Revolution, were built and operated by Joseph Tatnall in association with his son-in-law, Thomas Lea (1757–1833), and developed into a major industry of the region.

East of the bridge, their broken south walls rising straight from the water, are the few remaining parts of the old grist mill colony that bordered both sides of the Brandywine here in their flourishing period.

29. DERICKSON HOUSE (private), 1801 N. Market St., a two-and-a-half-story native stone house, built about 1771 by James Marshall, derives its title from Jacob Derickson, of the third generation of original Swedish settlers of that name, and is owned and occupied by Mr. and Mrs. Frederick Bringhurst, the latter a great-granddaughter of Jacob Derickson. The bold proportions of the entrance doorway suggest the influence of the Greek Revival style.

30. JOSEPH TATNALL HOUSE (private), 1803 N. Market St., represented in its original form the severe Quaker taste of the eighteenth century. This three-story stone house, greatly altered in recent years, was built in 1770 by Joseph Tatnall (1740–1813), English Quaker, son of Edward, the founder of the Wilmington family who, as one of the first master-carpenters of the town, knew a mellower tradition than his son's houses portrayed.

Generals Washington and Lafayette visited Joseph Tatnall here before the Battle of the Brandywine, and on later journeys through Wilmington stopped at the Tatnall home. On one occasion, after Washington became President, he had his chaise pull up at the house, and being told that the hardworking Quaker was in the mill, walked in upon him there.

In 1824 (October 6), when Lafayette came from Philadelphia to pay a visit to old friends in Delaware, he had the procession that escorted him halt before the Tatnall houses to pay his respects to members of the late Joseph's family. He was greeted by the son, Edward, who gave him a

basket of pears from trees grown by his father and named by Joseph Tatnall the "Washington Pear." Lafayete asked for Ann Tatnall whom he
remembered as a charming young daughter of Joseph. Ann, then Mrs.
Merritt Canby, had young daughters of her own, one of whom greeted the
distinguished guest. Another daughter was in school, for the good Quaker,
Principal Hilles, had refused to let her off, even at the request of her uncle,
Edward Tatnall, for the great occasion of Lafayette's visit—because the
permission "might interfere with discipline."

31. EDWARD TATNALL HOUSE (private), 1807 N. Market St., a
two-and-a-half-story stone mansion, was also built by Joseph Tatnall about
1790 for his own use, but he gave it to his son Edward when the latter
married. The rear portion with its walled-up doorway once overlooked the
Tatnall farm, the home of the first Edward, and is believed to be more
than two hundred years old. The slate roof was probably originally wood
shingled. The chimneys have not the usual breadth and flue size of those
of earlier periods. The front entrance blinds are carried up only to the
transom-rail, so as to light the hall.

32. WILLIAM LEA HOUSE (private), 1901 N. Market St., a two-and-
a-half-story stone mansion built in the early 19th century, is of Quaker
post-Colonial type, marked by the unbalanced treatment of the main façade
with the entrance to one side of the center axis. For many years this was
the home of the Leas, Brandywine Flour Mills proprietors. William Lea
(1805–76), was born and died in this house.

33. The pedimented entrance doorway of the WILLIAM SMITH
HOUSE (private), 1905 N. Market St., with its dog-ear architrave, tran-
som, and six-panel door is of extremely simple post-Colonial design. That
William Smith, a cordwainer, should erect a stone town house would indicate that shoemaking was a prosperous trade in 1801, the year Smith purchased the land from Joseph Smithell, grocer.

34. The CATHEDRAL CHURCH OF ST. JOHN, Protestant Episcopal, (open 9-5 weekdays; 7:30-5 Sun.), SW. corner Concord Ave. and N.
Market St., of Early English Gothic architecture, was erected in 1857. An
altar of white marble in the north transept is set against a marble background; to the left of the altar, in a carved marble recess, is the tabernacle. An arch of carved woodwork separates the sanctuary and presbytery.

A notorious tavern, the Green Tree Inn, razed in 1857, once occupied
the site, and tradition says the Cathedral's high altar is on the very spot
where stood the tavern bar. Alexis I. du Pont (1816–1857), killed in an
explosion at one of his company's powder mills, had built the church as a
memorial to his brother-in-law, Dr. Thomas Mackey Smith. Smith swallowed a poisonous draught in mistake for medicine. Du Pont read the
prayers for the dying at the death-bed, and was so impressed by the calm-
ness displayed by the doctor that he expressed a desire not only to join
the church, but also to build one as a memorial to Smith.

In 1936, the Chapel of the Holy Innocents, also used as a baptistery,
was completed in the south transept. Indefinite loan was obtained in 1937
of Farnese Investiture, 400-year old authenticated Titian picture valued at
about $250,000, which is hung under glass in the chapel. The loan was

made by an unnamed rector's wife who received it as a gift from the widow of an English art collector.

35. The OLD BRANDYWINE ACADEMY *(now a clubhouse)*, 5 Vandever Ave., a severely plain stone building, "Founded A.D. 1796," as the datestone above the door informs, was used formerly as a branch by the Wilmington Institute Free Library. The land was purchased from John Dickinson and John Welsh, the consideration in each deed being "the esteem he beareth his neighbors, a regard for the education of children, and of one cent in hand."

The wheel-bell cupola was not added until 1820. The first bell proved unsatisfactory and a new one was procured, which was rung joyfully when Lafayette rode through Brandywine Village October 6, 1824. Principal McNevin conducted the institution in 1830 as "an English and Classical Academy," and kept a bunch of switches in water in the cellar, the boy to be punished being required to go down and select the one for his own ordeal. When a new charter was secured in 1832, John M. Clayton was an incorporator. Under the Free School Act the Academy became the schoolhouse of District No. 3, New Castle County, and so continued until Brandywine Village was merged with Wilmington.

The building was early a community meeting-place, which might be used on Sundays as a place of worship for any sect except Roman Catholics. Mormons were permitted to hold meetings there in the 1840's and it was also used by the Millerites, who believed the world would come to an end in 1843.

36. The DELAWARE TRUST BUILDING, NE. corner 9th and Market Sts., constructed of steel, brick, and Indiana limestone, ranges in height from 13 stories at the Market St. end to 15 stories on King St. Characteristic of its modified Renaissance architecture is the cornice. The architects were Dennison and Hirons of New York. There is an automobile parking space in the basement for the use of tenants.

The section on Ninth Street was erected in 1921; additions were completed in 1930. The building houses offices of the Hercules Powder Companies, as well as the main office of the Delaware Trust Company developed by Alfred I. du Pont who later disposed of his holdings to a cousin, William du Pont. Hercules produces explosives, cellulose products, and naval stores.

37. WILMINGTON SAVINGS FUND BUILDING *(open bank hours)*, SE. corner 9th and Market Sts., is of classic design, its series of stone columns topped by Corinthian capitals. The Wyeth Mural, *Apotheosis of the Family,* covering the entire S. interior wall, is an allegory of home and its connotations, the work of Newell Convers Wyeth, Delaware artist. Large in conception, the subject of the mural moves through episodes of human activity dominated by the central group representing the Family and the Home. On either side stretches a landscape representing the succession of the seasons.

38. Torn down in 1948 for a parking lot was the DR. DIDIER HOUSE, 613 French Street, whose history is part of Wilmington's story when many citizens prominent in public affairs lived in that section. A three-story

mansion with large sideyard, exhibited little of its old-time character save the Flemish-bond brickwork and the water-tables; originally, the building was two stories, the Mansard roof being added in the 1890's. Its chief interest lies in the fact that it was from 1803 the residence of Dr. Pierre Didier (1740–1830), "Practitioner in Physick" and native of France. The doctor, a military surgeon on European battle-fields, having suffered several wounds, settled in Santo Domingo. He fled from there at the insurrection of the blacks in 1794, coming to Wilmington with many other French refugees. Here he practiced his profession chiefly among French families, including that of Éleuthére Irénée du Pont de Nemours, and lived to the age of 90. The obituary-writer of the *Delaware Journal* moralized that his ripe age was due to "temperance in eating and drinking—his food was simple in quality and moderate in quantity and his drink was water. Ye, who seek similar blessings, go and do likewise."

"The good Doctor," as the du Ponts called him, was buried in their family cemetery. The French Street property, left to E. I. du Pont, was subject, like a number of other centrally-located Wilmington properties, to a rent-charge of 25 shillings for 2,000 years beginning April 1, 1771, payable yearly "at one intire payment" to the Vestrymen and Wardens of the "Sweedes Lutheran Church called Trinity Church."

In a yard below the Didier house stood a draw-well that before the doctor's time gave rise to a tale of "the sailor's ghost." After the peace of 1783, French Kellum, a seaman, left Wilmington on a local brig bound for the West Indies. The vessel was unheard of for so many months that her owners were about to write off their loss. Then one evening about nine o'clock, the brig sailed up to the wharf. Kellum, hurrying to greet his family, slipped in the mud and decided to wash at the well. Ill-luck pursued him, however, for he fell into the well, the heavy lid dropping shut after him. As he climbed up, he shouted loudly, believing that in his awkward position he could not raise the lid. But this, by a supreme effort, he accomplished just as his wife and her landlady, terrified by the unearthly noises, made their way to the garden. The sight of her husband's face, with water dripping from his hair, was too much for the wife, who thought him a ghost risen from a watery death. She collapsed and the landlady ran crying for help. It was some time before the wife could be revived sufficiently to realize that she had her husband back, not a ghost to haunt her.

39. OLD TOWN HALL *(open 10-5, Mon.-Fri. 10-1 Sat.)*, 512 N. Market St., built 1798, was designed by Peter Bauduy, early French settler in Wilmington. Slight French influence is notable in Bauduy's design of the two-story brick building, which is of Georgian Colonial style. The front façade, dominated by the center pavilion, is laid in Flemish-bond. Above the arch-headed windows of the first floor is a stone belt course, punctuated by stone plaques, one above each window and one, bearing the date, above the doorway. The stone step at the entrance of this simple classical doorway is worn down perceptibly at the right from the tread of many feet. Notable features of the exterior are the stone keyblocks above the windows and the classical cornice with its modillions and pierced

ornament. The chimneys at the ends of the gables are joined by wooden balustrades instead of brickwork. Atop the hip roof is a captain's walk and a traditional belfry. The town bell, "from Uroupe," and clock were presented to the Borough in 1798, by Joseph Tatnall. The ancient bell is in the museum downstairs; the clock, now run by electricity, is still in place.

One of the first ceremonies at Old Town Hall was the formation of a procession to commemorate the death of George Washington; a public banquet celebrated the election of Thomas Jefferson; in 1812, at town meetings, defense of the Borough was planned; in 1824 a dinner was tendered Lafayette; and in 1832, the Chief Burgess and Borough Council turned over to the Mayor and Council of the newly-chartered *City*, the government of Wilmington. On the front steps, the first mayor, Richard H. Bayard, and those who followed him, welcomed distinguished guests, and in the dungeon-like basement cells suspects were fed on bread-and-water while awaiting trial. The green rear-terrace, then extending to King Street, was long defended symbolically by ante-bellum cannons.

After it was vacated in 1916 for the Public Building on Rodney Square, Old Town Hall was used for a short time as headquarters for the Red Cross. Purchased in 1917 by the Historical Society of Delaware, it became the museum and repository for the Society's valuable collections. In 1927 an Old Town Hall Association raised funds and made careful repairs to the building. A one-story annex with vaults in which to store priceless records owned by the Historical Society was erected in 1937-8.

Among the array of exhibits owned by the Historical Society and displayed in the Museum occupying the first or street floor are:

A portion of the eastern terminal stone of the famous Mason and Dixon Line, the coat-of-arms of the Lords Baltimore cut on one side and that of the Penns on the opposite side.

Chair used by Daniel Defoe, author of *Robinson Crusoe*.

Silver punch-strainer made from the first dollar earned by Benjamin Franklin.

A much larger than life-size wooden statue of George Washington, carved about 1776, long set up in Bowling Green, New York City, removed to other locations, and finally rescued by the late Coleman du Pont, from a position in front of a cigar-store, and presented by him to the Historical Society. This is regarded as the earliest known statue of the Father of His Country.

Flag carried at the Battle of the Brandywine and flags carried by Delaware regiments in various wars.

Sword and scarf worn by Major Kirkwood, leader of the Delaware Line in the Revolution. Tradition has it that the spots on the crimson scarf are from Kirkwood's death wound.

Document signed or in the handwriting of William Penn, including the Act of Union for annexing the "Three Lower Counties"—Delaware—to Pennsylvania, December 7, 1682.

Proclamation by "His Excellency, Caesar Rodney, President, Captain-General, and Commander in Chief of the Delaware State," naming May 6, 1779, as a "Day of Fasting, Humiliation, and Prayer."

Portrait of Colonel Samuel Boyer Davis, defender of Lewes in the War of 1812, painted by Thomas Sully for the State of Delaware.

Lottery wheel, used in draft of Delaware soldiers in the Civil War.

Binoculars of Admiral W. H. P. Blandy, used in the amphibious campaigns in World War II, given to the Society by the Admiral.

40. The DR. SIMMS HOUSE *(private)*, NE. corner 4th and King Sts., erected about 1820, shows in its second story the familiar black glazed headers of city houses of the period, and is one of the few recognizable dwellings in this once-ideal neighborhood of pre-Victorian homes and gardens. A sunken alley at the rear led, as the deeds state, to "two necessary houses, four feet square."

This building, for half a century, was the apothecary shop and residence of Dr. John Simms and his son, Dr. John Henry Simms, "botanic and eclectic physicians." The elder Simms, veteran of the War of 1812, established his shop here in 1840 when there was but one other drug store, that of the Bringhursts, in the city. Though most Wilmington business houses displayed the Stars and Stripes in their windows during the Civil War, Simms, sympathizing with the South, refused. One day his storewindow was broken by Union supporters, and a small American flag set there, which Simms left undisturbed for years.

The herbs used in the medicines were mixed with alcohol in the cellar, and the steeping done in copper kettles at a huge fireplace in the kitchen. The younger Simms, who continued the business, gained a reputation among travelers, and many patients came from other States for treatment, especially in affections of the lungs. Joshua L. Simms, another son, served (1872–5) as first Democratic Mayor of Wilmington after the Civil War.

41. SIGN OF THE SHIP TAVERN, SE. corner Third and Market Sts., built about 1738, is occupied by a retail shop. This three-story building of stuccoed brick is surmounted by an attic with a single dormer window. It was a famous inn of pre-Revolutionary days. On the Third Street side, the structure extends two feet beyond the building line. Beneath the Historic Marker erected by the State of Delaware is an original stone step, now flush with the pavement, that once afforded entrance to the tavern. In the cellar, a spring bubbles as of yore, the water of which is piped off, and in the front wall is a passageway that formerly led under Market Street. The wide original boards of the attic floor remain.

John Marshall, first proprietor, was still the occupant in the early days of the Revolution when the tavern received its best-known name. A traveling artist painted on the inn-sign an American sloop annihilating two British three-deckers, a taunting reference to an engagement on the Delaware River in which the American sloop-of-war *Randolph* defeated two British warships. Later, angry British sailors came to the inn with axes and destroyed both sign and post.

In 1789, Captain Patrick O'Flinn, an officer of the Revolution, became proprietor and changed the name to "The Happy Retreat." O'Flinn, church-elder as well as tavern-keeper, died in 1818, and was succeeded by General James Wolfe (*General* was his first name). The last use of the building as a tavern was in 1835. Among its guests were Washington,

Jefferson, Aaron Burr, Louis Philippe, and Commodore Oliver Hazard Perry.

42. ASBURY METHODIST EPISCOPAL CHURCH, SE. corner Third and Walnut Sts., pioneer of that denomination in Wilmington, was dedicated by Bishop Francis Asbury on October 10, 1789. A three-story structure with outer walls stuccoed and roof shingled, it has been greatly altered since its construction. The arched wooden doors are plain, and the tall windows on the second floor, the church auditorium, are arch-headed and fitted with tinted glass. Above the door, the white namestone gives the year of dedication. In the original building, high partitions divided the sexes, even husbands and wives. A modern pulpit was installed in 1840.

The congregation was organized in 1769, following the preaching of the first Methodist sermon in Wilmington by one-eyed Capt. Thomas Webb under the trees at what is now King and Eighth Streets. Then came Asbury and others. Tradition persists that timid souls of Wilmington wishing to hear the silver-tongued Asbury, but considering it a disgrace to be seen at a Methodist meeting, assembled far off to listen. Asbury's black servant, Harry, was put on the platform at the beginning of one meeting to give his experience, and it is said the unseen listeners were carried away by the eloquence of the man they thought was Asbury.

About 1800 a protest was printed in a local newspaper against the habits of "the infidel mob" in breaking the windows of Old Asbury, in stoning its preachers, and in "casting nauseous reptiles, insects, and other filth in at the windows among the female part of the congregation," and arrests were promised. In 1805, Asbury had a number of Negroes among its members, but "because benches were broken and the house defiled by dirt," it was resolved "that no black classes shall hereafter meet on the lower floor, and if they refuse to meet in the gallery, the sexton to inform them the door will not be opened for their reception." The Negro members then withdrew and formed their own congregation.

The only notable grave in the burial ground is that of Col. Allen McLane (1746–1829)—spelled Allan on the tombstone—a Delaware Revolutionary War hero. McLane, as captain of a partisan company of light dragoons, led a brilliant charge at Paulus Hook (Jersey City), was a major with Washington at Yorktown, and served as commandant of the Veteran Corps in the War of 1812. He was the father of U. S. Secretary of State Louis McLane.

43. The four-story brick CAPTAIN THOMAS MENDENHALL HOUSE (private), NW. corner Front and Walnut Sts., is one of the larger city residences of the beginning of the 19th century. It has a fine doorway and the sash of the second and third floors is original. The chimney is in the center of the ridge instead of the more usual location at the gable end.

44. SOUTH MARKET STREET BRIDGE, crossing Christina River about 500 feet S. of Front St., a steel, vertical-lift, double-leaf drawbridge, was erected in 1927. Until 1808, passage at this point was by ferry.

In the vicinity of the river front, east and west of the bridge, is a large industrial area, marking some of the earliest industries of the State.

To the west, at the foot of West St., is the **DRAVO CORPORATION** plant, one of the important centers on the Atlantic seaboard for ship assembly and launching during World War II. Here in the 100-acre yards along the Christina approximately 11,000 employees built and launched landing ships, destroyer escorts, sub-chasers, carfloats, lighters, barges and other vessels. Dravo is on the site of the Bethlehem Steel Company, formerly widely known as the Harlan and Hollingsworth Company, for nearly a century one of the important shipbuilding plants in the country. Built here in 1844 was the Bangor, first iron sea-going propeller-type ship constructed in America. Harlan's career as a shipbuilding company and plant ended in 1926. By that time 509 iron and steel ships of various types, notably iron-clads used in the Civil War, had been launched here; during World War I, 24 ships, total tonnage 158,179, were built, a record which gave the Harlan plant, staff and employees recognition comparable to Dravo in the 1940's.

Carbuilding was a Harlan pride. The first passenger coach was turned out four years after the first operation of railroad trains in America. *The Morris Run, Number One,* built in 1840, was, according to the contract, an "eight-wheeled Passenger and Ladies Accommodation Car," pointed to with pride as excelling any other car of its kind in the country.

East of the bridge, on the north bank, was the original plant and yard of the **CHARLES WARNER COMPANY**, a pioneer in the transportation of general merchandise by means of this stream. Now part of the Warner Company, of Philadelphia, one of the largest producers of sand, gravel, and lime in the country, the larger share of Warner operations in Delaware is carried on in a new plant on the south side of the Christina. Although the company owns 126 barges and nine tugs for transportation of its own products, the Warner Line of packets plying between Wilmington and Philadelphia, operated by them for over a century, was sold to the Bush Line in 1909. William Warner and John Warner who founded the company in 1794 were descended from a William Warner who married Christina, daughter of Sven Skute, the Swedish commander at Fort Casimir (New Castle) when it was retaken by the Dutch in 1655. Christina's son, William Warner, 3rd, married Mary Welton in 1732 and several years later came to Wilmington with the Shipleys and so established the Delaware family, making the present Warner grandchildren (1953) the eleventh generation from the Swedish Captain Skute and the first William Warner.

THE BUSH LINE, long at the foot of French Street, years ago bought by the **WILSON LINE**, at the foot of Fourth Street, was established 1774 by Captain Samuel Bush (1747–1831), son of Charles and Rebecca Bush, who came from Ireland and settled in Wilmington about 1737. Samuel followed a seafaring life until his sweetheart, Ann McKee, persuaded him in 1773 to stay ashore. He bought a sloop of 30 tons, called it the *Ann,* and used it to carry merchandise between Wilmington and Philadelphia. The outbreak of the Revolutionary War gave Captain Bush something to worry about in dodging British war vessels. In 1777, when Philadelphia was captured, Bush's sloop was pursued on one occasion until the owner was forced to scuttle it in a creek on the New Jersey shore. He raised the sloop when the British evacuated Philadelphia, and carried on business as usual, so much so that it was not long before the *Nancy,* double the tonnage of the *Ann,* and fitted to carry passengers was added. After that, a regular mercantile business was established in conjunction with the packet delivery.

East of the bridge, on the north bank at the foot of Poplar Street, is the shipyard and plant of the PUSEY AND JONES CORPORATION, still a busy industrial center founded in 1848 by Joshua L. Pusey (1820–91), and John Jones (1818–97). The first ship contract (an iron side-wheel steamer) was accepted in 1853; since then hundreds of vessels have been built at the Pusey and Jones shipyard, among them the steel-hulled racing yacht, *Volunteer,* which represented America in the International Cup Races in 1887, defeating the English yacht *Thistle.* The *Mahlon Betts,* claimed to be the first iron sailing vessel built in the United States, was also launched here.

In other departments, the Pusey and Jones Corporation has gained wide reputation, especially in the manufacture of papermaking machines, begun in 1853. The 23-ton anchors for Brooklyn Bridge were cast at this plant.

The Pusey family, thus identified with two leading shipbuilding plants on the Christina, came from Berkshire, England, in 1682, settling at Upland, Pa., before coming to Wilmington. Pennock Pusey (1825–1903) was the author of *Ebba Borjeson,* a novel of Swedish life in Delaware.

Farther downstream, at the foot of East Seventh Street, is the East Coast Warehouse Terminal in the former American Car and Foundry Company plant which was long known among local people as Jackson and Sharp's. Founded in 1863 by Job H. Jackson (1823–1901) and Jacob F. Sharp (1815–88), as a passenger-car and shipbuilding plant, it long enjoyed a world-wide reputation, especially in the construction of palatial private cars. Dom Pedro, Emperor of Brazil, and King Oscar II of Sweden, had their royal cars built here, and Dom Pedro paid a visit to Wilmington to inspect the plant. The first narrow-gauge cars made in America were constructed here in 1871. Stress is laid on the production of fine yachts and pleasure craft ranging up to 100 ft., mostly launched on the Brandywine, the shipways on the Christina being used for repairs of larger vessels.

45. ST. ANDREW'S PROTESTANT EPISCOPAL CHURCH, SW. corner 8th and Shipley Sts., a two-story building of local stone, later stuccoed and lined off to simulate coursed masonry, is noteworthy for its tiny churchyard, the only burial spot still in the central business section. Here the remains of Dr. John Lofland (1798–1849), "The Milford Bard," Delaware's fondly remembered poet, lay in a forgotten and unmarked grave. Lofland was buried a few feet from the grave of his sister, Mrs. Corry Chambers. In 1945 the Wilmington Poetry Society erected a bronze marker. To make room for an addition to the church, 1953–54, the bodies will be removed and re-interred under the church. St. Andrew's Church, built in 1829, was totally destroyed by fire January 25, 1840. The new church built on the site, dedicated in October of the same year, is the present building except for remodeling. The Rt. Rev. Alfred Lee, first Bishop

of the Diocese of Delaware (1841–97), in addition to his episcopal duties, served as Rector of St. Andrew's, 1843–87.

46. WASHINGTON'S HEADQUARTERS *(private)*, 303 West St., a three-story brick building, with new front but original two-story rear, was chosen because of its high location by the commander-in-chief for his headquarters immediately prior to the Battle of the Brandywine. The tablet on the front of the building, reciting its historical importance, was placed by the Delaware State Society of the Cincinnati, February 22, 1902.

Washington arrived in Wilmington on August 25, 1777, the day before the British General Howe landed at Head of Elk, Md. After a reconnoitering trip to Iron Hill with Lafayette and Greene, he lived at this house until September 8, when the Continentals marched to Chadd's Ford to fight the Battle of the Brandywine, September 11.

47. FRIENDS MEETING HOUSE *(open only for services)*, occupying with its burial ground the whole of the block bounded by West, Washington, 4th and 5th Sts., is a broad-gabled red brick building facing West St., erected in 1816 to replace a meeting house built in 1748 on the same plot. The original meeting house, built in 1738 by the first Quaker settlers in Willingtown, stood on the opposite side of West Street, where a portion of its wall, laid in Flemish bond with glazed black headers, can be seen as part of the wall of the vacated Friends School property.

The followers of Elias Hicks retained possession of the present meeting house when the Orthodox adherents removed in 1827 to Ninth and Tatnall Streets and in 1915 to Tenth and Harrison Streets. The congregations work in harmony. In summer when the West Street building is closed, both groups meet at the Harrison Street meeting house.

The remainder of the block is used as a burial ground, with graves marked by the usual low stone in the Quaker fashion. Among those buried here are John Dickinson, the "Penman of the Revolution," near whose grave is a Delaware Historical Marker; Governor Caleb P. Bennett; Jacob Alrichs, great-great-grandson of Peter Alrichs who, with his uncle, Jacob, was identified with the early history of New Amstel (New Castle); and Thomas Garrett, active in the "Underground Railroad." Leading Negroes of Wilmington drew the hearse to the grave when Garrett was buried. Here also are the graves of many early Quaker settlers of Wilmington, among them the Canbys, the Prices, and the Shipleys.

Benjamin Ferris (1780–1867), author of *A History of the Original Settlements on the Delaware,* rests here. Some portions of Ferris' book were used by Charles Reade, the famous English writer, in the text of his novel, *The Wandering Heir,* and Elizabeth Shipley's dream, first told by Ferris, is related in full by Reade in the same work.

The Wilmington Friends School, the oldest school in the State in continuous operation, had its origin in the first meeting house on the east side of West Street, and when the new house of worship was erected in 1748, the old building was used exclusively for school purposes, with a sun dial under the peak of the gable telling the time of day for the pupils. Up to 1786, only the "Three R's" were taught. To keep up with the standard of

the Old Academy which had opened on Market Street, a teacher was secured in Philadelphia to instruct in English grammar, Latin and Greek. A
new building was erected for girls in 1846; in 1883 the whole school was
enlarged; and in 1889 the older sections incorporated in a new building.
In 1937 this building, with all its quilt-like additions, was abandoned for a
new, large modern school building erected on a twenty-acre site near Rock
Manor, northwest of the city. Special buildings increase the facilities of the
school plant, and the high standard of education is maintained through all
grades and the successful college preparatory department.

48. ST. PETER'S ROMAN CATHOLIC PRO-CATHEDRAL, SE. cor-
ner 6th and West Sts., built of red brick, with white painted doorways, is
dominated by the bronze-topped tower rising from its principal entrance.
The original small building, the first Catholic church in Wilmington, was
built on the site in 1816 by the Rev. Patrick Kenny, early missionary priest.

Additions were made in 1832, and the church was well-established by
1868 when the Rt. Rev. Thomas A. Becker was assigned as first bishop to
the new Wilmington Diocese, formed from parts of the Philadelphia,
Baltimore, and Richmond Dioceses.

In 1925, the rectory and school, which had marred the simple lines of
the church, were razed, and the modern parochial school at Sixth and Tatnall Streets was erected. The modified Colonial rectory at Fifth and West
Streets was built the same year.

49. THE WOODWARD HOUSES *(private)*, 701–703 West St., were
built in 1745 and 1760 respectively. The house at 703 contains a hearthstone that was part of the platform upon which Thomas Jefferson stood
to read the Declaration of Independence to the public in Philadelphia.

50. COOL SPRING PARK, bounded by 10th St., Park Place, Van
Buren and Jackson Sts., with its many varieties of unusual and rare trees,
its wading pool and covered sand playground for children, provides a
welcome and quiet retreat from the solidly built-up environment.

A block west is Cool Spring Reservoir, giving the effect of a lake before
the houses that look out upon it from the west. These are on part of the
site of the former home of Caesar A. Rodney, nephew of the Signer, whose
estate, "Cool Spring" is the origin of the present name. Rodney's stone
dwelling house was famous for its hospitality. Letters to him from James
A. Bayard, Sr., mention with pleasure the "wine and woodcock" of "Cool
Spring." Caesar A. Rodney was U.S. Attorney General, 1807–11.
Elected to the Senate in 1823, he was appointed minister to Argentina
where he died June, 1824.

The RODNEY OAK, a huge white-oak now included in the estate of H.
Fletcher Brown, is best viewed from Franklin Street between Tenth and
Eleventh. Approximately 250 years old, with a girth of 13 feet, 10 inches,
and branches covering an area of almost 200 feet, it is the lone survivor
of a grove of hardwood trees that during the Revolutionary period was a
favorite picnic ground because of the view and the spring.

51. The Brandywine granite TILTON HOUSE (UNIVERSITY
CLUB) *(private)*, SW. corner 9th and Broom Sts., stands on Federal Hill,
so called because it was considered in 1798 as one of several sites suitable

for the nation's Capitol. The original portions were erected in 1802. Dr. James Tilton (1745–1822) acquired the plot in 1792. Tilton served as Surgeon-General of the U. S. Army during the War of 1812. When a tumor necessitated the amputation of his left leg, Tilton, then over 70 years old, watched the operation coolly and aided the surgeons.

52. RODNEY RESERVOIR, covering the square bounded by Rodney, Clayton, 8th, and 9th Sts., (capacity 7,500,000 gals.) on the highest ground in the city, is surmounted by a 40-foot steel OBSERVATION TOWER *(open 7:30-5 daily, winter; 7 a.m.-8 p.m., summer)*. On a clear day the view from the tower includes parts of three States and a stretch of the Delaware River from Bellevue to Port Penn, a distance of 20 miles.

53. SOLDIERS AND SAILORS MONUMENT, in the triangle formed by Delaware Ave., W. 14th, and N. Broom Sts., is a tall marble column in memory of Delaware's dead in the Civil War. The shaft is one of the columns of the Pennsylvania Bank Building, Philadelphia, razed in 1868. Sale of this monument was threatened by the sheriff after its unveiling in 1871 because a construction debt remained unpaid. Eli Crozier, known as "We The People" from his newspaper nom-de-plume, came to the rescue and raised sufficient money to release the monument.

54. WILMINGTON AND BRANDYWINE CEMETERY, N. side of Delaware Ave. between Madison and Adams Sts., extending to Brandywine Park Drive, was founded by Samuel Wollaston upon a portion of his farm, "Windsor," in 1843. Incorporated May 17, 1844, additions from time to time have brought its present area to 28 acres. The magnificent cedar of Lebanon, guarding the main entrance, was brought from Palestine by James Canby about 1850. Among the prominent Delawareans buried here are Commodore Jacob Jones (1768–1850), hero of the War of 1812 and later commander of the frigate *Constitution;* James Tilton (1745–1822), Surgeon-General, U.S.A.; General Thomas A. Smyth (1832–65), the last Union general officer to be killed in the Civil War. The remains of Dr. John McKinly (1721–96), first President of The Delaware State, were re-interred here in 1922 after removal from the Old First Presbyterian burial ground. In the Bayard Vault, the remains of Richard Bassett (1745–1815), Signer of the Constitution, U. S. Senator, and Governor of Delaware, and of James Asheton Bayard the elder (1767–1815), Bassett's son-in-law, U. S. Senator from Delaware, and a negotiator of the Treaty of Ghent, were re-interred in 1865, after first interment at Bohemia Manor, Maryland. Richard H. Bayard (1796–1868), first Mayor of Wilmington (1832–4), U. S. Senator, and Chief Justice of Delaware, who had the ashes of his ancestors removed here, was himself buried in the vault.

55. WASHINGTON MEMORIAL BRIDGE, spanning Brandywine Creek and gorge at Washington St., erected by the Levy Court of New Castle County, was dedicated on Memorial Day 1922, to "the Sons of Delaware who joined the forces of their Country in the Great World War."

Of reinforced concrete, it is supported by eight graceful arches, the largest, 250 feet in length, extending over the creek itself. Vance W.

Torbet was the architect and Benjamin H. Davis engineer. Most of the initial expense was met personally by Alfred I. du Pont, chairman of the Bridge Commission, who was later reimbursed. Six bronze tablets on the tall concrete monuments which break the lines of the bridge contain quotations from Washington, Lincoln, Theodore Roosevelt, Lowell, Tennyson, and Ruskin, and the names of the men from New Castle County who died in World War I, together with information pertaining to the bridge.

The TODD MEMORIAL, north of the bridge, is a granite shaft surmounted by a bronze figure of Victory, in memory of the men and women of Delaware who died in World War I. The memorial was erected by William H. Todd, successful shipbuilder who was born in Wilmington.

56. CANBY PARK extends somewhat in the form of an hourglass from Barry, Union, Sycamore, and Oak Sts. to Maryland Ave. and Richardson Park. Two-fifths of the area is a wooded rolling surface inclining to the two intersecting streams; the remainder is open and level. In the park are two bridle paths, two drinking fountains, picnic grounds, three fireplaces, natural springs, a swimming pool, four tennis courts, and trails.

57. The BANNING HOUSE (private), 809 S. Broom St., a large two-and-a-half-story mansion of stone, stuccoed over, since 1922 the rectory of St. Elizabeth's Roman Catholic Church, is typical of Delaware architecture of the early 19th century. Distinguishing features are its 20 rooms, its five separate cellars, its fine interior woodwork, and the wood balustrade on the roof joining the brick chimney tops. Greek characteristics are incorporated in the dormer window details.

Built in 1812 by Joseph Robinson, later owned by James T. Bird, father of Levi C. Bird (1842–1902), Wilmington lawyer, the property was sold in 1861 to Henry Geddes Banning (1816–1906), president of the National Bank of Delaware (1872–1905). His mother, Sarah Geddes, was the daughter of Captain Henry Geddes, an Irishman who came to Delaware and fell in love with Margaret Latimer, of the old Delaware family of that name. She refused to marry a British subject, and kept him waiting until he became a Delaware citizen and joined the American navy. Henry G. Banning married Emily Eschenburg, a great-granddaughter of Caesar A. Rodney. In the south parlor of this house Mrs. Banning organized the National Society, Colonial Dames of America, on May 19, 1892, and she was president of the Delaware Society as well as a national vice president until her death in 1897.

58. The razing of LATIMERIA, Maryland Ave. near Broom St., removed from the Wilmington scene an impressive mansion of faded charm and genteel shabbiness, facing the Christina from a rolling terrace. Its doors, shutters, mantels, now grace other homes. The two-and-a-half-story structure, whose original bricks were covered with brown stucco, had a portico with six slender columns. The entablature of the portico was without the usual architrave and frieze. Fan and sidelights were used in the doorway.

The hip roof was surmounted by a balustrade and pierced by two generously proportioned chimneys and dormer windows. An interior of beautifully carved woodwork, including chimney cupboards, and the delightful old garden without, were left undisturbed during the tenure of the last occupant, Miss Mary R. Latimer (1834–1929), who lived here most of her life.

The mansion, though named by John R. Latimer, wealthy tea-merchant of Philadelphia and China, was built by William Warner in 1815. Having purchased the land, Warner gave a dinner party to which the guests were requested to bring plans for the new house. All did except Victor du Pont, who arose to say:

> "My plan is best of all—
> Build not at all."

However, Warner chose the plan submitted by Victor's brother, Eleuthère Irénée du Pont, which may explain some of its French character-istics. The rear porch, a later addition, was of the Greek Revival period. Shortly after the house was built, Warner sold it to Robert Andrews, father of Col. John W. Andrews. John R. Latimer, the next owner, filled the house with china, pottery, furniture, and paintings collected during a resi-dence in China, and with treasured relics of the earlier Latimers. He died in 1865 and willed the property to his brother, Henry Latimer.

When Miss Latimer died at ninety-five years of age in 1929, a wealth of heirlooms, antique furnishings and decorations, the envy and despair of collectors, was distributed among relatives and friends in accordance with the terms of her will. These bequests included all the old silver and the crested blue china of generations of Latimers, as well as the family portraits.

59. PIERRE S. DU PONT HIGH SCHOOL *(open on application),* 34th and Van Buren Sts., named in honor of the well-known Delaware industrialist, notable contributor to public education, is designed in the classic Georgian style. The building, completed in 1935, is Wilmington's most elaborately equipped public school structure and accommodates more than 2,000 pupils.

WILMINGTON, PRESENT AND FUTURE

During and since World War II, Wilmington has lost some of its population to the fast developing suburban areas of northern New Castle County. Industry and business also have to some extent gone outside and new establishments, industrial and business, have chosen more sites outside than within the city limits. Supermarkets and shopping centers for the new suburban housing developments attract Wilmington residents as well as the suburban dwellers.

This withdrawal of consumer purchasing potential has promoted study of Wilmington's characteristics as a modern city, especially in merchandis-ing, and has resulted in more attention to parking facilities, planning, zon-ing, slum clearance. Wilmington Housing Authority has doubled its low-rent dwelling units, enabling the city to hold some low-income workers who otherwise would be tenants of substandard dwellings within and outside city lines. Sanitation, health and recreation programs have advanced greatly, public safety departments are highly efficient. New schools and churches have multiplied.

Wilmington provides services for large areas outside its limits: water, gas, electricity, street lighting. The State Highway Department and the county commission (Levy Court) provide others: road maintenance, police protection, sewer systems. But many suburban areas do not have all the services they need and Wilmington does not have enough revenue. City real estate, taxed by both city and county, bears the chief burden.

Modern rebuilding, on a sound plan, of some of the deteriorated areas, with more open spaces, will provide greatly increased values for tax assessment and increase the population of town-dwellers.

POINTS OF INTEREST IN THE ENVIRONS

Long Hook, *1.9 m.;* U. S. Lighthouse Depot, *4 m.;* Robinson House and ancient Block House (Naaman's), *7.5 m.;* Grubb House, *7.8 m.;* Buena Vista, *9.3 m. (see Tour 1).* The Blue Ball, *2.1 m.;* Lombardy, Bedford House, *2.4 m.;* Nemours Carillon Tower, *2.8 m. (see Tour 5).* The Buck, *3.5 m.;* Hoopes Reservoir Dam, *5.8 m.;* Friends Centre Meeting House, *7.6 m.;* Longwood, *12.4 (see Tour 6).* Henry Clay, old industrial village, *2.7 m.;* Du Pont Experimental Station, *2.9 m.;* Old Du Pont Powder Mills, Upper Hagley Yard, *3 m. (see Tour 6A).* Du Pont Family Cemetery, *3.8 m.;* Eleutherian Mills, *3.9 m.;* Christ Church Christiana Hundred, *4.3 m.;* Smith's Covered Bridge, *8.2 m. (see Tour 6B).* The Valley Garden, *4.9 m.;* Mount Cuba, *7.1 m.;* Helme Snuff Plant, *9.3 m. (see Tour 6C).* Brandywine Springs, *5.3 m.;* Hockessin Friends Meeting House, *9 m. (see Tour 7).* Coffee Run Catholic Cemetery, *6.4 m. (see Tour 7A).* Swedish Log House, *3.7 m.;* St. James Church, *7.3 m.;* Delaware Park, racetrack, *8.2 m.;* England House, *11 m. (see Tour 8).* Red Clay Presbyterian Church, *8 m.;* The Mermaid, *8.5 m.;* Christiana, *9.5 m.;* The Red Lion, *11.7 m. (see Tour 11);* Alfred I. du Pont Institute, *2.8 m. (see Tour 5).*

PART III

Tours

Preface to Tours

The Delaware Highway system of main and secondary roads is being rapidly expanded and improved. New roads, bypasses, interchanges; and roads under construction are plainly marked, but routes can be planned in advance by using the current official Highway Department maps and detour bulletins and maps furnished by mail or inquiry from the State Highway Division of Traffic and Planning, 152 South State Street, Dover. Maps may be had also at the Information Office of the Delaware Memorial Bridge, near the exit road from the Bridge on the north side.

An alternate route from the Memorial Bridge to Hare's Corner and junction with US 13 and State 40 there, is south on the first crossroad, which leads through the well preserved colonial town of New Castle *(see NEW CASTLE)*, with its architectural survivals in dwellings, churches, and public buildings.

The best route (1954) to the Chesapeake Bay Bridge is by US 13 to the north entrance of Smyrna, where State 300 branches west by a well-marked entrance. A new route by State 71 and State 4 will be met by Maryland's new Bay Bridge Route at the Delaware-Maryland Line west of Middletown in 1955–56.

From Delaware City to the south boundary of the State, the network of secondary roads east of US 13 abound with water scenes, wildlife haunts, secluded old homesteads, and unspoiled river and creekborders, as well as fishing and resort communities. Maps of inland waters for fishing and recreation in all parts of the State can be had by mail from the State Game and Fish Commission, Dover.

At the S. side of Wilmington's Canby Park *(see WILMINGTON)*, on the Newport Pike, is the site of one of the earliest mills in the State. Built by early settlers before 1687, it was bought by John Richardson in 1723 and descended from father to son until 1887. At the end of the first hundred years it was rebuilt. Not used as a mill in this century, it was finally torn down. A millstone and historic marker (R) indicate the site. On the hill above it is one of the two remaining stone dwelling houses built by the two earliest Richardsons, father and son.

Tour 1

(Chester, Pa.)—Wilmington—Dover—Delmar—(Salisbury, Md.); US 13.
Pennsylvania State Line-Maryland State Line, 105.1 *m.*
Pennsylvania R.R. parallels the entire route; the Baltimore and Ohio between the
Pennsylvania Line and Wilmington; Greyhound and other through bus lines follow
the route.
Roadbed paved throughout; dual highway between Wilmington and Dover; the road
bypasses many towns on the route.

Accommodations: First-class hotels in Wilmington; small hotels and tourist homes in
towns; few tourist or trailer camps; good motels.

US 13, the most direct route between Philadelphia, Pa., and Norfolk,
Va., traverses Delaware from end to end, passing through an industrial
and suburban section of hilly and rocky country north of Wilmington,
through gently rolling farmland in the middle of the State, and through
the nearly flat, sandy, pine-wooded and truck-raising expanse of Lower
Delaware lying in the Coastal Plain. The Delaware section of US 13 runs
more than one-half the length of the so-called Delmarva Peninsula, the
low-lying and water-bound region east of Chesapeake Bay that contains
the State of Delaware and the eastern shores of Maryland and Virginia.

Bordered by few famous buildings and no battlefields or natural won-
ders but by a countryside of comfortable farmsteads, busy towns and villages, and numerous vistas of quiet beauty, the route is notable for the
successive differences and contrasts, great and small, in the aspect of the
country and in the life of the people. Within 25 miles there may be differences in terrain, forestation, style or material of old houses, political color,
crops and farming methods, tempo of living, accent and expression of
speech. A farmer who lives in the southern part of the State may discuss
technically the latest aircraft model that flies above him from a nearby
military base and then speak of "housen" for houses, or of a chicken too
long killed as "dainty."

North and South, the 20th and the 17th century, the rocky Piedmont
and the broad salt marshes, meet along this route or are separated by no
great distance. Though the upper end of the US 13 country has a northern
flavor, the lower nine-tenths is more akin in many ways to the eastern
shore of Maryland, which is southern in essence and borders Delaware
for 130 miles on the west and south.

US 13 has superseded the waterways and the railroads as the main
artery of travel and transportation on the Peninsula. All year long a tide
of heavy trucks rolls northward over it, day and night, hauling fresh
vegetables, fruits, grain, chickens, milk, seafoods, lumber, canned foodstuffs, and other products of a fertile region. At times the lines of trucks
during a harvest season look like freight trains of boxcars loosely coupled.

SMYRNA

Empty trucks rumble southward at high speed. The progress of the season is accurately marked by the license plates on the trucks—in the space of two weeks asparagus is cut first in Virginia, then Maryland, then Delaware.

Section a. Pennsylvania Line to Wilmington, 8 m.

From the hills of this section of US 13, paralleling the Delaware River, there are intermittent views of the broad river and the factory smokestacks of the low-lying New Jersey shore. The route is almost solidly lined by unpretentious dwellings and villages suburban to Wilmington. The old houses are almost all of native stone quarried from the eastern edge of the hill country (R).

US 13 crosses the Pennsylvania Line, 0 m., about 3 miles southwest of Chester, Pa. (see Pa. Tour 35).

At 0.4 m. the highway is crossed overhead by the electrified main line of the Pennsylvania R.R. between New York and Washington.

The ROBINSON HOUSE (tearoom), 0.5 m. (R), facing Naaman's Creek, stands on a 1,000-acre tract patented in 1675 by Gov. Edmund Andros to six Swedes and Dutchmen. Along the creek, then much broader and deeper, gristmills and lumber mills were established and log houses

John Moll

built. A large steel mill now stands where once the woods stretched down to the nearby shore of the Delaware River.

The stone part of the house is said to have been erected about 1723. Another section is of wide weathered ship planks with flush joints. Across the front is a long portico of fluted columns, a later addition; the first floor contains much of the original woodwork, of fine craftsmanship. The house takes its name from Gen. Thomas Robinson, who acquired it in 1749 and was killed fighting Indians in the West.

As an inn on the King's Highway it was a favorite stopping place for notables during the congressional sessions at Philadelphia. From Aug. 23 to 25, 1777, Gen. George Washington was an anxious guest waiting to learn of the destination of the British forces commanded by Sir William Howe, which came up the Chesapeake and landed at the head of Elk River in Maryland. Gen. "Mad Anthony" Wayne was a frequent visitor, especially because he was a brother-in-law of Abraham Robinson, then proprietor, as well as guardian of the latter's niece Sally Robinson. The Robinson House so interested Henry Ford that he once tried to buy it for his early-American village at Dearborn, Mich. It is the property of the Worth Steel Co.

The small stone BLOCKHOUSE *(open by permission),* next to the Robinson House, is two stories with a hip roof, its walls whitewashed. It is now an annex to the tearoom. Legend presumes it was built in 1654 by Johan Rising, Governor of New Sweden, to protect the industrial settlement of mills and dwellings bordering the creek. Loopholes under the eaves permitted muskets to shoot out at marauders. Small windows were later cut through the thick stone walls, and an addition made the little building better suited for its peaceful use as a summer kitchen to the "big house."

Legend persists that Stuyvesant took it from the Swedes in 1655, but the Swedes built only log forts. The stone building was taken by the British in 1777. Revenge came in 1778 when "Light Horse Harry" Lee of Virginia led a detachment to the inn, and captured three officers from a British warship as they were having breakfast.

NAAMAN'S CREEK, flowing beneath the roadway here, was named for an Indian chief. Before the water power failed, grain was brought long distances to be turned into flour and meal and loaded on sloops to be taken to Philadelphia.

Until the middle of the 19th century the section was a popular duelling-ground, especially for Philadelphians, because of the ease of crossing the State Line and evading Pennsylvania law officers. In 1830 Midshipman Charles G. Hunter of the Navy fatally wounded William Miller of Philadelphia; President Jackson dismissed Hunter from the Navy, but he was later reinstated and served with honor in the Mexican War. In 1842 a political quarrel in Congress resulted in the wounding of Gen. James Watson Webb of New York by Thomas F. Marshall of Kentucky; it was said they were in deadly earnest, and the disgusted Marshall was with difficulty kept from taking another and more careful shot at Webb. The last duel known to have occurred here was in 1845 when two Philadelphians, Washington Keith and Morris Meredith, wounded each other and retired with honor satisfied.

The WORTH STEEL PLANT owned by Colorado Co., 0.7 m. (R), specializes in steel plates for tanks, boilers, and pipe lines. Here was the farm of Adolph Wertmuller (1751–1811), Swedish artist (see ART).

WORTHLAND, 1.1 m. (R), is a company village for steel employees.

The WREN'S NEST or Darley Mansion (R), 1.3 m. (private), a frame house painted white, was bought in 1850 by Felix O. C. Darley (1822–88), who was born in Philadelphia and was one of the best-known illustrators of his time. On commissions from the American Art Union, Darley illustrated the works of Irving, Cooper, Dickens, and Sims, Longfellow's Courtship of Miles Standish, Judd's Margaret, and the Library of Humorous American Works. He had a reputation for the execution of minute detail; did vignettes for banknotes, and, on order, made four drawings "representative of American life" for Prince Napoleon (1822–91), the younger son of Jerome Bonaparte and his second wife Catharine.

The present owner has a shop behind the house for making decorative metal articles, chiefly in wrought iron and copper.

At the Wren's Nest is the junction with a side road.

1. Right on this road to WOODS HAVEN SCHOOL (industrial) FOR WHITE GIRLS (R) 0.2 m. (visiting hours, Sun. 1:30-3:30), established in 1893.

The student-body varies between 50 and 100 girls between the ages of 11 and 21 years, committed for delinquencies. Usually 50 or more girls are out on parole, mostly in domestic service. The chief structure, the PHOEBE CURTIS BUILDING, of native stone, erected in 1932, houses classes through the 12th grade for girls able to do academic work. Others receive vocational and manual training.

2. Left on this road to MIRAFLORES (L), 0.2 m. *(private)*, a large Victorian house facing the river, the Delaware home for many years of John Edward O'Sullivan Addicks (1841–1919), Philadelphia-born millionaire, whose wealth had come largely from financing and building gas works in many cities. He was a noted political character who from 1889 to 1906 sought a U. S. Senatorship from Delaware.

ARCHMERE ACADEMY (L), 1.4 m. *(open to visitors)*, was founded in 1932 as a boys' boarding school under the direction of the Premonstratensian Fathers of the Roman Catholic Church. Enrollment is not restricted to Catholic students.

The handsomely landscaped estate of 30 acres overlooking the Delaware River was the home of John Jacob Raskob (1879–   ), vice-president of General Motors Corporations, former treasurer of E. I. du Pont de Nemours and Co., and chairman of the National Democratic Committee in 1928 when he and Pierre S. du Pont were prime backers of Alfred E. Smith for the Presidency. A devout Catholic, he presented Archmere to the Church. MAIN HALL, the former owner's residence, is the principal school building. Built in 1918, it is designed in the manner of an Italian Renaissance villa, and has a glass-covered patio of 2,000 square feet that can be entirely opened. The architects were McClure and Harper of New York City.

At 1.6 m. is the northern junction with Alternate US 13, called the Governor Printz Blvd. for Johan Printz, third Governor (1643–53) of the Swedes on the Delaware. It is a heavy traffic truck route.

Left on this highway, built in 1937 to avoid steep hills and congested city traffic; it rejoins US 13 south of Wilmington, and follows the ancient Indian trail along the river that was used by the Swedish settlers.

CLAYMONT, 1.7 m. (75 alt., 7,500 estimated pop. as a post office district), unincorporated, has no defined limits nor municipal government, and is considered a suburb of Wilmington. Claymont houses are mostly well-kept and unpretentious. Many of the old country places along the highway have suffered encroachment by stores, filling stations, and roadside markets.

Until 1852 the section was called simply Naaman's *(see above)*. The present name is said to have come from the nature of the soil, or perhaps from the Clayton family.

At 2.3 m. is the SITE OF THE QUEEN OF FRANCE TAVERN (R), occupied by a stucco-covered building erected after the burning of the old inn in 1872. During the Revolution a ball from a British sloop of war passed through a wall of the tavern. During the French Revolution the proprietor advertised the place with a sign on which was painted the bloody trunk of a beheaded woman, with the inscription, "To the Guillotined Queen of France." Public opinion made him remove the blood and change the inscription to read, "To the Woman Who Is Silent." About 1796 another innkeeper renamed the place "The Practical Farmer." After 1840 the inn became noted as a horseracing headquarters and for watermelon fairs attended by hundreds of Jerseymen and Pennsylvanians, the latter exchanging whiskey for the Jerseymen's melons. Cattle were brought for sale and exhibition.

At 2.3 *m.* is the junction with Grubb's Road.

Right on this road is ARDEN, 1.8 *m.* (193 alt., 1,300 pop.) *(see ARDEN).*

The GRUBB HOMESTEAD (R), **2.1** *m. (private),* a stone-and-log mansion set back from Grubb's Rd. in a grove of ancient honey locusts, is in an excellent state of preservation. This fine Colonial house, owned and occupied by the Grubb family for more than two and a quarter centuries, contains many old furnishings. The purchase of the furniture is recorded in a family ledger, still preserved.

John Grubb (1652–1708), the builder of the log section of the house, settled at Grubb's Landing in 1682 after having lived up the river for several years; he was a planter, a justice, and a member of the Colonial Assembly under Penn. His eldest son Emanuel was said to have been the first child of English parents born in Penn's province. About 1760 a later Grubb built the two-and-one-half-story stone wing, and the first house became the kitchen wing. The logs are now sheathed in boards; the old wing is a story and a half high, with a low kitchen ceiling and a fireplace so large that the back log was formerly dragged in by a horse; the log was unhooked, and the horse led out the opposite door. The "new" wing contains the original stairway, fine mantels, and wall paneling with dog-ear trim. The paneling is of walnut, unpainted but heavily varnished. The hardware and much of the wide flooring are original. The heavy front door is decorated with a pair of bull's-eye glass windows. Entries in the family ledger, which was used also for keeping the accounts in a Grubb-owned country store, run from 1746 to the time of the Revolution; they include the buying of the grandfather clock made by Thomas Wells, of Philadelphia, that still ticks slowly in a corner, and of the Chippendale chairs in the parlor.

Standing near the house is an old-time stone SLAVE QUARTER with loft and cellar. The old cow barn is also of stone in the local manner. In front of the house the great stump of a catalpa tree that fell recently has sent up a new green shoot to remind the family of the Battle of the Brandywine, Sept. 11, 1777, when a youthful Grubb rode a few miles northeast to see the fighting between Washington and the invading Howe; the tale is that the tree grew from a switch he broke to use on his horse and stuck in the ground on returning from the battle. The family has produced business and professional men that have gone away to live, but there has always been a Grubb living in the old house and farming the land about it, proudly keeping the place in unchanged order.

At the GEORGE LODGE HOUSE (L), 2.5 *m. (private),* built about 1840 of brick, now painted green, the novelist Anne Parrish lived for several years with her novelist brother Dillwyn Parrish. The scene of her *The Perennial Bachelor,* winner of the Harper's Prize for 1925, is northern Delaware.

The OLD LODGE HOUSE (R), 2.6 *m. (private),* was left perched high above the roadway when the final grading was done. No record has been found to tell when this little stone house was built on a 500-acre grant from Penn, but the front part is believed to have been erected by Daniel Buckley in 1700 or earlier. Recently razed for road widening.

BELLEVUE RESERVOIR (R), 3.8 *m. (open by permission),* a pretty little lake enclosed by rugged stone cliffs and wooded banks, owned by a suburban water company, is the old Bellevue Quarry from which came much of the granite that went into the building of the Delaware Breakwater (1828–32) at Cape Henlopen. A private canal admitted vessels from the river.

The WILLIAM DU PONT ESTATE (R), 4.3 *m. (private)*, overlooking the river, has a famous racing stable. There is a private race track on the grounds.

STATE HIGHWAY POLICE STATION No. 1 (R), 4.9 *m. (information and first aid service)*, was noted in 1932 for the mystery surrounding the disappearance of 145 cases of "choice" liquors that had been confiscated from a bootleg truck and stored in the police seizure room.

The TUSSEY HOUSE (R), 5 *m. (private)*, built in 1765 of stone, with hip roof and pent eaves, now covered with brown stucco, was where Capt. Thomas Webb came to preach in 1769; he was one of the first Methodists to enter the Colony. When preaching he wore a British Army uniform to remind his listeners that he fought under General Wolfe at Quebec in 1758, when he lost his right eye. Of him President John Adams remarked: "He is one of the most eloquent and fluent speakers I ever heard."

At 5.3 *m.* is the junction with Marsh Rd. and Lore Ave.

1. Right on Marsh Rd. to the junction with Carr Rd., **1.3** *m.;* L. on Carr Rd. to the SITE OF NEWARK UNION MEETING HOUSE, **1.9** *m.* (R), at the Newark Union M. E. Church. The meeting house was built about 1688 on a tract "New Wark" or "New Worke" patented to Valentine Hollingsworth *(see NEWARK)*. Monthly meetings were held here or alternately at Centre Meeting *(see Tour 6)* until 1707, weekly meetings continuing until 1754 when the building was moved to Centre Meeting as an outbuilding. The ancient graveyard remains here.

2. Left on Lore Ave., is HILLCREST, one of the earliest suburbs north of Wilmington, extending S. in cross streets beyond Marsh Road. Here in the 1890's and early 1900's a few professional people built good houses on spacious plots along tree-shaded roads, now closely built up.

On the W. side of Lighthouse Rd., S. of Lore Ave., in GORDON HEIGHTS, is MARCUS HOOK REAR RANGE *(open by permission)*, one of the beacons by which vessels on the river lay their courses to keep in the channel. Built of concrete during World War I the square tower has a powerful light 278 feet above the water. The wide view from the top on clear days includes the New Jersey shore, most of northern Delaware, and the William Penn statue on City Hall, Philadelphia.

The SHAW HOUSE (R), 5.4 *m. (private)*, on Penny Hill, built of stone by the Penny family in 1790, was the home of Robert Shaw (1859–1912), noted Delaware etcher and illustrator. Shaw was blinded for four years by his exacting work, later regained his sight, and took up water color. Among his most popular etchings, still hanging in many homes, are *Old Swedes Church, September Evening on the Brandywine, Immanuel Church, New Castle,* and *Old Market Street Bridge*.

At 5.7 *m.* is junction with side road. L on this to Merchandise Mart (R) on Printz Boulevard.

Across the Boulevard, on the SITE OF EDGEMOOR VILLAGE, are several new industrial plants. Once a town in its own right, Edgemoor was built in 1871 by the Edgemoor Iron Co. which fabricated iron for the Brooklyn Bridge, Philadelphia elevated railways, and framing for buildings at the Chicago Fair of 1893.

After liquidation of the firm in 1935 the whole village was razed—houses, stores, a school, and even a church. The site was called Verdritige Hook by the Swedes, whose houses, clustered along the river, were held without any title to the land save that by discovery and occupation. In the 19th century Du Pont powder wagons came here from the Brandywine to load ships *(see Tour 6A)*.

The U. S. LIGHTHOUSE DEPOT *(open by permission)*, **1.7** *m.*, on a wharf at the river shore, is the supply and repair base for all lighthouses, lightships, and buoys in the area of the Delaware River and Bay and along the Delaware seacoast to the Maryland line. The large wharf is usually covered with great steel buoys brought here for reconditioning; barnacles and rust are removed and bright red paint is applied to nun buoys, black paint to can buoys. Bells, horns, whistles, and lights are repaired or replaced. The warehouses contain all sorts of equipment, from expensive prism lenses of cut glass, for lighthouses, to soap and towels for lightship crews.

At 5.8 *m.* the highway crosses SHELLPOT CREEK, a tributary of the Brandywine Creek. The name is a corruption from the Swedish Sköldpadde Fallet *(Turtle Falls)*. The first gristmill was erected here soon after 1662 by John Stalcop, a Swede, aided by other Swedes and Dutchmen; mills flourished on the stream well into the 18th century. William Penn, writing in 1683, included the lower reaches of "Skilpot" Creek with the Christina, Brandywine, and Schuylkill as each having "room enough to lay up the Royal Navy of England."

Shellpot Park, for years a noted summer playground here, ceased to function after a fire in 1934 burned many of the amusement devices. Dance marathons were the last big attraction.

US 13 follows Market St. to 16th St.; L. on 16th St. to French St.; R. on French St. to 10th St.

WILMINGTON, **8** *m.* (80 alt, 110,356 pop.) *(see WILMINGTON)*.
Points of Interest. Old Swedes Church, The Rocks, Old Town Hall, Rodney Square, Du Pont and Nemours Buildings, Public Library, Delaware Art Center, Brandywine Park, and others.

Wilmington is at the junction with US 202 *(see Tour 5)*, State 2 *(see Tour 8)*, State 48 *(see Tour 7A)*, State 52 *(see Tour 6)*, and the Rising Sun Road *(see Tour 6A)*.

Section b. Wilmington to Hare's Corner, 6.6 m.

South of Wilmington, 0 *m.*, US 13 follows French St. to Front St.; R. on Front St. to Market St.; L. on Market St. across the Christina River.

South of the Christina River the highway leaves high, rocky hills and smoking factories and enters the lowlands of the Peninsula. This short section of US 13 is bordered by small suburban houses and many service stations that in recent years have filled most of the gaps between the large old brick farmsteads characteristic of lower New Castle County and northern Kent County.

LONG HOOK (R), 1.9 *m.*, inn and restaurant, part brick and part frame stuccoed, all painted yellow, stands on a rise overlooking the Christina Marsh (once called the Holland Marsh). Kent Manor Inn is a restaurant and tourist lodge, leased from the New Castle Historical Society, which now owns this property.

The oldest section of this house, a frame wing of wide vertical planks covering the structural timbers, contains a great fireplace and floorboards 22 inches wide. Peter Jacquet, son of Jean Paul Jacquet, vice-director (1655–7) of the Dutch colony on the Delaware, bought the property in 1722; his son Peter added a brick wing in 1763, as shown by his initials and the date in brick headers in the original south wall. Later additions, made about 1860, included an extension of the main wing and an additional story on both wings; the walls still show clearly the heights and lines of the original gables.

Another Peter Jacquet (1755–1834) was a major in the Revolution, serving from 1776 to the defeat of Cornwallis at Yorktown. The story is that he or another Jacquet was once sued for slander by Thomas Tatlow, a neighbor, whom he had accused of stealing wheat and had called a thief. Jacquet's attorney, the future Judge James Booth, told him he could not call a man that with impunity, but there were other names he could use.

"Write 'em down for me," said Jacquet.

The lawyer did so, and afterwards whenever Jacquet met Tatlow on the street he would read off the list of insults at the top of his voice.

The Jacquet family's traditional hospitality is recorded in 1679 in the *Journal* of Dankers and Sluyter, Dutch missionaries who spoke of the "medlar" plums from which the Jacquets made a liquor "even better than French brandy." There is a tradition that Washington and Lafayette were later entertained here. Even after the place was sold by the family about 1850 it continued to be noted for its social life.

At 2 *m.* is the southern junction (L) with Alternate US 13 *(see above)*.

At 2.7 *m.* was the entrance (L) to STOCKFORD *(private),* hidden at the end of a long wooded avenue, a large brick house in poor condition that was built about 1840 by John B. Newman on the farm formerly owned by John Stockton, who served in the Revolution and War of 1812. (Stockton's brick house still stands some distance east of Stockford.) After 1866 Stockford was the off-duty home of Maj. Gen. James Harrison Wilson (1837–1925), U. S. Army engineer, Civil War cavalry leader, military governor, and author, who married Newman's granddaughter, Ella Andrews. Stockford area is being converted (1953) into large motel park.

Wilson was born near Shawneetown, Ill., and was graduated from the U. S. Military Academy in the class of 1860. Strong in mind and body, self-confident, an executive as well as fighter, he rose with such meteoric rapidity after the outbreak of the Civil War that by 1864, at 27, he was Chief of Cavalry, Military Division of the Mississippi, with the rank of brevet major-general and a command about equal to that of Gen. Philip Sheridan under whom he had served in the Army of the Potomac. Wilson's charge resulting in the capture of Selma, Ala., April 2, 1865, has been regarded as of unexcelled brilliance from a tactical standpoint. A month later, in Georgia, a detachment of his men captured Jefferson Davis, President of the Confederacy.

LONG HOOK, NEAR WILMINGTON

In 1898 General Wilson volunteered for the Spanish-American War and afterwards was Governor of the Matanzas District of Cuba. In 1900 he led American and British forces against the Boxers in China. In 1902 he represented the Army at the coronation of King Edward VII and Queen Alexandra of England. The latter part of his life he devoted to writing. His works include biographies of Ulysses S. Grant, Charles A. Dana, and John A. Rawlins; his *Under the Old Flag* is autobiographical.

At 3.7 *m.* is the junction (L), with US 40, crossing the Delaware River.

Connecting the Delaware highway system with that of New Jersey, the new route uses the Delaware Memorial Bridge *(see TRANSPORTATION)* to Deepwater Point, New Jersey, where it joins US 130, N.J. 44 and the New Jersey Turnpike. The New Castle Ferry which formerly carried US 40 between Delaware and New Jersey has been discontinued.

On this route a short distance from the Bridge is an interchange with the Wilmington-New Castle road. Near the Bridge entrance (L), is an information office. On the river bank (R), the works and laboratory of Atlas Powder Company.

The DELAWARE STATE HOSPITAL (R), 3.8 *m. (visiting hours, Mon., Wed. and Sat., 1:30-4),* a group of large brick buildings on extensive grounds, is the principal State institution for the mentally ill, caring for about 1,000 committed patients. Since 1889 it has been known as Farnhurst, which was the name of the railroad station built nearby for the institution; the station has been removed. Here also was the New Castle County Almshouse until 1933 when the State Welfare Home at Smyrna was opened.

In recent years the hospital has acquired a high reputation for efficiency and use of modern therapeutic methods. It was one of the first State mental hospitals in the country to be approved by the American College of Surgeons and the American Medical Association. The hospital has a training school for nurses and operates a farm producing much of the food consumed on the premises. The MENTAL HYGIENE CLINIC, opened in 1931, treats persons not committed to the hospital and maintains a traveling service throughout the State. *(See Delaware Colony: Tour 2.)*

At 4.2 *m.* the highway crosses the tracks of the Delmarva Division of the Pennsylvania R.R., which runs the length of the Peninsula, about 200 miles. Rails of the Delaware R.R. reached the Maryland line at Delmar in 1859, and were extended by the New York, Philadelphia & Norfolk R.R. to Cape Charles, Va., in 1884.

At 5.3 *m.* is the junction with State 41 *(see Tour 7).*

NEW CASTLE COUNTY AIRPORT (R), 1,200 acres, is used jointly as a county airport and a U.S. Army Air Force Base. It has scheduled service by four commercial airlines, passenger, express, mail and freight. It is one of the largest mushroom-shipping points in the country. The Army Base is a Defense Wing of Air Force fighting units; training center for squadrons.

HARE'S CORNER, 6.6 *m.,* is the former junction with US 40 *(see Tour 4).* Left on this road, 2 *m.,* to New Castle, where the central town is a colonial survival of architectural worth and charm. *(See NEW CASTLE.)*

Hare's Corner was once a stage-stop and cattle market. Along the dusty roads herds were driven by farm boys whistling tunes and swishing willow branches. The Green Tree Inn, razed in 1931 to make way for the dual highway, stood at the northeast corner, where travelers alighted for refreshment while horses were watered or changed.

Section c. Hare's Corner to Dover, 39.1 m.

This section of US 13 runs 2 to 10 miles west of Delaware River and Bay, crossing many tidal creeks flowing eastward. The gently rolling countryside, tilled for nearly 300 years, is divided into farms that average 150-400 acres, larger than those found elsewhere in Delaware. About three-fourths of the farms are operated by tenants. Absentee landlords often own five or more farms each, usually inherited. The so-called "landed gentry" have virtually disappeared from the region since the collapse of the peach boom in the 1880's. The heavy clay soil, unsuited to truck crops, is devoted chiefly to wheat and corn and to pasture and forage crops. Timber is entirely hardwood, reduced to thin strips along streams for the most part. A large Negro population is the legacy of the slave system upon which agriculture in the region was almost wholly based in Colonial times; many slaves were freed before the Civil War and many Negroes have migrated north, but Negro labor is still the prime means of tilling the land. Owners and tenants are usually white.

John Moll

ODESSA

The old farmhouses are mostly of brick, with large kitchens and many outbuildings, nearly all set far back from the road. The farther south the road runs, the less the dialect and idioms of the people resemble the speech of northern Delaware. The barnyard of upper New Castle County becomes the "pound" of Kent County, for example, and the pitch and rhythm take on southern characteristics while retaining the R sounds.

The hillside that was formerly McCRONE'S WOODS, 0.1 *m.* (R), was the scene, on the afternoon of July 28, 1864, of a "Pic Nic Party" of well-known ladies and gentlemen from New Castle and the nearby countryside, a benefit affair for the avowed purpose of buying vegetables and other anti-scorbutics for the scurvy-ridden Confederate prisoners at Fort Delaware on Pea Patch Island in the Delaware River, 6 miles away. The commandant of the fort himself had issued the plea, which was read in many churches. The living conditions of the several thousand captured men outraged many Delawareans—especially the Southern-sympathizing Democrats. Application for permission to hold the picnic was made to the provost marshal, who sent back word that while he could not approve it, he "could not condemn it." Union troops had been used in Delaware to disarm "secessionists," but a benefit picnic was apparently safe.

Nevertheless the afternoon's amusement was abruptly stopped at 5 o'clock by the appearance of the provost marshal of the district and a captain with 60 men of the 114th Ohio Regiment, who had arrived from Wilmington by special train. The marshal called for the managers of the picnic, and addressed them, saying that he must arrest them for holding the picnic. He then paroled 26 young men "of the highest social standing" to appear at headquarters next day, and the picnic broke up peaceably except for the summary arrest of two young men who indulged in heated words with the officers. Other managers escaped arrest by being warned not to come to the picnic. Those who reported at headquarters were locked up for a sweltering day and night, and "not exempt from taunts and insults" were taken to the railroad station and thence to Fort McHenry, near Baltimore, where they were imprisoned until Aug. 6, when friends effected their release and they returned to Wilmington. This time there was a brass band to meet them.

STATE HIGHWAY POLICE STATION No. 2 (R), 0.9 *m.* *(information and first aid)*.

At 1 *m.* US 13 branches L. from US 40 *(see Tour 4)*.

BUENA VISTA (R), 2.7 *m.* *(private),* a plain brick house completed in 1846, has a recent large addition on the south; it stands at the end of a long avenue of trees. The house was erected by John Middleton Clayton (1796–1856), Chief Justice of Delaware, United States Senator and Secretary of State under President Zachary Taylor. Clayton named the place for the Mexican War battle out of tribute to Taylor's victory there in 1847.

Clayton was born in Dagsboro, Sussex County, of a family noted for mental ability, fine physique, and strong personality. His eloquence as a trial lawyer won him an unrivaled reputation in Delaware, and his statesmanship in Washington, sometimes undiplomatic but always vigorous, brought him international recognition. As Secretary of State he promoted American commerce and his program for opening trade relations with the Orient was used a few years later by Admiral Perry in the expedition to Japan. His most noted achievement was the Clayton-Bulwer Treaty with England in 1850, in which disputes were settled that were apparently leading to war. This treaty also contained pledges, skillfully worked in, that led to England's relinquishing territory on the Isthmus of Panama.

In the Capital, Clayton's fame as a statesman was equalled by his reputation as a host and epicure. More than six feet tall, well-built, his white hair always brushed into an unruffled pompadour, he would stand over a chafing-dish preparing diamondback terrapin according to his family recipe —adding an exact amount of fine sherry and cooking it just long enough. The terrapin were brought from Delaware in large quantities.

He died in 1856 after seeing the Delaware Railroad, which he promoted, carried nearly to the end of the State. Statues of him and Caesar Rodney were unveiled in 1934 in Statuary Hall in the Capitol, Washington, as two of Delaware's greatest sons. A portrait of him, probably made from a daguerreotype, hangs in the State House *(see Dover)*.

The present owner and occupant of Buena Vista is Clayton's greatnephew, the Hon. Clayton Douglass Buck, Governor of Delaware 1929–37. First as an engineer for Coleman du Pont in 1911 when the latter began construction of the $4,000,000 highway that he gave to Delaware, later as Chief Engineer of the State Highway Department, and finally as Governor, Buck was a developer of the road system that covers the State so completely that no spot is more than four miles from a paved highway.

Paintings at Buena Vista include a portrait of Queen Elizabeth made about 1580 by Nicholas Hilliard, and a number of portraits by Gilbert Stuart.

At 4.9 *m.* the road crosses RED LION CREEK, named after a nearby tavern *(see Tour 11).* It is the boundary between New Castle Hundred and Red Lion Hundred. In Delaware the term "hundred" has been used for a political division of a county since the late 17th century *(see GOVERNMENT).*

Red Lion Hundred, a wheat, dairy, and muskrat-trapping section, extending east to the wide marshes of the Delaware River, is the smallest hundred in the State (22 square miles). In 1850 its farms and orchards were the most productive and profitable in Delaware. The once-prosperous peach industry had its beginning here in the 1830's spreading down the Peninsula until about 1890 when the blight called the "yellows" destroyed the last great orchards. In 1845 an owner with 80,000 peach trees on his estate shipped the crop to Philadelphia and Baltimore on his own steamers *(see Tour 10).* This great productivity was no accident, but resulted from the application, to barren and nearly worthless land, of scientific-farming methods then far ahead of the times.

By 1800 successive crops of grain and tobacco, raised by slave labor, had exhausted the soil completely; old tobacco barns along the roads were falling down. Then during the digging of the Chesapeake and Delaware Canal in 1823–9 *(see below)* beds of marl were discovered, a substance containing decayed seashells from an early geologic era. A canal contractor spread some of the stuff on his land and found that its small content of carbonate of lime produced amazing results in the growth of his crops. For years thereafter thousands of cartloads were dug by Negroes from marl pits and spread on the farms—until the appearance of commercial lime put a stop to the heroic job of moving eight tons of marl to get one ton of lime.

Meanwhile some of the more prosperous farmers were sending sons to college to learn, among other things, methods of crop rotation and fertilization. The topsoil was restored to still greater fertility. Many substantial brick houses, with plenty of tenant houses for the slaves and free Negroes, were built along this road and other roads in the hundred, as in lower New Castle County generally. Slaveholding persisted but many slaves were being held as such only till the men reached the age of 25 and the women 21; then they were given their freedom to work for $10 or $15 a month while the landowners grew rich on the crops they raised. Civil War prices were sky-high, and profits became huge. Social life resembled that of a landed aristocracy and included dancing, fox hunting, and a good deal of drinking in spite of the prevailing Presbyterianism of the Scottish-Irish-English gentry.

After the Civil War the decline began; a depression and the collapse of the peach industry came together. There were no more slaves, and laborers were demanding higher wages. Prices of farm products fell. The Negroes began migrating to northern cities, and white labor was "scarce and common at that." As the tobacco barns had been falling down by

1800, so the frame tenant houses around the big houses were falling down by 1900. The mansions themselves contained tenants.

The rains are again carrying the thin topsoil into the gullies on many farms in Red Lion Hundred. A second cycle of the land is nearing completion.

At 6 *m.* is the junction with State 7 *(see Tour 11).*

At 6.3 *m.* the rectangular grove of lawn trees (L) is the SITE OF BROOKFIELD, built in 1860 but since burned, the home of Capt. Charles Corbit (1838–87), whose wild charge at Westminster, Md., June 29, 1863, delayed by nearly 24 hours the arrival of Gen. J. E. B. Stuart's cavalry at the Battle of Gettysburg. Stuart was further delayed by skirmishes in Pennsylvania, and did not reach General Lee in time to be of service to him. Regardless of its effect at Gettysburg, Captain Corbit's charge is an episode cherished in Delaware annals for its reckless bravery.

Corbit and his men were in Westminster as an advance guard of observation under Maj. N. B. Knight when word came to him that a column of Confederate cavalry was approaching. As the head of a column of cavalry was massing itself in the narrow road at the edge of the town, Corbit, at the head of his riders, sabres drawn, charged at full gallop into the packed enemy. His black horse was shot through the head and Corbit was captured. The southern cavalry, 6,000 in all, was still coming over the hill.

Stuart deployed his men and guns for what he thought was going to be a battle with a large force. Before he discovered the battle was over and had countermanded orders it was late in the evening and he pitched camp for the night. General Stuart sent for the Yankee captain and is reported to have asked:

"Captain, what men are these?"

"We're from Delaware, sir."

"From Delaware? Why, you should have been with us!"

(Confederate emissaries had appeared before the Delaware Legislature urging Delaware to join the Confederacy.)

WRANGLE HILL, 6.9 *m.,* a crossroads with an old brick house on a rise, is still so-called because of a feud between two early families who lived here.

DAMASCUS (R), 7.5 *m. (private),* a plain, commodious brick house built about 1790, was the home of Jesse Higgins (1761–1810), farmer, operator of a gristmill on Dragon Run, embanker of tidal meadows, publicist, and enemy of the legal profession. Believing that "an honest man cannot be a lawyer," he wrote a pamphlet called *Samson Against the Philistines* in which he held that arbitration could cheaply and effectively be substituted for lawsuits. (This is the thesis and function of the American Arbitration Association whose legal decisions are recognized in many States.) When the pamphlet was published in 1804, Delaware lawyers bought up the edition, whereupon William Duane, editor of the Washington *Aurora,* gave it wide publicity by republishing it. As a leader of the Jeffersonian Democrats of the day, Higgins engaged in a noted debate, at Glasgow Crossroads nearby, with James A. Bayard, the most famous Federalist in Delaware; as the two men took turns on the rostrum, the crowd of thousands cheered their respective champions.

At 7.6 *m.* the road crosses DRAGON RUN, flowing east through the large Dragon Swamp to the Delaware River. This almost bottomless swamp harbors snapping turtles of great size; but the name probably was given it by reason of its proximity to the village of St. Georges, thus carrying out some wit's fancy to perpetuate the legend of *St. George and the Dragon.* This swamp is a stronghold of the beautiful little wood duck (summerduck) that builds its nest in holes high up in trees. It is protected throughout the year by Federal law, relaxed 1941 to permit taking one a day.

LINDEN HILL (R), 8.1 *m. (private),* a large brick house with a long kitchen wing at right angles to the main section, is set back from the road in a grove of trees. It was built in 1836 by Anthony M. Higgins, who bought the worn-out farm in 1833, spread it with marl and lime, and by 1850 made it highly productive and himself a leader in the revival of Delaware agriculture.

Linden Hill was the birthplace of his son Anthony Higgins (1840–1912), United States Senator 1889–95 and arch-foe of J. Edward Addicks in his candidacy for a Senatorship from Delaware. Higgins was defense counsel in the case of Delaware *vs.* Neal, argued before the United States Supreme Court in 1880, which set a precedent establishing the right of a Negro accused of a crime to a trial by a "jury of his peers." In 1935 the Neal case was cited three times by Chief Justice Hughes in the decision of the Supreme Court that ordered new trials in Alabama for the "Scottsboro boys" and resulted in the acquittal of two of them in 1937 under circumstances similar to those of the Delaware case a half-century before.

Higgins, a Republican, was appointed by the Delaware court to defend William Neal, a Negro accused by a white woman of rape. In a former slave State it was assumed that the defense would be perfunctory, but at the trial Higgins made the startling request that the indictment be quashed because no Negroes were called for the jury. The motion was denied, and Neal was sentenced to be hanged. Thinking the case closed, Delawareans were again astonished when Higgins took an appeal to the Supreme Court of the United States, which set aside the verdict and remanded the case for a new trial. By this time the defense lawyer found himself bitterly denounced for trying to save the life of a "worthless nigger." At the second trial, in 1881, Negroes were summoned for jury duty; all were successfully challenged by the State, but they had been officially brought into the courtroom and a precedent had been set. This time Neal was acquitted; to guard against lynching after the trial he was spirited from the courthouse and out of the State.

At 8.5 *m.* is the junction with a side road.

Right on this road is KIRKWOOD, **2.7** (225 pop.), formerly St. Georges Station but renamed in 1862 in honor of Capt. Robert Kirkwood, officer in the Revolution. The village was a busy railroad shipping point until the advent of paved roads.

ST. GEORGES, 8.8 *m.* (265 pop.), keeps its charm despite widening and deepening of the canal passing through it, and the high-span bridge (1942) that overpasses it.

The village was laid out before 1730 at a milldam across the headwaters of St. Georges Creek, and a tavern was serving travelers by 1735. As late as 1762, when the King's Highway was officially surveyed through here, guests at the tavern were still complaining of the noise made by ducks on the creek marshes and the millpond. For more than a century the chief excitement in St. Georges was the arrival and departure of the two four-horse stages, north-bound and south-bound, that ceased running when the railroad was built down the State.

The SUTTON HOUSE *(private)*, Broad St., N. St. Georges was built in 1802 by John Sutton, merchant, grain buyer, and local financier, whose grandson, Dr. James N. Sutton, imported the first commercial lime and built a limekiln. The brick house, with a typical low kitchen-wing at right angles to the main structure and a brick-floored kitchen shed, is still owned and occupied by the family. There are nine fireplaces in the house; mantels and stairway are original. A towering holly tree in the yard was planted in 1802 by John Sutton and his bride.

In the second-story parlor, Dec. 13, 1864, Thomas J. Craven, executor of the large estate of Thomas Jamison, of Damascus Farm, was reading the will to Jamison's three daughters, who found they did not benefit from it as much as they expected. One of the girls asked to see the will, read a few minutes, and then thrust it into the coal stove. Craven dashed to the stove, upsetting the table with a lamp on it, but succeeded only in burning his hands. The lamp had set the room on fire and he had to put the blaze out. Then he rushed out to report what became the case of the burning of the Jamison will. After a two years' battle a lawyer's copy was accepted for probate and the case settled.

The CHESAPEAKE AND DELAWARE CANAL is crossed over the village by a fixed-span bridge replacing a lift bridge wrecked by a ship in 1939. Cutting 14 miles across the isthmus of the Peninsula from the Delaware River on the East, to Back Creek, an arm of Chesapeake Bay on the West, the C. and D. Canal, 27 feet deep, tidal and toll-free, is an important link in the Atlantic Intracoastal Waterway. Owned and operated by the Federal Government since 1919, the canal accommodates all but the largest ocean liners and battleships. It shortens the route from Baltimore to Philadelphia by 316 miles, to New York by 179 miles, and to European ports by about 100 miles. In case of war it is of strategic importance in the movement of ships, as it was in 1861 when troops and supplies from Philadelphia were brought through it to protect Washington against threatened invasion.

This waterway was predicted as early as 1661 by Augustine Herman, proprietor of Bohemia Manor, in a letter to Vice-Director Beekman of the Dutch settlements on the Delaware:

"The Minquaskil and the aforesaid Bohemia River run there within a league from each other, from where we shall in time have communication with each other by water, which may serve as encouragement to the inhabitants of New-Netherland."

In 1786 a group of public men including Benjamin Franklin, James Madison, and Benjamin Rush met in Wilmington to consider canal plans, but little was done until 1799, when Maryland chartered the Chesapeake and Delaware Canal Company with $500,000 capital stock and appointed a board of commissioners to work with Delaware and Pennsylvania authorities. Work was started in 1804 but ceased because of financial troubles. Final promotion grew active in 1823 and that year digging commenced in earnest.

For some distance east of St. Georges the route followed the bed of St. Georges Creek and its marshes; a high bank was built along the north side of the channel to hold in the water of this "lower level" and serve as a towpath for mules and drivers. Improper sluices in this bank flooded much lowland north of the canal, resulting in epidemics of mosquito-borne fevers that killed hundreds of Irish immigrants on the job and struck heavily all the adjacent countryside. West of St. Georges there arose gradually the ridge of the Peninsula divide, reaching a height of 100 feet at Summit Bridge (see Tour 9), the "Deep Cut."

When the new canal was opened in 1829 amid great celebration, having cost $2,200,000, its prosperity seemed assured. Tolls in 1831 ran to $2,600 a week. It was believed that Delaware City, at the east end, would rival Philadelphia as a port. Many parts of the East got their first cheap coal from barges that came down the Susquehanna River and its canals and thence through the C. and D. Canal to Delaware City, where steam tugs took them in tow to Philadelphia and other ports. Log-rafts acres in extent were laboriously broken into small sections at the locks and passed through one at a time.

Competition from the railroads was encountered almost as soon as the canal was opened, and when in 1832 the New Castle and Frenchtown R.R. put on a steam locomotive for the haul across the neck of the Peninsula, a line of passenger barges undertook the same job through the canal. The little railroad was soon ruined by competition from the Philadelphia, Wilmington and Baltimore R.R. around the head of Chesapeake Bay (see NEW CASTLE), but passenger steamer service between Baltimore and Philadelphia by the Ericsson Line lasted until the 1920's.

Out of the construction of the canal grew one of the most famous lawsuits in the history of Delaware. A contract had been made with a celebrated engineer named John Randel, Jr., of Albany, to plan and build the canal. In 1825, three years before the specified time for completion, the company, alleging neglect on Randel's part, engaged others to finish the work. Randel brought suit. Among his lawyers was young John M. Clayton (see BUENA VISTA above), to whom large credit was given for the $226,000 damages that were finally awarded the engineer in 1834.

The old canal had a life of its own. Captains of passing barges saluted each other with musical blasts from horns, while their wives hung out the wash on clothes-lines rigged abaft the deckhouse. Barge housekeeping in-

cluded the keeping of chickens and even pigs. Showboats from the Chesapeake circuit tied up here and at other canal towns, and many were the
floating emporiums traveling leisurely from place to place with tinware,
dress-goods, steel-traps, and other things too numerous to mention.

Wet excavation in the final deepening of the canal was done by great
pumping dredges that filled in marsh areas nearby and forced mud and
stones up the 100-foot bank of the Deep Cut to disposal areas a mile
away. Much of the dry excavation was done by machinery, though in the
winter of 1935-6, as in 1826, thousands of laborers worked with shovels
and wheelbarrows while powerful equipment stood idle. They were PWA
workers under the Relief Act of 1935, transported daily to the job by
train and truck from Baltimore and Wilmington.

When the St. Georges locks were being dug originally, a graveyard was
cut through—that of the Welsh-Episcopal church of Quinquinium, the
Indian name for a large area around the present village, where a congregation was organized before 1707. In 1937 the work exposed more bones,
which were reburied at Old St. Anne's Church near Middletown.

FIDDLER'S BRIDGE, 10.1 m., over Scott's Run, was once a narrow crossing where the swamp trees met densely overhead—a dark and gloomy
place. There is a tradition that a demented Negro fiddler used to sit on the
bridge rail and play doleful tunes. One night he fell in and was drowned.
For generations it has been said that if precisely at midnight a silver coin
is dropped into the water, the fiddler will play.

In the course of a houseparty held near Delaware City in the 1890's,
the hosts brought their guests to the bridge and related the legend. At
midnight the host, handing a coin to one of the girls, told her to drop it
into the black water. After a small splash and a moment of silence there
came from the darkness, unmistakably the slow and wistful playing of a
violin.

Not until later did the host confess he had planted an old colored fiddler in the swamp for the occasion.

At 10.8 m. is the junction with a side road.

Left on this road to LISTON RANGE REAR (L), 0.5 m., a tall black steel lighthouse standing four miles from the Delaware River. It is a range light which vessels keep over their bows coming up the river, over their sterns going down, in
order to keep in a certain section of the ship channel.

At BOYD'S CORNER, 12.6 m. is the junction with a road that follows more or less closely the "Old Man's Path"—a road cleared about
1673 by the Herman family to cross the peninsula between Bohemia
Manor and the homes of Casparus and Ephraim Herman on the Delaware
River (see Tour 10).

MACDONOUGH, 13.2 m. (20 pop.), formerly The Trap, a few old
houses on both sides of the highway and some fine trees, is the birthplace
of Commodore Thomas Macdonough (1783-1825), called the Hero of
Lake Champlain because of his capture of the entire British fleet in the
Battle of Plattsburgh, Sept. 11, 1814, though outnumbered both in men

and ships. Following Perry's victory on Lake Erie in 1813, Macdonough's smashing blow stopped the enemy invasion from Canada.

The MACDONOUGH HOUSE *(private)*, the naval officer's birthplace, is R.; it is a plain two-and-one-half story dwelling painted white with green trim, part brick, part frame. North of the house is a family graveyard within a brick wall. (The Commodore is buried at Middletown, Conn.)

On Macdonough's flagship, the *Saratoga,* many of the sailors were killed or wounded. A shot broke open a coop of game chickens on deck and a cock flew up into the rigging, flapped his wings, and crowed; the men cheered and fought harder. A pious man, especially in a crisis, Macdonough made his men kneel down and pray before the engagement. His letter reporting the battle to the Secretary of the Navy was this:

"Sir: The Almighty has been pleased to grant us a signal victory on Lake Champlain in the capture of one frigate, one Brig, and two sloops of war of the enemy."

Of the 16 ships captured, 12 were "gunboats," the rest the large vessels reported in the letter.

Coming of a military and naval family, Thomas Macdonough entered the Navy at 17 as a midshipman and saw plenty of excitement before the War of 1812. During the expedition against Tripolitan pirates he served under Stephen Decatur and was promoted for bravery and ability. In Liverpool in 1810 he was seized by a British press-gang and thrust on board a frigate. That night he took the clothes of a sleeping British sailor and asked permission to take a boat to "overhaul a cutter carrying rum." Permission was granted, but instead of pulling for the cutter he made off for his own ship, under fire when the deception was discovered. Later he recalled saying to himself with youthful bravado, "If I live through this I'll make England remember the day she impressed an American sailor!" This kind of impressment was one of the chief causes of the war in which two years later, on Lake Champlain, he avenged himself so spectacularly.

Idolized by the nation, Macdonough received grants of land from Vermont and New York; Congress gave him a gold medal and promoted him to the rank of captain (or commodore), then the highest in the Navy. In 1815 the Delaware Legislature made an appropriation to pay for the portrait of him, by Thomas Sully, that hangs in the Governor's office of the Legislative Hall in Dover. In 1925 the War Department erected a monument to him at Vergennes, Vt., to commemorate the building there of the American fleet on Lake Champlain. In 1937 was issued a postage stamp bearing his picture and Admiral Decatur's, one of 10 stamps in an Army-Navy series.

At 14.6 *m.* the dual roadway spreads apart to swing in a wide curve across the marshes and channel of DRAWYERS CREEK, which is typical of the twisting tidal streams that flow into the Delaware River and Bay. In earlier days there were landings on such streams wherever fastland came down to navigable water, for the loading and unloading of farm products and supplies. The railroad era blighted the landings and since the coming of paved roads there is hardly a trace of one to be found.

Like other creeks in Delaware, moreover, Drawyers has been filling up with silt washed down from the fields since most of the timber was cut off. The marshes also have been rising, and it is now only on storm tides that the boats of railbird hunters can be easily pushed over the thickening sedge—the gunner sitting in the bow, his pusher standing in the stern with his long pushpole. Until recent years this and similar marshes were famous for the September sport of "railbirdin'."

The name of the creek appeared as "Drawers" in a land title of 1667 and as "Drawers" or "Drayers" in so many subsequent land titles and other indentures that it was undoubtedly connected with the hauling of produce across the Peninsula over the Old Man's Path (*see above*). There is no evidence that the Swedish miller, Anders Dreijer, whose name has fascinated some historians, was ever on this creek.

DRAWYERS PRESBYTERIAN CHURCH (R) is at 14.9 *m.* (*grounds and cemetery always open; church usually closed except Sunday services at 2 p.m. 1st. Sunday in June*). This structure, one of the finest old churches of Delaware, is of brick in Georgian style on an elevation overlooking the creek valley.

It was begun in 1773 from English designs adapted by Robert May, on the site of a wooden church built in 1711 and called Appoquinimy. Robert May designed a number of notable houses in and near Odessa (*see below*), as well as in Philadelphia and elsewhere. The bricks, laid in Flemish bond and covered with ivy, were burned on the farm of Robert Meldrum, a member of the congregation. Altered only slightly inside, the old building is kept in excellent repair by the Friends of Old Drawyers, a society composed largely of descendants of members of the Colonial congregation.

A continuous cornice encloses pediments in the gable ends. There are two tiers of small-paned windows; those of the lower tier have segmental arches and 28 panes each, and all the windows have white raised-panel shutters. The all-white interior is entered through a fine pedimented doorway flanked by engaged columns. The box pews, each with a number gouged in a style surprisingly modern, and the pulpit were remodeled in 1833; above the pulpit is a golden dove and a canopied sounding board. The slave gallery on three sides now holds the overflow of the congregation—no Negroes have attended services here for many years though they are still numerous in the region. There is no choir stall but immediately in front of the pulpit is a "precentor's box" where sat the precentor with his tuning fork to give the key for hymns sung without musical accompaniment. Weekly services were discontinued in 1861.

The Presbyterian vigor emanating from the first and the present church was felt for miles around. Churches in Odessa, Port Penn, St. Georges, and Middletown are offshoots of Drawyers. When in 1777 the British were advancing from the head of Elk River, Md., toward Washington's

OLD DRAWYERS PRESBYTERIAN CHURCH, NEAR ODESSA

camp near Stanton, Dr. Thomas Read, first pastor of the new church, drew maps that were said to have enabled the Americans to evacuate the section and avoid fighting until the Battle of the Brandywine.

On Old Drawyers Sunday *(first in June: one service in afternoon)*. Formerly there were two services on this day when church and grounds were filled with sociable pilgrims attending the morning "preaching" and the afternoon meeting addressed by a layman usually discussing the history of the church. On this occasion, called by older visitors "Clover Sunday" because of the clover fields in full bloom, the surrounding countryside of rolling farmland and soft green marsh is at its best. Also in bloom is nearly a mile of pink rambler roses on the highway fences from the church northward along the dual highway.

Between the morning and afternoon meetings many visitors spread picnic lunches on the lawn under the ancient cedars, dining on fried chicken, deviled crabs, potato salad, preserves, and other Peninsula fare. While elders discussed the morning's preaching and other topics, young people strolled through the woods on the bluff above the marsh. Children were allowed to play games if they did not disturb the sleepers; tired old farmers, rather than snore during the afternoon meeting, slept now in the shade of the trees, newspapers over their faces to keep off flies and bumblebees.

ODESSA, 15.8 *m.* (52 alt., 467 pop.), important enough in the past to have several of the finest brick houses in the State, has almost no business activity except that of a cannery, a bank, and a small fire insurance company. Through travel no longer uses broad Main Street, the former King's Highway, but cuts straight across into farmland.

From 1721 a toll bridge over Appoquinimink Creek here was operated by a son of Capt. Edmund Cantwell, to whom in 1664 the English had granted the confiscated lands of Alexander D'Hinoyossa, Director of the Dutch settlement of New Amstel (New Castle). For 134 years the place, steadily rising in importance as a port, was called Cantwell's Bridge. From all the country around, including part of Maryland reached by an ancient cart-road, came more and more wheat, corn, tobacco and other products to be shipped on vessels down the creek to Delaware Bay and thence to distant ports. Tanneries manufactured large quantities of leather and enriched their owners. Fine houses were built from fortunes that shrewd Quakers managed to preserve through revolution and hard times.

By 1825 Cantwell's Bridge was a bustling market and shipping center. Large granaries along the wharves were being constantly filled and then emptied into the schooners, sloops, and finally the little steamers that went downstream on the rapid ebb tides. From 1820 to 1840 the shipments of grain amounted to 400,000 bushels annually. Agricultural fairs drew crowds from three States. Teamsters roistered at the hotel while soirées and houseparties held forth in paneled drawing rooms. The value of town lots boomed, and the south side of Main Street showed more and more comfortable houses—as contrasted with the north side, the property of a Scot named Osborne who had unaccountably disappeared. Young gentlemen raced carriages and sleighs down the street, while their elders bought up farms by the dozen and put tenants on them to grow grain, and later, peaches.

In 1855 came the collapse of the grain trade. The line of the Delaware R.R. was coming down the State, and it was proposed to carry it through Cantwell's Bridge. Trying to protect the shipping trade of the creek, the merchants and vessel-owners told the railroad to keep out. It went through Middletown, a crossroads three miles west, and it was soon carrying the grain and peaches. Even the hurried changing of the town's name that year to Odessa, for the Russian grain port on the Black Sea, could not prevent the gradual disappearance of the sloops and schooners from the wharves at the foot of the hill, though small steamers continued to run to Philadelphia. About the same time the supply of good oak tanbark ran out and the Corbit tanneries were closed. Nevertheless the town was not yet asleep, for the Civil War boomed trade in all the little agricultural centers temporarily, and in 1870 the population reached its high mark of 695. Thereafter the decline of farming was more than paralleled by the withering of the town.

Later the development of the Du Pont Blvd. as a main freighting route put Odessa back on a main transportation artery, and the almost lifeless village, having lost 35 percent of its people in 20 years, hoped for a commercial rebirth. But though it was formerly a port on the King's Highway and terminus on a trans-Peninsular route, it is now important to students of Colonial architecture, who turn east into Main Street at traffic light. Houses and buildings on this street have individual character that does not detract from the harmony of effect.

In 1938 H. Rodney Sharp of Wilmington, a former teacher in Odessa, bought Castle William (the Corbit House), the old schoolhouse, and other buildings, all of which he has authentically restored.

The DAVID WILSON MANSION *(open Tues. and Sat., 9-12, 1:30-4:30; adm. free)*, S. side of Main St. near 2d St., is a two-story brick Georgian Colonial house designed about 1769 for David Wilson by Robert May and Company of London. The house contains the Mary Corbit Warner Museum and the Corbit Library. House and museum were incorporated after Mrs. Warner's death in 1923.

The engaged columns of the classic doorway are characteristic of the period. In the paneled hall a handsome stairway rises to the second floor where the two front rooms, used as a museum, contain many of Mrs. Warner's possessions—family heirlooms of high value as well as miscellaneous objects of varying merit that were collected by her in America and abroad. Among the articles on display are several old chairs, a mahogany sugar-and-tea box shaped like a coffin, made in 1800 or earlier, and a mahogany washstand that closes and looks like a little bureau. There are also china and silverware. One room is furnished as a Colonial bedroom. The paneling of the house throughout is regarded as some of the finest in Delaware.

The Corbit Library of 9,000 volumes fills the handsome drawing room downstairs as well as a room added in 1937 to the rear of the house. Established in 1856 at the Odessa Public School by Dr. James P. Corbit, the library has been endowed by various members of the family and receives State support as well. It was moved to the Wilson Mansion from the school in 1924.

CORBIT HOUSE *(private)*, SW. cor. Main and 2d Sts. since 1773 has been the "great house" of Cantwell's Bridge and Odessa. Its noble Georgian Colonial façade faces the Appoquinimink, though the view was interrupted by buildings. It was built of brick on plans drawn or adapted by Robert May for William Corbit, born near Philadelphia, whose first wife was Mary Pennell, an heiress.

The few Victorian changes and additions were removed, 1940, when after careful research, the house was renovated and restored to its original perfection of exterior and interior which make it perhaps the finest example of its period in the State. The house is large and solid; the decoration inside and out bespeaks the wealth and taste that availed itself of the best English and American craftsmanship of the day. The doorway is elaborate, with columns, pediment, and delicate fanlight. Cornices and dormer windows carry extensive detail work and carving, and there is an unusual belt course of stone above the first floor windows. The roof is hipped and has a captain's walk with a white railing of intricate pattern. The interior is spacious, the rooms well-proportioned. Doorways have dog-eared corners and broken pediments. The noted reception room on the second floor, no longer marred by a bay window on one end, has a ceiling 10 feet 9 inches high, and walls paneled from floor to ceiling. Fluted pilasters rise at each side of a mantel to the beautifully carved

OLD PUBLIC SCHOOL, ODESSA

cornice; chair rails and window frames are in keeping with the rest of the woodwork.

For 150 years a succession of Corbits, Quakers all, lived here, amassed fortunes, and married into the first families of the country. Kitchens and quarters were always full of free Negroes who had been reared as house servants and coachmen; these were as proud of their situation as the family was of its own. Sons and daughters of the family were sent north to the best schools and colleges.

When the tanning business ceased to prosper, the Corbits raised peaches on farms bought with tanning profits. When the peach industry failed and Odessa lost its commerce, their Civil War bonds advanced in value and increased the family fortunes. Daniel Corbit, son of William, saw to all this in his day—and to his religious duties as well. Before the coming of the railroad down-State he drove the 22 miles to Wilmington once a month to attend what was then the nearest orthodox Quaker meeting.

The former ODESSA HOTEL *(private)*, NE. cor. Main and 2d Sts., was built of brick in 1822 by William Polk as a combination store and dwelling, but in 1824 it was opened as a hotel, continuing as that for about 75 years. The barroom was a favorite spot for traveling salesmen and for teamsters hauling grain to the wharf; from time to time the staid Quakers living nearby had the hotel's liquor license revoked in the hope there would be less noise and fewer drunks emerging from its hospitable doors. In 1936 the dilapidated old building was bought, repaired, and redecorated as a private house once more. Much of the original woodwork was retained by the new owner.

The OLD PUBLIC SCHOOL, NE. cor. Main and 4th Sts., stands well back from the street among old trees and high weeds, its front door boarded up; the present east wing with its odd square bell tower and octagonal cupola was built in 1844. The west section was added later, and housed the Corbit Library until it was removed to the David Wilson house (see above). The dividing line is very clear between the older and newer parts of the brick structure. The building was restored 1941.

FRIENDS MEETING HOUSE (Sun. Serv. 11 A.M.) Main St., W. of US 13, is a plain brick structure about 20 ft. square with a pitched roof and pent eaves across the gable end. The windows are shuttered tight with white shutters in which the boards run diagonally. The little meeting house was built in 1783 when the Duck Creek Meeting removed to Cantwell's Bridge as a more convenient place of worship. All went well until 1828, when the division occurred separating the congregation into Hicksites, followers of the rebellious Elias Hicks, and the Orthodox Quakers. The local meeting fell into the hands of the Hicksites, whereupon the conservative members quit the meeting house. It never prospered again as a place of worship, though for years one lone old Hicksite, John Alston, would walk stiffly up the street every First Day, enter the meeting house, sit for a time in meditation, then walk stiffly down the street again. After his death about 1880 the doors were closed; only recently in 1950 was the meeting house put to use again.

The Quakers in Delaware early caught the Abolition fever from the Pennsylvania Quakers, and in Odessa the Hicksites made their meeting house a station of the Underground Railroad. Braving the rage of the slaveholding countryside they hid runaway slaves from Delaware, Maryland, and Virginia in the loft of the little building, bringing them food until it seemed safe to send them on their way north, well fed and well clothed.

At the traffic light in Odessa is the junction with Main St.

Left on this street and across the causeway to FAIRVIEW (L), 1 m. (private), also known as the Elias Moore House, built in 1773 from plans of Robert May and Co. Its Georgian Colonial architecture is similar to that of the other brick houses by that firm in the neighborhood.

The DUNCAN BEARD HOUSE (R), 1.7 m. (private), a small dilapidated frame building, was built soon after 1767 by Duncan Beard, Scottish clockmaker, who until his death in 1797 made some of the finest grandfather clocks in America. Fifteen of them are known to exist, graceful in proportion and still good timekeepers. On the ornamental brass face of each clock there appear Beard's name and the word "Appoquinimink." He also made metal articles, including gun locks ordered by the convention that met in New Castle on Aug. 27, 1776 to adopt a constitution for the new State of Delaware. Beard belonged to a Masonic Lodge at Cantwell's Bridge, the first Masonic organization in Delaware, established in 1765, for which he made a tall clock, some candlesticks, and a chest; they were all destroyed when the Masonic Hall in Middletown burned in 1918. Beard was also a member of Drawyers Church *(see above)*.

For nearly three miles south of Odessa the boulevard leaves the old King's Highway, which went through the village and curved to the eastward, and cuts across country where no road had been before. Various other bends in the old road between Odessa and Dover are cut off by the boulevard in accordance with Coleman du Pont's version of the old maxim: "A straight road is the shortest distance between two points."

At 16.4 *m.* is the marked SITE OF THE TREATY OF PEACE made near the Appoquinimink in 1661 between Philip Calvert, Governor of Maryland, and a local chief named Pinna. Later the long struggle was begun between the Calverts and the Penns for possession of the lands along the Delaware *(see HISTORY)*.

At 16.7 *m.* the road crosses APPOQUINIMINK CREEK near its headwaters of Noxontown Pond *(see Tour 9)*. Though Delaware Bay is only four miles east, the creek travels about eight to get there. The marshes below Odessa are noted among black-duck and railbird hunters. The Indian name of the creek is traditionally translated as *wounded duck,* though better authority gives it as *place from which the village is seen.*

At 19.4. *m.* is the junction with a side road.

Left on this road to BLACKBIRD LANDING, 1.9 *m.,* where nothing remains of the granaries here that before 1860 held grain for shipment down Blackbird Creek.

UNION M. E. CHURCH (L), 20.7 *m. (open by permission),* a small brick building beside a grove of trees, was completed in 1848 on the site of Dickerson's Chapel, which was built in 1790. In the graveyard is a monument to Levi Scott (1802–82), born nearby, an itinerant preacher who became Bishop in 1852 and one of the most noted Methodists of Delaware. Bishop Scott liked to shoot squirrels; one of his friends, beaten at the sport, attributed the bishop's success to the fact that he always knelt when firing.

At 21.3 *m.* is the junction with State 71 *(see Tour 9)*.

BLACKBIRD, 22 *m.* (45 pop.), a hamlet and former stagecoach stop on the King's Highway, grew up around a gristmill established in 1780 at the head of Blackbird Creek. Traditionally the name was originally Blackbeard for Edward Teach, the pirate of the early 18th century, who is thought to have used the lower creek as a harbor and its banks as a hideaway for loot. There is no record of any having been found, despite much digging; in 1850, however, a farmer told his neighbors of a dream about buried treasure, and soon afterward, in midsummer, he left his crops standing in the field and moved to town with plenty of money to spend. In apparent disagreement with the Blackbeard legend are local land titles that show "Black Birds Creeke" as early as 1679, more than 30 years before Teach turned pirate.

At 25.1 *m.* is the junction with a side road.

Right on this road is DUCK CREEK VILLAGE, 1.7 *m.* (50 pop.), laid out about 1700 as the first settlement on the upper creek; for 150 years it was known as Salisbury. At this point on the old King's Highway a meeting house was built by the Quakers about 1705 and used until the place of worship was moved in 1783 to Cantwell's Bridge, now Odessa. A Church of England chapel was built here about 1740, and a Presbyterian church in 1773. The church buildings have all disappeared and only the graveyards remain, deep in weeds and age. Several old houses, mostly dilapidated, some occupied by Negroes, attract artists to the little backwater hamlet that is all but forgotten since the Du Pont Blvd. was built a half mile to eastward, forsaking the old King's Highway.

At 26.7 *m.* is the junction with a concrete side road.

Left on this road is the junction with an asphalt road, 0.3 *m.;* R. on this asphalt road to BRICK STORE LANDING, 2.5 *m.* on a bend of Duck Creek long since cut off from the main channel.

At this landing—once the most important shipping point for southern New Castle County, now forgotten except by local farmers and trappers—there still stands the old Brick Hotel, later called the BRICK STORE, that for years was the social and business headquarters of the region. Though the fine old building has been neglected and used for farm purposes, its 18-inch walls are apparently nearly as solid as the day the numerals "1767" (or 1761) were put in glazed header bricks in a gable end. The building is 50 feet long by 25 feet wide, and three-and-one-half stories high. The wall on the land side is laid in Flemish-bond brickwork. A great chimney rises at each end.

At low tide the soft black mud bottom of the creek is exposed where once vessels lay in 10 feet of water at the ebb; above the mud project great timbers of the rotting and sunken wharf where grain vessels and later fertilizer boats tied up for loading. The first floor of the building, entered only from the creek side, is said to have held the noisy barroom and busy kitchen of the hotel; the great kitchen fireplace is in ruins and the floor still shows signs of the sheep that in recent years had their winter quarters here. From the kitchen a narrow stair ascends to the former dining room, now used, with other rooms on this floor, as a granary for wheat raised on the farm. This room and the similar one at the other end each have a large fireplace; most of the pine paneling that until recently covered these chimney walls has been torn out for kindling wood. The heavy interior Dutch doors on great hinges are battened diagonally. Doorsills and all timbers visible are hand-hewn and very heavy. The removal of some fairly modern floor boards has disclosed the original wide boards also hewn with broadaxes.

The third floor, empty save for muskrat-trapping equipment, once was divided into bedrooms; windows are small and square. The ceiling has been removed so that there is now no floor for the attic, which was lighted only by a pair of small round openings at each side of both chimneys. Here may have been quarters for Negro servants, though legend says this attic was a dungeon for kidnapped slaves and free Negroes during the early 19th century, when cotton planters of the Southwest were offering such high prices for field hands that the kidnapping of Negroes was widespread throughout the border South. *(See TOUR 1A.)* In 1847 the first railroad south of the C. and D. Canal was built between here and Dulaney Manor, 8 miles west, to haul out timber to vessels.

At 1.2 *m.* on the concrete road is the junction with a gravel road; R. on this road to CLEARFIELD FARM (L), 0.3 *m. (private),* called New Bristol by Capt. David Clark, who built the brick house about 1755. Capt. William Clark, a son, raised a company in the Revolution and lost half his men in the Battle of Monmouth, N. J. A grandson, John Clark, the third owner, was a Colonel of Militia and Governor of Delaware 1817–20. The house is designed in the comfortable style of the period, with an exterior belt course of brick and the usual projecting water-table at the base of the walls. The main stairway is curious in its separation into two narrow parts that reach the second floor as enclosed stairways. Another curiosity is in the large enclosed summer kitchen, with brick floor, built long ago into the L formed by the house and the servants' wing; the roof of this kitchen shed would ordinarily have eliminated the three dormers on that side of the wing, but they were retained and look down darkly beneath the shed roof.

At 27.2 *m.* the road crosses DUCK CREEK (or Smyrna River), the boundary between New Castle and Kent Counties, flowing crookedly to Delaware Bay, seven miles northeast. Prior to 1820 it did not enter the bay at the present mouth but turned south for 13 miles and emptied into Little Duck Creek; that year a "thoroughfare" was cut across a mile of marshland and the route to the bay shortened by two-thirds.

SMYRNA (R), 27.8 *m.* (20 alt., 2,400 pop.), formerly Duck Creek Cross Roads, was named in 1806 for the chief seaport of Turkish Asia Minor. Why this name was picked is hard to tell, beyond the fact that commerce on the creek was booming and Smyrna was a good Biblical port name. The early village had its moment of official glory and suspense in 1792, when the General Assembly, turned out of the Courthouse at Dover by an irritated sheriff—while repairs to the building were being made—came hotfoot to Duck Creek Cross Roads, and at the tavern of Thomas Hale resolved to make this village the State capital. At the end of the session a calmer Assembly repealed the resolution. Adjoining the town is Lake Como, named after the Italian lake. Aside from these names the place is thoroughly American, from the filling stations and truckmen's lunch rooms that border US 13, here intended as a bypass, to the charming old town itself whose church spires show above the trees to the west of the boulevard. Traffic since 1923 has skimmed by the old town, hardly suspecting its presence, leaving Main Street to be used only by residents, visitors, and the farm families who come to do their dealing on Saturday night.

As at Odessa *(see above)*, the King's Highway, later the State Road, was the thoroughfare along which the village grew up. In the 1850's, at its peak as a shipping center, Smyrna was the most important port between Wilmington and Lewes. From the wharves at Smyrna Landing *(see Tour 12)* a mile down the creek, vessels set off for northern ports with grain, lumber, tanbark, staves, hides, peaches, and other produce of a region that extended well into Maryland on the west. Tanneries, shipyards, lime-kilns, and fruit-drying plants flourished, while merchants grew rich on the profits from their peach orchards and from their trade in grain, fertilizers, and manufactured goods.

Also like Odessa, Smyrna was mortally afraid of the railroad and in 1855 forbade its coming through the town, but in 1861 had a connection built to it. When shipping declined nevertheless, the town suffered but held on as an agricultural center, and the population increased to 2,455 in 1890.

The brick ENOCH SPRUANCE HOUSE *(private)*, S. side of Commerce St. bet. US 13 and Main St., is still owned (not occupied) by the Spruance family. The west section, built before 1791, for a time held the only bank between Wilmington and Dover; on Thursdays, when the directors met, customers would come great distances to do business. The two-story extension with dormer windows was added later. The window headings of the first floor are wooden, keystone and all, after the Delaware custom of the time. The porches are not original.

The former banking quarters are now the parlor—many down-State houses still have parlors. The door to this room, hung on handmade hinges, is very heavy and has a great lock. In the sitting room (still called that in Delaware) is a Duncan Beard grandfather clock *(see above)* with attachment for telling time in the dark: when a string inside is pulled, the clock repeats the last hour struck. The Franklin stove in the hall was bought in Philadelphia by Presley and Enoch Spruance, merchants of Smyrna, who were skeptical that those black stones called coal would really burn in it, as guaranteed. Among other articles in the house are candle-moulds, a flax carder, a long-handled waffle iron, and a number of samplers.

The ABRAHAM PIERCE HOUSE *(private)*, across the street, is a small brick dwelling of ancient but unknown age, though its brickwork and gambrel roof indicate that it was built in the middle of the 18th century. To the right of the added doorway and porch is a window with 15 lights in each sash. When a cellar was dug recently two cannon balls of unknown origin were found.

The LOCKWOOD HOUSE *(private)*, W. side of Main St., N. of Mt. Vernon St., a long two-story brick building, is said to have been used as militia barracks during the War of 1812.

The CUMMINS HOUSE *(private)*, E. side of Main St., N. of Mt. Vernon St., is a plain but massive brick house that is symbolic of the fortunes made in the grain and mercantile business of the early 19th century in Smyrna. It was built by John Cummins (1777–1833), who at 21 became a partner in the leading store, soon bought out the owner, and went into the grain trade as well. Within 20 years he became the greatest grain merchant in Delaware and had made Smyrna rank second only to Wilmington as a port. Returning from Wilmington, Philadelphia, New York, and Boston, his schooners brought manufactured goods for his wagons to distribute to towns and crossroads stores in two States. A few feet from the south side of the house is a small, square, brick building that was the office of this merchant, financier, and landowner. It is a survivor of the time when nearly every prosperous merchant, doctor, and lawyer down the State had his sanctum in a separate little building near his home; here a man could be away from his wife and Negro maids who might try to "straighten up" piles of papers, and here he could receive congenial callers.

The PRESLEY SPRUANCE HOUSE *(private)*, next door N., is another substantial brick house, painted yellow, erected about the same time as the Cummins House.

The JOHN BASSETT MOORE SCHOOL, S. side of South St. bet. US 13 and Delaware St., completed in 1936, is a good example of outstanding high schools in Delaware; it was named in honor of a Smyrna native, the Hon. John Bassett Moore (1860–1947), a member of The Hague Tribunal and the first American judge of the Permanent Court of International Justice. To the school library Judge Moore presented a complete set of his writings on international law, American history and diplomacy.

On the walls of the study hall are four murals painted in 1936 by members of the Federal Art Project, several of the talented young painters of Delaware. At one end of the room the painting depicts, on a formalized background, various types of high school boys and girls: the athlete, the future scientist, the future housewife, and others. The mural at the other end shows personages of Delaware history against a background of Delaware scenes. On a third wall are two Kent County landscapes, smaller in size. One of them is a scene at the fishing village of Leipsic *(see Tour 10)*, showing a man planing the gunwale of a boat while another lifts a bushel of oysters. The other is a corn-shucking scene, in which all half-dozen figures are white men; it would be difficult to find such a group in Kent County, where Negro farmhands predominate. An additional mural in panels representing scenes from Shakespeare's plays has been installed (1938) as a memorial to a former superintendent, C. W. W. Schantz.

At Smyrna is the junction with State 6 *(see Tour 12)*.

LAKE COMO, 28.2 *m.* (R), is a former millpond, 50 acres in area, owned by the town. Fishing conditions are under State regulation.

The STATE WELFARE HOME 28.5 *m. (visiting hours 2-4 on Sun. and Wed.),* a prominent group of brick buildings (R) in neo-Colonial style, was opened in 1933 to take the place of the almshouses in the three counties of Delaware. Planned to permit the addition of more buildings, an addition providing 120 beds was added in 1950. In 1953 there were 450 "guests" averaging 61 years of age; 38 percent were Negroes for whom certain floors are reserved. Maintenance averages $2.98 per day.

The Welfare Home and Hospital for the Chronically Ill is administered by the Board of Trustees of the Delaware State Welfare Home and Hospital, of four members. Until 1951, when the State Department of Public Welfare was created combining most of the welfare programs, the State Old Age Welfare Commission, set up by the 1931 Legislature administered both the Home and the Old Age Pension Fund. Because the responsibility for the Welfare Home in addition to its many other programs proved too burdensome for the Department, the special Board of Trustees was established in 1953.

In 1929, the late Alfred I. du Pont, powdermaker, financier, and noted philanthropist *(see Tour 5)*, set up a private fund from which pensions for two years were paid to about 1,100 persons over 65. After studying European pension systems he presented to the Legislature in 1931 a bill which became the law providing the combination of a pension system and the Welfare Home. In 1937 the Delaware plan was approved under the Federal Social Security Act, and an equal Federal appropriation now doubles the funds and the number of persons benefited.

The interiors of the MEDICAL CENTER and of other buildings are decorated so as to suggest an institution as little as possible. Walls are in warm colors, floors polished and windows bright, furniture and fireplaces are designed for pleasant comfort. In the Medical Center are the offices as well as a hospital and living quarters for white and Negro guests. To

BELMONT HALL, NEAR SMYRNA

the rear is the GUEST PAVILION with living quarters and an auditorium where church services and motion pictures are held. The architects were Massena and du Pont of Wilmington. The grounds along Lake Como comprise 56 acres.

At an early time the paupers of Delaware were required to wear red flannel letters on their right arms—"PN," "PK," or "PS" denoting paupers of New Castle, Kent, or Sussex Counties—and they were bound out to work in the fields. Almshouses were established soon after the Revolution.

At 28.6 *m.* (L) is BELMONT HALL *(private)*, set well back from the road in a large shady lawn, one of the noted old mansions of Delaware. In summer the heavy foliage almost completely hides from the highway the fine broad façade of the brick house with its handsome doorway surmounted by a gabled-heading and fine cornice; the roof, not pitched to the front and rear as usual, but sloping to the narrow ends, is topped by a captain's walk with white balustrade. In a Victorian day the outside of the house was painted brown and a front porch and bay window added; after a fire in 1920 damaged the upper part of the structure, the house was restored to approximately its early condition.

On a large grant called Pearman's Choice, the two parallel wings at right angles to the rear of the house are said to have been built about 1684. The main section with gabled front is said to have been built in 1753 by Thomas Collins, high sheriff of Kent County in 1767 and President of the Delaware State 1786–89. When the Revolution broke out he organized and helped to finance a brigade of militia; these soldiers gave him almost as much trouble as the Tories to be subdued in the region. A battalion of these rustics sent in 1777 to support Washington at Morristown, N. J., no sooner arrived there after taking four weeks on the way than they requested him to be allowed to go home. General Washington wrote a bitter letter to Colonel Collins expressing his opinion of soldiers who wanted to quit before doing any fighting, and Collins was able to persuade them to stay for active service. As Caesar Rodney, the Signer, once remarked to Washington, "He that can deal with militia may almost venture to deal with the devil."

The tradition is that Collins fortified his grounds with a stockade and kept a sentry on the roof, and one night a Tory or marauder crept up and shot the sentry at his post; the wounded man dragged himself to a room below and died in a great pool of blood. In the drawing-room fireplace, bullets were moulded by women of the house. Belmont Hall contains many family heirlooms. Much of the original woodwork remains, and some of the hardware bears the stamp of British manufacturers.

At 28.9 *m.* (L) is WOODLAWN *(private),* a brick Colonial house to which, about 1860, was added a frame front section with a tall-columned portico of Greek Revival style. The house and farm belonged to the Cummins family.

GARRISON'S LAKE, 32.1 *m.* (R), at the head of Little Duck Creek (L), contains bass and pike. *(Boats are usually available during fishing season at farms bordering the shores.)* This pond with its many snags showing above the surface is an example of the customary early method of damming streams without bothering to cut off the trees, which were left to drown and be blown over when the water loosened the roots.

At 33.6 *m.* is the junction with State 42.

Right on this road is CHESWOLD, **0.5** *m.* (400 pop.), a village that has grown up since the building of the railroad in 1856; until 1888 it was called Moorton. A distillery making apple and pear brandy is in this center of a fruit-growing region. Apple orchards cover thousands of acres and pear and peach orchards are also extensive.

A group of people locally called Moors has lived in the vicinity of Cheswold since Colonial days. Of unknown origin, they have skins varying from nearly white to dark yellow. Most of them are farmers, owning land. Generally quiet and industrious, they live by themselves, associating little with the whites and considering themselves superior to the Negroes. The public school attended by their children is classed as a Negro school but black children go elsewhere. The clan has its own church. A similar group of people, some claiming descent from the Nanticoke Indians, lives along the Indian River *(see Tour 15).*

The DELAWARE STATE COLLEGE (Negro), 37 *m.* (R), a group of large brick buildings at the end of a long paved lane, was opened in 1892 as a land-grant college. On the basis of Negro population in Delaware, the institution gets one-fifth of the Federal appropriations for the State, four-fifths going to the University of Delaware at Newark. The State supplies maintenance and has erected the college buildings, aided by gifts from Pierre S. du Pont through the Delaware School Auxiliary. The institution had two departments: the college, the only one for Negroes in Delaware, and the high school. Degrees conferred by the college include B.A. and B.S. in arts and science, and B.S. in education, home economics, agriculture, and industrial arts. The high school included the 10th, 11th, and the 12th grades only. In 1952 the high school closed when a public high school opened. The buildings are on a tract of 200 acres, 160 of which are used in the teaching of agriculture. SOLDIERS' FIELD, used for baseball and football games *(open to the public)*, covers 5 acres.

Buildings include LOOCKERMAN HALL, the brick homestead on the old farm, built by Nicholas Loockerman about 1740, now remodeled as a girls' dormitory; DELAWARE HALL, the academic and administration building, auditorium and gymnasium, erected in 1928 at a cost of $125,000; the TRADES BUILDING containing classrooms and laboratories, and the LIBRARY housing 4,000 volumes. There is a large dairy barn with a herd of cattle and modern equipment.

At 37.2 *m.* (L) is STATE HIGHWAY POLICE STATION NO. 3 *(information and first aid)*, of modified Greek Revival design; it housed the Delaware exhibit at the Philadelphia Sesqui-Centennial Exposition in 1926, and instead of being dismantled was moved here.

At 37.6 *m.* is the junction with US 113 *(see Tour 2)*.

SILVER LAKE, 38.1 *m.*, is a State sanctuary for waterfowl and other wildlife. The pair of imposing early-Georgian style brick mansions (R) on the south shore are the RICHARDSON HOUSES, built in 1935.

DOVER, 39.1 *m.* (20 alt., 6,500 pop.) *(see DOVER)*.

Points of Interest. The Green, State House, Legislative Hall, Hall of Records, old houses with gardens, State Museum, chicken-and-plum-pudding canning plant and others.

Dover is at the junction with State 8 *(see Tour 13)*.

Section d. Dover to the Maryland Line, 51.4 m.

South of Dover, 0 *m.* US 13 bears slightly westward, soon leaving the path of the old King's Highway and following the peninsular divide for about 20 miles. Farther south the landscape flattens in Sussex County to a level sandy plain; pine woods gradually supersede hardwoods; orchards and truck farms displace wheat fields and dairying. In this region, compared with the great farms of tidewater Delaware, farms are small and farm-tenancy is low. Much of this land was never tilled until after the building of the railroad in 1856–58; then the forests began to disappear under the axes of newcomers, crowded out of the old farming areas along Delaware Bay and the Chesapeake rivers. The southern portion of this section traverses a comparatively long-developed region along the navigable Nanticoke River, settled mostly by slave-holding Marylanders and Virginians in the late 18th and early 19th century.

CAMDEN, 3.6 *m.* (606 pop.), in an important fruit-growing countryside, is a quiet village with a number of plain, dignified, old brick houses.

FRIENDS' MEETING HOUSE (1805), CAMDEN

It is one of the few old Delaware towns not on navigable water, but before the coming of the railroad the place attained commercial importance chiefly through the use of the wharves at nearby Lebanon and Forest Landing on Jones Creek *(see Tour 2)*. Camden was laid out in 1783 by Daniel Mifflin, a Quaker, on a tract called Piccadilly.

The COOPER HOUSE *(private)*, near the N. entrance to the village (L), is a gray-painted brick house built in 1782. Its hand-carved pine paneling includes fine semi-circular cupboards on each side of the fireplace in the dining room. Doors have hand-wrought hinges and large box locks. In a closet on the second floor the original wooden pegs, used as clothes hangers, are still in place. There is a tradition that this house was a station on the Underground Railroad and a hiding place for Negroes who were concealed in a small, bunk-lined room above the kitchen; this was entered by a ladder, and a round window near the peak of the roof admitted light and air. Later owners sealed the opening in the kitchen ceiling and bricked in the window. Another story associated with the house is that a tunnel led to the adjoining house, built about the same time.

Almost opposite (R) is the DANIEL MIFFLIN HOUSE *(private)*, of tan-painted brick with yellow trim, built about 1796. Warner Mifflin, a brother of Daniel, was one of the first men in America to free his slaves unconditionally. There is a fanlight over the front door, and the interior contains much hand-carved paneling. The original white oak structural timbers have the bark still on them and are clamped with wooden pins.

On Commerce St. is (L) the FRIENDS MEETING HOUSE *(open by permission; meeting every First Day—Sun.—at 10:30)*, a plain two-story gambrel-roofed brick building in perfect condition. A marker near the peak in front bears the date 1805. Camden meeting is the only one still active in lower Delaware.

Only the front of the building is laid in Flemish-bond. The fine old door is framed by an architrave that projects beyond the side of the wall, an unusual feature in Delaware buildings of the time. Just under the peak is an odd little fanlight. Part of the interior woodwork has been renewed. On the second floor are old desks and other equipment left there in 1882 when the room was abandoned by the school long maintained by the Friends. The grave markers in the adjoining cemetery are taller than the usual very low stones of Quaker burial grounds. Upkeep of both meeting house and cemetery is guaranteed by a trust fund.

Right from Camden, on State 10, is WYOMING, **0.5** *m.* (911 pop.), a village (R) that developed after the coming of the railroad in 1856. It has a very large cannery and is in the center of one of the richest orchard and dairy regions in Delaware. Originally called West Camden, the place was early named Wyoming by the Rev. John J. Pearce, a Methodist minister from the Wyoming Valley of Pennsylvania.

At **8.2** *m.* on State 10, lying mostly south of the hamlet of Petersburg, is the 2,800-acre PETERSBURG SITE, a State recreation area, formerly of the Bureau of Agricultural Economics of the U. S. Department of Agriculture. This essentially hardwood timber tract was purchased in 1935-6 by the U. S. Resettlement Administration, which also acquired two other large tracts in Sussex County *(see Tour 16)*. Graded roads have been built through the area for access and fire control, and picnic sites and fireplaces are planned for public use.

At 6.8 *m.* is the junction with a side road.

Right on this road is WOODSIDE, **0.7** *m.* (157 pop.), which became a fruit and grain shipping-center when the railroad was built through this section.

At 9 *m.* is the junction with a side road.

1. Right on this road is VIOLA, **0.7** *m.* (134 pop.), laid out in 1856 when the railroad opened a station. It is on a grant known as Golden Thicket patented to William Shores in 1681.

2. Left on this road is CANTERBURY, **0.2** *m.* (30 pop.), once an important horse-changing station on the stage line down the Peninsula. The site was considered for a county seat before Dover was laid out.

At 11.5 *m.* is a marker (L) indicating the farm formerly known as BURBERRY'S BERRY, the home of Capt. Jonathan Caldwell, who served in Col. John Haslet's regiment in the Revolution. Because Captain Caldwell's men carried with them gamecocks of a celebrated "blue hen" strain developed in the county, and noted for their fighting ability, the Delaware soldiers were known as the "Blue Hen's Chickens." *(See HISTORY.)*

FELTON, 11.5 *m.* (463 pop.), a village of railroad origin, is a shipping point for fruits and vegetables. There is a cannery here.

HARRINGTON (R), 17.4 *m.* (2,241 pop.), is a spreading town that started as a railroad junction for the Delaware, Maryland and Virginia

R.R.; in 1862 it was named for Chancellor Samuel M. Harrington. Rail traffic has sharply decreased in recent years but the town has managed to survive as a rural trading center. In Harrington are two shirt factories, examples of the dozens of small plants that have come into the Peninsula to make shirts, dresses, trousers, underwear and other cheap apparel, taking advantage of tax exemptions, special power rates, a 10-hour day for the women employees, and comparative freedom from labor agitation. The town has a city manager, and is the center for the consolidation of 14 school districts.

Left from Harrington on State 14 to the junction with a side road, **3.5** *m.;* R. on this road is HOUSTON, **4.2** *m.* (322 pop.), a village of broad streets on the Delaware, Maryland and Virginia branch of the Pennsylvania R.R. A large LIBBY, McNEILL & LIBBY CANNERY operates here in summer, and an antique shop is well known throughout lower Delaware. The site was the Hunting Quarter tract patented to Luke Watson in 1681. In 1854 the village was named for John B. Houston (pronounced House-ton), a landowner.

At 18.3 *m.* is the entrance (R) to the KENT AND SUSSEX FAIR GROUNDS, annual scene *(late July and early Aug.)* of the only large agricultural fair in Delaware. At the fair are the usual sideshows and exhibits of livestock, produce, and handiwork, and dealers' displays of farm implements and machinery. The excellent RACE TRACK, with a large grandstand, is known throughout the East and nearby South for its harness racing. Thursday of fair week is Governor's Day when the Governor and his staff and hundreds of big and little politicians watch the races and hobnob with each other. On the last day, always a Saturday, automobile racing is the usual feature.

At 21.1 *m.* is the THARP HOUSE (R), built about 1835 by William Tharp, Governor of Delaware 1847–51. Part brick and part frame, ivied and mellow beneath old trees, this house in southern Kent County combines the brick construction typical of middle Delaware and the frame type usual in Sussex County to the south.

FARMINGTON (R), 21.2 *m.* (117 pop.), was first called Flatiron when in 1855 the railroad built a station at a crossroads. The Farmington post office was established three years later. In the 1880's the town had prosperous canning and fruit-evaporating industries, and a population of 300.

In this flat region of small sandy farms and pine woods, near no large town or navigable water, there flourished at the village between 1868 and 1878 a "select school" called Farmington Academy. Many of the boys who attended this school later became prominent. Among the alumni have been a college president, the founder of a law school, five professors, and several lawyers, doctors, judges, engineers, and preachers.

At 23.7 *m.* a stone marker (R) indicates the BOUNDARY BETWEEN KENT AND SUSSEX COUNTIES, a division of some importance.

In this region takes place the transition from the gently rolling land and hardwood groves of middle Delaware to the flat, sandy terrain of the lower peninsula stretching southward to Cape Charles. Here and to the

SATURDAY AFTERNOON, HARRINGTON

south the woods are predominantly of loblolly and spruce pine. Fresh-water swamps contain not so much swamp maple as gum, white cedar, and bald cypress; mistletoe in dull green bunches haunts the tops of the gums. Holly growing everywhere beneath the tall pines sometimes reaches a height of 50 ft. The latitude is that of northern Virginia, the climate is even milder.

Skunks and groundhogs (called woodchucks in the northern States), common in upper Delaware, exist only rarely south of here, though skunks have been extending their range a few miles southward every year. Turkey buzzards are very numerous; after a heavy rain, when the sun comes out, a dozen or more buzzards often perch in a line on fence-posts, stretching out their wings to dry. Gray foxes are almost as numerous as red ones, and annoy hounds by diving into brush piles like rabbits instead of leading the hounds a chase.

Though the speech of Sussex County as a whole has a pattern of ex-pressions, intonations, and rhythms very different from that of upper Delaware, this western side of the county has variations all its own. If a man asks another "Mung-ye comin' to church?" he means "Are you and your family coming to church?" In the singular sense the expression may be: "Mung-ye go fodder them mules"; that means "Somebody out of a group" go do it.

GREENWOOD (R), 25.7 m. (527 pop.), developed as a result of

the railroad, and became a center for shipping farm produce, taking trade away from the older village of St. Johnstown nearby *(see Tour 3)*. In the village are a dye-works and a garment factory.

Greenwood is at the junction with State 16 *(see Tour 3)*.

The new double US 13 south of Greenwood bypasses the towns. This tour diverges (R) on US 13A through the towns.

BRIDGEVILLE, 30.2 *m*. (1,500 pop.), is a thriving canning center, its activities continuing without pause from April asparagus to November pumpkins. Large nearby orchards bear apples and peaches shipped from Bridgeville or by truck direct from the plantations. This is one of the largest cantaloupe-shipping points of the Peninsula, and strawberries are shipped by truck and refrigerator car to many northern cities. A pork-packing plant is one of the few in Delaware doing an interstate business and is noted for its sausage and scrapple. A shirt factory employs women workers. The town is the birthplace of Edward Willis Redfield (1869–   ), the artist.

Bridgeville began with the erection of a bridge over a branch of the Nanticoke River in 1730, when the name Bridgebranch was given a few houses along what is now US 13. The present name was applied in 1810.

Recently Bridgeville had visions of an oil boom. Options were taken on hundreds of acres of farmland. In spite of a claim or two that some "oily mud" had been brought up, landowners by 1935 had returned to the cultivation of the surface rather than the probing of the depths.

At Market St. in Bridgeville is the junction with State 404 *(see Tour 14B)*, which unites with US 13 between Bridgeville and 31.7 *m*.

On Market St., across the railroad tracks (R), is the AUCTION YARD, an open field where during the summer auction sales of produce are held.

In the METHODIST CHURCHYARD, N. end of William St., is the grave of William Cannon (1809–1865), Governor of Delaware 1863–1865, a period when feeling in lower Delaware ran high between the Union and Confederate sympathizers. Soon after taking office he was threatened with impeachment. Democrats resented his action, as a Republican candidate, in securing Federal troops to "police" the polls in the election of 1862. But his courageous administration was the keystone of the State's Union stand.

At 31.3 *m*. is the junction with a side road.

Left on this road to a TOWNSEND APPLE ORCHARD, 3 *m*. The plantation, the largest in the region, contains 60,000 trees and covers about 1,000 acres *(in bloom late April or early May)*. At the height of the picking season *(Aug.–Oct.)* the spectacle is made vivid not only by the red fruit but also by the scores of pickers—black and white, men, women, and children, some of whom live in nearby barracks. The several kinds of apples are inspected for size and quality. A day's picking may run to 3,500 bushels; a normal crop yields about 200,000 bushels.

At 31.7 *m*. State 404 branches L. from US 13 *(see Tour 14B)*.

At 33.4 *m*. is the junction with State 18 *(see Tour 14)*.

HEARN'S MILLPOND, 34.9 *m*. (R) still furnishes power to a feed and flour mill. *(Boats available for fishing for bass and pike in season.)*

LAWRENCE, NEAR SEAFORD

At 36.3 *m.* (R) is LAWRENCE *(private)*, a large white-painted frame
mansion with smaller wings and a portico of tall square columns, built
about 1840 by Charles Wright, one of three brothers born a few miles
down the Nanticoke River, in Maryland; they came to Seaford and prospered as traders and shippers during the period of the town's first lusty
growth. Though the noted boxwood of the lawn has been removed, some
handsome old trees remain.

At 37.2 *m.* in the northern edge of Seaford is the northern junction
with State 20 *(see Tour 1A)*.

SEAFORD, 37.6 *m.* (25 alt., 3,200 pop.), is at the head of navigation
on the deep Nanticoke River about 40 miles from its mouth in lower
Chesapeake Bay. It is a busy town whose varied industries include the
making of baskets and other containers for fruits and vegetables, the mix-
ing of fertilizers, the canning of farm products, and the shucking and
packing of oysters. The largest industry is the Du Pont Nylon Plant.

As one of the two important Delaware towns on navigable streams
flowing into Chesapeake Bay, Seaford is similar to the many towns on the
Eastern Shore of Maryland that have depended largely upon water transportation and the seafood industry of the Bay. Oyster-packing, though
now decreasing in importance, is still carried on here from September to
May. From the 1870's to the 1900's dozens of rake-masted schooners made
weekly trips down the 60 miles of winding river to the oyster beds of the
lower Chesapeake. Nearly all of these vessels have disappeared from the

packing-house wharves, and most of the oysters are now hauled overland by truck from Delaware Bay. Formerly Seaford shipped thousands of shad that were caught in drift nets when they swam up the Nanticoke to mate and spawn in fresh water *(see below)*, but in recent years decreased numbers of shad in the Bay have met an increased barricade of pound nets in the mouth of the river, and few of the fine fish are shipped.

Since 1939, when E. I. du Pont de Nemours & Company opened here the first plant in the country for the manufacture of nylon yarn, Seaford has had a rapid but healthy economic growth.

Seaford was laid out in 1799 at what was then Hooper's Landing on the river; it was presumably named after Seaford, Sussex County, England, whence came some of the early settlers. Records before 1815 giving Seaford as the name seem to refute the tradition that the town was named after a horse brought from England that year by a surveyor named William Neal.

One of the early records of the town concerns what would now be called a "mercy killing": In 1818 Shadrach Cannon tried to pull his dog from under his house; the dog was rabid, and bit him. Within a few days Cannon became a raging madman and his doctor and friends decided to put him out of his misery, and "some of Seaford's best citizens were selected to smother him to death between two beds." (Doubtless this meant feather-beds.)

Seaford preserves the memory of Patty Cannon *(see Tour 1A)* more vividly than other towns that came within that outlaw's bailiwick. When she was finally arrested in 1829 it was the local magistrate that committed her to the Georgetown jail, and the story is that the town crier, calling the hours, bellowed: "Three o'clock and Pat Cannon's taken!"

After the Nat Turner massacre of August 1831 in Southampton County, Va., when more than 50 whites were murdered by a fanatical Negro preacher and his followers, Delaware shared with the entire South a foolish terror of a mass uprising of the slaves. On Election Day in 1831 most of the Seaford men had gone to vote at the district polls in Bridgeville, 7 miles north, when the rumor spread wildly that "The niggers are coming up the river!" It is recorded that a slave dealer ordered a slave to go to the masthead of one of his schooners for a better view downstream.

"Well, what do you see?" was the shout from below.

"Don't see nothin', sir."

"Look again!"

Nettled, the boy looked toward the blackened stumps of a burned-over piece of new-ground down the river, and shouted:

"I see thousands o' niggers a-comin' dis way!"

Unaware that the rumor had been started by some white pranksters, the dealer ran home, it is said, harnessed his best horse to his gig, threw in a bag of money, and left Seaford in a cloud of dust. This spectacle made a panic. Women gathered up children and a few essentials and followed in any kind of vehicle they could find, heading north. Some did not come back for hours or days.

Not long afterwards the ridiculed dealer bought up his last drove of

Delaware and Maryland slaves and took them south. He never came back again; other dealers took his place. The scare, however, was felt for years. Self-appointed vigilantes roamed the streets of Delaware towns dispersing groups of innocent Negroes, seizing their guns, even breaking up church meetings. The Legislature passed laws forbidding free Negroes as well as slaves to possess guns, and forbidding any Negro gathering to last beyond 10 P.M. Finally, like Sunday "blue laws," these statutes fell into disuse and the harassed Negroes were allowed to live in peace—as they had always tried to do.

Though the coming of the railroad in 1856 struck a hard blow to the Nanticoke River shipping, there was regular weekly—sometimes more frequent—steamer service between Seaford and Baltimore until well into the 20th century. Baltimore is only 80 miles northwest of Seaford, but the voyage down 60 miles of crooked river and up 100 miles of Chesapeake Bay took from 16 to 19 hours. Before that, when a man traveled by sailing vessel on a business trip to Baltimore, he was usually gone for two full weeks. (Automobiles go around the head of the bay to that city in four hours.) At times between 1825 and 1855 vessels from Norfolk, Va., arriving here (130 miles), connected with stages to Dona Landing near Dover (42 miles), whence another line of boats ran to Philadelphia (80 miles). This water-land-water route between North and South was killed by the railroad.

Seaford's prosperity as a manufacturing, canning, and trading center has given it many comfortable houses, including some well-designed new ones on the outskirts, but there are almost no old houses of distinction. The HOOPER HOUSE, behind a dwelling at Arch and High Sts., was built of brick by one of the Hoopers, it is said, who laid out the village in 1799. The remaining part of the original building is used for storage and garage purposes.

A new $2½ million feed mill on Nanticoke River near Porter St. will be completed before the end of 1954, to serve the extensive Delmarva Peninsula poultry industry. Seaford is also the center of petroleum products distribution by all the major oil companies for the peninsula south of the Chesapeake and Delaware canal. There is a small oyster-shucking-and-packing plant on the N. bank of the river at S. Cannon St. Annually more than 6,000 gallons of oysters are shucked at this plant, packed into tin cans, and shipped in refrigerated trucks and cars, chiefly to the Middle West. Shuckers of long experience and great dexterity work fast as they rapidly stab and open oyster after oyster.

The oldest church building in Seaford is ST. LUKE'S EPISCOPAL CHURCH, E. side of Front St. between King and Poplar Sts. *(Sun. services at 11; open by permission);* it was built in 1843 of brick with a square battlemented tower. Before the Civil War the slaveholding families in attendance were bitter against "Yankee meddling," and when the war broke out numerous young men joined the Confederate Army. During the war, however, Federal troops kept a suspicious watch on the whole region, and to express any sympathy with the South was to jeopardize one's property.

TESTING A BATCH OF TOMATOES   CANNING PLANT, BRIDGEVILLE

Credit: Waller Studio, Laurel

The SEAFORD CENTRAL SCHOOL, on the W. side of State 20 at the N. edge of town is an expansion of a 1928 building into a well-equipped modern school. Also in Seaford is Frederick Douglass School (Negro), named for the Eastern Shore slave who became a leader of his people. Both the original buildings were gifts of the late Pierre S. du Pont.

In Seaford is the junction with the Dulaney Mills Road, where the huge Du Pont nylon plant replaces the buildings of the old Dulaney estate described below. Fairfield house has been moved into Seaford for the Acorn Club. An airfield is part of the plant facilities.

Right on this road to FAIRVIEW (L), 1.5 *m. (private),* also called the Dulaney Place, on the shore of the Nanticoke River. Though the grounds of this once-noted plantation have been long neglected, the weatherboarded yellow frame house and outbuildings remain much as they were in 1849, when William W. Dulaney purchased the 500-acre place. (The tract was patented in 1682 as Nanticoke Manor under Maryland claims. In 1825 the plantation with a "good shingled dwelling" was bought by Peter Newton Rust of Westmoreland County, Va., who added the larger northeast portion of the house to the original structure.) The house is distinguished chiefly for its five handsome classic doorways—two of them under one portico—all presumably brought from Baltimore on the owner's vessel. The architect is thought to have been "Planner" Williams, a neighbor, who had a hand in most of the better country houses of the region.

During the period before the Civil War the "big house" beneath large trees was the center of the busy, self-contained plantation. An avenue of trees and "lazy-X" fences, painted white, led past the coach house, horse stables, and servants' quarters to the portico of the house, and thence down the slope, past a formal garden, to the plantation wharf. There, deep-draft sailing vessels and small steamers loaded grain, timber, railroad ties, hides, and other products of the estate, to be shipped to Balitimore. Near the wharf was a "seine ground" where the long shad seines were hauled out by Negro fishermen in the spring.

From the garden on the brow of the hill a long arbor of scuppernong grapes led down to a spring house where the milk was cooled, a half-mile from the cow barn. In the north yard was a row of beehives. A well with a huge sweep was near the kitchen, as well as a little "meal house" where all the bread and cakes were made. On a lane at the west were the domestic buildings including a frame SLAVE QUARTER (still standing) for house servants; the ash house, the ice house, and the smoke house. (It was Dulaney's custom to manumit his slaves after a number of years and give to each family a cabin and some land, so that there were seldom more than a dozen slaves at the "big house" quarters.) An odd building that looks like a child's playhouse—very small with miniature dormer windows—stands near the kitchen; it was formerly a BATH HOUSE down at the river's edge, used by the ladies during the long hot summer.

On Nov. 3, 1862 several steamers flying the United States flag came up to the wharf and disembarked several hundred troops from Baltimore under General Wool. They camped on the meadow, commandeered all the grain and cattle, and marched up the road to Seaford to police the elections held next day there and elsewhere; this procedure was bitterly resented by the area's Southern sympathizers including the Dulaneys, Martins, and Wrights.

At 37.8 *m*. US 13 crosses the **NANTICOKE RIVER.**

BLADES, 38.1 *m.*, is usually regarded as part of Seaford. The name came from a family and not, as some say, from the razors and pig-stickers said to have been used in Saturday-night scuffles.

In Blades is the southern junction with State 20.

Left on this road is CONCORD, 3 *m.* (150 pop.), a placid hamlet on Concord Pond at the head of tidewater on the Nanticoke River. Old, white, wooden houses are remnants of the era of high prosperity in the late 18th and early 19th centuries when mills flourished and the place was the center of bog-ore mining and iron furnaces. For a long period the smelting of bog ore was widespread in Sussex County and in Worcester County, Md., and hundreds of thousands of dollars were invested by northern capitalists *(see Millsboro: Tour 2).* George Morgan (1854–1936) was born here, author of *Patrick Henry* and other biographies, famous for his impromptu Delaware reminiscences.

DELMARVA CAMP (L), 42 *m. (first 2 weeks in Aug.; hotel and tent accommodations),* in a grove of trees, is the largest white camp-meeting in Delaware.

It is an example of the modernization, externally, of the old-time camp meetings popular on the Peninsula since the time of Asbury and other fervent dissenters of the 18th century. Where formerly the pine-and-hardwood grove was lighted with blazing pine knots on 6-foot-high firestands, there are now electric lights to illuminate the grounds. The early tents have been replaced by comfortable frame tents that each have a front room without a front wall, another room behind it, a kitchen shed in the rear, sleeping rooms above, and fancy jigsaw decorations. In the middle of the circle of about 60 tents is the TABERNACLE, a shed covering rows of pine benches and a rostrum, where services every evening are broadcast by a public-address system. There are no daytime religious meetings.

Before the day of the automobile, farm families camped here for the full two weeks; it was their opportunity to enjoy religion and sociability, to relax and make love. Nowadays everybody comes in a car, and may stay only for the evening services, which are attended more largely than ever. A fee is charged for "protected" parking—to prevent young people from using dark back seats for lovemaking. Many families still do their own cooking in their tents. Both privately and at the hotel the cooking is done by women of vast experience in preparing corn and beans, fried cymlin' (squash), chicken pot pie and fried chicken with gravy, corn bread and pones, beaten biscuits, large soda biscuits, and many other dishes native to the Peninsula. Desserts are huckleberry pie, cantaloupes, watermelons, or peaches and cream.

In the evenings the "old heads" like to sit in rocking chairs, talk with visitors, read papers, or watch the promenaders.

Religious fervor during the services is likely to burst out in "Amen, brother!" or "Praise the Lord!" and other shouts no less vigorous than in past times, though criticism is heard concerning the way the young folks go off and drink beer while the preaching is going on. After the preaching and hymn-singing there is more promenading until one by one the lights in the tents go out and the camp slumbers.

At 42.1 m. is the junction with a side road.

Right on this road is BETHEL, 2.5 m. (219 pop.), the ghost of a shipbuilding town on Broad Creek, a tributary of the Nanticoke River. Whitewashed picket fences surround the modest frame dwellings built very close to the oyster-shell streets that are nearly deserted these days but used to be alive with ship-captains, sailors, and ship-carpenters going to and from the docks and shipyards on the creek. The place is reminiscent of the little oystering and fishing villages of tidewater Maryland and Virginia. Old seafaring men and carpenters walk in the sun to try to ease the rheumatism brought on by years of exposure on Chesapeake Bay and the ocean beyond Cape Charles.

The village started in the early 19th century at a wharf built by Kendall Lewis, and was called Lewisville until 1880 when a post office was opened here. It was then already declining as an important shipping-point for Baltimore, but shipbuilding became a fine art here and attracted some of the best designers and riggers of the Chesapeake region who built the fine sailing vessels that in some cases still sail Chesapeake waters under full canvas.

A type of vessel developed at Lewisville and known as a "ram," had a flat bottom, straight deadrises, and carried three masts but no topmasts. Of the many ghost towns of Delaware, none is more ghostly or more charming than Bethel, a forgotten backwater of the great Bay.

Left in Bethel across Broad Creek to PORTSVILLE, 3.5 m. (50 pop.), also a ghost of the days of shipping and shipbuilding. At PORTSVILLE POND there is fishing (boats available in season). Beside the dam a water-power gristmill still runs. In 1930 some yellow stuff thought to be gold was discovered in the sand near here, and plans were made to wash the "ore" in the millrace. It was not gold, but it still makes conversation at the store. A Negro camp meeting is held here (early Sept.) in a spruce-pine grove (L).

LAUREL, 44.2 m. (25 alt., 2,700 pop.), at the head of navigation on Broad Creek, was laid out in 1802 and named for the laurel bushes grow-

SHIP CARPENTER'S HOUSE, BETHEL

ing thick on the banks of the stream. Thousands of crates of cucumbers and cantaloupes are shipped annually from here by truck, rail, and diesel boats. Other industries are basket-making, canning, and fertilizer-mixing. The town is too busy and "modern" to permit the survival of many old houses, but the tempo of living never suggests hurry or anxiety. During a week in October 1952, Laurel celebrated in pageant, drama, music the Sesqui-Centennial of its founding—a triumph of local talent and hospitality.

The town is built on a patent called Bachelor's Delight, part of 3,000 acres provided in 1711 by Maryland (this part of Delaware was claimed by Maryland) for the use of the Nanticoke Indians still living on the lower Eastern Shore. Within 50 years, however, nearly all had left the reservation and paddled up Chesapeake Bay and the Susquehanna River into Pennsylvania; afterwards members of the tribe would return from time to time in canoes to dig up their dead and take them northward for reburial. A group of persons who claim descent from the Nanticokes still live on Indian River (*see Tour 15*).

The AUCTION BLOCK *(9-4 daily)*, 8th St. near Central Ave., starts operation with strawberries about May 15 and continues into the fall. The block itself is a shed with two driveways into which farmers guide their produce-laden vehicles. In the long lines are trucks of all sizes and ages; carts, wagons, automobiles filled to their tops. Laurel Farmers Auction Market is operated by the Southern Delaware Truck Growers Association representing nearly 1,000 farmers of the surrounding region. Gross sales vary annually. Crop values range from $400,000 to nearly a million annually of cucumbers, cantaloupes, watermelons, tomatoes and berries.

The COLLINS HOUSE, Delaware Ave., N. Laurel, with a white-columned portico and gallery, was the home of Nathaniel Mitchell, Governor of Delaware 1805–8. The erection of buildings has marred the vista from the house to the creek at the foot of the slope. Part of RECORDS POND, N. edge of Laurel *(bass and pike fishing; boats available in season),* is Lovers' Lane, a nearly straight stretch of water two miles long where young couples like to drift between the wooded shores.

MEMORIAL LIBRARY, Fourth St. between Central and Delaware Aves. was presented to the town, Nov. 3, 1951, to house the public library, by Walter S. Carpenter, Jr., of Wilmington, and his three sons, in memory of the late Mrs. Carpenter, who was Mary Louise Wootten of Laurel. The gift included land and building with endowment toward maintenance.

Laurel is at the junction with State 24 *(see Tour 16).*

DELMAR, 51.4 *m.* (2,550 pop.; 1,200 in Del.), has two mayors, two town councils, and two separate school systems. State St., the principal business thoroughfare, is the Delaware-Maryland Line. The town, formerly almost wholly dependent upon railroad shops for its existence, has become a trading center and shipping point of some importance. When the Delaware Railroad reached the Maryland Line in 1859 the spot was a pine wilderness. Later the rails were extended down to Cape Charles by the New York, Philadelphia and Norfolk R.R., and the place grew up around the junction. In 1918 the whole line from Wilmington to Cape Charles was taken over by the Pennsylvania R.R. and is now called the Delmarva Division.

The Delaware-Maryland Boundary partly surveyed in 1750–51 by John Watson and William Parsons for Pennsylvania, and by John Emory and Thomas Jones for Maryland, was run from the Atlantic Ocean 35 miles westward to the center of the Peninsula, forming the southern boundary of Delaware. It was not until 1764 that Charles Mason and Jeremiah Dixon, after verifying the southern line, started from the western end and ran the other Delaware-Maryland boundary northward 100 miles to what is now Pennsylvania, and thence westward across the mountains toward the Ohio River. It was the latter boundary, between Maryland and Pennsylvania, that divided the free from the slave states before the Civil War. As sister slave states, the whole of Maryland and all but the northern tip of Delaware lay south of it.

Since 1950, despite the dividing state boundary, the school systems and other municipal facilities and services have been coordinated. Some new industries have also been established.

US 13A crosses the Maryland Line, 51.4 *m.,* about 7 miles north of Salisbury, Md. *(see MARYLAND GUIDE, page 420).*

Tour 1A

Seaford—Reliance; **5.6** *m.* State 20.
Paved roadbed.
Accommodations limited.

This route runs through flat, sandy, pine-wooded country in the southwest corner of Delaware. Farming consists chiefly of raising sweet potatoes, cucumbers, cantaloupes, strawberries, tomatoes, and other truck crops sold on the auction blocks of Seaford and Laurel.

State 20 branches west from US 13 *(see Tour 1, Sec. d.)* at the north edge of SEAFORD, 0 *m.* (25 alt., 3,200 pop.) *(see Tour 1, Sec. d.).*

RELIANCE, 5.6 *m.* (50 pop.), a remote and peaceful hamlet on the Maryland Line, was the headquarters of Lucretia (Patty) Cannon, kidnaper of free Negroes, tavern hostess, amateur wrestler, and by far the most famous outlaw, male or female, ever to range the Delmarva Peninsula. For many years after the end, in 1829, of her 40-year career, the hamlet was known as Johnson's Cross Roads for her ruffian son-in-law Joe Johnson, her partner at the tavern and in the Negro-snatching business. In 1882 the name of the place was changed to Reliance for respectability's sake.

A few yards west of the boundary is (R) the A. Hill Smith house *(private),* a two-story frame dwelling painted gray; built about 1885 on the SITE OF JOE JOHNSON'S TAVERN, and said to contain some of the tavern's original framing, it bears little resemblance to its notorious predecessor. The original building, also called Patty Cannon's Tavern, was much larger and had a long double veranda and a great outside chimney at each end.

On the first floor was the tavern barroom where the buxom, jovial, black-haired, and black-eyed hostess entertained travelers, local sports, and slave dealers from the deep South. Cash passed from the pocket of a dealer to the stocking of Mrs. Cannon, corn whiskey gurgled down to clinch the bargain, and off went another drove of Negroes, whimpering or sullen, to the slaver lying in the Nanticoke River at Cannon's Ferry or else at Sharptown, Md., just across the line. In the attic was the "nigger-keep" with its legendary bloodstained oak door and wrought-iron rings on the walls where shackled Negroes awaited purchase and shipment to Georgia, Alabama, Mississippi, or Louisiana. Behind the tavern was a woods where Patty kept Negroes chained in warm weather when no more could be packed into the dungeon. All these relics of doom have disappeared—the dungeon door was only recently cut up for firewood—but the memory of Patty Cannon is vivid.

Although many women refuse to discuss this "disgrace to white womanhood," Negro mothers use her name as a hobgoblin to make their children mind. "Less'n you young-uns quits dat squallin'," they warn solemnly, "Ole Patty goin' git you. She goin' ketch you some night an' chunk you in de head, fer she don't mess wid no bellerin' young-uns!"

According to a pamphlet published in 1841, Patty, the daughter of a barmaid and a young English nobleman, was born in Canada, and named Lucretia Hanley. Another story is that she was the black sheep of a good Sussex County family and the widow of Jesse (or Alonzo) Cannon whom she is believed to have poisoned. Certain it is that she combed the countryside for the terrified Negroes of two States. With Joe Johnson and her other thugs she made forays by day or night upon isolated cornfields or lonely shanties. She was but one of many border-South racketeers who were profiting from the high prices—sometimes as much as $1,000 a head —offered for field hands in the new cotton country. In the lower Peninsula, free Negroes were not popular, and the crime of kidnaping was winked at. Its penalty was set by the Delaware law of 1793 and consisted of 39 lashes, one hour in the pillory "with both of his or her ears nailed thereto," and the cutting off of the "soft part of the ears"—a punishment too severe to be enforced. Slave-stealing, however, was another matter; it brought quick punishment, and Patty rarely indulged in it.

The position of the tavern, on the State Line at the junction of three counties, enabled Patty and Joe to dodge quickly across a line and thumb noses at deputy sheriffs who from time to time mildly attempted to make arrests. The tavern itself was the exact opposite of an Underground Railway station. While Quakers in Camden, Odessa, and Wilmington were hiding runaway slaves and sending them north to freedom, Patty Cannon seized free Negroes and shipped them south into slavery. She even employed Negroes to lure others to the tavern on the pretext that they would be given passes north. They got leg irons instead.

Murder, by all accounts, came as natural to Patty Cannon as her back-slapping hospitality, her wit and her love of showing her great strength in "side-hold" wrestling bouts with all comers. She was believed to have killed more than one slave dealer for his money, using impartially a gun, a knife, or a club while the victim ate, drank, or slept. Her victims, black and white, male and female, murdered for various reasons, were supposed to number a score or more. One story widely encountered is that she would knock Negro children in the head when their crying annoyed her. (Several little skeletons were dug up nearby at the time of her arrest.)

One day in April 1829 a farmer was ploughing for Patty Cannon when his team sank into a low spot; digging he found "a blue-painted chest about three feet long and in it the bones of a man." A Negro servant of Patty's confessed that they belonged to a slave dealer named Bell who had vanished 10 years before, after he was heard to say he was carrying $15,000 in cash. According to the boy's story Patty shot him while he was eating supper, cut his body in two, and forced the servant to bury it. The boy directed the digging up of several more bodies—all of persons killed by her, he said. By a ruse the old woman was lured over the boundary into the arms of a Delaware deputy sheriff, since the bones were in this State. In Georgetown she was indicted on three charges of murder. She died in jail on May 11, 1829, before trial, and was buried in the jail yard. Nothing marks her grave, in what is now a parking lot. Two novels have dealt with her: *The Entailed Hat* (1884) by George Alfred Townsend, and *Patty Cannon Administers Justice* (1926) by R. W. Messenger.

At Reliance is the junction with a side road.

Left sharply on this road to WOODLAND, 4 *m.* (73 pop.), formerly Cannon's Ferry, on the northwestern shore of the Nanticoke River, a hamlet comprising a store, a small white Methodist church, a number of small frame dwellings, and a large mansion dominating the whole place. Ancient willows line the bank. The spot commands a good view of the handsome tidal river and its densely wooded shores. Small diesel freighters with oil or fertilizer pass occasionally on their way between Seaford and Baltimore. In winter there are oyster boats from Chesapeake Bay headed for the shucking houses at Seaford. On spring nights during the shad run the black surface of the water reflects the light from coal-oil lanterns riding on floats that mark the ends of drift nets. This part of the Nanticoke until about 1915 was noted for the thousands of fine shad caught annually, but pound nets at the mouth of the river and other factors have almost ruined the industry. There are still enough caught for local "shad-eatin's," however, and the annual Shad Supper (*a Sat. in April or May, 5-7 p.m., 50¢*) at the church is a benefit affair attended by hundreds.

CANNON HALL (*private*), facing the river just above the ferry slip, is to the R.; this large two-story frame mansion with a smaller wing was built about 1820 by Jacob Cannon (1781–1843). He never lived in it. He was engaged to be married, but the lady, it is said, jilted him at the last minute, and the house stood empty for more than 20 years. Later it became the property of the Nicholsons, who are buried with their kinsmen, the Cannons, in the little cemetery here. In the architecture of the house a strong Virginia-Chesapeake Bay influence is apparent in the proportions of the wings, the two large chimneys, the curved window-heads, the brick grillwork of the foundations, the cellarway with its gabled roof, the fine wainscoting and dentiled mantels.

Jacob Cannon and his brother Isaac acquired thousands of acres in the neighborhood. Shrewd merchants and traders, owning a fleet of sailing vessels going to Baltimore, they became hated for their usury and their acquisition of farm after farm by foreclosure. Jacob Cannon was said to have met his death in 1843 as the result of a petty dispute: he accused Owen O'Day, a former henchman of Patty Cannon's, of stealing a bee gum (section of a hollow tree containing bees) from one of his farms. O'Day shot Jacob as he stood on the ferry landing, and escaped under the eyes of condoning neighbors. Isaac Cannon died a month later.

At the Ferry Slip (L) paved with oyster shells, CANNON'S FERRY (*free bet. sunrise and sunset: blow horn*) connects Woodland with the terminus of a road extending southeast 5 miles to Laurel. The only cable ferry in Delaware, the boat is a small scow capable of holding two cars and driven by an automobile engine fastened on one side; until 1930 the power was supplied by the ferryman and his passengers using notched pull-sticks on the steel cable. The cable lies on the bottom when not in use, and the old pull-sticks are kept handy in case the motor fails.

A few days after a new ferryboat was put into use in December 1937, a sedan rolled off in midstream drowning a woman and child; safety precautions have since been rigidly enforced. The ferryman, employed by the State, lives in a State-owned house (R). He is not required to operate his craft at night but often does, tip or no tip.

South of Woodland the road skirts the river shore. At 5 *m.* is (L) WALNUT LANDING (*private*), formerly the Ellis place, a small house of Flemish-bond brickwork with recent frame additions; it stands on a wooded bluff overlooking a long downstream reach of the river. Thought to have been built before 1750, it was in ruins when the present owners restored it in 1936. It is one of the very few old brick houses in Sussex County, where clay was not available. Here as elsewhere the tradition is that the bricks came from England as ballast.

Across the Nanticoke a short way upstream is the SITE OF THE BOAZ BELL HOUSE, the home in the early 19th century of a retired West India ship captain. By legend his favorite stunt was to turn an iron pot over his head and walk across the bottom of the river—the pot acting as a diving bell.

◄◄◄◄◄◄◄◄◄◄◄◄◄◄◄◄◄◄◄◄◄◄ ☼ ►►►►►►►►►►►►►►►►►►►►►►►

Tour 2

Dover—Milford—Georgetown—Selbyville—(Berlin, Md.); US 113.
Junction with US 13—Maryland Line, **57** *m.*
Route used by Eastern Shore buses; by Delaware-Maryland buses between Milford and the Maryland Line; paralleled by the Pennsylvania R.R. between Milford and the Maryland Line.

Accommodations plentiful; small, fairly good hotels; tourist lodges chiefly in towns; few tourist or trailer camps; a few motels.
Roadbed paved throughout.

This Delaware section of US 113, the southern part of the Coleman du Pont Blvd., is an alternate route for US 13 between Dover and Pocomoke City, Md. The north portion passes through the tidewater eastern side of Kent County, crossing numerous streams that flow into Delaware Bay. The nearly flat landscape is made up of large farms devoted chiefly to grain, orchards, vineyards, and dairying. The timber has been mostly reduced to narrow strips along creeks and marshes; the open country is often characterized by thousands of dark-green cedars in single file, planted by birds along the fence rows. There is close kinship between life on the land and the salt-water activity of the nearby bay. Nearly every farmer has his seines, boats, crab nets, oyster tongs and other fishing gear, his old duck gun and his muskrat traps. Exposed from birth to hordes of mosquitoes from the salt marshes, the older people said they had developed a partial immunity to the stings—which indeed caused them little discomfort but raised large welts on outsiders. Work begun by the Civilian Conservation Corp and continued by the State Highway Department and Soil Conservation Commission, ditching and spraying bay marshes, has minimized the mosquito nuisance.

The south portion of this route swings away from the bay and ocean through the flat and sandy middle of Sussex County, where smaller farms alternate with patches or large areas of forest—mostly second-growth loblolly and Virginia ("spruce") pine, with some hardwood including oak and hickory. Here, interest lies in the historical background of an isolated farming region, the details of the present scene, and the lives and customs of the people. Much of this Sussex County midland region was solid forest until after the Civil War, and the slave system was not as firmly established as in the section nearer the navigable waterways.

Section a. Junction with US 13 to Junction with State 14, 19.8 m.

US 113 branches southeast from US 13, 0 *m.,* just N. of Dover.
DOVER, 1.5 *m.* (20 alt., 4,800 pop.) *(see DOVER).*

Points of Interest. Legislative Hall, State House, State Museum, chicken-and-plum-pudding plant, old private houses with gardens, and others.

At Dover is the junction with State 8 *(see Tour 13).*

DOVER AIR BASE, 3.1 *m.,* both sides of the highway on a 2,000 acre tract, is a key Military Air Transport Service (MATS) Base. Also maintained here are a fighter-interceptor wing of the East Coast Defense system, other Air Force units, and a commercial Airport. Scheduled airline service at the latter is passenger, express, and freight. Bus and taxi service connects with Dover. The Air Base is fast becoming a town itself. As most of the officers and the married enlisted men live off the base all available dwellings within commuting distance are in demand.

At 5.1 *m.* is the junction with a side road.

Right on this road is LEBANON, **1.3** *m.* (100 pop.), on the western bank of St. Jones Creek opposite the great creek swamp, a true ghost village whose prosperity rose and fell with commerce on this typical Delaware waterway. A score of frame houses and an ancient stable border a little street that is usually deserted. Though two main highways (US 113 and 113A) pass within a mile on either side, none of their modern speed penetrates this silent and nearly forgotten spot. The gasoline pump in front of the store is the expression of an unrealized hope rather than a sign of activity.

In the early 1850's the shipyards of Lebanon could not build enough schooners to carry away the products of a wide area: grain, fruit, lumber, cordwood, ship timber, staves, tanbark and other farm and forest wealth. Four vessels at once could load at the wharf. As late as the 1880's, despite the railroad 4 miles west, schooners left here for Gulf and West Indian ports as well as for Philadelphia, New York, and Boston. There was regular steamer service to Philadelphia, for freight and passengers, by a stanch little craft, the *Mary U. Githens,* from 1883 until she burned at her mooring here in 1912. Lebanon was, to some extent, the port of Dover, 4 miles up the crooked little stream.

The long wharves have rotted or burned. An occasional tomato or fertilizer boat, diesel-powered, ties up to the bank near the little iron drawbridge. In winter a trapper steps ashore from his old bateau with a sack of drowned muskrats over his shoulder, or a fisherman chugs past in his one-cylinder skiff.

The noted LOTUS LILY BEDS *(in bloom July 20 to Aug. 20; inquire at Lebanon for boats)* of Jones Creek are just north of Lebanon near the mouth of Moore's Gut, a tributary. With blue-green leaves larger than dinner plates, the pale yellow flowers of this species *(nelumbo lutea),* faintly fragrant, rise on stalks well above high tide. The lily, related to an Egyptian species, occurs in a number of states east of the Mississippi River.

Other lotus beds along the creek were destroyed about 1887 when dredges piled mud on them. The deepening of the channel in 1937 was again endangering the lilies to some extent.

Residents of the region have a number of stories concerning the lilies' origin. In one version the seeds were brought from Canada, in another version, from Egypt. One legend describes the finding in an unknown year of a sunken hulk of strange and curious design with Egyptian characters on her prow; lotus pods were said to have floated from the boat and taken root in the rich mud. If this was the ship of some nameless Egyptian Columbus, nothing remains of her to verify the story.

Right from the bridge in Lebanon on a dirt road along the creek and swamp to WILDCAT, 0.3 *m.* (R), at the mouth of Tidbury Branch. From Forest Landing, the decaying wharf of the plantation, a short avenue of trees leads up the lawn to the much-altered old frame house; it was built before the Revolution and still belongs to the Hunns, a family of Quaker Abolitionists who attended Camden Meeting *(see Tour 1)* before the Civil War. Beside the lane is a little old gambrel-roofed house, the sole survivor of several like structures that originally were granaries for the wheat shipped from Forest Landing. These later became cabins for Negroes who worked on the place. For years the Hunns' landing was almost as active as Lebanon. Prior to 1810 Nathaniel and Jonathan Hunn operated a sawmill at a pond (now dry) formed by damming Tidbury Branch.

At 6.8 *m.* is the junction with the Jones Neck road *(see Tour 2A).*

At 7 *m.* is the junction with State 9 *(see Tour 10).*

The long line of RED CEDARS, 7.3 *m.* (R), growing in the right-of-way of the road, owe their preservation to the Highway Act of 1917 which provides that "maintenance" shall include "the setting out and preserving of trees where desirable." Annually the State Highway Department spends several thousand dollars in landscaping main highways and planting many varieties of trees, shrubs, and flowers. Within the right-of-way trash of all kinds is removed and the grass borders are mowed at regular intervals. No advertising is permitted within the bounds of the roads.

This preservation of natural beauty is in accord with Coleman du Pont's policy in building the $4,000,000 highway he gave to the State *(see TRANSPORTATION).* During its construction he forbade his engineers to cut an oak that stood directly in the way of the concrete.

"But sir," they insisted, "an obstacle like that in the middle of a long straight piece of road would just be inviting cars to crash into it!"

Mr. du Pont was still firm, so one of the young men appealed to Mrs. du Pont, who agreed that beauty should be second to safety when the two were incompatible; the tree was removed.

ST. JONES CREEK, 8.3 *m.* ("Jones Creek" locally), is crossed by a drawbridge. The great salt marsh stretching fanwise to Delaware Bay, 3 miles east, is the habitat of muskrats, waterfowl, and other wildlife. The conical domes of dead vegetation are muskrat houses, or "beds" as they are called in Lower Delaware.

Since 1933 mosquito control has altered the conditions on wide areas of wildlife habitat, and is therefore being closely watched by conservationists, trappers, and public agencies including the U. S. Biological Survey *(see Tour 2C).*

At the south end of the bridge is the junction with a side road.

Right on this road is BARKER'S LANDING, 0.3 *m.,* also called Florence, a few houses and a cannery at a wharf on the creek. A CCC mosquito-control camp was established here in 1935.

The BARKER BURYING GROUND, 0.6 *m.* (R), is about 200 yards from the road in a field, its original 3-foot brick wall in ruins, its gravestones toppled over and half buried in briars and trash. In it is a stone bearing this inscription:

"In Memory of Mary Barker, wife of Joseph Barker and eldest daughter of His Excellency Thomas Collins, Esq., late Governor of the State of Delaware, who departed this life the 27th December, 1795, aged 30 years, 7 months & 2 days. Her death was occasioned by taking Peruvian bark, adulterated with litharge, which was purchased of an apothecary in Wilmington."

Thomas Collins was actually President of the Delaware State (1786–9); Mary Collins grew up at their home, Belmont Hall, just south of Smyrna (see Tour 1), and on marrying came here to live among the mosquitoes of St. Jones Creek. Apparently she contracted malaria and took the quinine-containing Peruvian bark, fatally adulterated with lead monoxide. What her husband did to the apothecary is not disclosed. Mosquito-borne fevers in eastern Delaware killed hundreds yearly, many of them young persons like Mary Collins Barker.

MAGNOLIA, 1.4 m. (173 pop.), is a quiet little village that originated about 1845, when merchants using Barker's Landing began to build houses here rather than along the marshy mosquito-infested shore. The village stands upon Caroone Manor, a 10,000-acre reserve that William Penn, when he arrived in 1682, ordered set aside for the Duke of York. (A similar tract was to be earmarked in each county for the Duke.) The part of it where Magnolia now stands was later sold to James Millechamp and was called "Millichop's Woods."

The MATTHEW LOWBER HOUSE, E. side of the main street, N. of the intersection, the oldest house in the village, is a white-painted brick dwelling built in 1774 with a frame section added about 1855. Standing in front of it are a pair of BRIDE AND GROOM TREES, sycamores planted by the newly married Lowbers in 1774, or 1775, following the sentimental and forward-looking custom of the day (see Coleman House: LEWES). One of these trees measures more than 15 feet in circumference.

At 10.8 m. is the junction with a side road.

Right on this road to the SITES OF LITTLE HEAVEN AND LITTLE HELL, 0.1 m., on the east side of US 113A. A roadside farm-produce stand is named Little Heaven, but there is nothing to mark Little Hell but a weeping willow tree.

The name Little Heaven was applied to a group of cabins built about 1870 by Jehu Reed and his son Jehu M. Reed for Irish laboring families brought here to work in their orchards (see below). Recently the Roman Catholic Church sold a lot at Little Heaven where it had originally intended to build a church.

About the time the cabins were built by the Reeds, a settlement for Negro families was established by Jonathan Willis, another large fruit grower. This soon acquired the name Little Hell. A brook between the two places was called the River Styx.

At 11.4 m. is (L) the junction with the Bowers Beach Rd. (see Tour 2B), and (R) the JEHU REED HOUSE (private), built of brick in 1771 and remodeled in 1868 in Victorian style. The house is a good example of the transformation that overtook many old Delaware country mansions between 1865 and 1880—the latter part of the second golden age of agriculture in the Colony and State.

Jehu Reed (1805–80), one of the most noted of an early group of scientific farmers (see RED LION HUNDRED: Tour 1), had grown wealthy on the sale of peaches, young grafted peach trees and other crops, including silk produced by silkworms feeding on his own mulberry trees. The Civil War boomed the price of everything he raised and in 1868 he began renovating the place.

After he finished rebuilding his extensive barns and stables, he enlarged

BARRATT'S CHAPEL

his home according to the best style of the day. To the simple and dignified two-and-one-half story Georgian Colonial house he added a heavy, square third story: the old brickwork is visible in the ends of the house. To the front of the house he added a porch, and on the broad new roof he placed an observatory with an ornamental iron railing (now gone) from which on clear days he might survey his lands and orchards. Windows, doorways, and woodwork were changed to conform with the current style.

BARRATT'S CHAPEL, (L) 12.6 *m. (always open; service at 2 p. m. every other Sun.; "Barratt's Day" service at 2, usually last Sun. in Sept.),* a plain two-story brick structure in a grove, beside a large cemetery, was built in 1780 by Philip Barratt (1730–84)—a landowner who donated the site —and Waitman Sipple, his father-in-law. Barratt and Sipple were among the many former members of the Church of England who had been converted to Methodism by Francis Asbury and other followers of John Wesley. Many babies are still named Wesley and Asbury in lower Delaware.

Barratt's Chapel is known and revered in Delaware and the Peninsula as the Cradle of Methodism. Here on Nov. 14, 1784, the Sacrament of the Lord's Supper was first administered in America by authorized Methodist preachers to Methodist communicants. Bishop Coke had been preaching, that Sunday, to a thousand persons in the church and grounds when, after the service (in Coke's words), "a plain, robust man came up to me in the pulpit and kissed me"—the apostolic salute. "I thought it could be no other than Mr. Asbury, and I was not deceived." The two called a meeting of preachers and made plans for the conference on Christmas Eve in Lovely Lane Church, Baltimore, where the organization of the Methodist Episcopal Church took place and Asbury was consecrated superintendent (though he immediately assumed the title of bishop).

From the time of the visit of John and Charles Wesley to Georgia in 1736–7 until the Revolution the efforts of the American Methodist missionaries had met great resistance from Church of England adherents; in some Colonies the former were even jailed. However, in Delaware, especially in Kent County, the itinerant preachers were warmly welcomed. Here in 1778 Asbury sought refuge at the home of Judge Thomas White when for a time the Methodists were being hounded as Tories because of some utterances by Wesley in England against the uprising in America. Legend has it that a number of men appeared at Judge White's door and asked him politely if he wanted them to ride the preacher out of the State on a rail. "Thank you, gentlemen," the Judge replied, "but I think I can attend to him." There was no further disturbance.

After the Revolution the Church of England collapsed as such in America and before it could reorganize as the Protestant Episcopal Church, the Wesleyan movement attained the great impetus that has made the Methodist Episcopal Church by far the largest denomination on the Peninsula.

The annual Barratt's Day service is attended by hundreds from all over the Peninsula and from neighboring States. A usual feature is a historical address by some authority on the building and its part in the development of the Methodist Church.

Little of the interior of the chapel is original. A gallery built for the Negroes runs around three sides; pews and pulpit are replacements. The bench on which Coke and Asbury sat during their historic first meeting is kept in a glass case on the platform. A metal star in the floor marks what is said to be the spot of their embrace and apostolic kiss.

FREDERICA (R), 13.8 m. (589 pop.), formerly Johnnycake Landing on the Murderkill, flanked by marsh on three sides, is one of the Delaware villages that developed from shipping and shipbuilding and declined when the railroad began to transport farm and forest products. There are some old brick and frame houses built along the King's Highway which ran through the town. In by-passing Frederica on its eastern side, the Coleman du Pont Boulevard was flung across an apparently bottomless swamp: 40-foot pilings disappeared like match sticks and 80-foot sounding rods followed the pilings. A fairly solid causeway was finally made ready for concrete after years of filling and settling.

First known as Indian Point, the village was built on a tract called St. Collum taken up in 1681 by Benoni Bishop who bought the Indian rights from the sachem, Saccarackett. Among purchasers of this land from Bishop's heirs in 1769–70 were Zachariah Goforth and Jonathan Emerson. When Emerson laid out streets in 1770, Goforth maintained in court a right to keep open a road through the new development to Johnnycake

LOWBER HOUSE, FREDERICA

Landing. Goforth, one of the early road builders of the Three Lower Counties, built other roads in this part of the country.

That Frederica was ever Johnnycake Landing is denied by some residents of the village in spite of the record that reinforces the tradition. Emerson may have bestowed the name Frederica when he laid out the streets; it apears as Frederica Landing in a record of 1796. The origin of the name is vague, though as the center of the Delaware Methodist revival of the 1770's and 1780's, Johnnycake Landing may have been changed to Frederica Landing to honor the Wesleys who had held a great revival in Frederica, Ga., in 1736.

The fine white oak that filled the woods nearby was an important factor in the shipbuilding industry that lasted here until about 1890. If a vessel was "Frederica-built" she was known to be stanch and sound. A crowd of a thousand persons would come to see the launching of a schooner at Lank's shipyard. Some of the vessels were more than 100 feet long with a draft of 8 feet. (The creek has since filled with silt and the U. S. Hydrographic chart of 1936 showed a depth of but 4½ feet at Frederica.) Small steamers plied between here and Philadelphia on regular overnight schedules with freight and passengers until 1929, the last such line serving a lower-Delaware town.

John W. Hall (1817–93), Governor of Delaware 1879–83, expanded the running of his general store in Frederica into the buying, selling, and shipping of all the products of the region, which went out of the Murderkill in his own fleet of about 30 vessels.

Much of the real estate in Frederica is entailed; holders of lots and houses pay rentals fixed generations ago. The perpetual leases are inherited like property.

The village has long been noted for its good cooking. Oysters and fish in their various Delaware styles attain here the old-time flavor and succulence.

The LOWBER HOUSE, W. side of Market St., N. of Main St. *(private)*, is an aged and decrepit brick building erected probably before 1750. It has Flemish-bond brickwork, arch-headed windows and doors, and a water-table around the base of the walls.

Right from Frederica on State 12 to the junction with the Harrington Rd., 0.7 *m.;* L. on this road to the junction with a side road, 3.4 *m.;* L. on this side road to MORDINGTON (L), 4 *m. (private),* on a bluff overlooking McColley's Millpond on a branch of the Murderkill. This fine Georgian brick house was erected in 1777 by the Douglass family who formerly operated a gristmill known as Mordington Mills, at the dam.

The first-floor plan of Mordington, unlike that of most old Delaware plantation houses, is two rooms instead of one room deep. A great chimney serves two fireplaces at one end of the house. As in many houses of the period, the keystone-type window caps are wooden because stone was not available. There is a broad beltcourse of brick entirely around the house at the second floor, and the cornice is handsome. Though the house contains much fine original woodwork, the graceful stairway is a newly made copy of the first one, which was sold. The doorway has been replaced by a gabled doorway from an old house in Berlin, Md. Large old trees shade the lawn. From between the roots of a great maple there grows an ancient York-and-Lancaster rose, bearing red-and-white striped blooms that symbolize the ending of the War of the Roses; the bush is believed to have been brought from England by the Douglass family.

Mordington is said to be haunted by the ghost of a comely slave girl who, locked in her room unjustly for punishment, jumped out of a window and was killed. Seven antique "squat-bottles" buried in a semicircle around the hearth of a former slave cabin nearby have been recently dug up; they are thought to have had some voodoo significance.

At 1.5 *m.* on State 12 is the junction with a side road; right on this road to the old brick BONWELL HOUSE (L), 2.9 *m. (private),* at the edge of Andrews Lake on another branch of the Murderkill. By tradition here lived in the 18th century a man called Quaker Bonwell, who once, the story goes, in a fit of anger killed a Negro boy working in his tannery. It is related that when Bonwell died his white neighbors refused to touch the body, which was finally given a Christian burial by Negroes to make sure his ghost would not rise to haunt them.

In spite of their precautions a specter did appear, the locally-famous Fence Rail Dog—a creature as long as a fence rail, with flaming red eyes and a great bushy tail over its back—that scared humans and horses into breakneck flight for home. For many years nobody has admitted having seen the Old Long Dog, as it is also called, but there are whites and Negroes who still do not feel comfortable, it is said, while walking the Felton Rd. at night.

At 14.2 *m.* on US 113 the highway crosses the MURDERKILL itself, flowing crookedly to Delaware Bay, 5 miles distant. There has been much debate in Delaware over the origin and meaning of this name. Its appearance on a map of 1704 and later maps as "Murther Kill" led to its popular spelling as Mother Creek from, it was supposed, the Dutch. *Murther,* however, was the English spelling of murder in the 17th century, and apparently was applied to the creek in this sense by the Dutch and Swedes.

On the map made by the Swedish engineer Peter Lindeström from his surveys of 1654–56 there is the name *Mordarekijhlen,* which is said by Amandus Johnson, a modern authority on the early Swedes in America, to be of three parts—the Swedish *mordare* for murder, the Dutch *kijhl* for creek, and the Swedish suffix *-en* which tied the whole word together.

In further support of this meaning is the deposition of Gerrit Van Sweeringen, one-time official of the Dutch Colonies on the Delaware, who described an expedition of Dutchmen in 1648 down the west side of Delaware Bay. After some misfortunes said to have been suffered near what is now Lewes, ". . . they went some 10 or 12 miles higher, where they landed again and traded with the Indians, trusting ye Indians to come into their stores ashore, and likewise aboard of their sloop, drinking and debauching with ye Indians till they were all at last barbarously murdered, and soe that place was christined with their blood and to this day called ye Murderers kill, that is Murders Creeke."

South of the Murderkill, within a narrow belt, the character of the woods changes from the hardwoods of the upper Peninsula to the predominantly evergreen region of loblolly and spruce pine that extends to Cape Charles. More and more holly appears as the soil becomes sandier and the winter climate milder and damper.

At 19.8 *m.* is the northern junction with State 14, the Lewes and Rehoboth road *(see Tour 2C).*

Section b. Junction with State 14 to Maryland Line, 37.2 m.

MILFORD (L), 1.4 *m.* (20 alt., 5,179 pop.) *(see MILFORD).*

Points of Interest. Parson Thorne House, Causey House, a noted dental laboratory, a yacht-building plant, and others.

HAVEN LAKE (R), 1.6 *m.,* a millpond formed by an ancient dam across the headwaters of the Mispillion River, is a State wildlife sanctuary where fishing is permitted *(boats available in season).* The name is said to be derived from Milford Haven, an estuary and the harbor of Milford, Wales.

To the L. is the PEARCE WOOLEN MILL *(open by permission),* using water power to prepare the wool in discarded clothing and other articles for reknitting into new garments. The old materials first go through a machine that breaks them into fine threads, then to machines that act like fine-tooth combs. After this garnetting process the material looks and feels much like raw wool. It is then sorted according to color so that it may be more successfully dyed by the purchasers of the wool.

The bridge over the main spillway of the lake is on the boundary between Kent and Sussex counties, a division of some significance *(see Tour 1).*

At 4.6 *m.* is the junction with a side road.

Left on this road is LINCOLN, 1 *m.* (400 pop.), a town laid out in 1865 by Col. Abel S. Small, of New York, on the line of the proposed railroad. When the railroad reached here in 1867, Colonel Small built stables for a future race track and laid out streets and parks on a grand scale for the "future metropolis of southern Delaware." The plans collapsed when Colonel Small died suddenly, but the village grew slowly, depending on farming and lumbering. Dogs and chickens are as safe on the broad avenues as in their own yards. A favorite pastime at the general store was to send a stranger looking for a "statue of Abe Lincoln" which does not exist.

The STATE FORESTRY DEPARTMENT NURSERY, 6.7 *m.* (R), a 4-acre plot with a frame building, is devoted to the production of forest-tree seedlings and transplants. From this nursery more than 125,000 young trees are distributed annually to landowners throughout the State. Seedlings are free for planting in State. Part of site is in soil-building crops. Complete tax exemption is offered for 30 years on reforested lands of 5 acres or more.

Besides white pine, Douglas fir, slash pine and other non-native trees, the nursery grows the important native timber species including loblolly pine, tulip poplar, black locust, and bald cypress. Experiments with English holly are being made to see whether it would be practical to establish groves of it for the production of holly sprays or branches, to supplement the native wild holly which has been threatened by careless methods of cutting. *(See AGRICULTURE.)*

CLENDANIEL'S POND, 6.9 *m.* (R), occasionally dry in past years, has been well restored.

A WOODLOT THINNING DEMONSTRATION of the Forestry Department, 7.6 *m.* (L), shows proper care of a stand of young loblolly pine.

At 9 *m.* is the junction with State 16 *(see Tour 3).*

At 9.1 *m.* the highway crosses the abandoned and trackless ROADBED OF THE QUEEN ANNE'S R.R., chartered in Maryland in 1894 and in Delaware in 1895 to run between Love Point, in Queen Anne's County, Md., and Lewes, Del. Ferries from Baltimore met trains at the Love Point pier on Chesapeake Bay. The trains traversed the 72 miles across the widest part of the Peninsula to Delaware Bay, where for a time a ferry ran between Lewes and Cape May, N. J. The rail line never made the profits predicted for it. In turn it became part of the Maryland, Delaware and Virginia R.R. Co., the Maryland and Delaware Coast Ry. Co., and the Maryland and Delaware Seacoast Ry. Co. Service was abandoned in 1924, and later much of the track was removed. Toward the end of operation the trains ran so infrequently that 4-foot pines grew between the rails, causing the engine to halt while the fireman chopped them down with an axe.

A PICNIC-GROUND AND CAMP SITE (L), 10.2 *m. (fireplaces for cooking, firewood, covered picnic tables, a pure water supply, and toilet facilities),* is on well-drained ground in the ELLENDALE SWAMP. The pleasant, shady site, maintained by the Forestry Department is one of an increasing number of such Delaware sites.

Along the highway right-of-way through a region of 993 acres of Ellendale State Forest are strips of swamp and woodland cared for by the Forestry Department in a manner to preserve the native flora. The State-owned borders of the forest are free from commercial signboards along a

3-mile stretch of wild beauty, an avenue straight as an arrow bordered by pines, cedars, tall hollies, and a lush undergrowth of land and water vegetation. Altogether the Ellendale Swamp and Forest comprise about 16 square miles, one-fourth cleared or tilled.

Although the swamp contains no big game it is a favorite with naturalists; the plant and animal life that abounds here includes many species of birds and plants native only to the South; among the birds are the prothonotary warbler and yellow-throated warbler, and among the plants are the muscadine grape, the swamp magnolia, and the white cedar. The prickly-pear grows in sunny patches of the dry woodland floor, mistletoe clings to high branches of hardwood trees, and wildflowers include several kinds of orchids.

Like most large fresh-water swamps the Ellendale (38-52 alt.) is on the divide between two drainage areas. Part of the run-off eventually finds its way into the Nanticoke River and thence to Chesapeake Bay, and part flows eastward toward Delaware Bay. Ditching and the clearing of natural streams has dried up much of the swamp, improving nearby farmland to some extent but exposing former peat bogs to the danger of underground fires.

At 13.6 *m.* is the junction with a side road.

Right on this road in the REDDEN STATE FOREST (2,820 acres) is a PICNIC SHELTER (L), 2.1 *m.* *(fireplace and firewood),* on the bank of Gravelly Branch of the Nanticoke River. The shelter, built in 1937 by the CCC, is of log construction with a large stone fireplace and chimney. The end with the fireplace is walled on three sides, the rest merely covered with a roof. The fire hazard is minimized by a concrete floor in the cabin and the clearing away of underbrush outside.

Through Redden Forest, the State Forester has maintained and improved a network of graded dirt roads, cleared logging trails, and foot trails that were made by CCC labor under the direction of the State Forestry Department. From the north side of the concrete road, a few yards east of the bridge over Gravelly Branch, a foot trail makes a two-mile loop along the stream, the gum swamp, and through the woods, a pleasant walk for nature students not afraid of harmless snakes.

At 13.9 *m.* is the junction with a side road.

Left on this road is REDDEN, 0.3 *m.* (52 pop.), a piney-woods hamlet that developed around a railroad station named in 1867 for John Redden, a local farmer. Sawmilling is still an industry here.

At 16.6 *m.* (L) is STATE HIGHWAY POLICE STATION No. 4 *(information and first aid).*

At 17 *m.* is the junction with State 18 *(see Tour 14).*

GEORGETOWN (L), 18.2 *m.* (50 alt., 2,000 pop.), is the seat and most central town of Sussex County. In the latitude of the Virginia mainland, the town's quiet and friendly appearance are typical of numberless southern courthouse towns that were established at crossroads as convenient centers for legal activity. The nearest navigable water is 8 miles away.

The white-columned brick courthouse on the Courthouse Square is the hub of Sussex County, and the radiating roads are the spokes. Into Georgetown come the people of the county, white, black, and yellow, from the

SUSSEX COUNTY COURTHOUSE, GEORGETOWN

towns, farms, and swamps, in all sorts of clothes and all sorts of vehicles —to serve on juries, attend court, transfer land titles, make wills, do their dealing in the stores of E. Market St., or just to stand around talking crops, politics, bird-dogs, and the weather.

Near the tree-shaded Square are the lawyers' offices, cluttered little snuggeries where lawyers have the latest *Delaware Code* alongside the musty law books that their fathers and grandfathers used before them. Here an elderly member of the Delaware Bar will receive his clients and cronies in a manner as informal as the surroundings. With one caller, the lawyer goes over a legal document and then spends a pleasant hour exchanging courthouse anecdotes; apropos of something or other, he quotes Shakespeare or Horace, and turning again to the law, expounds a precedent with scholarly force and clarity. Should the next caller be a tanned and worried farmer from Broad Creek Hundred, the lawyer drops into the rhythm and idiom of Sussex dialect, the kind of speech he uses in addressing juries, in language the farmer can best understand. The farmer does understand, and soon feels as comfortable as if he were in his own kitchen.

Georgetown is a pleasant place, full of the earthy flavor of the region. The legal, financial, and residential center is the Courthouse Square, flanked by the courthouse, the post office, the hotel, the banks, and the comfortable houses of prominent citizens; shady streets have their old cypress-shingled houses, their gardens, wistaria, and large magnolia trees.

The weekly *Sussex Countian,* formerly printed above the law office of its owner-editor, late Congressman Robert G. Houston, now owned and edited by his daughter, Mary Houston Robinson, is a live country paper of large circulation. The output of local plants in and near the town ranges from pearl buttons to blimps; includes flour, feed, bricks, millwork, clothing, aircraft parts and safety devises, baby chicks and broilers. Increase in employment at Georgetown and within 20 to 25 miles has spurred plans for new dwellings.

Throughout the Colonial period the county courts were at the Cape Henlopen settlement called Hoerekill under the Dutch, Whorekill and Lewes under the English. This coastal site was satisfactory while most of the people lived nearby, but it became more and more inconvenient to the settlers pressing westward toward the interior. In 1775 the boundary settlement with Maryland added wide southern and western strips to Sussex County, and the people there, accustomed to nearby county seats in Maryland, protested at having to travel 30 or 40 miles to Lewes. Consequently in 1791 an act was passed to purchase 100 acres of land in the center of the county "at the place called James Pettyjohn's old field," and to provide for the erection of a courthouse and jail. The next year the new village was named Georgetown in honor of George Mitchell, one of the commissioners appointed to look after the work.

As the town slowly developed around the courthouse, tanning and brick-making became the first small industries. A branch of the Farmers' State Bank was established in 1807. Private and public schools soon followed. In 1829 the notorious Patty Cannon died here in jail, indicted for murder *(see Tour 1A).* Here in 1841 was born the man whose novel

The Entailed Hat immortalized her—George Alfred Townsend. Meanwhile the Square was becoming a great place for markets, but more especially a public political arena for the whole county. On its greensward political campaigns reached their noisy height in torchlight processions and "speakin's." Here, on the Saturday night before the election of 1862, "Secesh threats" were made that may have been the chief reason why Republican leaders sent for Federal troops to "protect the polls" of Delaware on Nov. 4. On another occasion, when Union men stuck lighted candles on all the posts of the Circle, a horseman charged through the crowd and around the place, slashing off the candles with his riding whip and cheering, it is said, for Jeff Davis.

Before the days of rapid communication, the 2nd day after election was Return Day for the crowds of Sussex Countians who assembled in the Square to hear the announcers on the courthouse steps call out the results brought in by horsemen from the outlying hundreds, and to learn the national figures as they trickled in. The people brought their food along, or patronized the booths selling oyster sandwiches, fried chicken, or whiskey, and everyone was invited to cut himself a chunk of barbecued ox. Before the Civil War, invariably, and afterward usually, a great Democratic banner foretold the local results. An important ceremony was the "pole-raisin'"—the erection of a 40-foot pole topped by several ears of corn, emblematic of the Democratic Party.

In 1869 the Junction and Breakwater R.R. from Harrington to Lewes was built through here, bringing woodworking and canning industries that flourished for a generation. Of greater future significance to the town, however, was the completion in 1917, between here and the southern Maryland Line, of the first 20-mile stretch of the paved Coleman du Pont Blvd. (US 113) that was later to join Georgetown much closer than before to the outside world. To celebrate the Democratic victory of 1936 a revived Return Day was held here with speaking and an ox-roast—but the excitement of hearing the news was absent. Georgetown's festive spirit is aglow in the Christmas season, informally and in a Cotillion Society Ball.

Since World War II, Return Day is again an annual event with barbecue, Sussex specialties in food, festive decorations, general gaiety and social time. Returns are read in the Courthouse.

The SUSSEX COUNTY COURTHOUSE, SE. corner of the Square and E. Market St., built in 1839 on the site of the first Georgetown courthouse, was improved in 1914 by the addition of a portico and a handsome clock tower and cupola visible for miles. County offices occupy the first floor; on the second floor is the spacious courtroom. The $15,000 that the courthouse cost was raised in 1835 by a lottery authorized by the General Assembly. In former years the lawyers of Georgetown placed a great bowl of eggnog each Easter on the steps, and the public dipped in. The COURTHOUSE ANNEX, SW. corner Market and Race Sts., was built of brick in 1835 as the second county jail in Georgetown, was gutted by fire in 1865, rebuilt the next year and a third story added, abandoned as a jail in 1933 when the new County Jail was built south of town *(see below)*.

and improved and repaired in 1934 to house public offices. On the first floor are the county tax offices, on the second floor, local offices of the State Board of Education. The ORIGINAL GEORGETOWN COURTHOUSE *(private)*, W. side of S. Bedford St. near the Square, now a dwelling, is a plain structure covered with cypress shingles. It was built in 1793, on the site of the present courthouse, at the expense of private citizens who were reimbursed from the proceeds of a State-authorized lottery. In 1837 it was sold and moved to this spot.

The BRICK HOTEL, SW. corner of the Square and W. Market St., was built in 1836; the west wing was added in 1936. THE JUDGE'S *(private)*, NW. corner W. Market and Front Sts., is a fine old cypress-shingled house built by Judge Peter Robinson about 1810, and afterwards occupied by Judges Edward Wootten, Henry C. Conrad, and David T. Marvel. The little law office is a separate building in the same style at the corner of the grounds; the delicate cornices and other details are carried out even on the privy in the garden, as was customary on country estates. There are other old houses built in this same style on Bedford St. and other streets near the Square. Above Purnell's Store, E. side of N. Bedford St. near the Square, is the ARCHAEOLOGICAL COLLECTION *(open by permission)* of H. W. T. Purnell. Most of the hundreds of Indian relics here were found in Sussex County; they include arrowheads, axes, scrapers, mortars, shell beads, and bones from human skeletons. One of the arrowheads is made in a twist apparently for accuracy in flight.

Southeast from the town, reached by a new road is the large Georgetown Airport. Several plots of from twenty-five to seventy-six acres each are here leased to industries connected with aircraft. Among these are the All American Engineering Company hangar and two thousand feet of track for testing gear; the Arrow Safety Device Company; the General Development Corporation hangar and plant, manufacturing blimps for the United States Government. Southwest is one of the State's three modern comprehensive county high schools (Negro) for both academic and vocational training.

At 18.3 *m.* (L), was one of several Roadside Gardens, flower-and-shrubbery plots established by Mrs. Coleman du Pont (1863–1937), who strongly influenced Coleman du Pont's policy of combining engineering efficiency with beauty when he was building the State-long highway that bears Col. Du Pont's name. Sometime after Mrs. Du Pont's death the flower gardens she had established were abandoned because the Highway Department had greatly expanded its program of roadside planting.

The SUSSEX COUNTY JAIL, 20.2 *m.* (L), erected in 1931 to replace the Old Jail in Georgetown, is a one-story brick building of Colonial design standing behind the large yellow-and-white WARDEN'S RESIDENCE, which was formerly the county almshouse. The avenue of maples was handsome until the authorities cut off the tops; it was a Peninsula custom to poll shade trees in this manner.

Since 1717 the whipping-post has been a legally established institution in Delaware, the only state still preserving it as a common form of punishment. Until 1925 when an act of the legislature gave judges discretionary power as to its use, the laws of Delaware made whipping mandatory as a supplement to jail sentences for many felonies.

Larceny is the crime most commonly punished by whipping, with as many as 20 lashes. A majority of those whipped are punished for chicken stealing and similar crimes. For breaking and entering a dwelling at night, 20 to 40 lashes are legal as part of the sentence; for burglary with explosives at night, 15 to 25; for burning a vessel, mill, or granary, up to 20. Sixty lashes are the greatest number that may be applied to a man under one sentence; they may be distributed over two or more separate days. For burning a courthouse the penalty is a fine of $1,000, 60 lashes at the post, and up to 20 years in jail.

The prisoner sentenced to receive lashes is marched to the post, his body bare above the waist according to the statute which provides that "The punishment of whipping shall be inflicted publicly by strokes on the bare back well laid on." He faces the post with his arms encircling it and manacled to it. The warden reads the sentence aloud to the culprit and the onlookers standing outside the wire fence, then lays on the lashes at intervals of about three seconds, counting aloud each blow of the cat-o'-nine-tails.

The "cat" is a short handle with nine rawhide thongs about 18 inches long. Formerly the official applying the lash used a single whip of flexible wood, and a full-armed swing from the shoulder; now, using the cat, he must keep his upper arm against his body and swing with his forearm alone, to lessen the possible severity of the blows. Though prisoners are usually advised to tighten their back muscles to reduce the pain, the modern practice is not to strike very hard. Nevertheless, prisoners sentenced to be whipped frequently dread the public whipping—called "hugging old Susan"—more than the jail sentence of a year or more which always goes with it. More hardened criminals, knowing the softened stroke of the lash, sometimes exhibit bravado during punishment.

The whipping of women was ended by law in 1889.

One of the most celebrated cases of whipping in the State was the sentencing of four men in 1873 to receive 40 lashes each at New Castle for robbing the Bank of Delaware in Wilmington, besides one hour in the pillory and 10 years in jail. The fear they showed of the whipping-post, resulting in an attempt to bribe the sheriff not to whip them, has ever since been one of the chief arguments of those who have advocated the retention of the post as a crime-deterrent. The pillory was abolished in 1905 but the whipping-post survives repeated efforts, mostly by humanitarian bodies outside the State, to have it also done away with. It has been called "inhuman," "barbarous," and "ineffective," but protests against it are weak compared to the complacency with which most Delawareans regard it.

At 21.2 m. the highway crosses the ALMSHOUSE DITCH, wide and deep, its banks supporting large holly trees and other forest growth; its waters eventually reach Indian River and the ocean. Many ditches and canals like this one were made necessary by the lack of natural drainage from this swampy central part of the Peninsula. Some were dug by slave labor before the Civil War, others by ditch companies formed by landowners seeking to turn swamps into farmland.

Unprofitable farming in the late 19th and early 20th centuries resulted in the neglect of many of the ditches, including this one, and they became so clogged with silt, windfalls, and vegetation that the adjacent farmland was again unfit for tilling. Beginning in 1936 the Almshouse Ditch and many others were cleaned out and deepened by the CCC. Since then the State has developed a thorough ditching and ditch-cleaning program.

At 23.7 *m.* is the junction with a side road.

Left on this road through pine woods is the DELAWARE COLONY, 1 *m.* *(visiting hours, Wed. 1-5; annual Arbor Day a Sat. in April)*, the State institution for the feeble-minded. Founded in 1921 on a tract of 1,000 acres, it is administered by the Delaware Commission for Feeble-Minded.

The Colony cares for about 400 persons, mostly children; there are separate buildings for whites and Negroes, males and females. The plant includes administrative offices, training shops, a laundry, an infirmary, and farm and dairy equipment. The boys help to operate the truck-and-dairy farm of 400 acres and to care for the hogs and poultry. Girls operate the laundry. In the training shops are made brushes, brooms, shoes, toys, curtains, rugs, sweaters, and other articles used by the Colony or sold outside. Academic training through the fourth grade is given children able to assimilate it. The social development of the children is aided by singing, a drum corps, and supervised recreation. On Arbor Day, when the public is welcomed, a short play is usually given by the boys and girls.

BETTS' POND, 25.7 *m.,* crossed by causeway and bridge, is one of a chain of millponds forming the headwaters of Indian River.

MILLSBORO (L), 26.9 *m.* (15 alt., 479 pop.), on Indian River, 13 miles from the ocean as the crow flies, the principal town of the Indian River country of Delaware, is the capital of the Christmas holly industry of Delaware and one of the most important shipping centers for holly wreaths in the United States. The town is also a distributing point for hundreds of carloads of poultry feed and coal for the broiler chicken industry *(see Tour 16).* Here are manufactured crates, baskets, and other containers for berries, fruits, and vegetables that are shipped by truck and train from Millsboro and other points in Delaware and Maryland. A tomato cannery, a water-power flour-and-feed mill, and a hatchery add to the activity of this little but important place.

Despite the town's several enterprises, the main street with its one traffic light has all the appearance of a quiet southern crossroads village. Like other lower Delaware towns, Millsboro is given over on Saturday nights to the country people for their trading and social gathering, when every store awning has its groups of white and Negro men and boys, talking, laughing, and loafing, while the women "do the dealing." The Millsboro crowd, however, differs from that of any other Delaware town in the many "yellow people" or Moors from Indian River Hundred north of the river and other nearby regions *(see Tour 15).*

Under one of the wooden awnings a dreamy-eyed old yellowman with long drooping white mustaches, his skin the color of coffee mixed with rich cream, stands motionless for hours, nodding to friends as they pass by, but never saying a word. His aquiline nose bespeaks the Indian in him. Another group is composed of men of all hues telling stories; a white man pauses to laugh at a joke and exchange banter with his variously-colored friends. There is no friction betwen the races, but a clear and un-spoken understanding. The spirit of the fair prevails. Everyone knows everyone else, and a stranger's progress down the street is followed by all eyes. A storekeeper sets a stock radio out on the sidewalk and turns it on full blast. Every light is lighted. If the night is cool the town policeman wears his uniform coat; if it is hot he may remove his coat and recline in an easy chair outside the second-hand furniture store.

A storekeeper, before asking a farmer's wife what she wants, outdoes himself to inquire after the health of every member of her family. It is "How do, our folks?" at the start; and "Well, good-bye, our folks—come see us again!" at the end of the dealing. A half-hour spent in selling a new mower to a prosperous white man from Long Neck is followed by a half-hour spent in telling an aged Negro woman from "the Swamp" just how to make her old coal-oil lamp burn right. Out on the sidewalk, singing and whistling is heard everywhere. Dogs trot along in gangs under the leader-ship of a setter or "beadle-dog" (rabbit hound) that knows where some juicy morsel can be found.

Every December the holly market comes into sudden, short, but violent activity; at the sheds men wearing gloves and long white coats receive the wreaths made for miles around and pack them in wooden cases for ship-ment by rail and truck. Much loose holly and other evergreens are also shipped from here. (See AGRICULTURE.) A busy strawberry auction is held daily during late May and early June at the covered auction block on Railroad Ave. Long lines of vehicles of all kinds—wagons, trucks, old sedans packed full of crates—pull up to let the buyers lift lids and nod acceptance of prices asked. Drivers then unload their rigs into trucks or refrigerator cars for shipment north.

The pool at the base of Millsboro Dam is noted for the herring run in March and April, when in good seasons as many as a million have been taken in a few weeks. Fishing is usually done at night, the herring prefer-ring darkness to make their charge into the little bottleneck to spawn. As many boats work as can crowd on to the small area of fish-filled water—four men and a big dip net to a boat. Meanwhile trucks are backed down to the water's edge and are loaded under the street lamps for the haul across the Peninsula to factories on the Eastern Shore, where the herring are cleaned and pickled in brine for the trade in New York and other cities. The feverish fishing, the lights, the roar of motors, the cursing when there are no trucks at hand, the children on the banks scooping up herring in their hands, keep the village excited and sleepless until dawn.

As late as 1915 dozens of crabbers brought thousands of soft-shell crabs to Millsboro for shipment alive in boxes filled with wet grass. The alternate opening and closing of Indian River Inlet has since nearly ruined the industry, though a few soft crabs are still shipped from here. The new inlet now under construction is expected to revive the village as a prime market for crabs, fish, oysters, and clams taken in Indian River Bay and Rehoboth Bay *(see Tour 2C)*.

After Elisha Dickerson built his gristmill in 1792 at what was called Rock Hole, originally "Haul" (or river rockfish) on the north shore in Indian River Hundred, the increasing activity of the place led to the erection of a tavern and a few stores and houses. Shallow-draft sailing vessels left the landing at Rock Hole to call at down-river landings and pick up timber, grain, and other products for northern ports, returning with the storekeepers' stock-in-trade. In 1809 the name Rock Hole was changed to Millsborough while the south-shore settlement remained as Washington. A bog-iron furnace flourished for a while as the big industry of the place. In 1837, when a post office was opened, both sides of the river were called Millsborough, later shortened to Millsboro.

MILLSBORO POND, above the dam, contains bass and pike *(boats available for fishing in season)*.

The SITE OF MILLSBOROUGH FURNACE, S. bank of the river just below the dam, is thickly overgrown with honeysuckle, but a little scuffing exposes the remains of the brick foundation of the primitive blast furnace that William D. Waples established in 1817 and operated on bog ore until 1836. It was the last furnace of its kind in Delaware to survive the competition of better ores elsewhere. Here iron was made that an adjacent foundry manufactured into iron pipe for the old Croton Water Works of New York City, as well as castings for the Eastern Penitentiary at Philadelphia. The foundry ran until 1879 on imported bog iron.

Bog ore (limonite) resulted from the action of organic acids in swamps on iron compounds; the air oxidized these salts and iron hydroxides resulted. Men "raised" this ore and hauled it to the furnace, where a race and water wheel furnished power for the bellows that blew the charcoal fire to white heat. In 1833 an output of 600 tons of pigs and castings, produced with the aid of 180,000 bushels of charcoal and 7,000 bushels of oyster shells, was shipped to Boston, New York, Philadelphia, Baltimore, Washington, and Norfolk.

The HOUSTON-WHITE PLANT *(open by permission)*, Railroad Ave., is one of the largest Peninsula manufacturers of baskets and other containers for fruit and vegetables. Great gum logs are "cooked" in tanks and veneer peeled from them on heavy lathes. Basket-making machines clatter at high speed. The cylindrical cores of logs are often used by boatmen as rollers on which to haul out their craft. The basket industry here and elsewhere has nearly exhausted the supply of gum timber in Delaware, and most of it comes in from Maryland, Virginia, and North Carolina.

Millsboro is at the junction with State 24 *(see Tour 15)*.

DAGSBORO (L), 30.6 *m.* (474 pop.), an unhurried little village of shady streets and mellow old cypress-shingled houses with mossy roofs, is a distributing center for feed and coal consumed by the great broiler industry. There is a hatchery here. Dagsboro is the birthplace of John Middleton Clayton, Delaware statesman *(see BUENA VISTA: Tour 1)*.

Growing up around a gristmill at the head of Pepper Creek, a tributary of Indian River, this settlement was first called Blackfoot Town. About 1785 the name was changed to Dagsborough in honor of Gen. John Dagworthy (1721–84). The village stands upon Dagworthy's Conquest, a 20,000-acre tract granted him in 1759 by Maryland in appreciation of his services in command of Maryland volunteers in the French and Indian War and particularly in the conquest of Fort Duquesne (later Fort Pitt and now Pittsburgh, Pa.), Nov. 25, 1758.

Lieutenant Colonel Dagworthy brought news of the victory to Baltimore and a day of celebration was proclaimed. This was one of the three major victories that settled the struggle betwen the French and the English for the possession of America. Dagworthy got a cash bonus of £30 and this princely domain on the Eastern Shore. It was then considered by the Maryland Assembly as part of Worcester County, but when the boundary struggles between the Penns and the Calverts were being settled before the Revolution the final survey brought the tract within Sussex County, Del., and in 1774 the Penns confirmed Dagworthy's title.

Born and reared at Trenton, N. J., Dagworthy served with distinction as a captain of the "Jersey Blues" in the Canadian expedition of King George's War (forerunner of the French and Indian War), and in 1746 he was one of a group of officers who went to England bearing letters of recommendation from the New Jersey Council to the Duke of Newcastle. A result of this trip abroad was a royal commission as a captain in the British Army.

The full significance of this trophy appeared 10 years later to the great discomfiture of George Washington, a 24-year-old colonel commanding the Virginia forces during the French and Indian War. What enraged Washington was Dagworthy's flat refusal to take orders from him at Fort Cumberland, Md., where Dagworthy was in command of a garrison of Marylanders in 1756. Dagworthy, 11 years older than Washington, declared the latter was only a Virginia provincial officer and of inferior rank on the field to an officer holding a commission from the King of England.

General Braddock, before his death, upheld Dagworthy's claim to outrank the young Virginian. But Washington did not give up so easily, despite the fact that Governor Sharpe of Maryland was encouraging Dagworthy's defiance. That a man with only about 200 soldiers under him should defy the commander in chief of the Virginia forces led the irate Washington to write in a letter to Governor Dinwiddie of Virginia, Jan. 14, 1756:

"I am determined to resign the commission which you were generously pleased to offer me . . . rather than submit to the command of a person who has not such superlative merit as to balance the inequality of rank."

Colonel Washington then made a special trip in midwinter from Virginia to Boston to see Braddock's successor, General Shirley. There he was able to prevail upon the English commander in chief to reverse Braddock's ruling and let him outrank Dagworthy.

The feud was settled officially at least. Dagworthy did not take an appeal over Shirley's head but continued in command at Fort Cumberland.

Later as a lieutenant colonel he was put in command of Fort Frederick, where he had a battalion of 500 men with which to repulse the Indians in that frontier region. Governor Sharpe praised him for his success in holding his men together in the face of insufficient food, delayed pay, and other hardships.

After the French and Indian War Dagworthy returned to his Eastern Shore plantation now surrounded by the majestic sweep of Dagworthy's Conquest. (He had settled here before the war.) In his long, low plantation house *(see below)*, with his wife and numerous servants, he lived as a lord-of-the-manor, operating gristmills, sawmills and tanneries while his field Negroes cultivated hundreds of acres of cleared land. Quantities of cypress timber, lumber, and shingles were exported in his own vessels out of Indian River and up to Philadelphia and Trenton. In the region he was a prime supporter of the Church of England, helping to rebuild little Prince George's Chapel near his home and entertaining visiting missionaries with the famed hospitality of his mansion and household.

In 1774 John Penn appointed Dagworthy a justice for the county. Despite his royal commission in the British Army, Dagworthy took the side of the rebel patriots and in 1775 he accepted the commission of Brigadier General of Sussex County Militia. When a shipload of munitions for Maryland arrived in Indian River, Dagworthy sent the cargo across country to Chestertown under an armed guard. In 1777 Congress made him a bridgadier general in the Continental Army, though for some reason—perhaps his age, perhaps Washington's ill-will—his activity in the Revolution seems to have been limited to disarming the angry Tories who defied the patriots everywhere in the county.

When General Dagworthy died in 1784 he was buried under the chancel of Prince George's Chapel, a mile from his home *(see Tour 16)*.

On the farm of J. R. Baker on the Piney Neck Rd., at the northeast edge of Dagsboro, is the SITE OF THE DAGWORTHY MANSION, about one-quarter mile from the road. The long, comfortable frame house stood on a rise and faced south across a sloping lawn to Pepper Creek—the stream now hidden by woods. Except the few foundation bricks occasionally plowed up, nothing remains of the mansion which was destroyed by fire late in the 19th century. At a spot where a spring used to flow out of the meadow some scattered old bricks and hewn stones are said to be from the springhouse of the plantation. Growing all about are numbers of catalpa trees, descendants of the original trees of the species favored by early Colonial landscapers. In Dagworthy's time the place was one of the finest, if not the finest, in the county. Even as late as 1858 the following appeared in a newspaper as part of a letter from a traveler who visited the old mansion, then still standing:

"We rode up and looked at the remains of former grandeur, resembling in its palmiest days, I presume, the homes of English gentlemen. It is yet a beautiful spot, ornamented with pleasure grounds, and a great variety of shade trees."

Dagsboro is at the junction with State 26 *(see Tour 16)*.

FRANKFORD (L), 32.6 *m.* (615 pop.), a placid old village on Dagworthy's Conquest, started in 1808 as Long's Store on Vines Creek, an Indian River tributary. Later it became Gum's store after the succeeding storekeeper, Manaen Gum. The post office was opened in 1848 with the name of Frankford for a man named Frank who lived near a ford of the stream. Sawmilling was active here and a box and barrel factory in the 1870's and '80's. A tomato cannery runs during August and September.

Along the Du Pont Blvd. (US 113) at Frankford was one of the roadside gardens established by Mrs. Coleman du Pont *(see above)*.

Left from Frankford, **2.5** *m.,* on the Clarksville Rd., is OMAR, a cluster of frame houses around a country store, in an isolated section. It was called Waplesville until 1890.

In 1927 the hamlet was the SCENE OF THE HITCHENS MURDER in which a man was killed by his sister and her sons to collect a $2,000 life-insurance policy.

Drab enough in itself as the product of greed and spite in a poor and inbred backwoods community, the murder made headlines throughout the nation in 1934–35 when the 7-year mystery was suddenly broken. The jury's recommendation of mercy failing, the sister and one of her sons were hanged.

No woman had been hanged in Sussex County since the hanging of a Negro in 1869 for poisoning her baby. Though interest in the hanging of Mrs. May Carey rose high, little or no protest was made against the sentence because of sex. A second son was sentenced to life imprisonment. The third son, a boy at the time of the murder, who made the confession incriminating the others, received a sentence of 7 years. The Court, imposing sentence, described the crime as "one of the most vicious in the criminal annals of the State." Mother and son were hanged at the Sussex County Jail *(see above)* on June 7, 1935.

BLACKWATER PRESBYTERIAN CHURCH (R), **5** *m. (annual service 2nd Sun. in Oct.; annual Tunnell Family Reunion on a Sun. in Aug.),* was built in 1767 near the head of Blackwater Creek, an Indian River tributary. Although regular services were abandoned in 1907, this is one of the most cherished old Presbyterian churches in Delaware.

Painted gray, with green shutters, Old Blackwater is of frame construction, small, simple, and mellow with the years. One outside wall is of old matched boarding; other walls are of clapboards applied when the church was remodeled and repaired in 1893. Little of the original interior furnishings remain; there is said to be a floor of brick under the present board floor. Several large trees shade the church.

As late as 1839 Blackwater Church was one of the "united churches" that included Buckingham Church (Worcester County, Md.) and Laurel Church near Laurel. Until just before the Revolution, when the Maryland-Delaware Line was finally agreed upon, all three of these churches were considered in Maryland. There is yet a close bond between Blackwater and Buckingham. The first pastor was the Rev. Charles Tennent, whose brothers were organizers of Buckingham and New Castle churches, and whose father was a teacher at the Old Log College, now Princeton University. Records of the church are held by the Presbyterian Historical Society, Philadelphia.

SELBYVILLE (L), 36.7 *m.* (1,086 pop.), a place of comfortable houses and busy, well-kept streets, is one of the largest strawberry-shipping centers in the United States. About 100,000 crates are shipped annually by truck and refrigerator car to northern cities. Hundreds of barrels of strawberries in sugar are put into cold storage for sale to ice-cream manufacturers throughout the year; these are called cold-pack berries. Canneries here pack tomatoes and tomato juice as well as other products of this fertile region. Two lumber mills and the offices and shipping sheds of a large nursery add to the activity of this bustling little town near the Maryland Line.

Like many other Delaware towns, Selbyville had its origin in a gristmill and blacksmith shop, in this case not until the time of the Revolution; before the coming of the railroad no town could amount to much that was not on navigable water, and growth was slow. It was known as Sandy Branch until 1842, when Samson Selby opened a store here. He purchased his molasses, calico, muslin, whiskey, rum, tobacco, flour, and other goods in Philadelphia, and when he was asked where the winter's stock was to be sent, he is said to have replied, "It will have to be shipped by Indian River vessel and then hauled to where I'm opening a country store, so just mark it 'Selbyville'."

The town stands on land that belonged to the McCabe family. Matthew McCabe, the blacksmith, was a soldier in the Revolution. In 1817 or earlier the Long family dammed Sandy Branch, a tributary of Sinepuxent Bay, for a millpond to operate the gristmill and a sawmill. The forests were cut down and farmland spread, but the village's real development did not start until the Frankford and Breakwater R.R. reached here in 1873. (This line is now the Franklin City, Va., branch of the Pennsylvania R.R.)

At the STRAWBERRY AUCTION BLOCK, Church St. *(operating May 20-June 20)* growers from a 12-mile radius come to sell their berries to brokers' agents from the cities or to local commission men. Long rows of automobiles, trucks, and horse- or mule-drawn vehicles line up to pass slowly through the shed. The bidding is silent and only the auctioneer "crying the sale" appears to work hard for his living. There is much laughing and joking among the white and Negro drivers. Crap games and horseshoe pitching help to pass the time while the line inches along.

The local Negroes look forward eagerly to the sociability of the berry-field gangs as well as to the $6 or $7 a day that a fast picker may earn. Cooks and handymen by the score desert their employers for the fields. Farmers who do not grow berries have trouble finding help to thin or cultivate corn. Carloads of Negroes, brought up from the nearby Eastern Shore of Virginia to pick berries, are housed in vacant tenant houses, barn lofts, tents, or anything with a roof over it. Sanitary and living conditions are frequently bad; petty thievery and the robbing of henroosts are traced to the less respectable of the floaters.

Another large contingent of floating labor is brought in by labor agents in Wilmington, Baltimore, and Philadelphia who round up families of south-European extraction, chiefly Italians. These people likewise camp in anything offering some protection from the weather. The sun may be hot, but an excursion to the fields and the quick cash to be made are attractive to these families of peasant background who gladly leave city slums behind them and return year after year, often to the same employers. Many of them stay on to harvest cucumbers, cantaloupes, tomatoes, peaches, and apples. "Peach-plucks" is the old-time name applied to those working in the peach orchards.

The first strawberries planted near Selbyville were set out in 1871 by

FENWICK ISLAND LIGHT

D. J. Long. The coming of the railroad soon afterward resulted in a boom in strawberries that reached its peak in 1918, when 250,000 crates were shipped. Less than one-half as many berries are now sent away by highway trucks but Selbyville retains its place as an important strawberry center.

Along the highway here was one of the roadside gardens (L) established by Mrs. Coleman du Pont *(see above)*.

Left from Selbyville, **10.2** *m.*, is FENWICK ISLAND LIGHTHOUSE *(open by permission)*, about one-half mile from the ocean; it stands in Delaware against the Maryland Line. The 80-foot tower, painted white, has a prism lamp visible for 15 miles at sea. It was erected in 1857.

On the Maryland-Delaware Line, at the base of the lighthouse, is one of the few remaining FIVE MILE STONES placed along the boundary which was first surveyed in 1750–51 by a crew of Pennsylvania and Maryland surveyors *(see below and Tour 1, also HISTORY)*.

From the top of the lighthouse there is a fine view of the ocean, the beach, and the lagoons behind the beach. North of the road, in Delaware, is LITTLE ASSA-WOMAN BAY (originally spelled *Assawomet* from the Indian name); it is 4 miles long, one-half to one and one-half miles wide, and very shallow. South of the road in Maryland is BIG ASSAWOMAN BAY. The string of small dwellings along the beach in Delaware include squatters' summer cottages built upon State land *(see Tour 2C)*. The large settlement to the south on the ocean front is Ocean City, Md., 8 miles away.

Fenwick's Island itself is not an island but a narrow sandy peninsula 12 miles long, a part of the Coastal Barrier, joined to the mainland below Bethany Beach and extending south to Ocean City Inlet. A legend is that a man named Fenwick escaped from a pirate ship and swam to shore; later, to keep his cattle from straying, he cut a ditch across the narrow isthmus then connecting the peninsula with the mainland. This ditch, widened and deepened, is said to have become the Narrows, the waterway now crossed by a small bridge just west of the lighthouse.

At 37.2 *m.* US 113 crosses the Maryland Line, about 10*m.* north of Berlin, Md. *(see Maryland Tour 7)*. This east-west line was not first surveyed by Mason and Dixon, as is locally supposed, but by the earlier party of surveyors who started from Fenwick's Island *(see Tour 1)*.

Tour 2A

Junction with US 113—Jones Neck—Kitts Hammock; *3.2 m.* Jones Neck Rd. Roadbed paved throughout.

This short route passes through the low-lying farmland and woodland of historic Jones Neck (also called St. Jones Neck), extending eastward to Delaware Bay between St. Jones Creek and Little Creek.

JOHN DICKINSON HOUSE
Credit: Public Archives Commission

JONES NECK is one of the fertile necks along the bay shore of Kent County where large slave-worked plantations supported a rural aristocracy comparable to that which existed along the rivers and bays of the Eastern Shore of Maryland and Virginia to the west and south. While the interior of the Peninsula was still wilderness this eastern strip was settled late in the 17th century by immigrants from England and Wales, soon augmented by many from nearby Maryland. They and their descendants put the region under high cultivation. Transportation was largely by water. Sailing vessels built on the creek banks stopped at plantation landings to load grain, lumber, tobacco and other products for northern ports, and returning brought supplies and manufactured goods.

On the estates indentured white labor gave place to black slaves who tilled the fields and did the work in the "big houses." Fox hunting, duck shooting, balls, races, and picnics were the chief sports and diversions. As in Maryland, oysters, wild duck and diamondback terrapin were staples of diet rather than luxuries. (Elsewhere in Delaware were scattered plantations of economic and social eminence, but the average Delaware slaveholder owned but two or three families of Negroes and bossed them himself in the field—a hard-working man with little pretension to education or social graces.)

The spendthrift agriculture of the 18th century nearly exhausted the soil here by 1800. Better farming methods, including crop rotation and fertilization, learned about 1840, partially restored it and until after the Civil War fortunes were made in grain and peaches. Then came the peach blight down from Red Lion Hundred *(see Tour 10)* along with low prices for everything and the emigration northward of much of the cheap Negro labor. In the 1850's the railroad started the decline of the water commerce, and the shipbuilding. Tenants now occupy most of the old brick mansions of Jones Neck.

Largely influenced by Jones Neck and the bay region, Kent County was strongly pro-South at the beginning of the Civil War, and has remained steadily Democratic through several Republican State administrations. Kent still has a higher proportion of Negroes (21 percent) than either of the other counties.

The origin of the prefix *St.* to Jones Creek and Neck has long been a mystery. One of the several theories advanced in the past is that the name was imported by a Jones who accompanied William Penn to America in 1682 or followed soon afterwards.

While many by that name did come about that time, research indicates that the stream has been known as St. Jones Creek since 1671 when Robert Jones was granted land bordering it. Copies of land patents issued that year refer to *St. Jones his Creek, sd Jones his Creeke,* and *sd Jones his Line of marked Trees.* The spelling in these Duke of York patents shows many variations. "St. Jones" may have been a variation of *sd Jones* (said Jones). Or Robert Jones may have dedicated the stream to St. Jone (a Welsh way of spelling St. John), either because he came in from Maryland where a similar custom was followed by would-be lords-of-the-manor—Augustine Herman for example received a vague grant from the Calverts and called it St. Augustine Manor—or because Jones hailed from Wales where the naming of places for saints was notably common.

The population increasing in the St. Jones district, Gov. Edmund Andros in 1680 created St. Jones County out of the Whorekill and the county was known by that name until it officially became Kent upon the organization of the Province of Pennsylvania in November 1682. Toward the close of the year (Dec. 25) the name Jones for the county was abruptly abandoned when Penn directed that henceforth this upper part of the old Whorekill district should be called Kent County and the lower part Sussex. *(See LEWES.)*

At 0 *m.* the Jones Neck Rd. branches east from US 113, about 5 miles south of Dover *(see Tour 2)*.

DICKINSON MANSION (R), 0.3 *m.* was built on a 1,300-acre plantation by Samuel Dickinson who came from Talbot County, Maryland, in 1734 and became a Kent County judge. He moved to this new mansion in January 1740; here his family was reared and he was buried following his death on July 6, 1760. One of his sons born in Maryland was John Dickinson (1732–1808), "The Penman of the Revolution" whose brilliant legal mind and facile pen were prime forces in the establishment of the American nation. Named for him is Dickinson College, Carlisle, Pa., to which he left his library.

The brick mansion, with its Flemish-bond front facing south, is architecturally one of the best plantation houses of the region. Originally a two-story brick dwelling with a hip roof, a story and a half was added by 1803. In the following year a fire swept the old mansion and not much remained except the four walls. By 1806 the fire damage was corrected, including the addition of a gable roof on the mansion and a small brick kitchen wing at the west end. As Dickinson apparently intended that the mansion should be thenceforth used only by tenants, the interior woodwork was replaced in a plain substantial manner, omitting the former embellishments.

From the mansion a long lane went down to a landing on Jones Creek. The extensive slave quarters are gone; a slave burying-ground, a half-mile to the southeast, is said to contain the unmarked graves of 400 plantation Negroes. Through long years of tenant occupation the garden disappeared, except for a few old trees, and the mansion deteriorated to the point where a few more years would have witnessed its destruction. The Historic Activities Committee of the National Society of Colonial Dames of America in the State of Delaware, under chairmanship of Mrs. Charles Lee Reese, Jr., recognizing that the historic house would soon be lost to posterity raised $25,000 for its purchase and for partial repairs. On Constitution Day, September 17, 1952, the deed to the mansion was accepted by the State and the property turned over to the Public Archives Commission for restoration and administration as an historic site. A supplemental appropriation of $25,000 by the 1953 Legislature made complete restoration possible.

Here young Dickinson grew up as a rich planter's son enjoying the life of a country aristocrat; here he was taught by a private tutor who lived with the family, a young Irishman named William Killen, later first Chancellor of Delaware, 1792–1801. Dickinson studied law at the Middle Temple in London and was a successful lawyer in Philadelphia before he began devoting his brilliant conservative statesmanship to the cause of the rebellious Colonies.

When trouble with England was made acute by the Townshend Acts of 1767, he wrote, supposedly in this house, his *Letters from a Farmer in Pennsylvania* (Delaware then being the Three Lower Counties), which brought him fame in America and abroad. These pamphlets as well as his subsequent *Letters to the King* were an appeal-to-reason to avert or postpone a break with England. Unlike Patrick Henry's incendiary speeches, Dickinson's patriotism took the form of a calm analysis of the problem from the legal and economic standpoint. His thesis was that England would enjoy a more profitable trade with the Colonies if she did not belabor them with taxes.

This unfulfilled hope for conciliation cost him popularity when in July 1776 as a delegate from Pennsylvania he absented himself from the vote on Richard Henry Lee's resolution for independence, voted against the Declaration of Independence, and then declined to sign that document. Previously he had suggested separation if the American grievances

KENT COUNTY'S FIRST COURTHOUSE, TOWN POINT

were not redressed, but he wished to make a last peaceful gesture.

Once the decision was made, however, Colonel Dickinson and Colonel Thomas McKean, also of Delaware, were among the few members of the Continental Congress to take up arms in the field. In 1781–82 Dickinson's prestige was sufficiently restored for him to serve as President of Delaware, after which he resigned to become President of Pennsylvania—such a thing being possible then.

Dickinson's passion for justice and order in government reached its flower in the Constitutional Congress of 1787 where his counsel halted fruitless bickering and clarified many problems. After the Constitution was finally drawn up he campaigned with pamphlets signed "Fabius" for its adoption by the States, and had the satisfaction of seeing Delaware ratify it first of all.

His last years were spent in Wilmington, where he joined the Friends' Meeting; he and his rich Quaker wife, the former Mary Norris of Philadelphia, had been married by a magistrate, but became benefactors of many Quaker institutions. His grave is in the yard of the Friends' Meeting House at 4th and West Streets, where his gravestone is the usual Quaker marker not a foot high. A portrait of him hangs in the State House in Dover.

A younger brother, Philemon Dickinson (1739–1809), also spent his youth at Kingston-Upon-Hull, living the same life, taught by the same tutor. After being graduated in 1759 from the College of Philadelphia (now the University of Pennsylvania) he managed for a while his family's enormous plantations in Delaware and in two counties of the Eastern Shore of Maryland. Later he returned to Philadelphia to read law in John's office. A resident of New Jersey at the time of the Revolution, he rose to be a major general and commander-in-chief of the New Jersey militia, and in 1777 his command drove the British forces from Staten Island. In 1782 he was elected to Congress from Delaware, where he owned land, and from 1790 to 1793 he filled the unexpired term of a Senator from New Jersey.

At 0.9 *m.* on the Kitts Hammock Rd. is the junction with a side road.

Left on this road to BYFIELD, **0.8** *m.* (L), believed to be the birthplace of Caesar Rodney (1728–84) whose 80-mile horseback ride from here to Philadelphia, July 1-2, 1776 to cast his vote for Richard Henry Lee's resolution for independence has become the most noted episode of Delaware history. His vote and Thomas McKean's overrode the negative vote of George Read, a conservative like Dickinson *(see above),* and enabled Delaware on July 2 to be one of the 12 Colonies whose delegates voted for the Declaration of Independence. This document was signed by Rodney, McKean, and later on by Read along with delegates from the other Colonies, including those from New York, which as a Colony did not vote for it originally.

In 1923 an equestrian statue of Rodney on his famous ride was erected in Rodney Square, Wilmington *(see WILMINGTON).* In 1934 a statue of him and one of John M. Clayton *(see BUENA VISTA, Tour 1)* were placed in Statuary Hall in the Capitol at Washington, D. C., as Delaware's two most important native sons.

The rutted lane, hubdeep in winter, leads to a slight elevation on which stands the sagging ruin of a frame house that replaced the original house of Byfield. The 800-acre plantation belonged originally to the Jones family *(see above),* later becoming the property of William Rodeney (1652–1708) who came to America about 1681 and was six times a member of the Delaware Assembly under Penn. His son Daniel sold it to a brother, Caesar Rodney, the Signer's father, in 1731, some 3 years after Caesar, Jr.'s birth. It is not definitely known that the parents were living at Byfield before buying it, hence the doubt as to its being the birthplace of the noted patriot. However, Caesar Rodney grew up here, inherited the farm, and was buried here. In 1887 what were thought to be his bones were dug up and reinterred in Christ churchyard, Dover. The family graveyard at Byfield was almost effaced by years of neglect and some doubt was expressed at the time that the bones removed were the right ones.

At 1.9 *m.* on the main road is the junction with an avenue of maples.

Right on this private dirt lane, often impassable, to TOWN POINT, **1.5** *m.,* on Jones Creek, an ancient, small, plain house in lonely crumbling decay, the first story brick, the second story frame. It is probably the "Towne Point" mentioned in an early deed as "the first seat on said creek," standing in 1680 as the house of Edward Pack, an early magistrate, who held here the first courts of St. Jones County.

A few years later Pack sold for 1,200 pounds of tobacco "all the land, dwelling-house and tobacco-house" to William Darvall, also a magistrate or justice, under Penn. Darvall was granted a salary of "40 pounds in current money" to run a ferry here—on condition that he employ a man to keep a tavern, sell "all liquors at retail," and "dispose of all manner of trade whatsoever." In this way the authorities sought to establish the nucleus of a town—hence the name "Towne Point"—

in this wilderness region which was lagging far behind the sections around New Castle to the north and Lewes to the south. The courts of St. Jones County (later Kent) met here only until 1690, however, when they were transferred to the tavern of William Maxwell. Not far from the latter a courthouse was erected about 1697 where the present courthouse stands in Dover *(see DOVER)*.

At 3.2 *m.* on the main road is KITTS HAMMOCK on Delaware Bay where it is widest—nearly 30 miles broad. For years simply a small grove of trees on the shore, this ancient fishing and "pleasuring" ground now consists of a string of small cottages and boarding houses. In recent years hook-and-line fishing in the bay has been popular here. Bathing is possible only at high stages of the tide when the mud flats are covered to a shallow depth. This was one of the worst mosquito-ridden spots in Delaware before the advent of mosquito control; even "smothers" of damp seaweed could not make enough acrid smoke to protect picnickers.

For 250 years the shallow bay flats here have been noted fishing and oyster grounds. Colonial planters detailed the best fishermen among their Negroes to go to the beach with seines and tongs to catch the quantities of fish and oysters that were a regular diet for all slaves as well as their masters. Oxcart loads of bay trout and bluefish went back home to be barreled in brine for winter use.

Nowadays, though city anglers may blister in the sun, farmers of the region still find sport in hauling seines at night when the fish run best and cannot see the nets. Whiskey helps to counteract mosquito bites, and whether or not many fish are caught everyone has a good time. (Other favorite nocturnal sports of Kent Countians are 'coon hunting and fox hunting.)

It is said that Kitts Hammock was originally "Kidd's Hammock" for Capt. William Kidd, the 17th century pirate *(see LEWES, also Tour 12)*. A hammock (variant, hummock), a wooded knoll or high fast land in a marsh or near a beach is spelled *hammock* in all Delaware original deeds for such tracts.

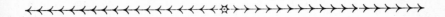

Tour 2B

Junction with US 113—Murderkill Neck—Bowers Beach; 3 *m.*

Main road paved throughout.

This short route traverses Murderkill Neck, which extends between St. Jones Creek and the Murderkill to Delaware Bay.

At 0 *m.* the Bowers Beach Rd. branches east from US 113, about 11 miles south of Dover *(see Tour 2)*.

At 0.4 *m.* is the junction with a side road.

Right on this road to a fork and a private lane, 1.1 *m.;* straight ahead on the
lane to a farmhouse, 2 *m.,* owned by S. Warren Hall, where permission should
be asked to visit the LARGEST TREE IN DELAWARE, one-half mile south, a white
oak that measures 22 feet, 5 inches in girth at a point 5 feet above the ground. It
has been damaged by storms, but steps are being taken for its preservation as one
of the greatest trees in the United States, and a public road to it is planned by the
State.

At 2 *m.* on the main road is the junction with a side road.

Left on this road to the KING CRAB PLANT, 1.5 *m. (open by permission),* at
Warren's Landing on St. Jones Creek, where king (horseshoe) crabs are dried and
ground up for fertilizer or livestock feed. The industry was first undertaken here
by Jehu Reed *(see Tour 2)* who enriched poor land with crab fertilizer till it produced huge crops of peaches.
In the late spring hundreds of thousands of these grotesque creatures with heavy
shells and spiny tails, survivors of a prehistoric era of marine life, come from the
ocean to the Delaware Bay shallows to mate and lay eggs. At night they come
swarming in to Bowers Beach. Barefoot men and boys walk through the water
towing boats or small scows behind them like aquatic express-wagons. Seeing a
crab or feeling a hard shell underfoot, the crabber picks it up and tosses it into his
boat, watching out for its lashing tail (king crabs have no biting claws). The
night's catch is put into wire-netting pens in the water where the crabs are kept
until taken by scows up the creek to the plant. Here on a long wharf made of cedar
poles the crabs are stacked by the tens of thousands to dry in the sun until October.
Then they are pulverized or broken in small pieces in crushers. Sometimes they are
merely smashed alive and thrown to hogs or chickens which soon strip the shells
bare of flesh. In summer the odor from the crab plant is powerful. It takes about
1,500 king crabs to make a ton of fertilizer. The price paid for the crabs varies
from $1 to $3 a hundred. Females make richer fertilizer and bring the higher price.

At 3 *m.* on the main road is a typical example of MOSQUITO CONTROL
DITCHING (R) on a salt marsh of Murderkill Creek.
BOWERS BEACH, 3 *m.* (284 pop.), on Delaware Bay, in winter is
an oyster village and in summer a noted salt-water anglers' resort. It is
always a place of piquant activity, color, and smell. *(May–Oct., boats and
tackle for hire; hotel accommodations and cottages for rent.)*
Bowers Beach was named for the family who owned the site from 1734
to 1847. Its main thoroughfare is the mouth of Murderkill Creek which
here meets the bay one-half mile below the mouth of Jones Creek; the
Murderkill is usually full of power boats and oyster schooners, either
under way about their business or made fast to the long wharves. Besides
oystering, a winter activity of the permanent residents is muskrat trapping on the marshes of both streams. In summer the population doubles
or trebles, and on a busy Sunday as many as a thousand anglers may go
out to the bay on fishing boats. This fleet comprises about 200 power
craft, 25-65 feet long, mostly with cabins or awnings covering part of
the decks. Many of them were built on local ways by local boatbuilders.
There are also commercial fishing boats whose crews use nets. Auction
sales of fish take place on the wharves before dawn at irregular intervals,
when commission merchants load trucks for northern markets.
Fishing parties usually put out to the bay about 5, cruise for fishing
during the morning, and return to the wharves by 1 or 2. (Anglers who

KING CRABS, WARREN'S LANDING, NEAR BOWERS BEACH

insist on staying out longer are disliked as "stickers.") Fish caught are mostly croaker (hardhead) and sea trout, though a day's catch is likely to include flounder, drum (channel bass), bluefish, shark and other species. An average day's catch under favorable conditions for an 8-man party is 400 fish.

Many fishermen from distant points carry their catch home in specially built ice chests on their cars. In the absence of a legal limit on the daily catch—now being urged by conservationists—a pair of anglers often go home with a washtub full of fish. Most of the anglers are Pennsylvanians who arrive before light, go fishing, and leave in the afternoon. One of the most businesslike groups is the contingent of Pennsylvania coal miners who come by motor truck straight from the mines in their blackened working clothes; on the fishing grounds they attend strictly to work and catch as many fish as possible. Back at the wharf they load the fish on their trucks, ice them down, and hurry north 150 miles to sell their catch in regions where fresh seafood is a rare delicacy. The revenue to boat owners from fishing parties on the Delaware side of the bay is a good return on an estimated $1.5 million invested in wharfage, power boats, and equipment. They say: "Come empty-handed! Head home with a great catch."

Bowers Beach is one of the Delaware Bay villages recently discovered by artists, who come to paint the scene along the Murderkill wharves: the packed masses of craft ranging from shiny new power boats to old oyster schooners tied up at shucking houses; the piles of oyster shells and the nets hung up to dry; and the tall quiet-spoken boat captains in white caps and faded blue shirts, with fine sun-wrinkles at their eyes from the glare on the water. There are also the flaming red faces of city fishermen who have sat too long on the afterdeck out on the smooth, blue bay.

"Big Thursday" *(2nd in Aug.)* at Bowers Beach has been a Delaware institution since the memorable day in 1852 when the new oyster ban was lifted. A law had been put into effect that year to prohibit the taking of oysters between May 1 and August 10. The people of the county, accustomed to eating their oysters throughout the year, winter and summer alike, impatiently waited until the opening day arrived. Falling that year on Thursday the day was a gala festival of tonging oysters and eating them raw or roasted, of fiddling and dancing, of talking and drinking and sleeping. When at last the covered wagons or hayracks departed they were loaded not only with oyster-stuffed men, women, and children but also with baskets of oysters in the shell carefully packed in wet marsh grass for storage in cool cellars for future use.

Even since then Big Thursday has continued to be a celebration for the rural population of Kent County. Even the subsequent postponing of the oyster season until September 1 made little difference in the size of the crowds that enjoyed their day in August year after year. Then, instead of wagons, automobiles and trucks bring farm families from nearby necks along the bay or from piney-woods regions near the Maryland Line. Farm work is slack: corn is too big for cultivating, and tomatoes and other crops have not reached their peak. It is a good time to take a breathing spell from hot fields and hotter kitchens.

In election years Big Thursday crowds made an irresistible appeal to candidates for office. In a state where a farmer in overalls naturally addresses a United States Senator by his nickname, and the Senator just as naturally calls the farmer by his, gatherings like this are not to be neglected. The Delaware farmer feels that he should get some oratory, at least, in exchange for his vote, and he enjoys good old-fashioned campaign speeches. His stomach is full, his shoes are loosened or off, and he settles back comfortably to listen. Since World War II the fête is declining.

"Black Saturday" *(next after Big Thursday)* at Bowers Beach is the Negro equivalent of Big Thursday. It was set aside by the landowners in 1852 or soon afterwards as a holiday for slaves and free Negroes who also wanted to celebrate the opening of the oyster season.

Like Big Thursday, Black Saturday survived as a day of rest and amusement, with much eating, sleeping, and promenading in fine clothes. Men wore the latest Harlem styles or sweat-stained overalls. Women displayed long evening gowns all day long. Courting was usually in evidence, as at the white affair, but on Black Saturday, sometimes resulted in fighting. On both Thursday and Saturday State troopers helped with routing and parking vehicles and dealt with offenders against order. Big Thursday and Black Saturday will soon be known only in the history of Delaware folkways, because of a more active civic life and newer recreations.

Tour 2C

Milford—Rehoboth—Maryland Line; State 14. Rehoboth bypass, 14A.
Junction with US 113—Bethany Beach, 38.8 *m.*
Road paved throughout.

Accommodations in towns and in resorts during the season.

This section of State 14 parallels lower Delaware Bay and the Atlantic Ocean. Between Milford and Rehoboth, through level farmland with pine and oak woods, the route runs several miles inland to skirt the broad salt marshes of the bay. South of Rehoboth the highway follows the sand dunes and marsh of the Coastal Barrier that separates the lagoons of Rehoboth Bay and Indian River Bay from the ocean. Salt-water towns and resorts are on or are reached from this route.

At 0 *m.* State 14 branches southeast from US 113, just north of Milford *(see MILFORD).*

For 20 miles the highway follows generally the route of the Colonial traces and wagon roads that became the King's Highway between New Castle and Lewes, for a century the two most important places in Delaware. The road was crooked, however, and very sandy, and even after the railroad finally reached Lewes in 1869, the maritime southeastern part of Delaware remained isolated and provincial; of those who traveled, many never stopped at Wilmington in their lives—going always by ship or train to Philadelphia when obliged to visit "the city." The first real intimacy between this region and the rest of the State dates from the building of this concrete highway. Philadelphia is still the metropolis, but Wilmington is now only two hours away.

SUNNYBRAE (L), 0.4 *m. (private),* is a large brick Georgian-style house built in 1934, an example of a new trend on the lower Peninsula: the building of country residences by non-farmers.

At 1.2 *m.* is the junction with State 14 West.

Right on this road, N. Front St. extended, is MILFORD, **0.5** *m.* (20 alt., 5,200 pop.) *(see MILFORD).*
Points of Interest. Parson Thorne House, Causey House, a noted dental laboratory, a wood-veneer plant, boatyards, and others.

At 1.4 *m.* State 14 crosses the MISPILLION RIVER on a drawbridge. The stream is the boundary between Kent and Sussex Counties.

At 1.9 *m.* is the junction with State 36.

Left on this road to site of former FORT SAULSBURY (R), **5.4** *m.,* a United States Coast Artillery defense unit established during World War I and named in honor of U. S. Senator Willard Saulsbury (1820–92), whose son, another U. S. Senator Willard Saulsbury, proposed the measure which resulted in the fort. The fort was garrisoned by a detachment from Fort Du Pont under a non-commissioned officer. Two batteries hidden within grassy emplacements were named in honor of Col. David Hall and Col. John Haslet of the Delaware Revolutionary forces.

At **5.8** *m.* on the side road is a drawbridge over CEDAR CREEK CANAL *(power boats available for fishing in Delaware Bay)*. Nearby is CEDAR BEACH, a small summer settlement.

The DIAMOND STATE NURSERY (R), 2.9 *m. (open by permission)*, borders State 14 for two miles. In spring and summer the abundance of flowers makes this a colorful spot, especially early in May when many acres of azaleas are in bloom. Precise rows of evergreens and shrubbery stretch into the distance. This 1,200-acre nursery, supplying mail order firms and department stores, is one of several on the Peninsula, where the light and sandy soil responds quickly to fertilizers and produces plants far ahead of those set out in the North.

At 5.6 *m.* is the junction with a side road.

Right on this road to the ruins of the old BRICK GRANARY, 0.4 *m.* (L), on Cedar Creek, from which grain was shipped before Milford was laid out. Cedar Creek Village, now vanished, was once a thriving center of farming, shipping, and milling. Several millponds west of here on the creek and its branches still furnish power for gristmills. The first building of St. Matthew's Church, a mission of the Church of England, was built nearby in 1707, the first of the sect in Sussex County. A second building was erected in 1770, and services were continued until 1854; later this building was moved to Milford and used as a sawmill. The congregation had lasted a century and a half before dying out or moving away.

At 5.8 *m.* the highway crosses CEDAR CREEK, so named because of the great numbers of southern white cedars (locally termed "soft cedar" or "cedar-cypress") growing along its swampy banks. The tall, straight, smooth trunks of the white cedar make good masts and the finest kind of hull planking. The seasoned wood is light but tough.

At 6.6 *m.* is the junction with a paved road.

Left on this road is SLAUGHTER BEACH, 3.7 *m.*, on Delaware Bay, a summer community of about 75 small cottages and a hotel, deserted in winter. A few party-boats from their moorings in Slaughter Creek, behind the resort, put out to the bay through Cedar Creek Canal. Big Thursday *(2d in Aug.)* is an annual celebration here as at Bowers Beach and Oak Orchard, when the country people for miles around spend a day at the shore during a lull in the summer's farm activity. The original excuse for Big Thursday was the opening of the oyster season, but that has been nearly forgotten and the day now bears no relation to oysters *(see BOWERS BEACH: Tour 2B)*.

The origin of the name of the creek and beach is not certainly known. Settlers may have brought it from Gloucestershire, England, where it is an ancient place name and family name. Slaughter is still a fairly common name in Delaware. A local tradition gives, however, a bloody explanation: In early Colonial days the Indians had become so hostile toward the whites that a massacre seemed likely to overtake all but one man whom the savages respected for some reason. This man, named Brabant, borrowed a cannon from a vessel that was stranded on the beach. A call was sounded for a general meeting. To the Indians Brabant explained that the voice of the Great Spirit was about to speak with a loud noise, and any "bad" chiefs might be punished. He then had all the conspirators line up in front of the cannon, which duly spoke, killing or maiming all the troublemakers and preserving peace in Slaughter Neck for some time afterwards.

John Lofland, the Milford Bard *(see MILFORD)* said of this story: "It is part of the unwritten history of Delaware which has been handed down by tradition, as Strabo informs us the history of Creation was by a Chaldean shepherd."

In recent years several Indian burial pits and camp sites have been excavated along Slaughter Creek by archaeologists who have found here the bones of bear, deer, turkeys, geese, and other wild game, besides tons of oyster shells and bits of pottery and other artifacts.

WAPLES POND, 10.6 *m.*, placidly laps both sides of the causeway embankment. Black snags still poking above the water are the remains of the forest that was drowned to make the pond at the head of Primehook Neck. The old frame building (L) across the pond is the last WAPLES'S MILL, long since abandoned. Another old building in decay was the Waples-owned STORE of political note in Broadkill Hundred. Not far downstream are the ruins of an ancient brick gristmill. Not a few Delaware towns have developed at sites no more favorable at the start than this spot.

At 13.1 *m.* is the junction (R) with State 16 *(see Tour 3)*, and (L) with the Broadkill Beach Rd.

Left on the Broadkill Beach Rd. to the junction with a side road, **1.2** *m.;* L. on the side road to the HENLOPEN GAME FARM, **2.9** *m. (open to visitors),* where large numbers of bobwhite partridges (quail) and English ringneck pheasants are raised annually. Gas-fired brooders warm hundreds of baby bobwhites until they are old enough to live outdoors. The usual custom is to have bantam hens hatch and hover bobwhites.

At **2.8** *m.* on the Broadkill Beach Road is the PETERFIELD DRAIN DITCH, in which was a large tide gate (L), one of several gates that regulate water-levels on 5,000 acres of the PRIMEHOOK MARSH. In fall, winter, and spring these gates maintain water for ducks and muskrats; in summer they are partly or entirely opened to drain away stagnant water and to allow tides to pass in and out and flush the network of ditches. This gate was torn out by a "sorehead" in 1939.

At **3.9** *m.* is the site of the former SOD MONUMENT (R) memorializing the work of the CCC in ditching marshes under the Delaware Mosquito Control Commission. The monument was begun on Dec. 5, 1935, the second anniversary of the commencement, near this spot, of the work which has largely abated the plague of salt-marsh mosquitoes in the State. In January 1938 more than 2,000 miles of ditches had been dug on about one-half of the tidal marsh area. Farm families no longer huddle around "smothers" of smoldering green leaves, and farm animals are no longer driven to bellowing madness by swarms of stinging insects.

In a ceremony that December day in 1935 each CCC worker in turn placed on the rising conical mound a thick sod he had dug on a marsh somewhere in line of work. On each subsequent anniversary the ceremony was then repeated on this bleak and isolated moor in the presence of the working personnel, the Army officers of the camps, Mosquito Control Commissioners, and guests. Annually there was placed within the mound a sealed copper box containing a copy of the annual work report. (The monument has been removed.)

The first serious mosquito-control work in Delaware was undertaken previously by private citizens at Rehoboth, notably Mrs. Henry B. Thompson and members of a women's club. Later the town took over the work, which set a precedent to be followed by the state-wide use of the CCC under the direction of W. S. Corkran as executive officer and engineer. The marsh methods developed by the Delaware authorities have been studied and applied by agencies in other parts of the country. The work in Delaware, as elsewhere, has been closely watched by muskrat trappers, duck hunters, naturalists, and organizations devoted to the conservation of wildlife resources. Whatever the ultimate effect on wildlife may be, mosquito-breeding has been nearly eliminated on tidal marshes. No oils or poison sprays have been used where ditching provides a tidal ebb and flow to flush out the larvae. Studies of wildlife habitat have paralleled the operations on the marshes, especially where conditions have been changed.

BROADKILL BEACH, 4.1 *m.,* is a summer bathing-and-fishing resort of small frame cottages strung along the treeless dunes bordering Delaware Bay. The one street, running behind the row of houses, has a row of small garages on the east side and the flat salt marsh on the west. Even the store is closed in winter. The beach itself has long been a favorite spot for farmers who come here at night with seines to fish until dawn. Cheered by occasional nips at a bottle and their own singing, they prefer their form of sport to the city-fisherman's use of a rod aboard a boat in the hot sun.

The weatherbeaten old CONWELL HOUSE (R), 14.1 *m. (private),* is typical of the old houses of eastern Sussex County. The simple rectangular two-and-one-half story house, with large chimneys, has a story-and-a-half wing with the same front line. The whole house is sheathed in the long bald-cypress shingles characteristic of the oldest buildings of the regions near the Great Pocomoke Swamp *(see Tour 15).* The deep and lustrous gray of the shingles, now unfortunately covered with asbestos ones, was part of the air of melancholy worn by this survivor of the 18th century.

At this house lived Aletta Clowes Clarke (1767–1832), wife of Miers Clarke, both members of old Broadkill Hundred families. Below are excerpts from a diary she kept from 1789 to 1793:

1789

Oct. 31. I went to see my sister. She told me of two dreams she had dreamed. In one she was dressed in white, and her company told her she did not look as if she belonged in this world. In the other her child was born, and she was to die three days afterward.

Dec. 1. I went to my sister's to get help about sizeing up a web.

Dec. 2. I got the piece out that I had in the loom, and got it to work.

Dec. 4. I wove on it all day. Just at night Mrs. Russel sent for me. About 10 o'clock at night she was delivered of a daughter. About 12 I got home.

Dec. 5. In the morning my Brother came over and said that Sister Sally was taken with an ague, and was very sick. I went right away to see her, and found her sickness most violent. Her violent sickness brought on her labour. On Sunday the 6th at sunrise she was delivered of a son. Not being well I went home.

Dec. 7. This morning . . . it pleased God to take her into His safe keeping. She was 20 years and 6 months old this day lacking 3 days.

Dec. 31. Negroes a Christmasing.

1790

Feb. 28. Mary Lewis died. Her husband died nine days before. They lived about 1 mile from me. The sickliest time that I ever knew, there is hardly an individual without complaint.

March 17. I hear there are 4 more of the Chace family dead, I am told that out of 10 there are but 3 left. Lord have mercy. Thy arrows fly not at random.

May 24. A great meeting on the Beach, Cakes, Raisins, Meat, Bread, Rum, Wine, & all such things there to sell.

1791

June 13. A great day of frolic on the Beach. I hear there were a great many there and a great disturbance. Many were hurt.

June 16. King's negro dies with the smallpox.

1792

Jan. 22. Snowing all day and very cold. The snow was so deep that people could not pass the Causeway. There were three lodged here all night.

May 8. Rainy weather. Very busy with the goslins.

May 9. My little girl Sarah was born. Grandma and Sally Draper went home.

June 24. Warm. Musquitoes very thick.

Huge letters painted on a drawbridge at 14.6 *m.* spell BROADKILL RIVER. Many Delawareans do not accept the term "river," saying the stream has always been called Broadkill Creek. Actually the use of any word after "Broadkill" is redundant, since the Dutch word *kil* meant creek or small river. Thousands of dollars' worth of muskrats are caught each winter on the Broadkill marshes.

While a store was kept here by Samuel Paynter (Governor of Delaware 1824–7) and by his descendants and successors, the Drawbridge was a shipping community of some importance. Vessels whose home port was here or at Milton, several crooked miles upstream, ran regularly to Philadelphia with grain, timber, and other products until the early 1900's. Some pine mine-props and other rough timber are still occasionally swung aboard small vessels here by crude derricks.

At 15.3 *m.,* on the northeast corner of the junction with a side road, is an OAK STUMP (L), the site of an accident in 1897 that is still remembered by older residents. In the summer of that year a Negro named Jim Coursey, aloft in the tree, sawed off the limb he was sitting on. Though his employer ruined a fine young stallion racing for the doctor, the Negro died of a broken neck.

OVERBROOK, 17.1 *m.,* is not even a hamlet, but the center of a farming community bearing the name, and a former station on the defunct Queen Anne's R.R. This line between Chesapeake Bay and Delaware Bay was famous in the late 1890's for its excursions to Lewes, where passengers boarded a steamer for Cape May; it was abandoned in 1924.

This neighborhood is the home of some of Sussex County's most ardent fox hunters, who follow by day or night their packs of dogs across country, through pine woods and gum thickets. The hunters go on foot or in automobiles, seldom on horseback; many say they are just as satisfied to hear the hounds giving tongue as to see the chase itself. The average pack is five or six hounds and there is considerable rivalry among the owners. On crisp moonlights nights in the fall the baying of hounds may be heard the length and breadth of Delaware, but in this region it is particularly loud and long.

The RED MILL POND (R), 17.9 *m.,* once known as Coolspring Pond, has been known by its present name for several generations. *(Boats are available in season for bass and pike fishing).* Clear of stumps and snags, and rimmed by pine woods, this is one of the loveliest lakes in Delaware. A red-painted gristmill (L), was rebuilt on the site of one burned in 1927.

NASSAU, 19.1 *m.* (75 pop.), on the Lewes and Rehoboth Branch of the Pennsylvania R.R., is a shipping point for milk, fruit, and produce.

FARM HOMESTEAD, SUSSEX COUNTY
Credit: Waller Studio, Laurel

Large apple orchards bordering the road are known locally as "tree farms." Shortly after the Civil War Nassau was booming, but the railway pushed on to Lewes and the place settled into its present sleepy state.

At 19.9 *m.* is the junction (R) with State 18 *(see Tour 14)*, which is united with State 14 between this point and WESCOAT'S CORNER, 20.5 *m.*, where State 18 branches L.

As early as 1725 a public house on the King's Highway was kept at this corner. Local militia trained here, and it is said that an early county pillory and whipping post were at the roadside here before being removed to nearby Lewes. For years the place was called Quakertown, then Prettymanville for the family by that name. The Wescoats had operated a wagon-building shop here, and after the Prettyman store was abandoned, the point became Wescoat's Corner. The RHODES SHANKLAND HOUSE *(private)*, a small shingled dwelling (L), is believed to have been built about 1767. Shankland was a sheriff of the county and member of a Quaker family prominent in the region before 1700.

At 21.9 *m.* is the junction with a side road.

Right on this road to the junction with another road, 0.6 *m.*; R. on this road on the farm (L) of Ralph G. Rust, 1.1 *m.*, is a weathered cypress-shingled structure, 50 by 25 feet, now a barn; it was formerly St. PETER'S CHURCH in Lewes *(see*

LEWES), erected in 1808. In 1853, when the present church in Lewes was being erected, the parish gave this old building, in payment of a debt, to Harbeson Hickman, who moved it to a farm near here. During World War I a later owner refused an offer of $1,000 for the massive black walnut timbers to be made into gunstocks. In 1935 the steeple was removed and the old building brought here.

At 22.6 *m.* is the junction (R) with State 24 *(see Tour 15).*

At 23 *m.* is the junction with a side road.

Right on this road is MIDWAY, **0.3** *m.* (75 pop.), midway on the old dirt road between Lewes and Rehoboth, but bypassed by the new concrete road. In the old days of crooked sandy roads and coughing Maxwells and Model T's, Midway was a welcome sight to weary tourists bound for the seashore after six or eight hours on the road from Wilmington.

At 24.3 *m.* is the junction with a private road, surfaced soil (may be poor driving in wet weather).

Right on this lane to the MARSH FAMILY CEMETERY, 1 *m.,* a well-kept, ironfenced plot in a grove of stately pines and oaks, one of the two largest private burying-grounds in the State. (The other is the Du Pont Family Cemetery on the bank of the Brandywine: *see Tour 6B.)* Here are the graves of more than 125 members of the Marsh family; the earliest headstone, that of Peter Marsh, records 1769 as the year of his death. The cemetery was established on part of the Young Hope patent which "Peter Marsh, yeoman" bought from "Richard Hinman, Gent." in 1730. One of the early Marsh plantation houses, perhaps the original one, now restored and enlarged, is The Homestead at Henlopen Acres *(see REHOBOTH).* Nearly every plantation of lower Delaware had a private burying-ground, but most of these plots, unlike this one, are abandoned jungles of briars and toppled gravestones. Each spring the ploughs go closer until finally, in some cases, fences and jungles and tombstones disappear and growing corn brings oblivion.

At 24.5 *m.* State 14A (R), bypasses Rehoboth Beach, to Dewey Beach.

At 25.4 *m.* the road crosses the LEWES AND REHOBOTH CANAL, about 9 miles long, opened in 1913 to connect Delaware Bay and Rehoboth Bay as part of an inland waterway to Chincoteague Bay, Md.-Va., a total distance of about 40 miles. The great expectations of water traffic never materialized, though for a decade the canal was used by motorboats towing barges of tomatoes from landings on Rehoboth Bay and Indian River to a cannery at Rehoboth. Paved roads put an end to this, and the landings are rotting away. Since the depth of Rehoboth Bay averages even less than the canal's controlling depth of about 6 feet, the waterway is little used except by small yachts coming to Rehoboth. The northern terminus is at Lewes (Roosevelt Inlet).

REHOBOTH, 26 *m.* (10 alt., 2,500 winter pop.) *(see REHOBOTH).*

Points of Interest. The Beach, the Boardwalk, the Pines; usual seashore amusement places; sports including bathing, fishing, sailing, golf, tennis, riding.

At 26 *m.* on Rehoboth Ave. is the junction with Bayard Ave.; right on this dual street is the continuation of State 14.

At 26.5 *m.* at the southern town limits of Rehoboth, the highway crosses SILVER LAKE ("Newbold's Freshwater Lake" on early maps), draining into the **ATLANTIC OCEAN** (L) through bordering sand dunes. This is a State wildlife refuge, where in fall, winter, and spring wild ducks and geese feed on the heavy growth of widgeon grass.

REHOBOTH-BY-THE-SEA, 27 *m.*, a development of the local land boom of 1925–29, was arrested by the depression when only a few houses had been built along the several miles of streets laid out by the promoters. Building has since been resumed to some extent. The large and expensive Craft House *(private)* built about 1940 of hand-split cypress shingles has a really fine view of the surf; it is the most imposing structure in this section if not in the entire Rehoboth area *(see REHOBOTH)*.

DEWEY BEACH, 27.6 *m.*, a straggling group of small summer cottages on the sand dunes facing the ocean, is one of the oldest resort settlements on the Delaware Coast. It developed around the REHOBOTH LIFE-SAVING (now COAST GUARD) STATION established here in 1879, and in 1898 became one of the numerous namesakes of Admiral George Dewey, hero of the Battle of Manila Bay.

At several wharves (R) on Rehoboth Bay, many small pleasure boats are moored in summer. The sailboats for hire are mostly locally-built of a design native to the waters of the eastern Peninsula—the "Chincoteague deadrise sailing bateau," a name that someone has suggested should be set to music. Their hulls and rigs appear somewhat primitive at first sight but these shoal-water craft are seldom bested in races with the most expensive and carefully-rigged boats of similar size. The "Chincoteaguers" are of two styles: "one-stickers" with a single mast and sail, and "two-stickers" with a tall mast forward and a short one aft. The native white cedar masts are stepped at raking angles without any stays at all, depending on sheer thickness and toughness against breaking. Mainsails and spankers are rigged with sprits; the jib-head peak is raised several feet higher than the masthead by means of a gaff hauled up alongside the mainmast. The speed of these craft is further due to the rakish hull design, developed by generations of oyster-tongers—a V-bottom with a sharp bow and graceful curves toward the stern. Gunwales are low, as they were when the tongers stood in the boat and worked over the side.

REHOBOTH INDIAN BEACH, 28.5 *m.* (L), a group of neat cottages of trim design, was established in 1936 by residents of Washington, D.C. A white picket fence surrounds this development.

For the 12 miles between Rehoboth and Bethany Beach this Ocean Highway section of State 14 takes a north and south course behind the curving dunes of the ocean beach; south of Dewey Beach the road follows the narrow strip of the Coastal Barrier separating the ocean from the brackish lagoons on the west. The breakers (L) are only occasionally visible. (Army anti-aircraft firing ranges are along this road.)

Surf fishing is more and more popular along the whole ocean side. At night, beach parties, picnics, clam bakes, and hot-dog roasts are indicated by driftwood fires lighting up circles of faces and reclining blanketed figures, while the hollows among the dunes are sought by scores of romantic couples.

Most of this Coastal Barrier strip is State-owned land, and though it is the only remaining primitive wilderness in Delaware suitable for general recreation, it has become dotted with squatters' habitations of all sorts, from old houseboats hauled out on the edge of the bay marshes to cottages of much greater value. The State has not yet (1938) taken steps to evict the squatters.

REHOBOTH BAY (R), beyond the marshy strip, stretches more than 4 miles along the road and about 3 miles westward to the horizon of purple-green pine woods. Averaging 4 feet deep, shallower in many places, this bay is the most northerly of similar shallow lagoons along the whole east coast of the Peninsula. Old records and maps show that it had this Biblical name late in the 17th century. With Indian River Bay *(see below)* it was noted in early Colonial times for oysters, clams, fish, and waterfowl.

Every fall this eastern side of Rehoboth Bay is lined with dozens of blinds containing duck hunters and often their Chesapeake Bay dogs or other retrievers. Marsh ducks include native and Canadian black ducks, pintail (sprig), teal, widgeon, and mallard. The flocks of diving ducks—canvasback, redhead, bluebill (blackhead), and others—have almost vanished from these waters; there has been almost no marine vegetation on the bottoms in recent years and most of the remaining diving ducks, Canada geese, and swans pass on down the coast without stopping. Previous to the Federal ban on the use of live decoys (1935), hundreds of domesticated Canada geese were tethered in front of blinds to lure the wild flocks to the guns. The usual practice was not to let the wild geese rise, but to wait until they bunched up and then shoot as many as possible on the water. Few geese have been thus killed since the disuse of live decoys.

At 31.9 *m.* is (L) the INDIAN RIVER COAST GUARD STATION *(open by permission)*, until the completion of this road in 1934 the most remote and inaccessible station on the Delaware coast. Only a vague sandy trail wound among the dunes from Rehoboth. Sailboats on Rehoboth Bay were used to make the trip to the mainland for provisions, and in recent years the beach has been navigated in automobiles with half-deflated tires.

Members of a station crew patrol the beach watching for ships or persons in need of aid. There is always a lookout standing (he is not allowed to sit) in the little tower on top of the building. Here, as at all Coast Guard stations, everything is shining, from the surfboat in the boatroom to the top of the kitchen stove; the first duty after breakfast is sweeping, dusting, scrubbing, polishing, or painting. There are regular drills with the boats, breeches-buoy, signal flags, and other equipment. Between duties the members of the crew sit around reading, talking, or playing "high-low-jack-and-the-game" (pitch) with a worn deck of cards. On cold winter days there is always a big pot of coffee on the stove for men coming in after beach patrols. At any time the order may come to rescue with boat or breeches-buoy the crew of a dismasted lumber schooner or of a coal barge whose towline has parted in a gale. A surfman or a boatswain's mate may be drowned, but that is all in the day's work.

Near the site of this station after easterly storms, for more than a century, old coins have been picked up on the wash of the beach. Most are Irish coppers of the period 1780–90. A few gold coins have also been found. Hunting for coins has become a great sport for summer vacationists, who are usually rewarded for their efforts if the storm has been severe enough to churn up the sand. It is supposed the coins came from the strong-box of a vessel wrecked off the coast—perhaps the *Faithful Steward,* filled with Irish immigrants, which foundered in 1785 while bound for Philadelphia. Another storm-sent bounty is the huge quantity of clams that the waves sometimes cast up in windrows. Usually too full of sand to be eaten, they are steamed and the juice extracted and strained. An occasional sight on the beach is a loon or a duck whose feathers are glued down with bilge oil, crawling up from the breakers to try to clean itself, but doomed to die in a few days.

BURTON'S ISLAND, 33.3 *m.* (R) is identified by its several tall wind-whipped trees and two small buildings, about a mile inside the Coastal Barrier, between Rehoboth Bay and Indian River Bay. By tradition it was joined to Long Neck, the arm of the mainland that extends out behind it, until the owner cut ditches to keep his cattle on the island. The shallow flats nearby were famous for the great numbers of soft-shell crabs found in the grass that used to grow on the bottom but has since disappeared. Scores of crabbers made a good living catching them and selling them in the Millsboro market at one cent apiece. There are still quantities of hard crabs, but the lack of vegetation causes a dearth of small marine life which supplies their food, and the crabs do not outgrow their shells fast enough to maintain a reliable supply of soft crabs for the market.

INDIAN RIVER INLET, 33.7 *m.,* the common inlet for the two bays, was first bridged in 1934, when a fixed timber bridge was built for this new highway. The Charles W. Cullen swing span drawbridge, built 1938–39, has 14 foot clearance above high water over the inlet which is 500 feet wide and 12 feet deep. The south end, destroyed by a storm, Feb. 10, 1948, was reconstructed by June 9, 1951. Here is a fishing center with about 100 party boats available. State-owned lands around the Inlet have been developed as Indian River Inlet Park for swimming, fishing and other recreation. Restaurant, picnic sites, and sanitary facilities are conveniently located.

The new Indian River Inlet is the result of years of dissatisfaction with a natural channel that not only was subject to alternate opening and closing but also had a habit of migrating back and forth along the coast under the influence of storms and tides. This capricious behavior was intensified after the digging of the Assawoman Canal about 1890, which drained bay water southward, and the digging of the Lewes and Rehoboth Canal which robbed the bays of more water that would have gone out through the inlet and helped to keep it open. A climax came in the 1920's when after a dry spell the inlet was closed entirely for several years, killing all marine vegetation, ruining the seafood industry, and backing up stagnant, mosquito-breeding water on marshes and low shores. After some individuals had tried in desperation to dynamite a channel, the State began dredging off and on for several years, but the sand kept filling in almost as fast as the dredge could dig it out. Although for decades the need of a good inlet had been felt, nothing was achieved until 1935–6 when the Mosquito Control Office at Lewes made a report estimating the value of a permanent channel to mosquito-control, the seafood industry, rod fishing, wild-life, and water transport. Under mosquito-control auspices, mass-meetings were addressed by members of Congress and by crabbers and watermen. The District U. S. Engineer was authorized to make a survey, and in 1937 approved the project. The Federal appropriation was made later that year.

For two centuries small sailing vessels traded in and out of Indian River Inlet on flood tides, bringing merchandise and fertilizer from Philadelphia and other ports, and going out with grain and forest products picked up at plantation landings. Early shipments included tobacco and flax in the early 18th century, iron castings and pig-iron from Millsboro Furnace in the first decades of the 19th century. Many of the little vessels were built at yards on Indian River. Sometimes lighters would meet deep-draft vessels outside the inlet and bring cargoes up the 15 miles of bay and river to Millsboro (see Tour 2). Before the era of railroads and paved highways, the inlet was the heart-valve of the 150 or 200 square miles of the Rehoboth Bay-Indian River region. Its permanent improvement is the most dramatic event in the history of these waters since June 20, 1814, when the British frigate Nieman anchored outside and sent several barges into the bay with about 60 men, who stole provisions along the shores and burned several vessels loaded with lumber before returning to their ship.

INDIAN RIVER BAY (R) borders the highway for about 3 miles south of the inlet. Westward it extends about 7 miles, receiving the fresh waters of Indian River and Pepper Creek as its most important tributaries. In most ways it is similar to Rehoboth Bay with which it is connected by the Ditches near Burton's Island.

The NATIONAL GUARD CAMP (R), 38.1 m. (encampment during Aug.), having a group of frame buildings on very low ground, is a summer training headquarters for National Guard units of Delaware and neighboring states. The establishment includes barracks, hangars, a flying field, and a parade ground. The Delaware Guard is an anti-aircraft unit whose practice by day and night attracts hundreds of visitors. By night the sky is cut by brilliant searchlight beams trying to pick up "enemy" airplanes towing targets for the artillery. Balloons are sent up by the dozen to be smashed by streaming red incendiary bullets from machine guns. There is an annual Governor's Day when the Governor and his staff review the troops at dress parade. The camp is always given the name of the Governor currently in office.   •

Across the road from the camp are the BETHANY BEACH COAST GUARD STATION (abandoned) and the BETHANY BEACH NAVAL RADIO STATION (no admittance). This radio station is one of three —the others are at Cape Henlopen and Cape May—that function primarily in furnishing ships their positions off the Capes and nearby coast. By tuning the antennae at each station the direction of the ship is found from the three points. The stations plot these three lines on a chart.

Where the lines cross is the ship's position, which is flashed back to her in latitude and longitude within a minute after her request. Two bearings would be technically sufficient to establish the position, but the bearing from the third station is an additional check for accuracy. Code signals from the stations and from ships come out of private radio receivers in piercing blasts that often ruin the reception of programs within a radius of many miles.

BETHANY BEACH, 38.8 m. (118 winter pop.), is a small ocean resort of well-kept, comfortable summer cottages and boarding houses, with a short boardwalk extending along the beach front. The white sand beach is gently sloping, and the surf bathing and fishing are unexcelled on the Delaware coast. Life guards are on duty during the season.

Most of the residents are quiet families who own cottages or rent them by the season. The place retains a good deal of the religious atmosphere of its beginnings at the turn of the century. By the terms of the deed for the resort, the sale of alcoholic beverages on any piece of property would forfeit the lot back to the developers. Hence no beer, wine, or liquor is sold in Bethany Beach, but drinking on private property is not restricted unless it results in disorderly conduct. There are no ferris wheels, rifle ranges, or games of chance.

In 1898 this site was picked out from others up and down the Atlantic Coast by several members of the Christian Church Disciples of Scranton, Pa., who were appointed to select a spot for the summer activities of the Christian Missionary Society of Maryland, Delaware and the District of Columbia. Later forming the Bethany Beach Improvement Co., this group agreed to purchase the land and develop it, and to provide transportation from the railroad to the isolated place, provided that the society would purchase not less than 100 lots and give "moral support." On July 12, 1901 Bethany Beach was formally opened and the Tabernacle dedicated. Transportation from the railroad at Rehoboth was provided by the little steamboat *Atlantic* across Rehoboth Bay, Indian River Bay, and up White's Creek to Ocean View, whence horse-drawn carryalls covered the last 2 miles to the beach. Later a ditch was dredged a mile long between the Assawoman Canal and the resort, so that boats could land at the spot. Both canal and ditch have since shoaled up so that only rowboats can now approach Bethany Beach this way.

The TABERNACLE, (R), on State 14, was completed late in the summer of 1901. Its octagonal form, nearly 100 feet in diameter, makes this one of the most distinctive buildings in Delaware. Here in June are held the annual meetings of the still vigorous Christian Missionary Society.

At Bethany Beach is the junction with State 26 *(see Tour 16)*.

South from Bethany Beach State 14 passes through more State lands between the ocean dunes (L) and Little Assawoman Bay (R).

At 44.6 m. is Fenwick Island Light *(see page 393)* at the Maryland Line, about 8 m. north of Ocean City, Maryland.

◄◄◄◄◄◄◄◄◄◄◄◄◄◄◄◄◄◄◄◄◄✿►►►►►►►►►►►►►►►►►►►►►

Tour 3

Junction with State 14—Milton—Greenwood—(Denton, Md.); State 16.
Junction with State 14 to the Maryland Line, 26.7 *m.*

Roadbed paved throughout.
Accommodations limited.

State 16 is an east-west highway crossing lower Delaware and following closely the abandoned route of the Queen Anne's R.R. It is the shorter
of two main routes between the Cape Henlopen region and the Matapeake-
Annapolis ferries *(see also Tour 14).* Some of the country along the way
is fertile and prosperous; other stretches of arrow-straight road pass
slowly recovering poor soil and cut-over timberland, part of which, W. of
Oakley (L) is now State-owned Owens forest tract, 170 acres.

At 0 *m.* State 16 branches west from State 14 *(see Tour 2C)* about 12
miles northwest of Rehoboth.

At 1.4 *m.* is a farmhouse (L) owned by H. Ernest Conwell *(apply here
for permission to enter the farm).*

Left on a private dirt lane to the CLOWES FAMILY CEMETERY, **0.6** *m.,* on high
ground at what was formerly Heaviloe's Landing on the Broadkill. As at other
abandoned family graveyards in Delaware, a few tombstones still stand here in a
tangle of weeds and honeysuckle. The ancient BRICK VAULT that distinguishes this
graveyard is a crumbling brick cave about 15 feet long, 8 feet wide, and 7 feet
high, with an arched roof almost entirely underground. Though the Clowes family
Bible mentions at least three bodies that were placed in it from 1769 on, the vault
is apparently empty. Why they were removed—if they were removed—is not disclosed. But there is a legend concerning this fine example of the bricklayers' art in
a region where there was little ostentation before or after death.

The tradition is that by an old English custom, the body of John Clowes (1730–
90), Justice of the Delaware Supreme Court 1781–90, could not be buried in a
grave until his debts were settled from his estate, and it was placed temporarily in
this vault built for the purpose; later, when everything was settled, his body was
buried nearby in the regular manner and marked by a tombstone still visible.

Evidence against the legend is in the family Bible, in which John Clowes himself wrote that his *father* was buried in 1769 in an "open grave" and later that year
"was Intered in a New Vault built since his death at Mr. Heavelo's Landing."
This was 21 years before the death of Justice Clowes. The Bible also states that the
Justice "objected being laid in the Vault" and "was buried at the South Corner of
the Vault." That is precisely where his tombstone still stands.

MILTON (L), 2.7 *m.* (30 alt., 1,321 pop.), only 7 miles from Delaware Bay in a direct line but many more by the convoluted Broadkill,
is one of the little old Delaware towns that prospered through shipbuilding and shipping in the 19th century. The shipyards have long ago
disappeared from the foot of Union and Federal Sts., but the town
benefits from growing industrial activity at the edges: a cannery, several

factories making cheap cotton garments, small button factories, and other more-or-less steady employers of local labor. The business section displays a rare lot of the permanent store awnings, wood or metal roofed, that used to shade the sidewalk in front of nearly every store in lower Delaware, but have disappeared from many main streets. The old part of the town contains many old cypress-shingled houses characteristic of eastern Sussex County. Some of the newest houses are on the shores of Milton Pond, which still furnishes water-power for one of the largest grist and flour mills in the county. Milton was on the now-defunct Queen Anne's R.R. (later called the Maryland & Delaware Coast Ry.), and still receives freight service from the Pennsylvania R.R. at Ellendale, 6 miles west, over the only piece of Queen Anne's trackage that has not been torn up.

In 1686 James Gray received the patent for a 1,000-acre tract on which the present town stands; later the site of South Milton belonged to the Conwell family and the site of North Milton (above the stream) to the Perry family. The little settlement growing up at the head of navigation was known as Osborne's Landing, Conwell's Landing, Upper Landing, and Head of Broadkill. In 1807 the name "Head of Broadkill" was changed by act of Legislature to Milton—after the great English poet, it is said. By 1809, besides a shipyard, there were seven granaries and four stores; tanyards were later established. Shipbuilding reached its peak between the Civil War period and 1880, during which time there were on the stocks usually three or four schooners that measured as much as 125 feet in length. The stream was so narrow that there had to be excavations made on the opposite side to receive the vessels as they were launched ("lanched") down the ways. By 1887 shipbuilding had almost ceased, but six vessels plied regularly to Philadelphia and five to New York with grain, produce, lumber, cordwood, and other products. At present the only boats calling Milton their home port are several party-boats (cabin cruisers) that take out salt-water fishing parties on the bay.

The principal street of Milton, formerly Main St., became Federal St. (south of the river) and Union St. (north of the river) during the Civil War, though many residents were sympathetic toward the South. Mill St. is known to older residents as Puddin' Hill—the name derived, it is said, from the famous puddings that Mrs. Fowler, wife of a shipbuilder, used to make on certain days. On "Puddin' Day" the husband would bring home some of his friends for supper, their mouths watering for the feast they knew would be served. Another curious name is that by which Milton Pond has long been called by some residents: Lake Fanganiszky. No one seems to know the exact origin of this Polish-sounding word.

Milton since 1934 has had an annual Old Home Week *(usually the 2d week-end in Aug.),* celebrated with a parade, baseball games, and a special church service.

CONWELL'S BOXWOOD NURSERY *(open by permission),* N. Milton, on a hot day smells like an 18th-century Peninsula garden. Besides acres of young boxwood bushes set out in rows, there have been temporarily transplanted near the office many boxwoods of great size and age, brought from old country places of Delaware, Maryland, and Virginia to be sold to new owners. The delicate "balling-up" of great quantities of earth in burlap around the roots of a tree being made ready for shipment is an engineering feat. The GOVERNOR HAZZARD HOUSE *(private)*, E. side of Union St., N. Milton a two-and-a-half story gray shingled dwelling set back among old trees, was built by John Hazzard about 1790, and was the home of his son David Hazzard (1781–1864), Governor of Delaware 1830–33. Set in the pavement at the SW. corner of Union and Broad Sts. is a MILLSTONE bearing the points of the compass, said to have been placed there by a Government surveyor about 1850. On the SITE OF MILTON ACADEMY, at the corner of Chestnut and Coulter Sts., between 1822 and 1880 almost without interruption, a private school was maintained that drew children and young ladies and gentlemen from villages and farms for miles around. The PETER PARKER HOUSE *(private)*, E. side of Chestnut St., N. Milton, is a well-preserved example of an elderly eastern Sussex house. It was built about 1835, is shingled, has dormer windows, and a wing at the rear instead of at one end. The house contains much of the original woodwork. The design of the boxwood garden has been retained, and at the rear of the house is an old shingled "meat house" with batten shutters and a mossy roof.

At 5 *m.* on State 16 large APPLE AND PEACH ORCHARDS border the road.

A 100-foot FOREST FIRE TOWER, 7.1 *m.* (L), overlooks many square miles of forest land, including the Ellendale Swamp south of the road *(see Tour 2)*.

ELLENDALE (321 pop.), a village notable for its wide streets, is still a primary lumber and timber center of Delaware, though greatly crippled industrially by the decreasing supply of marketable pine and oak trees. There is much young pine timber in the nearby swamp and elsewhere, but the practice is to cut the trees long before they reach the size of the trees that used to furnish the planks and wide boards for which the region was famous. Many of the residents raise chickens or drive truckloads of produce to northern markets.

The village was laid out in 1867 by Dr. John S. Prettyman, who sought to start a community at the railhead of a branch of the railroad which had reached this point; he named it Ellendale after Ellen, his wife. Most of the residents of Federalsburg (formerly Fleatown), one mile north, moved to the new town rising by the side of the steel rails.

The village has like other small communities of Sussex County a lively interest in current opportunities for economic and civic improvement.

At 9.9 *m.* is the junction with US 113 *(see Tour 2)*.

OAKLEY, 12.7 *m.,* is a country store (R).

At 17.4 *m.* is the SITE OF ST. JOHNSTOWN, a bustling stage-stop, the center for the first school of the region, and a trading center of some importance before the Revolution. In 1858 the railroad came down a mile to the west, and the village of Greenwood started to grow up beside the track. Just as Ellendale swallowed Fleatown *(see above)*, so Greenwood swallowed St. Johnstown. There is nothing left of it.

At 17.5 *m.* is the junction with State 36.

Right on this road to the AMISH SCHOOL (L) 1 *m.* *(private)*, where little boys wear blue overalls and the little girls wear long-sleeved high-necked dresses, long stockings, and little bonnets. They are children of farmers of German extraction who came here in this century from Pennsylvania. They are attentive to their own business, industrious, frugal, and suspicious of "worldliness," and they prefer to employ a teacher rather than allow their children to attend the public schools.

At 18 *m.* is the junction with US 13 *(see Tour 1)*.

GREENWOOD, 18.4 *m.* (746 pop.) *(see Tour 1)*.

At 23.8 *m.* is (R) TODD'S CHURCH (Methodist Episcopal), a white-painted frame structure whose Greek Revival lines and proportions make it one of the most charming rural church buildings in the State. It was erected in 1858.

At 24.6 *m.* is MARSHYHOPE CREEK, an important tributary of the Nanticoke River *(see Tour 14B)*.

HICKMAN, 26.6 *m.* (100 pop.). is a village that grew up at a station on the Queen Anne's R.R. in the 1890's, flourished for a few years, and declined with the railroad.

At 26.7 *m.* State 16 crosses the Maryland-Delaware Line, 8 miles southeast of Denton, Md.

Tour 4

(Deepwater Point, N. J.)—Hare's Corner—(Elkton, Md.); US 40.
East side of Delaware River—Maryland Line, 18.4 *m.*

Near Deepwater Point, N. J., US 40 joins the eastern approach, 0 *m.*, of the Delaware Memorial Bridge, crosses the 2-mile suspension span and continues W. through an underpass (where there is an interchange with the New Castle or River Road) to open country.

At 4.6 *m.* is a second interchange and the junction with US 13 *(see Tour 1)*. Between this junction and Hare's Corner, US 40 coincides with US 13.

*Section a. Alternate Route Delaware R. Bridge—New Castle—
Hare's Corner, 4.5 m.*

At the Interchange of US 40 with the New Castle (River) Road, 0 *m.*, follow signs to head S. on this road.

South on this road is BOOTHHURST *(private)*, 0.5 *m.* (R), in a tract of natural woodland, containing ancient white oaks. An early brick farmhouse was enlarged in 1842 in English Cottage Gothic by James Rogers, Attorney General of Delaware. Old ice house is studio of present owner, L. R. Rogers, artist.

NEW CASTLE, 2 *m.* (10 alt., 5,400 pop.) *(see NEW CASTLE, also see "New Castle on the Delaware," a book of the American Guide Series)*.

At the fork keep L. to first cross street (Chestnut) ; left on this street one block to Second St.; turn R. on 2nd St. which leads into the center of the old part of the town and dead ends at Delaware St.

Points of Interest. Old Court House, Amstel House, Immanuel Church, old Dutch House, the Read House, and other Colonial buildings.

To leave New Castle follow Delaware St. W. leading onto State 273. At 6th St. is the junction with the River-Bay Rd., L. *(see Tour 10).*
At 3.3 *m.* is the junction with State 41 *(see Tour 7).*
This route follows fairly closely old New Castle and Frenchtown R. R. on which a locomotive ran in Sept. 1832 *(see TRANSPORTATION).*

BELLANCA FIELD (L) adjoins the factory of the Bellanca Aircraft Corporation *(open by permission),* manufacturer of aircraft parts and several types of planes, and contractors to the United States and foreign governments.

NEW CASTLE COMMON, 3.4 *m.* (R) is a tract of 1,068 acres divided into farms from which the revenue, for more than two and one-half centuries, has gone to the town of New Castle.

From earliest days of settlement the Dutch and the Swedes set aside certain areas for the public to use for pasturage, for the production of public revenue and so on. When the English took over the Delaware Colony in 1664 community ownership of the tracts was confirmed. William Penn, becoming the Proprietary in 1682, reconfirmed the reservation, but there were so many complaints of abuses that in 1701 he ordered that the land "hitherto reputed and called New Castle Common" be established in one convenient tract of 1,000 acres. Still the abuses and encroachments kept on, and in 1764 a charter was secured from Thomas and Richard Penn, sons of William, setting up a board of trustees with power to protect the property.

But because this charter did not empower the trustees to lease the land to farmers who would till it on shares, in 1791 two Penns, both named John, heirs of the Proprietary, signed away all claim to the land to permit the incorporation of the Trustees of the Common under the laws of the State of Delaware; in the deed they provided against the selling of the land or the diversion of any of its income. The next year (1792) the charter from the State established the system under which the Common farms have since been leased. Gross income varies; was $57,000 in 1953. After deducting the cost of building repairs, insurance, and the county taxes, New Castle obtains enough income for town expenses to materially benefit its taxpayers. In 1885 the Trustees of the Common procured an act of the legislature abrogating that part of the Penn's deed forbidding the sale of any Common land; however, except for some small parts sold for rights-of-way and other public or semipublic uses, none has been sold other than that taken by the County for the airport. New Castle is still protected on the west from unsightly developments.

At HARE'S CORNER, 4.5 *m.,* is the northern junction with US 13 *(see Tour 1).* US 40 is united with US 13 between Hare's Corner and State Road.

Section b. Hare's Corner to the Maryland Line, 11 m.

At STATE ROAD, *1 m.,* formerly a station of the Pennsylvania R.R., is the southern junction with US 13 *(see Tour 1, Sec. c).* Between this point and New Castle the present rail line follows the roadbed of the old New Castle and Frenchtown R.R. West of here the New Castle and Frenchtown was unable to compete with the railroad built around the head of Chesapeake Bay, and was abandoned in 1857.

At 3.7 *m.* is the junction with State 7 *(see Tour 11).*

GLASGOW, 8.9 *m.* (100 pop.), is a small hamlet containing several old brick houses and the PENCADER PRESBYTERIAN CHURCH, erected in 1852; its congregation was organized in the early 1700's by residents of Welsh Tract *(see Tour 9).* During a few recent years one of the handsomest old houses was an outpost of the Elkton marriage industry; a large illuminated sign on the lawn bore the words:

MARRIAGE INFORMATION FREE

INQUIRE WITHIN

The sign was removed when a Delaware law of 1936 prohibited all marriage advertising within the State.

The early name of the hamlet was Aikentown for Matthew Aiken who laid out the streets and kept a noted tavern that was the headquarters of the invading British General William Howe, Sept. 3 to 8, 1777. Howe used the early Presbyterian Church as a hospital for his sick and wounded men after the skirmish at Cooch's Bridge *(see Tour 9).* When the canal feeder was being dug, one of the earliest banks in Delaware was established here; it soon failed. In the first half of the 19th century Glasgow was a noted political arena, debates between party champions attracting thousands of persons from Delaware and Maryland.

At Glasgow is the junction with State 896 *(see Tour 9).*

At 10.4 *m.* a marker indicates the excavations of 1804–5 for a FEEDER CANAL intended to conduct water from Elk River in Maryland to a proposed ship canal between the Elk and the Christina Creek in Delaware. After an expenditure of $100,000, work was abandoned when the route of the present Chesapeake and Delaware Canal was fixed to the south. "Feeders" were necessary to supply water to the upper level of a lock canal, since a lockful of water was lost every time a boat passed into or out of it.

US 40 crosses the Maryland Line, 11 *m.,* about 3 miles east of Elkton, Md.

Tour 5

(West Chester, Pa.)—Wilmington; US 202.
Pennsylvania Line to Wilmington, 6.5 *m.*

Route used by The Short Line (bus).
Roadbed paved throughout.

Accommodations in Wilmington.

In high, hilly farming and dairy country with old stone houses and barns, US 202 (the Concord Pike) crosses the Pennsylvania Line, 0 *m.*, about 10 miles south of West Chester, Pa. *(see Pa. Tour 4).*

What was formerly PERRY'S TAVERN, 0.8 *m.* (L) is still in use as a roadhouse, now mansard-roofed and stuccoed. Before 1820 and for many years afterwards it was a popular inn and a stage-stop.

At 0.8 *m.* is the junction with Naaman's Rd.

Left on latter, **0.3** *m.* is Brandywine Raceway; 20-night pari-mutuel harness meet, Aug.-Sept. At **2.5** *m.* is junction with State 261; left on latter to CHESTER-BETHEL M. E. CHURCH, **2.9** *m.* (L), a small stone structure, now used as an implement shed; it was built in 1799 on the site of Cloud's Chapel, a log church erected in 1780. Among the early preachers here were Capt. Thomas Webb, a pioneer evangelist *(see Tour 1, Sec. a),* and Francis Asbury. In 1849 this was one of many evangelical churches that split over the question of musical accompaniment to singing. The younger members founded Siloam Church just across the Pennsylvania Line, but by 1859 the parent body could no longer resist buying a small melodeon organ for itself. Services in the old stone building ceased in 1873 when the new church was built adjacent to it.

TALLEYVILLE, 2.2 *m.* (400 alt., 250 pop.), named for the Talley family resident in this farming section since Colonial days, has long been a center of fox hunting. Like their ancestors before them, the Talleys and their neighbors, scorning pretension or formality, follow home-raised hounds on home-raised horses that are also used for farm work.

The ALFRED I. DU PONT SCHOOL (R) named for the donor *(see below)* of site and building was turned over to the State by his will. With several additions and a new 24-room elementary school, east on the Faulk Road, the school has grown in 23 years from 275 pupils to 1,500; from 8 teachers to 60 in elementary grades through junior high school.

At 4.1 *m.* the gray stone mansion (L) is LOMBARDY *(private),* purchased in 1793 by Gunning Bedford, Jr. (1747–1812), who served in the Continental Congress from 1783 to 1787 and was a member of the Constitutional Convention and a signer of the Constitution. In 1789 President Washington appointed him first judge of the United States District Court for Delaware.

The former BLUE BALL TAVERN *(private)*, 4.4 *m.* (R), now a dwelling, was built before 1800 and was another lively drinking spot of early days. Built of stone, it has been covered with buff stucco. In front there still stands a pole with a large blue-painted wooden ball on top, the sign of the old hostelry. Near the tavern was a toll house of the old Concord Turnpike which was incorporated in 1811 and ran between Wilmington and West Chester, Pa. It was not taken over by New Castle County and made free until 1911.

At 4.4 *m.* is the junction with the Rockland Rd.

Right on this road to NEMOURS, 0.7 *m.* and the endowed hospital for crippled children on the grand and beautiful estate (L) of Alfred I. du Pont (1864–1935), powdermaker, financier and philanthropist. On the 300-acre property there are the chateau of Nemours itself, a carillon tower, and the several hospital buildings of Nemours Foundation. The hospital and laboratory, the center of orthopedic work and research are financed by the entire $60,000,000 residue of Mr. Du Pont's fortune. Surrounding the estate is a high stone wall topped with varicolored pieces of broken glass set points up in cement, after the fashion of walls around old French chateaux.

Visible for miles is the 210-foot CARILLON TOWER *(carillon peals lasting 10 min. at noon and 4:30; Westminster chimes every quarter-hour 8 a.m.-8 p.m.).* The top of the tower, 552 feet above sea level, is by far the highest pinnacle in Delaware. The Nemours Carillon was completed in 1936 after Mr. Du Pont's death as a memorial to his parents, Eleuthère Irénée (2d) and Charlotte Shepard Henderson Du Pont. The main shaft of the tower is of pink North Carolina granite, with imposing base and quoins of gray Vermont granite. The cupola containing the chimes, set back from the body of the tower, is decorated with four supporting stone eagles. The carillon itself comprises 31 bells weighing 25 tons. Within the bronze entrance doors is a hall, lighted by stained-glass windows. At a height of 160 feet in the tower is an observation platform reached by an elevator. There is also a spiral stairway leading up the tower. Beneath the tower is a crypt that is to be the permanent tomb of Mr. Du Pont. Close by the tower is buried a mongrel dog named Yip that adopted Mr. Du Pont on a golf course; the dog became his constant companion and survived him only a few days.

The residence of Nemours, built in 1908, is of formal French chateau style throughout, the exterior finished in Indiana limestone. The house and gardens were designed as a memorial to Mr. Du Pont's parents, to the early Du Ponts in America and their French ancestors, and to King Louis XVI and Queen Marie Antoinette whom they served. The colonnade, grand basin, fountains and statuary, pool and water courses, urns and lawns, all suggest the Garden of Versailles.

The main approach, through wrought-iron entrance gates, proceeds to the forecourt leading to the chateau. The front terrace is flanked by two white marble sphinxes formerly at the Chateau de Sceaux, home of Jean Baptiste Colbert. Behind the sunken gardens, on an eminence, stands a classic "temple of love." On the grounds are iron gates that belonged to Catherine the Great of Russia, as well as gates from Wimbledon Manor in England that are considered masterpieces of design and workmanship. Architects for the chateau were Carrère and Hastings of New York, designers of the New York Public Library and other monumental buildings. Architects for the Carillon Tower were Massena and Du Pont of Wilmington, who have done most of the landscaping and architectural work since 1930, including the sunken gardens, the "temple of love," and work on the interior of the chateau.

Alfred I. du Pont became noted as a philanthropist. The Delaware Old Age Pension Fund *(see State Welfare Home; Tour 1, Sec. c)* grew out of a pension system that he established from his private means. His concern for the unfortunate was a characteristic from his youth. *(See WILMINGTON; also Tour 6A).*

At 4.7 *m.* is the junction with Augustine Cut-Off.

Right on this road to FRIENDS SCHOOL *(open to visitors)*, 0.5 *m.* (R), a private, non-sectarian, preparatory school for boys and girls, administered by the two Monthly Meetings of Friends in Wilmington. Since 1937 the school has occupied this large field-stone building whose Georgian-Colonial aspects suggest an early Quaker meeting house; E. William Martin was the architect. The 127 rooms can accommodate 375 day students. Grounds of 20 acres are flanked by the Alapocas Woods, a Wilmington park. Established in 1748, Friends School is the oldest educational institution in Delaware *(see WILMINGTON)*.

At 5 *m.* on US 202 there is a good view of the city of Wilmington, the Delaware River, and the New Jersey shore.

US 202 follows Concord Ave. to Baynard Blvd.; R. on Baynard Blvd. across the Brandywine Bridge; straight ahead on Washington St. to 11th St.

WILMINGTON, 6.5 *m.* (80 alt., 1-0,356 pop.) *(see WILMING- TON)*.

Points of Interest. Old Swedes Church, The Rocks, Old Town Hall, Rodney Square, Du Pont and Nemours Buildings, Public Library, Delaware Art Center, Brandywine Park, and others.

Wilmington is at the junction with US 13 *(see Tour 1)*, State 2 *(see Tour 8)*, State 48 *(see Tour 7A)*, State 52 *(see Tour 6)*, and the Rising Sun Rd. *(see Tour 6A)*.

Tour 6

Wilmington—Centreville—(Longwood, Pa.); State 52 in Del. and Pa.
Wilmington to Pennsylvania Line, 7.8 m.; to Longwood Gardens, 12.4 m.

The Short Line (bus) follows the route.
Roadbed paved throughout.
Accommodations in Wilmington; tourist lodges near Longwood.

Between Wilmington and the Pennsylvania Line, State 52 (the Kennett Pike) passes through pleasant rolling country composed almost entirely of estates belonging to members or connections of the Du Pont family; the large houses, often hidden from the road by trees or low hills, are set amid parks and pastures, woods and tilled fields. This is a fox-hunting country, with fences of rails or stone. There are no billboards or other commercial eyesores along the road. Besides the recently built houses, there are many ancient stone houses typical of the region. The highway itself, for 100 years a toll road, was widened and paved with concrete by Pierre S. du Pont, owner of Longwood.

WILMINGTON, 0 *m.* (80 alt., 110,356 pop.) *(see WILMINGTON).*

Points of Interest. Old Swedes Church, The Rocks, Old Town Hall, Rodney Square, Du Pont and Nemours Buildings, Public Library, Delaware Art Center, Brandywine Park, and others.

From Tenth and Market Sts., 0 *m.*, the route follows 10th St. W. to Delaware Ave.; R. on Delaware Ave. to Pennsylvania Ave.; L. on Pennsylvania Ave.

GOODSTAY *(private)*, 2 *m.* (L), is the home of Mrs. Ellen C. du Pont Wheelwright, daughter of Coleman du Pont. The rambling stone and frame structure contains one of the best small collections of modern art in Delaware. Among the noted artists represented are Charles W. Hawthorne and John Noble.

The WILMINGTON COUNTRY CLUB *(private)*, 2.1 *m.* (L), is the successor to the Young America Cricket Club, founded in 1883, and the Delaware Field Club, organized in 1885. The present club, whose membership of over 1,000 includes at least 50 millionaires, was incorporated in 1901 when it engaged its first golf professional who was known as a "coach and general overseer." The property now is valued at nearly a million dollars.

The club house, brown stuccoed and white frame, was erected in 1925 to replace a building destroyed by fire in 1924. Many social functions are held in it, including, in several recent years, the Wilmington Assembly Ball. This is said to have been the first building of its kind in the country to be equipped with a system that constantly circulates air through every locker. In a separate building are five squash courts.

The club occupies a tract of 135 acres which includes an 18-hole golf course, 14 grass tennis courts and two composition courts. On these courts are played the Delaware State Lawn Tennis Championships *(June)* held annually since 1908.

Other events *(open to the public as spectators)* are: Women's Golf Tournament *(May)*; Women's Invitation Golf Tournament *(June)*; Wilmington Country Club Invitation Tournament for Mitchell Trophy *(June)*; 36-hole medal play *(Memorial Day and July 4)*.

At 2.2 *m.*, at the junction with Rising Sun Lane *(see Tour 6A)*, is ST. AMOUR *(private)*, the huge, stone castle-like home (R) of Lammot du Pont, president (1926–1940) of E. I. du Pont de Nemours & Co., Inc., and one of the founders of the American Liberty League. St. Amour was built in 1892 by his mother, Mary Belin du Pont, eight years after her husband, Lammot du Pont, was killed in an explosion at the company's high-explosives plant at Gibbstown, N. J.

At 2.4 *m.* the adjoining estates (R) are those of Mrs. Mary Chichester du Pont and Ernest du Pont.

At 2.6 *m.* the stone building (R) on a bank sloping down to an athletic field is the ALEXIS I. DU PONT SCHOOL, a public school unique in Delaware because of its $60,000 endowment fund, one of Pierre S. du Pont's many educational benefactions in this State. Erected on land donated by E. I. du Pont de Nemours & Co., the school was named by Francis G. du Pont in honor of his father. The younger du Pont had been instrumental in obtaining the site. Other gifts to this school by Pierre S. du Pont for improvements and equipment totalled $133,000. He created the endowment fund at a time when appropriations from the State for the maintenance of public schools were inadequate. The State now is generous in its care of schools, including this one, but as this fund belongs to the Alexis I. du Pont School, it remains for whatever purposes the school board chooses. This building is the high school of the Alexis I. du Pont Special District. The elementary school of the district is a short distance beyond the Greenville Post Office, ahead (R). The building is one of the outstanding modern schools designed by the architect G. Morris Whiteside II.

Across the road is WESTOVER HILLS (L), an expensive residential section. Its unofficial name just after the crash of 1929 was "Leftover Bills."

At 2.7 m., the junction with Breck's Lane, is the SITE OF THE TOLL GATE, one of two on the Kennett Pike. The gates on this road, the last toll road in Delaware, were removed in 1919. In its early years this road was regarded as the shortest and best route to tidewater from the rich farming section of Pennsylvania bordering Delaware. The Wilmington and Kennett Turnpike Co., incorporated in 1811, built the original road at a cost of $30,000. Pierre S. du Pont, who widened and rebuilt the highway, paid double the par value for the company's stock, assumed a debt of $10,000 against it, and built the present highway out of his own pocket at $85,000 a mile.

During the years of the pike's existence as a private commercial enterprise, it was constantly necessary, as the city spread, to move the toll gate further into the open country. Added reason for this migration was that a number of thrifty citizens made the pleasing discovery that with the opening of additional side roads, they could drive their rigs on to the pike without having to pay toll.

While horses provided motive power, the gates were quiet, leisurely places, centers for tipped-back chairs and rural gossip. All this vanished as automobiles appeared and with them the necessity for faster toll collections and swift change-making. The last years of the Kennett Pike Toll gates were busy ones for the attendants. Nearly forgotten now are the toll exemptions for funerals and churchgoers, provided in the highway company's articles of incorporation. No matter what or where a Sunday driver's ultimate destination might be, he passed through free if he but nodded yes to the gate-keeper's inquiring "Going to church?"

At 2.7 m. is the junction with State 100, the Montchanin Rd. *(see Tour 6B)*.

At 3.1 m. is the junction with the Barley Mill Rd.

Left on this road to a fork, **0.5** m.; R. at the fork to the EDGAR M. HOOPES RESERVOIR DAM (R), **2.7** m. *(a public walk leads up a hillside to the summit of the* *dam; no trespassing permitted on the water or the banks).* The concrete dam, 135 feet high and 970 feet long, was built 1929–32 across a narrow valley. Submerging many former farms and roads, the artificial lake is 1.67 miles long and averages 0.25 miles wide; the maximum depth is 100 feet. The total cost of this 2 billion-gallon water supply for Wilmington was $3,000,000. The water forms a "stand-by" reserve for future needs, and has been used only when the Brandywine pumping station in Wilmington was temporarily shut down. Water is brought to Wilmington by pipe systems to the Porter Reservoir. The spillway empties into Red Clay Creek.

Large country houses on surrounding hills overlook the handsome little lake and its wooded and reforested shores. Many points and coves give the illusion that the lake is natural. It is very popular as an objective for summer evening drives from Wilmington by roads commanding a view of the water *(see Tour 6C).* Here the ascent to the top of the dam is steep, and must be made on foot.

A bronze tablet at the southeast end of the top of the dam bears the names of the construction authorities and the dedication of the reservoir to Col. Edgar M. Hoopes, Jr. (1888–1931), a former chief engineer of the Wilmington Board of Water Commissioners. At the foot of the dam the Old Mill Pumping Station is named for the Old Mill, a summer home of Coleman du Pont that once stood on a site now flooded.

At 3.5 *m.* the plastered stone house (R) was formerly known as the BUCK TAVERN and is now used as a residence *(private).* An inscription "P & R II, 1821" on the front of the building near the roof, presumably indicates the year of construction, but it is said there is an earlier date at the west end covered by cement. There is a tradition that the building was used as a headquarters by couriers who maintained liaison between Union troops at Gettysburg, Pa., and troops encamped in this section during the Civil War. The naming of the tavern is attributed to a trivial incident. When the near, or buck, ox of a passing yoke became engulfed in quicksand, people from the surrounding country were summoned to help extricate the animal, the place from then on becoming known as the Buck Tavern.

At GREENVILLE POST OFFICE, 3.6 *m.,* are a coal and lumber yard and a post office, shopping center and elementary school. It is on the Reading R.R.

At 4.3 *m.* is an entrance (L) to DOGWOOD *(private),* the estate of Eugene E. du Pont. The curiously shaped hedge pear tree at the entrance probably was twisted in youth by a gale. More than 200 years old, the tree was a recognized landmark under which travelers rested as long ago as 1790. Modern tree surgery, as evidenced in the wide strip of white cement winding about the tree, has prolonged its life.

At 4.5 *m.* is the junction with State 82 *(see Tour 6C).*

CHEVANNES *(private),* 4.6 *m.* (L), was built for Mrs. B. G. du Pont, first wife of Alfred I. du Pont *(see Tour 5).* The house is of French-Norman style and its main part and gardens are a reproduction of the home at Chevannes, France, of the first Pierre Samuel du Pont de Nemours, founder of the American line of the du Pont family. Albert E. Ives was the architect.

As family historian, Mrs. du Pont, owner of Chevannes, was the author of several books, the first of which was a *History of the Du Pont Company, 1802–1902.*

At *5 m.* the gatehouse (R) is an entrance to WINTERTHUR *(see below)*, the Delaware estate of Henry F. du Pont, and previously of his father Col. Henry A. du Pont (1838–1926), United States Senator 1906–17, who named it after the small city in Switzerland. Once the Antoine Bidermann farm *(see Tour 6A)*, the estate has expanded until it extends about a mile and one-half along the Kennett Pike and includes several thousand acres, one of the largest and grandest estates in America. On it are a private golf course, a station on the Reading R.R. (of which the elder du Pont was president), a post office *(open to the public; see Tour 6B)*, numerous employees' houses, and enormous dairy barns for the noted herd of Holstein cattle established by Colonel du Pont.

A long driveway leads to the residence on a knoll hidden from the highway. The house built by Colonel du Pont about 1885 was remodeled in the French Chateau style and greatly enlarged in 1931 by the present owner at a cost of more than $2,000,000. The mansion, of masonry and cream-colored stucco, includes a main section of three and one-half stories flanked by five-and-one-half-story wings. These wings, rising to the same height as the central portion, are built on a lower slope of the hillside. The architect was Albert E. Ives of Wilmington. The principal rooms and many of the 40 bedrooms are decorated in the manner of the various periods in American history from the 17th through the early 19th century; Charles O. Cornelius, Associate Curator of American Art in the Metropolitan Museum of Art, New York, served as consultant in the decoration. The collection of rare antiques, paintings, and curiosa include many articles bought at auction in competition with bidders from the Boston, the Metropolitan, and other museums. Of particular importance is the collection of Duncan Phyfe furniture which was loaned to the Metropolitan for exhibition while the house was being built. The Lowestoft china includes sets said to have been used by Washington and Jefferson. There is a noted collection of early-American silver.

The house is now the Henry Francis du Pont Museum, providing a panorama of colonial and early state interiors, 1690–1840. Tickets of admission may be had for a specific date by writing well in advance to Secretary of the museum, Winterthur, Del.; fee $2 per person; luncheon at cafeteria may be reserved at same time. Tour of rooms takes full day.

At *5.6 m.*, at the junction with the Old Kennett Rd., is the LOWER BRANDYWINE PRESBYTERIAN CHURCH (L), built in 1859 by a congregation organized in 1720. The early history of the church was marked by a prolonged controversy; some persons favored a site on the west bank of the Brandywine while others wished the church to be built on the east side of the stream. The dispute continued until the original building, in Pennsylvania, became unfit for use a few years before the Revolution. In 1774 this site was selected for a new church, and a small log building was erected.

Here in 1828, during the pastorate of the Rev. Thomas Love, a meeting of the Presbytery was held that established a precedent. For the first time in its history the Presbytery was entertained without the use of alcoholic spirits.

Near this junction is the SITE OF A KENNETT PIKE TOLL GATE *(see above)*.

Left on the old Kennett Rd. to DAUNEPORT *(private)*, 0.7 *m.*, the estate (L) of Amy E. du Pont, a noted horsewoman and a pioneer in Delaware in the breeding of hackney horses. The white mansion, completed in 1933, was modeled after Mount Vernon. The architect was Mrs. Mary Craig of Santa Barbara, Calif.

At 0.9 *m.* on the Old Kennett Rd. is the junction with Owl's Nest Rd.

1. Right on this road to OWL'S NEST *(private)*, 1.1 *m.*, the estate (L) of Eugene du Pont. Constructed of stone and wood in the style of an English-Tudor manor house, it is hidden from the road by trees and shrubbery. Here on June 30, 1937, took place the reception that followed the wedding at nearby Christ Church *(see Tour 6B)* of Mr. and Mrs. du Pont's daughter Ethel and Franklin D. Roosevelt, Jr., son of the President. President Roosevelt, his family, and members of the Cabinet were among the 1,300 guests invited to the reception. From a carved oak gallery in the two-story main hall of the house the new Mrs. Roosevelt tossed her bridal bouquet. In the fields nearby were vast parking areas, and a large tent served as headquarters for the reporters, photographers, and telegraph operators assigned to cover the event. Secret Service men, State Police, and soldiers from Fort Du Pont were on duty. It rained hard that day, and tractors were used to pull automobiles out of the mud. Plans for traffic control between church and house were deranged by the lining of roads by hundreds of automobiles whose occupants hoped to catch sight of the bride and groom, their families, and other celebrities. A carnival spirit prevailed; peddlers sold balloons, souvenirs, hot dogs, and ice cream along the way.

2. Left on Owl's Nest Rd. to the VICMEAD HUNT CLUB *(private)* 1.7 *m.* (R). The stone and stucco clubhouse, formerly a farmhouse, is the headquarters of the only recognized hunt in Delaware. Organized in 1920, the club takes its name from those of two of its founders, Mrs. Victor du Pont and the former Mrs. Hollyday S. Meeds. The property occupies more than 100 acres and has kennels for hounds and a stable for hunting horses. Across the road are trapshooting facilities for club members. The clubhouse used to be in the center of the hunting country, but the building of many new houses and paved roads in recent years has forced the club members to haul their hunters in vans to new foxhunting country south of the Chesapeake and Delaware Canal.

At 6.7 *m.* is the junction with a side road.

Right on this road to the junction with a crossroad, 0.6 *m.;* L. on the crossroad a few yards; L. on a private lane to CAMP LANDIS for the blind, 1 *m. (open to visitors May-Sept.),* comprising several one-story frame buildings painted gray, on a hillside near a woods; it was established in 1930 by Mrs. Irénée du Pont and administered by the Delaware Commission for the Blind. At this camp, one of the first of its kind in the country, nearly every blind man, woman, and child in Delaware spends two weeks as a guest. Certain periods are reserved for Negroes. Blind persons employed at the Blind Shop in Wilmington continue here their chair-caning and other work. Recreation includes Braille reading, games, and music. From the verandas ropes are strung through the woods for the guidance of walkers.

At 0.9 *m.* on the main side road is the old FRIENDS CENTRE MEETING HOUSE (L), built in 1796 and still used on the last Sunday (First Day) of each month as a place of worship for the Quaker congregation. The severe lines of the old brick structure with its front porch, its gaunt carriage sheds at either side, and its worn stepping-stones on which meeting-goers of past generations alighted from their horses or carriages, are typical of meeting house architecture in this section of the country.

The interior is divided by a frame partition that once separated the sexes. The hard wooden benches are held together by wooden pegs. A small table also reveals the same careful construction. Not until recent years has it become necessary to replace sections of the original floor.

In the rear of the meeting house, enclosed by a wall of brick, is a little burying ground, bordered at one end by a wooded area. There are low grave markers and clumps of old boxwood.

Like that of Lower Brandywine Presbyterian Church, the choice of this site also was debated. Proximity to the Brandywine, which was often a deep, turbulent, and dangerous stream, created a difference of opinion between those living on the Brandywine's east and west banks. In winter the ford across the stream was unsafe and the journey to the First Day meeting frequently was a hazardous one. The first Centreville Monthly Meeting, organized before 1690, built a small wooden church in 1708. The actual meeting alternated between that building, the meeting at Newark Union in Brandywine Hundred *(see Tour 1, Sec. a)*, and the meeting at Hockessin *(see Tour 7)*. For a time the Centreville Meeting was abandoned but the deeding of six acres of land in 1794 led to construction, two years later, of the present brick meeting house.

Diagonally opposite the meeting house is (R) the small stucco covered CENTREVILLE SCHOOLHOUSE *(private)*, now used as a residence. A log school had been built on the meeting house ground before 1800. It was replaced in 1818 by a small brick structure. In 1854, Antoine Bidermann *(see Tour 6A)* who had come to Delaware in connection with the Du Pont industry of that period, gave $1,000 toward construction of the present building.

CENTREVILLE, 6.8 *m.* (438 alt., 210 pop.), a small neat village, stands on what is usually calculated to be the highest point in Delaware. In its early days the settlement, though far from being the geographical center of Delaware, was truly a center for Pennsylvania and Delaware farmers who patronized the proportionately large number of taverns and inns here. As much as a wagonload of liquor in a week was consumed at these drinking places by thirsty travelers.

In the cupola of the white painted structure (R), an old unused SCHOOL, a bell that once summoned lagging students to class still hangs in place. Below it is the date "1863." At the side of the road, just outside the fenced school property, is a nearly illegible milestone with the inscription "7 to W."

At 7.6 *m.* the three-story, white painted brick house beyond the stone wall (L) is former residence of D. O. HASTINGS *(private)*, U. S. Senator 1929–36. Although he had announced that he wished to retire from public office at the expiration of his term in 1936, Senator Hastings, a Republican, was drafted by his party as a candidate for the election of that year. He campaigned vigorously, but was unsuccessful in the election and a Democrat was swept into office. Senator Hastings became nationally known for his denunciation of New Deal measures and policies during the first Roosevelt administration. He now lives nearby on Twaddell Mill Road and practices law in Wilmington.

This house is on the estate of Mr. and Mrs. Harry W. Lunger; Mrs. Lunger is a daughter of Philip F. du Pont.

At 7.8 *m.* State 52 crosses the PENNSYLVANIA LINE. The old stone house (R) stands in two states and is known as the LINE HOUSE.

At 8.5 *m.* on Pa. State 52 the large, stone mansion on the hill (L) is that of Mrs. Philip F. du Pont. Mr. du Pont left more than $10,000,000 to his alma mater, the University of Virginia, when he died in 1928.

FAIRVILLE, 8.7 *m.* (100 pop.), is a small hamlet.

MENDENHALL, 9.6 *m.*, is a station on the Pennsylvania R.R. Northwest of this point, the character of the road changes; instead of large estates on either side, there are small homes and farms.

At HAMORTON, 10.9 *m.,* is a junction with US 1 which unites with State 52 between Hamorton and a point at 11.7 *m.* The houses of a Colonial-style village (R), mostly of stone, are occupied by Longwood employees and their families. Houses of other members of the staff, which includes engineers, farmers, gardeners, and servants, are the comfortable-looking, well-kept homes on either side of the highway.

At 11.7 *m.* US 1 branches L. and a sign on State 52 indicates the private entrance to Longwood.

LONGWOOD MEETING HOUSE (L), 11.8 *m. (annual meeting in June),* a simple frame structure, is regarded as a nursery for the cause of Abolition. Belonging to the Pennsylvania Yearly Meeting of Progressive Friends, organized in 1853, this building was dedicated in 1855. Except during 1861 when no meeting was held, the meeting house has echoed each year to the oratory of men and women who have discussed national topics including slavery, militarism, suffrage, child labor, single-tax, and prohibition. Speakers here have included Theodore Tilton (1835–1907), Robert Purvis, Henry George (1839–97), Lucy Stone (1818–93), Susan B. Anthony (1820–1906), Lucretia Mott (1793–1880), and Mary A. Livermore (1821–1905).

The name "Longwood" was not applied until just before the Civil War when the surrounding long woods sheltered Negro slaves who were fleeing north from Delaware, Maryland, and farther south. This Underground Station was run by a group of Wilmington, Hamorton, and Kennett Square Quakers.

At 12.4 *m.* (R) is the public automobile entrance to parking space for LONGWOOD *(open, free, 11-5 on weekdays and this includes Saturdays; and on Sundays and holidays a "hospital fee" of 50 cents is charged; there is a free organ recital on Sundays, 3-5; daylight saving time observed May–Sept.).* Longwood is the estate of Pierre S. du Pont. The gardens and conservatories—the latter includes two acres under glass—comprise what has been called the finest privately-owned horticultural collection in the world.

In 1701 George Pierce acquired this site, known afterward as Evergreen Glade, with a 500-acre tract, from William Penn. In 1725 Pierce deeded the place to his son, Joshua, whence it passed to Caleb Pierce, and, in 1800, to Caleb's twin sons. When Mr. Du Pont acquired it in 1906, the park and garden here were known as Pierce's Park. Then, as now, the place was open to the public.

Since the completion of the conservatories and gardens in 1921, Longwood has been visited by more than 100,000 persons each year. Some parts of the greenhouse and grounds are closed to the public. Visitors enjoying the extensive open parts of both are requested to accord to the owners of Longwood the same courtesy and right of privacy that they would to any other considerate hosts.

In the conservatories are many varieties of orchids, peach trees "pleached" on trellises, oranges, bananas, cacti, and rare azaleas from Belgium. Seasonal displays are striking: From January to April the blooming flowers include amaryllis, daffodils, hyacinths, tulips, and lilies; in April and May, azaleas and rhododendrons; about Thanksgiving Day, chrysanthemums, and at Christmas time, poinsettias.

The conservatory houses a large pipe organ, containing more than 200 stops and 10,000 pipes. More than 300,000 gallons of fuel oil are required annually to heat the place.

Facing the conservatory entrance are the fountains, completed in 1932; their display is most effective at night when red, blue, green, amber, and white lights, with all the variations and blends of those colors, tint the cascading water. Part of the general fountain plan is a tower in which chimes strike the quarter hour. Their tone is particularly sweet when the sound is muted by the gushing water.

The fountain system comprises two canals, both 18 feet wide and 275 feet long, a 260-foot circular basin, a rectangular basin on a low hill, and a waterfall. In the upper canal are 14 single and 14 display jets. There are 12 display jets in the rectangular basin from which water leaps 40 to 100 ft. The fountains are illuminated by 800 powerful light units. Three pumps, each with a capacity of 4,000 gallons per minute, return the water falling from the fountains. Displays usually follow concerts or recitals, held either in the conservatory or in the open air theater. The best point from which to view the fountains is the paved terrace at the entrance to the conservatory.

The Longwood open air theater, completed in 1927, is built on a terrace and has a seating capacity of 2,200. A vine-covered stone wall is a background for the stage; neatly clipped arbor vitae and boxwood form the wings at either side. A line of fountains takes the place of the usual curtain separating actors and spectators. Footlights are so placed as to give the effect of light streaming up from the ground. Back-stage space includes completely-equipped dressing rooms.

Near the estate is a monument unveiled in 1925 honoring Hannah Freeman (1730–1802), last of the Lenni-Lenape Indians in this section. The marker, mounted on a water-worn stone taken from the nearby Pocopson Creek, was erected on the site of her birthplace.

Longwood has its own fire fighting, construction, and maintenance systems. A modest brick mansion *(private)*, part of which was built in 1730, is occupied by Mr. Pierre S. du Pont. Mrs. Du Pont died in 1944.

Mr. du Pont, owner of Longwood, past president of E. I. du Pont de Nemours & Co., Inc. (1915–19), elder brother of Lammot and Irénée du Pont and generally considered head of the du Pont clan, was born in Wilmington in 1870, a son of Lammot and Mary Belin du Pont. He was educated at the Penn Charter School, Philadelphia, and at the Massachusetts Institute of Technology, Cambridge. He went to work for the du Pont Company at Carney's Point, N. J., in 1890.

When he was 32 he and his cousins, Alfred I. and Coleman, assumed control of the du Pont Company. As president through the war years, Mr. du Pont guided the firm while du Pont powder was being supplied to the Allied troops and later to the American Expeditionary Force in Europe.

In 1915 Mr. Du Pont married his first cousin, Alice Belin, daughter of his mother's brother, Henry Belin, of Scranton, Pa.

In 1917 he was a successful defendant in the famous suit instituted by Alfred I. du Pont and others in the U. S. District Court *(see WIL-MINGTON)*.

After the death by influenza in 1918 of Lewes A. Mason, a Delaware youth who had come to Longwood as a chauffeur and endeared himself to the Du Ponts, Mr. Du Pont sponsored the erection of the Chester County Hospital, West Chester, Pa., as a memorial to Mason. The cost was $1,-200,000. The 50-cent fee charged at Longwood on Sundays and holidays goes to this and another hospital in Chester County, and to three hospitals in Wilmington.

Like his ancestor of the same name, Mr. Du Pont has been intensely interested in public education. In 1919 when, from an educational standpoint, Delaware ranked thirty-third nationally, Mr. Du Pont formed the Service Citizens of Delaware, an organization that enlisted experts in making an educational survey of the State. Out of this grew the Delaware School Auxiliary to administer his gift of $9,000,000, with which, under a new State educational code, school districts were helped in financing the erection of new buildings *(see EDUCATION)*. In 1921 he ended a term as vice-president of the Delaware State Board of Education. After the Du Ponts had acquired large interests in the General Motors Corporation, Mr. Du Pont served as president of that corporation from 1920 to 1923.

When Mr. Du Pont served as State Tax Commissioner, 1925 to 1937, he paid salaries from his own means to specialists in carrying out a vigorous and systematic roundup of delinquent State income taxes. By 1926 the Delaware School Auxiliary Association, which he financed to a large extent, had erected 84 Negro schools and 19 schools for white pupils throughout the State.

Objecting to Prohibition because he believed it impracticable and that it attempted too-close supervision of the manners and morals of a free people, he became active, as did Mrs. Du Pont, in the Association Against the Prohibition Amendment. At his own expense he conducted a State-wide wet-and-dry poll.

In 1928, in appreciation of many services to the French people, including hospitalization during World War I, Mr. Du Pont was honored by the French Government at a ceremony in Washington at which he was made an officer of the Legion of Honor.

In 1930 he received the Chemical Markets Medal for services he had rendered to chemistry in America and publicly opposed a plan under way in Wilmington to erect a statue of him. When Delaware ratified the repeal of the 18th Amendment Mr. Du Pont helped draft the State liquor-control law. His activity against Prohibition led to his appointment in 1933 as State Liquor Commissioner, an office that made him a virtual czar of the State's tavern keepers and liquor dealers, inasmuch as there were no other members of the commission. During the Depression he maintained work-relief units at his own expense and served on the New Castle County Temporary Emergency Relief Commission.

For many years Mr. Du Pont has contributed large sums to plans for encouraging thrift among his personal employees, rewarding them for long or especially good service, and providing income for disability and retirement.

Tour 6A

Junction with State 52—Henry Clay—Old Upper Hagley Powder Mills; Rising Sun Lane, 0.8 m.

Roadbed paved throughout.

This short route follows the curving west bank of the Brandywine, flowing unharnessed where formerly the rushing waters were diverted into races to run mills on the rocky, wooded banks. In this quiet sylvan setting are industrial landmarks, both old and new, of significance in the beginnings and the present development of the Du Pont chemical business.

Rising Sun Lane branches northeast from State 52 (the Kennett Pike), 0 *m.*, at the Wilmington city limits about 2 miles northwest of the center of the city.

At 0.3 *m.* on Rising Sun Lane is the junction with New Bridge Rd.

Right on this road across an iron bridge to the EXPERIMENTAL STATION OF E. I. DU PONT DE NEMOURS AND CO. (R), **0.4** *m. (no admittance)*. First group of many-windowed brick buildings stands on the site of the Lower Hagley Powder Mills whence wagons hauled powder over New Bridge Rd. to a loading wharf at Edgemoor *(see Tour 1)*. Ahead are the multiple buildings of the $30 million laboratories having the largest staff of its kind in the United States—where they work out new chemical products and improvements in old ones. The finest laboratory equipment is supplemented by a vast scientific library. By the terms of the company's contract with its well-paid scientists, all rights to their discoveries are retained by the company. At the PAINT FARM on the grounds various materials covered with paint and varnish are exposed to the weather for months or years to test the durability of the finishes.

The new buildings use grounds of the DU PONT COUNTRY CLUB *(private)* for employees, their families and friends, has a large, well-equipped clubhouse, two 18-hole golf courses, and other recreation facilities. It was established in 1921 by the company. The new clubhouse and grounds are on Rockland Road N. of Nemours.

HENRY CLAY, 0.5 *m.* (200 pop. est.), on both sides of the creek, is a slumbering village of old stone houses either whitewashed or in pastel tints of yellow or blue; in the 19th century it was a thriving quarter for

OLD WOOLEN MILL, NEAR WILMINGTON

hundreds of persons employed in the mills nearby. When Du Pont explosives were no longer made in Delaware, old powder makers, smoking pipes, sat on sunny front porches with their wives or grandchildren, dreaming of old times when the powder wagons rumbled by. Their conversation turned sooner or later to the great explosions that roared up without warning and broke the windows in the houses. Just as the old residents of seafaring towns talk of relatives drowned at sea, the old people of Henry Clay talked of fathers, uncles, or cousins killed in the explosions of mills or powder wagons.

Now the most of these old laborers, mechanics, and gang bosses have died or moved out of Du Pont family owned houses that have been repaired, equipped, and redecorated for rental to more affluent families who wish to live in this historic and lovely spot within easy distance of the downtown offices.

At 0.6 *m.* is BRECK'S MILL (R), on the creek bank, acquired early in the 19th century by Alfred Victor du Pont and operated as a woolen mill. For years it has served for informal parties of the Du Pont family. Here a family orchestra used to rehearse, and amateur dramatics have been staged for charity. During World War I the old stone building was the Hagley Community Center for munitions workers.

At 0.7 *m.* (L) the yellow-washed STONE HOUSE *(private)*, with a marble stone above the door inscribed "C. I. D. 1823," was built by Charles Irénée du Pont (1797–1869), grandson of Pierre Samuel du Pont de Nemours. Charles I. du Pont operated woolen mills with his brother Alfred Victor; was interested in agriculture, and helped organize the Delaware Railroad. Lafayette was a guest at his first marriage and kissed the bride, the former Dorcas Van Dyke, daughter of U. S. Senator Nicholas Van Dyke of New Castle. His second wife was Ann Ridgely of Dover.

The OLD UPPER HAGLEY YARD of the Du Pont powder mills, 0.8 *m.* *(private)*, is the principal reliquary of the first century of the Du Pont industry. For a mile or more northward along this bank of the Brandywine the site of early powdermaking has become divided into the private estates of the Du Pont family. Now (1953) the Eleutherian Mills—Hagley Foundation is converting 160 acres here into an historical center to perpetuate the Du Pont industry's early history and development. When the project is completed winding roads will extend through this beautiful valley; footpaths will connect the several museums with old buildings and sites. Recreation facilities will contribute to enjoyment of the unusual museum. Scattered along this beautiful and peaceful hillside, where birds sing and flowers bloom, are the sites or ruins of many structures where powder was made to kill men and game and to blast out ways for tunnels, bridges, and dams through the world. Among the buildings were storehouses, charring houses where willow wood was turned into charcoal, saltpeter refineries, machine shops, blacksmith shops, wheelwright shops, sawing and planing mills, and keg-making shops. Many of these will be restored.

Most vital—and most lethal—of all, however, were the powder mills themselves along the bank, between the creek and the now-empty millrace that furnished water power, built in pairs with a single great wooden drive-shaft to a pair. In ruins, about 20 of these mills remain—small, square structures with 3-foot thick stone walls, patterned after the French powder mills in which Eleuthère Irénée du Pont de Nemours learned the business. Only the walls on three sides remain. The roofs and the sides facing the Brandywine, built of light, flimsy construction, rotted away long ago. The roofs slanted toward the creek. In case of explosion from lightning or friction the mills were mortars: they would fire off wooden fronts and roofs and contents over the water, doing the least possible damage. New roofs and front walls were then put back in place upon the heavy masonry. Many of these mills were built in the period 1802–50. (The Historic American Buildings Survey in 1936 made drawings of one built in 1824.)

Du Pont territory extended for three miles on either side of the creek; outsiders were stopped for their own safety by no-admittance signs. Here powder was produced for every important battle in which the United States has engaged from the War of 1812 until World War I. During the World War little powder was made at the Hagley Yards, and all powdermaking operations ceased here in 1921.

The story of the Du Ponts in Wilmington starts in Paris, where in 1739 Pierre Samuel du Pont (who became de Nemours) was born, a son of

Samuel du Pont and Anne Alexandrine de Montchanin. He studied medicine but turned to economic and political philosophy, working with the Economists Turgot and Quesnay in their attempt to restore the finances of France, and simplify the taxation system by substituting a single land tax for the complex and oppressive taxes levied by the government. When Turgot was dismissed from the ministry in 1776, Pierre Samuel du Pont retired to his estate near Nemours. His son Eleuthère Irénée, of scientific bent, went to work in the laboratory of the great physicist Antoine Laurent Lavoisier. At the arsenal of Essonne he learned the processes by which saltpeter, charcoal, and sulphur were purified, pressed, polished, and grained into black powder.

In the French Revolution the father was shorn of his offices one by one until, at 52, he started a political newspaper expressing the policies he advocated. The publication was suppressed in 1797. In 1800 he brought his family to America to establish Pontiana, a colony to demonstrate his idealistic economic concepts.

Thomas Jefferson, who as Ambassador to France had become a friend of Du Pont, was not impressed by the idea for the colony. Together they planned the development of a democratic system of education. Meanwhile the sons Eleuthère Irénée and Victor had little to occupy their time and, it is related, Irénée went gunning with Col. Louis de Toussard, who had come to America with French troops during the American Revolution. Irénée found that American powder was both bad and expensive. He and his father went back to France and obtained sufficient financial backing to make a start in the powder business. The French Government allowed him to inspect French factories, drawings and formulae were given him, and he was promised a graining machine to do the work of ten men.

On his return to America in 1801, Irénée chose the Brandywine Creek in Delaware as power and the land of Jacob Broom as the site—where in 1795 Broom had built one of the first cotton mills in the country. The choice proved excellent: the water power was strong, and the banks were filled with willow trees for making charcoal. In the nearby small French colony, besides Colonel Toussard, lived the architect and artist Peter Bauduy, who also urged the site and invested money in the venture. In 1802 Irénée built his house "Eleutherian Mills" on the hillside overlooking the mills (see Tour 6B).

Because of difficulties it was not until 1804 that the first run of powder was made. In New York a star salesman was Victor du Pont, who obtained the first good customers. Bauduy was another active salesman and there were soon orders from the Federal Government despite prejudice against the du Ponts who for years were considered "foreigners." Profits went back into the business. Du Pont powder was used in fighting the Tripolitan pirates. John Jacob Astor's American Fur Co. bought 25,000 pounds of powder a year. With the War of 1812 came the first of many expansions of the powdermaking plant.

French investors protested that they were not getting enough return for their investments, and one of them, Jacques Bidermann, sent his son Antoine across to investigate. Young Bidermann was pleased at what the

OLD POWDER MILL ON THE BRANDYWINE

firm was doing, and married Evelina, Irénée's daughter. Soon he lined up with his father-in-law to force out Bauduy, who sued the firm and started a rival powder plant, failing in both efforts.

In 1817, having lived to see his two sons make him a very proud father, the aged Pierre Samuel du Pont de Nemours died. Victor died in 1827, and Eleuthère Irénée kept on at the business until his death in 1834; the firm was about to emerge from debt, and was making a million pounds of powder annually. The "foreign" Du Pont family, quiet and industrious, was now fully accepted in Wilmington society. The company presidency of Antoine Bidermann from 1834 to 1837 was the single exception to the rule that a Du Pont must be the president.

There was a peculiar form of partnership in the firm. There were no formal titles. The oldest Du Pont ruled. The extensive landholdings were held in common. As each male Du Pont married, the company built him a house and charged no rent. The partners drew no salary but were credited on the books with shares of the profits. Sums for personal needs were drawn from the cash box as needed. One clerk was bookkeeper, cashier, and paymaster.

The Du Pont men regarded the company as their religion and their life. All were on terms of intimacy with the workmen, superintending operations at the yard with them and sometimes dying with them in explosions. One day a Du Pont saw sparks coming from a drive shaft; ordering workmen to run away, he went down to the creek, dipped his tall silk hat full of water, and threw it over the hot spot.

The firm weathered depressions largely because wars created further demand for the products. Shortly after the panic of 1837 began to pinch, the Mexican War came along. Profits from British purchases during the Crimean War tided the firm over the panic of 1857. A great boom came with the Civil War, though the firm had difficulty in getting its money from the Government. Thenceforth the railroad-building era provided a tremendous market for du Pont explosives, and prosperity increased. The Spanish-American War brought more profits, with smokeless powder added to the company's line. In 1899 the partnership became a corporation.

After the death in 1902 of Eugene du Pont, at the time president, most of the family stockholders wanted to sell the company. Young Alfred Irénée du Pont *(see Tour 5)*, a chemist who had been working in the mills, enlisted his cousins Coleman and Pierre Samuel du Pont, both of whom had gone away to work because they could not get ahead fast enough at home, and together they issued new stock without having to raise the cash to buy the company.

On July 4, 1902, a celebration was held here at the Upper Hagley Yard to commemorate the firm's 100th anniversary; there were music, dancing, and fireworks. Present were the three men who were to guide the company through a new and fabulous era; Alfred, Coleman, and Pierre du Pont were even then planning to move their offices into town *(see WIL-MINGTON)*.

The manufacture of powder continuing here for another 20 years, in 1915 an explosion added 30 more names to those who had met sudden death at the spot. As at the time of the Civil War, enemy spies were suspected. Mills were in ruins and even in Wilmington window panes were broken. The company, as always, made provision "to restore everything but life" to the families of the dead.

Tour 6B

Junction with State 52—Montchanin—(Chadd's Ford, Pa.) ; State 100.
Junction with State 52—Pennsylvania Line, 5.2 m.

Roadbed paved throughout.

State 100, or the Creek Rd., running about one mile west of the Brandywine, passes for nearly its entire length through handsome rolling country of large estates and mansions that belong mostly to the Du Ponts, their family connections, and families whose wealth has come from employment or investment in E. I. du Pont de Nemours and Co. Few wire fences are seen, but there are plenty of rail fences and old stone walls between fields and along the road.

State 100 branches north from State 52, the Kennett Pike *(see Tour 6)*, 0 *m.*, about 2.5 miles northwest of the center of Wilmington.

At 0.8 *m.* is the junction with the Buck Rd.

Right on this road to the DU PONT FAMILY CEMETERY (L) 0.3 *m. (private)*, enclosed by an iron fence and stone wall, on the hillside overlooking the site of the first Du Pont powder mills on the Brandywine. It contains scores of graves and is one of the two largest private burying grounds in Delaware. (The other is the Marsh family cemetery near Rehoboth: *see Tour 2C.)* The plot, nearly hidden from the road by shrubbery, is shaded by old trees.

Every generation of the family in America is represented here. The oldest gravestone is that of Pierre Samuel du Pont de Nemours (1739–1817), a plain horizontal slab. Most of the markers are simple marble headstones, some bearing a line or two about the career of the deceased person. One of the two shafts is a broken Greek column symbolizing the death of Lammot du Pont (1831–84), killed in an explosion at Gibbstown, N. J.; he was the father of the current president of the company *(see Tour 6A)*. The inscription on the headstone of Thomas Coleman du Pont (1863–1930), financier, road-builder, and Senator, reads:

> Unselfish, kind, generous, his achievements
> made smooth the path of many dearly loved.

The grave of one of the most noted members of the clan, Alfred I. du Pont, is not here. His body lies at the base of his Carillon Tower visible across the Brandywine *(see Tour 5)*.

At 0.4 *m.* is the entrance (L) to ELEUTHERIAN MILLS *(private)*, the Crowninshield estate on the Brandywine. The 95-acre property of Jacob Broom, cottonmiller and signer of the Constitution, was bought in 1802 by Eleuthère Irénée du Pont as the site for the powder mills he and his brother Victor planned to build. That year he built a house for his family newly-arrived from France—the center section of the present stone-and-stucco mansion of Eleutherian Mills on the steep bluff above the creek. His son Henry du Pont, grandfather of the present owner (the former Louise du Pont), added the two smaller wings to the three-story house in 1843. The architecture of the house clearly reflects the taste of the builder in the simplicity of design and detail. A porch with delicate iron-grillwork, originally facing the driveway, has been removed and placed on the creek side of the house for the lovely view of the Brandywine valley below. The house is furnished throughout in early-American style; many of the pieces of old furniture are of great value. There is a collection of early American prints and lithographs, including a rare set of colored drawings of old steam locomotives. Below the house the ruins of powder mills have become parts of terraced gardens; other "ruins" are artificial. Various kinds of Scottish heather are among the garden specialties that annually attract members of the Garden Club of America.

A few yards southwest of the house is the small one-and-a-half story ORIGINAL OFFICE BUILDING of the powder company, built in 1802 of native stone. It has been made into a guest house for Eleutherian Mills. Beyond this is a large stone building, once a COAL HOUSE where willow trees were reduced to charcoal, an essential ingredient of black powder. Still visible are the holes in the walls that gave access to the furnaces. Stored in the building is a Conestoga powder-wagon built in 1802 and perfectly preserved; it is supposed to be one of the wagons that laboriously hauled black powder through the wilderness to Commodore Perry for use in fighting the British on Lake Erie in the War of 1812.

On the hillside below the coal house is a little two-story stone house, built early in the 18th century, whose walls show the original yellow mortar between the stones. Here Eleuthère Irénée du Pont and his family spent the winter of 1802–3, awaiting completion of the larger house on the hill. He complained of the "damp air of the creek." Originally there were four rooms on the first floor, but as remodeled, the building has but one large downstairs room with a large open fireplace. This little house is also furnished with early American pieces.

At **0.8** *m.* is CHRIST CHURCH CHRISTIANA HUNDRED *(Episcopal: Sun. services at 11),* built in 1856 of Brandywine granite in Gothic style. Du Ponts and other country families have worshipped at this spot, however, since 1848, when Episcopal services first were held in a building erected for the Brandywine Manufacturers' Sunday School, incorporated in 1817. A Sunday school had been founded the previous year by E. I. du Pont and his daughter, Mrs. Ferdinand Bauduy. The building and congregation are affiliated with the Protestant Episcopal Diocese of Delaware.

In this simple little building with carved oak pews, columns, and groined arches, many baptisms, confirmations, weddings, and funerals of the Du Pont family have taken place. The most noted recent wedding here, that of Ethel du Pont and Franklin Delano Roosevelt, Jr. *(see Tour 6),* was performed by the Rev. Endicott Peabody, D.D., headmaster of Groton School in Connecticut, which the Roosevelts attended, and by the Rev. Frederick T. Ashton, rector of this church.

At 1 *m.* on State 100 is an entrance (R) to DILWYNE FARMS *(private),* the estate and tile-roofed home of the late R. R. M. Carpenter, an executive of the Du Pont Company. On the estate is an old SODA HOUSE, formerly used in making powder, which the owner has made into a sound-equipped theater where motion pictures are sometimes shown to invited guests before release to first-run commercial theaters. Mr. Carpenter was a noted big-game hunter, and a large room in the soda house contains the mounted heads of wild beasts killed by him in North America, Africa, and elsewhere. His estate on the Bohemia River near Cecilton, Md., is a feeding ground for thousands of wild Canada geese that spend the winter grazing on sprouting wheat *(see MARYLAND GUIDE).*

MONTCHANIN, 1.4 *m.* (R), is a quiet hamlet with a post office and railroad station. It was named in honor of Anne Alexandrine de Montchanin, mother of Pierre Samuel du Pont, the emigrant, by Col. Henry A. du Pont of Winterthur, who was president of the Wilmington and Northern R.R. before it was acquired by the Reading System. Colonel du Pont also gave the names Granogue and Guyencourt *(see below)* to stations on the line, after places in France associated with the family. For the Du Pont-Roosevelt wedding in 1937, President Roosevelt's special train was switched to a siding here *(see above and Tour 6).*

At 2.3 *m.* is the junction with an improved lane.

Left on this lane **0.2** *m.* to a small shingled building that is WINTERTHUR STATION AND POST OFFICE on the Reading R.R., which here crosses Winterthur, the estate of Henry F. du Pont *(see Tour 6).* Though the lane is privately maintained and the facilities at the station are used chiefly by the owner and employees of the estate, the public has free access.

At 2.5 *m.* is the junction with a crossroad, where State 100 turns L.

Right on this road is ROCKLAND, 1 *m.,* on the Brandywine, scene of a paper mill and a number of old stone houses.

GUYENCOURT, 3.3 *m.* (R) is a Reading R.R. station. A post office here, serving nearby estates, was discontinued in 1937.

SMITH'S BRIDGE, BEAVER VALLEY

At 3.9 *m.* is an entrance (R) to GRANOGUE *(private)*, the large stone residence of Irénée du Pont, brother of Pierre S. and Lammot du Pont, and past president (1919–26) of E. I. du Pont de Nemours and Co. The house is on a hilltop and has a view of hills and valleys for miles around. The Reading R.R. tracks almost encircle the base of the hill.

At 4.1 *m.* is the junction with the Beaver Valley Rd.

Right on this road to GRANOGUE STATION AND POST OFFICE, **0.8** *m.* (R), adjoining the Granogue estate *(see above)* of Irénée du Pont. Several old stone houses cluster nearby.

At **1.4** *m.* on the Beaver Valley Rd. is SMITH'S BRIDGE over Brandywine Creek. It was built in 1839, has a span of 139 feet and (1953) is the one remaining covered bridge still in use in the State. The purpose of the roof and sides was to protect the floor planking from the weather. A car passing through makes echoes like rumbling thunder.

At 5 *m.* on State 100 is (L) the entrance to MEADOWS-ON-THE-BRANDYWINE *(private)*, the estate of Norman P. Rood. The Wilmington Horse Show for many years was held here in the narrow valley bordered by wooded hills. The show, under the direction of Deborah Rood, daughter of the owner of the estate, had become one of the most important in the East. Following Mr. Rood's death the estate was sold.

The BRANDYWINE CREEK is visible to the R.

State 100 crosses the Pennsylvania Line, 5.2 *m.,* 3 miles south of Chadd's Ford, Pa.

Tour 6C

Junction with State 52—Yorklyn—(Kennett Square, Pa.); State 82.
Junction with State 52—Pennsylvania Line, 5.6 *m.*
Roadbed paved throughout.

This route passes through a hilly, wooded region of large estates alternating with small farms—a grain, dairy, and fox-hunting country.

State 82, the Yorklyn Rd., branches west from State 52, the Kennett Pike, 0 *m.*, about 4 miles northwest of Wilmington.

At 0.4 *m.* is the junction with a paved private lane.

Left on this lane to the VALLEY GARDEN, **0.1** *m. (open except Sat. and Sun. in April and May),* the property of Mrs. Ellen C. du Pont Wheelwright of Goodstay *(see Tour 6).* One of the show places in the vicinity of Wilmington, this "naturalistic treatment of a neglected stream" in a little valley was landscaped for Mrs. Wheelwright's mother, Mrs. Coleman du Pont (1863–1937), by Wheelwright and Stevenson of Philadelphia; Robert Wheelwright, a partner, became the husband of the present owner. The firm was employed to restore The Rocks on the Christiana River, landing-place of the Swedes *(see WILMINGTON),* and has landscaped stretches of the Du Pont Blvd.

One quarter mile long and several hundred yards wide, confined by wooded ridges on either side, the Valley Garden was developed along the course of a little brook that cut a deep gash through a pasture and barnyard. The barnyard and farm buildings gave place to grass, flowers, shrubs, and trees. The brook was dammed at intervals to make small ponds now bordered with iris. An old apple-and-pear orchard was left to bloom at the west end of the valley. Daffodils, tulips, hyacinths, and other flowering bulbs form carpets of bright color in spring and fall. The native dogwood, alder, and shadblow are supplemented by many varieties of exotic and naturalized flowering plants. Peacocks strut about, startling visitors from time to time with their raucous cries. A driveway one-half mile long encircles the valley.

About three-fourths of all the trees, plants, and bulbs were transplanted here in 1930 from Mrs. Coleman du Pont's Old Mill Garden a mile to the west, before the site was submerged by the Hoopes Reservoir. (The Old Mill itself, a stone building erected in 1732, restored and equipped by the Du Ponts as a summer home, was also condemned for the reservoir.)

At 0.8 *m.* the highway crosses the northeast end of the Edgar M. Hoopes Reservoir *(see Tour 6),* on a causeway.

THE OLD WALNUT GREEN SCHOOLHOUSE *(private)* at 1.2 *m.* is a small stone structure built about 1780 and used as a school in 1790. In 1918 this old white landmark was rehabilitated and a wooden addition made by Mrs. Henry B. Thompson, a nearby resident, whose efforts have saved from oblivion other more important buildings including the Old Town Hall and Bank of Delaware *(see WILMINGTON);* she was a daughter of Maj. Gen. James H. Wilson, Civil War cavalry leader *(see STOCKFORD: Tour 1).*

At 2.1 *m.* is the junction with a paved road.

Left on this road to MOUNT CUBA, 0.5 *m.*, a tiny hamlet of old stone houses and an abandoned sawmill. Its name was derived from an estate called Cuba Rock owned by Cornelius Hallahan, a well-to-do Irishman who came to America in 1730 and purchased a 250-acre tract on Red Clay Creek from Letitia Penn, a daughter of William Penn. That year one of the earliest Roman Catholic services in Delaware was held on his estate.

Mount Cuba was a legendary headquarters of Sandy Flash, a locally-famous highwayman of southeastern Pennsylvania. Tradition says his real name was Capt. James Fitzgerald, a deserter from the British army at the Battle of the Brandywine. As portrayed in Bayard Taylor's *The Story of Kennett*, a romantic novel in which all the characters were said to represent real persons, Sandy Flash was a Robin Hood type of fellow. His accomplice was Deborah Smith who worked in various prosperous homes and informed Flash of her employers' movements, especially when they carried cash with them on journeys. He was finally captured and hanged, it is said, through the agency of Deborah Smith, who had quarreled with him. Another headquarters of the outlaw is said to have been the Crooked Billet House on the Kennett Pike near Wilmington.

Northwest of 2.5 *m.* the Yorklyn road follows the winding and rocky RED CLAY CREEK. In recent years the water itself has been colored red— not from the banks but from chemicals dumped into the stream by a vulcanized-fibre plant at Yorklyn. Since the pollution of the water there have been no fish in the creek. An ancient COVERED BRIDGE, 3.3 *m.* (L), still in place across the stream, has been closed to traffic since 1922 and is now used only as a footpath to the houses on the opposite bank. At 3.5 *m.* the road itself formerly crossed another covered bridge now replaced by the modern sturdy cement span. A series of hills 300 feet high (L) is the nearest thing in Delaware to a mountain range.

YORKLYN, 4.8 *m.* (176 alt., 335 pop.), on Red Clay Creek, is an industrial center whose old stone houses are flanked by a snuff mill, a paper plant, and a vulcanized fiber plant. Part of the site in 1684 was on William Penn's extensive Staning Manor. The hamlet was known as Auburn Mills before the name Yorklyn was applied. In 1708 the Quakers established a meeting here and in 1783 a road was laid out connecting the settlement with the Hockessin Friends' Meeting House *(see Tour 7)*.

The HELME SNUFF PLANT *(no admittance)* is housed in old and new buildings (L) that fill the surrounding air with a pungent odor. One building has a stone with the inscription, "John Garrett—1782." Another bears the date "1846." Though the era of the silver snuffbox is gone, the old Yorklyn mills have worked steadily through the years. The latest available national production total, including that of Yorklyn, is for the year 1933 when 46 million pounds of snuff were ground, a gain of 12 million pounds over the figure for 1908.

Here John Garrett, Jr., established the water-power mill that was to lay the foundations of the Garrett fortune, now valued at $17,000,000; many thousand claimants have been waging legal warfare over this estate since the death in 1930 of Mrs. Henrietta Garrett, of Philadelphia. The manufacture of snuff in this country was for generations largely controlled by the Garrett family until they relinquished the business in 1895.

SNUFF MILL, YORKLYN

Except for the introduction of machinery to speed production, the process of refining snuff from tobacco is much the same today as it was generations ago. After the tobacco is removed from its hogshead containers, it is shaken by hand and bundled. Later the bundles are dipped in water and the tobacco is piled up for casing. It then is ground by machinery into small pieces, repacked and sent to the curing room, high in the mill building. During the seven to nine weeks in which the tobacco remains in that room, it ferments and gains strength. When sufficient time has elapsed, it is run through cylinders and is sent, a second time, to the curing room, for further refining and strengthening. After the tobacco is given a thorough drying in big cylinders, comes the last stage in the process, grinding the tobacco into snuff. Boxing, labeling and stamping make the product ready for the market.

ANTIQUE AUTO MUSEUM (L), 4.9 *m.,* of Mr. T. Clarence Marshall *(no admission charge).* On exhibit are forty or more automobiles dating from 1900. Included are 25 Stanley Steamers, all in running condition. Also included in the collection are a Doble Steamer, only 30 of which were manufactured; Locomobile Steamers, Pierce Arrows, Packards, Fords, and a Baker Electric.

State 82 crosses the Pennsylvania Line, 5.6 *m.,* about 4 miles southeast of Kennett Square, Pa.

Tour 7

(Lancaster, Pa.)—Hockessin—Marshallton—Newport—New Castle; State 41. The old Newport and Gap Turnpike.

Pennsylvania Line—Junction US 40, 12 m.

Roadbed paved throughout.

State 41 across northern Delaware is, in summer, a heavily-traveled route between the Middle West and the New Jersey ocean resorts. Within its brief course it descends from one of the highest elevations in Delaware —356 feet at the State border—to the tidal level of the Delaware River and its marshes. The crisp air of the rocky hills averages 5° to 10° cooler, all year round, than at New Castle, and the tempo of life and speech at the northern end of the route contrasts noticeably with the slower rhythm of the humid lowlands. Old stone houses of the hills give place to the warmer-toned brick buildings of tidewater, where stone was not available.

Between Pennsylvania and Newport the route is that of the old Newport and Gap Turnpike, running from the rich grain country of southeastern Pennsylvania to navigation on the Christiana Creek (or River). The Pennsylvania section was authorized in 1807 and the Delaware section in 1808; it was the first of the toll turnpikes in the State, and one of the first highways to be improved with stone. Until the railroad era, a steady stream of heavy wagons rumbled over it bringing grain down to the vessels at Newport and Christiana.

State 41 crosses the Pennsylvania Line, 0 *m.*, 4 miles southeast of Avondale, Pa. *(see Pa. Tour 29)*.

At 0.8 *m.* is the junction with the Valley Rd.

Left on this road to a fork, **0.5** *m.*
1. Right **0.6** *m.* at the fork to (L) HOCKESSIN FRIENDS' MEETING HOUSE *(First Day meetings at 10)*. Erected in 1738 and enlarged in 1745, this low stone building with frame addition commands a superb view of the green Hockessin Valley. Still here are the high stepping-blocks, where the dignified Quakers alighted from their carriages, and the long carriage-sheds at the rear. Across the road (R) the ancient cemetery, with its little Quaker headstones, contains magnificent boxwood that is scarcely matched in Delaware except by that in the graveyard of Little Creek Meeting House *(see Tour 13)* in Kent County.

HOCKESSIN (Ind., *place of many foxes)*, 1.2 *m.* (350 alt., 354 pop.), one of the highest settlements in Delaware, is a neat village built on a long hillside. Industries are the growing of mushrooms in numerous dark and odorous mushroom houses, and the mining of kaolin or China clay from large deep pits. The clay is shipped to pottery makers elsewhere. The village is on the Landenburg Branch of the B. & O. R.R., but passenger service has been discontinued.

The tract where Hockessin stands was part of Letitia Manor, a 15,000-acre estate given by William Penn to his daughter Letitia in 1701. It was soon broken up and sold to settlers.

At 2.5 *m.* (R) the line of great white pines leads to SUNNY HILLS SCHOOL, a private, non-sectarian, "progressive"-type country day and boarding school for boys and girls from the nursery through high school; it was established in 1930 on this hilltop farm of 80 acres.

At 2.7 *m.* (L) is the junction with State 48 *(see Tour 7A)*, the old Lancaster Pike.

At 4.7 *m.* (R) is the EMILY P. BISSELL SANITARIUM, the State institution for persons suffering from tuberculosis. The name was Brandywine Sanitarium until changed by the 1953 Legislature to honor the good friend of the institution. The Bissell Sanitarium includes the Edgewood Sanitarium (for Negroes) under one administration. The latter is housed near the main building, which was recently constructed with all modern equipment and facilities at a cost of two and a half million dollars. The total bed capacity is 800. South of the entrance on the left side of the main highway is SUNNYBROOK NURSERY SCHOOL for blind children. This was formerly the Sunnybrook Cottage for tubercular children.

The T.B. sanitariums receive part of their support from the sale of Christmas Seals, originated in this country in 1907 by Miss Emily P. Bissell of Wilmington, who was trying to raise funds for anti-tuberculosis work in Delaware, and developed a plan that had been used in Denmark for the purpose. The annual sale of Christmas Seals pours some millions into the "warchest" of the National Tuberculosis Association. At Brandywine Sanitarium in 1937 a bronze plaque in honor of Miss Bissell, who was still active in the work, was erected by the association on the site of the little frame building that was supported by 1907 receipts.

At 5.2 *m.* is the junction with a side road.

Left on this road to the SITE OF BRANDYWINE SPRINGS HOTEL, **0.1** *m.* (R), where a jungle of briars and trees has recaptured the hilltop that from 1827 to 1845 was a noted resort. A huge hotel, having columns reaching to the roof above the triple veranda, was surrounded by great stables, ice houses, meat houses, and quarters for the Negro hotel servants and the personal servants of the guests. Enclosed and covered springs of chalybeate (iron-containing) water were ostensibly the attractions that brought hundreds of aristocratic families and many famous personages for short or long summer holidays. The noted spa appealed especially to the tobacco and cotton planters of Virginia, the Carolinas, Georgia, and Tennessee, some of whom arrived in four-horse coaches followed by other vehicles containing black valets and ladies' maids, and mountains of baggage. Other families came by steamboat up the Chesapeake to Frenchtown, Md., and thence by stage. While the gentlemen relaxed in white linen clothes, drinking mint juleps and Bourbon whiskey, their ladies gossiped, displayed their needlework, or walked under the great old oaks. Southern belles danced tirelessly with their young gentlemen, or rode horseback with them.

In 1832 the place was bought by Matthew Newkirk, a wealthy Philadelphian, who spent money lavishly in remodeling the hotel and beautifying the grounds, and placed white marble statuary under the trees. Guests of this period included Henry Clay, Daniel Webster, James Buchanan, Jefferson Davis, and Robert E. Lee.

In 1951 the State Park Commission acquired 57 acres at a cost of $45,000 and in 1953 the State appropriated $67,500 to start landscaping the park and developing it into a recreational area. The fine old trees and other natural features will be preserved. A landscape architect and horticulturist will be in charge. One of the consultants was New York State Park Commissioner Robert Moses.

At the foot of the wooded hillside is the COUNCIL OAK, more than 15 feet in girth, under which Washington and Lafayette are said to have met before the Battle of the Brandywine, Sept. 11, 1777.

MARSHALLTON, 6.6 *m.* (1,500 pop.) *(see Tour 8)* is at the junction with State 2 *(see Tour 8)*.

At 6.9 *m.* (R) KRUSE SCHOOL (State industrial for colored girls) occupying several stuccoed buildings, was incorporated in 1920 to care for delinquent Negro girls 14 to 21 years old. The school activities include education through high school for those able to assimilate it, and domestic arts. Many of the students are paroled to work in private homes.

BELVIDERE, 7 *m.,* is a Negro village of long existence. One of the few Negro Roman Catholic congregations in Delaware attend the Chapel of Our Mother of Mercy, in charge of the St. Joseph's Society, better known as the Josephite Fathers.

NEWPORT, 8.2 *m.* (20 alt., 1,171 pop.), on the Christiana River and the main line of the Pennsylvania R.R., is one of the old towns of New Castle County. Several 18th-century houses still stand, overshadowed by factories along the creek, as the Christiana is called locally. The largest industry is the manufacture of paint pigments; smaller plants turn out fibre products, awnings, burial vaults, pottery clay, and other products.

The village was laid out in 1735 by John Justis, who called it Newport Ayre. Like Christiana and Wilmington, Newport became important as a flour-milling and grain-shipping center. Grain wagons from Pennsylvania and Maryland discharged their loads into granaries, mills, and vessels, and loaded up with merchandise for the return trip. In 1825 Newport was at its flood tide of prosperity, with five stores and six taverns. In 1837 the railroad passed through, but the village never grew to rival Wilmington, as it hoped, becoming instead a suburb of that city. Newport was the birthplace of Oliver Evans (1755–1819), who has been called the "first great American inventor." He built steam engines as early as 1802, and used steam power to run boats, vehicles, and a dredging machine; his power-driven equipment revolutionized the handling of grain first in Delaware and then throughout the country.

The former INN, NW. cor. James and Market Sts., a yellow-stuccoed brick building containing stores, was one of Newport's busiest taverns. Former Governor John Penn of Pennsylvania, here in 1788, was amused by a "war of words between two rustics completely drunk," but he praised the accommodations. The old DOUBLE HOUSE (*private*), next to the Inn on Market St., has walls of Flemish-bond brick. The MYERS or PARKIN HOUSE (*private*), SE. cor. Market and Johns Sts., part of it built during the middle of the 18th century, is a carefully preserved brick house of great charm, with long, low proportions. Heavy pent eaves extend along the front. Though the house seems to have been built in sections at successive intervals, the architectural style is 18th century throughout; there is fine woodwork inside. The GALLOWAY HOUSE (*private*), W. side of Johns St., S. of Market St., is a little gambrel-roofed brick house built about 1730 upon a stone foundation. The woodwork matches that of the Myers house so exactly that the same artisan must have worked on both houses.

At 10.7 *m.* is the junction with US 13 (*see Tour 1*).

(R) is 1500-acre New Castle County Airport with busy landings and take-offs of military and commercial planes. The 332nd Fighter-Intercepter Squadron here has the safest flying record of any Air Force squadron in Eastern U. S. and jet-propelled two-seater used has lowest accident rate of any jet plane in the Air Force. The primary purpose of this Air Force installation at New Castle Airport is to provide air defense of vital Delaware River industrial area. On part of the field Atlantic Aviation Service, Inc. maintains complete non-scheduled and charter service (*see Du Pont Airport, Tour 7A*). A US Weather Bureau station operates at the Airport.

Between this point and New Castle the farms on both sides of the road are part of New Castle Common, from which the revenue goes to the town of New Castle (*see Tour 4*).

At 12 *m.* is the junction with State 273 (*see Tour 4*), at the western edge of New Castle (*see NEW CASTLE*).

◄◄◄◄◄◄◄◄◄◄◄◄◄◄◄◄◄◄◄◄◄◄◄☼►►►►►►►►►►►►►►►►►►►►►►►

Tour 7A

Junction with State 41—Wilmington—(Deepwater Point, N. J.); State 48.
Junction with US 40 via New Castle Avenue—Delaware River Shore, 13.2 *m.*
Roadbed paved throughout.

Accommodations in Wilmington.

This route, known west of Wilmington as the Lancaster Pike, runs through hilly Piedmont country.

State 48 branches southeast from State 41, 0 *m. (see Tour 7),* the Newport and Gap Turnpike, 1.5 *m.* southeast of Hockessin.

COFFEE RUN CEMETERY, 0.8 *m.* (R), enclosed by an iron fence, was established in 1786 or earlier and is believed to have been the first Roman Catholic burial ground in the State *(see MT. CUBA: Tour 6C).* Within the enclosure, to the L. of the entrance, is the SITE OF ST. MARY'S CHURCH (Coffee Run Church), the first Roman Catholic Church in Delaware; it was a log structure which Father Kenny *(see below)* used also as living quarters before the completion of his stone rectory adjoining. With the church as his base, he attended five other missions in Delaware and nearby Maryland and Pennsylvania, and almost unaided kept Catholicism alive in the region during that early period. After the erection of other churches nearby, services in the church he built here were discontinued in 1884 and the building decayed until it was finally razed in 1908. Wooden cross and iron bell were saved. Under a restoration program begun 1952, the Knights of Columbus have built a tiny chapel on the early site.

The FATHER KENNY HOUSE (R), 0.9 *m. (private),* a two-and-one-half-story dwelling of stone and frame, bears a marble marker in the east wing inscribed "P K 1812." It was built by the Rev. Patrick Kenny (1761–1840), born in Dublin, Ireland, who came to America in 1804 and became a pioneer Roman Catholic priest in Delaware.

At 1 *m.* the road crosses small COFFEE RUN. One story as to the origin of the name is that the water was coffee-colored; another, that tramps used the water in making coffee.

At 2 *m.* is the junction with a side road.

Right on this road to the EXPERIMENTAL STATION (L) of the Hercules Powder Co., **0.3** *m. (no admittance),* a group of buff-colored tile and brick buildings. On the property, for the use of employees and their friends, are a clubhouse, golf course, and tennis courts. The Hercules company has had a nominally separate existence from the Du Pont company since 1912, when it was ordered severed from the latter under anti-trust proceedings. Hercules specializes in sporting powder and commercial explosives, none of which is manufactured in Delaware.

At 3.9 *m.* is the DU PONT AIRPORT (L); the small building (R) bear-

ing formerly, the large letters "WDUP" (now removed) served for some
years as a combined radio beacon and short wave broadcasting station.

The privately-developed 100-acre field, rated a commercial airport by
the Department of Commerce is the property of Henry Belin du Pont, a
well-known sportsman-aviator. Parts of the airport are leased from Mr.
Du Pont by Atlantic Aviation Service, Inc., which has a complete non-
scheduled air-carrier and charter service; and by All American Engineering
Company, which maintains an aeronautical research and development plant.
The airfield's two main runways are 2,600 and 2,110 feet long. The field
is lighted at night according to Federal regulations.

At 4.9 *m.* is SILVERBROOK CEMETERY (R). Beneath a 5-foot monument
there are buried in one grave 10 identified and several unidentified bodies
of victims of a Du Pont powder explosion on the Brandywine *(see Tour
6A)*. The cause of death is not specified on the stone, only "Died November 30, 1915."

Near here is the SITE OF A TOLL GATE for the Lancaster Pike, which
was completed in 1817 between Wilmington and the older Newport and
Gap Turnpike *(see Tour 7)*, and was one of the first highways in the
State to be surfaced with stone. It was a private enterprise until taken over
by the County in 1877.

State 48 follows Lancaster Ave. to Union St.; L. on Union St. to 4th
St.; R. on 4th St. to Market St.

WILMINGTON, 7.2 *m.* (80 alt., 110,356 pop.) *(see WILMING-
TON)*.

Points of Interest. Old Swedes Church, The Rocks, Old Town Hall, Rodney
Square, Du Pont and Nemours Buildings, Public Library, Delaware Art Center,
Brandywine Park, and others.

At Wilmington is the junction with US 13 *(see Tour 1)*, US 202 *(see
Tour 5)*, State 2 *(see Tour 8)*, State 52 *(see Tour 6)*, and the Rising Sun
Rd. *(see Tour 6A)*.

Southeast of Market St., State 48 follows 4th St. to a lift bridge over the
Christiana River. Near the approach to this bridge (L) is the Wilson Line
steamboat office. Across the bridge Christiana Ave. (L) runs east to the
entrance of the Wilmington Marine Terminal *(see Wilmington)*. Heald St.
(R) branches right at the fork to join US 13. At the fork (L) on New
Castle Ave. to interchange for Delaware Memorial Bridge, 13.2 *m.* to
Deepwater Point, N.J. New Castle Ave., also known as the "Wilmington-
New Castle Road" and the "River Road," runs straight to New Castle, 6 *m.*
(see NEW CASTLE).

← ← ← ← ← ← ← ← ← ← ← ← ← ← ← ← ← ← ← ⚙ → → → → → → → → → → → → → → → →

Tour 8

Wilmington—Newark—(Elkton, Md.); State 2.
Wilmington—Maryland Line, 15.4 m.
The route is paralleled by the Pennsylvania R.R., and the B. & O. R.R., and followed by the Delaware Bus Co.
Roadbed paved throughout.

Accommodations in towns.

State 2 runs across the northern part of Delaware, skirting the fall line where the foothills of the Appalachian Piedmont merge into the coastal plain of the Delmarva Peninsula. For nearly three centuries the rich soil of this region has yielded a good living to farmers; dairying is an important industry here.

WILMINGTON, 0 *m.* (80 alt., 106,597 pop.) *(see WILMINGTON).*

Points of Interest. Old Swedes Church, The Rocks, Old Town Hall, Rodney Square, Du Pont and Nemours Buildings, Public Library, Delaware Art Center, Brandywine Park, and others.

Wilmington is at the junction with US 13 *(see Tour 1),* US 202 *(see Tour 5),* State 48 *(see Tour 7A),* State 52 *(see Tour 6),* and the Rising Sun Rd. *(see Tour 6A).*

From Pennsylvania Ave. *(see Tour 6),* State 2 follows Union St. out of the city.

ELSMERE, 1.8 *m.* (5,314 pop.), is a residential outpost of Wilmington stretching along the highway.

At PRICE'S CORNER, 3.6 *m.,* is the junction with three side roads.

1. Right sharply on the first side road to the FERRIS SCHOOL FOR BOYS (L), 1.2 *m.* *(visiting hours, 1st and 3d Sun. of each month, 1-3:30)* housed in several brick buildings grouped around a yellow-stuccoed farmhouse. This school for delinquent boys was opened 1886 under a bequest from John Ferris, and taken over by the State in 1919. An excellent program of care, retraining, and rehabilitation on a 190-acre farm provided for about 100 white and Negro boys.

2. Right on the third side road to the NEW CASTLE COUNTY WORKHOUSE (L), 0.5 *m.* *(visiting hours, Mon. and Wed. 1:30-4 and Sat. 9-4),* a group of large brick buildings. This institution was authorized by the State in 1899; prisoners were transferred from the old jail at New Castle in 1901. All New Castle County prisoners, and long-term (10 years or more) prisoners from the two lower counties are confined here. The prison is supported by appropriations from the three counties and by income from the prison shops and farm of 500 acres. Here, as at the other county jails, stands a whipping post *(see Tour 2, Sec. b).*

At 0.7 *m.* on this side road is (L) the GREENBANK MILL *(open by permission),* one of the few water-powered gristmills still running in Delaware; it is a three-story frame building with a smaller stone mill building attached. Red Clay Creek furnishes power for two turbines which turn burrs and other machinery for the grinding of feed and meal. The frame building, now clapboarded outside, was built in 1790; some of its early machinery was purchased from Oliver Evans of Newport, noted millwright and inventor of that time. The stone wing of the building was erected in 1812 as a woolen mill on the site formerly occupied by a log mill known as the "Swedes' Mill."

The whitewashed LOG HOUSE (R), 3.7 m. (now a roadside market), is believed to have been built in the 17th century. The house has one and one-half stories, and measures about 18 by 24 feet; it is of the "crib" type of construction with logs notched at the ends and laid horizontally on each other. The logs are roughly squared and still show the marks of axe or adze. The interior is lathed and plastered, with paneling and partitions of plain wide boards. A long low fireplace, stone outside but brick inside, is on the ground floor, with a smaller one of brick upstairs.

The land on which the house stands was granted in 1678 to Johan Anderson Stalkofta (Swedish, steel coat), or Stalcop, who came to New Sweden not later than 1644. A son, John Stalcop, gave the land on which Old Swedes Church was erected (see WILMINGTON). The Swedes were familiar with the crib type of log house construction in old Sweden, and it was natural for them to employ it here. English settlers copied it from the Swedes, for the English at first planted the logs in the ground, like a fence or stockade, to form the walls of their houses—a practice then used in England for the ruder sort of timber construction.

At 3.9 m. is the junction with State 41 (see Tour 7).

MARSHALLTON, 4.9 m. (about 1,500 pop.), is an unincorporated village strung along the highway for about two miles. It was named for John Marshall, who established a rolling mill here in 1836. This industry flourished for more than half a century, but at present a vulcanized-fibre plant occupies the old rolling mill building. Within the village, near the bridge over Red Clay Creek, is the marked SITE OF EARTHWORKS thrown up by Washington's army in 1777 prior to the Battle of the Brandywine.

At 5.8 m. is the junction with State 7 (see Tour 11).

ST. JAMES' EPISCOPAL CHURCH (L), 7.3 m. (open by permission; Sun. services at 11), was built in 1820 of native stone that has since been plastered over; the belfry was added in the late 1890's. Except for this and minor additions, the exterior of the church is of Greek Revival design. The interior is of early 19th century construction with old box pews on the ground floor and unpainted pews in the gallery that is built on three sides. The church and yard are enclosed by a low stone wall, begun in 1817. Large trees shade the churchyard and also provide a refuge for blackbirds, which became so troublesome that a recent rector tried to drive them away by discharging roman candles, but succeeded only in setting the church on fire.

The earliest stone in the churchyard bears the date 1726. As early as 1708, a large part of the Anglican congregation at New Castle came from this White Clay Creek neighborhood. In 1717 James Robinson gave about 10 acres of land for a "Church and Schoolhouse," and in that year was completed the first church, a frame structure measuring 32 by 22 feet; it was called St. James or White Clay Creek, and at the time was said to be "as fair and complete an oratory, as any not made of Brick within this Governmt." In 1764 the White Clay Creek Church had about 60 families —"an orderly and religious people"—and was in a "flourishing condition," in contrast to the New Castle church, which was "but very thin of people." The latter persisted in considering the St. James Church an appendage or "chapel of ease" to New Castle, but the country congregation even prior to 1729 stoutly maintained its independent status. In the 1760's the St. James group built a new brick church in Newport, then deemed a better situation than the old one. However, sentiment and property rights kept alive interest in this old site and the present building was erected.

At 8.2 *m.* is (L) the main entrance to DELAWARE PARK, opened in 1937 as one of the finest race tracks in the East *(race meet held for one month in summer),* and the first track built in Delaware since the legalizing of racetrack betting in 1933.

There are a one-mile flat-racing track and two steeplechase tracks. The grandstand, seating 8,000 persons, is entirely covered, and there is standing room for several thousand more spectators between the stand and track. This area is sloped and terraced for an unimpeded view of the racing, and the whole property is landscaped and planted.

The only betting allowed is that done with pari-mutuel machines within the grounds. A 20-cent tax on admissions, as well as 3 percent of total sums wagered, go to the State.

WHITE CLAY CREEK PRESBYTERIAN CHURCH (R), 10.5 *m. (Sun. services at 11)* stands at the foot of Polly Drummond Hill, formerly Meeting House Hill. This rather large, plain, two-story brick structure was erected in 1855 to replace the previous building which had stood for 103 years. The stone wall enclosing a part of the ground was built in 1785.

At the church is the junction with a side road.

1. Right on this road up Polly Drummond Hill is the old three-story ANDREW GRAY HOUSE (R), 0.4 *m. (private),* built of native stone probably in the last quarter of the 18th century, although one wing may be older. Few changes had evidently been made in the house from the time of its erection until the present owner, former Judge Hugh M. Morris, purchased it. In the restoration made in recent years the fine old features have been retained—the main stairway with delicate spindles, the many mantels, some ornate, some plain, the woodwork with molded trim, the floorboards with numerous knots, the battened doors and shutters, the traceried fanlight and the enormous kitchen fireplace.

At 1 *m.* at the top of Polly Drummond Hill, is the junction with a dirt lane; R. on this lane a few hundred feet is the SITE OF THE FIRST WHITE CLAY CREEK PRESBYTERIAN CHURCH (L). The tombstones bear later dates than the earliest (1734) in the cemetery of the nearby present church.

There was a meeting house here as early as 1723; in that year the Presbytery met here and suspended the pastor for "prophaning the Lord's Day by washing himself in a Creek." In 1739 the famous evangelist George Whitefield held a "four days meeting" here, and is said to have preached—without benefit of amplifiers—to an open-air audience of 8,000—a vast gathering for those days.

2. Left on the side road from State 2 is the old ENGLAND MANOR HOUSE AND MILL, 0.5 *m.* (L). The brick manor house is on a small elevation with a terrace and garden sloping down to the shaded banks of White Clay Creek. The mill is at the foot of this elevation.

The front or upper part of the house bears the date 1747, and its design and construction are of the finest colonial type. Pent eaves are a feature of the front of the house, and the effect is repeated by extending the cornice across the gable ends. The walls, slightly thicker at the base, are stepped back at the first floor line by a molded brick water table. Larger than usual, the brick are laid in Flemish-bond with black glazed headers. Small recesses appear at fairly regular intervals in the outside walls, where headers have been omitted, obviously by intention but without apparent reason. In the lower part of the house smaller size brick are used, with the Flemish-bond only on the front wall. The gable end has tapered barge boards, typical of Delaware architecture, and bears the marks of built-in Dutch ovens which have since been removed. The house is built on a high stone foundation. Especially notable are the low, wide doors and the hand-riven shingles.

The interior has been greatly altered, but retains many original features—a mantel-cupboard in the corner of one room, HL and strap hinges, battened doors, old window panes, old hand-split laths, and fireplaces and mantels, one of which is unusually large and occupies almost the entire side of the room.

The superstructure of the barn, across the road, is of modern boards, but the 8-foot stone foundation is dated 1748.

The house and mill are on part of a 600-acre tract of land purchased in 1726 by John England, who in 1723 had come from England to manage the Principio Iron Works in Maryland, and is thought to have bought this and other nearby parcels of land with the hope that they might contain iron ore. Not later than 1734 he constructed the first dam, race, and mill on the site of the present one, now called the OLD RED MILL, but formerly England's Mill. The mill is said to have been rebuilt about 1747, but the stone lower story of the present mill has the inscription "I E/1789" cut on one of the stones. The present wooden upper story, in spite of its faded red paint, was probably built later; but hand-wrought nails indicate that it too is very old.

The old undershot mill wheel was replaced some years ago by a sideshot water turbine, developing 43 horsepower, which turns a set of old millstones and other more modern machinery, and, until an electric transmission line came down this road, generated electricity for the miller's use. Many thousands of barrels of high-grade flour have been ground on this site during the past two centuries. The diverted waters of the White Clay still flow noisily through the race, but now only grind feed for local trade.

The house and mill remained in the possession of the England family until 1839. Since then the house has been owned by the Eastburn family, but the mill has changed hands many times.

On a farm adjoining White Clay Church, Capt. Robert Kirkwood, Revolutionary soldier, was born.

Near site of old ROSEVILLE MILL, 10.8 *m.* (R), the road has been straightened (1953) by new bridge from the once busy industrial community of Roseville. Here, west of the bridge, the creek descends rapidly over a bed of stones, forming one of those water-power sites so highly prized before the advent of steam and electricity. Before the Revolution the waters of the White Clay were dammed at this point; a mill on this site, owned by Capt. James Black, was used to grind meal and flour for the neighboring farmers. Prospering, half a century later it was described as a "merchant mill"—one which sold its flour on the market instead of grinding at a fixed toll for local farmers, as did the smaller "custom" mills. In 1828 there was a cotton-manufacturing plant here that operated until it burned after the Civil War. Site is now Roseville Park, residence community.

At 12.7 *m.* in the eastern end of Newark is the junction with Chapel St.

R. on Chapel St. which becomes Paper Mill Rd., to where covered wooden PAPER MILL BRIDGE, **0.5** *m.,* built in 1861 over White Clay Creek, has been replaced by a cement span. Before 1816 travelers forded the stream here.

At **0.6** *m.* is (L) the CURTIS PAPER PLANT *(open by permission),* a spread-out group of low brick buildings to the right of the milldam. The plant specializes in rag-content book and cover paper, importing some of the rags from Europe. Paper-making, Newark's oldest manufacturing enterprise, and one of the earliest in the state, was begun on this site by the Meteer family not later than 1798. The Curtis brothers, paper makers from New England, purchased the property in 1848 and rebuilt it. Again in 1887 the mill was rebuilt and its capacity enlarged. Originally called the Millford Mills, the name was later changed to the Nonantum Mills. The Curtis family continued to conduct the enterprise until 1926.

Across the road from the paper mill is the S. MINOT CURTIS HOUSE *(private),* a two-and-one-half-story brick dwelling with frame additions, painted yellow. Believed to be quite old, it stands on land deeded by William Penn in 1684. The name ELLIOTT HEIGHTS is applied to the group of modern dwellings which line the road here.

At MILFORD CROSSROADS, **2.5** *m.,* is the LOUVIERS BUILDING, new offices-in-the-country of the Du Pont Company **(L)**. Pushmobile Derby track **(R)**. At fork— R. straight ahead to wooded field **(L)** **3.2** *m.* where Mason and Dixon set up a post in June, 1764, preparatory to surveying the Mason-Dixon Line *(see Tour 9)*. The post, referred to in their journal as "the post marked West," has long since disappeared. It marked the parallel of latitude precisely 15 miles south of the southern-most point of Philadelphia, which parallel, after a long dispute between the Penns of Pennsylvania and the Calverts of Maryland, had been agreed upon as a dividing line between the two Provinces. Had "the begining of the fortieth degree of North-erne Latitude," which Penn's charter specified as the southern boundary of Penn-sylvania, meant 40° N. lat., as the Calverts claimed, Philadelphia would be in Maryland; had it meant 39° N. lat., as the Penns contended, Baltimore would be in Pennsylvania. From "the post marked West" the two English surveyors extended their line due west along this parallel, to form the official boundary between Pennsylvania and Maryland.

At **3.4** *m.* on this road is the junction with a farm lane; R. on this lane to FOX-DEN GUERNSEY FARM, **3.8** *m. (of interest to dairymen and cattle breeders).* Champion Guernsey cows of the Foxden herd are the leaders in the State. The herd of about 60 registered Guernseys are scientifically fed and are tested for disease, stabled in sanitary and fireproof quarters, and thoroughly cleaned and disinfected before being led to automatic milkers. The milk, once bottled for retail sale, is now sold only in bulk.

At **4.2** *m.* across an open field **(L)** now owned by S. Hallock du Pont was the notable china clay plant and diggings, founded 1912 by a native of Switzerland, Victor E. Ullman, who produced high grade clay used in making dishes and other chinaware articles. The 300-acre tract of land is underlain with veins of kaolin, as are similar tracts at Hockessin and other nearby places *(see Tour 7)*. The clay was shipped from Newark for manufacture elsewhere.

NEWARK, 13.2 *m.* (135 alt., 6,731 pop.) *(see NEWARK)*.

Points of Interest. University of Delaware, the Newark Academy Building, the new Haskell Laboratory of the Du Pont Company, a $2 million center (1954) *(open by permission)* for expanding research on safeguarding the health of its em-ployees and users of its products—on State 2, S.W. 3 *m.* of town. The Stine Labora-tory on the same site, an animal medicine and nutrition research center; Chrysler Tank Arsenal, paper mills, vulcanized fibre plants, and others.

At Newark is the junction with State 896 *(see Tour 9)*.

At the B. & O. R.R. tracks, Main St., is the junction with State 273.

Straight ahead on State 273 to HEAD OF CHRISTIANA PRESBYTERIAN CHURCH, **1.9** *m.* (L), locally called "Head of Christine," a large brick building erected in 1858 on the site of a log structure (1708) and a second church, of brick, erected in 1750. The annual Poultry Supper *(Oct.)* has been held here for nearly a century.

In the four-and-one-half-acre cemetery are graves of several pastors, including the Rev. George Gillespie, installed in 1713 and author in 1735 of a *Treatise Against Deists or Free Thinkers;* under his direction the second building was erected. Another stone marks the grave of the Rev. James L. Vallandigham, pastor 1853–96. (During the church's first 190 years there were only seven pastors.) The burning of the second building in 1858 was said to have been caused by boys who were smoking out a fox from beneath the flooring.

At 13.6 *m.* on State 2 is the junction with a side road.

Right on this road to a fence (L) **1.5** *m.* that runs through a field and a clump of trees to the B. & O. R.R. tracks; across the tracks is a path through a woods to the Maryland Line, about 100 yards; here at the left of the path is the PRISMATIC STONE *(see B on WEDGE MAP)*, erected in 1849 by Col. J. D. Graham of the U. S. War Department. It marks the southern point of The Wedge *(see Tour 9)*, and the point at which the line drawn due north from the Tangent Point intersects the 12-mile radius arc that is Delaware's northern boundary.

State 2 crosses the Maryland Line, 15.4 *m.*, 4 miles northeast of Elkton, Md.

At 15.5 *m.* is the junction with a private lane.

Left on the lane to a barn (R) **0.1** *m.;* in the pasture between the barn and the Penna. R.R. tracks are two stones which mark the TANGENT POINT *(see A on WEDGE MAP)*, at which the straight line between Delaware and Maryland running up the Peninsula touches the 12-mile-radius arc. The first stone, bearing the arms of the Penns and the Calverts, was placed by Mason and Dixon in 1765, and beside it stands a newer stone marking the relocation of the tangent point by Colonel Graham in 1849 *(see Tour 9)*. The Delaware-Maryland boundary between here and the Prismatic Stone, 1.5 miles north, is not a straight line but a curve, part of the 12-mile-radius arc which forms the northern boundary of Delaware. Few even of the large-scale maps portray it thus.

"The post marked West" *(see MILFORD CROSSROADS, page 455)* was replaced June, 1953, by a Brandywine granite shaft erected by Mr. S. Hallock du Pont, owner of the farm. Research data assembled by Mr. William T. Mahoney, the enthusiastic promoter of this history project, enabled Civil Engineer Leroy Haitsch to make the surveys determining the approximate site of the original Mason and Dixon post.

◄◄◄◄◄◄◄◄◄◄◄◄◄◄◄◄◄◄◄◄✿➤➤➤➤➤➤➤➤➤➤➤➤➤➤➤➤➤➤➤➤

Tour 9

(New London, Pa.)—Newark—Middletown—Junction US 13; State 896 and 71.

Pennsylvania Line—Junction US 13, 27.4 m.

Roadbed paved throughout.

Accommodations in towns and motels.

This route follows the watershed divide of the upper end of the Delmarva Peninsula. Headwaters along the way flow eastward toward the Delaware River, or westward toward the Chesapeake. The pleasant rolling countryside of western New Castle County is a grain and dairy section, its soil among the richest in the State.

State 896 crosses the Pennsylvania-Maryland Line, 0 *m.*, about 7 miles southeast of New London, Pa., and runs for a fraction of a mile through Maryland.

At 0 *m.* is the junction with a side road.

Left on this road to a farmhouse (L) 0.1 *m.;* opposite the house, on the bank of a brook, a 2-foot granite shaft marks the NORTHEAST CORNER OF MARYLAND *(see C on WEDGE MAP),* defined in 1765 by the English surveyors Charles Mason and Jeremiah Dixon, who thence ran the Pennsylvania-Maryland Boundary Line, called the Mason-Dixon Line, due west 230 miles almost to the Ohio River.

The stone set up in 1765 was replaced by Colonial boundary commissioners in 1768 with a more elaborate "crown stone" *(see Tangent Stone: Tour 8).* The latter was no longer in place—local tradition said it had been carried away for a chimney piece—when Lieutenant Colonel Graham of the United States Engineers re-established the point in 1849. In digging the hole for his marker he found a stone like others planted by Mason and Dixon. The present stone, Graham's, has the date 1849 on the north side, the letter P (for Pennsylvania) on the north and east sides, and the letter M (for Maryland) on the south and west sides. An accurate indication of present-day sovereignty would require a triangular stone with P on the north, M on the west, and because The Wedge *(see below)* has been adjudged part of Delaware, the letter D on the east side.

At 0.2 *m.* State 896 crosses the Maryland-Delaware Line.

Between this point and 0.5 *m.* the route traverses THE WEDGE, an 800-acre triangular piece of land lying between the due-north line and the 12-mile arc and north of their intersection at the Prismatic Stone *(see Tour 8).* Its ownership for many years was disputed between Pennsylvania and Delaware. Mason-and-Dixon's surveys designated it as part of Pennsylvania, as did those by Colonel Graham in 1849, but their conclusions were not accepted by Delaware and in 1893 a joint commission from both States finally awarded the tiny no-man's-land to Delaware. The commission's action was ratified by Pennsylvania in 1897 and by Delaware and Congress in 1921. Before the dispute was settled, duels, prize fights, and similar

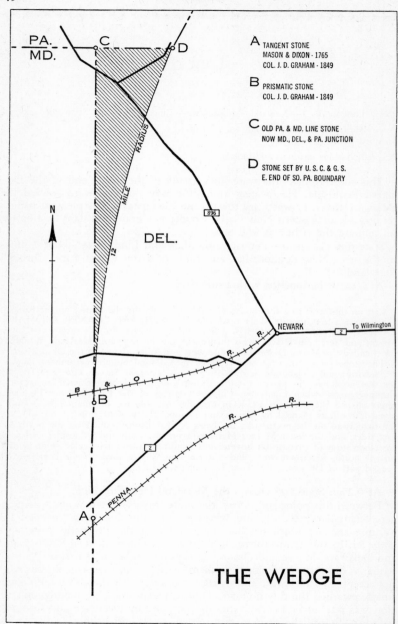

A TANGENT STONE
   MASON & DIXON · 1765
   COL. J. D. GRAHAM · 1849

B PRISMATIC STONE
   COL. J. D. GRAHAM · 1849

C OLD PA. & MD. LINE STONE
   NOW MD., DEL., & PA. JUNCTION

D STONE SET BY U. S. C. & G. S.
   E. END OF SO. PA. BOUNDARY

PA.
MD.

N

DEL.

12 MILE RADIUS

896

NEWARK

To Wilmington

2

B   &   O

B

R.

R.

R.

R.

2

PENNA.

A

THE WEDGE

illegal activities were carried on with impunity in The Wedge. When in 1846 a resident of the area, William Smith, was elected to the Delaware legislature, he was facetiously addressed by his colleagues as "the gentleman from Pennsylvania."

In 1892, in anticipation of the award of The Wedge to Delaware, the Mason-Dixon Line was extended east to the arc of Delaware's northern boundary, about 0.8 miles. This extension is the northern boundary of The Wedge, now constituting a small step-like protuberance from the smooth curve of the Delaware boundary. *(For explanation of this curved State boundary unique in the United States, see HISTORY.)*

At 0.5 *m.* is the junction with a side road.

Left on this road to a crossroads, **0.7** *m.;* in a field (R) stands a dark granite monument 5 feet high, marking the eastern end of the present extended Mason-Dixon Line. *(See D on WEDGE MAP.)*

NEWARK, 3.4 *m.* (135 alt., 6,731 pop.) *(see NEWARK).*

Points of Interest. University of Delaware, the Newark Academy Building, vulcanized fibre plants, paper mills, and others.

At Newark is the junction with State 2 *(see Tour 8).*

At 5.7 *m.* is the junction with a side road.

Right on this road to WELSH TRACT BAPTIST CHURCH (L), **0.2** *m.* *(meetings 3d Sun. in the month; open by permission),* erected in 1746 as successor to the first Baptist church in Delaware, a log structure built in 1706. The congregation now belonging to the Primitive Baptist group, was organized in Wales in 1701. That year the members emigrated to America and in 1703 bought from William Penn a tract of 30,000 acres that has since been called WELSH TRACT, about one-fourth of it lying in Cecil County, Md. The elevation of Iron Hill is said to have attracted them, and to this part of New Castle County the name Pencader Hundred was given; *pencader* is supposed to have meant "highest place" in the Welsh tongue. The present building is simple in line, one story in height, with a hipped roof, and is built of brick laid in Flemish-bond. The bricks are said to have been imported from England, unloaded at New Castle, and brought here in panniers on muleback. The date is on a stone set into the top of the front wall. The present white-painted, brown-trimmed pews are of the 19th century. The oldest communion service consists of two pewter plates and two pewter cups and saucers in use about 1830.

The yard is enclosed by a whitewashed stone wall built at various times from 1827 on, and is shaded by huge old oaks growing just outside. A grassy lawn sloping down to the Christiana Creek attracts picnickers on summer days. Across the road are whitewashed carriage sheds and the ancient little whitewashed stone house of the caretaker.

Some of the early 18th-century grave stones are rough-hewn from brown stone, and show the marks of the chipping tools. Celtic words are crudely lettered on them. A soldier of Oliver Cromwell's "Ironsides" regiment is supposed to be buried here. Visitors are told that the mother of Jefferson Davis is also buried here—an untrue but sturdy legend based apparently on a gravestone inscribed "Hannah Davis, died 1854, aged 71 years." Jefferson Davis's mother was Jane Cook Davis. However, his great-grandparents John and Anne Davis (or Davies), lived in this vicinity.

At 6.3 *m.* the main road arrives at junction with crossroad.

WELSH TRACT BAPTIST CHURCH, NEAR NEWARK

L. on latter Cooch House *(private)* at Cooch's Bridge on Christiana Creek, built 1760 by Thos. Cooch, still occupied by the Cooch family; was originally of brick and was two stories high; now it is covered with yellow plaster. A third story was added to the front part of the house about 1865. The columns of the side porch, originally the front porch, were cut from old shipmasts; those of the present front porch were made by an itinerant Irish carpenter before the Civil War. The house contains some of the original woodwork and many pieces of antique furniture and other heirlooms.

At the gateway is a large monument memorializing the SITE OF THE ONLY MILITARY FIGHT OF THE REVOLUTION ON DELAWARE SOIL—the skirmish of Cooch's Bridge on Sept. 3, 1777 between Washington's troops and the British during the latter's advance northeastward from the head of Chesapeake Bay to Philadelphia. Tradition declares that here the Stars and Stripes was first unfurled in battle. Lord Cornwallis, the British commander, made the Cooch house his headquarters at the time, without considering the wishes of the patriot owner, Thomas Cooch, who had come from England in 1746, and was a colonel in the Revolutionary Army. His son held the rank of major general of Delaware militia.

At the south end of the concrete bridge is the junction with a side road.

Right on this road to the junction with a side road, 1.1 *m.;* R. on this road to the SUMMIT OF IRON HILL (334 alt.), 1.8 *m.,* commanding a view, in clear weather, of four States, the Delaware River and Chesapeake Bay, and the five tall steel bridges over the Chesapeake and Delaware Canal to the southward. An airplane beacon light on the hill marks the New York-Washington air lane.

Iron Hill is the highest hill but not the highest elevation in Delaware—Centreville stands on a plateau a hundred feet higher. The British troops under Cornwallis camped on the hill in 1777, and American troops under Caesar Rodney in 1814. From before 1661 to 1891 iron ore was mined in varying quantities here, in the latter 19th century by a "benching" process in which layers of ore were broken off by spikes and wedges; the ore was shipped thence to Principio Furnace, Md., for smelting. Swedish records of a Minquas Indian fort on a "high hill" about 12 miles from New Castle are interpreted on the marker as referring to Iron Hill, but the long Swedish miles would place the fort in Maryland on the Susquehanna River, where its site has been identified.

At the time of the Cooch's Bridge skirmish the British and Hessian lines were extended along this route as far south as the hamlet of GLASGOW, 9.7 *m. (see Tour 4).*

At 10.4 *m.* the New Castle and Frenchtown R.R. crossed this road *(see NEW CASTLE).*

At 14.4 *m.* is the junction with State 71. Straight ahead on State 71 now the route.

The CHESAPEAKE AND DELAWARE CANAL is crossed here by a tall lift bridge *(see TRANSPORTATION).* This is the Deep Cut, through which tidewater flows east or west 100 feet below the bridge.

The old brick house with handsome arched dormer windows (R) on the south side of the canal was THE BUCK or Carson's Tavern; it is now on the Government's canal reservation. Washington stopped here several times on trips between Chesapeake Bay and New Castle, and the Hessian

General Knyphausen made this his headquarters on Sept. 2, 1777. A tavern patron of the Revolutionary era describes the hospitality of the Buck as "indifferent for bed and table—good for horses."

SUMMIT BRIDGE, 14.8 *m.* (53 pop.), is a tiny hamlet formerly noted for its saloons, still to some extent a farmers' trading center.

MOUNT PLEASANT, 16.7 *m.* (201 pop.), in flat country, is a hamlet and freight station of the Pennsylvania R.R. serving as a point for shipping grain and distributing fertilizers. Canada geese from the Chesapeake feeding grounds to the west frequently visit the young-wheat fields of this section during the winter months, though never in such numbers as to attract sportsmen from a distance. Farmers occasionally shoot them from pits or corn shocks. This is the only section of Delaware sought as a feeding ground by geese from the Chesapeake, though the eastern edge of Sussex County is followed by the coastal migratory flyway *(see Tour 2C)*.

MIDDLETOWN, 21.2 *m.* (30 alt., 1,755 pop.), is a comfortable town inhabited largely by the owners, widows of owners, and the agents of the great flat farms that surround the place and extend over into Maryland. It is one of the few old Delaware towns not on a navigable waterway.

Middletown was originally a tavern stop about midway on the ancient cartroad between the head of navigation on the Bohemia River, in Maryland, and the Appoquinimink Creek. As grain merchants and others settled here, a village gradually developed around the tavern. From 1850 to 1875 the town boomed from the profits created by the short-lived peach industry and other huge crops. Then the "yellows" wrecked the peach orchards here as the blight started down the Peninsula, and by 1900 agriculture had ceased to be the bonanza that permitted elderly farmers to turn over their farms to tenants and retire to shady streets. The town has an efficient government; it operates its own electric plant, that serves nearby communities as well, and yields a profit to the town in spite of the low rates charged.

The old MIDDLETOWN ACADEMY, W. side of Broad St. near Crawford St., a two-and-one-half story yellow-stuccoed brick structure, was erected in 1826 and used, chiefly as a private school for the children of country gentlemen, until it became the district public school in 1876. It ceased to serve as a school building in 1929, when the present Middletown School was built. The building, still owned privately and administered by trustees, is dilapidated; the wooden spire on the belfry points at a crazy angle, and the playground is now high in grass where generations of children used to scamper on the bare earth during recess from what they called the "Yellow Prison."

The first principal was the Rev. John Wilson, engaged in 1827 at a salary of $400 a year. A pupil who studied the "English branches" exclusive of mathematics paid $8 a session; including mathematics, $10. "Good boarding can be had in respectable families in the village at the rate of $40 per session," the announcement said, concluding with the remark that "a few boarders can be accommodated in the family of the principal."

The large brick, mansard-roofed MIDDLETOWN HOTEL, SW. cor. Main and Broad Sts., is supposed to contain part of the walls of a popular tavern built in 1761 by David Witherspoon. One night when David Witherspoon, Jr., was the tavern-keeper, James Knight, noted as a duellist, came in drunk and demanded liquor. Witherspoon, it is said, refused to serve him, whereupon Knight drew his pistol and snapped the hammer twice. While it was missing fire, Witherspoon reached above the bar, took down a horse pistol, shot and killed Knight.

In the TOWN HALL, W. side of Broad St. near Green St., is the headquarters of Union Lodge No. 5, A.F. & A.M., the oldest Masonic lodge in Delaware, organized at nearby Cantwell's Bridge (now Odessa) at least as early as 1765. The lodge's minutes are extant from 1766. An entry for Sept. 25, 1777 says: "The lodge did not meet last month on account of the enemy landing at Elk." A famed early member was Duncan Beard, clockmaker and silversmith *(see ODESSA)*.

At the traffic light is the junction with State 4.

Right on this street and road to COCHRAN GRANGE *(private)*, **1.2** *m.* (L), the home of John P. Cochran (1809–98), Governor of Delaware 1875–79. Completed in 1845, this large brick mansion has a portico of tall square columns with a fanlighted doorway, and a smaller two-story wing; both wings have the square boxlike lines characteristic of the period. The nearly flat roof of the main wing is surmounted by a glass-enclosed observatory—in this house and others like it, a symbol and expression of wealth. Nothing in Delaware agriculture before or since has quite matched the spectacle of well-groomed ladies and gentlemen taking their ease in the observatories on top of their fine houses, watching their Negroes at work in the broad grain fields and peach orchards, or merely enjoying the view in the pride of possession.

In this section called The Levels, once the richest land in Delaware, some farms contain 500 acres or more. Until the 1880's or 1890's most of these fertile estates were occupied and managed by their owners. Now more than 83 percent of the farms in this Middletown region are operated by tenants—the highest proportion of tenancy in the State, which averages 34 percent.

In most cases the overseers simply received share-leases instead of salaries, moved their families into the big houses, and continued to raise wheat and corn exactly as they had done before. The heavy soil is unsuited to raising melons, berries, broiler chickens and the other quick cash crops that enable down-State farmers to buy small farms. Few tenants in this section can accumulate enough capital from their share of the wheat and corn to buy a 500-acre farm, but they can usually make a living from the dairy herds they are allowed to keep. The owners and heirs, on the other hand, consider themselves lucky if their share of the crops pays for the taxes, insurance, and upkeep. The chief problem of a Middletown or Odessa farm agent—who may have charge of 20 big farms—is to secure tenants who will produce enough grain to meet fixed expenses and overhead. The heirs of the old estates like Cochran Grange go to the cities to make a living. Roof-top observatories are forgotten.

At 22.2 *m.* on State 71 is (R) OLD ST. ANNE'S EPISCOPAL CHURCH *(annual services 3d Sun. in June, 8 and 11 a.m.; open by permission)*, erected in 1768 and well preserved as one of the most prized old church buildings in Delaware. Shaded by great oaks, it is a plain brick structure with no external ornament except a cove cornice carried horizontally across the gable ends under a pent of shingles, and a Palladian window at the east end. The small entrance porch is a later addition.

The altar and white-painted box pews with doors are characteristic of the period, as is the unpainted slave gallery, divided into stalls and built

COCHRAN GRANGE, NEAR MIDDLETOWN

along the sides. The ivy on the exterior walls has grown from plants said to have been brought from England by Bishop Doane. One of the oaks, "Old St. Anne's Oak," measures 17 feet in girth and is believed to be 300 years old.

A treasured possession of the church is a small piece of a communion-table cover embroidered with the silk letters "A R" *(Anne Regina)*, presented by Queen Anne of England to the original "congregation of Appoquinimy" in 1705, when a log church was built here or nearby. Also belonging to Old St. Anne's is a silver beaker made by Johannes Nys of Philadelphia between 1700 and 1723, the only such vessel he is known to have made, and a silver paten and chalice given to the church in 1759.

The annual Old St. Anne's Sunday celebration is typical of other old country church services in Delaware. Special services on the annual day in 1955 will commemorate the two hundred and fiftieth anniversary of the original St. Anne's congregation of 1705. Restoration of the church building of 1768 in authentic form and detail, in progress for several years, will be completed at that time.

Here, as at other outposts of the Church of England in Colonial days, the first priests were missionaries sent out by the Society for the Propagation of the Gospel in Foreign Parts. The Rev. Thomas Jenkins, the first missionary sent to St. Anne's, went there fearing "the rage and scorn of . . . those numerous crowd of Heathen called Quakers," but fell a victim to more deadly enemies. As a fellow priest reported in 1709: "Poor brother Jenkins at Apoquinimy was baited to death by musquitoes and blood thirsty Gal Knippers, which would not let him rest night nor day till he got a fever, came to Philadelphia, and died immediately. These places must be served by itinerants, and it is hardly possible for anybody to abide there, that is not born there, till he is musquito proof." The first really settled minister was the Rev. Philip Reading who came in 1746 and survived both the mosquitoes and the buzzing of Revolutionary hornets about his loyal Tory head until his death in 1778. He is buried near the south entrance to the churchyard.

Regular services were discontinued in 1872 and a new church, also called St. Anne's, was built in the nearby center of Middletown.

At 22.6 *m.* is the junction with a side road.

Left on this road to the entrance to ST. ANDREW'S SCHOOL, 0.9 *m.;* in a group of stone buildings of collegiate Gothic design, it was established in 1929 by A. Felix du Pont as a school for boys and placed under the jurisdiction of the Episcopal Diocese of Delaware. The school property of 350 acres borders Noxontown Pond and Silver Lake, millponds at the head of Appoquinimink Creek. A policy of the school is that the boys make the beds, wait on the tables, and do other work usually done by servants in private schools. Attendance is not limited to Episcopalians. Hanging in the main school building are paintings by two noted Delaware artists: scenes from Ivanhoe by Frank E. Schoonover, and a painting by Stanley Arthurs depicting the Delaware militia under Caesar Rodney encamped on the nearby Noxon farm in September 1777 *(see below).* The architect for the school buildings was Arthur H. Brockie of Philadelphia.

At 1.4 *m.* on the main side road is (L) the two-and-one-half-story brick NOXON HOUSE *(private),* overlooking Noxontown Pond, built in 1740 by a planter and gristmiller named Thomas Noxon (or Nixon) whose mills were at the dam below and at other nearby sites. Large country fairs were held here in Colonial and later times, and it is said the spot was nicknamed Oxentown because of the livestock brought here for sale or exhibit. As late as 1855 vessels ascended the Appoquinimink to the dam to take on cargoes of flour, meal, grain, lumber, and other products.

At 25.4 *m.* is the junction with a side road.

Right on this road is TOWNSEND, 0.5 *m.* (421 pop.), a marketing center of a farming area and a railway junction of decreased importance. Before 1850 it was called Charley Town after Charles Lloyd, a Negro living in one of the several Negro shanties that then comprised the settlement. The railroad station was named Townsend about 1855 for Samuel Townsend, a local landowner. The family name is pronounced Towns'nd, but the town is locally called Towns-end—a variation originated, it is said, by train conductors announcing the stop here.

NEW DISCOVERY, 26.5 *m.,* a Negro settlement strung along the highway for about one mile, is indicative of the importance of this slaveholding countryside of lower New Castle County in Colonial and pre-Civil War days. As late as 1920 most of the roads in Delaware south of Wilmington were bordered by Negro settlements like this, but owing to the widening of the roads and the migration of the Negroes northward to the cities, comparatively few such roadside communities remain.

At 27.1 *m.* State 71 forms a junction with US 13 *(see Tour 1, Sec. c)* just north of Blackbird.

Tour 10

New Castle—Delaware City—Port Penn—Leipsic—Little Creek—Junction with US 113; Unnumbered roads and State 9, 51.5 m.
Roadbed paved or improved throughout.

Accommodations in towns.

This little-used route follows Delaware River and Bay for about one-half the length of the shore of Delaware, passing through a tidewater countryside of farms and towns in one of the earliest-settled regions of the State. Between New Castle and Port Penn the river is usually in sight; south of Port Penn the bay is seldom visible but is never more than 6 miles distant.

On this route filling stations are few and no billboards appear against the quiet landscape of fields and occasional sparse woods, or of marsh and creek and river. Muskrat houses dot the tidal marshes; about 80,000 "rats" are trapped annually in this river-and-bay strip of New Castle and Kent counties, one of the important fur-producing areas of the United States. The marshes along the route have a variety of plant and animal life and are visited in the fall by gunners and all year round by nature-lovers. Bordering the road are miles of trimmed or untrimmed osage-orange and Virginia thorn hedges.

There are many plain, dignified old brick mansions, never far from navigable waters; some are in good repair, others crumble amid wood-grown lawns, untended boxwood, scratching hound dogs, and the legal entanglements of the heirs. Delicate mantels and stairways bespeak the taste of the landowners who drew wealth from the heavy, fertile soil, and enjoyed their dancing parties, fox hunting, and duck shooting. Their sons and grandsons benefited from the growing of Delaware peaches that started in this section and lasted until the great orchards were blighted after the Civil War. Thereafter farming declined as prices and fertility went down and wages rose. Most of the old houses are occupied by white tenants who till the big farms with the aid of Negro labor, and in growing the traditional crops of wheat, corn, and hay usually take from the soil more than they put back. Dairying sometimes gives the tenant a margin of profit, but the agent employed by the absentee heirs is pleased if the revenue from a farm pays taxes and insurance.

The villages, once proud little ports, are in the backwaters of the life and commerce that have passed them by for generations. Upturn is in progress, though old merchants and fishermen sit around talking about the days of peaches or sturgeon; the young men go elsewhere to make a living. After 1860 the vessel lines serving the villages succumbed to competition

John Moll

OYSTER BOATS AT LITTLE CREEK

with the railroad, and commercial fishing in the river was almost destroyed
after 1900 by pollution from industrial centers to the north.

NEW CASTLE, 0 *m.* (10 alt., 5,400 pop.) *(see NEW CASTLE).*

Points of Interest. Old Court House, Amstel House, Immanuel Church, Old
Dutch House, the Read House, and other Colonial buildings.

This route branches south from US 40 *(see Tour 4)* at 6th St.; S. on
6th St. to South St.; R. on South St. to 7th St.; L. on 7th St. (the River
Rd.).

DOBBINSVILLE, 1 *m.,* a row of brick tenements at the outskirts of
New Castle, was erected in the 1870's by Richard J. Dobbins for employees of the old Tasker Iron Works. Tenants now are mostly laborers in the
yard gangs of nearby manufacturing plants.

At 2.2 *m.* is the junction with a side road.

Left on this road to the DELAWARE RAYON PLANT *(no admission),* now making
artificial silk, but during World War I a Bethlehem Steel plant that loaded thousands of heavy artillery shells. The workers, including many women, were called
"powder monkeys"—their skins stained a deep yellow from picric acid.

At **0.3** *m.* on this road is DEEMER'S BEACH on the Delaware River shore
(bathing facilities and amusement devices).

At 2.4 *m.* (R) is a small lighthouse called NEW CASTLE RANGE, REAR.
Pilots on vessels coming up the river keep this light and the front range

light on the shore in a line over the bow in order to stay in the ship channel; ships going downstream line up the two lights over the stern.

At 3.5 *m.* (L) is the old RIFLE RANGE of the Delaware National Guard; the meadow slopes to the target pits near the shore. It is used at irregular intervals.

At 5.9 *m.* the road crosses RED LION CREEK.

LEXINGTON *(King's College),* 7 *m.* (R), behind a high hedge, a large rectangular brick mansion with colonnaded portico, was named by Henry Clay, when he was brought here by Sen. John M. Clayton in 1847 to see the great peach orchards of the owner, Major Philip Reybold, the "Peach King" of Delaware and the Eastern Shore of Maryland. After a dinner attended by other Whig leaders as well as by most of Reybold's twelve sons and daughters, the party was taken on an inspection trip through the orchards, and two choice baskets of peaches were picked for Clay. Later Major Reybold asked Clay to name the great estate with its new mansion. The Kentuckian is said to have replied: "Major, your beautiful house and countryside remind me of Ashland, my own home near Lexington. I therefore suggest, sir, that you name your estate 'Lexington'."

Reybold's career is an important chapter in the history of Delaware. Born in Philadelphia, the son of a butcher, he was orphaned at 10. In 1810 with a partner he came to Red Lion Hundred and bought a farm; the partner defaulted and the farm was lost with all Reybold's savings. He rented the same farm and soon bought it again with profits from sheep and from castor oil pressed from beans he grew as an experiment. He raised grain and beef cattle and bought one run-down farm after another, restoring fertility by spreading the sour land with marl—earth containing rotted sea shells—which he excavated as contractor for the Chesapeake and Delaware Canal east of St. Georges. On the canal job he made another fortune supplying beef and bread to all the thousands of laborers on the whole 14-mile cut. More profits came from making bricks from clay deposits on his land.

Agriculture, however, was his chief love, and by 1845 he and his five sons had 117,000 peach trees in bearing in two States. He shipped the fruit to Philadelphia and New York on his own steamers, and when the prices did not suit him he ordered entire shiploads dumped overboard. After spreading the fame of Delaware peaches throughout the United States and making more money than any Delaware farmer ever made before or since, Major Reybold died in 1854 when he was 71.

There were small peach orchards in Delaware in the early 18th century, and numerous large orchards for the next century, particularly in Sussex County; the fruit was small and was usually turned into peach brandy, or dried for home use. The boom of 1840–80 was made possible by the discovery that "budded" trees—trees raised from peach stones and grafted with buds from fine living trees—produced superior fruit. The method was brought to Red Lion Hundred in 1832 by Isaac Reeves, of New Jersey, who owned a farm now part of the Fort Du Pont reservation *(see below).* Major Reybold took up peach-raising in 1835; in 1875 the center of the industry was Middletown, in 1880 Smyrna, and in 1890 it was Seaford. By that time the "yellows" blight had struck, and there was not an orchard left in this Red Lion Hundred section, and all the orchards of the Peninsula were doomed. Not until well into the 20th century were sprays developed to control the disease; once again great orchards are being set out in Delaware.

At 7.6 *m.* (R) is ST. JAMES PROTECTORY, a Roman Catholic home for orphan boys.

At a junction, 7.7 *m.,* the route turns L.

DELAWARE CITY, 9.7 *m.* (10 alt., 1,365 pop.), is a river town of broad, tree-shaded streets, old brick hotels that have been closed as such for decades, and one of the most charming waterfronts in Delaware. On lower Clinton St. the row of stores of varying heights, built in a solid line, has not changed appreciably in 40 years. A few small boats of shallow draft lie at the wharf on the former basin of what was once the main entrance to the Chesapeake and Delaware Canal.

The Steamboat Wharf no longer resounds with the thump of peach baskets or the laughter of rich farmers boarding the *Major Reybold* or the *Thomas Clyde* for Philadelphia. No more passenger trains come in on the branch rail line, and the trolley tracks have been torn up; some of the residents commute to Wilmington by bus or automobile. Old shad and sturgeon skiffs blister in the sun on the old towpath, nets rot away in dark barn lofts. Soldiers from Fort Du Pont stroll with their town girls in grassy Battery Park where the whole community used to gather at evenings to see the *Lord Baltimore* or the *William Penn* enter the locks on the way from Philadelphia to Baltimore. Hip-booted fishermen, gunners, or trappers—according to the season—were included in this picture of 1938.

Delaware City superficially resembles other Delaware tidewater villages that flourished for 40 or 50 years on shipbuilding and the transportation of grain and forest products, and then were withered by the railroad. But these places are only fitfully disturbed by ambition. Delaware City is different. There is always, going on in the vicinity, or planned for the future, some large undertaking that may restore prosperity.

For 25 years a river wharf here had been called Newbold's Landing. But when the fine wide streets were laid out in 1826 at the junction of the Delaware River and the Chesapeake and Delaware Canal then being dug across the Peninsula, Daniel and William Newbold, who drew the plans, gave the proposed town the grandiose name of Delaware City in expectation of future glory; the main street was named for Governor De Witt Clinton of New York, chief promoter of the Erie Canal, and a lot of less than an acre sold for $4,000.

Then this first boom subsided and the Newbolds sold out to Manuel Eyre, another promoter; on July 4, 1827 a great dinner was held in the street at a table a block long; companies of militia paraded and important men spoke. The next year a brick hotel and other buildings were erected on Clinton St., and an optimistic little town greeted in 1829 the opening of the canal. Lock tenders and toll-receivers were soon busy locking through the barges of lumber, coal, lime, and grain. Large stables arose on the canal bank for the mules that plodded along the towpath pulling boats. But the canal brought no great development because the railroads soon began to compete seriously.

Peaches came next, hauled down Clinton St. in six-ox and six-mule wagons to "The Major's Wharf" on the river where the baskets were stacked three tiers high and a hundred yards long to be loaded on three steamboats at one time. But the peach growers did not live in the town or spend much money here, and though they sent their children to the private Delaware City Academy established in 1856, these farmers habitually boarded the steamboat and spent their money in Philadelphia. In 1860 the population reached its record peak of 1,355. About 1865 the Delaware City Bank had been founded. The various little home-operated plants from 1840 to 1890 turned out wagons, carriages, mincemeat, metal goods, canned goods, and fertilizer.

When peaches were no longer shipped, new hopes were raised by the development in 1898 of Fort Du Pont across the canal. Some residents found work there during construction, and later the stores began to sell candy and tobacco to soldiers off duty from "The Post." Meanwhile the shad and sturgeon fishing industry was employing many men and dozens of skiffs. Shad by the carload went off every spring, and 400-pound sturgeons gave up buckets of roe that brought a dollar a pound from the caviar packers in Philadelphia and New York. In the fall and spring the town's weather-beaten market gunners brought in thousands of ducks from the river marshes nearby; in late February, when the ice was coming down the river, they dressed in white clothes, rowed out through the floes in white "iceboats," and sculled down on rafts of sleeping black ducks which they slaughtered with huge white-painted swivel guns mounted in the bow. Uncounted cripples escaped to die, but barrels of ducks were shipped from Delaware City year after year until the sale of migratory game birds was stopped by law in 1918.

By this time there was talk of a sea-level ship canal to take the place of the old two-level lock canal. The climax came when in 1919 the Government bought out the canal company. That October a second great canal celebration was held on Clinton St. From a flag-draped platform, Army officers and Senators of several States spoke of the great ships that would use the waterway, and the people of Delaware City prepared once more for their era of growth and prosperity.

When the tidal canal was opened in 1927, however, the eastern entrance was not at Delaware City at all, but was cut through open fields and marsh two miles below the town. The distance might as well have been 20 miles for all the benefit the town got from the waterway; small freighters and yachts passed through without stopping—Delaware City heard them blow for the bridge if the wind was south, and that was all. Stunned, the town could only plead to keep its old canal entrance, now tidal and joining the main canal 2 miles to the southwest. Dredging the old canal entrance to establish it as a yacht basin was in prospect (1953). Yachtsmen sometimes find their way in here to get provisions and fuel or to see the stranded old town.

The deepening of the Chesapeake and Delaware Canal for ocean-going ships between 1935 and 1938 meant that still larger vessels might pass by, out of sight and without pausing. The pollution of the river has reduced the fleet of shad and sturgeon boats to only a few each spring. The people, however, still have hope. As late as 1929 they packed the Town Hall to hear a promoter describe the "Ideal City" that would shortly arise on 9,000 acres of adjacent farmland for which he had "secured options." Ideal City has not yet been built, nor has the promoter been seen here since.

BATTERY PARK, foot of Clinton St., is at the old entrance of the canal, where boats were locked in and out and tolls paid. The old stone-walled LOCK, preserved along the southern side of the park, contains some water and small boats are stored in it. The river end is closed by an embankment, but there is access for boats between the river and the old basin by a small channel just south of the lock. Near the lock stands an ancient iron DIVING BELL, within which a man could be lowered to the bed of the canal to make repairs to the lock gates. From the park there is a good view of Fort Delaware (see below), a mile east on Pea Patch Island.

Opposite Battery Park on Clinton St. is the former DELAWARE CITY HOTEL (private), later called the Lower Hotel, built of brick by Manuel Eyre in 1828 and since covered with buff stucco. This large and well-proportioned building with its delicate dormer windows is a monumental relic of Delaware City's early optimism. Until the advent of Prohibition it was one of the noted taverns of the countryside. Another well-known hotel was the red-brick building formerly the CENTRAL HOTEL, SE. cor. Clinton and Front Sts.

The MAXWELL HOUSE (private), NW. cor. Adams and Williams Sts., a large white frame dwelling, was erected about 1850 by Capt. George Maxwell, a steamboat captain, who designed the interior as much like a ship as possible and built a lookout box on the roof for a fine view up and down the river.

At 10.1 m. on the River Rd. is the entrance (L) to FORT DU PONT SITE. Expanded during World War II as an army air engineer base and fortification for the Delaware River, the fort was decommissioned in December, 1945. In 1946 the 320 acre site and 65 buildings were given the State, and made into a State health center, opened October 28, 1948.

Fort Du Pont was the headquarters of the harbor defenses of the Delaware River and Bay, and the only regularly garrisoned fort in the area. Other fortifications under its authority was Fort Delaware and Fort Saulsbury (see Tour 2C), where detachments were posted. The 270-acre reservation of Fort Du Pont, fronting the river, comprised a parade ground, officers' quarters, a hospital, large brick-and-frame barracks for enlisted men, stables, a moving picture theater (open to public nightly and Sun. at 2:30, adm. 20¢), and the other usual buildings of an Army post.

Long garrisoned solely by Coast Artillery regiments, Fort Du Pont has been predominantly an engineer post since 1922 when the First Engineers arrived for permanent station. This unit has had an honored record in four wars since its nucleus was organized as Company A at West Point in 1846.

They served first in the Mexican War, took part in many engagements in
the Civil War, participated in the capture of Santiago in the Spanish War,
and for active battle service in the World War the entire regiment was
twice decorated by France.

Since then the activities have included duty in Nicaragua (1929–31)
and the development of pontoon equipment. Nearby waterways are proving grounds of pontoon bridges for the transport of heavy motorized
equipment. More spectacular has been the floating of officers' quarters
intact across the river from abandoned Fort Mott, N. J., to new sites here.
During the Mississippi Valley floods of 1937 the First Engineers aided in
emergency construction and rescue duty.

An auxiliary battery for Fort Delaware was placed on this shore in 1863,
more guns were mounted between 1872 and 1876, but the present fortifications were established beginning in 1899, when the new fort was named
for Rear Admiral Samuel Francis du Pont (1803–65) of Delaware, a
Civil War naval officer.

Boats may be hired at Delaware City to visit OLD FORT DELAWARE on Pea
Patch Island—opposite Delaware City. This island ceded to the United States in
1813, was returned to the State in 1945. It has been converted into a State park and
recreation area. Scheduled boat service was expected to be established by the summer
of 1954. The following history was written in 1938.

On a marshy island in midstream, is the grim and bleak gray mass of Fort Delaware, a huge granite pentagon commanding a southward sweep of river and bay.
Tiers of empty gun ports look out from casements in the walls and jutting bastions
above an encircling moat filled with dark water. On the earth-covered upper battle-
ments trees have grown fantastically, their roots twining into dungeon ventilators,
their branches twisted by gales. Only the flag and the Monday wash of a non-
commissioned officer's wife flutter gaily in the breeze to relieve the sullen melancholy of the great old fortress. The silence is usually heavy and unbroken. A small
detachment of soldiers from Fort Du Pont is stationed here, to warn off trespassers,
to paint mines and other equipment, and to care for the modern guns.

Visitors are guided through the main sally port into the spacious courtyard
within, where three-story brick buildings—formerly barracks, officers' quarters, and
guard rooms—stand with their tops at a level with the top of the masonry battle-
ments. Great rooms are empty that during the Civil War rang with the footsteps
and shouted orders of the garrison of nearly 300 men and officers. Irregularly garrisoned since then, Fort Delaware attained its greatest importance during those
four years when a Confederate invasion was feared, 131 guns were in place, and
barracks on the island held thousands of Confederate prisoners of war. Within the
granite ramparts the guide's flashlight shines into damp and black dungeons, where
prisoners who defied authority or plotted to escape were confined in the fetid air.
In the occasional niches in the corridor walls, guards were stationed. Here and
there an arched ceiling has fallen into a mass of bricks on the floor.

At one time during the latter part of the war 12,000 prisoners were quartered in
the wooden barracks to the north and west of the fort within a barbed wire stockade, under the cannon trained on them day and night. Sleeping in three tiers on
rough planks, they were tortured by mosquitoes in summer and half frozen in winter; mortality from cholera was as high as 331 in one month. The ground was too
marshy to bury the bodies here, and except when river ice prevented a crossing,
they were taken for burial to the New Jersey shore, where the 85-foot Confederate
Monument marks Finn's Point National Cemetery (see NEW JERSEY GUIDE).
Despite all precautions hundreds of prisoners escaped to the Delaware State shore,
where Confederate sympathizers harbored them and sent them south. Those in con-

FORT DELAWARE, PEA PATCH ISLAND

finement tried to amuse themselves playing poker, making toys, and reading or studying; from their soup bones they fashioned elaborate sets of delicately carved knives, forks, and other small objects. Before the war ended, about 700 Confederate prisoners took the oath of allegiance to the United States, and many were doing guard duty over their former comrades.

The legend of the origin of Pea Patch Island is that a vessel loaded with peas foundered on a bar in the river, the peas sprouted, catching floating debris, and little by little the island was formed. Testimony that "in 1773 the island was only the size of a man's hat" appears in the record of the suit brought by the State of Delaware in 1839 against a New Jersey resident who claimed the island. In 1814, when an Army captain with 100 soldiers and 30 laborers had taken possession, dykes had to be built to keep the tide out of much of the area. In 1831 the first small fort was burned at a $100,000 loss, and work on a new fort was suspended for four years while the suit was in progress. In 1843 the suit was decided in favor of the State of Delaware, represented by John M. Clayton, and a valid deed was given the Government.

In 1846 a tidal wave swept the island clean, and in 1848 work began on the present fortress. It took nearly three years to settle the foundation of 6,000 piles— 45-foot tree trunks disappeared and others had to be driven down on top of them. In 1860 the new fortifications were finished, having cost more than $1,000,000, and the work of mounting the guns commenced at the outbreak of the Civil War. Within recent years these guns were removed and with hundreds of cannon balls were sold for scrap iron.

Opposite the entrance of Fort Du Pont on the River Rd. is POLK-TOWN (pronounced Poketown), a Negro section of Delaware City named for the Polk family, white landowners. It was the scene of Ella Middleton Tybout's *Poketown People,* a volume of Negro dialect stories.

At 10.9 *m.* on the north bank of the canal is the old frame JOHN REY-BOLD FARMHOUSE (L) where a Hungarian immigrant boy named Michael I. Pupin (1858–1935) learned his first English as a farmhand and mule-driver in 1874. Later Pupin became a famous inventor and professor of electro-mechanics at Columbia University, but in his autobiography *From Immigrant to Inventor* he writes of the kindness of the tenant farmer and his wife who gave him sympathy and counsel in the strange country. One of his memories was that the prosperous farmers wore chin whiskers but no mustaches. On the adjacent Government property is a majestic holly tree whose trunk is 6 feet 8 inches in girth.

At 11 *m.* the road crosses a great steel lift bridge over the CHESA-PEAKE AND DELAWARE CANAL *(see TRANSPORTATION).*

For three miles south of the canal the River Rd. passes through great areas of marsh, formerly embanked against tides but now subject to regu-lar tidal ebb and flow east of the causeway. In late fall these marshes and the marshes farther south along this route are leased for railbird and black duck shooting, in the winter for muskrat trapping. All summer and into September numbers of tropical white herons (egrets) as well as the native great blue herons wade through the reeds and cattails spearing frogs and other small creatures. In August, great expanses of marsh are gay with pink and white marshmallows.

PORT PENN, 14 *m.* (252 pop.), on Delaware River at the head of Delaware Bay, is an old village of wistful and lonely charm, long resigned to being the ghost of its robust youth and vigorous middle age. The green river-marshes extend nearly to the backyards of old brick and frame houses and taverns that were standing when Port Penn was an important shipping-point for grain and a port of entry with a custom house. As one of the best deep-water ports of the Delaware shore, the village was often full of deck-hands who joined the drivers of grain wagons in roistering in the taverns. Later, Port Penn became noted as a center for shad and sturgeon fishing and continued as such for decades until pollution of the water from the north paralyzed the industry after 1920. A few hard-bitten fishermen, whose ancestors "followed the bay" before them, still go out hoping that by some miracle they will encounter a run of fish like old times, but they usually return in disgust with only a few shad flopping in the bottom of the skiff. A tomato cannery is operated here in summer.

Tradition says that William Penn once landed here for a supply of water —hence the name. No record of his stopping here has been found. Since the name Port Penn does not appear on maps prior to 1780, it is probable that the name was first applied in 1774 when the Philadelphia port au-thorities ordered piers built in this vicinity. Another legend without appar-ent basis is that the Polish Count Casimir Pulaski, a general in the Amer-ican Revolution, built a house and lived in Port Penn.

Among the old dwellings is the brick STEWART HOUSE *(private),* on the S. side of the Presbyterian Church. Erected about 1750, it has been the home of most of the seven Drs. David Stewart who from century to century maintained the medical tradition of their family. The house is said to have been hit by a cannon ball from a British man-of-war during the invasion of the river in 1813.

East by water from Port Penn to REEDY ISLAND, **0.5** *m.,* on which was the REEDY ISLAND DETENTION STATION of the U. S. Public Health Service where no person could land without authorization. Built upon 6-foot stilts on the marshy island, to guard against high tides, a hospital, barracks, doctor's quarters, a delousing room, and other buildings permitted the plant to be put into service at any time as a quarantine station, as it was at times since its establishment in 1893. The station was remodeled and re-equipped in 1935 at a cost of $100,000 and served for a year once more as the main quarantine station of the Delaware River, but after 1936 it has had the status of an occasional detention station, with only a skeleton crew and without a resident doctor, and operated under the authority of the present main quarantine station at Marcus Hook, Pa.

Abandoned by the Health Service, the island has recently been cleared of buildings. There is hope that it will be developed as a wildlife refuge.

AUGUSTINE BEACH, 14.6 *m.,* locally called The Piers, is a little "pleasuring ground" on the upper bay that used to be crowded on summer week-ends by farm families and excursionists coming by the *Thomas Clyde* from Philadelphia. The place has declined since the boat stopped running in the 1920's; the pier is wrecked, the empty amusement buildings stand in the shade of the large grove of trees. Young people of the countryside long came to bathe at high tide in the shallow brackish water, using the bath houses for hire at the water's edge. They held impromptu dances in the old dance hall and drank beer in the large brick HOTEL (R), erected in 1814 and for years a social center of the region. In election years the annual late summer Farmer's Day Picnic here was always attended by politicians eager to "get amongst the people." On that occasion automobiles filled the lot where buggies, double-carriages, and dearborns used to stand in rows. The resort is ripe for restoration as a county recreation area.

The spot takes its name from Augustine Herman, Bohemian surveyor and adventurer, who made a map of the Delaware-Chesapeake region for Cecil Calvert, second Lord Baltimore. The map so pleased Baltimore that he gave Herman in 1662 a great tract of land lying mostly in Maryland but including a strip of what is now Delaware extending to Delaware River and Bay. Herman called it Bohemia Manor *(see MARYLAND GUIDE).* The eastern part, however, was claimed by the authorities at New York after 1664, who would patent to Herman only a few hundred acres in this vicinity, and then only if he would improve the land. This he did by settling his sons Casparus and Ephraim on Reedy Island Neck *(see below).*

At 15.4 *m.* the road crosses AUGUSTINE CREEK at the northern edge of REEDY ISLAND NECK, where Casparus and Ephraim Herman lived for a time. Near here was the beginning of the cart road cut through the woods by the Hermans for 22 miles westward to Augustine Herman's home on the upper Bohemia River in Maryland. This road was in use in 1679. With Augustine Herman's road between the Appoquinimink Creek *(see ODESSA)* and the Bohemia River, it was one of the first vehicle roads in what is now Delaware.

At 16.4 *m.*, where the route turns R., is the junction with a side road.

Left on this road to BAYVIEW BEACH, 0.5 *m.*, a cluster of small frame summer cottages on the bay shore near the range light called LISTON RANGE FRONT.

At a junction, 16.9 *m.*, the route turns L.

The long lane to LONG ISLAND FARM *(private)* is (L) at 18.3 *m.* From her green-painted dwelling here Mrs. Catherine Fox (1856–1936), the "Muskrat Queen of Delaware," ruled autocratically over her marshy kingdom on Delaware Bay. Even during her life she had become legendary. From the house she kept close watch on the trappers she employed on her more than 1,000 acres of marsh which would yield 10,000 muskrats as a single winter's catch. The trappers could never fathom her mysterious ability to tell how many "rats" they should bring up for skinning on any certain day; if the day's catch was smaller than Mrs. Fox expected there was sure to be trouble. Fur buyers could never cheat her, for she knew grading as well as prices. Invitations to shoot ducks on Long Island Farm were highly valued not only for the fine sport there but also for the entertainment provided by Mrs. Fox's jovial humor and sprightly conversation.

The route crosses APPOQUINIMINK CREEK, 18.8 *m.*

At a junction, 20.3 *m.*, the route turns L.

At THOMAS CORNER, 20.5 *m.*, a Negro settlement, the route turns R.

At a junction, 21.3 *m.*, the route turns L.

The HUGUENOT HOUSE *(private),* 24.5 *m.*, a large two-story brick house (R) with hooded doorway, was built in 1711 by Elias Naudain, 2d, who was born in London and was the son of a French Huguenot refugee. The Naudains became the owners of large estates in this region. The house, in its somewhat heavy solidity and plain exterior, is a good example of Delaware's early-Colonial architecture. Inside, the rather primitive paneling is in keeping with the age of the house and the luxury of the day. Paneled walls have arched doorways. Tenants occupy the house.

At 25.6 *m.* the road crosses BLACKBIRD CREEK, into which the pirate Blackbeard is supposed to have sailed to hide his plunder *(see Tour 1, Sec. c).*

At 26.2 *m.* is TAYLOR'S BRIDGE, a hamlet of a store and a few dwellings overlooking the great marshes of Blackbird Creek. The 135-foot steel lighthouse to the L. is REEDY ISLAND RANGE, REAR.

Here the route turns R.

Left (straight ahead) from Taylor's Bridge on a side road to the LISTON HOUSE *(private),* 2.7 *m.* (L), a small gambrel-roofed house of Flemish-bond brickwork erected in 1739 by Edmund Liston, son of Morris Liston who had come to America before 1675 and acquired a large acreage by patents under the Duke of York, and from William Penn in 1702. In 1747 Edmund Liston and his neighbor James Hart complained to the Philadelphia authorities that a boatload of "Spanish Pirates" had landed here on the bay shore, plundered their houses, and stolen their Negroes. The leader wore a "laced hat" and by his speech and fair skin they thought he was an Englishman. The whole bay and ocean shore of Delaware was still being harassed by petty freebooters who, eluding the expeditions sent down from Philadelphia, robbed tidewater plantations of everything movable and slaughtered fat pigs and cattle for fresh meat supplies. The Liston House has been much altered inside.

John Moll

LEIPSIC ON LITTLE DUCK CREEK

At 30.6 *m.* on the Bay Rd. is FLEMING'S LANDING at a bridge across DUCK CREEK (Smyrna River), the boundary between New Castle and Kent Counties. The old course of the creek turned south just west of the bay shore and flowed crookedly 13 miles through marsh to enter the bay, but sometime before 1740 a mile-long "thoroughfare" was cut through to the bay to save time for vessels using this once-busy waterway between Smyrna Landing and northern ports.

At 31.7 *m.* is the junction with a side road.

Left on this road to the RUINS OF THE BRICK HOTEL, 1.1 *m.* (R), in which the marble door sills and window caps and the remains of fine paneling give some indication of its appearance in 1812 or earlier.

At 34.6 *m.* is the junction with State 6 *(see Tour 12)*.

At 38 *m.* is the junction with State 9; L. (straight ahead) on State 9, now the route.

LEIPSIC (pronounced Lipsic), 39.7 *m.* (254 pop.), is a little old village on the edge of the greatest tidal marsh area of Delaware—that of northeast Kent County. From the south shore of Little Duck Creek—also called the Leipsic River—Delaware Bay is only 7 miles away as the crow flies but much farther as the creek goes twisting through the vast wet flats.

Everything about Leipsic—even the rich muddy-salty smell of the air—is eloquent of the marshes and bay whence some of the people derive their living. There is little activity on the narrow streets between the small frame houses with their low fences. The women keep house and attend to their children and chickens while the men spend their days on oyster vessels in the bay, or prowling the marshes to take muskrats out of traps, or in summer overhauling the boats to be ready for the oyster season in the fall. Fishing and crabbing are commercial occupations as well as sport and trucks call regularly for the catch. A good many of the small population work at industries in Smyrna and Dover and come home at night to one of the most peaceful municipal communities in Delaware.

Wharf scenes in Leipsic may include in winter power boats (replacing rake-masted schooners) with men forking oysters from their decks into trucks backed down to the vessel-side. Hip-booted trappers come in with boatloads of drowned muskrats to skin them, stretch the hides on pointed shingles, and bargain with fur buyers, who once regarded this region as one of the greatest fur markets in the United States. Other watermen bring in snapping turtles weighing 5 to 20 pounds apiece that have been caught in baited live traps or speared with heavy barbed "turkle-progs." Muskrat "meats," snapper soup, fish, and oysters are staples of diet, varied by wild ducks in the fall. Before the enforcement of game laws, no Fourth-of-July dinner in Leipsic was complete without a mess of fledgeling black ducks caught on the marshes with long-handled crab nets.

Fishing-party boats are not for hire in Leipsic because the river winds miles through marshes before reaching the bay where sportsmen can come direct by road. Small boats are available for river fishing and pleasure trips through the salt marshes.

Customs survive in Leipsic that have long since disappeared from places in closer touch with the world. For instance, when someone dies, a member of the family goes around knocking on all doors to show at each house a piece of paper bearing the time and place of the funeral. A strange family just settled here receives this visit along with everybody else, as a matter of course, for everybody is invited. As in many fishing villages throughout the Peninsula, no Negroes were tolerated in town after dark; a story is related of a scuffle that once took place between the races when all the Negroes were pitched into the creek to swim to the other side or drown.

When a village here was laid out by Jacob Stout in 1723 it was called Fast Landing because the site was the nearest solid ground up the creek from the bay. In 1814, despite a legislative act changing the name to Vienna, the place was named Leipsic for the fur-shipping center of Leipsic, Germany. Between 1836 and the coming of the railroad era in 1855, the village was a busy little port; it had shipyards and shipped lumber, grain, and oysters to Philadelphia. Long before the last steamboat stopped running on semi-weekly schedule to Philadelphia in the 1920's, however, Leipsic was declining as a port. Very little of the income from fur, hay, or oysters is spent here.

At 41.6 m. on State 9 is the Lane (R) to WHEEL OF FORTUNE (private), a typical pre-Revolutionary manor house of eastern Kent County,

John Moll

WHEEL OF FORTUNE, MANOR HOUSE, NEAR LEIPSIC

two and one-half stories in height, and built of brick on an L-shaped plan. The exterior walls are laid in Flemish-bond brick with glazed headers. The front and side porches are later additions. Unlike most other old plantation houses of lower Delaware occupied by tenant farmers, this house has been kept in good repair by its owner. The interior paneling with its dog-ear trim is especially notable.

At 42.7 *m.* is the lane (R) to PLEASANTON ABBEY *(private)*, a brick mansion built about 1750 by Henry Stevens. Architectural features of the exterior include Flemish-bond brickwork, a moulded brick water table, a fine cornice, and the wooden window headings characteristic of many Delaware houses of the period.

An ardent Tory during the Revolution, Stevens was suspected by the patriots of harboring other and more militant Tories in his house. One night, by tradition, he and his beautiful French wife were entertaining some pro-British friends (or soldiers) when a servant announced the arrival of a patriot searching party. Only one place occurred to him where the party might not look, and he told his friends to climb up into the chimney. The searchers looked everywhere but the chimney, and after they left the sooty Tories came down again in safety.

At 44.3 *m.* (L) is the OCTAGONAL SCHOOLHOUSE, locally called the

Eight-Square Schoolhouse, standing under old cedars at the edge of a woods. This odd little building was erected of stone in 1836 as a public school, and continued as such until the early 20th century. Inside were two circles of desks, the outer circle for boys facing the wall, the inner circle for girls facing the center. In recent years the old structure has been used occasionally as a community meeting-house.

At 46.3 *m.* is the junction with State 8 *(see Tour 13)*.

At 46.7 *m.* is the junction with a side road.

Left on this road and causeway across the marsh to PORT MAHON, 3 *m.*, a light-house and wharf on Delaware Bay; this deep-water anchorage was named early in the 19th century after Port Mahon, capital of the Spanish island of Minorca in the Mediterranean Sea. The inaccessibility of the landing prevented much use of it by vessels until 1936, when the present long causeway was built from the mainland. New wharves are used by party-boats taking anglers to the fishing grounds on the bay, and by oyster schooners that formerly had to struggle with tides and sandbars in going up to Leipsic or Little Creek to unload their cargoes. Trucks come down to the bay itself at Port Mahon.

In May and June the Delaware oyster fleet cruises back and forth on the State-owned seed grounds off Port Mahon, dredging seed oysters to be planted on the leased beds elsewhere in the bay. They are all sailing vessels and make a handsome sight, running with mainsail, foresail, and jib all set and drawing, their low, white-painted hulls gleaming in the sun, their decks piled high with oysters. Amidships on each side of a vessel is a dredge (pronounced *drudge* by the oystermen), a metal frame let down by chains and dragged on the bottom to scrape up the oysters, which are hauled up overside and dumped from time to time. A law forbids the use of power boats on the seed beds in order to give the poor man a fair chance. Power is used on private grounds in harvesting the crop. Less than a dozen schooners and some power-boats now comprise the dwindling oyster fleet of Delaware, vastly outnumbered by the New Jersey fleet that operates on the larger and better grounds east of the ship channel. Since Colonial days the oystermen of the two States have had frequent pitched battles, and police interference was required as late as 1932.

LITTLE CREEK, 47.2 *m.* (223 pop.), on the north shore of Little Creek, 2 miles from Delaware Bay, was once the busy center of the oyster industry, and its chief charm is still the scene at its wharves. The "party-boats" that are its principal source of revenue now dominate that salty scene. The few oyster schooners that still come in here to discharge cargo or to lay up in off-seasons make a quiet background of rigging and white-tipped masts for the dozens of power cruisers that from May to October carry parties of anglers out to the bay. *(Meals, lodging, bait, and tackle are available in the village.)* Party boats usually leave for the bay at day-break and return in the afternoon; they are so numerous they fill the channel. Little Creek ranks with Bowers Beach and Lewes as one of the noted salt-water fishing resorts on the Delaware shore. In winter many of the residents engage in trapping, commercial fishing, and dredging for oysters, clams, and crabs.

Before 1837, when John Bell built a wharf and opened a store here, there was not much at Little Creek Landing except the Colonial NOWELL HOUSE (L), built of stone brought in by vessel. In April 1813 the neighborhood was surprised by the arrival in the creek of a boatload of men from the British schooner *Pilgrim,* sent to secure food supplies by the warship *Poictiers,* then blockading the bay. The people refused to furnish

the supplies and the landing party spent the next 36 hours taking whatever they could find, until they were finally driven off by the enraged
farmers and fishermen.

At 47.3 *m.* on State 9, just south of the creek bridge, is the junction
with a side road.

Right on this road was CHERBOURG *(now destroyed)*, **0.6** *m.*, an old brick house
built in an odd-shaped plan at the end of an avenue of poplars. An early Georgian-
Colonial front wing, very small but with a great chimney, was connected at the rear
to a later and larger addition that extended on a parallel axis beyond the west wall
of the original wing. The first section of the house is believed to have been built
by John Marim about 1715. From the Marim family Cherbourg passed to the
Comegys family, and was the home of Cornelius P. Comegys, a lieutenant colonel
in the War of 1812, Governor of Delaware 1837–41. Behind the house was a large
circular brick barn, very unusual in Delaware.

All materials from Cherbourg when it was taken down, were saved for restoring
Delaware survivals of the same period.

At 51.3 *m.* is the junction with the Jones Neck Rd. *(see Tour 2A).*
At 51.5 *m.* is the junction with US 113 *(see Tour 2).*

Tour 11

(Lancaster, Pa.)—Stanton—Christiana—Junction with US 13; State 7.
Pennsylvania Line—Junction with US 13, 16.1 *m.*
Roadbed paved throughout.

Accommodations in towns.

State 7, its northern part called the Limestone Rd., runs through a hilly
piedmont region with rapid streams and old stone houses, thence through
the nearly level tidewater lowlands of the Peninsula plain where the old
houses are of brick. The two regions differ in rhythm and atmosphere: at
the northern end of the route the highly specialized mushroom industry
(see Tour 7) contrasts sharply with the southern end where large fields of
corn and wheat are tilled largely by Negro labor. Many of the farms bordering Pike and Mill creeks in the upper section have been bought in
recent years by members and connections of the Du Pont family as a fox-
hunting preserve for the Vicmead Hunt Club *(see Tour 6),* and pink-
coated horsemen and bowler-hatted horsewomen follow the hounds
through the hills and valleys every Saturday, rain or shine, during the
hunting season, jumping the rail panels and splashing across streams.

State 7 crosses the Pennsylvania Line, 0 *m.,* about 4 miles southeast of
Avondale, Pa. *(see Pa. Tour 29).*

At BALDWIN'S CORNERS, 1 *m.,* is the SITE OF MUDFORD (or
Tweed's) TAVERN, one of the stopping places of thirsty teamsters hauling
grain over the Limestone Rd. in pre-railroad days.

The former MERMAID TAVERN *(private)*, 3.5 *m.* (R), now a dwelling, was a noted oasis as early as 1740, when the stone part is believed to have been built. Both stone and frame sections of the long two-and-one-half story structure have been much altered inside and out, but many original details remain. There are traces of the old bar, which was hinged so that it could be raised to make a partition separating the liquor supply from the barroom when desirable. Some of the Mermaid's flooring is of "ark planks" from the heavy wagons or "arks" that broke down after years of hauling grain from Pennsylvania and Maryland to vessels at Christiana or Newport. A large stable, a wheelwright shop, and a blacksmith shop disappeared with the coming of the iron horse, but the Mermaid continued to be a focus of local activities; it was a post office for many years, and still preserved is the old ballot box that was used here when the tavern was the polling place of Mill Creek Hundred. The century-old Farmers Mutual Insurance Co. of Delaware was organized here in 1839 and held its meetings here until 1850. The room above the old carriage shed was long used for meetings of Harmony Grange, organized here in 1874.

At 4.3 *m.*, GRAVEYARD HILL (L) is topped by a lone Siberian pine which, by local tradition, stands guard over the body of a Revolutionary patriot buried upright with ax and musket in hand, ready to meet the invading British. Another version makes the corpse an Indian chief and the invaders the white men. The view from the hilltop is as fine as any in northern Delaware.

At 5.4 *m.*, the foot of a knoll on which a buff-colored frame house stands, is the SITE OF AN OAK TREE under whose shade, it is related, Washington and some of his officers stopped and were served tea.

MILLTOWN, 5.5 *m.*, at the fall line of Mill Creek, is a few buildings clustered around a mill-building erected of rubble in 1815 and now used as a barn. The mill replaced Robinson's Mill, described in 1742 as being then in a bad state of repair. The old two-story BALL HOUSE *(private)*, buff-plastered, is (L) the birthplace of Dr. Lewis Heisler Ball (1861–1933), U. S. Senator 1903–5.

At 5.6 *m.* is the junction with three side roads.

Left sharply to DEL-CASTLE FARM, 1.4 *m.* (L), a part of the New Castle County Workhouse property, producing food for prison consumption.

At 1.6 *m.* on this road is (R) RED CLAY CREEK PRESBYTERIAN CHURCH *(Sun. services at 11; open by permission)*, a large white rectangular structure of the modified classic type popular for church architecture when it was built in 1853; it has since been stuccoed over. Some of the stone came from an earlier church building that stood further up the hill in the cemetery. One of the stones in the south end of the interior attic wall has the date 1761 rudely carved on it. In the east yard is a tulip poplar tree about 17 feet in girth. An old gravestone (1766) bears this legend:

> When I am dead and in my grave
> And all my bones are rotten
> Remember me when this you see
> Lest I should be forgotten.

At 5.7 *m.* on State 7 is (L) the MURRAY HOUSE *(private)*, consisting of a stone wing erected in the late 18th century and a smaller gambrel-roofed wing of stucco-covered logs, with a chimney dated 1741.

At 6.2 m. is the junction with State 2 *(see Tour 8)*.

STANTON, 7.2 m. (20 alt., 400 pop.), a village near the confluence of Red Clay and White Clay creeks, is one of the oldest settlements in the region. As late as 1768 it was called Cuckoldstown; why this indelicate name was given it, no one seems to know. The place was later named for Stephen Stanton, a local property-owner. Grist and sawmills used the water power of the creeks at least as early as 1679. Washington, expecting Howe to march from the Head of Elk to Philadelphia this way, camped here with his army Aug. 28-Sept. 8, 1777, but the British detoured to the west through Newark *(see Tour 9)*, and Washington moved his men toward Brandywine Springs. In the 19th century there were cotton and woolen mills here, but there are no important industries in Stanton now.

The large BRICK HOUSE, SE. cor. of the main intersection, was a tavern, kept in 1797 by Peter Springer. The TATNALL or BYRNES HOUSE *(private)*, E. side of Old Mill Rd., formerly a busy thoroughfare to the mills, was built about 1750 of brick in the Dutch Colonial style. To the R. is the STANTON MEETING HOUSE *(meetings no longer held)*, erected in 1873 to replace an earlier one. The meeting was organized in 1781 as White Clay Creek Meeting. In 1834 it was recorded that "The number of Friends residing in the neighborhood being very small, it is difficult to maintain a school in that place." Next door is the old stone building used as the school. At the stuccoed-brick MARSHALL HOUSE *(private)*, on State 7, (R) according to tradition, Washington and his aides were eating a meal when the sound of British cannon caused them to leave in haste.

At 7.5 m. is an entrance to DELAWARE PARK (R) and its racetrack *(see Tour 8)*.

Opposite the entrance, the ridge (L) is the SITE OF WASHINGTON'S FORTIFICATIONS occupied by his army Sept. 7-8, 1777; he is said to have had cannon "as thick as they could stand" and with pickets posted as far south as Christiana Bridge.

The BOYCE HOUSE *(private)*, 8.1 m. (L), built before 1775 on the bank of White Clay Creek, is a large two-story brick dwelling with a basement kitchen opening at grade on the creek bank. With its broad chimneys, brick belt course, and water table, it is a notable example of Georgian Colonial architecture. On Sept. 6, 1777 the American officers were ordered to a meeting here. A great sycamore tree stands on the lawn. Across the creek from the house is BREAD AND CHEESE ISLAND, noted as such on the 1656 map of the Swedish engineer Peter Lindeström.

CHRISTIANA, 10.7 m. (20 alt., 411 pop.), another quiet village, was once an important shipping point on the Christina Creek, whose name, originally Christine Bridge, became Christiana in Colonial days. Market town and news center (via sloops and stages) it was also a craft center during most of the eighteenth century. Here James, Joseph and Alexander Kinkead made their tall beautiful clocks, now collectors' items.

There was a bridge across the Christiana here as early as 1686. As the back-country filled up, more and more vessels ascended from the Delaware River to load the grain, produce, and high-grade flour milled on the banks of this and other streams nearby; it was shipped to Philadelphia and thence often abroad. In 1756 with "70 or 80 houses" Christiana had vastly more activity than now. In 1785 a line of stage boats sailed between here and Philadelphia, and later a semi-weekly packet service was established.

Many famous travelers stopped at "Christiana Bridge." Mason and Dixon met here in 1765 to discuss boundaries with the commissioners of Maryland and Pennsylvania. George Washington frequently dined, breakfasted, lodged, and baited his horses here. Reaching the bridge one day in September 1787 on his way home from the Constitutional Convention in Philadelphia, he found that rains made the creek alarmingly high but the long-used bridge carried his horses and chariot safely on. Further along beyond the Delaware line, one of his horses fell through another flooded bridge. Mill hands sprang to the rescue and soon had the horses and chariot on their way.

Changes in transportation routes brought the decline of Christiana: first the Chesapeake and Delaware Canal in 1829, followed by the New Castle and Frenchtown R.R. in 1832, the rail line around Chesapeake Bay by Elkton, and more recently the motor routes of US 13 and US 40, avoiding the village by several miles.

CHRISTIANA PRESBYTERIAN CHURCH, W. side of State 7 just N. of the main intersection, built in 1858, is on the site of a church erected in 1745. An old pewter communion service is a treasured possession. Col. Samuel Patterson, a miller and an officer in the Revolution, is buried here. The old CHRISTIANA HOTEL, NW. corner of the intersection, was built in the 18th century. The yellow-painted building with pent eaves, E. side of State 7 just S. of the intersection, is the former SHANNON HOTEL, erected before the Revolution. William Shannon, a locally famed host, is said to have entertained Washington here.

At the traffic light is the junction with State 273 and the Cooch's Bridge Rd.

1. Right on State 273 to the SITE OF TALBOT'S FORT, **0.4** *m.* (R), marked by a bronze tablet. The fort was built in 1684 by Col. George Talbot, a cousin of Lord Baltimore, to defend the latter's claim to this territory along the Delaware River as part of the Maryland grant. During the two years that the little fort was garrisoned by Maryland soldiers and sympathizers, Talbot raged and roared, cursing and threatening to dispossess those who "would not forthwith yield Obedience to ye Lord Baltimore & Own him to be their Propor [proprietor] and pay rent to him."

OGLETOWN, **2.2** *m.*, is a hamlet named for Thomas Ogle who acquired land here in 1739. The small, old, brick house (R) was successively the shop of a clockmaker named Le Huray (died 1834), a tavern, and a store. *(Destroyed 1953.)*

At **2.9** *m.* on State 273 is the NEWARK BOX TOE PLANT *(open by permission)*, making felt shells for box-toes; these are shipped mostly to the Middle West, and built into shoes of all kinds.

2. Right on the Cooch's Bridge Rd. to the junction with a side road, **0.6** *m.*; L. on this road to the old PATTERSON or BUFORD MILL, **0.3** *m.* (L), a large brick and stone structure built in 1795 by Joseph Israel, to whom Samuel Patterson sold the property in 1784. Grain was ground on the site as early as 1705 by Col. John French. The present mill building has been idle since 1924. Mill and dam are owned

by the Pennsylvania R.R., which operates here its CHRISTEEN PUMPING STATION; the water of the pond, after a softening process, is forced 11 miles through pipes to the Todd's Cut Yard, north of Wilmington, for use in locomotive boilers. Across the road is the MILLER'S HOUSE *(private)*; its rear wing in Flemish-bond brickwork was erected prior to 1740.

At 11 *m.* on State 7 is (L) the LEWDEN HOUSE *(private)*, on the bank of the Christina, a handsome brick Georgian Colonial house built in 1770, enlarged in 1815, and recently restored. The fine old stairway, mantels, paneling, cupboards, and battened doors have been carefully preserved. From 1695, when John Lewden bought the tract called Fishing Place, until recently, the portion of the estate where the house stands was in the continuous possession of one family. During a short period the house was used as a store.

At 13.1 *m.* is the junction with US 40 *(see Tour 4)*.

THE BEAR, 13.2 *m.,* is a hamlet of a few houses where formerly the Bear Tavern, long since gone, was a welcome stop for travelers on the King's Highway. Even the station on the Pennsylvania R.R. has been removed from this nearly forgotten spot.

RED LION, 14.9 *m.,* in Red Lion Hundred, is another old crossroads where a tavern welcomed travelers. A Red Lion Inn is mentioned as long ago as 1765; it stood at nearby Pigeon Run, and its accommodations were described by a Revolutionary soldier as "tolerable." This inn burned, and after the Revolution a French Huguenot woman named Elisse Roussier opened a new RED LION (R)—the present white-painted brick-and-frame dwelling *(private)* facing State 71. President Washington, returning from Philadelphia to Mount Vernon in March 1791, noted in his diary that he gave his horses "a bite of Hay at the Red Lyon," and noticing that one was "lame and otherwise much indisposed," had him bled and afterwards led to the Buck Tavern *(see Tour 9)*. Across the road is another old brick building with fanlighted doorway, formerly a store. The Red Lion Inn sign and an original brick wall are restored at Winterthur Museum.

At 16.1 *m.* is the junction with US 13 *(see Tour 1, Sec. c)*.

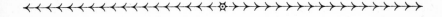

Tour 12

Woodland Beach—Smyrna—Clayton—(Millington, Md.) ; State 6.
Woodland Beach—Maryland Line, 17.2 m.
Roadbed paved throughout.

Accommodations in towns.

State 6 runs along the upper end of Kent County across the State between Delaware Bay and Maryland. It crosses great marshes near the bay
and old farms of waning fertility that were in the heart of the Delaware
peach bonanza as it moved down the Peninsula in the 1860's. Much of the
country west of Smyrna, lacking navigable streams and poorly drained,
was cleared of forest only after the building of the Delaware R.R. in
1855 made it practicable to get the timber out.

WOODLAND BEACH, 0 *m.*, is a small fishing, bathing, and picnicking resort *(boats and fishing equipment for hire)* in a grove occupying a
high-and-dry spot on the bay shore of marshy BOMBAY HOOK ISLAND
(pronounced Bumba Hook), which is separated from the mainland by the
winding channel of Old Duck Creek. Summer residents live in small cottages and boarding houses. Hundreds of week-end anglers from the cities
join the farm families who come for the day. In election years the beach is
a favorite place for political rallies accompanied by ox-roasts, speeches,
and great conviviality. Relief from mosquitoes depends on the continuance
of mosquito-control work on the marshes. In stormy weather in the fall
there is some duck shooting on marshes not included in the new Federal
game refuge *(see below)*.

By legend this lonely and windswept beach was chosen by Captain William Kidd as a cache for plunder; digging for it, however, has been in
vain. In Colonial times the shallow water off here was a noted seine-ground
for planters and their slave fishermen.

After the Civil War the place took on new life when steamers brought
excursionists from Philadelphia and Wilmington. In the 1880's the brilliantly decorated steamer *Republic,* sidewheeling to Cape May, paused
near here to take aboard vacationists who had left Baltimore by steamboat
at daybreak, crossed Chesapeake Bay and ascended Chester River to Chestertown, and thence come by train to Bombay Hook Landing. Not until
after dark would they arrive at Cape May, a scant 100 miles from Baltimore by airline distance. The Baltimore and Delaware Bay R.R., completed
in 1873, has long been obliterated.

Most of Bombay Hook Island south of here is within the BOMBAY
HOOK MIGRATORY WATERFOWL REFUGE *(no shooting permit-
ted)*, which borders the bay for 12 miles, averages 4 miles wide, and contains about 14,000 acres of marsh, with some dry land. Since it was established in 1935 by the U. S. Bureau of Biological Survey, the refuge has become one of the most important waterfowl sanctuaries on the Atlantic Flyway, attracting thousands of migrants in fall, winter, and spring. Among
the score of visiting species are Canadian black duck, mallard, pintail, teal,
Canada geese and snow geese. Species nesting here include black duck,
wood duck, and blue-wing teal. The natural food supply is excellent. A
series of fresh-water lakes is under construction (1953) with the aid of a
dyke project of the U. S. Department of the Interior.

A tract of land on the island was granted in 1675 to Peter Bayard of
Bohemia Manor, who agreed to pay the Duke of York a quitrent of six
bushels of wheat annually. The name is a corruption from the Dutch
"Bompies" or "Bompties" Hook.

At 2.9 *m.* on State 6 is the junction with a paved road *(see Tour 10).*
At 7.3 *m.* is the junction with a side road.

Right on this road is SMYRNA LANDING, 0.3 *m.*, a hamlet of one tree-shaded street at the head of navigation on Duck Creek. A fertilizer plant here still imports its basic materials by water, but there is almost no other activity in this once-busy shipping and shipbuilding center that reached its greatest importance in the 1850's. Dozens of steam and sailing vessels loaded grain, lumber, shiptimber, tanbark, and other products that they carried up Delaware River; they brought back lime, manufactured goods, and general merchandise that the merchants of Smyrna distributed in Delaware and Maryland. Regular freight and passenger steamers ran between here and Philadelphia for more than 75 years. Scores of sailing vessels were launched from the ways of Smyrna Landing—the largest one, 120 feet long, in 1871. The sole surviving GRANARY (L), a sagging frame structure, is a relic of more prosperous days.

SMYRNA, 8 *m.* (20 alt., 2,346 pop.) *(see Tour 1, Sec. c)* is at the junction with US 13 *(see Tour 1).*
At 9.1 *m.* is the junction with State 300 *(see Tour 12A).*
CLAYTON, 9.8 *m.* (824 pop.), is a quiet town at the junction of the Oxford (Md.) Branch of the Pennsylvania R.R. In 1920 the railroad offices and repair shops were removed, leaving the place with few industries besides a cannery and a cold-storage plant.

In 1855 the cross-roads railroad station here was called Smyrna Station, later changed to Clayton in honor of John M. Clayton, a prime promoter of the Delaware R.R. *(see BUENA VISTA: Tour 1, Sec. c).* The site of the new village supposedly belonged to Richard Tibbitt, who sold the lots, but on his death ownership of the whole tract was claimed by William Wertenby, of San Francisco, on the ground that Tibbitt had only a life interest in it. Two noted lawyers fought the case: for the defendants, Reverdy Johnson of Maryland, and for Wertenby, Thomas F. Bayard of Delaware, later Secretary of State under Cleveland. When Wertenby won, he gave Bayard one-fourth of the tract as a fee, and on that one-fourth almost the whole town was erected.

Right from Clayton on Clayton Ave., to ST. JOSEPH'S INDUSTRIAL SCHOOL, 0.3 *m.* (L), an institution for Negro boys, established in 1896 by the St. Joseph's Society of the Sacred Heart of the Roman Catholic Church. Frame buildings on the tract of 400 acres include a chapel, dormitories, and workshops where instruction is given in printing, farming, poultry-raising, carpentry, and other manual arts. Boys of good character between the ages of 10 and 14 are admitted for a period of 5 years, and receive academic education through the first 2 years of high school.

At 11.2 *m.* (R) is the pre-Revolutionary HOFFECKER HOUSE *(private),* two and one-half stories in height. The facade of this small house, typical of other old brick houses in the region, has two windows flanking a doorway in the first story, and three windows in the second story.
At 13.5 *m.* is the junction with a dirt lane.

Right on this lane to AIRY MOUNT *(private),* 0.4 *m.*, one of the old plantation houses of Deer Park, a 2,250-acre tract bought in 1733 under a Maryland patent by Benjamin Blackiston for 45 pounds and 2 shillings. The long, two-and-one-half story house is built in two sections of similar proportions; the pre-Revolutionary east section is of brick, the west section is of frame construction and was apparently added later. The plain interior woodwork is very old. Under the window-sills in the "parlor" are drawers in which, it is said, money was kept when this brick section of the house was used as a bank about 1800. A great old sycamore tree shades the kitchen wing. A tall white silo nearby contrasts oddly with the antiquity of Airy Mount.

BLACKISTON, 13.9 *m.,* is a few houses, a garage, and a blacksmith shop.

At 15.9 *m.* (L) the small gray frame structure is BLACKISTON M. E. CHURCH on the site of the original chapel designed by Bishop Francis Asbury and erected in 1787.

At 16.8 *m.* (L) is the HAZELL HOUSE *(private),* also on the former Deer Park tract of the Blackistons; this small two-story brick house, with belt course, and a wing of frame construction, is painted white. The small Gothic porch is an addition, but the interior contains much of the original woodwork and hardware. About 100 yards behind the house is a small stream that is a headwater of the Chester River of Maryland.

At 17.2 *m.* State 6 crosses the Maryland Line, 4 miles east of Millington, Md.

Tour 12A

Junction with State 6—Kenton—(Sudlersville, Md.) ; State 300.
Junction with State 6—Maryland Line, 11 m.
Roadbed paved throughout.

State 300 runs across the fertile farmlands of northwestern Kent County through Kenton Hundred, partitioned from Duck Creek and Little Duck Creek hundreds in 1869. In 1683 the Manor of Freith was surveyed in this region as the 10,000-acre tract which William Penn ordered reserved for his family in this county, supplementing similar tracts in other counties. Like other manors of his, this one was soon broken up and sold to settlers. A tract of 3,000 acres in this area was patented in 1714 to the Bristol Naval Store Co-Partnership Co. of Bristol, England, for raising hemp to make rigging for ships. The Dulaney and Blackiston families also had large holdings in this section. Most of the land, however, stayed in hardwood timber until the railroad furnished means of exporting lumber and then farm produce.

At 0 *m.* State 300 branches southwest from State 6 *(see Tour 12),* at the western edge of Smyrna.

At 0.3 *m.* (L) is BANNISTER HALL *(private),* a large yellow frame house set well back from the road at the end of an avenue bordered by tree-filled lawns. The house has the square lines and the cupola characteristic of Delaware country mansions of the Victorian period. It was erected 1865 by John Anthony with labor, tools, and equipment brought from his former home town of Troy, N. Y. A short distance behind Bannister Hall is the original residence of the plantation, the small brick BAYNARD HOUSE of two stories, erected about 1750. Numerous outbuildings give the appearance of a small village.

At the small WHITE HOUSE (*private*), 2.4 *m.* (L), a tavern before the era of the railroad, a kind soul known simply as Aunt Betsy offered refreshment to teamsters hauling produce to Smyrna Landing on Duck Creek (*see Tour 12*). The 18th-century house is of brick, white-stuccoed. Farms in this neighborhood had names like Rippling Brook, Springfield, and Pushmatahaville.

At 4.5 *m.* (R) is BRYN ZION BAPTIST CHURCH (*occasional services*), erected of brick in 1771, now covered with brown stucco. In 1871 the original windows and pews were replaced by the present ones. The building shows its age, but its plain lines and simple pitched roof have considerable charm. The congregation is an offshoot of the Welsh Tract church. An old cemetery surrounds the structure.

KENTON, 5.5 *m.* (231 pop.), is a small trading center on the Oxford Branch of the Pennsylvania R.R. A cannery here operates only in summer. Originally the name was Lewis Cross-Roads but the place was soon called Grogtown, presumably because of the drinking facilities for travelers going between Maryland and the ports of Smyrna Landing and Leipsic. The green-painted brick PRETTYMAN HOUSE (*private*), E. cor. of the junction with State 42, was built about 1775; it has a watertable and belt course. The former KENTON HOTEL, SE. side of State 300 just SW. of the junction, is a frame structure erected in 1809 by Philip Lewis; it is a liquor store. Tavern-keeping declined after the building of the branch rail line through the village, but the shipping of grain and produce gave Kenton some importance until motor trucks began transporting the crops directly from the fields.

At 6.9 *m.* (R) is the DOWNS HOUSE (*private*). Except for an added porch and cornice, it remains virtually unaltered since it was built, according to a dated brick, in 1773. The house is unusually large in comparison with other Georgian Colonial brick residences of the region. The moulded brick watertable is especially fine. The original lead roof is said to have been sold during the Revolution to the American authorities for melting into bullets. A small kitchen wing is very old. The house contains the original paneling, flooring, and hardware. The estate name is Aspendale.

DOWNS' CHAPEL, 9 *m.*, is a hamlet with a crossroads store; Downs' Chapel itself (L) is a small brick structure with a belfry, erected in 1927 on the site of a chapel built in 1880.

At 10.5 *m.* is the junction with a dirt lane.

Right on this lane to the CLARK HOUSE (*private*), 0.3 *m.*, now occupied by the Ford family. The gray-painted dwelling has a center section of brick that was built in the 18th century and is now flanked by two frame sections. To the rear of the house, L. of the stables, a lane leads to a bluff above Jamison's Ditch, 0.5 *m.,* the grassy spot said to have been the SITE OF CHENEY CLOW'S FORT.

The story of Clow's "fort" and his "rebellion" is a mixture of record and legend. He is described as a captain in the British army before the Revolution and an ardent Tory during the war. Whether or not he was the leader of the numerous roving Tory marauders who harassed the patriots from time to time during the war, is not certain. He did refuse to take the oath of allegiance required of suspected enemies of the new country, and one night in 1782 a Sheriff's posse went to arrest him at his house in the backwoods near the Maryland Line. They shouted the order to surrender, and were answered by a fusillade from the darkened house. The posse fired back and the siege was on. The rapidity of the shots from the house indicated several defenders, but when the door was finally battered in the only persons found were Captain Clow and his wounded wife, who had been loading spare muskets for him.

Clow surrendered, dressed himself in his British uniform, and started back to Dover with his captors. Halfway there they were met by a company of militia who demanded that Clow be turned over to them for hanging; the posse refused to do so, and managed to get him to jail. Clow was charged with treason and brought to trial Dec. 10, 1782, but he convinced the jury that as an enemy officer he was entitled to be treated as a prisoner of war, and he was acquitted. Remanded to jail, he was next charged with the murder of one of the posse who had been killed during the siege of the "fort." This time he was convicted and sentenced to be hanged, but it was not until 1788 that the date of execution was set, at Clow's own request, by the reluctant Governor Thomas Collins. On the day of the execution, it is said, Caesar Rodney declared he never before wished to be Governor, but wished he was then so he could pardon Clow. The bitterness of the Whigs prevailed, and Captain Clow was hanged. His wife, who had spent six years pleading for his pardon, took his body and buried it no one knows where. Then a "great revulsion of feeling" took place in the county at the way a brave man had been treated.

At 11 *m.* State 300 crosses the Maryland Line, becoming Md. State 300, about 6 miles east of Sudlersville.

Tour 13

Junction with State 9—Dover—Marydel—(Goldsboro, Md.); State 8.
Junction with State 9—Maryland Line, 17 m.

Roadbed paved throughout.

State 8 runs across the middle of Kent County in central Delaware between the edge of the Delaware Bay marshes and the Maryland Line.

Section a. Junction with State 9 to Dover, 4.4 m.

East of Dover the tidewater countryside of Little Creek and East Dover hundreds was settled in the late 17th century. Old brick plantation houses, occupied by tenant farmers, stand among large fields whose fertility has usually diminished under careless tilling after the failure of the peach crops in the late 19th century. Negro quarters have disappeared from the once well-kept estates of slaveholding gentry who, like their neighbors of Jones Neck *(see Tour 2A)*, enjoyed dancing and fox hunting and traveled behind black coachmen in livery. Only narrow strips of woods survive near the streams or swamps.

State 8 branches west from State 9 *(see Tour 10)*, 0 *m.*, just north of Little Creek.

At 0.8 *m.* on State 8 is the junction with Quaker Lane, a private dirt road.

Right on this lane to the RUINS OF LITTLE CREEK QUAKER MEETING-HOUSE, **0.5** *m.*, built of brick in 1802 to succeed a meeting-house that was erected nearby in 1771; though the "Friends of Little Creek in Kent County" had had their own congregation since 1711 when they received permission to separate from Duck Creek Meeting near Smyrna. Because the number of Quaker families decreased in the vicinity, Little Creek Meeting suspended regular worship about 1865 and thereafter the congregation attended Camden Meeting *(see Tour 1, Sec. d.)*, 7 miles southwest. In 1888 this building was sold and has since been used as a farm catchall; parts of the fine paneling are still in place. Across the lane (R) is the old GRAVEYARD surrounded by a high wall and fragrant with red cedars and magnificent boxwood trees. Small headstones include those of the Cowgills (pronounced kógle) and other quiet and dignified old families of the region.

At 3.6 *m.* is the junction with US 113 *(see Tour 2)*.
DOVER, 4.4 *m.* (20 alt., 6,223 pop.) *(see DOVER)*.

Points of Interest. The Green, State House, Legislative Hall, old private houses with gardens, a noted chicken-and-plum-pudding plant, the State Museum and others.

At Dover is the junction with US 13 *(see Tour 1)*.

Section b. Dover to the Maryland Line, 12.6 m.

West of Dover the route rises to cross the 50-foot plateau drained only by the little headwaters of streams flowing either east or west. This section, like most of the whole western side of Delaware, was not fully developed as a grain, fruit, and dairy region until the railroad came down the State in the 1850's. Toward the Maryland border much of West Dover Hundred has never become anything but cutover timberland; drainage ditches have helped somewhat, and many little farms grow berries, rye, and apples.

At 1.9 *m.* (R) on State 8 is the MAPLEDALE COUNTRY CLUB *(private)*, with a small club house and a 9-hole golf course.

At 4.1 *m.* is the junction with a side road.

Left on latter to the ROSE VALLEY CHEESE PLANT *(open by permission)*, **0.8** *m.* (L), where 200-pound cheeses are made from milk produced on the farms of the Amish Mennonites of the section. When these people began to come down here from southeastern Pennsylvania, about 1900, they brought with them their jealously-guarded recipes for making cheese—secrets brought in turn from Switzerland. The cheese factory and the sawmill (R) are run co-operatively. The Amish have a

much closer connection with their relatives in Pennsylvania than with their Delaware neighbors, and most of the cheese is shipped north to Reading and Philadelphia, though they drive to Dover each week in their closed carriages to sell cream,
cakes, butter, eggs, and other produce to housewives. Their appearance is distinctive: they use no buttons on their clothes; the men wear black suits, black hats,
and beards but shave the upper lip; the women wear bonnets and many petticoats;
children dress exactly like their parents. In Switzerland, their ancestors, to avoid a
tax on buttons and mustaches, began the practice of fastening their clothing with
hooks and eyes and of shaving the upper lip. They do not drive automobiles and
politely decline to be photographed; they will not hold public office, nor send
their children to the public schools, but maintain a small school of their own. Families number about 25.

An earlier Mennonite settlement in Delaware was made in 1661 at the Hoerekill
(now Lewes) under charter from the burgomasters of Amsterdam, Holland, to
Pieter Plockhoy; this group was disrupted in 1664 by Capt. Robert Carr when the
British seized the Dutch settlements on the Delaware *(see LEWES)*.

At 6.4 *m.,* PEARSON'S CORNER, is the junction with State 44.

Right on this road is HARTLY, 3.3 *m.* (101 pop.), a village on the Oxford
Branch of the Pennsylvania R.R. There is little activity except a cannery running in
summer. Hartly grew up at the crossroads station at a spot known previously as
Arthurville and Butterpot, the latter name arising, it is said, from the crock that a
woman set in the nearby stream to cool her newly-made butter; young men would
go from house to house singing, "Butterpot gals, ain't you comin' out tonight?" to
the tune of *Carolina Gals.*

MARYDEL, 12.5 *m.,* is a hamlet in two States, as its name indicates.
Near here in 1877, James Gordon Bennett (1841–1918), owner of the
New York *Herald,* fought a bloodless pistol duel with Fred May, a New
York socialite of the day, who had been reported engaged to Bennett's
sister. The sudden breaking of the "engagement" provoked Bennett to
challenge the other, and their seconds chose this isolated spot on a State
line to prevent interference by the law.

At 12.6 *m.* State 8 crosses the Maryland Line, 6.5 miles northeast of
Goldsboro, Md.

Tour 14

Lewes Beach—Lewes—Georgetown—(Federalsburg, Md.); State 18.
Lewes Beach—Maryland Line, 35.7 m.
Roadbed paved throughout.
Accommodations in towns.

Between Delaware Bay and the western Maryland-Delaware Line, State
18 runs across the flat, sandy plain of Sussex County marked by small
farms and squared-off blocks of loblolly pine timber. Cornfields alternate

with fields planted with tomatoes, peas, and other cannery crops. Along the road the occasional sheds covering heavy machinery are "bean-viners" to which lima-bean vines are brought by the wagonload to be thrashed. The beans are packed in water-filled containers and rushed to the canneries. The strong sour smell around a bean-viner arises from the great heaps of fermenting vines that have been thrown out by the machine. Other crops of the section are asparagus, broccoli, apples, and peaches.

LEWES BEACH, 0 *m.*, is a summer resort of several hotels and boarding houses and scores of cottages built on the sand dunes along the curve of Delaware Bay; it is separated from Lewes by the salt meadows of Lewes Common and the Lewes-Rehoboth Canal. A short boardwalk runs along the beach front. There is excellent salt-water fishing, bathing, and sailing. Party boats for fishing set out from the Canal Basin at Lewes. The headquarters of the Lewes Yacht Club is at the northwest end of the resort at the Roosevelt Inlet; sailing races are held on week-ends throughout the season *(see LEWES).*

At 0.1 *m.* is the junction with Cape Henlopen Drive *(see Tour 14A).*
LEWES, 0.6 *m.* (15 alt., 2,904 pop.) *(see LEWES).*

Points of Interest. Old cypress-shingled houses, the Zwaanendael House, The DeVries Monument, fishing-boat wharves, and others.

At 1.5 *m.* (R) is the SITE OF THE ORIGINAL CCC MOSQUITO-CONTROL CAMP in Delaware, established in 1933 in a section of the State where men and beasts had suffered and died from the mosquito plague since earliest settlement. In 1937 this camp was disbanded after mosquito breeding had been abated by the ditching or flooding of all the salt-marsh areas in southeastern Sussex County *(see Tour 2C).*

At 2 *m.* (R) is OLD EBENEZER CEMETERY, one of the oldest burying-grounds in Delaware. The earliest marker is for the infant Rhodes Shankland, buried in 1700.

At WESCOAT'S CORNER, 2.7 *m.*, is the eastern junction with State 14 *(see Tour 2C),* which unites with State 18 between this point and 3.3 *m.*

BELLTOWN, 3.6 *m.* (300 pop. est.) is an all-Negro village, with a school, church, stores, and a beauty parlor. Some of the houses shine with paint or whitewash and have well-swept front yards of bare earth, set off by beds of bright red cannas. Other dwellings are paintless tumbledown shacks surrounded by tin cans and refuse. Nearly every family has a flock of chickens and a pig or two. The village has no governing body of its own, but the people sometimes gather in the schoolhouse to discuss a problem affecting them. A favorite form of entertainment is a "quartet contest" held in church or school; groups of four to six male or female singers from several towns take turns singing spirituals and other songs before judges. Tickets to the entertainment are often bought by white neighbors, some of whom attend and are shown to seats at the front of the hall.

In the mornings, most of the adult population leaves on foot or in old automobiles for work in Lewes or in the nearby apple and peach orchards.

At night files of Negroes, sometime singing, plod home to Belltown—
a procession that is a century-old ritual.

Belltown was named for Jake (Jigger) Bell, a free Negro, who about
1840 gave a plot of land for a church and sold lots for the establishment
of a town. The village, though supporting the church, soon became noted
for its "Devil-Worshippers"—a sect led by Arnsy Maull, whose voodoo
art is still remembered and probably still followed to some extent; his
clientele included whites as well as Negroes for miles around. His "cunjurs"
had the required power, it is said, to cure a misery or kill an enemy. The
Devil Worshippers had a prolonged initiation period: a neophyte had to
spend seven Sundays in the woods in solitary communion with the Devil,
who on the seventh Sunday took possession of his soul and gave him
supernatural powers.

Arnsy Maull on his death bed repudiated this dark religion, ordering his
followers, so the story goes, to get long whips and lash the air so as to
"drive off the Devil and let the Lord in!" This they did all night, accom-
panying the cracks of the blacksnake whips with prayers and exhortations.
Arnsy's son Silas, an old man, disclaims any belief in Devil Worship but
sells "charms" and "cures" made of herbs and other things *(see FOLK-
LORE AND CUSTOMS)*. Silas died 1940.

At 7.1 *m.* is the junction with a side road.

Right on this road to COOL SPRING PRESBYTERIAN CHURCH (R), 0.3 *m.* *(usually
closed; annual service on a Sun. in Oct.)* The present white frame building, erected
in 1855, is said to be the third that has stood on or near this site since the organizing of Cool Spring congregation prior to 1728. With the Lewes church it was one
of the earliest establishments of the sect in Delaware.

At 7.7 *m.* is the junction with a side road.

Left on this road to the junction with another road, 0.4 *m.;* L. on this road to
the little gambrel-roofed MARTIN HOUSE (L), 0.5 *m.* *(private),* unpainted and in
poor condition but older than the typical Colonial houses of eastern Sussex County,
which have pitched roofs and cypress-shingled side walls. The wide weatherboards,
the ancient battened front door of short planks fitted in herringbone style and held
together with hand-wrought nails, the roof design and other details, indicate the
house was built about the end of the 17th century or early in the 18th century.

HARBESON, 9.8 *m.* (L), is a hamlet of neat frame buildings; it was
named for Harbeson Hickman, a landowner of the region, when the railroad station was established here in 1869. Much timber and lumber were
formerly shipped from here.

Casual motorists passing through Harbeson during the 1937 Christmas
season were surprised to see hundreds of cars blocking the single street
and the highway. The attraction proved to be illuminated decorations resulting from rivalry between the residents and culminating in a display
unprecedented in this Protestant region—a large and complete crèche,
built in a front yard, equipped with animals and figures and brilliantly
lighted. Farmers drove 15 miles to see it.

At 14.6 *m.* (R) is a large meadow comprising the SITE OF A RACE-
TRACK AND FAIRGROUNDS used for several years before it was abandoned
early in the 20th century.

GEORGETOWN, 16 *m.* (50 alt., 2,000 pop.) *(see Tour 2).*

At 17 *m.* is the junction with US 113 *(see Tour 2).*

At 20.7 *m.* (R) is a State FORESTRY DEMONSTRATION STAND of both thinned and unthinned pine timber.

COLLINS MILLPOND, 24 *m.* (R), contains bald cypress trees, a southern species of timber here approaching its northern limit. The water-power mill here is the successor to several that have occupied the site since Colonial days.

At 26.4 *m.* is the junction with State 404 *(see Tour 14B).*

At 28 *m.* is the junction with US 13 *(see Tour 1, Sec. d).*

CANNON, 29.6 *m.,* is a hamlet that grew up about a station on the Delaware R.R. after 1879. The station has been closed for several years, and a general store houses the express agency.

At ATLANTA, 33.7 *m.,* a cannery packs tomatoes and sweet potatoes. Until 1917 the brandy still operated by Fred Brown was a favorite spot for local connoisseurs of Sussex County apple and peach brandy. Before 1873 the place was called Horsey's Cross Roads for a storekeeper named Nathaniel Horsey.

At 35.7 *m.* State 18 crosses the Maryland Line, 4 miles east of Federalsburg, Md.

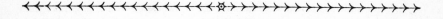

Tour 14A

Lewes Beach—Cape Henlopen; Cape Henlopen Dr.
Junction with State 18—Cape Henlopen, 2.6 m.
Roadbed improved throughout.

This road runs through the salt meadows, scrub pines, and sand dunes of the LEWES COMMONS, confirmed to the people of Sussex County by William Penn in 1682 *(see LEWES)* and since used for pasturing cattle, harvesting marsh hay and firewood, trapping, and gunning. The town treasury receives some revenue from the leasing of land to fish-oil plants and sand companies.

The Cape Henlopen Drive branches east from State 18 *(see Tour 14)* at Lewes Beach, 0 *m. (see Tour 14).*

At 0.6 *m.* (L) is the LEWES COAST GUARD STATION *(open by permission)* with its private pier extending 1,500 feet into the bay so that the crew may launch boats in any sea. Because of the many pleasure and commercial craft using the great roadstead of Delaware Bay, this station is one of the most important on the Atlantic coast; calls for help average 150 annually and service includes anything from rescuing the occupants of a capsized sloop to towing in a disabled power vessel wallowing in a gale. Breeches-buoy and signal drills are held regularly. Nearby is an old building that before the establishment of the station in 1884 was the headquarters of the volunteer "Vigilantes" who went to the aid of vessels in distress off this treacherous beach.

FISH PRODUCTS CO. and CONSOLIDATED FISHERIES CO. (L), 1-1.2 *m.* *(open by permission)* are two large and strong smelling factories on the bay shore where oil is rendered from the inedible menhaden fish. Many large diesel trawlers drag purse seines in the open sea along 200 miles of coast to catch millions of barrels of the fish. These are brought to the plants and cooked in huge vats. The oil is shipped by rail to refineries that prepare it for use in paint, oilcloth, linoleum, soap, etc. Much of it is used by steel mills for tempering steel. The residue is dried, pulverized and shipped to feed mills to be mixed into poultry and animal feed.

Consolidated Fisheries Co. is the oldest plant. Fish Products Co., established 1939, has 600 employees, 40 percent white, 60 percent colored.

The menhaden fishing fleets in Delaware waters have long been famous. In 1953 the U.S. Fish and Wildlife Service reported a total fish catch by Lewes boats of 360 million lbs., making Lewes the leading U.S. fish port.

The oily, mealy, bony menhaden which is unpalatable as table food is rich in vitamins and minerals. Its use in poultry and animal feed spares products valuable as human food and so plays a substantial part in the total food economy and is one more ocean source of industrial materials.

At 1.2 *m.* is the junction with a side road.

Right on this road to the SAND WORKS, **0.5** *m.,* where elevators dump sand from the great Lewes Common Dunes into freight cars. Raw sand is shipped short distances only, because of transportation cost. Graded sand, however, bringing a higher price, is shipped as far as the Mississippi. Vibrating sieves separate the various grades used for water-filtering, sand-blasting, filler for fertilizer, and other purposes. The amount of royalty paid the town of Lewes by the sand concerns has been a bitterly-argued issue for years.

At 1.6 *m.* (L) is the ruined and long abandoned IRON PIER, built by Federal Government between 1870 and 1890 but never completed. Extending out 2,000 feet, it was nearing completion, the story goes, when an accident occurred. By an old method, the last auger-tipped piles were ready to be screwed into the bottom of the bay, and a span of six horses, all groomed for the occasion, stood by the capstan. The driver, however, having celebrated at a saloon, got his gees and haws mixed and drove his team off the end of the pier into the water. The driver was saved but the horses were drowned, and the last piles were never set. Storms have since demolished more than one-half of the rusty old skeleton.

At 2.6 *m.* the road ends in limited PARKING SPACE at POINT O' CAPES. In summer both the ocean and bay shores of the Point are lined with salt-water anglers casting into the rising tide. At night the driftwood fires of beach parties flicker brightly as vacationists roast hot dogs, drink beer, or make love. These fires, however, are innocuous compared to the fires that pirates and outlaws used to build to lure ships on the Hen-and-Chickens Shoals, and then loot the wreckage. One fellow, by legend, hung a lantern from his mule's neck to fool skippers who tried to run by this "lighthouse" and instead piled up on the shoals.

The GREAT SAND HILL (R) rises 100 feet, gleaming in the sun. Its eastern slope down which Lewes children rolled colored hard-boiled eggs on Easter Monday is now U. S. fortified area. Under its brow spreads Fort Miles. Egg-rolling now is done on a different part of the hill.

The shifting sands of this noted landmark have been steadily creeping back over the scrub pines that grow behind it; their dead wind-twisted branches reach above the sand like ghosts. The top of the sand hill is the SITE OF CAPE HENLOPEN LIGHT, a 45-foot hexagonal stone tower, painted white and completed in 1767 to succeed a lighthouse erected in 1725. During the Revolution the light was extinguished by patriots in the hope of wrecking British vessels, but the British themselves landed and burned out the inside, and it was not restored and relighted until 1784. In 1924, the foundation was so weakened that it was abandoned. On April 13, 1926, a heavy storm finished the job of undermining the tower and it toppled towards the sea. Pieces of its masonry are favorite material for fireplaces, and many a Lewes or Rehoboth mantel has a painting of the lighthouse above it.

From the top of the Sand Hill is a broad view all around the compass:

To the west are the spires of Lewes; to the southwest, the great marshy flats of GORDON'S POND; to the south, the long line of dunes down the coast to Rehoboth in the distance, and to the east, the Atlantic Ocean with the waves breaking over the HEN-AND-CHICKENS SHOALS in the foreground, and the OVERFALLS LIGHTSHIP riding at anchor 4 miles offshore, steadfastly guarding the shoals.

To the northeast, on a clear day, the dim line on the horizon is CAPE MAY, 13 miles away; sometimes in hot weather the whole town appears suspended upside down in the air—a startling mirage. On clear nights the lights of the New Jersey resort glow faintly.

To the north is the great sweep of DELAWARE BAY beyond the mile-and-one-half long HARBOR OF REFUGE BREAKWATER with its archipelago of ICE BREAKERS at the farther end, built in the 1890's.

To the northwest, close in the foreground, is the mile-long DELAWARE BREAKWATER with the BREAKWATER LIGHT, a red lighthouse, on its eastern end. It was built (1828–35) of Brandywine granite to form the Breakwater Harbor, where in storms dozens of vessels find shelter.

A small but seaworthy steamer cruising anywhere near the Cape may be either of the two pilot boats—the *Delaware* or the *Philadelphia*—ready to answer the signal that means a vessel wants a pilot for the Delaware River *(see LEWES)*.

The Great Sand Hill, always a vantage-point, has often been a grandstand. During the 60 years of piracy that plagued this coast after 1685, many Lewestowners would come here to watch craft that flew the French and Spanish flags, as well as the Jolly Roger, as they pounced upon shipping or fought each other. During the Revolution they watched from here a cat-and-mouse engagement between the schooner of Capt. Nehemiah

Fields, of Lewes, and the tender of the British brig *Roebuck*. Chasing the schooner, the armed tender went aground on the Hen-and-Chickens Shoals. The parent ship could not approach to defend it, and Captain Fields, coming about, had great sport for two hours as he sailed back and forth and raked the helpless enemy until the rising tide permitted the *Roebuck* to rescue her tender. Fields later joined the British. In April 1813 the Sand Hill was a good place to watch the bombardment of Lewes. In recent years it was a perch from which to watch the boats trying to find the sunken *De Braak* and its treasure *(see LEWES)*.

Near the base of the hill were salt wells, dug to collect seeping water that contained more salt than did the sea water. Large metal pans were used to boil the water until there was nothing left but a residue mostly salt. As early as 1832 more than 1,000 barrels of salt were reclaimed annually by this primitive method in Sussex County along the coast.

The Cape itself has had various names, official and unofficial, since Henry Hudson sailed to it in 1609, and called it a "point of land." In 1620 Capt. Cornelis Mey (or May), of the Dutch West India Co., thinking he was a discoverer, named this cape "Cornelis" and the north one "Cape May." Cape May stuck; but Cape "Cornelis" (or "Cornelius") was called "Cape James" as early as 1629 and was occasionally so called at late as 1794. William Penn in 1682 directed that the name be confirmed as Cape James, but before the close of the 17th century the Dutch name Hinlopen given in Mey's time to the "False Cape" (Fenwick's Island), 25 miles south, became attached to the real cape so securely that not even the years of boundary disputes between the Penns and the Calverts could change it henceforth. Since 1800 all maps give it the name Hinlopen or Henlopen *(see HISTORY)*.

Tour 14B

Junction with State 18—Bridgeville—(Denton, Md.) ; State 404.
Junction with State 18—Maryland Line, 11.4 m.

Roadbed paved throughout.

State 404 in both Delaware and Maryland is part of a popular route across the Peninsula between ocean resorts and the cities of Baltimore and Washington by way of the Matapeake-Annapolis ferries. In Delaware, State 404 runs through the flat farming country and pine woods of Sussex County.

State 404 branches northwest from State 18 *(see Tour 14)*, 0 *m.*, at a point about 10 miles west of Georgetown.

At 1.7 *m.* is the junction with US 13 *(see Tour 1, Sec. d.)*, which unites with State 404 between this point and BRIDGEVILLE, 3.2 *m.* (1468 pop.) *(see Tour 1, Sec. d.)*, where State 404 branches L.

At 9.8 *m.* the road crosses MARSHYHOPE CREEK, a tributary of the Nanticoke River flowing into lower Chesapeake Bay. In the spring of 1934 the creek, choked by windfalls and swamp growth and swollen by heavy rains, suddenly swept down upon Federalsburg, Md., and desolated the lower portions of the town by a flood that reached second floors. Boats were sent from Lewes, Oak Orchard, and other Delaware points to help in salvage work; the people of Federalsburg considered this only fair, since most of the water came out of Delaware, where the swamp conditions were worse. To help prevent future floods and to drain farmland, part of the upper creek and its feeders were cleaned out and later more work was done to clear the bed of the stream below this point where it had been silted up for several miles.

The Marshyhope Swamp here is typical of the headwaters of Chesapeake tributaries rising in Delaware. In the jungles beside these sluggish black waters is nearly every variety of animal and vegetable life native to the Peninsula.

At 11.4 *m.* is the WOODENHAWK INTERSTATE FOREST FIRE TOWER (L), straddling the Maryland-Delaware line; this tall structural-steel affair has a lookout box at the top where a fire warden stands guard during the spring and fall months when most fires occur. The tower is maintained and the warden paid jointly by the States of Delaware and Maryland.

State 404 crosses the Maryland Line, 11.4 *m.*, about 9 miles southwest of Denton, Md.

Tour 15

Junction with State 14—Millsboro—Gumboro—(Pittsville, Md.); State 24 and 26.
Junction with State 14—Maryland Line, 27.4 *m.*
Roadbed paved throughout.

Accommodations in towns.

Running between the Cape Henlopen region and the southern Maryland-Delaware Line, this route crosses the level farmlands and pinelands of southeastern Delaware, passing to the westward of Rehoboth Bay, In-

dian River Bay, and the Great Pocomoke (or Cypress) Swamp. Along the
north shore of Indian River the highway traverses the country of the so-
called Moors and Nanticoke Indians.

Until penetrated in recent years by paved roads this whole region was
one of the most isolated sections of isolated Sussex County. In spite of the
roads, automobiles, newspapers, radios, and the buses that haul white children 5 or 10 miles to large consolidated schools, the aspect and atmosphere
of the region have changed very little since it was settled, in the late 17th
and early 18th centuries, chiefly by Englishmen and Eastern Shore Virginians. Teachers fondly despaired of making children say "it" for *hit,*
"houses" for *housen,* "take" for *carry,* and "carry" for *tote.* A sparrow was
a *sporry* in some spots, a harrow a *horry.* Other expressions through this
area that are still heard, are:

"Hit favors rain right smart."

"He belongs to be here by now."

"The road is so norry I cain't hardly shun the ruts."

"I always was a dear lover of scrapple."

"He never seen me till I wavered at him, then he struck a-runnin'."

Friendliness, sociability, curiosity, humor, self-respect, and general good
will are as deeply rooted here as anywhere else in Delaware. The expression "our folks" heard throughout the region is the essense of this mental
climate. "Now don't be in a hurry, our folks, we're layin' off to have supper by and by. . . . Got to be a-travelin'? Well, our folks, come see us
again when you've got more time!"

There are middle-aged and old persons who have never gone to
school more than a few months in their lives, and some, both white and
colored, who cannot read or write. Some can figure only by their own
occult system of making little marks on paper or in the dust; the result,
though slow in coming, is usually correct—as a muskrat buyer finds out if
he tries to cheat a backwoods mathematician. The once substantial gentry
of educated landowners, mostly Tories during one war and Southern sympathizers in another, has largely disappeared; no class-consciousness seems
to exist apart from the matter of race, and there it takes the form of mutual good feeling. Farm tenancy is fairly high, but many tenants, white
and colored, succeed in buying the farms they occupy. Farmers help each
other on all occasions from plowing to soy-bean thrashing and hog-killing.

State 24 branches southwest from State 14 *(see Tour 2C),* 0 *m.,* about
3.5 miles south of Lewes and west of Rehoboth.

At 2.5 *m.* the highway crosses LOVE CREEK, a tributary of Rehoboth
Bay. In summer the bridge rails are lined with vacationists crabbing with
hand lines and dip nets.

At 4.7 *m.* is the junction with a side road.

Left on this road down ANGOLA NECK, a largely wooded peninsula extending
4 miles southeast between Rehoboth Bay and Herring Creek. The Marsh and Robinson families had large plantations here in the early 18th century. The last 3 miles
of road *(sandy)* runs through unbroken pine forest without a house in sight—one
of the largest wooded areas in the State. Wild azaleas and other flowering shrubs
and plants bloom in summer in the semi-darkness of the forest floor; the winter

DAGWORTHY BURTON'S STORE, ANGOLA
(Closed after Mr. Burton's death in 1941)

woods are brightened with red-berried holly and the flashing streaks of cardinals, robins, bluejays, bluebirds, and other migrants from the North. At the lower end of the neck are small cabins used in summer by campers and in late fall by duck hunters. The marshes along the shores are the haunts of muskrats, wild ducks, several kinds of herons, and shore birds of many species.

This has been called Angola Neck since the 17th century, when Delaware began to receive its share of the thousands of Negro slaves exported from Angola, Portuguese West Africa. It is still traditional here that Angola natives ("Gullahs" in South Carolina) made the most useful plantation workers.

ANGOLA, 5.4 *m.*, consists of a store and several houses; the red-painted ones are occupied by the Negroes of the Burton estate. For a century or more a dam has backed up the headwaters of Herring Creek here (R) to form BURTON'S MILLPOND *(boats for fishing in season)*; the gristmill has been gone for many years.

The little red STORE (R) was one of the few typical old-fashioned rural stores left in lower Delaware, with a stock of staple groceries, overalls and other clothing, horse collars, hames, and a wide assortment of chewing and smoking tobacco. A "Winter King" iron chunk stove stood the year round in a box of sand in the middle of the room. Public notices of auction sales, tax collections hung on the walls. Chairs were set about hospitably. Dagworthy Burton, born 1851, when retired from the management of his land but not from his store, took his ease in white linen in summer. (He was postmaster of Angola P. O. from 1886 to its discontinuance 1937.) Usually there were two or three little Negroes playing at his feet or asleep in the corner. When they stared at the penny candy until they had to swallow, "Mistuh D" growled, got up from his chair, and gave them each a sourball or a stick of licorice. The entrance of a customer meant a sale perhaps, but a social visit primarily. After a transaction the caller never left immediately.

At 5.5 *m.* is the junction with a side road.

Right on this road to the junction with another road, **1.9** *m.;* R. on this road to ST. GEORGE'S CHAPEL *(Episcopal; Sun. services usually at 9:30; Rogation Day exercises and service 5th Sun. after Easter),* **2.5** *m.* (L). Within its fenced and walled churchyard, filled with the gravestones of the Burtons, Robinsons, Hazzards, Prettymans, Josephs, and other families of the neighborhood, this old brick church is a symbol of the religious zeal of the Church-of-England planters who took up the largest tracts in Indian River Hundred in the early years of colonization. In 1719 an "oak frame church" was erected here, and in 1728 the Rev. William Beckett, missionary, reported that 200 persons, white and black, were communicants. After the wooden building burned in 1792, another church building, of brick made on the premises, was erected in 1794, with raised, wine-glass pulpit, a sounding-board, box pews, and a slave gallery on three sides. In 1883 the roof was changed to a steep Gothic pitch, windows were altered, galleries removed, and the whole interior made to conform with the style of that period. Later a square brick bell tower was added at the entrance. Despite these changes the church retains much charm in this quiet spot at the edge of a pine woods.

After the Revolution and the rise of Methodism, St. George's-Indian River shared with other Episcopal churches in lower Delaware a heavy loss in membership, but unlike most of them this church has maintained regular weekly services almost continuously for two centuries. On Rogation Day there is usually a costume pageant representing the early members giving thanks for the harvest and beseeching another good year for the farmers.

At **2.7** *m.* on side road (L) is charming little Beaver Park.

At 6.4 *m.* on State 24 there is often a CHARCOAL "PIT" in the woods (R); it is not a pit at all, but a large conical mound like an Eskimo igloo, giving off acrid pine smoke. To build it, several cords of 4-foot sticks are stacked on end in two tiers around a hollow center. Pine needles ("shats") and a coating of clay are spread over the whole surface save for a small opening at the top; a trench is dug around the base, and holes are punched through the shell to permit dehydration without combustion. Knots of fat-pine lightwood are ignited and dropped down through the hole at the apex, the hole is closed up, and the "pit" becomes a slow oven for a week. Then the clay is removed and the charcoal drawn. The blue-tinged "pigeon-wing" coal, considered the best, rings like a bell when tapped with a stick.

Thousands of bushels of charcoal were used at the bog-iron furnace at Millsboro in the early 1800's to smelt the bog ore. Just before the Civil War the charcoal industry was revived and recently as many as 60 pits have been smoking. The product is shipped north for filtering rum and whiskey, hardening tool steel, etc. During Prohibition much Indian-River-Hundred charcoal went into moonshine rye whiskey and apple brandy.

At 7.8 *m.* is the northern junction with State 5 and the Long Neck Rd.

1. Right on State 5 to the junction with a side road, 2 *m.;* R. on this road to the VOTING GROUND, 2.4 *m.* (L), a clearing and a disused schoolhouse in the woods, the polling place for Indian River Hundred. Here on election days assemble crowds of white, Negro, and Moor voters and their children. Many remain the entire day loafing, talking local politics, and visiting with each other. The Negroes and Moors especially come in their best holiday clothes and their gayest holiday mood, happily aware that election day is the climax of their sudden importance to the white electioneers that for weeks have been working to round up the votes. A tall Negro girl promenades in a bright blue evening dress and high-heeled slippers, laughing and joking with her more plainly dressed escort. Booths set up at the edge of the woods do a big trade in oyster sandwiches, clam fritters, fried chicken, pies, and coffee if the day is cold, or soft drinks if it is warm. Mouth organs, banjos, and accordions ("cardeens") make music in the hands of celebrants seated on running boards, and someone takes a few buck-and-wing steps. The sandy road is choked from morning till evening with cars and horse- or mule-drawn rigs of all styles.

In 1946 the polling place for the Hundred was moved to another unused building, old Hollymount School. At crossroad 3 *m.* ahead, turn L. to school at 4.4 *m.*

At 3.5 *m.* on State 5 is (R) the INDIAN MISSION M.P. CHURCH *(Sun. services at 10:30)*, a neat white frame structure where a white preacher serves a large and highly respected congregation of Moors or yellow people, some of whom belong to the Nanticoke Indian Association *(see below)*. Children attending this church go to separate schools: parents belonging to the Association will not permit their children to be taught with other yellow children despite blood ties that make everyone kin to nearly everyone else in the community. However, some of the non-Association families of this church go on alternate Sundays to a nearby Negro church where nobody claims to be an Indian, "to listen to a man of our own race." A number of the graves here are decorated with large conch shells picked up on the ocean beach. Indian Mission Church is under Baltimore jurisdiction.

2. Left on the Long Neck Rd. down LONG NECK, which extends 6 miles eastward between Indian River Bay and Rehoboth Bay. Like Angola Neck, Long Neck was taken up in the late 17th century by a few large landholders—in this case the Burtons from nearby Accomac County on the Eastern Shore of Virginia, a prolific family who soon possessed most of the neck and much land elsewhere in Indian River Hundred. They cut the magnificent virgin oak and loblolly pine, tilled the cleared fields with scores of slaves, and shipped forest and plantation products on their own sailing vessels out of Indian River Inlet to the ocean and up the coast to Philadelphia and other ports. The Burton family still owns land on Long Neck. The population here is still more than one-half Negro.

Among the place-names on the neck is that of HOSS-GOIN'-OVER, a swamp of bottomless depth where, by legend, a horse being ridden along a trail became suddenly frightened and leaped over into the bog, disappearing with its rider forever.

At 1 *m.* on the Long Neck Rd. are the RUINS OF THE CHAPEL OF THE HOLY COMFORTER (L) in the corner of a cutover timber tract. The little church was built by families of Long Neck and consecrated in 1847 by the Rt. Rev. Alfred Lee, first Episcopal Bishop of Delaware. Last repaired in 1880, it has long been abandoned. The roof has fallen and the little Gothic porch and belfry are about to fall into the tangle of brush and young pines.

At 3.5 *m.* on this road is the lane (R) to the WHITE HOUSE *(private)*, a small early-Virginian type brick dwelling on Indian River Bay; it was erected in 1722 by Woolsey Burton whose body lies in a little walled graveyard near the west end of the house. Other graveyards contain the graves of generations of more recent Burtons and their Negroes. The house was gutted by fire in 1934 and rebuilt within the original thick walls. As the Flemish-bond brickwork shows, there were originally two arch-head doorways on both the north and south sides. A single doorway was later cut in the middle of each of these walls.

For about 7 miles southwest of the junction with the Long Neck Rd.,
State 24 runs through the heart of "DOWN SOCKUM"— so termed because
at one time there seemed to be more persons named Sockum (Ind.
sachem?) than there were Harmons, Clarks, Wrights, Streets, Johnsons.
Norwoods, or other families of this distinctive community along the north
shore of Indian River.

Some in this section call themselves Moors, some call themselves Negroes, and a few call themselves Indians—terms having apparently little to
do with their color, which may be anything from rich cream to almost
black. Yet all these mixed-blood people have a quality that sets them off
from both the whites and the recognized Negroes. A few have brown hair
or blue eyes. Flat noses and kinky hair are scarce among them. Most individuals have one or more of these features: red-brown skin, high cheek-
bones, straight black hair, and aquiline noses, bespeaking the Indian in
them that some proudly claim and that some admit having, but disdain as
a "mess o' foolishness." Everyone has a friendly, polite, and level gaze,
without hint of self-assertion or servility. As a landowning class primarily,
they have been their own masters for generations. The United States Census and most Sussex Countians consider these people Negroes, and many
of the people themselves say they have Negro blood, neither deploring it
nor boasting of it. When one of them by some chance was summoned for
jury duty at Georgetown, he asked to be excused, saying he did not think
the white men would want him next to them in the box. The judge excused him. Negroes are not called to sit on juries in Sussex County.

The name "Moors," by which the several hundred people of the community are most often called, has its origin in a legend still current. It is
just that "A long time ago a Spanish ship was wrecked off the coast and
the shipwrecked sailors married Indian women." No record of this has
been found, but the early 18th century was a lusty period of privateers
and pirates off the Delaware Capes.

The other story is that related by an old woman named Lydia Clark,
called twice by the State in 1855 to testify against Levin Sockum, a "Moor"
storekeeper accused by Nathaniel Burton, a white man, of "selling ammunition to a free mulatto" named Isaac Harmon and of "possessing a
gun." Burton invoked the long-neglected law of 1832 forbidding the sale
of arms or ammunition to Negroes. As Sockum's "kinswoman," Lydia
Clark gave testimony that in the first trial established Harmon a Negro
and in the second trial established Sockum a Negro; Sockum was convicted both times and each time paid a fine of $20. The woman's testi-
mony amounted to this:

Before the Revolution there was living in the hundred an Irishwoman
named Requa who bought a handsome Negro slave from a ship in Lewes
and had children by him; the children could not marry whites and would
not marry Negroes, so they intermarried with the remnants of the Nanticoke Indians who still remained on Indian River after most of the tribe
had left the Peninsula.

The prosecuting attorney, later a judge, recalled that Harmon was "by
far the handsomest man in the courtroom, with perfect Caucasian features,

rosy cheeks, and hazel eyes." Lydia Clark he described thus: "Though only a halfbreed she was almost as perfect a type of the Indian as I ever saw; she was as spry as a young girl in her movements and of intelligence as bright as a new dollar." (In 1938 she was recalled by a man who was born nearby in 1846: "Old Lydie was tall and thin and wore a man's plug hat.")

The social lines these people draw among themselves often baffle their white neighbors and the State authorities alike. Though the Delaware school system is officially divided into white and Negro schools, there are four separate kinds in this region. Within a few miles of one another there are white schools, Negro schools, a school listed as a Moor school, and the Nanticoke Indian school. Children attending the latter are apparently no different in color or otherwise from their cousins outside the Nanticoke Indian Association, Inc.

This split in the community has developed over their common Indian ancestry, which most of the people laugh at. A few of them however, ridiculed by whites, Negroes, and sometimes even by their own brothers and sisters, have maintained a tradition of Indian blood and kept socially to themselves, discouraging marriages with "dark people." As early as 1890 they were supporting their Warwick Indian School, and until 1937 they maintained a school at their own expense except for one year when their teacher was paid by a special act of Legislature. For years the State school authorities have been hard put to it to make the schools in the region fit the caste system. The "Moors" would not send their children to a Negro school, and so in 1921 the Harmon School was established for them. The "Indians" would not send their children to the "Moor" school, and so in 1937 the State took over the little Nanticoke Indian School, for children "entitled to membership in . . . the Nanticoke Indian Association." The law states that "No white or colored child shall be permitted to attend any school for Moors or any school for Indians." Though the census does not recognize any Indians or Moors in the county, the State does, and allows the people to classify themselves. In case of a dispute, there is provision for it to be settled by a committee of the Resident County Judge, the State Registrar of Vital Statistics, and a member of the State School Board living in the county.

The Nanticoke Indian Association was incorporated in 1922 on the encouragement and guidance of Dr. Frank G. Speck, of the Department of Anthropology of the University of Pennsylvania, who was impressed by the efforts of a few families to keep up traditions of Indian ancestry in spite of ridicule and the loss of tribal language, customs, and dress since the final Nanticoke emigration to Pennsylvania about 1750. He taught them Indian dances *(see RIVERDALE below)* and helped draw up a constitution providing simply that for eligibility to membership, "Indian ancestry must be proved." It was never his intention, he has stated, for the Association to limit members to the handful that comprise it—about 35 persons of all ages.

At 9.4 *m.* on State 24 is the HARMON SCHOOL (L), also called the Moor School, attended by most of the children of the community. Though

CHIEF CLARK, RIVERDALE

This Sioux-type headdress was worn only on the western plains, never by the Nanticokes. Charley Clark having picked it up in Philadelphia is none-the-less proud of it.

the building is typical of the schools built for the Negroes of Delaware by Pierre S. du Pont, Negro children are not permitted to attend this one *(see above)*. But other Moor children attend the regular Negro schools by preference.

At the Harmon School is the southern junction with State 5 (L) and the junction with an unmarked road.

1. Right on the unmarked road to the junction with another road, 1.3 *m.;* R. on this road to a farmhouse (R), 1.4 *m.;* R. by trail about 0.5 *m.* to the GRAVE OF LYDIA CLARK in a dense pine forest. The inscription on the stone is:

> In memory of
> LYDIA CLARK
> Who died Dec. 26, 1856
> Aged about 75 years.
> The last one of the Aborigines
> of the Country, a person of
> truth and a witness against
> the arrogant Negros that
> assumed to be what they
> ware not.

Here lies the body of the old woman who related to a jury the tradition that her people were descended from an African Negro, an Irishwoman, and the Nanticoke Indians. The gravestone, it is said, was put up by Nathaniel Burton out of gratitude for her testimony.

2. Left on State 5 is OAK ORCHARD, 2 *m.,* a small summer resort of cottages and boarding-houses on the pine-wooded shore of Indian River. Locally it is called "The Archard." A short boardwalk edges the river. Bathers wade far out before the water is more than waist-deep. Elderly farm women wearing long bathing suits and sunbonnets splash and laugh as they enjoy a Saturday afternoon's fun with their families. Farther out, motorboats and sailboats crisscross each other's paths. Picnic tables in the grove are laden with food as cars are unpacked. Camping trailers from long distances stand about unhooked. Children run around in droves, shrieking and shouting as they pile off a big blue school bus that has brought them to a Sunday school picnic. Shops and stands sell ice cream, hot dogs, and soft-shell crab sandwiches. On Saturday nights the little dance hall on a pier is packed with summer residents and young farm people. Only white persons patronize "The Archard." The largest crowds come on Big Thursday *(2d in Aug.; see Tour 2B)*.

Right from Oak Orchard along the river to RIVERDALE PARK, 2.6 *m.,* much like Oak Orchard except that there are more new cottages standing along the wooded shore and in the woods extending back from it. A large clearing (R), filled with small cabins, was formerly the scene of the annual Thanksgiving-Day pow-wow of the Nanticoke Indian Association *(not held since 1936)*. Large crowds listened to an address of welcome by the Nanticoke chief in his ceremonial headdress and regalia, and watched a dozen or more young members of the Association dance around a council fire in home-made garments to the beating of a drum. Sometimes a visiting full-blood Indian made a speech in an Indian tongue, then repeated it in English.

At the edge of the road (R) is a large stone MONUMENT TO LYDIA CLARK erected by the Colonial Dames of Delaware; on it the year of her death is erroneously given as 1859. On a pier (L) a combined grocery-store and dance pavilion bears the large sign:

> CHIEF CLARK
> STORE

This is only one of the enterprises of Charles Cullen Clark, "Little Owl," who owns several farms and owns or has sold most of Riverdale. He is the great-grandson of Lydia Clark. By custom, only white persons patronize Riverdale Park.

At 10.1 *m.* on State 24 is the NANTICOKE INDIAN SCHOOL (L), a small frame building built and owned by the Nanticoke Indian Association but now administered by the State Board of Education. "Moors" are not permitted to attend this school *(see above)*.

At 10.2 *m.* is the junction with a side road.

Left on this road is ROSEDALE BEACH, 0.8 *m.,* a resort and amusement park run by Negroes for Negroes, Moors, and Indians. The popular bathing is varied by an occasional public baptism in the river. During the annual Negro camp-meeting at Antioch A.M.E. Church near Dagsboro *(see Tour 16),* the beach is crowded in the daytime with Negroes enjoying a respite from preaching.

At 12.8 *m.* the highway crosses SWAN CREEK, a tributary of Indian River.

At 13.1 *m.* is INDIAN SWAN ORCHARD, an extensive apple and peach plantation bordering both sides of the road, part of the large Sussex County holdings of former U. S. Senator John G. Townsend, Jr. Most of the fruit is shipped north by truck. He owns the large broiler industry here.

At 14.7 *m.* in Millsboro is the junction with State 30.

Right on this road to a goup of tall loblolly pine trees, **0.2** *m.* (L), whose tops become billows of purple wistaria in season *(late April or Early May),* a brilliant and startling sight against the dark green boughs.

At 14.8 *m.* the highway crosses the dam at the head of INDIAN RIVER. MILLSBORO, 15 *m.* (15 alt., 479 pop.) *(see Tour 2).*

At 15.5 *m.* is the junction with US 113 *(see Tour 2).*

PHILLIPS HILL, 18.3 *m.* (R) is a typical old-style plantation settlement comprising a large white frame house, a small Colonial cypress-shingled dwelling originally the main residence, a store, and numerous outbuildings and quarters, all painted white.

At 19 *m.* is the junction with a side road.

Right on this road to CAREY'S CAMPGROUND, 1.2 *m. (white; camp-meeting held a week or longer in Aug.).* In a grove of oaks, about 50 mossy-roofed frame "tents," each of one and one-half stories, form a circle around the Promenade, in the center of which is the Tabernacle or shed with its rough benches; during revival meetings the dirt floor is covered with sawdust from a nearby "steam mill." ("You won't mind the hard seats, our folks, if your hearts are with me!") A day's meals cost a dollar-a-head at the Boarding Tent, a building where great platters of food are set on the table and everyone helps himself. Families arrive on Saturday with trailer-loads of furniture, bedding, cooking utensils, clothing, homegrown vegetables, melons, poultry, and other supplies, and presently the little cabins become comfortable living quarters ready for the opening of camp on the morrow. The tabernacle and tents are lighted by electricity instead of the primitive fire-stands, which were elevated boxes of sand with blazing fat-pine lightwood knots. In the early days here the food was cooked in pots hung from poles resting on crotches; the fire was protected by "harbors" of brush made windproof and fire-proof by a covering of pine "shats" and clay. Carey's Camp, one of the oldest in the State, was founded prior to 1830.

At MISSION, 20 *m.,* a crossroads with a store and a few houses, is an old whitewashed LOG CORNCRIB (L), typical of a vanishing style. Most of the corncribs in the region were made of bald cypress or white cedar logs from the Great Pocomoke Swamp.

At a junction (straight ahead) with an unmarked highway, 20.6 *m.*, now the route, State 24 branches R. *(see Tour 16).*

At 21.6 *m.* is a junction (L) with State 26 *(see Tour 16).* Right (straight ahead) on State 26, now the route.

At 22.5 *m.* State 26 crosses the POCOMOKE RIVER, flowing sluggishly southward through its great swamp to tidewater in Maryland. After passing within 7 miles of Chincoteague Bay on the Atlantic side of the Peninsula, it finally empties into Chesapeake Bay below the Maryland-Virginia Line.

GUMBORO, 25 *m.* (200 pop.) is an isolated little village whose site in 1840 was a dense forest at the edge of the swamp. Houses and a store or two were built near a sawmill. The place is said to have taken its name from a large white-gum tree that stood by the woods road, but some residents believe the name is "Gumburr" from the prickly seed-balls of the gum trees. GUMBORO SCHOOL is a substantial brick structure built in 1929.

Gumborough was the original spelling of the hundred that was partitioned from Broad Creek and Dagsborough hundreds in 1873. Gumborough Hundred was part of Dagworthy's Conquest, the baronial 20,000-acre estate granted in 1759 to Gen. John Dagworthy by the Colony of Maryland *(see DAGSBORO: Tour 2).* Many land titles in what is now southern and western Delaware—a region long claimed by Maryland—were not reassigned to Delaware until 1775.

Left from Gumboro to the GREAT POCOMOKE SWAMP, 1 *m.* (40 alt.), also known as the Big Cypress Swamp. (It is divided into areas called locally the Cedar Swamp, the Gum Swamp, or the Burnt Swamp.) Altogether this largest freshwater swamp of the Delmarva Peninsula includes about 50 square miles, mostly in Delaware, a small part in Maryland.

Originally the great "Delaware Everglades" contained thousands of acres of bald cypress timber, here approaching its northern limit on the Atlantic coast. Of the large old-growth cypresses only a scattered few survive deep in the almost impenetrable jungle along the Pocomoke River itself, their trunks rising smooth and straight to lofty crowns, their knees (here called "nine-pins") standing like elves above the black water. Great stands of gum have disappeared into the cooking vats of basket factories to be made into the veneer containers for the Peninsula's fruit and vegetables. White cedar still grows tall and slim from the bog, and the dryer hummocks support loblolly pine and holly. Big blue huckleberries are gathered by the hundreds of gallons by swamp people who know how to choose their footing. ("If you don't know how to travel the old swamp, you'll likely go ka-sow-jup, head and years!")

There are no rattlesnakes, but the occasional water-moccasins and copperheads are not to be trifled with. Bears survived here a full century after extinction everywhere else on the Peninsula; rusty hand-forged bear traps are still found from time to time by dealers in old iron, visiting nearby farms. Once in a while there has been a report that dogs raised a deer, which everyone at once turned out to kill. Game laws here mean no more than liquor laws; the people of the Great Swamp have run their moonshine stills for generations, and these stills are another reason why strangers have to watch their step.

A causeway runs for miles through a watery waste of blackened snags—the result of the terrible fire of 1930, said to have started from an exploding still. It burned for 8 months while hundreds of volunteers struggled to control it. They could not, because it burned underground that dry year through the accumulated peat of ages, and burst forth anywhere and everywhere—even in the middle of nearby cornfields. Not only was standing timber burned, but the destruction of the peat bed, many feet deep, meant the destruction of the buried cypress for which the swamp was most noted.

From prehistoric times, gales blew down generations of old trees. Above the sunken windfalls new cypresses grew up, to plunge in turn into the ooze of sphagnum moss and rotting vegetation. Slowly the swamp closed above layer upon layer of great trees, preserving them perfectly by chemical action. From the days of "Dagworthy's Conquest" men cut the growing timber for shingles until it was nearly gone; then they began to mine cypress. Tons of soggy peat were scooped from above the tree-trunks. Oxen floundered and wheezed, chains pulled taut, men cursed, and the logs were dragged out to where crosscut saws could be used.

Men with holly-wood mauls and heavy iron blades called "frows" rived the cypress cylinders into shingle blocks and then draw-knifed them into the 30-inch shingles that would wear out but never decay. Nearly all the mossy old houses of southeastern Delaware and nearby Maryland are sheathed with these lustrous hand-riven Pocomoke cypress shingles. Some have worn as thin as cardboard after 150 years of weather, but are still as sound as the day they were nailed on hand-hewn oak frame. Since the first drainage ditches were dug through the swamp in 1867 there have been successive peat fires, but the fire of 1930 put an end to all shingle-making, which was already dying from competition from western redwood shingles not hand-shaved but sawed in mills. Old-time Pocomoke shingle-makers scorn these modern 18-inch shingles as trash: "You cain't expect a sawed shingle to last—hit just ain't no 'mount fer nothin'."

In 1936 a large-scale ditching project attempted to reclaim more of the unburned swampland for farming by digging a 20-foot-wide canal to divert water from the Pocomoke River to Indian River, with many miles of feeder ditches. The water level was lowered to some extent but the great swamp is still here, a stubborn, melancholy wilderness whose mists rise like the ghosts of its vanished cypresses while the buzzards wheel overhead. On dark cloudy days there may be heard from the depths of the swamp, it is said, the sound of the "Old Man" riving out his shingles, hour after hour, as he used to do. He is a ghost too.

At 27.4 *m.* is the junction with the Line Rd. Here State 26 crosses the Maryland Line, about 4 miles north of Pittsville, Md.

Left on the Line Rd. to BETHEL M.E. CHURCH, 2.1 *m.* (L). On the wooded north bank of the road, west of the building, are several old GRAVES WITH SHIN-GLE ROOFS, almost hidden by undergrowth. They are the only remaining examples of the once-popular local custom of placing a small pitched roof close over a grave to keep off the rain. Some of the old graveyards in this section have cypress slabs instead of gravestones.

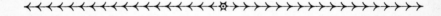

Tour 16

Bethany Beach—Dagsboro—Laurel—(Sharptown, Md.); State 26 and 24.
Bethany Beach—Maryland Line, 38.8 m.
Roadbed paved throughout.

Accommodations in towns.

Roughly paralleling the Maryland Border on the south, this route runs across the southern end of Delaware between the Atlantic Ocean and the western Delaware-Maryland Line. In much of this low-lying region, natural drainage is virtually non-existent, so flat is the land. Fields are bounded not so often by fences as by ditches in varying stages of neglect—the vestiges of the wide, deep ditches and canals dug with great labor before and after the Civil War in the attempt to make the cut-over timberland fit for farming; some ditches have been cleaned out by CCC and WPA labor. Great areas of these lowlands, however, have remained sour and soggy, and abandoned farms are fast being recaptured by second-growth pine and scrub oak.

State 26 branches west from State 14 at BETHANY BEACH *(see Tour 2C)*, 0 *m.*

At 1.3 *m.* the highway crosses the ASSAWOMAN CANAL (originally "Assawomet" from the Indian name). Occasionally a rowboat passes through the semi-darkness of overhanging pine trees and trailing vines, startling "shike-pokes" (little green herons) that flap slowly ahead of the intruder. Half-sunken boats lie rotting along the banks. Sandbars extend nearly across in places. Seldom is the water more than 2 feet deep.

The Assawoman Canal is far from being the important intracoastal waterway its sponsors predicted in the 1880's when the Federal Government agreed to dig it 4 miles long and 6 feet deep to connect Indian River Bay on the north with Little Assawoman Bay on the south, as a link in an inside route along the ocean side of the Peninsula between Delaware Bay and Chincoteague Bay. The water traffic did not materialize, the sand washed in, and soon the canal was not navigable. As a drainage ditch, however, it proved very beneficial to half-drowned farmland.

OCEAN VIEW, 1.8 *m.* (10 alt., 450 pop.), a small rambling village, has no view of the ocean whatever. It is related that when this settlement on White's Creek was known as Hall's Store, a boy climbed to the top of the tallest pine tree in the place, happened to look eastward, and exclaimed, "I can see the ocean from here!"

The annual Ocean View Homecoming Celebration *(1st Thurs. in Aug.)* is attended by crowds of former residents, their families and friends from several States. Held first in 1908, the affair includes informal picnicking, much visiting among long-separated friends or relatives, and scheduled speeches and concerts. The historian reads a piece about the past celebrations, and the poet reads the annual poem written for the occasion. Young people go bathing at nearby Bethany Beach.

From a backwoods community dependent on poor-to-fair farmland and on the fishing and crabbing of Indian River Bay, Ocean View since about 1925 has become the highly prosperous center of one of the most impor tant sections of the United States for the production of broiler chickens In 1937, it was estimated, 17 million broilers were raised in Baltimore Hundred, this extreme southeastern corner of Delaware.

At first the broiler industry here and elsewhere in the State trucked live chickens to the New York, Baltimore, Washington, Norfolk, Philadelphia and Pittsburgh markets. After 1938, dressing plants were rapidly established. Dressed broilers are now shipped to market packed in ice. The dealers are constantly telephoning New York for the latest prices, or speeding from one broiler farm to another to bid on marketable "crops" of 1,000, 40,000, or 100,000 chickens. Feed and coal trucks rush about with the thousands of tons of material needed for the 14 weeks it takes to turn baby chicks into broilers. This big business hums along side by side with little farms from whose wet soil it is difficult to wrest a living.

State 26 and nearby side roads in the region are lined with frame brooder houses—some of which are 700 feet in length—divided into compartments in each of which a small stove warms 500 baby chicks until they are old enough to run out to the adjoining fenced lots where young rye, clover, and other forage crops stay green all winter in this mild climate. Well-drained plots are chosen, since dampness spreads disease. Only a small fraction of the feed is produced in the vicinity; hundreds of carloads of mixed dry feed are imported from the north and west. Nor can the region supply more than a few of the baby chicks required: local hatcheries run largely on eggs from other States, and growers purchase millions of baby chicks from New England. Many broilers are raised on shares; dealers, landowners, and banks advance feed, fuel, and equipment to the growers. It is the latter who suffer most when the price of chickens drops below the cost of production.

At 1.9 *m.* is the junction with a side road.

Left on this road to the junction with another road, **3.7** *m.;* L. on this road down Miller Neck through the ASSAWOMAN SITE. This and the Trappe Pond Site *(see below),* as well as the Petersburg Site *(see Tour 1, Sec. d),* are included in the Delaware Forestry Project of the Land Utilization Division under the U. S. Department of Agriculture. The Assawoman Site comprises 1,200 acres lying on both sides of Miller Creek and on both sides of the shallow brackish lagoon called Little Assawoman Bay; this bay, 4 miles long and averaging one mile wide is separated from the ocean by the narrow sandy Barrier Reef.

Naturally isolated and unproductive for farming, these farm and forest lands were purchased by the Federal Government in 1935–6 and families moved from sagging, leaking houses to more fertile land elsewhere. Abandoned fields are planted in young trees or allowed to grow up in native pine. New graded roads reach the shores of creek and bay after winding through acres of pine and holly, from which the fire-menace of underbrush has been cleared. Small ponds are planted in widgeon grass and other natural feed for waterfowl; tiny artificial islands are nesting places for wood ducks and black ducks. At **7.5** *m.* within the Assawoman project bounds is STRAWBERRY LANDING RECREATION AREA *(shelter house with fireplace, firewood, and latrine; bathhouses; fishing and crabbing).* The bathing beach has a sandy bottom. A similar recreation area is at Mulberry Point on the bay.

At 2.4 *m.* (L) on State 26 is the LORD BALTIMORE CONSOLIDATED SCHOOL, erected in 1933; this large brick building with a Greek colonnaded portico is an astonishing sight in the midst of this piney-woods farmland. Pupils are brought in buses from villages and farmhouses within a wide radius. The large auditorium is a civic center for the region.

MILLVILLE, 3.1 *m.* (270 pop.) is a hamlet in the broiler country. It grew up around a "steam mill" (sawmill) operated by Capt. Peter Townsend in the late 19th century.

CLARKSVILLE, 5 *m.,* is a cluster of houses and a store or two.

At 6.8 *m.* is the junction with a side road.

Right on this road to CAMP OTONKA, 1.2 *m.*, at Sandy Landing on Indian River Bay, a girls' summer camp operated by the Young Women's Christian Association of Delaware *(July and Aug.)*. The brown-stained frame buildings on a wooded bluff command a good view of the bay, one and one-half miles wide here. Bathing, boating, and crabbing are campers' sports. Before the railroad era, Sandy Landing was a shipping point of some importance for the farm and forest products that went out of Indian River Inlet on shallow-draft schooners. Some of these vessels were built just east of here at the mouth of Blackwater Creek.

Until 1775, when the Pennsylvania-Maryland boundary dispute was finally settled, a sort of unofficial compromise made Indian River and Bay a median line in the disputed area. North of the river, the Penns controlled most of the patenting of land; south of it, most of the deeds were granted under the Lords Baltimore. In 1744 the Maryland Assembly ordered a town called Baltimore to be laid out on 50 acres of land in Worcester County—on Indian River. The county surveyor for some reason refused to survey the lots, and the next year another act ordered the town to be laid out on "a more commodious and navigable part of the river."

If this Baltimore was ever laid out, much less built upon, the records do not show it. (Perhaps the Maryland surveyor was scared off by those holding patents from the Penns.) Indian River was certainly too shallow to have a seaport on it. Nor is it clear why another "Baltimore" was planned for this remote region, when Baltimore Town, now the city of Baltimore, had been established on the Patapsco in 1730 by act of Assembly. The answer may lie somewhere in the ancient jealousy of the Eastern Shore toward the counties west of Chesapeake Bay. But the name Baltimore Hundred has stuck to this part of Sussex County through the years.

At 8.5 *m.* State 26 crosses VINES CREEK, a handsome little estuary of Indian River Bay, winding through marsh and pine woods.

At 10.6 *m.* (R) is PRINCE GEORGE'S CHAPEL *(Episcopal; annual Harvest Home service on 1st Sun. in Oct.; open by permission)*, one of the most beloved old country churches of Delaware; it was erected in 1757 on the site of an earlier building. Both this and its predecessor were chapels of ease in St. Martin's parish, Worcester County, Md. The interior of Prince George's Chapel is preserved almost entirely in its original condition; the heart-pine woodwork has never been painted and its rich brown color glows from the barrel-vaulted ceiling and the walls. There is no altar, but a small table. Part of the slave-gallery has been removed. The outside shingles were put on when general repairs were made in 1929. Regular services were discontinued about 1870. At the annual autumn service all sorts of foodstuffs for charity are piled at the chancel rail. The church is in the care of the rector of St. Paul's Church, Georgetown.

In the churchyard is a large monument erected in 1908 by the State of Delaware to Gen. John Dagworthy, "gallant soldier of three wars," whose body, by his own request, is buried beneath the chancel of the church *(see DAGSBORO: Tour 2)*. On one side of the yard are the gravestones of other parishioners; on the other side there are no stones to mark the many graves of Negroes who attended Prince George's with their masters and mistresses. The presence of the Negro graves would be long forgotten but for the little ceremony that takes place here once a year: on Decoration Day a few solemn Negroes join in a prayer over the graves of their slave ancestors, leave some flowers, and depart.

At 10.9 *m.* is the junction with a side road.

Left on this road to the large brick JOHN M. CLAYTON CONSOLIDATED SCHOOL, 1 *m.* (R), erected in 1933 to serve a large part of Dagsboro Hundred.

At 1.2 *m.* (R) on this road is ANTIOCH A.M.E. CAMPGROUND *(Negro campmeeting opens Sat. before 2d Sun. in Aug., lasting 8 days; adm. 10 cents).* Several thousand Negroes from Delaware and Maryland and some from other States attend this large old-fashioned campmeeting. In the pine grove a circle of "tents" made of pine shiplaps surrounds the promenade with the tabernacle in the center. Families bring enough food, furnishings, and clothing to make their tents bright and comfortable living-quarters. These tents house only a small part of the revival crowd, most of whom come and go daily. The road outside the camp is jammed with cars bumper to bumper before and after the evening meetings.

By day, those who do not have to work spend their time bathing and frolicking at Rosedale Beach on Indian River *(see Tour 15).* It is night that brings Antioch to life. Then the front porch of each tent is brightly lighted with shaded floor-lamps or table-lamps; old men and women sit in rocking-chairs bowing to friends promenading by, or cupping an ear toward the preacher in the "tab'nacle." Under this long shed the benches are filled with those most anxious to "get de spirit right." Across in front of the rostrum runs one long board, the mourners' bench for converts later on. Hundreds keep on promenading, talking, and laughing as the preacher starts out to arouse his seated congregation to a perspiring religious fervor. Sometimes the "spirit" is slow in coming, and several preachers take turns "zortin' " the listeners. The one who "hollers his sermon the loudest" is most likely to be the first to get the audience to shouting: "Amen," or "I know it, brother!" and "Hain't it so!" Hell fire is the recurrent theme. When everybody finally "gets happy" enough to suit the preacher he has six or eight good voices take up an old-time spiritual, and soon the whole tabernacle audience and most of the prom-enaders outside, even the wisecracking youngsters, are swaying and shuffling in rhythm. Verses are sung over and over with a gradually accelerating tempo until sometimes the combined sound rises to a high moaning scream echoing through the pine forest. White persons are welcome and the preacher in charge takes pride in passing the plate to them personally—with a blessing for the liberal giver.

For those with no tents to cook in, there is a boarding tent where a dozen chickens are boiled in one big iron pot, a bushel of sugar-corn in another, and gallons of lima beans in a third. Watermelons are plentiful, though there are never any watermelon patches near the campground. Disorderly conduct on the grounds is vigilantly suppressed by a strong-arm committee.

DAGSBORO, 11 *m.* (198 pop.) *(see Tour 2).*

At 11.9 *m.* is the junction with US 113 by-passing the center of Dags-boro *(see Tour 2).*

At 17.6 *m.* is a junction (R) with an unmarked highway. Right on this now the route.

At 18.6 *m.* is a junction with State 24 *(see Tour 15);* L. on State 24 now the route.

At 25.2 *m.* is the junction with a side road.

Left on this road to the TRAPPE POND SITE *(picnic shelters, boat landings, bathing, fishing),* 1 *m.,* a part of the Delaware Forestry Project of the Land Uti-lization Division of the U. S. Department of Agriculture. When the Federal Gov-ernment purchased the tract of about 800 acres in 1936, Trappe Pond was dry. The dam was rebuilt and the woodland lake restored—a place of wild beauty with its pine-and-cypress shaded shores, its coves, points, and little island jungles, all deep in the surrounding forest. Wildlife abounds. Several miles of new graded road encircle the 2-mile long pond. Work in developing this wilderness recreation area is still in progress.

At 2.7 *m.* (L) on this road is TRUSSEM POND *(boats for bass and pike fishing in season),* an old millpond in whose dark water cypress trees stand with their elfin knees (called "nine-pins" locally) looking weird and mystical. Hidden snags pre-vent the use of outboard motors.

CHRIST CHURCH, BROAD CREEK, NEAR LAUREL

At 28.7 *m.* on State 24 is the junction with a side road.

Right on this road to CHRIST EPISCOPAL CHURCH, BROAD CREEK HUNDRED, 0.5 *m.* (R), on the pine-wooded shore of CHIPMAN'S POND. *(Open twice yearly: all-day meeting on a Sun. in May with sermon at 2:30, and a Rogation service on the 3rd Sun. in Sept., 2:30).*

Christ Church was erected in 1771 upon ground that until 1775 was claimed by Maryland. For some years after the settlement of the boundary the church continued as a chapel of ease in Stepney parish of Somerset County, Md. The plain building has never been altered, and except for the window sashes has never been painted. Because of the lasting qualities of the fine-grained, resinous heart pine of which it was constructed, inside and out, it remains today in almost perfect condition, a notable example of Georgian Colonial church architecture. The roof has been renewed from time to time, and the two front doors replace those of earlier times.

Inside, the light from the many-paned, arched windows falls upon the rich brown patina of the old woodwork, box pews and paneling, beneath a barrel-vaulted ceiling. Instead of a formal altar there is a plain table within a railing and a wooden cross above. High on one side of the room is the pulpit with a canopy above it. There is a slave gallery above the entrance.

The church possesses two pewter alms basins and a pewter paten bearing the name of the maker, Gleason; it also has two old silver chalices with ebony bases. A Bible said to have been presented by George III's queen in 1777 has disappeared. Parish records of 1792 list a membership of 476 adults, white and black, including 109 communicants. The rise of Methodism in the 19th century made such inroads on the congregation that regular services ceased in 1850. The church is in the care of the rector of St. Philip's Church, Laurel.

LAUREL, 30.8 *m.* (25 alt., 2,700 pop.) *(see Tour 1, Sec. d)*, is at the junction with US 13 *(see Tour 1, Sec. d).*

At 37.7 *m.* on State 24 is the junction with a side road.

Left on this road is COLUMBIA, 1.5 *m.,* a trading center of a distinctive farming community about four miles square in the southwestern corner of Delaware. Former names of the community have been Owens' Store, Mount Hermon, and the Cooper Neighborhood.

The spirit of co-operation has been developed in this section to a degree unsurpassed elsewhere in Delaware. Almost all the farmers are owners. They co-operate in everything, 365 days in the year. Twice a week eggs and vegetables are hauled to nearby towns; each farmer has his turn to drive the truck with the produce of all the farms. When there is corn to shuck, wood to cut, or hogs to butcher, no one fails to help. Each family is almost as much concerned with the neighbors' everyday life as with its own. Once when a preacher insisted that services be held every Sunday, a prominent member of the congregation arose and said: "Brother, you got to give us every other Sunday to go see how folkses' hogs are growing!" On Sunday it is not unusual for 40 or 50 persons to dine at the home of a popular family; all the women pitch in days beforehand to help, bringing dishes and pickles and pies. The crowd eats in sittings: first several groups of men and then several groups of women and children, until all are filled and gasping for breath.

A local chapter of the National Grange includes 90 percent of the eligible population, many of whom are members of the Senior Order United American Mechanics, also meeting weekly in the GRANGE HALL. A canning plant and cantaloupe grading plant are run co-operatively, and a sawmill runs at times. The most important annual social event is the Cooper Family Reunion *(a day in July)* attended by hundreds from far and near; second only to this is the annual Oyster Supper at MOUNT HERMON M.P. CHURCH *(on a fall or winter night).* School buses take the annual Sunday-School Picnic to some shore resort. Every month the Mount Hermon Ladies Aid Society, which has not missed a meeting in 40 years, meets at the home of a member where a business session is followed by prayers and refreshments of homemade cake and ice cream.

At 3.8 *m.* on this side road is the junction with another road; R. on this road to the original STONE MARKING THE SOUTHWEST CORNER OF DELAWARE, 5 *m.,* placed here in 1764 by Charles Mason and Jeremiah Dixon at the western end of Delaware's southern boundary which had been surveyed in 1750–1 by another surveying party *(see Tour 1, Sec. d).* From this point Mason and Dixon ran the western boundary of Delaware northward 100 miles to what is now the Pennsylvania-Maryland Border *(see Tours 8 and 9).*

At 38.8 *m.* State 24 crosses the Maryland Line, 2 miles southeast of Sharptown, Md.

PART IV

Appendices

Chronology

1609 August 28. Henry Hudson, in service of Dutch East India Company, discovers Delaware Bay and River.

1610 August 27. Capt. Samuel Argall names present Cape Henlopen, Cape la Warre, for Governor of Virginia, Sir Thomas West, Lord de la Warre.

1614 Capt. Cornelis Hendricksen ransoms from Indians near site of Wilmington the first three white men known to have trodden Delaware soil.

1631 April. Expedition from Holland sent by David Peterson de Vries for the patroons settles 28 colonists at Swanendael (site of Lewes).

1632 December 6. De Vries arrives at Swanendael to find the settlement completely wiped out by Indians.

1638 March 29 (or earlier). First Swedish expedition commanded by Peter Minuit arrives at The Rocks, site of Wilmington, establishing first permanent settlement on Delaware soil.
May 6. Dutch at New Amsterdam protest right of Swedes to trade or settle on the river.

1640 April 17. Reorus Torkillus, first Lutheran preacher to have a charge in this country, arrives at Fort Christina.

1643 February 15. Johan Printz arrives at Fort Christina as Governor of New Sweden.

1651 July-August. Peter Stuyvesant, Dutch Director of New Netherland, builds Forth Casimir at Sand Hook (New Castle).

1653 September-October. Johan Printz returns to Sweden with 25 soldiers and settlers.

1654 May 21. Johan Classon Rising, new Swedish Governor, captures Fort Casimir and names it Fort Trinity.

1655 September 1. Peter Stuyvesant recaptures Fort Trinity and renames it Fort Casimir.
September 15. Fort Christina and all Swedish claims surrendered to Dutch.
November 29. Jean Paul Jacquet appointed by Stuyvesant vice-director on South River at Fort Casimir.

1657 April 21. Jacob Alrichs arrives at Fort Casimir as director for the burgomasters of Amsterdam, who name the place New Amstel.

1659 September 6. Col. Nathaniel Utie presents, at New Amstel, Lord Baltimore's claim to Dutch settlements on South River.
December 30. Jacob Alrichs dies, after having appointed Alexander D'Hinoyossa his successor.

1663 July. Peter Cornelius Plockhoy establishes a Mennonite colony of "41 souls" at Swanendael, near present Lewes.

1664 October. Sir Robert Carr seizes the Delaware territory for the Duke of York.

1667 Crane Hook Church built by Swedes near mouth of Christina Creek.

1669 December 20. Count Konigsmark, "The Long Finn," is condemned for insurrection in the first trial by jury on the Delaware.

1673 Dutch regain control and establish courts at New Castle and Hoorn-kill, or Hoerekill (Lewes).

1674 Dutch possessions in North America again pass to British.

1676 September 22. Duke of York's laws established and courts at Whore-kill (Hoerekill, later Lewes) are continued.

1680 St. Jones' County formed by dividing territory south of Bombay Hook.

1682 October 28. William Penn, new Quaker proprietary, welcomed at New Castle.
November 2. First court under Penn meets at New Castle.
December 4. Representatives of the three Lower Counties attend Penn's first Assembly at Upland (Chester).
December 25. Deale and St. Jones Counties, the two parts of Hoorn-kill, later Whorekill, renamed Sussex and Kent Counties respectively.

1683 May 30. First conference between William Penn and Lord Baltimore, upon the bounds of their respective provinces, proves fruitless.

1686 May 26. Maryland Council appropriates supplies for men at Talbot's Fort at Christina Bridge to enforce Lord Baltimore's claim to territory.

1698 August 27. Pirates land at Lewes and pillage town.

1699 June 4. Swedish church at Christina dedicated on Trinity Sunday.
Crew of brigantine *Sweepstakes* mutinies at New Castle and seizes the ship which is "piratically taken away."

1700 April. Captain Kidd visits Delaware Bay and trades with Lewes residents.

1701 First survey of boundary circle is made with "ye end of ye horse dyke" in New Castle as center.

1704 November. Three Lower Counties under charter of 1701 convene in first separate Assembly at New Castle.

1709 May 7. Lewes plundered by French privateer.

1711 Gustavus Hesselius, first notable painter in America, arrives at Old Swedes Church (Wilmington).

1717 General Assembly at New Castle appoints commissioners to lay out town of Dover as county seat of Kent.

1718 July 30. William Penn dies; Hannah Penn, his wife, is made executrix for proprietaries.

1722 Home of Col. John French in New Castle destroyed by fire. Legislative minutes and other records burned in the house.

1730 Andrew Justison, father-in-law of Thomas Willing, has first streets of Willingtown surveyed.

1734 Voting for members of General Assembly made compulsory for citizens of Three Lower Counties, under penalty of 20 shillings.

1735 August 9. William Shipley, "Father of Wilmington," buys land in Willingtown.

1738 Autumn. First Friends' Meeting-house in Willingtown, erected at High (Fourth) and West Streets.

1739 November 16. Willingtown becomes by charter the Borough of Wilmington. Population 610.

1740 Scotch-Irish residents of Wilmington erect First Presbyterian Church.
March 31. Land is purchased in Wilmington on Market Street above Third for erection of gaol, stocks, and whipping-post.
September 8. William Shipley chosen Chief Burgess at first election in Wilmington.

1748 Summer. Quakers help other Wilmington residents erect redoubt on site of Fort Christina, to repulse expected attack by French and Spanish privateers.

1750 November 15. Boundary commissioners fix upon the Court House as center of twelve-mile circle about New Castle.

1751 The seal of the three counties with the inscription "Delloware" is replaced with a new great seal of silver, containing arms of King of Great Britain and "Counties on Delaware."

1754 David Ferris and Joseph Tatnall are members of library company formed in Wilmington.

1761 At Wilmington, James Adams establishes first printing press in Delaware.

1767 November 30. First of John Dickinson's *Letters from a Farmer in Pennsylvania to the inhabitants of the British Colonies* appears.

1769 June 3. Scientists, from point near Cape Henlopen, observe transit of Venus over the Sun.
November 10. John Penn, representing Thomas and Richard Penn, proprietaries, signs charter for Newark Academy.

1774 August 22. Caesar Rodney, Thomas McKean, and George Read appointed delegates to first Continental Congress.

1775 Population of State 37,219; of Wilmington 1,229.
December 22. Friendship Fire Company, first in State, organized at Wilmington.

1776 January 19. John Haslet is commissioned colonel of the Delaware Regiment.
May 8-9. Schooner *Wasp* and several row-galleys harass British frigates *Roebuck* and *Liverpool* opposite mouth of Christina Creek, until they retire down the river.
June. 1,000 Tories assemble in Cedar Creek Hundred; disperse after conference with members of Council of Safety.

June 3. "Flying Camp" is established; Col. Samuel Patterson in command.

July 1-2. Caesar Rodney rides from Dover to Philadelphia to break tie between McKean and Read in Delaware's vote on Declaration of Independence.

September 10. Convention at New Castle frames first Constitution for "The Delaware State."

October 28. First Legislature under new Constitution meets at New Castle.

1777 January 17. Legislature adopts design for Great Seal of The Delaware State.

April 5. David Hall is commissioned Colonel of the new Delaware Regiment.

May 12. Dover supersedes New Castle as seat of government.

August 24-25. Main body of Continental Army, under personal command of General Washington, passes through Wilmington.

August 26. General Anthony Wayne, under orders from Washington, comes to Wilmington.

September 3. Battle of Cooch's Bridge, only Revolutionary War engagement on Delaware soil.

September 13. Vessel with Delaware documents, monies, and private valuables is seized under guns of fort at Wilmington; President John McKinly taken prisoner.

October 20. First meeting of General Assembly at Dover.

1778 September 12. Freeborn Garrettson, Methodist missionary, preaches from Academy steps in Dover.

1779 February 1. Assembly ratifies Articles of Confederation; authorizes Washington to quarter Pulaski's cavalry within State.

1780 August 16. Casualties in the Delaware Regiment at Battle of Camden, S.C. reach 265; remnants organized into two companies under Captain Robert Kirkwood.

1781 July 10. Thomas McKean of Delaware elected President of Continental Congress.

November 15. State schooner *Vigilant* ordered to protect trade on Delaware Bay and River.

1782 September 11-12. British ships in Delaware Bay attack French ships *La Gloire* and *L'Aigle;* Louis Philippe, Comte de Sègur and other French officers and soldiers escape to Delaware shore with one-half million livres in gold to pay French soldiers of Lafayette.

1783 September 13. Richard Allen, later A.M.E. bishop, first Negro to preach in Wilmington.

1784 November 14. Francis Asbury meets Thomas Coke and Richard Whatcoat at Barratt's Chapel near Frederica. Outcome is organization of Methodist Episcopal Church at the Baltimore conference of Methodist societies in Christmas week of 1784.

1787 February 3. John Fitch granted exclusive rights by Delaware Legislature to use steamboat invented by him.

November 10. Oliver Evans granted exclusive rights by Legislature to manufacture and sell steam-carriage invented by him.

December 7. Delaware is first State to ratify United States Constitution.

1789 February 3. The Medical Society of Delaware is incorporated.

1790 Population of State (U.S. Census) 59,096.

August 5. John Fitch's steamboat makes scheduled trip from Philadelphia to Wilmington and "Christeen" Bridge.

1791 Heirs of Penn sue through Thomas McKean for quit rents and proprietary land.

Robert Coram, Wilmington schoolmaster, publishes *Plan for the General Establishment of Schools Throughout the United States.*

Outbreak of revolution in Santo Domingo brings many French refugees to Wilmington.

October 29. Assembly designates Georgetown as county seat of Sussex.

1792 June 12. Second State Constitution adopted.

October. William Cobbett, later noted English writer and reformer, arrives in Wilmington, where he teaches school.

1793 Wilmington becomes a port for ships and many Philadelphians avoiding the yellow fever epidemic in Philadelphia.

1795 First cotton factory opened in Old Academy, Wilmington, by Jacob Broom.

February 9. Bank of Delaware, in Wilmington, chartered. (First bank in State.)

1796 Legislature creates public school fund of all money from marriage and tavern licenses.

1797 May 12. Vice President Thomas Jefferson stays overnight at Patrick O'Flynn's Tavern, Wilmington.

1798 Yellow fever, brought to Wilmington by refugees from Philadelphia, claims 250 victims.

May 25. British sloop-of-war *DeBraak* sinks off Lewes with loss of 40 lives and cargo, reputed to be gold valued at $1,000,000.

1799 February 1. Assembly permits "free black persons and free mulattoes" to testify in criminal cases.

1800 Population 64,273.

Custom House moved from New Castle to Wilmington.

1802 June. Eleuthère Irénée du Pont de Nemours buys land on the Brandywine and begins to manufacture gunpowder.

1803 January 10. Vice President Aaron Burr is detained in Wilmington three days by deep snow.

1805 July 25. Thousands attend first Methodist camp-meeting in Delaware, three miles south of Smyrna.

1806 February 5. Robert Montgomery Bird, author and dramatist, born at New Castle.

1807 January 20. President Jefferson appoints Caesar A. Rodney, Attorney-General of the United States.

1810 Population 72,674.

1811 By Act of Apportionment by Congress, number of Delaware Representatives in Congress is increased from one to two.

1813 March. Fort Union constructed at "The Rocks" (landing place of Swedes).
April 6. Lewes bombarded 22 hours by British fleet; "one chicken killed, and one pig wounded, leg broken."
May 27. Pea-patch Island ceded to United States for erection of fortifications.
August 11. Dr. James Tilton, of Wilmington, appointed Physician General of United States Army.
September 13. "United Church of Africans," Wilmington, first church in United States organized and entirely controlled by Negroes, is legally recorded.

1814 February 4. Commodore Oliver Hazard Perry, hero of Lake Erie, visits Wilmington.
September 11. Commodore Thomas Macdonough, native of Delaware, victorious over British Fleet on Lake Champlain.
December 24. James A. Bayard signs Treaty of Peace at Ghent.

1820 Population 72,749.

1822 February 22. Dam broken and mills damaged when Brandywine rises 20 feet.

1823 January 27. Caesar A. Rodney appointed Minister Plenipotentiary to Buenos Aires.

1824 January 20. "The African school society of Wilmington" incorporated by Negroes for the education of their children.
April 23. The Strand, New Castle, devastated by "great fire," entailing loss of $100,000.
October 6. General Lafayette feted in Wilmington.

1828 May 23. Congress makes first appropriation of $250,000 to construct Delaware Breakwater at Lewes.

1829 February 12. First general free school law of Delaware is enacted; counties divided into school districts.
April 18. Louis McLane of Delaware appointed Minister to Great Britain.
July 22. Martin Van Buren attends Louis McLane dinner in Wilmington Town Hall.
October 17. Chesapeake and Delaware Canal opened.

1830 Population 76,748.

1831 Joseph Bancroft establishes Bancroft Cotton Mills at Rockford, on the Brandywine.
February 8. $100,000 fire almost destroys Fort Delaware.

July 4. One and one-half miles of New Castle and Frenchtown Railroad officially opened. (Horse cars used.)

December 2. Third State Constitution framed.

1832 January 18. Legislature grants City Charter to Wilmington.

March 7. Richard H. Bayard chosen first Mayor of Wilmington.

September 10. First steam locomotive used on New Castle and Frenchtown Railroad.

1833 May 29. Louis McLane of Delaware, U.S. Secretary of Treasury, is appointed U. S. Secretary of State.

June 28. President Andrew Jackson is given reception at City Hall, Wilmington.

1834 May 8. Opening ceremonies of Delaware College at Newark.

1835 February 11. Leigslature authorizes lottery to raise money for State and school purposes.

1839 April 2. Hezekiah Niles, editor of *Niles' Register,* dies in Wilmington.

1840 Population 78,085.

October 20. Daniel Webster addresses Whig meeting of 6,000 persons in Wilmington.

1841 March 11. Charles Dickens visits Wilmington.

1844 May. The *Bangor,* first iron seagoing propellor steamer constructed in United States, launched at Wilmington.

1846 June 5. Tornado wreaks damage in Wilmington; two killed, buildings unroofed, trees uprooted.

1847 February 19. Legislature passes first local option law in State. (Court of Errors and Appeals declares law unconstitutional on ground that it *had been* submitted to the people.)

April 8. Delaware Regiment leaves for Mexico.

August 23. Henry Clay visits John M. Clayton; greeted at New Castle wharf by large crowd.

1848 May 29. Chief Justice Roger B. Taney of U.S. Supreme Court and U.S. District Judge Willard Hall, at New Castle, fine Thomas Garrett, Quaker Abolitionist of Wilmington, $5,400 for aiding fugitive slaves.

June 10. Congressman Abraham Lincoln, campaigning for Zachary Taylor, addresses Delawareans from balcony of Athenaeum (Fourth Street Market House) at Wilmington.

1849 January 21. Dr. John Lofland known far and wide as "The Milford Bard," dies in Wilmington and is buried in St. Andrew's Churchyard.

March 7. John M. Clayton appointed Secretary of State of United States.

1850 Population 91,532.

April 19. John M. Clayton signs Bulwer-Clayton Treaty between Britain and United States.

1851 May 12. President Millard Fillmore and Cabinet visit Wilmington.

1853 April 29. Richard Tucker, Negro, wins $10,000 in Delaware Lottery.

July 15. President Franklin Pierce and Secretary of War Jefferson Davis speak at City Hall, Wilmington.

1854 May 30. Three wagon loads of du Pont powder explode on 14th Street near Market, Wilmington. (Five killed and several wounded.)

1855 June 1. Prohibition becomes effective by legislative act. (Repealed January 30, 1857.)

1856 January 1. First train over Delaware Railroad runs to Dover.

1860 Population 112,216.
December 3. John Bassett Moore born at Smyrna.

1861 January 3. Hon. Henry Dickinson of Mississippi addresses Assembly and invites Delaware to secede from Union.
April. Civil War begins. Troops from Philadelphia garrison Fort Delaware, which becomes prison camp of importance.
May 11. Henry du Pont commissioned Major-General of Delaware troops.
June 27. Peace Convention at Dover favors peaceable recognition of Confederacy.
November 21. Dr. Watson F. Quimby, of Wilmington, patents an apparatus, with parachute attached, for navigating the air.

1862 April 3. Flags captured at Port Royal by Admiral S. F. du Pont hung on walls of City Hall, Wilmington.
November 4. William Cannon, former Democrat, elected Governor on Union ticket.
December 22. U.S. Senator Willard Saulsbury offers resolutions in Senate to investigate armed interference at Delaware polls.

1863 March 2. Explosion at du Pont powder packing plant, at Hagley Yard on Brandywine; 17 killed.

1864 May 31. Historical Society of Delaware organized, with Judge Willard Hall president.
June 29. First horse cars run on tracks of Wilmington City Railway.

1865 April 9. Brigadier-General Thomas A. Smyth dies three days after receiving mortal wound at Farmville, Va. (Buried in Wilmington and Brandywine Cemetery, April 17.)

1870 Population 125,216.

1871 April 20. Masonic Temple and Grand Opera House dedicated in Wilmington.
October 9. Earthquake shakes Wilmington and vicinity.

1873 February 6. President Ulysses S. Grant entertained in Wilmington by Governor and Legislature.

1874 Spring. Michael Pupin (noted electrical engineer and physicist) comes to Delaware as immigrant boy, and works on farm as muledriver.

1878 April. First telephone installed in Wilmington.

1880 Population 146,608.

1881 January 4. Robert Ingersoll speaks at Grand Opera House, Wilmington, to approximately 600 people; subject "What Must We Do to be Saved?"

April 13. Moses America is first Negro drawn for jury service in Del.

1882 December 23. First electric street lights installed in Wilmington.

1883 June 1. Municipal Court in Wilmington established by act of Legislature.

1885 March 5. Senator Thomas F. Bayard appointed U. S. Secretary of State.

1887 September 30. *Volunteer*, steel-hulled racing yacht built in Wilmington, defeats *Thistle*, in International Cup Race.

1888 January 24. First trip over Wilmington electric street railway.

1889 February 26. Law passed forbidding punishment of women at whipping-post or pillory.

September 10-12. Many ships wrecked and 40 lives lost at Delaware Breakwater during storm.

1890 Population 168,493.

1891 September 12. 700 workmen made idle by fire at Delaware Iron Company's plant at New Castle; $300,000 damage.

August 16. Delmar nearly destroyed by fire.

1893 March 31. Thomas F. Bayard appointed first Ambassador to Great Britain.

April 8. President Grover Cleveland visits Ambassador Bayard in Wilmington.

1895 May 9. General Assembly adopts Peach Blossom as Floral Emblem of Delaware.

May 9. General Assembly adjourns without electing a U.S. Senator, the first of a series of deadlocks occasioned by the candidacy of J. Edward Addicks.

June 15. Single-tax campaign starts in Delaware.

October 3. Liberty Bell exhibited at Wilmington on way to exposition at Atlanta.

October 18. First Arbor Day celebration in Wilmington.

November 3. Henry George, author of *Progress and Poverty*, addresses meeting at Opera House, Wilmington.

1897 June 4. Fourth Constitution of State adopted; property qualifications required of voters abolished.

1898 April 26. First Delaware Regiment encamps at Middletown to undergo training for war.

1900 Population 184,735.

Howard Pyle, nationally known illustrator, opens his school of art at Wilmington.

February 9. Robert Ingersoll indicted for blasphemy as per instructions of Chief Justice Joseph P. Comegys.

June 12. Frank Stephens purchases 163 acres near Grubb's Corner to found the Single Tax village of Arden.

June 27. Ordinance passed in Wilmington requiring register of vital statistics.

1901 February 12. Legislature ratifies 13th, 14th, and 15th Amendments to U. S. Constitution.

September 3. Monument unveiled at Cooch's Bridge to commemorate first (claimed) unfurling of American Flag in Battle, September 3, 1777.

November 22-25. Prisoners transferred from old county jail at New Castle to New Castle County Workhouse at Greenbank.

December 24. George K. Rudert, a Wilmington jeweler, operates an automobile in Wilmington.

1902 Delaware not represented in U. S. Senate because of deadlock.

1903 Night of June 22. George White, Negro, taken from Workhouse and burned at stake. (First and only lynching in Delaware.)

1905 March 20. Act abolishes use of pillory in Delaware. (Last State to do so.)

1908 May 30. Monument in memory of Brigadier General John Dagworthy, in graveyard of Prince George's Church, near Dagsboro, is unveiled.

1909 March 18. Legislature transfers title of Chesapeake and Delaware Canal to Federal Government.

1910 Population 202,322.

1911 State Legislature modifies corporation law to permit incorporation of Du Pont Boulevard Corporation.

1912 July 24. State Flag is adopted, its background of Colonial blue surrounding a diamond of buff in which is placed Coat of Arms of State, with words "December 7, 1787" below.

1916 July 25. Delaware National Guardsmen sent to Deming, New Mexico.

1917 State Highway Department created.

1918 August 29. First Delaware troops embark from Hoboken, N. J., for France.

September 29. Edward Thomas Demby, Negro, native of Wilmington, appointed Suffragan Bishop of Protestant Episcopal Church in Arkansas and Southwest. (First Colored Bishop of the American Church with jurisdiction in United States.)

1920 Population 223,003.

December 9. All city volunteer fire companies fight fire for 26 hours at Wilmington Leather Co.; loss $2,250,000.

1921 Wilmington volunteer fire companies merge into paid Fire Department.

March. New School Code, basis of present educational system, is enacted.

March 21. Assembly ratifies boundary survey of 1892 settling boundary dispute with Pennsylvania.

1923 May 5. Public Library dedicated at Tenth and Market Streets, Wilmington.

1924 January 11. Jefferson S. Coage, Wilmington Negro, is appointed to investigate conditions in Virgin Islands.

1925 May 31. Crown Prince Gustavus Adolphus and Crown Princess Louise of Sweden visit Old Swedes (Holy Trinity) Church, Wilmington.

1930 Population 238,380.

1936 October 29. President Franklin D. Roosevelt, from rear platform of B. & O. train, addresses largest gathering of citizens ever assembled in Delaware, at Delaware Avenue Station, Wilmington.

1937 March 27. Postmaster General James A. Farley dedicates new Post Office at Wilmington.

June 26. Delaware Park opens at Stanton, the State Constitution having been amended (1935) to permit pari-mutuel betting.

June 30. Franklin D. Roosevelt, Jr. and Ethel du Pont married at Christ Church in Christiana Hundred.

1938 June 27. Tercentenary Celebration of the Landing of the Swedes, first permanent settlement on Delaware's soil.

1940 Population 266,505.

1941 Wholesale arrests (500) for Blue Law violations made by Attorney General to find out whether these laws were enforceable.

December 7. The Pearl Harbor attack coincided with Delaware Day, anniversary of Delaware's ratification of the Federal Constitution.

1945 Pension system for State employees inaugurated.

1946 President Truman signed bill authorizing Delaware River Bridge.

1947 November 29. Scheduled passenger, express and freight service opened at the New Castle County Airport.

1948 March. Fort Delaware with its site, Pea Patch Island in the Delaware River, was officially returned to the State.

October. The Governor Bacon Health Center was opened at the site of Fort Du Pont; site and buildings were transferred to the State, 1947.

1949 Revised public school program including State-supported uniform salary schedule for teachers and all personnel was established.

1950 Population 318,085.
State Museum of Arts and History opened at Dover.

1951 Separate State Supreme Court was created by Constitutional amendment; also Constitutional provision for county zoning.

June 17. Tercentenary of New Castle's founding by the Dutch was celebrated; delegates from the embassies of nine European governments attended.

August 16. The $46 million Delaware Memorial Bridge opened to traffic.

1953 The General Assembly directed all schools to teach Delaware State government and the Delaware and Federal Constitutions.

Bibliography

"The search for the hidden items of Delaware history is an elusive quest—at once a source of charm and despair. He who seeks for knowledge outside the beaten path must himself be a pioneer, go back to original sources and bit by bit piece his picture together like a fragment of literary mosaic." Thus wrote Judge Richard S. Rodney in the opening paragraph of his valuable pamphlet, *Colonial Finances in Delaware* (1928). As far back as 1906, Prof. Edgar Dawson, in the *Annual Report* of the American Historical Association, had declared, "There is probably no State in the Union where one would find less material for writing its history than in Delaware." Such difficulties, however, do not mean that matters on the records which have been lost and destroyed cannot be reconstructed from other sources within and without the State, but it partly explains why a meticulous researcher will often find valuable fugitive facts where they are least expected to be.

The following are selected from the large list of sources used for this guide, as those most likely to afford the reader a broad background.

DESCRIPTION AND TRAVEL

Borah, Leo A. *Diamond Delaware, Colonial Still.* National Geographic Magazine. 67: 367-398. Sept. 1935. Includes 15 natural color photographs by B. A. Stewart. Has inaccuracies.

Journal-Every Evening, Wilmington, Del. *Delaware Today and Tomorrow.* 2-27-1937: supplement. 48 p.

Murphy, Henry C., transl. *Journal of a Voyage to New York and a Tour in Several of the American Colonies, 1679–80, by Jaspar Dankers and Peter Sluyter.* Brooklyn, Long Island Historical Society, 1867. 440 p. Valuable notes on Delaware.

Murphy, Henry C., transl. *Voyages from Holland to America, A. D. 1632 to 1644, by David Peterson De Vries.* New York, Billin & Brothers, 1853. 199 p. illus.

Rothrock, J. T. *Vacation Cruising in Chesapeake and Delaware Bays.* Philadelphia, Lippincott, 1884. 262 p.

Smithers, William W. *A Coaching Trip through Delaware, June 20th-25th, 1892.* Wilmington, Mercantile Printing Co., 1892. 29 p.

NATURAL SETTING

Benson, Adolph B. *Peter Kalm's Travels in North America.* The English version of 1770 revised from the original Swedish and edited by Adolph Benson. New York, Wilson-Erickson, 1937. 2 v.

Booth, James C., ed. *Memoir of the Geological Survey of the State of Delaware, &c.* Dover, S. Kimmey, 1841. 188 p.

Brandt, Francis B. *The Majestic Delaware, the Nation's Foremost Historical River*. Philadelphia, Brandt & Gummere, 1929, 192 p.

Ecological Society of America. *The Naturalist's Guide to the Americas*. Baltimore, Williams & Wilkins Co., 1926. 761 p. "Delaware" by Frank Morton Jones, pp. 398-401.

Small, John K. *Peninsula Delmarva. Journal of the New York Botanical Garden*. 30: 62-71. March 1929.

Vallandigham, Edward Noble. *Delaware and the Eastern Shore. Some Aspects of a Peninsula Pleasant and Well Beloved*. Philadelphia, Lippincott, 1922. 229 p.

ARCHAEOLOGY AND INDIANS

Archaeological Society of Delaware. Mimeographed bulletins from May 1933 to October 1953 contain numerous scholarly articles pertaining to Delaware Indians and archaeological material.

Johnson, Amandus. *Geographia Americae with An Account of the Delaware Indians, Based on Surveys and Notes Made in 1654–1656 by Peter Lindeström*. Translated from the original manuscript with notes, introduction and an appendix of Indian geographical names with their meanings by Amandus Johnson. Philadelphia, Swedish Colonial Society, 1925. 418 p. illus., maps..

Dunlap, A. R. and Weslager, C. A. *Indian Place Names in Delaware*, gives full treatment to each place-name from comprehensive authentic sources, with bibliography, map list, and index.

GENERAL HISTORY

Andrews, Charles M. *The Colonial Period of American History*. New Haven, Yale University Press, 1937. 3 v.

Bevan, Wilson Lloyd, ed.; Edwin Melvin Williams, historian. *History of Delaware, Past and Present*. New York, Lewis Historical Publishing Company, 1929. 4 v. illus. Volumes 3 and 4 are devoted to biographies.

Björnson, Marion L. (Mrs. Henry Clay Reed). *The Underground Railroad in Delaware*. Newark, Del., June 1928. 76 p. Thesis toward degree of M.A. in history, University of Pennsylvania.

Booth, Elizabeth. *Reminiscences*. New Castle, Del., privately printed, 1884. 367 p.

Buchanan, Roberdeau. *Life of the Hon. Thomas McKean*. Lancaster, Pa., 1890. 136 p.

Conrad, Henry C. *History of the State of Delware; from the Earliest Settlements to the Year 1907*. Wilmington, Author per Wickersham Co., Lancaster, Pa., 1908. 3 v. illus., map. Often appears to follow the *History of Delaware* by J. T. Scharf.

Delaware, General Assembly. *Memorial Services in Honor of Peter Minuit, First Governor of New Netherlands, 1626–1632, and of New Sweden, 1638*. Dover, Delawarean Power Print, 1895. 43 p.

Delaware. General Assembly. *Original Land Titles in Delaware*. Commonly known as the *Duke of York Record*, &c. Wilmington, Sunday Star Print, 1903. 199 p.

Documents Relative to the Colonial History of the State of New York. 12 v. Vols. 1, 2, 3, 4, 5 ed. by E. B. O'Callaghan. Albany, Weed, Parsons and Co., 1853–61. Vol. 12, with subtitle *Documents Relating to the History of the Dutch and Swedish Settlements on the Delaware,* ed. by B. Fernow, was printed in Albany by the Argus Co. in 1877.

Ferris, Benjamin. *A History of the Original Settlements on the Delaware,* &c. *To which is added an Account of the Ecclesiastical Affairs of the Swedish Settlers and a History of Wilmington, &c.* Wilmington, Wilson & Heald, 1846. 312 p. illus., map.

Harkness' Magazine. John C. Harkness, ed. Quarterly, v. 1-4, September 1872– January 1877.

Historic Markers Commission of Delaware. *Guide to Historic Markers in Delaware.* Wilmington, Historic Markers Commission of Delaware, 1933. 59 p. illus., map.

Houston, John W. *Address on the History of the Boundaries of the State of Delaware.* Wilmington, Historical Society of Delaware, 1879. 108 p.

Kinsman, F. J., and George Gray. *Addresses* (in) *Celebration of the Three Hundredth Anniversary of the Landing of the De Vries Colony at Lewes, Delaware, September 22d, A. D. 1909.* Wilmington, Historical Society of Delaware, 1909. 26 p.

Kinsman, Frederick Joseph. *Salve Mater.* New York, London, Longmans, Green & Co., 1920. 302 p.

Myers, Albert Cook, ed. *Narratives of Early Pennsylvania, West New Jersey, and Delaware, 1630–1707.* New York, Scribners, 1912. 476 p. map.

Powell, Walter A. *A History of Delaware: General History from the First Discoveries to 1925* (and) *History of Education.* Boston, Christopher Publishing House, 1928. 475 p.

Read, William Thompson. *Life and Correspondence of George Read.* Philadelphia, Lippincott, 1870. 575 p.

Reed, Henry Clay. *Readings in Delaware History, Economic Development.* Newark, University of Delaware, 1936. 104 p. (Mimeographed.)

Rodney, Richard S. *Early Relations of Delaware and Pennsylvania.* Wilmington, Historical Society of Delaware, 1930. 32 p.

Rodney, Richard S. *Colonial Leader, Colonel John French of New Castle.* Address delivered at the annual meeting of the Society of Colonial Wars in Pennsylvania, March 14, 1935, in Philadelphia. v. 4, no. 8, of the Society's publications. 18 p.

Runk, J. M. & Co. *Biographical and Genealogical History of the State of Delaware.* Chambersburg, Pa., 1899. 2 v.

Ryden, George Herbert, ed. *Letters to and from Caesar Rodney, 1756–1784.* Philadelphia, University of Pennsylvania Press, 1933. 483 p. Ms. supplement in Wilmington (Del.) Institute Free Library.

Scharf, J. T. *History of Delaware, 1609–1888.* Philadelphia, L. J. Richards & Co., 1888. 2 v. illus., maps. The first written general history of Delaware and a compilation of great value, notwithstanding its numerous errors.

Turner, C. H. B., comp. *Rodney's Diary and Other Delaware Records.* Philadelphia, Allen, Lane & Scott, 1911. 148 p.

Vandegrift, Lewis C. *Memoir of Commodore Thomas Macdonough.* Wilmington, Historical Society of Delaware, 1895. 14 p.

Vincent, Francis. *A History of the State of Delaware, from Its First Settlement until the Present Time,* &c. Philadelphia, John Campbell, 1870. 478 p. Only the first volume of this projected history was completed.

GOVERNMENT

Charter to William Penn, and Laws of the Province of Pennsylvania, Passed between the Years 1682 and 1700. Commonly called the *Duke of York's Book of Laws.* Published under the direction of John Blair Linn, Secretary of the Commonwealth. Compiled and edited by Staughton George, Benjamin M. Nead, Thomas McCamant. Harrisburg, Lane S. Hart, State printer, 1879. 614 p.

DeValinger, Leon, Jr. "The Development of Local Government in Delaware, 1638–1682." Newark, Del., 1935. 221 mimeographed p. Thesis submitted to Faculty of University of Delaware in partial fulfillment of the requirements for degree of Master of Arts.

Dickinson, John. *Letters from a Farmer in Pennsylvania to the Inhabitants of the British Colonies.* New York, Outlook Co., 1913. 146 p.

Dickinson, John. *Political Writings.* Wilmington, Bonsal & Niles, 1801. 2 v.

Johnson, Amandus, transl. *The Instruction for Johan Printz, Governor of New Sweden.* With introduction, notes, and appendices, and a special introduction by John Frederick Lewis. Philadelphia, Swedish Colonial Society, 1930. 287 p. illus., map, etc.

Maxey, Chester Collins. *County Administration: a Study Based upon County Government in the State of Delaware.* With introduction by Charles A. Beard. New York, Macmillan, 1919. 203 p.

Messersmith, George Strausser. *The Government of Delaware.* New York, Cincinnati, American Book Company, (1908). 296 p. illus.

Rodney, Richard Seymour. "Early Delaware Judges." (Manuscript in possession of the author.)

AGRICULTURE, INDUSTRY, COMMERCE, AND LABOR

Conrad, Henry C. *Old Delaware Clockmakers.* Wilmington, Historical Society of Delaware, 1898. 34 p.

Clark, Victor S. *History of Manufactures in the United States, 1607–1860.* Washington, Carnegie Institute of Washington, 1928. 2 v.

Commission of Packing and Marketing. *Delaware Food Products: Report of the Commission,* &c. Dover, Del., 1933. 112 p.

Delaware State Board of Agriculture, Bureau of Markets. *Delaware.* n.p., 1936c. 77 p. illus.

Delaware State Program. *What Delaware Makes and Spends.* Wilmington, Clearing House, 1920. 55 p. "The story of State revenue and expenditures."

Du Pont, B. G. *E. I. du Pont de Nemours and Company, a History 1802–1902.* Boston, Houghton Mifflin, 1920. 196 p. illus.

Hanna, Mary Alice. *Trade of the Delaware District, before the Revolution.*

Northampton, Mass., Smith College, 1917. (Smith College. Studies in History, v. 2, no. 4.)

Rodney, Richard S. *Colonial Finances in Delaware.* Wilmington, Wilmington Trust Co., 1928. 68 p. illus.

Sterrett, W(illiam) D(ent). *Report on Forest Conditions in Delaware and a Forest Policy for the State.* Delaware College Agricultural Experiment Station. Bulletin 82. Dec. 1908. 58 p.

TRANSPORTATION

Delaware State Program. *The Story of Roads in Delaware from the Days of the Beasts of Burden to the Road of Tomorrow.* Wilmington, Clearing House, 1919. 53 p.

RACIAL ELEMENTS

Johnson, Amandus. *The Swedish Settlements on the Delaware, Their History and Relation to the Indians, Dutch and English, 1638–1664, &c.* New York, University of Pennsylvania Press per D. Appleton & Co., agents, 1911. 2 v. illus., maps.

Louhi, Evert Alexander. *The Delaware Finns, or The First Permanent Settlements in Pennsylvania, Delaware and West New Jersey and Eastern Part of Maryland.* New York, Humanity Press, 1925. 331 p.

Ward, Christopher (Longstreth). *Dutch and Swedes on the Delaware, 1609–64.* Philadelphia, University of Pennsylvania Press, 1930. 393 p.

EDUCATION

Carpenter, T. Leslie. *Record of Musical Societies in Wilmington, Delaware, 1800–1933.* Mimeograph copy.

Conner, William H. *The First Hundred Years* (of Delaware College). Alumni News. Centenary Number, May 1934. Newark, University of Delaware. P. 5-8.

Cooper, Richard Watson, and Hermann. *The One-Teacher School in Delaware, a Study in Attendance.* Newark, University of Delaware Press, 1925. 434 p. illus., maps.

Coram, Robert. *Political Inquiries: to Which is Added, A Plan for the General Establishment of Schools throughout the United States.* Wilmington, Andrews and Brynberg, 1791. 108 p.

Hayward, Harry. *The Educational Problem of Delaware.* Delaware Magazine, March 1912, v. 4:735-748.

Morgan, George. *The Colonial Origin of Newark Academy and of Other Classical Schools* &c. Newark, University of Delaware Press, 1934. 112 p.

Morgan, George. *Sunny Days at Dear Old Delaware: What I Remember of My Experiences There in 1871–1875.* University of Delaware, Delaware Notes, eighth series, p. 84-106. 1934.

Powell, Lyman P. *The History of Education in Delaware.* No. 15 in *Contributions to American Educational History,* ed. by Herbert B. Adams. Washington, Government Printing Office, 1893. 186 p. (U. S. Dept. of Interior. Bureau of Education. Circular of Information, no. 3.)

Rodney, Richard S. *The Development of Education in New Castle*. n.p., n.d. 17 p. pamphlet.

Weeks, Stephen B. *History of Public School Education in Delaware*. Washington, Government Printing Office, 1917. 181 p. (U. S. Dept. of Interior. Bureau of Education. Bulletin 18.)

RELIGION

Barratt, Norris S. *Barratt's Chapel and Methodism; Historical Address Delivered before the Forty-Third Wilmington Annual Conference, &c. March 17, 1911*. Wilmington, Historical Society of Delaware, 1911. 62 p.

Bumstead, W. F. *Diocese of Delaware, Its Historical Parish and Mission Churches*. With foreword by Rt. Rev. Philip Cook. n.p., 1934. 50 p. illus.

Burr, Horace, (transl. and ed.). *The Records of Holy Trinity (Old Swedes) Church, Wilmington, Delaware, from 1697–1773, with Abstracts of English Records from 1773–1810*. Wilmington, Historical Society of Delaware, 1890. 772 p.

Catholic Historical Book of Delaware; Issued in Commemoration of the Centenary of St. Peter's Cathedral, Wilmington, Delaware. Wilmington, J. V. Brennan Co., 1916. 56 p.

Dulaney, Henry S., editor. *History and Directory of Pastors of the Asbury Methodist Episcopal Church*. Wilmington, Del., n.p., 1903. 71 p. P. 5-21: History of the Asbury M. E. Church, Wilmington, Del., by John D. C. Hanna.

Edwards, Morgan. *History of the Baptists in Delaware*. Pennsylvania Magazine of History and Biography. v. 9, 1885; April, p. 45-61; July, p. 197-213.

Higgins, Anthony. *Historical Address Delivered before the "Friends of Old Drawyers" Presbyterian Church, near Odessa, Delaware, on Sunday, June 7, A.D. 1908 &c*. Wilmington, Historical Society of Delaware, 1908. 20 p.

Holcomb, Thomas. *Sketch of Early Ecclesiastical Affairs in New Castle, Delaware, and History of Immanuel Church* (New Castle, Del.). Wilmington, Del., Delaware Publishing Co., 1890. 254 p.

Jacobs, Henry Eyster. *A History of the Evangelical Lutheran Church in the United States*. New York, Christian Literature Co., 1893. 539 p. Valuable references to Delaware.

Pusey, Pennock. *Crane Hook Church, Predecessor of Old Swedes Church &c*. Wilmington, Historical Society of Delaware, 1895. 14 p.

Records of the Welsh Tract Baptist Meeting, Pencader Hundred, New Castle County, Delaware, 1701 to 1828. In 2 parts. Wilmington, Historical Society of Delaware, 1904. 237 p.

Rodney, Richard S. *Delaware's Greatest Glory*. Americana XXI, no. 2: 176-192. April 1927. An address at Old Drawyers Presbyterian Church, July 7, 1925, on Delaware's part in framing and adopting the Federal Constitution.

Ryden, George Herbert. *Relation of the Newark Academy of Delaware to the Presbyterian Church and to the Higher Education in the American Colonies*. University of Delaware. Delaware Notes, ninth series, 114 p.

Vallandigham, James Laird, Rev. and Gayley, Samuel A. *History of the*

Presbytery of New Castle from its Organization, March 13, 1717 to 1888. Philadelphia, Presbyterian Publishing Co., n.d. 24 p.

Waterson, Elizabeth. *Churches in Delaware during the Revolution with a Brief Account of Their Settlement and Growth.* Wilmington, Historical Society of Delaware, 1925. 117 p.

SOCIAL WELFARE

Delaware. General Service Board. Organizing Committee. *Program for the Study and Development of Civic and Social Questions in Delaware, and a Brief Survey of Present Practices, Conditions, and Progress in this State.* (Wilmington, Del., 1915.) 146 p.

LITERATURE AND THE PRESS

Foust, Clement E. *Life and Dramatic Works of Robert Montgomery Bird.* New York, Knickerbocker Press, 1919. 725 p.

Hawkins, Dorothy Lawson. "James Adams, the First Printer of Delaware." (In Papers of the Bibliographical Society of America. Chicago, University of Chicago Press, 1934. v. 28, pt. 1, p. 28-63.)

HOWARD PYLE

Abbott, Charles D. *Howard Pyle, a Chronicle by Charles D. Abbott.* With an introduction by N. C. Wyeth and many illustrations from Howard Pyle's works. New York, Harper, 1925. 249 p.

Morse, Willard S., and Gertrude Brinckle, comp. *A Record of Howard Pyle's Illustrations and Writings.* Wilmington, Society of the Fine Arts, 1921. 225 p.

PAINTING

Du Pont, Jean Kane Foulke. "Painters of Delaware." (Manuscript in possession of author.)

ARCHITECTURE

Bennett, George Fletcher. *Early Architecture of Delaware.* With introduction and text by Joseph L. Copeland. Wilmington, Historical Press, Inc., 1932. 215 p. illus.

Embury, Aymar, II. *Early American Churches.* Garden City, N. Y., Doubleday, Page & Co., 1914. 189 p. plates.

Embury, Aymar, II. *Farm Houses of New Netherland.* New York, Russell F. Whitehead, 1916. 16 p. illus. (V. 1, no. 3, *The White Pine Series of Architectural Monographs.)*

Faris, John Thomson. *Historic Shrines of America, Being the Story of One Hundred and Twenty-one Historic Buildings and the Pioneers Who Made Them Notable.* New York, George H. Doran Co., 1918. 421 p.

Grosvenor, Jewett A. *An Architectural Monograph on the Wooden Architecture of the Lower Delaware Valley.* (St. Paul, Minn., White Pine Bureau), 1920. 16 p. illus. (V. 6, no. 3, *The White Pine Series of Architectural Monographs.)*

Hammond, John Martin. *Colonial Mansions of Maryland and Delaware.* Philadelphia, Lippincott, 1914. 304 p. illus.

Hollister, Paul Merrick. *Famous Colonial Houses.* Illustrated by James Preston, with introduction by Julian Street. Philadelphia, David McKay Co., 1921. 170 p. plates.

Lathrop, Elise. *Historic Houses of Early America.* New York, R. M. McBride & Co., 1927. 464 p. illus.

Upjohn, Hobart Brown. *Churches in Eight American Colonies Differ.ng in Elements of Design.* Photographs by Kenneth Clark, measured drawings from the G. F. Lindsay Collection. New York, R. F. Whitehead, 1925. 8 p. illus.

United States Department of the Interior, Office of National Parks, Buildings and Reservations, Historic American Buildings Survey. *Survey No. 9, 1-6.* Wilmington and New Castle Buildings. Plans drawn by Albert Kruse and other Delaware Architects. Washington, D.C., Government Printing Office, 1934. 38 sheets.

Wallace, Philip B. *Colonial Churches and Meeting Houses, Pennsylvania, New Jersey and Delaware.* With measured drawings by William Allen Dunn and introduction by Horace Wells Sellars. New York, Architectural Book Publishing Co., 1931. 291 p. illus.

CITIES, TOWNS, AND VILLAGES

Cooch, Francis A. *Little Known History of Newark, Delaware, and Its Environs.* With an introduction by George H. Ryden. Newark, Del., Press of Kells, 1936. 297 p. illus.

Cooper, Alexander B. *Fort Casimir, the Starting Point in the History of New Castle in the State of Delaware.* Wilmington, Historical Society of Delaware, 1905. 39 p. maps.

Delaware. Works Progress Administration. Federal Writers' Project. *New Castle on the Delaware.* Wilmington, New Castle Historical Society, 1937. 2d ed. 150 p.

Every Evening (newspaper). *History of Wilmington, Delaware.* Wilmington, 1894. 276 p. illus.

Handy, Egbert G. and Vallandigham, Jas. L., Jr. *Newark, Delaware: Past and Present.* Newark, Delaware Ledger Print, 1882. 91 p.

Janvier, Anne R. *Stories of Old New Castle.* n.p., n.d. 43 p.

Lewes Tercentenary Commission. *Dedication of Zwaanendael House, 1631–1931.* Lewes, Del., Saturday, May 7, 1932. n.p. 11 p. pamphlet. illus. Not entirely accurate.

Lincoln, Anna T. *Wilmington, Delaware, Three Centuries under Four Flags, 1609–1937.* Rutland, Vt., Tuttle Publishing Co., 1937. 411 p.

Lore, Charles B. *History of Odessa.* Address at the St. Paul's Methodist Episcopal Church, Odessa, November 18, 1901. n.p. 18 p.

Montgomery, Elizabeth. *Reminiscences of Wilmington, in Familiar Village Tales, Ancient and New.* Philadelphia, T. K. Collins, Jr., 1851. 367 p.

Powell, Walter A. *Annals of a Village in Kent County, Delaware, about the Middle of the Nineteenth Century.* n.p., 1934. 46 p.

Ségur, Louis Philippe, Comte de. *Memoirs and Recollections.* London, Printed for Henry Colburn, 1825. 442 p. Pp. 307-323: Delaware Bay, Wilmington, Dover in period of 1782.

Vincent, Francis. *History of Wilmington. Harkness Magazine.* v. 1, no. 2, Dec. 1872 to v. 4, no. 16, Jan. 1877, the last issue of the quarterly. 50 p.

Johnston, George. *History of Cecil County, Maryland, and the Early Settlements around the Head of the Chesapeake Bay and on the Delaware River.* Philadelphia, Dickson & Gillen, 1881. 548 p. map.

"Penn Manuscripts: Papers Relating to the Three Lower Counties." Vol. 15, 1629–1774. (Library of Historical Society of Pennsylvania.) For other ms. in same library see *Annual Report* of American Historical Association for 1906, v. 2, p. 148.

Turner, C. H. B. *Some Records of Sussex County.* Philadelphia, Allen, Lane & Scott, 1909. 387 p.

SUPPLEMENT TO BIBLIOGRAPHY (*See Literature*)

Able, Augustus H. "Fiction as a Mirror of Delaware Life," in *Delaware History* (magazine). Wilmington, 1948.

Caldwell, R. G. *The Penitentiary Movement in Delaware, 1776–1829.* Wilmington, 1947.

Canby, Henry Seidel. *The Brandywine.* Farrar & Rinehart, New York, 1941.

Colonial Dames. *Portraits in Delaware 1700–1850.* Ill. Wilmington, 1951.

Cooch, Edward W. *The Battle of Cooch's Bridge.* Wilmington, 1940; *Delaware Historic Events,* 1946.

Dolan, Paul. *The Organization of State Administration in Delaware.* Johns Hopkins Press, 1951.

Hindes, Ruthanna. *George Alfred Townsend.* Wilmington, 1946.

Hist. Soc. of Delaware. *Delaware History* (magazine), semi-annual, 1946.

Liberman, Cy. and Rosbrow, James M. *The Delaware Citizen.* Wilmington, 1952. An exposition of Delaware's government.

Library of Congress. *Old New Castle and Modern Delaware.* U.S. Gov. Printing Office, 1951. Ill. catalog Delaware Exhibit, June-Nov., 1951.

Lunt, D. *The Bounds of Delaware.* Wilmington, 1947. Penn-Baltimore controversy.

Munroe, John A. *Delaware Becomes a State.* University of Del. Press, 1953.

New Castle Historical Society. *New Castle on the Delaware.* Wilmington, 1950.

Reed, H. C., Ed. *Delaware, A History of the First State.* Vols. I, II, N. Y., 1947.

Ridgely, M. L., Ed. *The Ridgelys of Delaware and Their Circle.* Portland, Me., 1949.

Tatnall, R. R. *Flora of Delaware and the Eastern Shore.* Wilmington, 1946.

Weslager, C. A. *Delaware's Forgotten Folk.* Philadelphia, 1943; *Delaware's Buried Past,* 1944; *Delaware's Forgotten River* (The Christiana) 1944.

Wildes, Harry Emerson. *The Delaware.* Farrar & Rinehart, New York, 1940.

Wooten, B. and Higgins, A. *New Castle on the Delaware 1651–1939.* Boston, 1939.

Wuorinen, John H. *The Finns on the Delaware 1638–1655.* New York, 1938.

Zebley, Frank R. *The Churches of Delaware.* Wilmington, 1947.

KEY

━━━━━━ 13 ━━━━━━ U. S. HIGHWAYS

━━━━━━ 41 ━━━━━━ STATE HIGHWAYS

RESERVATIONS

SECTIONAL DIVISION OF STATE MAP

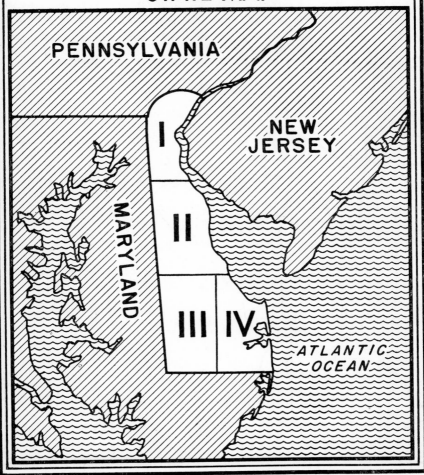

PENNSYLVANIA

NEW JERSEY

MARYLAND

I

II

III IV

ATLANTIC OCEAN

SECTION I

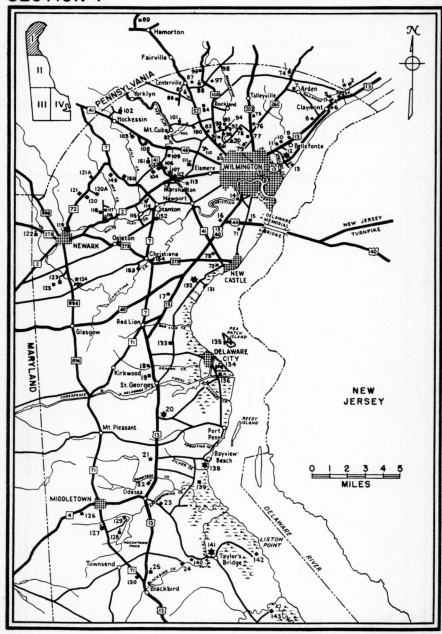

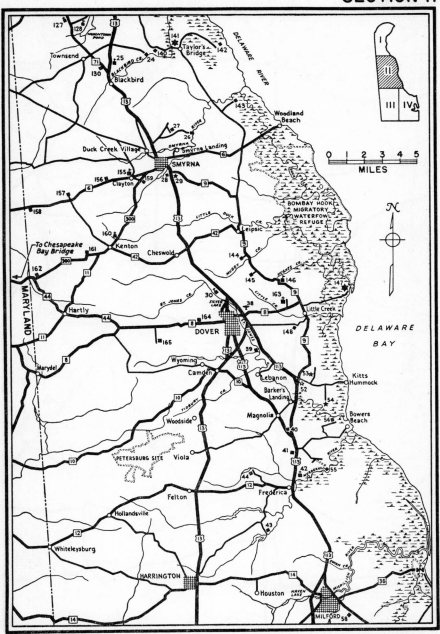

SECTION III

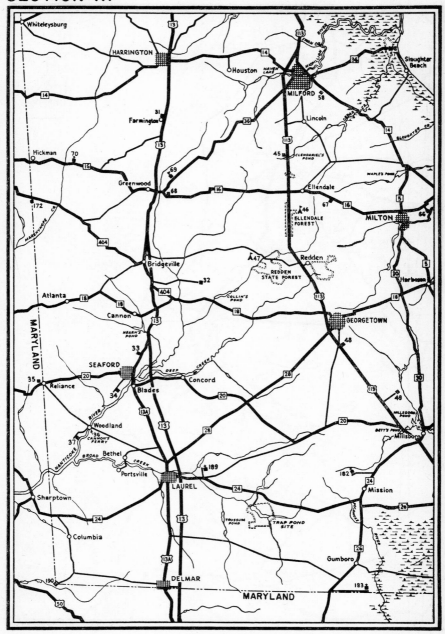

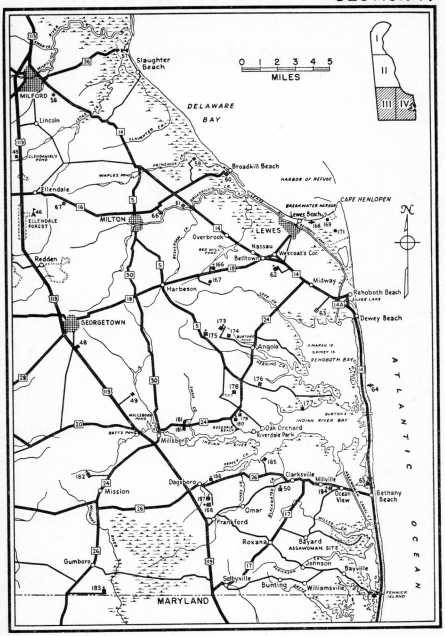

Index to Map Sections

Index

[Houses, ships, etc., are assembled under those heads.]
[Italic figures refer to main descriptions.]